Fundamental Programming

D1403783

LEARNING RESOURCE CENTER
JOLIET JUNIOR COLLEGE
JOLIET, ILLINOIS 60436

Fundamental Programming

J. Denbigh Starkey
Washington State University

Rockford J. Ross
Montana State University

West Publishing Company
St. Paul • New York • Los Angeles • San Francisco

Cover photography by Michel Tcherevkoff for Alleghany.

COPYRIGHT © 1984 By WEST PUBLISHING CO.
                    50 West Kellogg Boulevard
                    P.O. Box 43526
                    St. Paul, Minnesota 55165

Library of Congress Cataloging in Publication Data

Starkey, J. Denbigh.
    Fundamental programming.

    Includes index.
    1. Electronic digital computers — Programming. I. Ross,
Rockford. II. Title.
QA76.6.S715 1984   001.64′2   84-2293
ISBN 0-314-77801-2

To Jean
and
To Cheryl

Contents

Preface

Our purpose in writing this book was to present an introduction to programming in true textbook form. What we wanted was a textbook that could be used by students and instructors alike with the confidence that the issues fundamental to programming were covered in a thorough and integrated fashion. We wanted to ensure that students were not left dangling by incomplete discussions or topics devoid of application, and that instructors would not be forced to refer to other sources to fill in gaps left in the book. What we did *not* want was yet another programming language manual (many fine language manuals already exist) or a book that only discussed the fundamental issues of programming in isolated sections without integrating these concepts into the everyday development of programs. Learning the details of a programming language is relatively easy; the challenging part is learning how to program.

In striving towards our goals we have held to one basic tenet: students learn best by example. Each new programming concept introduced is discussed as it is needed within the framework of a complete top-down development of a program. Related issues, such as program efficiency and correctness, are integrated within this discussion rather than being relegated to isolated sections. Thus, this is a large book, not because it encompasses so much new material, but because of the novel and thorough presentation of the fundamental topics.

PHILOSOPHY

In determining the content of the book we had a definite pedagogical model in mind. This model stemmed from the startling observation that when students were asked to design a substantial program independently, many would return with a program consisting primarily of one or two large routines with little modularity — programs that were difficult to read and difficult to modify. Furthermore, when asked simple questions about the efficiency or correctness of their programs, the students were often at a loss for answers. This was true in spite of our efforts at teaching structured design, correctness, and efficiency of programs. What had gone wrong? The answer was surprisingly simple: we weren't practicing what we preached. Traditional textbooks used in the introductory courses either did not cover these topics well or they covered them in isolated sections of the text. Furthermore, procedures and functions were normally introduced late in these textbooks, almost as an afterthought, as the "right way" to program. Students were mistakenly led to believe that procedures and functions were difficult topics of more bother than they were worth; it's no wonder that they were avoiding their use later. In designing our book, then, our philosophy was to introduce programming in a way that would reinforce proper programming style and habits from the start. We do this as follows:

(1) Case Studies. The central pedagogical tool we use is the case study. These are programming problems for which complete, working programs are designed in a top-down, structured fashion as new programming concepts are introduced. The problem of exploring new concepts in isolation from practical experience is thus avoided. In all there are 51 complete case studies in the book.

(2) Use of a Pseudolanguage. The solutions to the case studies are developed in a structured, top-down fashion in a simple pseudolanguage. This allows us to concentrate on programming rather than the distracting details of a real language as the programs are developed. Students should learn that program development in a pseudolanguage is a completely separate process (now widely practiced in industry) from the implementation of the resulting program in some particular programming language. Once a program has been designed in the pseudolanguage, it is easy to translate it into any of the usual procedural languages like Pascal, FORTRAN, BASIC, Ada, or C.

(3) Immediate Introduction of Procedures and Functions. From the first case study on we teach that programs are collections of short, well-defined procedures and functions, which are organized and called from an initial procedure (main program). The crucial concepts of procedures, functions, parameters, and modular program design are thus ingrained into the habits and practice of students from the beginning. Students learn these topics without problem, and their later programming practices are greatly enhanced as a result.

(4) Inclusion of Program Correctness. As part of each case study we include an integrated discussion of program correctness. This starts out quite simply with the early case studies but eventually includes the notions of a program walkthrough, semi-formal verification steps (particularly for loops), program testing, choosing proper test data, robustness, and debugging techniques. Students receive a practical knowledge of the concepts of program verification and are provided a sound basis for advanced courses on the topic.

(5) Integrated Discussion of Program Efficiency. The execution time efficiency (time complexity) and storage space requirements (space complexity) of the programs are discussed for each relevant case study. Time complexity is determined by doing a count of the number of statements executed, and space complexity is determined by counting the number of storage cells used. These simple, intuitive approaches are accurate and practical. Students continuing on in computer science will have a basis for advanced study of these topics, while those terminating after this class will understand practical methods for determining program efficiency.

BOOK ORGANIZATION

All chapters except the first follow a specific format designed to implement our philosophy. Each has three major sections, **Getting Acquainted, In Retrospect,** and **The Challenge.** In the Getting Acquainted section, simple case studies introducing the new programming concepts of the chapter are studied. All of these case studies should be covered because the procedures and functions developed there are often used in later case studies. In Retrospect summarizes these new concepts and provides a place to turn to for review. The Challenge presents more challenging case studies involving the new concepts of the chapter. Four groups of exercises are integrated into each chapter, and answers to some of these are found in appendix A, **Answers to Selected Exercises.**

The first chapter of the text is different from the other chapters; it describes a model computer and the simple operations that a computer can perform, providing the motivation for the rest of the book by answering the question, "Why must we write programs?". It was carefully written so that students could read it on their own during the first week of class as the instructor tended to other matters (such as describing how to use the computer).

We hope that you will find this book as easy and pleasant to use as we have. However, you will probably find parts that you dislike or disagree with. We would be delighted to receive any comments you may have, and corrections will be gratefully accepted and included in future printings or editions.

IN GRATITUDE

Those to whom we are most indebted for the form and content of this book are the thousands of students in the introductory programming course at Washington State University over the past two years. Their questions, comments, sharp-eyed ability to catch errors, and enthusiasm for the material kept us going. Also to be thanked are the many reviewers who helped us through various stages of the book:

Gabriel Barta
(University of New Hampshire)
Rodney M. Bates
(Kansas State University)
Leland L. Beck
(San Diego State University)
Don Cartlidge
(New Mexico State University)
Cecelia R. Daly
(University of Nebraska)
Nancy Duffrin
(SUNY at Stony Brook)
Arthur C. Fleck
(University of Iowa)
Tamar E. Granor
(University of Pennsylvania)
James L. Hein
(Portland State University)

Rachelle Heller
(University of Maryland)
Leon Levine
(University of California, Los Angeles)
Gene Mahalko
(University of North Dakota)
Lawrence H. Miller
(University of California, Los Angeles)
Ralph Moore
(Modesto Junior College, California)
Keith R. Pierce
(University of Minnesota)
Alan L. Schwartz
(University of Missouri, St. Louis)
Robert F. Simmons
(University of Texas, Austin)
Stephen F. Weiss
(University of North Carolina, Chapel Hill)

Their careful evaluations and widespread support for the book were indeed helpful. The many instructors who labored in front of the classes with rough drafts of the book receive our appreciation, too.

Although many helped us along the way, there are others whose help was particularly important. Roger Hirsch first interested us in writing the book, without his encouragement we might never have started. Shirley Farmer was unflagging in her typing of the manuscript (even when her eyes said "Oh no, not chapter 4 again!") We also thank Mike Langston, whose enthusiasm for the book and personal friendship as a colleague did not temper his constructive criticism of our efforts. Then there are all those at West Publishing Company, who probably never saw so many deadlines come and go before and yet continued to provide the necessary support to keep the project moving. Editor Pete Marshall, production editor Deanna Quinn, and marketing coordinator Renée Grevious worked so intensely with us that they now seem more like friends than business associates. We also thank Pamela McMurry for carefully copyediting our manuscript; she not only read for syntactic errors but for a true understanding of the material.

Then there are the few without whose support the project definitely would have been doomed: our families. To those who missed us on family occasions, holidays, and weekends, yet continued to stand by as the project seemed to extend indefinitely — well, what can we say? Without you there would be no book.

J. Denbigh Starkey
Rockford J. Ross

To the Student

This book has been designed with you in mind. We have given numerous examples of all important programming concepts and provided exercises to reinforce your learning. If you study this material carefully you will be well prepared for advanced courses in computer science; if this is the only course that you plan to take, you will have a sound understanding of the programming process to apply in later life. For example, it may well be that the most useful things that a future engineer learns from this book are program correctness and efficiency if he or she is later involved in projects where the successful design of a program by members of a team is crucial, or where the speed of a particular software component of a system is important. Similarly, business students may later find that they are responsible for decisions about the purchase or use of programs, and a practical, working knowledge of the concepts of program design, efficiency, and correctness may be far more important than actual programming skills. In short, these topics are of concern not only to computer professionals but to all who will be involved with computers in the future.

To use this book most effectively, you should read the chapters in the order given. The first chapter answers the question, "Why must computers be programmed?" You can read it as you are becoming used to the actual computer you are using; this chapter contains no programming assignments. In subsequent chapters you should study each of the case studies in the Getting Acquainted sections in succession. The order is important because later case studies build on earlier ones. The In Retrospect section of each chapter is especially for you. You should read it carefully and then use it as a reference whenever you need to review a particular topic. The Challenge section contains advanced case studies exploring the new topics of the chapter. Later introductory case studies do not depend on previous Challenge case studies, but the Challenge case studies give you a more intimate look at the programming process.

Whether you are a computer science student or a student from another discipline we have designed this book to be useful to you now and later as a reference. And one warning: if you have learned to program previously on your own, try to forget what you learned. We have seen many sad cases of students coming in with previous programming experience who start well but end up doing poorly because they never shook their previously learned bad habits! Using this book you will learn to be a complete programmer.

Fundamental Programming

| CHAPTER 1 |

Getting Ready

Learning to program is exciting. In fact, programming is a mixture of art, craft, and science that nearly everyone finds intriguing. It's a good thing that this is so, because computers are finding their way into nearly all aspects of our lives, and soon almost everyone will need a basic understanding of computers. On the other hand, many students face their first programming course with apprehension and awe. We as authors are aware of this, and we understand the worries that some students may experience. In this first chapter we will work our way carefully and gently into the realm of programming. In fact, we will not even write programs in this chapter. Instead, we will discuss the motivations for programming. Careful reading of this chapter is a worthwhile investment, because once you understand the concepts presented here, the ideas of the later chapters will be easier to grasp. The time spent reading chapter 1 can also be used for becoming acquainted with the actual computer you will use for learning programming. Then, by the time you reach chapter 2, you will be ready to begin designing your first programs.

Computers are a relatively new phenomenon. The first ones were invented primarily for military and scientific applications during the late 1930s and the 1940s. It wasn't until the latter part of the 1950s and the 1960s that large *mainframe computers* found widespread use in business corporations. Continued improvements in technology in the 1970s allowed computers to become smaller, faster, and much less expensive. The resulting medium-sized and reasonably priced *minicomputers* were soon in use in nearly all businesses of moderate size. Today we have small *microcomputers*, or *personal computers*, that have all the power of those first military computers but fit conveniently on the top of a desk. Now, the smallest businesses, public schools, and even families can afford a computer. Computer brand names such as Apple, Commodore, DEC, Hewlett Packard, IBM, and TRS-80, to list a few, are becoming household names.

During this brief history many different programming languages were developed for programming these computers. (A *programming language* is simply a language that is used for writing procedures to direct the computer to perform certain desired calculations.) Most of these early languages were not widely accepted and have been forgotten. Some that are in use today include Algol, Basic, Cobol, Fortran, Pascal, and PL/I. Other languages continue to be developed, including an important new language called Ada. These languages are examples of *high level programming languages*, or *procedural languages*. To be able to program one of today's computers we must learn at least one of these procedural languages. All modern computers are capable of being programmed in such procedural languages, although any particular computer will probably be set up to handle only a few of these languages.

With so many different computers on the market and so many different programming languages to choose from, we might wonder where to begin learning to program. Regardless of which computer we learn to program, we most certainly will confront a new and different computer later. And regardless of which programming language we first use, we are likely to need to learn a different one later. It almost looks as though we can't win! The most confusing questions facing beginning programmers are often: Where do I begin? and How can I possibly learn about all of these things? Fortunately we can easily lay these initial worries to rest.

Observation 1. For the purpose of programming in a procedural language, all computers are the same.

Observation 1 really makes the world a lot simpler! Except for rare, special purpose computers, it doesn't matter whether we have access to a multimillion dollar supercomputer or an inexpensive microcomputer as we learn to program. Even the brand of the computer is of no consequence. The process of programming is always the same. If we learn to program using one computer, we will know how to write programs for any computer!

Observation 2. All procedural programming languages are similar.

Again, Observation 2 really simplifies life. In essence it says that once we learn to program, we will be able to learn any of the procedural programming languages without difficulty! Programming languages are not nearly as difficult to learn as natural languages such as German, Finnish, or Cantonese. Also, whereas knowing one foreign language, say German, does not help us much in learning another foreign language, say Cantonese, knowing one programming language makes learning another one quite simple.

Observations 1 and 2 play key roles throughout this book. Rather than worry about features of any particular computer, we will discuss only those concepts that are common to all computers and are necessary for an understanding of programming. And, instead of designing programs in one of the existing programming languages, we will do our initial thinking and design work in a *model programming language* (i.e., a programming language that really does not exist but that embodies the common features of all procedural languages). This way, we won't be tied to any particular computer or programming language. Once we understand the underlying general computer model and learn to do our thinking, planning, and design of programs in the model programming language, it doesn't matter which computer or which language we run into in the future—we'll be ready!

To summarize these thoughts and provide the motivation for the organization of the rest of the book, the four fundamental concepts that we must learn in order to have a firm grasp of programming are listed below:

1. *The computer model.* Programs are designed and written to be executed on a computer. We need to understand the basic concepts that are common to all computers in order to understand the fundamental concepts of programming.
2. *Program design.* The formulation of a problem in terms of simple statements that can be executed by our computer is the first step in programming. It is also the most crucial step. It requires careful thought and the application of proven methods for dividing the original problem into smaller and simpler pieces on the way to a solution. Program design is done in the model programming language to keep the design independent from any particular programming language.
3. *Program implementation.* With a program design in hand, the next step is to implement (write) the program in an actual programming language, so we need to learn one real programming language.
4. *Program execution.* Once our program has been implemented in a real programming language, it must be run on a real computer.

In this chapter we will describe our computer model and introduce some basic features of the model programming language *mpl*.

Modern computers are complex devices. Fortunately, we need to know very little about the workings of a real computer to understand programming. This is as it should be. The intricacies of a computer should be *transparent* to the programmer; that is, the computer should simply carry out program instructions without requiring the programmer to be aware of the details of computer circuitry. However, to understand programming we *do* need to understand the basic design of a computer. This will help us see, for example, why we cannot simply issue the directive "print this month's paychecks" to make the computer calculate and print the payroll, or "play chess" to make the computer play chess. Instead, we must expend considerable effort in designing programs to do these things using much simpler statements.

**1.2
THE MODEL
COMPUTER**

For our needs, we will look at only those features that are common to all computers and that are necessary for understanding programming. This idea of describing a complex device or phenomenon in simple terms is called *abstraction:* we abstract only the features that are important to us and ignore the others. An abstraction can be thought of as a simplified model of the real thing, in this case, a model of a real computer. Our model, illustrated in figure 1–1, is representative of all modern computers. It consists of a *processor*, a *store*, an *input device*, and an *output device*. The processor is the central component of the computer where program instructions are carried out, or *executed*. The store is where values used by the program are kept. The input device is where the programmer enters his/her programs and the data for the programs, and the output device is where the answers generated by the program are printed. These four components are described in more detail in the following sections.

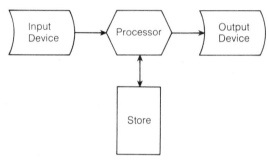

FIGURE 1–1. THE COMPUTER MODEL

THE PROCESSOR

The processor derives its name from its function: based on instructions supplied by the programmer, the processor processes given data values to produce new values. As shown in figure 1–2, the processor has a number of different units for accomplishing these tasks. The first is the *program unit*, where the list of instructions (the *program*) is kept. There are other units for adding, subtracting, multiplying, and dividing two values. There is also a unit for exponentiating (raising a value to some power, for example, 10^3). Finally, there is a unit for comparing two values. For now we will be interested only in the five *arithmetic units* in the processor: the adder, subtracter, multiplier, divider, and exponentiater. The comparison unit will be discussed later.

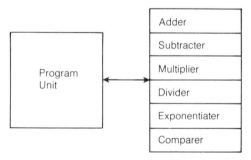

FIGURE 1–2. THE PROCESSOR

First, consider how few arithmetic operations this processor can actually carry out: we can only add, subtract, multiply, divide, and exponentiate two values with our computer. Even the cheapest calculators on the market can do more than that—most of them have at least a square root function, too! What gives the computer its power, then? *We do!* That is the subject of this book. We must learn to program the computer to do complex tasks based on the simple arithmetic and compare operations that the processor is able to carry out. When we need to do some new computation, for example, averaging a list of numbers, we must design and write a *routine* for doing this task based on the simple arithmetic operations available to us.

In other words, we cannot issue directives like "compute the payroll" or "play chess" to our computer because the processor is too simple for this. There is no circuit or unit that computes the payroll or figures out chess moves. Instead we must design and write programs based on the simple operations of addition, subtraction, multiplication, division, exponentiation, and comparison to do these more involved tasks. (Actually, few real computers even have an exponentiation unit. We equip our model computer with an exponentiation unit because most real programming languages have an exponentiation operator.)

We can design an unlimited number of new procedures to run on our computer. On the other hand, the number of functions that calculators can perform is limited by the number of keys they contain (this, of course, does not apply to programmable calculators, which are becoming more and more like computers). This is what makes computers so much more powerful than calculators. Our goal is to extend the power of the computer by designing and writing programs using the elementary operations available in the processor. This is the process of programming.

In order to understand how a computer is programmed, we must see how the arithmetic units in the processor function. The processor uses these five arithmetic units to evaluate *arithmetic expressions*. For example, the arithmetic expression $2 + 2$ is evaluated by the adder to produce 4. The + operator signals the processor to enter the values on either side of the + into the adder to produce the result. The other operators work similarly. Table 1–1 gives the list of operators that the processor recognizes and can process. The + and − symbols are familiar to us. The others may not be so familiar. The * is used to represent multiplication instead of the symbol ×, which could be confused with the letter x. The symbol for divide is /; this allows us to write expressions involving division on a single line, for example,

1/2   instead of $\frac{1}{2}$

The exponentiation symbol ↑ is used for the same reason: we can write 10^3 as 10 ↑ 3 on a single line.

TABLE 1–1. ARITHMETIC OPERATORS

+	Addition
−	Subtraction
*	Multiplication
/	Division
↑	Exponentiation

Example   Table 1–2 gives a series of simple arithmetic expressions and their values as computed
1.1   by the arithmetic units of the processor.

TABLE 1–2. ARITHMETIC EXPRESSIONS AND VALUES

Expression	Computed Value	Expression	Computed Value
3 + 5	8	−2 * 3	−6
5 − 3	2	−2 * −3	6
3 − 5	−2	4 / 2	2
2 * 13	26	4 ↑ 2	16
13 * 2	26	3.2 * 1.1	3.52
7 / 4	1.75	2 ↑ 2	4

These expressions are all evaluated as we would expect. Notice that the processor can distinguish whether the symbol − is used to mean "negative number" or "subtract." For example, the expression −2 * 3 in the above table evaluates to −6 (we read this expression as "multiply negative two times three").

Actually, the processor is able to process more complex arithmetic expressions such as

2 + 3 + 4

which is evaluated in the processor to produce 9. Since the adder can add only two numbers at a time, however, each + operator is handled separately: first the 2 is added to the 3 to get 5, and then this 5 is added to the 4 to get 9. The processor evaluates this more complicated expression from left to right. If we did not want the processor to handle the expression from left to right, we could use parentheses to cause the processor to evaluate the expression in a different order. We simply rewrite the expression as

2 + (3 + 4)

using parentheses to indicate which subexpression is to be evaluated first. In this case, the processor first adds the 3 and 4 to get 7 and then adds the 2 to this 7 to get 9.

The use of parentheses in the above example does not change the final result of the expression; in both cases the computed value is 9. (Some readers will remember that this occurs because addition satisfies the associative law.) Sometimes, however, parentheses will affect the value of an expression. Consider the arithmetic expression

2 + 3 * 4

If we rewrite this expression as

(2 + 3) * 4

then the processor will first use the adder on 2 and 3 to produce 5; this 5 and the 4 will then be processed by the multiplier to produce the value 20. On the other hand, if we rewrite the expression as

2 + (3 * 4)

the 3 and the 4 will first be multiplied to produce 12, and then the 2 and this 12 will be added to produce 14. In this case, the differing use of parentheses causes the processor to evaluate the expressions in different orders and gives different results.

What happens if we direct the processor to evaluate the expression

2 + 3 * 4

without parentheses? In this case the processor does not evaluate the expression from left to right; precedence is given to the multiplication operator over the addition operator, and the expression is evaluated as if it had been parenthesized as

2 + (3 * 4)

to yield the result 14.

The processor has *precedence rules* that it follows when evaluating arithmetic expressions. Expressions in parentheses are evaluated first. (If a parenthesized subexpression also contains parentheses, the subexpression surrounded by the innermost set of parentheses is evaluated first.) Exponentiation, the operation with the highest precedence, is performed next. Multiplication and division have the same precedence, just below exponentiation. Finally, addition and subtraction have the same precedence but are lower than that of multiplication or division. When there are two or more operators at the same parentheses level and with the same precedence, the leftmost of these operators is evaluated first. (That is, in case of ties, the processor evaluates expressions from left to right.) Table 1–3 shows the precedence rules used by the processor when evaluating arithmetic expressions. Examples will help us understand these rules.

TABLE 1-3. PRECEDENCE CHART FOR ARITHMETIC EXPRESSIONS

1.	(,)	expressions in parentheses are evaluated first; innermost parentheses have priority.
2.	↑	exponentiation is the arithmetic operation with highest precedence.
3.	*, /	multiplication and division have the same precedence.
4.	+, −	addition and subtraction have the same precedence.

The expression 3 + 2 − 1 is processed to yield the value 4. Since + and − have the same precedence level, the 3 and 2 are first added to get 5, then the 1 is subtracted to yield 4. This can be illustrated as

Example 1.2

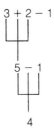

This graphical representation of the evaluation of an expression is called an *evaluation chart*; it is a particularly convenient way of describing the order of evaluation. We will use evaluation charts in subsequent examples, also.

Example
  1.3   The evaluation chart for (3 + 2) * 2 / 5 is

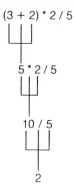

Example
  1.4   The evaluation chart for 2 * (3 + 7) / 2 is

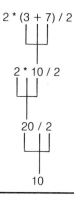

The only part of the processor that we have not yet discussed is the comparison unit, which allows us to compare values. We will discuss this unit after learning about the store.

THE STORE

We now turn our attention to the store. The store is conceptually a very simple device used for holding values as the processor executes a program. It consists of a series of *storage cells* as shown in figure 1–3. Each cell in the store

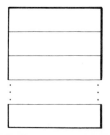

FIGURE 1–3. THE STORE

can hold a single value, such as 25, −57.3, 0, or 3.14159. In order to keep track of which storage cells contain which values, we are allowed to name individual cells. We can then refer to the contents of a particular cell by using the cell's name. Figure 1–4 illustrates the store when some of the cells have been given names and contain numeric values. In this figure the cell named *cat* has the value 45. Rather than saying "the cell named *cat* has the value 45" each time, we shorten this to "*cat* has the value 45" or, even more simply, "*cat* = 45." In this way the actual storage cell becomes transparent to us: we identify the cell and its contents with the cell name.

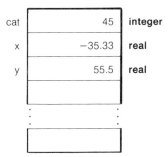

FIGURE 1–4. THE STORE WITH CELL NAMES AND VALUES

Notice also in figure 1–4 that some of the numeric values in the cells are whole numbers (numbers with no decimal point) and some are fractional numbers (numbers with a decimal point). In our model, as well as in the real computers we are modeling, these two types of numbers are handled differently, so we must be careful to distinguish between them. Formally, we refer to whole numbers as *integers* and to fractional numbers as *reals*. There is no category for fractions like ¼; all fractional numbers must be written in decimal form because the processor is not capable of handling fractions.

The Variables Instruction

While each memory cell can hold either integer or real values, the processor must know which type of value each storage cell currently contains so that arithmetic on these values can be done properly. One of our responsibilities as programmers is to supply both the names of storage cells we wish to use and the type of value we intend to store in each cell. We will do this in each procedure we write by using a **variables** instruction. For example, a typical declaration of the names and types of storage cells might be

```
variables
    cats: integer
    x, y : real
```

When the processor encounters this instruction, it will name the first three cells of the store *cats*, *x*, and *y*, respectively. The cell named *cats* can hold only integer values, whereas the cells named *x* and *y* are designated to hold only real values. After processing this **variables** instruction, the processor would set up the store to look like

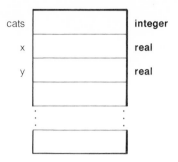

The **integer** and **real** designations after each storage cell indicate the type of value the cell can contain. The cell names *cats*, *x*, and *y* are called *variables*, because the storage cells they stand for can hold different values at different times; that is, the values associated with *cats*, *x*, and *y* can vary throughout the course of the program, as we shall see in later examples.

This example illustrates a few points we should note about the use of the **variables** instruction:

• *cats*, *x*, and *y* have no values. The **variables** declaration does *not* put values into the memory cells; it only names them and sets up the types of values that the cells can contain. We will soon learn about using assignment statements to assign values to these cells.

• The choices for variable names are arbitrary, but it is helpful to choose names that reflect the meanings of the values we wish to store.

• Although this particular use of the **variables** instruction causes *cats* to be assigned the first cell, *x* the second cell, and *y* the third cell, we really don't care which cells are assigned which names. All we care about is that the processor knows which cell has which name, so that we can refer to the cells by name.

• In each routine we write, we will need to use a **variables** instruction to establish the names and types of all the storage cells we plan to use. When a routine is executed by the processor, storage cells are established with the names given in the **variables** instruction. When execution is complete, the names, types, and values of the storage cells declared in that routine "disappear." The cells are then free to receive new names, types, and values when a new routine is executed.

The Assignment Statement

To assign values to the storage cells established in a **variables** instruction, we can use an *assignment statement*. For example, the assignment statement

cats ← 20

assigns the value 20 to the storage cell *cats*. Similarly, the statement

y ← 3.14159

puts the value 3.14159 into the cell named *y*. In executing an assignment statement, the processor takes the value on the right of the ← symbol and stores it into the cell whose name is given on the left side of the ← symbol. After the two assignment statements shown above are executed, the store looks like

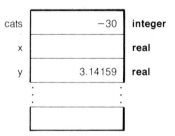

Notice that x still has no assigned value; we say that x is *undefined*. (Immediately after a **variables** instruction is executed, all of the newly named cells have undefined values, since, as we pointed out earlier, the **variables** instruction assigns only names, not values, to the cells.)

The assignment statement allows great flexibility. We can give the storage cells values that we will use in subsequent calculations. Later we can easily change the value in a cell by simply issuing another assignment statement. For example, if the store appears as last shown and we issue the statement

> cats ← −30

the store would now appear as

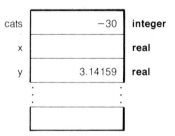

A natural question to ask about the use of assignment statements is What happens if we assign a real value to an integer cell? or What happens if we assign an integer value to a real cell? In the first case, when our model processor handles an assignment statement such as

> cats ← 12.721

it recognizes that the variable *cats* can contain only integer values, so it *truncates* the value 12.721 to 12 and stores 12 into the cell named *cats*. In other words, if a real value is to be stored into an integer cell, the processor takes only the whole number portion of the value and discards the fractional part. It does *not* round the value. If an integer value is to be assigned to a real cell, the processor simply adds a decimal point to the end of the integer before storing it into the real cell. For example,

> x ← 25

would result in 25.0 being stored into x. Thus, execution of the two assignment statements

> cats ← 12.721
> x ← 25

would result in the store

cats	12	**integer**
x	25.0	**real**
y	3.14159	**real**

Although we can change the values stored in the cells, we cannot change the cell types nor can we rename the cells once we have set them up with a **variables** instruction.

The assignment statement is actually more flexible than we have so far described. We are allowed to write statements of the form

variable ← *arithmetic expression*

where on the left of the ← symbol we have a variable that has been previously declared in a **variables** instruction and on the right of the ← symbol we have any arithmetic expression. For example, having declared x to be a real variable, we can issue the instruction

x ← (3.0 + 5.0 + 7.0)/2.0

The processor first evaluates the expression

(3.0 + 5.0 + 7.0)/2.0

to get 7.5, and then the 7.5 is stored into x. The evaluation chart for this assignment statement looks like

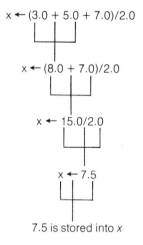

7.5 is stored into x

If the store contained the values last shown, then it would contain the following values after execution of the above assignment statement:

cats	12	**integer**
x	7.5	**real**
y	3.14159	**real**
⋮	⋮	

If the expression on the right side of the assignment statement evaluates to a real number, but the variable on the left side has type **integer,** then, as usual, the real number is truncated before it is stored into the variable. Similarly, if the result of the arithmetic expression is an integer and it is to be stored into a real variable, a decimal point is added to the integer number.

A related question that comes to mind is What happens if we mix integer and real values in an arithmetic expression to the right of ←? An example of this might be

$$x \leftarrow 7 / 4 * 3.2$$

In the model computer and the model programming language we are developing, we will assume that every operation results in the most accurate possible answer. Thus, the evaluation tree for this expression is

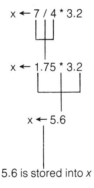

$$x \leftarrow 7 / 4 * 3.2$$

$$x \leftarrow 1.75 * 3.2$$

$$x \leftarrow 5.6$$

5.6 is stored into *x*

As a result of this assignment statement, the store would now look like

cats	12	**integer**
x	5.6	**real**
y	3.14159	**real**
⋮	⋮	

This is, however, one point of difference among real programming languages. In some languages, the result of dividing two integers is the truncated quotient—in our example, 7/4 would result in 1 instead of 1.75. You must be very careful to determine exactly how such expressions are handled in any programming language you use. If you are not sure, the best policy is to not mix integer and real values in an arithmetic expression.

Arithmetic expressions may also include cell names (variables). For example, if the store is as last shown and the processor executes the statement

y ← x * 3

then 16.8 will be stored into y. The processor first substitutes the current value of x for the x appearing in the arithmetic expression and then does the arithmetic. The evaluation chart for this assignment statement is

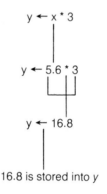

The store now looks like

cats	12	**integer**
x	5.6	**real**
y	16.8	**real**

Since the expression on the right of the ← is evaluated before the result is stored into the variable on the left, we can also write assignment statements like

cats ← cats + 1

Here the variable *cats* appears on both sides of the assignment arrow. We read this as "Take the current value in *cats*, add 1 to it, and place the result into *cats*." The evaluation chart of this assignment statement would be

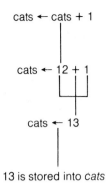

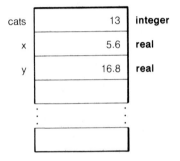

13 is stored into *cats*

The store now appears as

cats	13	**integer**
x	5.6	**real**
y	16.8	**real**

We will often use this type of assignment statement for counting. If for some reason we are using a program to count the number of cats, we can do this by first setting *cats* to zero with the statement.

cats ← 0

and then issuing the command

cats ← cats + 1

whenever our program is to count one more cat. At the end of the program, the variable *cats* will contain the number of cats we have counted.

More examples of the use of the assignment statement follow.

With the **variables** statement

Example 1.5

    variables
       average: **real**
       score1, score2, score3, score4 : **integer**

and the assignment statements

    score1 ← 75
    score2 ← 100
    score3 ← 88
    score4 ← 95

we cause the store to look like

average		**real**
score1	75	**integer**
score2	100	**integer**
score3	88	**integer**
score4	95	**integer**

score1, score2, score3, and *score4* all have values as a result of the assignment statements, but *average* is still undefined. If we now wish to assign the average of the four scores to the variable *average,* we can do this with the statement

average ← (score1 + score2 + score3 + score4) / 4

The evaluation chart for this assignment statement is

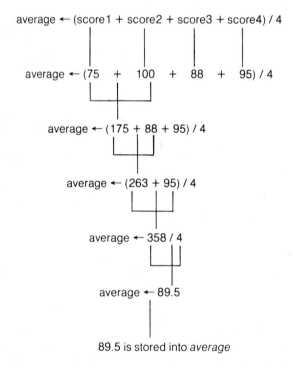

89.5 is stored into *average*

After the processor has executed this assignment statement, the store looks like

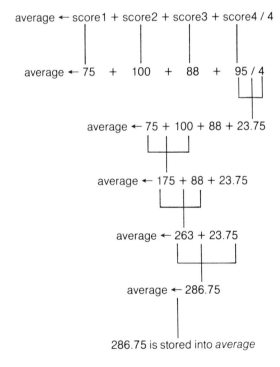

average	89.5	**real**
score1	75	**integer**
score2	100	**integer**
score3	88	**integer**
score4	95	**integer**

Just to refresh our memory, let's see what would have happened if we had issued the assignment statement

average ← score1 + score2 + score3 + score4 / 4

instead of the one above. (Notice that we have eliminated the parentheses from the arithmetic expression to the right of the ←.) From the hierarchy of arithmetic operators (see table 1–3) we can see that the evaluation chart for this assignment statement would be

average ← score1 + score2 + score3 + score4 / 4

average ← 75 + 100 + 88 + 95 / 4

average ← 75 + 100 + 88 + 23.75

average ← 175 + 88 + 23.75

average ← 263 + 23.75

average ← 286.75

286.75 is stored into *average*

Here we have not computed the average at all. When writing an arithmetic expression we must be careful to specify exactly what we mean, using parentheses when necessary. The processor is not "smart." It only does what we instruct it to do and cannot second-guess us.

Also notice our choice of variable names, which indicates that we want to calculate the average of four scores. But these names have absolutely no meaning to the processor: it does not know or care what value we place in the variable named *average*. It would compute the same value from the following statements:

variables
    aardvarks: **real**
    cornflakes, x, r2d2, c3po : **integer**

cornflakes ← 75
x ← 100
r2d2 ← 88
c3po ← 95
aardvarks ← (cornflakes + x + r2d2 + c3po) / 4

However, we humans have no clue as to what is to be computed just from reading these statements. If we were the ones who wrote these statements, within a few weeks even we would forget what we meant! This underscores an important principle of programming: *When picking variable names, choose names that indicate the values being represented.*

Example 1.6

With the statements

variables
    area, radius : **real**

radius ← 23.2

we set up the store to look like

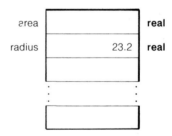

If we now issue the statement

area ← 3.14 * radius ↑ 2

the store will look like

area	1690.0736	**real**
radius	23.2	**real**

Since exponentiation has a higher priority than multiplication, the evaluation chart for this assignment statement is

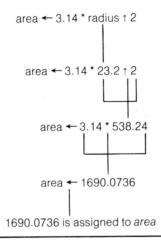

area ← 3.14 * radius ↑ 2

area ← 3.14 * 23.2 ↑ 2

area ← 3.14 * 538.24

area ← 1690.0736

1690.0736 is assigned to *area*

To summarize, the store is just a series of cells for storing (remembering) values needed for calculations within the processor. The cells are named with the **variables** statement; the values in the cells are then referred to by the cell names. Assignment statements can be used to assign values to the cells. We usually refer to storage cells as variables, because we can change the cell values whenever we wish.

THE PROCESSOR — COMPARISON UNIT

We now understand better how the computer performs arithmetic. The processor is capable of evaluating arithmetic expressions by using the five arithmetic units it contains: the adder, subtracter, multiplier, divider, and exponentiater. Computed values are assigned to cells of the store as the processor executes assignment statements. We might think that this is all that is necessary to provide the computer with its potentially great power: we as programmers could provide various combinations of assignment statements to compute nearly anything we wished—areas of rectangles, average scores and grades for students, and so forth. This, however, is not true. The computer would be almost powerless without the comparison unit (see figure 1-2 on page 4).

In all nontrivial programs, comparisons must be made. Examples are easy to think of. We must decide whether a student's average score is greater than some value in order to decide whether to pass the student; to determine the proper withholding tax, we must decide what income bracket a computed salary lies in; when searching for a particular entry in a file, we must decide whether we have found it. Each of these computations requires comparing values. This is done in the comparison unit of the processor, which operates in a way similar to the way the arithmetic units operate.

Recall our previous example where the average of four scores was computed with the assignment statement

Example 1.7

average ← (score1 + score2 + score3 + score4) / 4

Afterwards the store looked like

average	89.5	**real**
score1	75	**integer**
score2	100	**integer**
score3	88	**integer**
score4	95	**integer**

Now we would like to determine whether the computed average is a passing score. If we have previously decided that 65.0 or above is passing, then we can have the processor decide whether *average* is greater than or equal to 65.0 by having it evaluate the expession

　　average $\geqslant$ 65.0

We can think of the processor working this way: the value in *average,* the value 65.0, and the greater than or equal to symbol ($\geqslant$) are each supplied to the camparison unit. The comparison unit then determines whether average is greater than or equal to 65.0. The evaluation chart for this expression is

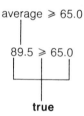

The comparison unit in this case returns the value **true** because 89.5 is indeed greater than or equal to 65.0.

　　If the value in average were 57.3 instead of 89.5, the evaluation chart for

　　average $\geqslant$ 65.0

would be

average $\geqslant$ 65.0
|
57.3 $\geqslant$ 65.0

false

In this case the comparison unit would return the value **false** because 57.3 is *not* greater than or equal to 65.0.

　　The symbol $\geqslant$ in the above example is called a *relational operator,* and the relation average ⩾ 65.0

is called a *conditional expression*. Simple conditional expressions have the form

> *value1* **relational operator** *value2*

where *value1* and *value2* are either variables or constants. Evaluation of conditional expressions by the comparison unit results in either **true** or **false** in every instance, because *value1* either stands in the expressed relation to *value2* (**true**) or it does not (**false**).

The relational operators that can be processed by the comparison unit are given in table 1–4. We can compare two values to see if the first value is less than, less than or equal to, equal to, not equal to, greater than, or greater than or equal to the second value.

TABLE 1–4. RELATIONAL OPERATORS

<	Less Than
⩽	Less Than or Equal To
=	Equal To
≠	Not Equal To
>	Greater Than
⩾	Greater Than or Equal To

Assume that the store contains the following values:

Example 1.8

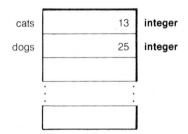

Then the expression

> cats = 13

has the evaluation chart

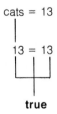

The expression

> 100 < dogs

has the evaluation chart

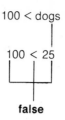

100 < dogs

100 < 25

false

The expression

dogs ≠ cats

has the evaluation chart

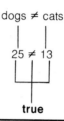

dogs ≠ cats

25 ≠ 13

true

Expressions evaluated by the comparison unit are called conditional expressions, because evaluation of these expressions yeilds either **true** or **false**, depending on the conditions (values) of the variables and constants in the expressions.

Conditional expressions can contain more than one relational operator.

Example 1.9   Assume again that the store looks like

average	89.5	**real**
score1	75	**integer**
score2	100	**integer**
score3	88	**integer**
score4	95	**integer**

If we wish to assign a letter grade to the average we have computed instead of just deciding whether it is a passing score (see example 1.7), the situation is somewhat more complex. For example, assume that the letter grade B is to be awarded if the average is at least 85.0 but not 92.0 or larger. In other words, we wish to test the condition that 85.0 is less than or equal to *average* and *average* is less than 92.0. This would be written mathematically as

$$85.0 \leq average < 92.0$$

However, this expression cannot be evaluated by the comparison unit, which can only handle two values at a time. If we tried to write the evaluation chart for this expression to see how the comparison unit would attempt to process it we would get

$$85.0 \leqslant \text{average} < 92.0$$
$$|$$
$$85.0 \leqslant 89.5 < 92.0$$

$$\textbf{true} < 92.0$$

$$???$$

Since the comparison unit can handle only two values at a time, it evaluates the first two to begin with. This results in the expression

true < 92.0

which makes no sense at all: **true** has absolutely no relationship to 92.0.

To write these more involved conditional expressions, then, we need a different method. Remember how we stated this expression in words: "85.0 is less than or equal to *average* and *average* is less than 92.0." This statement has two parts, which we can separate as

85.0 is less than or equal to *average*

> **and**

average is less than 92.0

In this case **and** is called a *logical operator,* because (logically) if the first expression is true *and* the second expression is true, then the entire compound expression is true. That is, in order for *average* to lie between 85.0 and 92.0, both expressions must be true. However, if either expression (or both) is false, then (logically) the entire expression is false. We can rewrite the above expression as

(85.0 $\leqslant$ average) **and** (average $<$ 92.0)

in terms of our relational operators. This expression can now be evaluated by the comparison unit as

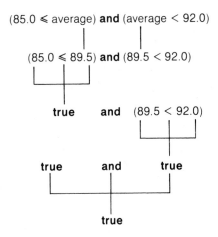

Notice that when the **and** is finally evaluated (recall that expressions in parentheses are evaluated first) the comparison unit no longer "remembers" what the two expressions were, but it has computed the fact that both expressions were true. Since the first expression is true *and* the second expression is true it follows (regardless of what those two expressions were) that the entire compound expression is true. The result computed by the comparison unit for

true and true

is thus **true.**

What if the value of *average* were 96.3 instead of 89.5? Then the evaluation chart would be

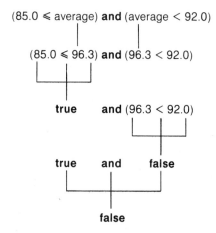

Whenever at least one of the values on either side of the **and** is false, then the entire compound expression is false, regardless of what the original expressions were.

This example shows how compound conditional expressions can be constructed using the logical operator **and:** two conditional expressions joined by **and** will be evaluated by the processor to the value **true** if—and only if—both of the conditional expressions first evaluate to **true.** If either or both of the conditional expressions evaluate to **false,** then the entire expression is **false.** We can show this symbolically using evaluation charts. If we let *exp1* and *exp2* be any valid conditional expressions, then we have:

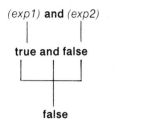

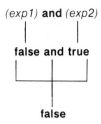

These four charts represent all possible situations in which the logical operator **and** may appear.

Another logical operator that can be processed by the comparison unit is **or.** Often we will not need to know whether both of two conditional expressions are true but only whether one **or** the other is true (or both).

Suppose that a program is being designed to process patients' records for a doctor so that a notice can be sent to parents of 5- and 10-year-olds when it is time for their children to receive immunization shots. As each child's record is processed, we must ask the question Is this child's age 5 or 10? If it is either 5 or 10, then the immunization notice must be sent. In terms of conditional expressions we would write this as

Example 1.10

  (age = 5) **or** (age = 10)

where the variable *age* was previously declared in a **variables** statement as

  variables
    age : **integer**

If the value of *age* is 10 (i.e., the child whose record is being processed is 10 years old), then the evaluation chart for this expression is

$$\begin{array}{c}
(age = 5)\ \textbf{or}\ (age = 10)\\
(10 = 5)\ \textbf{or}\ (10 = 10)\\
\textbf{false}\quad \textbf{or}\quad (10 = 10)\\
\textbf{false}\quad \textbf{or}\quad \textbf{true}\\
\textbf{true}
\end{array}$$

The comparison unit evaluates this compound conditional expression to **true** because at least one of the simple conditional expressions on either side of the **or** is true.

What if *age* is 7? In this case the evaluation chart would be

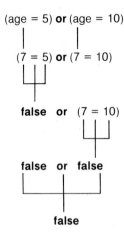

Here, the entire expression evaluates to **false** because neither the first simple conditional expression nor the second is true.

As in the case of the logical operator **and, or** is evaluated after the conditional expressions on both sides of the **or** have been evaluated. Regardless of what these conditional expressions are, if at least one of them evaluates to **true,** then the entire expression evaluates to **true.** If both evaluate to **false,** then (regardless of what those expressions are) the entire expression evaluates to **false.**

There are four situations that can arise whenever the logical operator **or** is applied to two conditional expressions. If the expressions on both sides of the **or** evaluate to **true,** then the entire expression connected by the **or** would be true (this could happen, for example, if we are checking whether a number is even **or** greater than zero; clearly a number could satisfy both of these conditions). If the expressions on both sides of the **or** evaluate to **false,** the entire expression connected by the **or** should be false. Finally, there are two situations in which the expression on one side (left or right) of the **or** evaluates to **true** but the expression on the other side (right or left) evaluates to **false;** in these cases the entire expression connected by the **or** is true. This can be shown by evaluation charts:

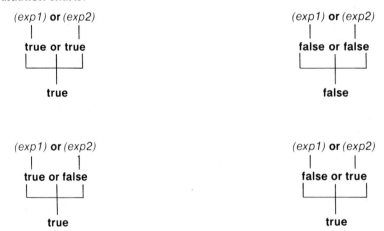

A final logical operator that is sometimes needed is **not.**

Example 1.11

Using the setting of the previous example, suppose that for some reason letters are to be sent to all patients who are *not* 5 or 10 years old. Then for each patient we could have the processor evaluate the expression

not ((age = 5) **or** (age = 10))

The **not** is placed *in front of* the expression to be negated. If the age of a patient is 7, the evaluation chart for this expression would be

not ((age = 5) **or** (age = 10))

not ((7 = 5) **or** (7 = 10))

not(**false   or**   (7 = 10))

not(**false   or   false**)

not   false

true

In other words, it is true that 7 is not 5 or 10, so this entire expression evaluates to **true**.

As shown in this example, the **not** logical operator negates the computed value of a conditional expression. **not true** is (logically) **false,** whereas **not false** is (logically) **true.** The evaluation charts for **not** are quite simple and are shown below, where *exp* is any conditional expression:

not (*exp*)

not true

false

not (*exp*)

not false

true

The previous example also shows us that it is possible to write arbitrarily long and involved conditional expressions using parentheses as well as the **and, or,** and **not** logical operators. Such complex conditional expressions are rarely needed, however.

Arithmetic expressions can also be compared.

Example   If the store looks like
1.12

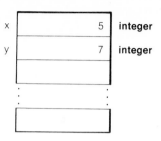

we can write the expression

x * y + 2 < 31 + x

which will be properly evaluated by the processor. Notice that before

x * y + 2

and

31 + x

can be compared, their values must be computed. In our model computer we will assume that the processor gives precedence to arithmetic operators over relational and logical operators. Then the evaluation chart for this expression is

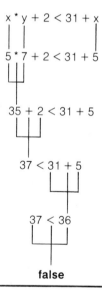

We can now give the complete precedence chart used by our model processor in evaluating all expressions (see table 1–5). The actual operator precedence charts for real programming languages vary widely, especially for the **and, or,** and **not** logical operators. We have chosen this particular precedence scheme for our model programming language, because expressions written under these precedence constraints will be properly evaluated in most real programming languages. Nonetheless, it is important that you become well acquainted with the operator precedence chart of each real programming language you use.

TABLE 1-5. COMPLETE OPERATOR PRECEDENCE CHART FOR *MPL*

1.	(,)	expressions in parentheses are evaluated first; innermost parentheses take priority.
2.	↑	exponentiation is the operator with the highest precedence.
3.	*, /	multiplication and division have the same precedence level.
4.	+, −	addition and subtraction are the arithmetic operators with the lowest precedence.
5.	<, ≤, > ≥, =, ≠ **and, or, not**	relational operators and logical operators have the same precedence; they are the last operators to be executed in an expression.

In the examples and discussions so far we have learned that the processor can handle conditional expressions by using the comparison unit. We also mentioned at the beginning of this section that comparisons are an essential part of programming. How do we use conditional expressions to perform comparisons in programs? Actually, we will use them in many ways. In chapter 3, for example, we will learn to write statements like

if (age = 5) **or** (age = 10)
    then {statements to be executed if the condition is true go here}
    endif

This **if** statement is quite easy to understand. When the processor sees the **if** statement it first has the comparison unit evaluate the conditional expression

    (age = 5) **or** (age = 10)

If this expression evaluates to **true,** the processor will execute the statements following the **then.** Otherwise, if the expression evaluates to **false,** the processor will skip all of the statements in the group following the **then.** The **if** statement is just one of a number of statements we will learn for controlling the execution of our programs. In essence it means, "If the stated condition is true, then do these statements, otherwise skip them." It gives us a way of directing the processor to selectively execute certain statements based on the current values of program variables.

We can also use an assignment statement to assign the value of a conditional expression to a variable. However, since the value of a conditional expression is either **true** or **false,** we cannot use variables of type **integer** or **real** to hold these values. We need a new variable type that we will call **truth value.** Variables of type **truth value** can hold just two different values: **true** or **false.**

Suppose that the store now looks like

*Example
1.13*

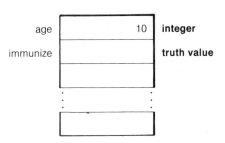

We assume that we have already done some processing that assigned the value 10 to *age*. The variable *immunize* is still undefined. Both *age* and *immunize* were declared in the statement

variables
 age : **integer**
 immunize : **truth value**

Given the value of *age* in the store, if the processor now executes the assignment statement

immunize ← (age = 5) **or** (age = 10)

immunize will be assigned the value **true** and the store will now look like

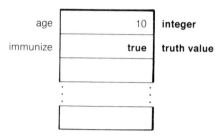

The evaluation chart for this assignment statement is

immunize ← (age = 5) **or** (age = 10)

immunize ← (10 = 5) **or** (10 = 10)

immunize ← **false or** (10 = 10)

immunize ← **false or true**

immunize ← **true**

true is stored into *immunize*

THE INPUT AND OUTPUT DEVICES

Look again at the diagram of our model computer (figure 1–1). The last components to be discussed are the input and output devices. These devices provide the processor with links to the outside world. Values can be read from the input device and placed into storage cells by the processor for use in later calculations. Also, values currently in storage cells, such as the results of calculations performed in the processor, can be printed at the output device. The operation that the processor performs when reading a value from the input device and placing it into the store is called an *input operation.* Printing the value of a storage cell at the output device is called an *output operation.*

The Input Device

An input statement directs the processor to read a value from the input device and place it into a storage location.

Assume that the processor has processed the statement

variables
    area, length, width : **real**

causing the store to look like

Example 1.14

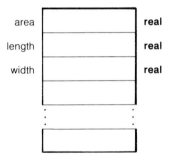

Then upon encountering the statement

input length, width

the processor will read two values from the input device. The first value will be assigned to the variable *length,* and the second value will be assigned to the variable *width.* So if

5.3   6.72

are the values at the input device when the **input** statement is executed by the processor, the store will become

```
area   ┌─────────┐ real
       │         │
length ├─────5.3─┤ real
       │         │
width  ├────6.72─┤ real
       │         │
       ├─────────┤
       │   :   : │
       │   :   : │
       └─────────┘
```

If the processor then executes the statement

area ← length * width

the variable *area* would take on the value 35.616 and the store would look like

area	35.616	**real**
length	5.3	**real**
width	6.72	**real**
	⋮	

At this point you may be somewhat puzzled about the use of the **input** statement. If its only purpose is to assign values to storage cells, how is it different from the assignment statement? The difference is crucial—the **input** statement is what makes our programs *general*. For example, if we wrote a program that calculated the area of a rectangle using the statements

```
length ← 3.0
width ← 2.5
area ← length * width
```

we would have to change the program every time we wished to compute the area of a different rectangle. That is, we would have to replace the statements

```
length ← 3.0
width ← 2.5
```

with different ones, for example,

```
length ← 7.2
width ← 7.1
```

There are many reasons why changing the program like this is undesirable: it takes time, it is a source of human error, and, most important, there is a better way.

Consider our first example in this section, where we used the statements

```
input length, width
area ← length * width
```

To calculate the area of the rectangle with length 3.0 and width 2.5 we would only need to supply the values 3.0 and 2.5 at the input device as the processor executes the program. If we later wished to calculate the area of the rectangle with length 7.2 and width 7.1, we could have the processor execute the same program, but this time we would supply the values 7.2 and 7.1 at the input device. In other words, the **input** statement allows us to apply our program to different sets of data *without making any modifications to the program*. This is what makes a program general.

Except for the generality added by the **input** statement, it acts just like the assignment statement. If a value is placed into a variable by an **input** statement, it remains there until an assignment statement or another **input** statement changes that value.

Assume that the store has been organized by the statement

Example
1.15

> **variables**
>> dogs, pumpkins : **integer**

to look like

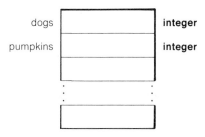

Then the statement

> **input** pumpkins, dogs

would cause the processor to pick up two values supplied at the input device and place them into *pumpkins* and *dogs,* respectively. If the two values at the input device were

>> 5   25

then after execution of the **input** statement the store would look like

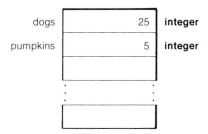

Afterwards, execution of the statement

> dogs ← dogs − pumpkins

would change the store to look like

dogs   20   **integer**
pumpkins   5   **integer**

Subsequent execution of the statement

> **input** pumpkins

would cause the processor to pick up the next value supplied at the input device and place it into *pumpkins*. If this value were 13, then the store would become

dogs	20	**integer**
pumpkins	13	**integer**
	⋮	

In summary, the **input** statement has the form

input *variable1, variable2, . . ., variableN*

where *variable1, variable2, . . ., variableN* must be variable names that have been previously declared in a **variables** statement. Upon encountering such an **input** statement, the processor retrieves the first value it can find at the input device and places it into *variable1*, the second value is placed into *variable2*, and so on. It is the responsibility of the programmer to ensure that there are enough values at the input device and that these values match the type (e.g., **integer** or **real**) of the variables into which they are to be read.

The Output Device

The **output** statement directs the processor to print messages and the values of certain variables at the output device. In real-world situations, this is our only means of viewing the results of the calculations performed in our programs. In this book we pretend that we can see variable values by drawing a diagram of the store and listing the contents of each storage cell. Of course, this is not possible when dealing with real computers. It is also not desirable. What we really want is to have just those values that interest us displayed at a screen or printed on paper. The **output** statement allows us to do this.

Example 1.16   Assume that the store currently looks like

length	3.0	**real**
width	2.5	**real**
area	7.5	**real**
	⋮	

If we wish the processor to print the value of *area* we use the statement

output area

The processor will then print the value currently in the cell named *area* at the output device. That is,

7.5

will appear on the output device. If we wished to see the values of *length, width,* and *area* all together, we could write

output length, width, area

This would result in

3.0 2.5 7.5

being printed at the output device.

Thus we see how the **output** statement is used to print variable values at the output device. The form of the **output** statement is

output *variable1, variable2, . . ., variableN*

The results printed on the output device as a result of executing an **output** statement of this form are

value1 value2. . .valueN

where *value1* is the value of *variable1, value2* is the value of *variable2,* and so on.

One problem remains in our use of the **output** statement. Since just the variable values are printed, we have no way of correlating the values with what they stand for. The output

3.0 2.5 7.5

gives no clue to what these values mean. But, you might think, if we know that these values were printed by

output length, width, area

then we know that 3.0 is the length, 2.5 is the width, and 7.5 is the area. This is true, but it requires us to look back in our program to find the statement that printed these values, and this may not be a simple task if there are other **output** statements in the program.

Fortunately, there is a better way to print our results—we are allowed to print messages as well as variable values.

If the store looks like

Example 1.17

length	3.0	**real**
width	2.5	**real**
area	7.5	**real**
⋮	⋮	

then the statement

>   **output** 'length ', length, ' times width ', width, ' = ', area

when executed by the processor will cause

>   length 3.0 times width 2.5 = 7.5

to be printed on the output device. The messages in the single quotation marks are printed just as they appear. Names not in quotes are assumed to be variables and their *values* are printed.

The **output** statement thus has the more general form

>   **output** *item1, item2, . . ., itemN*

where each item is either a message (any combination of characters) in single quotes or the name of a variable. Each message is printed literally, character by character. When a variable appears in the **output** statement, the *value* (not the name) of the variable is printed.

At this point we should clarify two common misconceptions about the **output** statement. One concerns the use of messages to label variable values. Some beginning students believe that the computer can correlate the labels and the values. For example, the statement

>   **output** 'length ', length, ' times width ', width, ' = ', area

was used in the previous example to demonstrate the use of message labels. We might think that somehow the computer knows that a word in quotes (e.g., 'length') corresponds to the variable length of the same name (e.g., length). This is not so. The processor simply causes each item in the output list to be printed in order regardless of what it is. This statement produced the output

>   length 3.0 times width 2.5 = 7.5

as we saw earlier. On the other hand, the statement

>   **output** 'width ', length, ' times length ', area, ' = ', width

would cause

>   width 3.0 times length 7.5 = 2.5

to be printed, and

>   **output** 'width ', area, ' times length ', width, ' = ', length

would cause

>   width 7.5 times length 2.5 = 3.0

to appear at the output device. Of course, these last two printed messages make no sense to us, but the processor executes these **output** instructions without any problem—it prints the first item in the output list, then the second item, then the third, and so on, just as it was instructed. Again we must stress this point: we as programmers are responsible for supplying meaningful and proper instructions to the processor.

A second misconception concerns the contents of the store after an output statement has been executed. Remember this: the **output** statement does not

erase the variable values in the store when it prints them, it only prints a copy
of each value. If the store looked like

length	3.0	**real**
width	2.5	**real**
area	7.5	**real**

and the processor executed the statement

> **output** 'length ', length, ' times width ', width, ' = ', area

and printed

> length 3.0 times width 2.5 = 7.5

at the output device, the store would be unchanged:

length	3.0	**real**
width	2.5	**real**
area	7.5	**real**

To summarize, the input and output devices provide us with our only link
to the internal values of the store and the results computed by our programs.
We can supply values at the input device to be read directly into the store
when the processor executes an **input** statement. This gives our programs
generality, because we can use the same programs with different input data.
The **output** statement is used to print the results of our computations at the
output device.

So far we have described only the functional characteristics of our model
input and output devices—their use in inputting new data values and outputting results. We have purposely neglected the physical properties of such devices, since there are many different kinds available in actual computing environments. From our model you should form ideas about what real input and
output devices *do*, not what they *are*. In many cases the input devices and the
output devices for a particular computer are completely different and separate
from each other. In other instances the input device and the output device may
be the same unit, such as a video terminal screen. Regardless of their physical
properties, however, the purpose of such devices is to input data and output

results. Our model input and output devices abstract these properties and are sufficient for our needs.

SUMMARY OF THE MODEL COMPUTER

In this section we have described our model computer. Its central component is a processor that carries out simple instructions that we as programmers must supply. The processor can evaluate arithmetic expressions involving only addition, subtraction, multiplication, division, and exponentiation. It can also compare two values. The results of these computations can be saved in the store through the use of assignment statements.

Even though our model computer may appear quite primitive and limited, it is an accurate representation of all common computers, the kind called *digital computers*. From small personal computers costing a few hundred dollars to multimillion dollar supercomputers, there are no differences in their basic structures. This is why our model computer will be sufficient for us to use as a basis for understanding programming.

1.3 THE PROGRAMMING PROCESS

The purpose of presenting the model computer in the previous section was to make it clear just how simple computers really are in terms of the operations they can perform. Because the operations of a computer are so simple, programs telling the computer what to do must be written using simple instructions. We have seen a few of these instructions already: the **variables** statement instructs the processor to name certain storage cells for later use; the assignment statement instructs the processor to perform elementary arithmetic and comparison operations; the **input** statement directs the processor to read values from an input device into storage cells; and the **output** statement directs the processor to print messages and variable values at an output device for humans to read. Every procedural programming language has instructions equivalent to these. Programming is the process of designing sequences of such instructions to cause the processor to carry out desired tasks.

PROGRAMS

Given the limited expressive power of the simple instructions we have learned, it will come as no surprise to learn that programs to do substantial tasks, such as computing the payroll for a large organization or playing chess, take a good deal of effort to design. In fact, if large programs had to be written as one long sequence of simple assignment, **input,** and **output** statements, the programming process would be unmanageable. Instead, modern programming languages allow the programmer to group instructions for smaller subtasks of the program into logical units, or routines, called *functions* and *procedures*. Each function and procedure can be designed separately, then they can all be gathered into a large single program.

For example, a program to compute statistics for test results might consist of one procedure to input the list of student names and scores, a function to compute the class average, another function to compute the standard deviation, a different procedure to sort the names and scores into numeric order by test score, and one last procedure to print the ordered list of students and scores as well as the average and standard deviation. Each of these procedures and functions represents a separate, relatively small portion of the original program and can be designed with comparative ease. To mesh these procedures and functions together into a program, an *initial procedure* is written; the initial procedure calls on each of the other procedures and functions in succession to produce the desired test statistics. It is called the initial procedure because it is the procedure that the processor will begin executing first, before all the other procedures and functions in the program. The initial procedure organizes the program by ensuring that each of the other procedures and functions of the program is executed in proper order.

FUNCTIONS AND PROCEDURES

Functions and procedures are the building blocks of programs. What is the difference between them? Essentially, it is this: functions extend the *operation set* of our programming language, whereas procedures extend the *statement set* of our programming language.

Functions

To understand the nature of a function better, let's consider one of the arithmetic functions (usually called an arithmetic operator) provided directly in our programming language. Addition is a function that takes two values and computes their sum. If we write

$3 + 8$

the result 11 is computed. That is, as a function, addition has the form

$\_ + \_$

where we can choose any two values to fill in the blanks. Pictorially, this looks like

The values of x and y supplied to the addition function are called the *arguments* or *parameters* of addition. For any two values we supply for x and y, the sum will be computed.

We would like to have functions available that are more sophisticated than the primitive arithmetic operators supplied in our programming language. For example, a function *sum* to accept an arbitrarily long list of integers and compute their sum would be useful in adding test scores in preparation for calculating the average, in summing deposits and withdrawals to determine the balance of a bank account, and in many other situations.

A simpler example would be a function that computes the average of four integers. If we called this function *average4* we would want it to work like the function +, i.e., we would want to be able to supply any four values to *average4* and have this function compute the average of these four values. Pictorially, this looks like

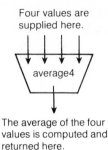

Four values are
supplied here.

average4

The average of the four
values is computed and
returned here.

We could use our new function *average4* in a statement like

ave ← average4(4, 15, 7, 12)

which would compute the average of the four numbers 4, 15, 7, and 12 and place the result into variable *ave*, or we could use it in

input a, b, c, d
ave ← average4(a, b, c, d)

which would compute and store into variable *ave* the average of the four values input for *a*, *b*, *c*, and *d*. Similarly, if we had four quiz scores lying between 0 and 10 and we wished to compute their average as a percentage, the statements

input score1, score2, score3, score4
percentage ← average4(score1, score2, score3, score4) * 10

would do this for us. In other words, each new function we design can be used in any place that an arithmetic expression involving the function + could be used (for example, in larger arithmetic expressions occurring within assignment statements, in **output** statements, or in conditional expressions).

Of course, we cannot escape the fact that all computations, regardless of how complex they are, must eventually be expressed in terms of the simple operations supplied in the processor. This means that the design of function *average4* would need to include a statement like

average4 ← (u + v + w + x)/4

which uses the common operators (functions) + and / to compute the average of any four values supplied to *u*, *v*, *w*, and *x* and assigns the result to the name of the function (*average4*).

Procedures

Procedures are different than functions in that procedures are intended to extend the set of statements, rather than the set of operations, available in our language. For example, we may wish to have a statement that would sort an arbitrary list of names into alphabetical order (this would be useful in many applications). Unfortunately, such statements do not exist in programming languages, because there is no internal circuit for sorting in the computer. Instead, we must design a procedure to do the sorting using the simple instructions that are already available. Once the sorting procedure has been designed, however, it can be used in different programs.

A simpler example that is related to the sorting problem is a procedure to swap two values: if variable *a* contains 5 and variable *b* contains 10 and we include the new statement

swap(a, b)

in our program, then upon completion of that statement the value in *a* should be 10 and the value in *b* 5. However, since there is no such statement in our programming language (because the processor contains no circuits to swap two values), we need to design procedure *swap* ourselves based on the simple instructions that are available. That is, inside procedure *swap* there would have to be statements like

temp ← x
x ← y
y ← temp

so that for any two values supplied for *x* and *y*, *x*'s value would first be stored into *temp*, then *y*'s value placed into *x*, and then the value in *temp* (*x*'s old value) placed into *y*, effectively swapping the values in *x* and *y*.

The statement

swap(a, b)

can thus be expressed pictorially as

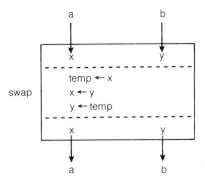

Notice the differences between this procedure and a function. A function computes a single value that can be used in an arithmetic expression, a conditional expression, or in an **output** statement. On the other hand, the purpose of a procedure like *swap* is not to compute a single value but to perform a task that often changes the parameters sent to the procedure. In *swap*, for example, the values sent to *swap* are exchanged and sent back. These fundamental differences between procedures and functions will become clearer as we begin to design programs.

An Example—Procedure Circle

In spite of their differences, the basic structure of procedures and functions is the same. Although you will not need to know the design details of a complete procedure or function until chapter 2, we give here an example of a simple procedure (containing no parameters) for computing the area of a circle. This example will use all the *mpl* statements we have learned so far.

```
circle : procedure
    storage specification
      variables
          radius, area : real
      end storage specification
    begin circle
      input radius
      area ← 3.14159 * radius ↑ 2
      output 'the area of the circle with radius ', radius, ' is ', area
      end circle
```

Notice that this procedure is named *circle* in a **procedure** statement. Two **real** variables *radius* and *area* are declared in the **variables** statement. The execution part of the procedure is delimited by the statements

```
begin circle
    .
    .
    .
end circle
```

The computations are carried out in this *computation section* of the procedure. First a value for variable radius is input from the input device. Then this value is used in computing the area of the circle in the assignment statement. Finally the computed area is printed in the **output** statement, and the procedure is finished.

There is no need for you to completely understand this procedure at this time. We will begin developing complete programs in the next chapter. The procedure *circle* would not even execute without an initial procedure to call on it. For now, just notice the roles played in this procedure by the four statements we have discussed in this chapter: the **variables** statement, assignment statement, **input** statement, and **output** statement.

In summary, the programming process can be thought of as a *divide and conquer* strategy. Instead of tackling a large (and unmanageable) problem all at once, we will first identify independent subproblems and design concise procedures and functions to solve them. A function will be used when the subproblem requires the computation of a single new value. A procedure will be used whenever the subproblem requires the alteration of parameter values or input or output. A separate initial procedure will also be designed to organize the calls to the other procedures and functions in such a way that the entire problem is properly solved. Of course, in identifying the subproblems for some new program we will often isolate a particular subproblem for which we have previously designed a procedure or function; in these cases, we can use the old procedure or function directly in the new program.

THE MODEL PROGRAMMING LANGUAGE

As we are beginning to see, in order to have a computer do useful work for us, we will need to learn to design programs that the computer can execute. Learning the individual instructions of some programming language, such as the **variables,** assignment, **input,** and **output** statements we have seen in this chapter, is the easier part of learning to program. The more challenging part is learning how to combine these instructions to form a correct program; we call this process programming. Although the names of individual instructions vary from one programming language to the other, the program design process is the same *regardless of which procedural programming language is used* (recall observation 2 on page 2).

This means that the programming language we learn is of less importance than learning to program. For this reason we will use a *model programming language (mpl)* for designing programs in this book. The instructions developed for *mpl* represent the latest known features available in modern programming languages, and, in fact, *mpl* instructions have direct counterparts in most real programming languages. Using a model programming language like *mpl* frees us from having to worry about the petty details of precise punctuation and spelling required in real programming languages and allows us to concentrate on the difficult part—program design.

Learning to design programs in an environment free from the constraints of a particular programming language has another benefit—it prepares us to program equally well in any of the actual procedural programming languages available:

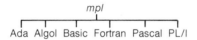

We first think about the problem at hand and design a program solution in *mpl*. Then, when we are completely satisfied with our program, we translate it directly into the programming language required, i.e., we follow these steps:

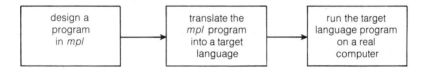

When learning a different language (e.g., Ada) we need only learn the translation step again. This is usually an easy task.

In summary, we just need to keep a clear picture in our minds of the purpose of our model programming language. It is a tool, a vehicle for thinking about the design of programs. Since it is just a tool for the mind, there is no strict form it must follow. In real programming languages we must be concerned about even the slightest details of punctuation when we write a program. In *mpl* we have much more flexibility. In fact, we are not at all concerned that you learn *mpl* in exactly the form we define it. The important thing is that you learn to design programs using instructions known to be particularly helpful in programming, the kind represented in *mpl*. In other words, as you design programs in conjunction with this text, it is not important whether your programs take on the flavor of the actual programming language you are using instead of pure *mpl*, as long as your designs make use of programming language structures similar to those presented in *mpl*.

The use of a model programming language like *mpl*, sometimes referred to as a *pseudolanguage*, for designing programs is gaining wide acceptance in the real world, especially for large programs. By learning the same technique here, you will be better prepared for the type of programming currently practiced in the real world.

1.4 | REVIEW EXERCISES
EXERCISES

1.1 Diagram the model computer. When you are finished, compare your diagram with the one in this chapter.

1.2 Diagram the processor of the model computer. Explain in your own words what each part does. When you are finished, compare your diagram with the one in this chapter.

1.3 Explain the purpose of the store in the model computer.

1.4 List the operations that the model computer can perform.

1.5 Give the precedence chart for the operations of the model computer.

1.6 In your own words, describe why we cannot issue commands to the model computer like "compute the area of a rectangle with length 3.5 and width 5.7" or "compute my income tax, favorably."

1.7 How will the store be organized after the following statement is executed by the processor?

variables
    x, apples : **integer**
    y : **truth value**
    corn : **integer**
    zero, whatsit : **real**

1.8 Give the evaluation chart for each of the following arithmetic expressions.

  (a) $3 + 2 - 5$ (b) $3 * 5 * 2$

  (c) $3 + 7 / 4$ (d) $3 * 7 / 4$

  (e) $(3 + 7) / 4$ (f) $(3 * 7) / 4$

  (g) $3 \uparrow 2 + 4 \uparrow 2$ (h) $(3 \uparrow 2 + 4) \uparrow 2$

1.9 Give the evaluation chart for each of the following arithmetic expressions.

  (a) $((5.2 + 7.3) * 3.2) / 5.0$ (b) $(5.2 + 7.3 * 3.2) / 5.0$

  (c) $5.2 + 7.3 * 3.2 / 5.0$ (d) $(5.2 + 7.3) * 3.2 / 5.0$

  (e) $(5.2 + 7.3) * (3.2 / 5.0)$ (f) $5.2 + 7.3 * (3.2 / 5.0)$

1.10 Give the evaluation chart for each of the following conditional expressions.

  (a) $3 < 5$ (b) $(3 < 5)$ **and** $(5 < 10)$

  (c) $(3 \neq 6)$ **or** $(7 > 7)$ (d) **not** $((3 < 5)$ **and** $(5 < 10))$

1.11 Assume that the store is as shown below:

x	10	integer
y	7	integer
q		integer
z		real
t		truth value

(a) After the processor executes the following three statements, what will the store look like?

$y \leftarrow y / x$

$z \leftarrow y / x$

$t \leftarrow x > y$

(b) Given the store as modified by (a), what will the store look like after the processor executes the following three statements?

$x \leftarrow x \uparrow 3$

$q \leftarrow y + y * y$

$t \leftarrow (x > y)$ **and** $(q > y)$

(c) Given the store as modified by (b) what will the store look like after the following four statements are executed?

$z \leftarrow z * (x + 4) / 2$

$y \leftarrow x * z / 3$

$q \leftarrow x + y + z$

$t \leftarrow (x \geqslant y)$ **and** (**not** $q > y$))

1.12 Give the proper arithmetic expression in *mpl* for the following mathematical expressions:

(a) $3.14159r^2$ (b) $i(1 + r)^n$

(c) $ax^3 + bx^2 - cx + 5.37$ (d) $-bx^2 + by^2$

(e) $\dfrac{a + b + c}{3}$ (f) $\dfrac{-b + \sqrt{b^2 - 4ac}}{2a}$

1.13 Explain what the term *divide and conquer* means with respect to the programming process.

1.14 Explain the logical differences between a procedure and a function.

1.15 What role does the initial procedure play in a program?

| CHAPTER 2 |

Simple Programs

NEW CONCEPTS: Programs, Functions, Procedures,
Parameters, Top-down programming

We have learned enough in chapter 1 to begin writing programs in earnest. In fact, the entire thrust of the book from now on will be program design based on a series of problems, called *case studies*, for which solutions (programs) in *mpl* will be carefully developed.

In this chapter and the remaining ones, the case studies have been organized into two parts — an introductory section entitled Getting Acquainted, which presents new programming concepts, and an advanced section called The Challenge, which illustrates the use of newly learned programming concepts in more involved programs. A special section, In Retrospect, follows the Getting Acquainted section; it is a comprehensive summary of the new concepts of the chapter. There are sets of exercises immediately after both the In Retrospect and Challenge sections. Solutions to some of these are given at the end of the book.

We recommend that you read all of the case studies in the Getting Acquainted sections carefully, since each of these studies introduces new programming concepts and later case studies are often built on these studies. The case studies of The Challenge section are optional, but you are advised to examine at least one of them in each chapter, to reinforce the new concepts learned in the chapter.

The topics of this chapter are program structure and program design. We will see that a program consists of an initial procedure that provides the organization of the program and one or more other procedures and/or functions that carry out various subtasks of the original problem. We will also learn how parameters are used for communication between the various routines (procedures and functions) of a program.

The case studies of this section are quite simple. Their purpose is to demonstrate the basic structure of a program, tying together the ideas learned in chapter 1. Each case study will be introduced by a problem description, followed by an input specifications paragraph describing the data that will be supplied at the input device for processing by the program. As we shall see, each program will consist of an initial procedure and one or more procedures and/or functions that communicate with each other via parameters. The fundamental concepts of procedures, functions, and parameters will be the foundation on which all programs are built.

**Case Study
2.1** | Compute the Average of Three Numbers

> ***Problem Description:*** Given three integers, compute their average as a truncated integer and print the result.
>
> ***Input Specifications:*** There will be one input line containing three integers.

First Solution — A Simple Initial Procedure

This problem appears to be very easy. We already know how to compute the average of three integer values in *mpl*. The arithmetic expression

$(a + b + c) / 3$

will do this for any three values contained in the variables *a*, *b*, and *c*. Even though this calculation is our goal, however, we can't rush things! There are a number of steps we must follow in constructing a program to eventually perform this simple calculation. First of all, we need to declare the three variables *a*, *b*, and *c*, as well as a fourth variable, *average*, (to which the result of the calculation will be assigned) in the **storage specification** statement:

> **storage specification**
>   **variables**
>   a, b, c, average : **integer**
>   **end storage specification**

Execution of this statement by the processor would cause the store to look like

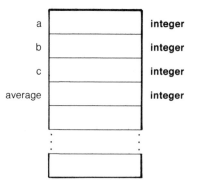

where *a*, *b*, *c*, and *average* are undefined (they have no values yet).

Our next concern, then, is where to get the values for *a*, *b*, and *c* so that we can compute their average. The input specifications tell us that three values will be provided at the input device, so we will need to include the statement

 input a, b, c

in our program. For example, if the three values to be input were

 75 86 81

then execution of the **input** statement would cause the store to look like

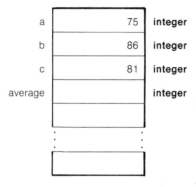

a	75	integer
b	86	integer
c	81	integer
average		integer

Now, since the **input** statement will take care of reading values into *a*, *b*, and *c*, we need to follow this statement with the assignment statement

 average ← (a + b + c) / 3

in order to compute the average. For example, if the store were as last shown, this assignment statement would be evaluated as

 average ← (75 + 86 + 81) / 3

where the values for *a*, *b*, and *c* as given in the store have been substituted into the arithmetic expression on the right, giving 80.6666... (an infinitely long result). Since *average* is an integer variable, however, this result would be truncated before being stored into variable *average*, giving the store

a	75	integer
b	86	integer
c	81	integer
average	80	integer

Printing the computed average is the last task our program must perform. This can be done, as we know from chapter 1, with the statement

 output 'the average is ', average

We can now group all of our statements together in an initial procedure, which we call *average of three.*

---

average of three : **initial procedure**
{computes the truncated average of three integer values}

    storage specification
      variables
          a, b, c, average : **integer**
    end storage specification

    begin average of three
      input a, b, c
      average ← (a + b + c) / 3
      output 'the average is ', average
    end average of three

CASE STUDY 2.1 — REFINEMENT 1

The phrase in brackets ({, }) is just a comment describing what the program does. The comment is not executed by the processor; it is for the benefit of people reading the program.

In this program the initial procedure is the only procedure (recall that the initial procedure is the procedure where the processor begins execution). This initial procedure is actually an entire program for computing the average of three integers. We arrived at this procedure by thinking about the problem description and by writing down examples of how the procedure should work. (Using scratch paper to write down brief examples as we have done is a tremendous help in designing programs.)

In our book, since all of our programs will appear neat and well written, it might seem that it is possible to develop programs without much effort and without any false starts. Don't worry. Even though we authors have been programming for some time we still make many attempts at (and refinements to) our programs before we have a finished product. Actually, it has been shown that this careful design step on paper is important to the development of good programs. So, while at first it might seem that we are spending far too much time working with pen and paper and far too little time using the actual computer, you can be assured that this is the right way to program.

Second Solution — Use a Simple Function

Having just described at length the care that must be taken in developing a program, perhaps we should critically examine the program we have just developed to see whether it really is satisfactory. This program is not very general. It will, without modification, compute the average of any three integers supplied at the input device, but is this really general? Suppose that we had just computed the final class scores for three students and we now wished to compute the class average by averaging their three final scores. The program we just developed would not work in this application, because it must always read the three values to be averaged from the input device. In other words, if we had other calculations to perform to produce *a*, *b*, and *c* before *a*, *b*, and *c* were averaged, then we would need to write a new program for this application, even though the underlying function required to compute the average is the same.

In this simple case study, computation of the average of three integers is easy enough to be written on a single line, and the effort of including this line in a new program is minimal. However, it is the principle that we are trying to illustrate here. Most problems to be solved on a computer are not as simple as the average of three numbers, and the best way to handle such problems is to design a separate *mpl* function or procedure for each identifiable subtask. Once a separate routine is designed and written, it can be used over and over again in different programs that require it. In each case we can be sure that no new errors have crept in from rewriting and retyping the instructions every time they were needed.

However, a more important reason for designing programs around separate functions and procedures to solve specific subtasks is that this leads to an organized, disciplined style of programming that is much more productive than writing a single large initial procedure to solve the entire problem all at once. So, even though this case study culminates in a small program (as will most of the case studies in this book) we will nonetheless present this disciplined approach to programming in order to prepare you for real-world programming situations.

To demonstrate this modular style of programming we will rewrite our initial procedure:

---

average of three : **initial procedure**
   {prints the truncated average of three integer values}

   storage specification
      variables
         a, b, c, average : **integer**
      end storage specification

   begin average of three
      input a, b, c
      average ← average3(a, b, c)
      output 'the average is ', average
      end average of three

   where average3 computes the average of three integers

CASE STUDY 2.1 — REFINEMENT 2

The only difference between this version and refinement 1 is that the assignment statement

   average ← (a + b + c) / 3

has been replaced by

   average ← average3(a, b, c)

We no longer compute the average of *a*, *b*, and *c* directly in the initial procedure. Instead, *average3* is a function to which we supply the values of the three integer variables *a*, *b*, and *c* and expect to get their average in return. Just how the average is computed by function *average3* is of no concern to us in the initial procedure, as long as the result is correct.

Having completed the development of the initial procedure, we turn our attention to the design of function *average3*. We must develop the internal structure of the "black box" given below, which illustrates what happens when the statement

average ← average3(a, b, c)

of the initial procedure is executed by the processor.

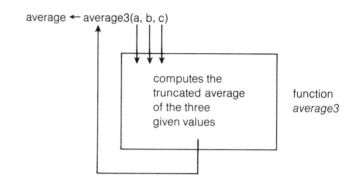

The three values in *a*, *b*, and *c* are sent to function *average3*, and a single integer value (the average of the three values sent) will be computed and returned. This returned value will replace the function call

average3(a, b, c)

and therefore be assigned to variable *average*.

The first step in writing the function *average3* is to identify this function to the processor with the *function header statement*

average3 : **integer function**

which simply states that the group of *mpl* statements following this header statement will compute and return a single integer value.

Next, since function *average3* will be sent three integer values for which it is to compute the average, it must have three "containers" for those values. We call these containers *parameters* and describe them in a **parameters** statement:

parameters
x, y, z : **in only integer**

The parameters *x*, *y*, and *z* look like variables, and they can be treated almost like variables, but their purpose is different. Parameters are used in procedures and functions to communicate with other procedures and functions. The **parameters** statement in our function *average3*, for example, indicates to the processor that *average3* expects three values to be supplied to the containers (parameters) *x*, *y*, and *z* whenever function *average3* is called upon by another procedure or function. When *average3* is included in a statement like

average ← average3(a, b, c)

(as in the initial procedure of the last refinement), the processor executes function *average3*, and in the process, *a's* value is sent to *x*, *b's* value is sent to y, and c's value is sent to z. The parameters x, y, and z are called **in only** parameters of type **integer,** because they expect to receive integer values sent into function *average3*, but the values sent in are not modified or changed in any way. That is, values come in to function *average3* via the parameters x, y, and z, but no values are sent back out through x, y, and z to the routine that called on *average3*. Hence x, y, and z have the **in only** designation. (We will later see examples of **in out** parameters, where the parameters' values come into a procedure, are modified, and then are sent back out to the calling procedure in their modified form.)

With the parameters x, y, and z, we can include the assignment statement

average3 ← (x + y + z) / 3

in *average3*. When the processor executes this statement, the values in the parameters x, y, and z, which were sent to *average3* from the initial procedure, will be added, divided by 3 and then stored into *average3*. Notice that *average3* is not the name of a variable, but the name of the function we are designing. The last task of any function is to assign a value to the name of the function; when the processor returns to the location in the program from which the function was called, that function call is replaced by the value computed in the function.

The entire function *average3* looks like

---

average3 : **integer function**
  {computes the truncated average of three integers}

  storage specification
    parameters
      x, y, z : **in only integer**
    end storage specification

  begin average3
    average3 ← (x + y + z) / 3
    end average3

CASE STUDY 2.1 — REFINEMENT 3

Except for the function header statement and the **parameters** statement, function *average3* has the same basic form as the initial procedure. Unlike the initial procedure, however, it cannot be executed by itself. Instead, *average3* must be included as part of a program that contains an initial procedure. The processor will begin execution with the initial procedure and will only process function *average3* when it is called upon in some other statement that it is currently executing.

When the processor executes the statement

  average ← average3(a, b, c)

in the initial procedure, the effect is as illustrated below:

Example 2.1

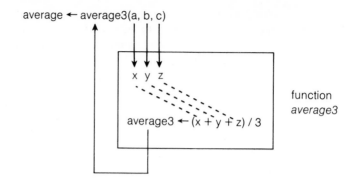

average ← average3(a, b, c)

function
average3

The value in *a* is sent to *x*, the value in *b* is sent to *y*, and the value in *c* is sent to *z*. Then the sum of *x*, *y*, and *z* is divided by 3, and the result is stored into *average3*, the name of the function. At this point the function terminates, and the value computed in *average3* is returned to the initial procedure, replacing the function call

average3(a, b, c)

Function *average3* is completely unaware of the names of the values it is sent (in this case *a*, *b*, and *c*).

Like the hardware operations +, −, *, /, and ↑, *average3* is now an operator, or function, in its own right and can be called on more than once in the same program (or in different programs), receiving different values each time. For example, in a different program we may need to use function *average3* in the statement

weightedaverage ← average3(s1, s2, s3) * 10

where *s1*, *s2*, and *s3* are variables whose values have previously been computed. Function *average3* would work here without any modifications:

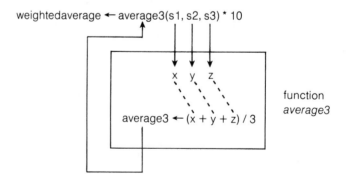

weightedaverage ← average3(s1, s2, s3) * 10

function
average3

The value in *s1* would be passed to *x*, the value in *s2* to *y*, and the value in *s3* to *z*. The average of the three values in *x*, *y*, and *z* would be computed in function *average3* and returned to the calling point

average3(s1, s2, s3)

where this value would be multiplied by 10 and the result stored into variable *weightedaverage*.

This second solution to our problem, then, is a program consisting of the initial procedure *average of three* given in refinement 2 and the function *average3* given in refinement 3. To run the program on a computer we would have to gather both of these routines into a single package (a program) and submit this package as a unit to the computer:

```
average of three : initial procedure
    {prints the truncated average of three integer values}

    storage specification
        variables
            a, b, c, average : integer
        end storage specification

    begin average of three
        input a, b, c
        average ← average3(a, b, c)
        output 'the average is ', average
        end average of three

    where average3 computes the truncated average of three integers

average3 : integer function
    {computes the truncated average of three integers}

    storage specification
        parameters
            x, y, z : in only integer
        end storage specification

    begin average3
        average3 ← (x + y + z) / 3
        end average3
```

CASE STUDY 2.1 — REFINEMENT 4

We will not usually gather all of the parts to a program together at the end of a case study as we have done here, since we usually want to consider only one routine at a time when we are doing top-down program design. Just remember that in order to execute a program on a computer, all of the procedures and functions required must be grouped together into a single unit — the program.

Correctness

Having designed a program we must convince ourselves that it is correct. That is, we must determine whether it will compute the correct answers for any input values we might give it. The process of program design is not really complete until this verification step is done.

One way to help determine that a program is correct is to test it with some input values to see if the expected results are computed. Of course, we cannot be sure that a program is correct by simply testing it with a few values. Testing is just one of the methods used in verifying a program's correctness. To test this program we would need to translate it into a real programming language and then run it on a real computer; we suggest that you do this.

However, before testing the program on a real computer there is one important check that can be applied to the design to convince us that it works. This check is called a *program walkthrough*. In a program walkthrough, some input values are chosen and the programmer steps through the program, simulating the processor by executing each statement just as the processor would.

A walkthrough can uncover important design flaws before the programming effort gets as far as translating the program design from *mpl* into an actual programming language. In fact, it is best to have a friend do this walkthrough, because the friend is more likely to catch problems that you might overlook because you are so familiar with your program. We will demonstrate a program walkthrough here.

Example　For our walkthrough, assume that the program of refinement 4 has been submitted to
2.2　the computer for execution and that the three integers

　　85 73 92

have been supplied at the input device. The processor always begins execution with the initial procedure of a program, so in this case processing starts with *average of three.* The first statement there is

variables
　　a, b, c, average : **integer**

in the **storage specification** section; this causes the store to be set up as

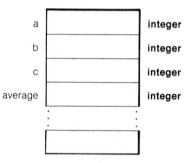

After processing the **variables** statement, the processor moves on to the computation section of the initial procedure following

　　begin average of three

where the first statement encountered is

　　input a, b, c

Execution of this statement by the processor causes the first value at the input device to be placed into *a*, the second value into *b*, and the third into *c*, resulting in the store

a	85	**integer**
b	73	**integer**
c	92	**integer**
average		**integer**

Having completed execution of the **input** statement the processor moves on to the statement

average ← average3(a, b, c)

which calls function *average3*. After verifying that function *average3* has indeed been included in this program, the processor remembers where it is in the initial procedure and then proceeds to execute function *average3*.

The function header statement

average3 : **integer function**

tells the processor that a storage cell of type **integer** must be reserved for the function name *average3*, because a value is always placed into the function name upon termination of the function. This causes the store to look like

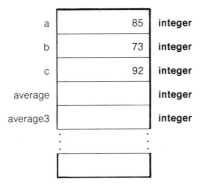

a	85	integer
b	73	integer
c	92	integer
average		integer
average3		integer

The processor next encounters the **storage specification** section of function *average3,* where it processes the **parameters** statement

parameters
x, y, z : **in only integer**

Since these are **in only** parameters, the processor must reserve space for them in the store so that they can contain the values sent from the initial procedure. The store now looks like

a	85	integer
b	73	integer
c	92	integer
average		integer
average3		integer
x		integer
y		integer
z		integer

As the final step in processing the **parameters** statement, the processor takes the values in a, b, and c (a, b, and c are the *arguments*, or *actual parameters* sent to *average3* when it was called in the initial procedure) and copies these values into the parameters (called the *formal parameters*) x, y, and z of *average3*. Since a was the first actual parameter listed in the statement

average ← average3(a, b, c)

of the initial procedure, it is copied into x, the first formal parameter appearing in the **parameters** statement. Similarly the second and third actual parameters (b and c) appearing in the call to *average3* are copied into the second and third formal parameters listed in *average3* (y and z, respectively), thus resulting in the store

a	85	integer
b	73	integer
c	92	integer
average		integer
average3		integer
x	85	integer
y	73	integer
z	92	integer

At this point the processor is working in function *average3* and can no longer "see" the variables a, b, c and *average* of the initial procedure, even though these variables are still in the store. Only the storage cells *average3*, x, y, and z for the function name and the parameters of function *average3* can be accessed by the processor while it is processing *average3*.

Now the processor resumes execution with the first statement of the computation section of *average3* following

begin average3

which is

average3 ← (x + y + z) / 3

The adder and divider are used to produce the result

83.3333...

which must be stored into the function name *average3*. Since *average3* is of type **integer,** the result is truncated giving

a	85	**integer**
b	73	**integer**
c	92	**integer**
average		**integer**
average3	83	**integer**
x	85	**integer**
y	73	**integer**
z	92	**integer**

Having executed this statement, the processor moves on to the next statement

end average3

which is the end of function *average3*. At this point, execution of *average3* is terminated and the processor resumes execution of the initial procedure by going back to the statement where function *average3* was called:

average ← average3(a, b, c)

Now, however, the value of *average3*(*a, b, c*), 83, has been computed and stored in the cell *average3*. So the processor replaces *average3*(*a, b, c*) with 83 upon returning to the initial procedure making this statement equivalent to

average ← 83

At the same time, since the processor has finished executing function *average3* and has returned to executing the initial procedure, all of the storage cells used by function *average3* disappear. Thus, just before completing the assignment

average ← 83

The store looks like

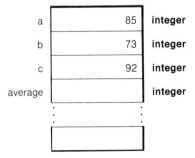

So, after the statement

average ← 83

has finally been executed by the processor, the store looks like

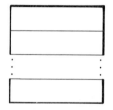

and the processor moves on to execute the next statement

> **output** 'the average is ', average

This causes the message

> the average is 83

to be printed at the output device, since 83 is the value in variable *average*.
The last statement to be executed by the processor is

> **end** average of three

which causes termination of program execution, and all values in the store disappear

in preparation for the execution of some other program. The only result produced by this program is the output line

> the average is 83

which is what the program was intended to produce.

Again, we stress that a successful walkthrough or test of a program with one set of input values is by no means proof that the program is really correct and will work for all input values. In this case, however, we will be satisfied with the single walkthrough given in this example as sufficient evidence that our program works.

Summary — Case Study 2.1

In this case study we have seen the programming style we will be following in this book. Each time a program is to be designed, we will take a description of the problem to be solved and the input to be processed and design a program in *mpl* to solve the problem in a top-down fashion. We will usually begin by designing the initial procedure, and whenever we run into an involved calculation, we will assume that a separate function or procedure exists to do this calculation, put a line in the initial procedure calling on that function or procedure and then continue with the design of the initial procedure. After completing the design of the initial procedure, we can then begin working on the design of any function or procedure whose existence we assumed in the initial procedure. Being able to concentrate on separate small pieces of the program without needing to keep the entire program in mind greatly simplifies the programming process.

Designing a new function like *average3* is like creating a new operator (like +, for example) that can be used often in one program or included in other programs without modification. The major difference between a software (programmed) function like *average3* and a hardware (wired-in) function like + is that a software function must specify just one fixed type for each parameter (although there can be different types of parameters within the same function), whereas hardware functions can often take more than one type (for example, + can be applied to either integers or reals).

The parameters of a function or procedure are called *formal parameters*, and the values actually sent to these formal parameters when the function or procedure is invoked (i.e., called on) are called *actual parameters*. The types (e.g., integer or real) of the actual and formal parameters must match.

When a function or procedure is called from another routine, the processor sets up a new storage cell for each **in only** formal parameter and then copies the actual parameter values into the corresponding formal parameter cells before proceeding with the execution of that function or procedure. Since **in only** formal parameters are only copies of the actual parameters, any changes that might be made to the formal parameters as the function is executed will not affect the actual parameters. That is, changing the copies does not change the originals; this is why these parameters are called **in only**: values can be sent into the function through **in only** parameters, but no values can be sent back out to the calling routine through these parameters.

While the processor is executing a particular function, variables declared in other procedures and functions cannot be accessed or used in any way, even though some of these values may already be in the store. The only way of transferring values between different routines is via parameters and function names. Each time a function or procedure finishes executing, all of the storage cells set aside for that function or procedure are released and their values become undefined again.

The next case study is a similar example involving a function.

Area of a Rectangle

Case Study 2.2

> *Problem Description:* Compute and print the area of a rectangle.
>
> *Input Specifications:* Two real values, one for the length and one for the width of a rectangle.

This problem looks much different than the previous case study, but in reality it is very similar. In fact, the organization of this program will be identical to that of the last program.

The Solution — A Function With In Only Parameters

The initial procedure will read the length and width from the input device, call on a function to compute the area, and then print the area. We will need two variables to hold the real input values, which we might as well call *length* and *width*:

> **variables**
>   length, width : **real**

Including this **variables** statement in the **storage specification** section and organizing the initial procedure like the one in the preceding case study we get the initial procedure shown in refinement 1.

---

rectangle area : **initial procedure**
    {prints the area of a rectangle}

    storage specification
      variables
        length, width : **real**
    end storage specification

    begin rectangle area
      input length, width
      output 'length ', length, ' times width ', width, ' = ', rectangle(length, width)
    end rectangle area

    where rectangle computes the area of a rectangle

CASE STUDY 2.2 — REFINEMENT 1

Notice here that the function *rectangle* is called directly in the **output** statement: evaluation of function *rectangle* will result in a value that will be printed directly by the **output** statement.

Refinement 2 gives function rectangle. Recall that the area of a rectangle is found by multiplying its length by its width.

---

rectangle : **real function**
    {computes the area of a rectangle}

    storage specification
      parameters
        length, width : **in only real**
    end storage specification

    begin rectangle
      rectangle ← length * width
    end rectangle

CASE STUDY 2.2 — REFINEMENT 2

In this case the formal parameters in the function *rectangle* have the same names (*length* and *width*) as the actual parameters sent to *rectangle* when it was called in refinement 1. This makes no difference, because the names of formal and actual parameters have no relationship to one another. For example, refinement 2 could be replaced by refinement 3 (where the parameter names have been changed from *length* and *width* to *x* and *y*) without affecting the program.

rectangle : **real function**
{computes the area of a rectangle}

  storage specification
    parameters
      x, y : **in only real**
    end storage specification

  begin rectangle
    rectangle ← x * y
    end rectangle

CASE STUDY 2.2 — REFINEMENT 3

Correctness

We will now do a walkthrough of this program (refinements 1 and 2) to convince ourselves that it works.

The entire program consists of the initial procedure *rectangle area* and the function *rectangle.* The processor always starts with the initial procedure. First, the **variables** statement is executed to set up the store. At first *length* and *width* are undefined (have no values). The **input** statement is then executed. If the values

    3.5 7.2

are provided at the input device, then after the processor executes the statement

    input length, width

the store looks like

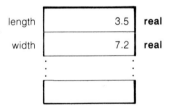

Now, the processor executes

    output 'length ', length, ' times width ', width, ' = ', rectangle(length, width)

Before anything can be printed, function *rectangle* must be invoked, because it appears in this list of items to be printed. A storage cell must therefore be reserved for the function name, *rectangle,* and since *rectangle* has formal parameters of the type **in only real,** cells must be set aside in the store for these formal parameters, and the values of the actual parameters must be copied into these formal parameters. So, upon invoking function *rectangle,* the processor must set up the store to look like

Example 2.3

length	3.5	real
width	7.2	real
rectangle		real
length	3.5	real
width	7.2	real

The processor is able to keep track of the fact that the last three cells, *rectangle, length,* and *width,* belong to the function *rectangle* and that the first two cells, *length* and *width,* belong to the initial procedure. After properly establishing the store, the processor executes the only assignment statement in the computation section of function *rectangle*

rectangle ← length * width

causing the store to look like

length	3.5	real
width	7.2	real
rectangle	25.2	real
length	3.5	real
width	7.2	real

This is the end of function *rectangle,* so now the statement in the initial procedure that initially invoked rectangle,

output 'length ', length, ' times width ', width, ' = ', rectangle(length, width)

can be completed. The value returned by the function *rectangle* (in the cell named *rectangle*) is 25.2, so 25.2 is substituted in the **output** statement to give

output 'length ', length, ' times width ', width, ' = ', 25.2

Since *rectangle* has now finished executing, all of its storage cells are released and the store only contains the variables of the initial procedure again:

length	3.5	real
width	7.2	real

Therefore, the **output** statement causes

length 3.5 times width 7.2 = 25.2

to be printed at the output device, where the values of *length* and *width* (the variables in the initial procedure) have been substituted in the **output** statement.

Again, do not forget that a program walkthrough is not enough to prove that a program is correct. In this case, however, because our program is so simple, we are confident that it is correct.

Summary — Case Study 2.2

This case study and the previous one were very similar in their organization. This pattern of an initial procedure to input the necessary data values, call on other routines to process these values, and then print their results will become very familiar.

In this case study we chose names for the formal parameters of function *rectangle* (*length* and *width*) that were the same as those used in the initial procedure. This causes the processor no confusion, as it keeps track of which storage cells are accessible from any procedure or function. From the processor's point of view, the names of formal parameters and the corresponding actual parameters have absolutely no relationship to one another.

Swap Two Values

Case Study 2.3

> *Problem Description:* Input two integer values, print them in the order in which they were input, then print them in the opposite order.
>
> *Input Specifications:* Two integers.

This might seem like an odd problem, because it can easily be solved with the statements

```
input x, y
output x, y
output y, x
```

assuming that *x* and *y* are properly declared variables. However, what we really want to do here is to develop a procedure called *swap* that will be useful in later case studies, when we want to exchange the values of any two integer variables *x* and *y*.

The Solution — Procedure Swap With In Out Parameters

In designing the initial procedure, we assume that procedure *swap* has already been developed so that we can use it in the sequence of statements

```
input x, y
output x, y
swap(x, y)
output x, y
```

After x and y have been input and printed, x and y are sent as actual parameters to procedure *swap*. Following execution of procedure *swap*, the values in x and y should have been exchanged, so that when x and y are finally output again, the values printed will be the opposite of those printed by the first **output** statement. This gives us the complete initial procedure:

```
test swap : initial procedure
    {tests the swap procedure}

    storage specification
        variables
            x, y : integer
        end storage specification

    begin test swap
        input x, y
        output 'x = ', x, ' and y = ', y
        swap(x, y)
        output 'Now x = ', x, ' and y = ', y
    end test swap

    where swap exchanges the values in x and y

    CASE STUDY 2.3 — REFINEMENT 1
```

This initial procedure has the same general form as the others we have written. Values are input, they are processed by another routine, and then the results are printed. The new feature of this initial procedure is in the way *swap* is called. In previous case studies we used functions that returned a single computed value in the name of the function, as in

```
average ← average3(x, y, z)
```

swap, however, does not return a single computed value; it takes x's value and puts it into y and takes y's value and puts it into x. If $x = 10$ and $y = 15$ before $swap(x, y)$ has been called, then x must be 15 and y must be 10 after $swap(x, y)$ has been called. Thus, we just write the procedure call to *swap* as if it were a new *mpl* statement

```
swap(x, y)
```

which can be paraphrased "swap x and y."

In order for procedure *swap* to work properly, it needs to change the values of the actual parameters (x and y) sent to it. This is an important departure from the way we have handled parameters up to this point. In the functions of our previous case studies, the formal parameters were of type **in only,** which meant that any changes we made to these formal parameters had no effect on the values of the actual parameters sent to the function. This is because formal **in only** parameters are just copies of the actual parameter values sent, not the original values themselves. For procedure *swap*, however, we need a different kind of parameter — one called **in out** — which gives the procedure access to the original values sent (not just copies) so that changes to the formal parameters cause the same changes in the actual parameters. That way, when x and y are sent as actual parameters to procedure *swap*, the formal parameters to which x and y are sent can be changed, and these same changes will be made to x and y in the initial procedure.

Pictorially, *swap* appears to the initial procedure as a black box to which *x* and *y* are sent, processed, and returned in exchanged order:

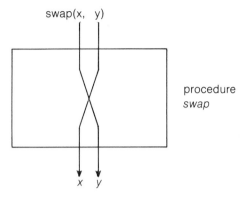

swap(x, y)

procedure
swap

x *y*

Using **in out** parameters, we make our first attempt at procedure *swap*. If we call the formal parameters of *swap a* and *b*, then we must put *b*'s value into *a* and *a*'s value into *b*. This thinking could lead us to the following design for procedure *swap*.

swap : **procedure**
　　{exchanges the values in two integer parameters}

　storage specification
　　　parameters
　　　　　a, b : **in out integer**
　　　end storage specification

　begin swap
　　　a ← b
　　　b ← a
　　end swap

CASE STUDY 2.3 — REFINEMENT 2

Unfortunately, as the next example shows, this version of procedure *swap* is incorrect!

Without looking at the entire program, just assume that *a* is 10 and *b* is 15 when we execute the two statements

　a ← b
　b ← a

Example 2.4

At first the store looks like

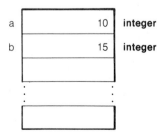

a　|　10　| **integer**
b　|　15　| **integer**

After the processor executes $a \leftarrow b$ we have

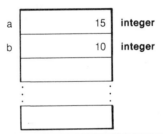

| a | 15 | integer |
| b | 15 | integer |

Then when it executes $b \leftarrow a$ we finish with

| a | 15 | integer |
| b | 15 | integer |

which is wrong, obviously, (although many a person has written *swap* this way). What we really want in the store upon completion of *swap* is

| a | 15 | integer |
| b | 10 | integer |

To fix *swap* we need an extra storage cell that we will call *temp* (for temporary storage cell), where we can save the original value of *a*. Then we can store *b* into *a*, because we have a copy of *a* in *temp*. Then the value of *temp* can be placed into *b*. This gives the correct version of *swap:*

```
swap : procedure
    {exchanges the values in two integer parameters}

    storage specification
        parameters
            a, b : in out integer
        variables
            temp : integer
        end storage specification

    begin swap
        temp ← a
        a ← b
        b ← temp
    end swap

CASE STUDY 2.3 — REFINEMENT 3
```

Notice that this version of *swap* has not only parameters but also a variable, *temp*, which is defined in a **variables** statement. We call *temp* a *local variable* because it belongs locally to this procedure. When *swap* is called, a storage cell is set aside for the variable *temp*. When *swap* is finished, the cell for *temp* disappears — it is no longer in the store. Both the parameters and the variables require cells in the store, so both are declared in the **storage specification** part of procedure *swap*.

Correctness

To assure ourselves that our most recent refinement of procedure *swap* works properly, we will do a walkthrough of the entire program.

Starting with the initial procedure in refinement 1, we see that the **variables** statement would be executed first. Then, if the values *Example 2.5*

     10 15

are at the input device, the statement

   input x, y

causes the store to be

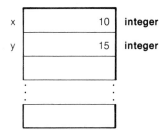

The first **output** statement of the initial procedure is executed next, causing

   x = 10 and y = 15

to be printed. Then procedure *swap* of refinement 3 is invoked by the initial procedure in the statement

   swap(x, y)

Since *x* is the first actual parameter, it is matched up with the first formal parameter, *a*, in *swap*. Similarly, *y* is matched up with *b*. Because the formal parameters *a* and *b* are of type **in out** they become identified with the actual parameters *x* and *y*. After calling *swap*, the store looks like

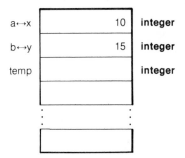

Thus, when we use *a* (or *b*) in procedure *swap,* we are actually using the same cell as *x* (or *y*) of the initial procedure; **in out** parameters take over the same storage cells as the actual parameters passed to them for the time that the procedure is in execution. Notice also that a new cell has been designated for the local variable *temp.* Since *swap* is a procedure rather than a function, no storage cell is set aside for the name *swap.* No values are ever returned in the name of a procedure.

As the processor continues executing *swap,* the first statement executed after the **storage specifications** section is

temp ← a

which causes the store to look like

a↔x	10	**integer**
b↔y	15	**integer**
temp	10	**integer**

Execution of the next two statements

a ← b

b ← temp

changes the store to

a↔x	15	**integer**
b↔y	10	**integer**
temp	10	**integer**

Since procedure *swap* is now finished, the storage cells it used disappear, and upon return to the initial procedure the store looks like

x	15	**integer**
y	10	**integer**

Now, the last statement of the initial procedure (the **output** statement) is executed

output 'Now x = ', x, ' and y = ', y

This causes

Now x = 15 and y = 10

to appear on the output device, showing that procedure *swap* works for this input.

Summary — Case Study 2.3

In this case study we have seen our first example of a procedure (other than the initial procedure). Once we have designed a new procedure like *swap*, we can use it over and over again in the same program or in different programs. It is like having a new *mpl* statement. Just as we have used the assignment, **input,** and **output** statements, we can also use the new statement

swap(—, —)

where we can fill in the blanks with any two integer variables. The variables must be defined and we must include the *swap* procedure in any program in which we wish to use it, but we do not need to redesign *swap* for each program.

In designing procedure *swap* we discovered that we needed a new kind of parameter, called an **in out** parameter. **in out** parameters are different from **in only** parameters in that changes to formal **in out** parameters cause the same changes in the corresponding actual parameters. These differences can most readily be demonstrated by an example.

Assume that in procedure *swap* of refinement 3 we replace the declaration

Example 2.6

a, b : **in out integer**

with the declaration

a, b : **in only integer.**

thus changing the parameters from **in out** to **in only.** A walkthrough of the program will demonstrate that this will cause the program to execute incorrectly.

Let's assume that the processor has begun executing the initial procedure and that the variables *x* and *y* have been initialized by the **input** statement to 10 and 15, respectively. Afterwards, we have the store

When *swap(x, y)* is called from the initial procedure, the formal parameters *a* and *b* of procedure *swap* will be given their own storage cells, since they are now **in only,** and the values of *x* and *y* will be copied into them, giving

x	10	integer
y	15	integer
a	10	integer
b	15	integer
temp		integer

Now, as the processor executes procedure *swap,* the three statements

```
temp ← a
a ← b
b ← temp
```

will successfully swap the values of *a* and *b,* giving

x	10	integer
y	15	integer
a	15	integer
b	10	integer
temp	10	integer

At this point, however, everything goes wrong. Since execution of procedure *swap* is now complete, processing will resume with the initial procedure, and all storage cells associated with the call to *swap* will be discarded, leaving the store

x	10	integer
y	15	integer

Thus the values of *x* and *y* have not been changed by the call to *swap.*

Compare this example with the walkthrough of the correct version to see the difference between **in only** and **in out** parameters.

Another new concept introduced in this case study was the use of a variable in a routine other than the initial procedure. In procedure *swap* we needed the variable *temp* to make the procedure work properly. Some beginning programmers confuse parameters and variables: why, for example, is *temp* a variable in procedure *swap* rather than another parameter like *a* or *b*? The answer is simple: parameters are only used when they are needed to communicate values to and/or from a procedure or function. For procedure *swap* to work, it must be given the two values it is supposed to exchange, so they are communicated to and from *swap* as formal **in out** parameters that we call *a* and *b*. To perform the exchange, however, we discovered that we needed an additional cell to hold the value of parameter *a* temporarily. This temporary cell can be a variable; there is no need for it to be communicated to procedure *swap* from the calling routine or vice versa, so it does not need to be a parameter. This cell is used internally within procedure *swap*, and its existence does not even need to be known outside of *swap*. For this reason we declared the cell *temp* in a **variables** statement within procedure *swap*.

The concepts of procedures, **in out** parameters, and local variables will continue to be used in future case studies.

In this section of each chapter we will review the important concepts presented in the previous Getting Acquainted section. In this chapter, top-down program design, program structure, procedures, functions, parameters, and program correctness were the primary topics.

2.2 IN RETROSPECT

TOP-DOWN PROGRAM DESIGN

In the Getting Acquainted section of this chapter we designed our first programs. As simple as these programs were, they introduced the most important topic of the book: top-down program design. We will tackle every problem we encounter in the fashion presented in these early case studies, starting with the problem statement and organizing the solution in an initial procedure. In designing the initial procedure, as we encounter subproblems that seem to be substantial tasks in themselves, we will relegate these tasks to other procedures and functions, just pretending for the moment that these procedures and functions have already been written and work correctly. After the initial procedure is complete, we will then go back and design each individual procedure and function whose existence we assumed. Since each procedure and function called in the initial procedure represents a subproblem of the original problem, we can design these procedures and functions just as we did the initial procedure, organizing the solution to a subproblem in such a way that any substantial subtasks of this subproblem are relegated to yet other procedures and functions.

The beauty of this top-down approach to programming is that we can concentrate on just one simple subproblem of the original problem at any one time, rather than needing to keep track of the solution of the original large problem all at once. (For the simple programs we have designed so far, it would actually have been easier to have written the solutions as single initial procedures instead of calling other functions or procedures. However, few real-life problems are this simple, so we will continue to use this top-down programming approach for our case studies — regardless of how simple the problems are — in order to cultivate good programming habits that will be useful in real-life problems.)

Another benefit of this top-down style of program design is that many of the procedures and functions we design will be useful in completely different applications, so we will not have to redesign the routines to solve old sub-problems arising in other applications. For example, procedure *swap* developed in case study 2.3 will be used again in sorting programs.

As we have seen, there are three crucial notions to be mastered for top-down program development: procedures, functions, and parameters. Procedures and functions are the fundamental building blocks of programs. Parameters are the means of communicating among procedures and functions. It is imperative that you master these concepts early and apply them in every program. They are reviewed in the next few sections, which will be a reference to turn to whenever you have questions about these concepts.

FUNCTIONS AND PROCEDURES

Some beginning students get confused about the differences between functions and procedures. Since these differences are fundamental, it is important that you master them.

Functions

Functions are used whenever the computation of a single new value is relatively complicated. The value computed by a function can be assigned to a variable, used in an arithmetic or conditional expression, or included in an **output** statement. A function might be used, for example, to compute the sum, average, or standard deviation of a list of numbers.

Once a function has been designed, it can be treated like a new operator in the language. For example, just as we can use the + operator in the assignment statement

$$y \leftarrow 5 * (a + b)$$

in *mpl*, if we have designed a function called *minimum* to compute the minimum value of three integers, we could use function *minimum* in the assignment statement

$$y \leftarrow 5 * minimum(a, b, c)$$

In this case function *minimum* would compute the smallest value among *a*, *b*, and *c*, and this result would be multiplied by 5 and assigned to *y*. Similarly, since the statement

output x, a + b, y

is proper, the statement

output x, minimum(a, b, c), y

would also be proper. That is, whenever we can use an expression involving one of the standard arithmetic operators, we can also use any numeric function we have designed, because a function, just like one of the standard operators, computes a single value.

Since a function computes a single new value that replaces the function name wherever the function is called, a function should never change the values of the parameters it is sent. For this reason we advise that only parameters of type **in only** be used in functions. In fact, some programming languages (e.g., Ada) will not allow functions to use **in out** parameters because this leads to the possibility that the parameter values might be changed.

Since the purpose of a function is to compute a single new functional value, any change in one of the actual parameters sent to a function is an unwanted *side effect*. After the function has finished executing, we want the values we sent to the function to be the same. For example, if we had designed function *minimum* as described above to compute the minimum of three integer values, and we included the statements

```
min ← minimum(a, b, c)
output 'the minimum of ', a, ' ', b, ' and ', c, ' is ', min
```

in our program, then we would want *minimum* to compute and return the minimum value in *a*, *b*, and *c*, but we would not want the side effect of having any of the values of *a*, *b*, or *c* changed by function *minimum*. For similar reasons, a function should generally never include **input** or **output** statements since, again, these cause side effects beyond the stated purpose of the function — just computing and returning a single new value in the name of the function.

In summary, a function call can be visualized as

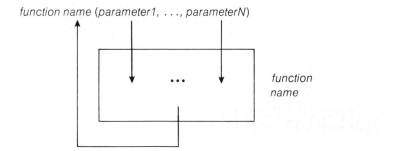

function name (parameter1, . . ., parameterN)

function name

where the box represents the computations done in the function itself. Values are sent into the function, but only one value is returned from the function — it is computed as the value of the function and it replaces the function reference in the calling routine, illustrated by the arrow leaving the box.

Procedures

In contrast to functions, procedures are not intended to compute just a single new value. Instead, a procedure is used when we reach a point where a substantial subtask must be carried out, such as swapping two values, sorting a list of numbers into ascending order, or multiplying two matrices. In this respect a procedure is like a separate program — it is really a subprogram of the original program.

Once a procedure has been developed, it is invoked (called) on a separate line in some procedure or function, as in

swap(x, y)

Thus each new procedure we develop essentially gives us a new statement for our programming language; in this case

swap(___ , ___)

is the new statement where we can fill in the blanks with any two integer variables.

No value is returned in the name of a procedure (unlike a function, where the *only* value returned should be in the name of the function), so the parameters are the only lines of communication between a procedure and the routine that called it. Thus a procedure may use any kind of parameters: **in only, in out,** and a new kind we will learn about, **out only.**

Finally, a procedure is free to use any *mpl* statement. Procedures may input values, output values, and change the values of their parameters.

Differences between Functions and Procedures

You should memorize the following points, which summarize the differences between functions and procedures.

1. Functions are used to compute a single new value; procedures are used to accomplish a separate subtask of the original problem.
2. Functions extend the operator set of a programming language; procedures extend the statement set of the language.
3. Functions should use just type **in only** parameters; procedures can use any mixture of **in only, in out,** and **out only** parameters.
4. Functions should avoid **input** and **output** statements and any other action that may cause side effects beyond the one purpose of computing and returning a single new value in the name of the function; procedures may include any statement.

Memorizing these points will make it easier for you to design programs, because you will know when to use functions and when to use procedures, and you will know how to apply them properly.

PROGRAM STRUCTURE

Every *mpl* program we design will consist of an initial procedure and a collection of other procedures and functions. The initial procedure and all other procedures and functions have the following structure:

name : |header|

    storage specification
      |declaration of storage|
    end storage specification

    begin *name*
      |statements of computation section|
      end *name*

    where |descriptions of other routines invoked|

There are three possible forms for the {header}: **initial procedure** for the initial procedure; **procedure** for all other procedures; and *type* **function** for any function, where *type* is any *mpl* type, such as integer or **real.** The *name* on the {header} of the routine is chosen by the programmer and should indicate what the routine is to accomplish.

The **storage specification** section describes all storage requirements for a procedure or function, including parameters and variables. When a routine begins execution, all storage cells described in the **storage specification** section will be reserved in the store, and when the routine is exited, all storage cells associated with that routine will be removed and lost. Whenever a function is called, one additional storage cell is reserved and named with the function name. When execution of the function is complete, this cell is also removed along with the others established in the **storage specification** section of the function, but only after the value in the function name has been returned to the calling routine, replacing the function call.

The statements in the computation section of any function or procedure should all be simple to understand. Complex subtasks should be relegated to other procedures or functions and described in **where** statements following the computation section of the calling routine.

PARAMETERS

Parameters are the means of communication among procedures and functions. *Mpl* procedures and functions are modeled in such a way that they cannot use the contents of variables in another routine unless these variable values are sent to them as actual parameters.

We have so far seen two kinds of parameters, **in out** and **in only.** In later chapters we will need a third kind called **out only,** so for completeness we will describe all three here.

To understand the differences between these three types of parameters, it helps to realize that the words **in** and **out** refer to values coming into or going out of the procedure or function using one of these parameters. Within a procedure or function, a formal parameter that is **in only** will receive a value into the routine using that parameter, but it will not be able to send a value out of the routine in that parameter. An **out only** formal parameter is the opposite. It cannot receive a value into the procedure or function where it is used, but that procedure or function will be able to pass a value out of the routine through this parameter. When a procedure or function is called, any **out only** parameters are initially undefined, but values can be assigned to such parameters before termination of that routine. Finally we have **in out** parameters, which combine the features of **in only** and **out only** parameters. When a procedure or function that uses **in out** formal parameters is called, these parameters can be used to accept values into the routine, and, upon termination of the routine, they can be used to send values out of the routine.

We will give examples to show how the processor treats each of these different kinds of parameters, but first we will review the terms *actual parameter* and *formal parameter*.

Actual and Formal Parameters

The term *formal parameter* refers to parameters declared in a procedure or function in a **parameters** statement. Formal parameters are the placeholders or containers of a procedure or function that expect to receive values from and/ or send values back to a routine where the procedure or function is called. *Actual parameters*, on the other hand, are the values or variables supplied to the formal parameters of a procedure or function when it is called from a routine.

For example, look at the following program skeleton, which contains an initial procedure and a function called *minimum*. Function *minimum* is used twice in the initial procedure.

```
tryit : initial procedure

    storage specification
        variables
            min, a, b, c : integer
        end storage specification

    begin tryit
        .
        .
        .
        min ← minimum(a, b, c)
        .
        .
        .
        output minimum(5, a + b, min)
        .
        .
        .
        end tryit

minimum : integer function

    storage specification
        parameters
            x, y, z : in only integer
        end storage specification

    begin minimum
        .
        .
        .
        end minimum
```

The formal parameters of function *minimum* are *x*, *y*, and *z*. The first time *minimum* is used in the initial procedure, the actual parameters sent to *minimum* are *a*, *b*, and *c*. Actual parameter *a* corresponds to formal parameter *x*, actual parameter *b* to *y*, and actual parameter *c* to *z*. The assignments of actual parameters to formal parameters are made strictly in the order of appearance. It is up to the programmer to ensure that the types (e.g. integer or real) of the actual and formal parameters match.

In the second call to function *minimum* the actual parameters are 5, the computed value of *a* + *b*, and *min*. Formal parameter *x* of function *minimum* will thus be 5, *y* will have the value of *a* + *b*, and *z* will have the value in *min* as function *minimum* executes this time.

One final point that should be absolutely clear in your mind is that the names of actual and formal parameters have absolutely no relationship to one another as far as the processor is concerned. Given the function *minimum* outlined above, the initial procedure could invoke *minimum* with the statement

```
min ← minimum(x, y, z)
```

(assuming that x, y, and z are properly declared variables in the initial procedure). In this case the actual parameters x, y, and z in this statement have the same names as the formal parameters x, y, and z of function *minimum*. In fact, the initial procedure could include the statement

min ← minimum(z, x, y)

without confusing the processor. In this case the first actual parameter, z, of this call to *minimum* would match up with the first formal parameter, x, of function *minimum*. Similarly, the actual parameter x would match up with the formal parameter y, and the actual parameter y would match up with the formal parameter z. Although this looks confusing to the programmer and should therefore be avoided where possible, the processor will not be stymied by the similarity of the names of the formal and actual parameters. Such situations indeed arise when a group of programmers works on one program, with each programmer responsible for a different procedure or function.

In Only Parameters

When a procedure or function containing an **in only** formal parameter is called, a separate storage cell is reserved for this parameter and a copy of the corresponding actual parameter is placed into that cell.

Assume that the processor is executing the nonsense program given below

Example 2.7

```
goforit : initial procedure

    storage specification
        variables
            a, b, : integer
        end storage specification

    begin goforit
        a ← 5
        b ← 10
        output messup(a, 8, a + b)
        end goforit

    where messup does some strange things

messup : integer function

    storage specification
        parameters
            x, y, z : in only integer
        end storage specification

    begin messup
        x ← x + 1
        messup ← x + y * z
        end messup
```

Upon executing the initial procedure, the processor first establishes two storage cells named a and b and then assigns 5 to a and 10 to b, giving the store

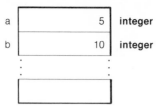

At this point the **output** statement of the initial procedure is encountered; this causes a call to function *messup.* The formal parameters of *messup* are **in only,** so separate storage cells are reserved for these parameters during execution of *messup,* and copies of the actual parameters are initially placed into these cells, giving the store

a	5	integer
b	10	integer
messup		integer
x	5	integer
y	8	integer
z	15	integer

Remember that a cell is also reserved for the function name.

After execution of the two assignment statements in function *messup* the store will then look like

a	5	integer
b	10	integer
messup	126	integer
x	6	integer
y	8	integer
z	15	integer

Notice that the change to the formal parameter *x* did not cause a change to the corresponding actual parameter *a,* because the copied value in *x* was changed, not the original in *a.* Thus, upon return to the initial procedure, the computed functional value of *messup* (126) is printed in the **output** statement and the store looks like

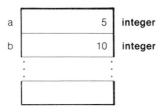

The variables *a* and *b*, which were used as actual parameters to function *messup*, have not been altered. In fact, since the formal parameters of function *messup* are **in only,** there is no way that the values of the actual parameters *a* and *b* could have been changed by function *messup*.

If a formal parameter in a procedure or function is **in only,** then the corresponding actual parameter in the calling routine may be a variable, a constant, (e.g., 5), an expression (e.g., $a + b$), or another function call. If the actual parameter is a variable, the value of that variable is copied into the formal parameter. If the actual parameter is a constant or an expression, then the value of that constant or expression is copied into the formal parameter. If the actual parameter is a function, that function is first executed, then its returned value is copied into the formal parameter.

In Out Parameters

When a procedure or function containing an **in out** formal parameter is called, the formal parameter shares the same storage cell as the corresponding actual parameter. Thus, any changes to the value of a formal **in out** parameter during execution of a procedure or function will cause changes both to the formal parameter in the called routine and to the actual parameter in the calling routine.

Consider the following program consisting of the initial procedure *fusser* and the procedure *mixit.*

Example 2.8

```
fusser : initial procedure

    storage specification
        variables
            a, b : integer
        end storage specification

    begin fusser
        a ← 5
        b ← 10
        mixit(a, b)
        output a, b
        end fusser

    where mixit does just that
```

mixit : **procedure**

   storage specification
     parameters
       x : **in only integer**
       y : **in out integer**
     end storage specification

   begin mixit
     output x, y
     x $\leftarrow$ x + 1
     y $\leftarrow$ y + 1
     output x, y
   end mixit

When the processor begins execution of this program, it sets up the store with two integer cells named *a* and *b* as specified in the initial procedure. The first two assignment statements of the initial procedure put a 5 into *a* and a 10 into *b*, resulting in the store

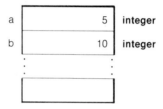

At this point procedure *mixit* is called, and *a* and *b* are passed as actual parameters to *mixit.* So, after the **parameters** statement of *mixit* is processed, the store looks like

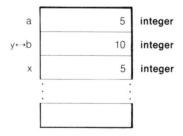

Since the formal parameter *x* is **in only,** it is set up with its own cell containing a copy of the corresponding actual parameter *a*, whereas the formal parameter *y* takes on the same cell as its corresponding actual parameter *b*, because *y* is **in out.** The $\leftrightarrow$ symbol in the cell label

   y$\leftrightarrow$b

indicates that changes to *y* will affect *b* and that *y* can "see" *b*'s value initially.
   The first **output** statement of *mixit* causes

   5   10

to be printed. Then 1 is added to both *x* and *y*, giving

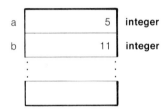

Notice that a change to the formal parameter *x* did not cause any change to its corresponding actual parameter *a*, because *x* as an **in only** parameter has its own cell. However, since *y* is an **in out** parameter and shares its storage cell with *b*, the change to *y* has caused the same change to occur to the corresponding actual parameter *b*.

When the second **output** statement of *mixit* is processed,

    6   11

is printed. This is the last statement of the procedure, so all values in the store corresponding to *mixit* disappear when control is returned to the initial procedure, leaving the store looking like

Here we see that *a*'s value has not been changed, but *b*'s value has. Thus, the final **output** statement in the initial procedure prints

    5   11

If a formal parameter in a procedure or function is **in out,** then *the corresponding actual parameter can only be a variable.* The way we have modeled the store, constants and expressions occupy no storage cells and so cannot be passed as actual parameters to formal **in out** parameters, because formal **in out** parameters take on the same storage cells as the corresponding actual parameters. (It would hardly make sense, anyway, to consider passing a constant (e.g., 5) to a formal **in out** parameter with the possibility that the formal parameter could be changed, thereby changing the value of the constant 5. Most Fortran processors do allow this, however.)

Because of possible side effects, formal **in out** parameters should generally not be used in functions.

Out Only Parameters

One other kind of parameter we have mentioned but not yet used in any case study is the **out only** parameter. If a formal parameter in a procedure is **out**

only, then that formal parameter will take on the same storage cell as the actual parameter sent to it. In this way an **out only** parameter is exactly the same as an **in out** parameter. However, the big difference between **in out** and **out only** parameters is that an **out only** parameter is not allowed to view or use any value in the cell of the corresponding actual parameter when the procedure is initially called. Essentially, this means that no value can be sent into the procedure via an **out only** parameter, but a value can be (and should be) sent back out to the calling routine through such a parameter.

This may seem strange at first, but **out only** parameters find use, for example, in procedures whose sole purpose is to input a set of values and return these values to the calling routine. This could also be done with **in out** parameters, of course, but using the **out only** designation for a parameter ensures that the procedure cannot use that parameter without first giving it its own value in the procedure, since that procedure is not allowed to use any value already in the associated cell when the procedure is called.

Example 2.9

Look again at the program of the previous example (initial procedure *fusser* and procedure *mixit*) in the section on **in out** parameters. Changing *y* from an **in out** to an **out only** parameter would cause an error in procedure *mixit*. The store would look like

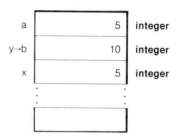

after the processor handled the **parameters** statement of *mixit*, where the notation

$$y \rightarrow b$$

indicates that changes to the formal **out only** parameter *y* will result in the same changes to *b*, but that *y* cannot see the value in *b* when procedure *mixit* is first called (even though there is a 10 there). Thus, the first **output** statement in *mixit*

output x, y

would cause an error, because as far as the processor is concerned the formal **out only** parameter *y* is undefined at this point. If in *mixit* we removed this **output** statement and replaced the statement

$$y \leftarrow y + 1$$

with

$$y \leftarrow 11$$

to initialize *y* in *mixit*, then the procedure would work fine.

A more likely situation involving **out only** parameters is demonstrated in the following program, which includes a procedure called *readin*, which inputs two integer values.

showit : **initial procedure**

    storage specification
      variables
          a, b : **integer**
      end storage specification

    begin showit
      readin(a, b)
      output a, b
      end showit

    where readin inputs two integer values

readin : **procedure**

    storage specification
      parameters
          x, y : **out only integer**
      end storage specification

    begin readin
      input x, y
      end readin

When the processor begins execution of *showit,* the store is set up with two integer variables, *a* and *b*.

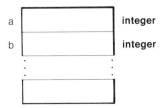

The first step of *showit* is calling the procedure *readin;* the undefined variables *a* and *b* are sent to procedure *readin* as actual parameters. As the processor begins executing *readin,* the actual parameters *a* and *b* are matched to the formal parameters *x* and *y,* giving the store

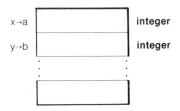

If 33 and 41 are at the input device when the **input** statement of procedure *readin* is executed, then the store will look like

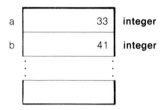

When the processor quits *readin* and returns to *showit*, the store will be

so the **output** statement of *showit* will cause

    33   41

to be printed.

Of course, this simple example seems silly, because the call to *readin* in the initial procedure could be replaced by

    input a, b

and procedure *readin* could be eliminated. However, in later case studies when large lists or tables of information must be input, it will be useful to do this in a procedure, using **out only** parameters to transfer the data to the calling routine.

For the same reasons cited for **in out** parameters, the actual parameters corresponding to formal **out only** parameters can only be variables, not constants, expressions, or other function calls. Also, because of possible side effects, **out only** parameters should generally not be used in functions.

Summary of In Only, In Out, and Out Only Parameters

Parameters are the only means for passing information among procedures and functions in *mpl*. It would therefore be helpful to memorize the following points about the different kinds of parameters:

1. Formal **in out** parameters are the most general. They can use the values sent into the routine in the corresponding actual parameters, and they can modify and return different values to the calling routine in the actual parameters. **in out** parameters should be used whenever communication both from and to the calling routine is required. The corresponding actual parameters must be variables, and the types of the actual and formal parameters must be the same.

2. Formal **in only** parameters receive copies of the corresponding actual parameters. Therefore, changes to the formal parameters do not affect the corresponding actual parameters. **in only** parameters should be used whenever communication from the calling routine is required but no communication

back to the calling routine is necessary, and whenever the procedure or function called should not be able to tamper with the actual parameter values sent.
3. Formal **out only** parameters cannot receive values through the corresponding actual parameters, but they can be used to send values back out to the calling routine through the corresponding actual parameters. **out only** parameters should be used when we want to communicate values back to a calling routine and we also want to ensure that values are actually assigned to the formal parameters in a procedure before these parameters are used within that procedure.
4. Generally, functions should use **in only** parameters, since functions should not cause side effects by changing the values of the actual parameters sent to the function. Procedures can use any of the parameter types.

When a procedure or function calls on a second procedure or function, the formal parameters of the first routine can be used as actual parameters to the second.

LOCAL VARIABLES

A procedure or function can also use variables that have been defined within that procedure or function in a **variables** declaration statement. These variables can only be used locally in the routine in which they were defined (unless they are passed as parameters to another routine). In general, parameters should be passed among procedures and functions only when they are required. Other storage cells needed only locally for computations within a function or procedure should be declared as variables in a **variables** statement and should not be passed as parameters.

PROGRAM VERIFICATION

Program verification, the process of ensuring that a program will always work correctly regardless of the input values, is a difficult and complex subject. In fact, it has been proved that one cannot write a program to examine all programs to determine whether they are correct. However, there are some relatively simple methods that can be used to help assure us that a program is correct; two of these methods are program walkthroughs and program testing.

A program walkthrough is done after the *mpl* design of the program is complete and before the program is translated into an actual programming language and run on a real computer. As we have demonstrated in the case studies in this chapter, a walkthrough is done by picking some appropriate input values and then executing the program just as the processor would. Program walkthroughs are useful in detecting *logic errors* (incorrect program design because of faulty thinking in developing a solution) as well as simple typographical errors (e.g., inadvertantly writing an *x* instead of a *y* in an **output** statement). A careful program walkthrough by you, or preferably by a friend who has not seen the program before, can give you confidence in the program design. However, it must continually be stressed that a program walkthrough does not prove that a program is correct, because it is normally impossible to do the walkthrough for all possible input values to the program.

After a program that has been designed in *mpl* is finally translated into an actual programming language, it should be tested with different input values.

This testing method is the same as the walkthrough method, except that the computer, not a human, executes the program. A larger variety of input values can be tested this way, but it is still generally impossible to test the program with every possible set of different input values. Also, the programmer must verify that the program output from each test is correct, a process that may require a calculator and some sweat.

We will refine these verification methods and introduce new methods in later chapters.

BATCH VS. INTERACTIVE PROGRAMMING

Before moving on, we should discuss the two general environments in which programs are designed to be executed. One is, for historical reasons, called the *batch* mode, and the other is called the *interactive* mode. Programs run in the batch mode are submitted to the computer along with the necessary input data and then left to be executed whenever the computer is ready. The programmer (or program user) can leave and come back later to pick up the program output.

In contrast, programs that run interactively require that the programmer (or program user) remain at a terminal, supplying data on demand as the program executes. This is the usual mode of program execution on personal computers and on many of the larger computers used for instruction in programming language classes. Computer games are the most obvious examples of interactive programs. Other more serious interactive programs use a video screen to list the various subtasks that the program can perform and ask you to select one by typing an appropriate number on the keyboard. Then, as the program executes, it continues to request information from you as it does its job. The program pauses each time it needs you to type information, and it will not proceed until you do type something. Thus, in order for an interactive program to execute successfully, you must interact with it, supplying input values when requested.

The biggest difference between batch and interactive programs lies in the input of data. In a batch program all the data must be provided at the input device before execution of the program begins. For example, if a program is to sort a list of names into alphabetic order, then the list of names must be provided at the input device before the program is executed. The programmer does not need to be present as this list of names is input and sorted.

In an interactive program, data is requested from a person as the program is executed. This brings up a key point about the way an interactive program must be designed: before each **input** statement in an interactive program, there must be an **output** statement to tell the program user what data to input next. During execution of an interactive program, the processor executes an **output** statement before each **input** statement, printing an appropriate message. Then, as the processor executes the following **input** statement, it pauses until the person at the video terminal responds by typing some appropriate data.

Each of the case studies we have designed so far has been designed as if it were to be run in batch mode. To modify these programs to run interactively, we only need to insert an appropriate **output** statement before each **input** statement.

If the program of case study 2.2 is to be executed interactively, we should include the *Example* statement *2.10*

output 'please enter the length and width of the rectangle'

just before the statement

input length, width

in the initial procedure. When the processor executes this modified program interactively, it processes the new **output** statement first, printing

please enter the length and width of the rectangle

for the program user to read; it then pauses at the **input** statement waiting for two numbers to be entered at the keyboard. After the numbers have been entered, the program continues executing exactly as was described in case study 2.2.

To summarize, the differences between batch and interactive programs are really not substantial. In an interactive program, special attention must be paid to the messages printed at the screen in order to make the program appear friendly and helpful to its user, but the actual design of the program itself is no different than that of a similar batch program. Therefore, we will continue to design the programs of our case studies around the batch concept. If you wish to run these programs interactively, you must include the proper **output** statements before each **input** statement as you translate the *mpl* program into your real programming language.

2.3 WARMUP EXERCISES

FOR REVIEW

2.1 Describe in your own words the top-down program design method and the role procedures and functions play in this method.

2.2 Which of the following statements are true?

(a) A function must always assign a value to the name of the function.

(b) There are essentially no conceptual differences between procedures and functions.

(c) A new function is like an extension to the operator set of a programming language.

(d) A new procedure is like an extension to the set of statements in a programming language.

(e) A function can be used anywhere a variable can be used in a program.

(f) A procedure can have a value assigned to its name.

(g) Functions should generally use only **in out** parameters.

(h) Procedures can use any kind of formal parameters.

2.3   In the use of functions, what are side effects? Give an example of a program that contains a function with side effects.

2.4   Explain the terms *actual parameter* and *formal parameter.*

2.5   Describe in your own words the uses of and differences among **in only, in out,** and **out only** parameters.

2.6   Indicate whether each of the following properties is true for **in only, in out,** and/or **out only** formal parameters.

   (a)   should not be used in functions
   (b)   may be used in procedures
   (c)   if changed, causes changes to the corresponding actual parameter
   (d)   if changed, will not cause changes to the corresponding actual parameter
   (e)   does not allow access to the original value of the corresponding actual parameter
   (f)   may have constants, expressions, or other function calls as corresponding actual parameters
   (g)   only allows variables as corresponding actual parameters
   (h)   allows values to be communicated from and to the calling routine
   (i)   allows values to be communicated in only one direction, from the calling routine to the called routine
   (j)   allows values to be communicated in only one direction, from the called routine to the calling routine

2.7   Describe in your own words the differences between variables and formal parameters, and explain why both might be needed in a procedure or function.

2.8   What is a program walkthrough? What is a program test? What is the difference between the two?

2.9   Explain why a program walkthrough or test cannot demonstrate beyond doubt that a program is correct.

2.10 Explain the terms *batch* and *interactive* as they relate to programs. What changes are needed to turn a batch program into an interactive program?

A DEEPER LOOK

2.11 In case study 2.2 we used **in only** parameters in function *rectangle.* What would have happened if we had declared these parameters to be **in out** instead? Would the program still have worked? Explain.

2.12 The questions of this exercise refer to the following program:

gandalf : **initial procedure**

    storage specification
      variables
          w, x, y, z : **integer**
      end storage specification

    begin gandalf
      x ← 2
      y ← 4
      z ← x + y
      output x, y, z
      gollum(x, y, z, w)
      output x, y, z, w
    end gandalf

    where gollum is defined below

gollum : **procedure**

    storage specification
      parameters
          v, w : **in out integer**
          x : **in only integer**
          y : **out only integer**
      end storage specification

    begin gollum
      v ← x + w
      x ← v
      y ← x + w
    end gollum

(a)   Do a walkthrough of the program. (Keep careful track of the store during this walkthrough, or you may get lost.) What values are printed by the two **output** statements?

(b)   What would the output of the program be if the **parameters** statement of procedure *gollum* were changed to

    parameters
      v : **out only integer**
      w : **in out integer**
      x : **in only integer**
      y : **out only integer**

(c)   What would the output of the program be if the **parameters** statement of procedure *gollum* were changed to

    parameters
      v : **in out integer**
      w : **out only integer**
      x : **in only integer**
      y : **out only integer**

(d)   What would the output of the program be if the **parameters** statement of procedure *gollum* were changed to

> **parameters**
>   v, w : **in only integer**
>   x, y : **in out integer**

2.13   Consider the following *mpl* program

peter : **initial procedure**

> **storage specification**
> **variables**
>   x, y, z : **real**
> **end storage specification**

> **begin** peter
>   x ← −4.5
>   y ← 2.0
>   rabbit (x, y, z)
>   **output** x, y, z
>   **end** peter

where rabbit is defined below

rabbit : **procedure**

> **storage specification**
> **parameters**
>   a, b : |parameter declaration|
>   c : **out only real**
> **end storage specification**

> **begin** rabbit
>   a ← a + b
>   c ← 2 * b + a
>   **end** rabbit

What will be printed by this program if |parameter declaration| is replaced by

(a)   **in only real**

(b)   **in out real**

TO PROGRAM

2.14   Design a program in *mpl* to compute the volume of a cube, where the length of each side of the cube is a real value input from the standard input device. Do a detailed walkthrough of your program with an input of 1.2.

2.15   A motorist is driving over the speed limit and is stopped by the police. Write an *mpl* program that inputs the driver's speed and computes the cost of the speeding ticket, given that the fine is $6 for each mph over 55.

2.16   Design an *mpl* procedure that rotates the values of three integer variables, *a*, *b*, and *c*, so that the value of *a* is placed into *b*, *b* goes into *c*, and *c* goes into *a*. Can this be done with only one local variable in *mpl*? As usual, you should write an initial procedure to call and test your procedure *rotate*. Do a detailed walkthrough of your program using your own input data.

2.17 Assume that there are three kinds of seating at a football stadium. Seats near the 50 yard line cost $25, those in the end zone cost $15, and other seats are $20. Design an *mpl* program that inputs three integers giving the number of $25, $20, and $15 tickets sold for a game, and computes the total income from the game.

2.18 Design an *mpl* program that reads in five integers and prints them out in reverse order. For example, if the input is

13   2   −7   64   −2

then the output will be

−2   64   −7   2   13

Use a separate procedure to perform a reversal of the formal parameters.

There are three case studies in this first challenge section. The first two deal with the problem of computing simple and compound interest. The final case study gives an example of a function that includes a call to another function. In none of these case studies will we include a section on program correctness. Instead, you should choose some appropriate values and perform a program walkthrough on each of the resulting programs to convince yourself that they are correct.

**2.4
THE
CHALLENGE**

Computing Simple Interest

Case Study 2.4

> ***Problem Description:*** Compute the interest earned on a simple interest savings certificate given the initial amount invested, the annual interest rate, and the duration in years and days of the investment.
>
> ***Input Specifications:*** First two reals, giving the initial amount invested and the annual interest rate, and then two integers giving the number of years and extra days of the investment period.

When money is invested using simple interest, the interest earned is not eligible for interest. For example, if we invest $100 at 5% interest for 3 years, the interest earned would be 5% per year on $100, or $5 per year, for a total of $15. If the money is not invested for an exact number of years, the additional days will earn interest at the rate of 1/365 the annual interest rate for each extra day. We will develop the formula for computing simple interest and use it in our function *interest*, which will compute the interest earned on the initial investment.

The Solution — A Function to Compute Simple Interest

First, we will design the initial procedure, which has the same basic organization as the other initial procedures we have written:

```
simple interest : initial procedure
     {prints the simple interest earned on an investment}

     storage specification
        variables
             initial, annualrate, earned : real
             years, days : integer
        end storage specification

     begin simple interest
        input initial, annualrate, years, days
        earned ← interest(initial, annualrate, years, days)
        output 'the interest earned is : ', earned
        end simple interest

     where interest computes the interest earned
```

CASE STUDY 2.4 — REFINEMENT 1

We now turn our attention to the function *interest*, which will not be quite as easy to design as the functions we have encountered previously. Our top-down method of programming is very useful here — we have deferred writing function *interest* until we can concentrate on it alone. When function *interest* is written, the program will be complete. Notice that the initial procedure does not make any assumptions about how interest is computed in function *interest*. If we wanted to compute compound interest instead of simple interest, we could use the same initial procedure and just design a different version of function *interest*.

To design function *interest* we must develop the formula for computing simple interest. From the preceding discussion, we know that the interest earned each year is

   initial * annualrate/100

and for each additional day the interest is

   1/365 * initial * annualrate/100

We assume that the annual interest rate is given in percent, for example, 11.5 (11.5%), so it must be divided by 100 to get the correct decimal form, for example, 0.115. The total interest earned is computed by multiplying the first expression by the number of years the money has been invested, multiplying the second expression by the number of additional days for which the money was invested, and then adding the two results:

   (initial * annualrate/100) * years + (1/365 * initial * annualrate/100) * days

We can factor this expression and rewrite it as

   (initial * annualrate/100) * (years + days/365)

With this formula we can now write the *mpl* function for computing the interest earned.

interest : **real function**
    {computes interest earned using simple interest}

    storage specification
      parameters
        initial, annualrate : **in only real**
        years, days : **in only integer**
    end storage specification

    begin interest
      interest ← (initial * annualrate/100) * (years + days/365)
    end interest

CASE STUDY 2.4 — REFINEMENT 2

Notice that the formal parameter names in this function match the actual parameter names used when this function is invoked in the initial procedure. Once more, we stress that this is not necessary.

Summary — Case Study 2.4

The top-down method of program design was very helpful here; It allowed us to design function *interest*, which took concentrated effort, without worrying about the rest of the program which uses function *interest*. Similarly, when we designed the initial procedure we deferred working on the interest function, assuming that the function existed and that it worked.

Computing Compound Interest

Case Study 2.5

> ***Problem Description:*** Repeat case study 2.4, computing compound interest instead of simple interest.
>
> ***Input Specifications:*** Same as case study 2.4

The Solution — A Function to Compute Compound Interest

Comparing this case study with the last one, we see that the only difference is in the way we compute the interest, which was isolated in the previous case study in function *interest*. Thus we can use the initial procedure from case study 2.4 to solve this new problem (although we should probably change its name from *simple interest* to *compound interest*). So, we just need to develop a new version of function *interest* here.

When interest is compounded, the interest rate is applied to all of the money currently owned, including the interest earned in previous years (this is the difference between compound interest and simple interest). After one year the investor owns the initial amount invested (*initial*) and also the interest earned on that amount:

initial + initial * annualrate/100

We will rewrite this formula as

current = initial * (1 + annualrate/100)   (1)

After the second year, the interest will be earned on *current*, and the total amount invested will be

current + current * annualrate/100

which can be written as

current * (1 + annualrate/100)

Using this expression and replacing current with its original value from equation (1) gives

initial * (1 + annualrate/100) * (1 + annualrate/100)

which is the same as

initial * (1 + annualrate/100)^2

Similarly, after three years, the total value of the investment is

initial * (1 + annualrate/100)^3

In general, the value of the investment after *n* years is

initial * (1 + annualrate/100)^n

If there are also *d* extra days when the money is invested, the total accumulation will be

initial * (1 + annualrate/100)$^{n+d/365}$

The interest earned can be found by subtracting the initial investment from this accumulated sum:

initial * (1 + annualrate/100) ↑ (years + days/365) − initial

where we have translated the formula into *mpl*. We use this formula to give us the compound interest function shown below in refinement 1.

---

interest : **real function**
  {computes interest earned using compound interest}

  storage specification
    parameters
      initial, annualrate : **in only real**
      years, days : **in only integer**
    end storage specification

  begin interest
    interest ← initial * (1 + annualrate/100) ↑ (years + days/365) − initial
    end interest

CASE STUDY 2.5 — REFINEMENT 1

Summary — Case Study 2.5

Because we used the top-down method when we designed the program to compute simple interest, we were able to compute compound interest by reusing the same initial procedure and changing only one line in function *interest*.

Computing the Area of a Trapezoid

Problem Description: Given real numbers *a*, *b*, and *h*, compute the area of a trapezoid with parallel sides of length *a* and *b*, and height (the distance between the parallel sides) *h*.

Input Specification: One input line containing three real numbers for *a*, *b*, and *h*.

The Solution — Use Function Rectangle of Case Study 2.2

The problem here is very similar to case study 2.2, where we computed the area of a rectangle. The initial procedure will be:

```
trapezoid area: initial procedure
    {prints the area of a trapezoid}

    storage specification
        variables
            a, b, h : real
        end storage specification

    begin trapezoid area
        input a, b, h
        output trapezoid(a, b, h)
        end trapezoid area

    where trapezoid computes the area of a trapezoid
```

CASE STUDY 2.6 — REFINEMENT 1

The interesting part of this program is developing function *trapezoid*. A trapezoid is shown below:

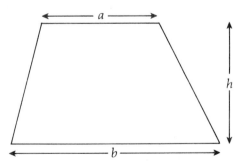

The area of this shape can be found by superimposing a rectangle on the trapezoid as shown:

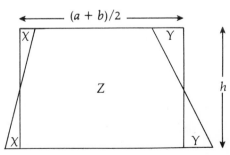

By comparing the common area (marked Z) and the areas of the two pairs of triangles X, X and Y, Y, we see that the rectangle has the same area as the original trapezoid. The width of the rectangle is the same as the height of the trapezoid (h), and the length of the rectangle is the average of a and b, $((a + b)/2)$.

One way to design function *trapezoid*, then, is to use function *rectangle*, which we developed in case study 2.2, calling function *rectangle* from within function *trapezoid*. This leads to the function shown in refinement 2 below.

---

trapezoid : **real function**
    |computes the area of a trapezoid with sides a and b and height h|

    storage specification
        parameters
            a, b, h : **in only real**
        end storage specification

    begin trapezoid
        trapezoid ← rectangle(h, (a + b)/2)
    end trapezoid

    where rectangle was defined in case study 2.2, refinement 2

CASE STUDY 2.6 — REFINEMENT 2

Notice that function *rectangle* is called in the statement

    trapezoid ← rectangle(h, (a + b)/2)

where the expression

    (a + b)/2

is one of the actual parameters sent to function *rectangle*. As we discussed in the In Retrospect section, we can use an expression as an actual parameter to function *rectangle* because the formal parameters of function *rectangle* are **in only**. Before *rectangle* is actually called, this expression is evaluated and the result is substituted for the expression. For example, if a is 10.0 and b is 15.0, then

    (10.0 + 15.0)/2

would evaluate to 12.5, and the call to *rectangle* would actually be

    trapezoid ← rectangle (h, 12.5)

This is the first time we have seen an initial procedure (*trapezoid area*) call on a function (*trapezoid*) that calls on yet another function (*rectangle*) to compute its result. The *calling sequence* is:

    trapezoid area
      ↓
    trapezoid
      ↓
    rectangle

As our case studies become more involved, extended calling sequences like this will become commonplace.

Improved Solution — Computing the Area of a Trapezoid Directly

Refinement 2 illustrates the idea of a procedure or function other than the initial procedure calling on a function, but it is cumbersome. Since the area of the trapezoid can be calculated directly with the statement

trapezoid ← h * (a + b)/2

we should probably do it this way, which is simpler than using function *rectangle*. This gives our final refinement for function *trapezoid*:

trapezoid : **real function**
  {computes the area of a trapezoid with sides a and b and height h}

  storage specification
    parameters
      a, b, h : **in only real**
    end storage specification

  begin trapezoid
    trapezoid ← h * (a + b)/2
  end trapezoid

CASE STUDY 2.6 — REFINEMENT 3

Summary — Case Study 2.6

In this case study we have designed two different solutions to the problem. As our problems become more complex, there will generally be many different ways to solve them. The first solution used the initial procedure *trapezoid area*, which called on function *trapezoid*, which in turn called on function *rectangle*. To execute this version of the program, these three routines would have to be gathered into a single package and submitted to the processor. The second solution was simpler, consisting of just two routines, the initial procedure and the modified trapezoid function, which computed the area of the trapezoid directly.

2.19 Design an *mpl* program to input the radius of a circle and compute and output its area and circumference. Your program should call two real functions, *area* and *circumference*, directly from the initial procedure. Perform a detailed walkthrough of your program.

2.20 Design an *mpl* program to compute the volume of a cylinder, given two real input values for radius and height. Design two versions of a function *cylvol*, one that computes the volume directly and one that uses the function *area* from the preceding exercise. Do a walkthrough for both versions.

2.21 What is printed by the following program?

**2.5
WORKING OUT**

```
bertrand : initial procedure

    storage specification
        variables
            x, y, z : integer
        end storage specification

    begin bertrand
        x ← 2
        y ← 4
        russell(x, x, x + y, z)
        output x, y, z
        end bertrand

    where russell is defined below

russell : procedure

    storage specification
        parameters
            a, b : in out integer
            c : in only integer
            d : out only integer
        end storage specification

    begin russell
        a ← b + c
        d ← a + b + c
        end russell
```

2.22   What would have been output if in the last exercise we had changed
       the formal parameters *a* and *b* from **in out** to **in only** in procedure *russell?*

2.23   In exercise 2.17 you were to design a function to compute the income
       from a football game. Now assume that for each ticket sold there is an
       additional income (on average) of $3.50 from sales of hot dogs, pro-
       grams, and so forth. Modify your original program to include this in-
       come and compute the total income.

2.24   Consider the following *mpl* program

```
alan : initial procedure

    storage specification
        variables
            x : integer
        end storage specification

    begin alan
        x ← 2
        output turing(x, x)
        output x
        end alan

    where turing is defined below
```

turing : **integer function**

    storage specification
      parameters
        a, b : {parameter declaration}
      end storage specification

    begin turing
      a ← a + b
      turing ← a + b
    end turing

For each of the following forms of {parameter declaration}, state whether the function will finish execution properly, and if so, what the program output will be and whether any side effects occur.

(a)   {parameter declaration} is **in only integer**

(b)   {parameter declaration} is **in out integer**

(c)   {parameter declaration} is **out only integer**

2.25   If you throw a ball up into the air with velocity v feet/second, the time before it gets back down again is about $v/16$ seconds. During its flight it will have traveled about $v * v/32$ feet. Design an *mpl* program to input a real value v and output the flight time and distance traveled for that starting velocity. Design two versions of the program, one with two real functions named *time* and *distance*, each with a single parameter v, and one with a single procedure with three parameters, v, *time*, and *distance*, where *time* and *distance* are declared as **out only real.** Perform a walkthrough for each version.

2.26   Design an *mpl* program to calculate the square root of any positive real number, n. Use a modification of a technique called *Newton's method:* estimate the value of the square root of n and save it in a variable named *guess*. If you then calculate the value of the expression

(guess ↑ 2 + n)/(2 * guess)

you should get an improved estimate, which becomes the new value of *guess*. Repeat this process five times. The value in *guess* should then be a good approximation of the square root of n.

Your program should input n and use $n/2$ as the first estimate of the square root of n.

| CHAPTER 3 |

Making Decisions

In this chapter we explore two important new statements: the **if** and the **case** statements. They will allow us to direct the processor to execute entirely different groups of statements based on certain conditions. Both statements use the processor's ability to compare values with its comparison unit. Before reading the case studies of this chapter, you may find it helpful to review conditional expressions in section 1.2 of chapter 1.

3.1
GETTING
ACQUAINTED

The case studies in this section provide a comprehensive look at variations of the **if** and **case** statements. Although not every procedural programming language includes both of these statements, they have proven to be very useful programming aids, so we have included them in our model programming language. These statements are easily simulated in languages where there are no direct counterparts, so you are encouraged to use the **if** and **case** statements freely as you design programs in *mpl*, regardless of which real procedural programming language you eventually use to implement your programs.

Case Study
3.1

Find the Larger
of Two Values

> ***Problem Description:*** Given two integers *a* and *b*, find the maximum of *a* and *b*.
>
> ***Input Specifications:*** One input line containing two integer values, one for *a* and one for *b*.

The Solution — If-Then-Else

The initial procedure for the program to solve this problem is trivial; we have seen it in other guises many times before and will see it many times again. It is given below in refinement 1.

```
max value : initial procedure
    {prints the larger of two input values}

    storage specification
        variables
            a, b : integer
        end storage specification

    begin max value
        input a, b
        output maximum(a, b)
        end max value

    where maximum(a, b) computes the maximum of a and b

CASE STUDY 3.1 — REFINEMENT 1
```

The design of function *maximum*, however, presents a new twist. The value returned by *maximum(a, b)* is to be the larger of *a* and *b*. How can we decide which of *a* and *b* is larger? We need to tell the processor, "If *a* is greater than *b*, then return the value of *a*. Otherwise, return the value of *b*, because *b* must be the larger value." The **if–then–else** statement allows us to do just that. Given two initialized integer variables *a* and *b*, we know that the processor can determine whether the expression

$$a > b$$

evaluates to **true** or **false,** so we can use the statement form

```
if a > b
    then {a is the larger}
    else {b is the larger}
    endif
```

to determine whether a or b is larger. If $a > b$ is true, the processor executes the **then** clause, otherwise the **else** clause is executed. This leads us to the following function for *maximum*.

```
maximum : integer function
    {computes the larger of a and b}

    storage specification
        parameters
            a, b : in only integer
        end storage specification

    begin maximum
        if a > b
            then maximum ← a
            else maximum ← b
            endif
        end maximum
```

CASE STUDY 3.1 — REFINEMENT 2

Correctness

In earlier case studies we have satisfied ourselves that a program was correct by performing a program walkthrough with some representative input values. This time we will assume that you can draw diagrams of the store yourself, so we will just do a restricted walkthrough.

Function *maximum* is the important part of this program to check out. Given two values a and b, will it always return the larger of the two?

Let $a = 5$ and $b = 15$. The **if** statement of function *maximum* becomes

```
if 5 > 15
    then maximum ← 5
    else maximum ← 15
    endif
```

Example 3.1

Since the expression $5 > 15$ evaluates to **false,** the **else** clause (not the **then** clause) is executed by the processor, causing 15 to be assigned to the function name *maximum* before control is returned to the initial procedure.

This choice of values for a and b indicates that function *maximum* will work properly when b is larger than a. What happens if a is larger than b? Let's pick $a = 0$ and $b = -5$. Then the **if** statement of function *maximum* becomes

```
if 0 > −5
    then maximum ← 0
    else maximum ← −5
    endif
```

In this case the expression $0 > -5$ evaluates to **true,** so the **then** clause is executed, causing the value 0 to be assigned to the function name *maximum.* The **else** clause is skipped. At this point function *maximum* terminates and control returns to the initial procedure with the proper value (0) in *maximum*.

There is one other condition we should check. What if $a = b$? Choosing $a = 5$ and $b = 5$, the **if** statement becomes

if 5 > 5
    then maximum ← 5
    else maximum ← 5
    endif

The expression 5 > 5 evaluates to **false**, so the **else** clause is executed and a 5 is stored into **maximum**. When the two values are equal, either one of them can be considered the larger, so function *maximum* works in this case, also.

In the case studies of chapter 2, we were able to do a walkthrough with just one set of representative input values. Whenever we use an **if** statement in a program, one set of input values is not enough to use as a program check. Instead, we need to choose enough sets of input values to check each possible execution path in the program. In this case study, for example, we picked one set of data to test the **then** clause of the **if** statement and another set to test the **else** clause. We must also be concerned with *special data values*. For example, in this case study special values include those where $a = b$. Since we had our minds fixed on picking the larger of a and b, we could easily have overlooked the possibility that those two values could be equal. These special value situations are the cause of many program logic errors, so it is important that you begin to identify special values and check your programs using these values.

The program check we did in the above example was not a complete program walkthrough and so was not absolutely convincing. For example, some remaining questions are whether the formal parameters of function *maximum* properly match the actual parameters passed from the initial procedure, and whether we have chosen the right kind of parameter (**in only**). You should do a complete program walkthrough to convince yourself that these parts of the program are correct.

Summary — Case Study 3.1

The basic form of the new **if–then–else** statement used in this case study is

if *condition*
    then {statements to do if the condition is true}
    else {statements to do if the condition is false}
    endif

The condition following the **if** is first evaluated by the processor to determine whether it is true or false. If the condition is true, the processor executes the statements following the **then** and skips the statements following **else**. If the condition is false, the processor executes the statements following the **else** after skipping the statements following **then**.

In function **maximum** there is only one statement after **then** and only one after **else**. Other situations will arise where more statements are needed, as in

```
if x < y
    then low ← x
         high ← y
    else low ← y
         high ← x
endif
```

which would assign the larger of x and y to *high* and the smaller to *low*.

The **if–then–else** is a *control statement*. Control statements are used to direct the processor to execute one group of statements instead of another or to control how many times a certain group of statements is executed. We will continue to see new kinds of control statements in this chapter and the next.

Compute the Largest of Three Values

Case Study 3.2

> *Problem Description:* Given three integers, a, b, and c, compute the maximum of a, b, and c.
>
> *Input Specifications:* One input line, containing three integer values for a, b, and c.

The initial procedure is again in our old standard form; it is very similar to the initial procedure in case study 3.1.

```
maxof3 : initial procedure
    {prints the largest of three input values}

    storage specification
        variables
            a, b, c : integer
        end storage specification

    begin maxof3
        input a, b, c
        output max(a, b, c)
        end maxof3

    where max computes the maximum of three integers
```

CASE STUDY 3.2 — REFINEMENT 1

Function *max*, which is called in the **output** statement of the initial procedure, will require more thought to design than was needed for function *maximum* of case study 3.1. In this instance, we must find the maximum of three integers rather than two. We will certainly need an **if** statement, but there are so many ways to approach this problem that it might be difficult to decide which approach to take.

First Solution — Nested If-Then-Else

Our first attempt at function *max* is this: compare a to b. If a is larger than b, then we don't need to worry about b anymore, because it can't be the largest;

the race is between a and c. However, if *a* is not larger than *b*, we don't need to worry about *a*; the race is between *b* and *c*. Let's write this down:

```
if a > b
    then {decide which of a and c is larger}
    else {decide which of b and c is larger}
    endif
```

This demonstrates another application of top-down programming. Here we have given the overall structure of the **if–then–else**, without filling in the details of what goes on within the **then** or the **else** clauses. Instead, we have just written what we want to do in words. Later we can concentrate on the **then** and **else** parts alone, forgetting that they are part of an **if–then–else**.

Now, let's do the segment

{decide which of a and c is larger}

by itself. In case study 3.1 we saw how to do this:

```
if a > c
    then max ← a
    else max ← c
    endif
```

The segment

{decide which of b and c is larger}

is similar:

```
if b > c
    then max ← b
    else max ← c
    endif
```

Now that we have finished these two segments we can plug them into

```
if a > b
    then {decide which of a and c is larger}
    else {decide which of b and c is larger}
    endif
```

to get

```
if a > b
    then if a > c
            then max ← a
            else max ← c
            endif
    else if b > c
            then max ← b
            else max ← c
            endif
    endif
```

Our top-down design has thus led us to the following design for function *max*.

```
max : integer function
   {computes the maximum of a, b, and c}

   storage specification
      parameters
         a, b, c : in only integer
      end storage specification
   begin max
      if a > b
         then if a > c
                 then max ← a
                 else max ← c
              endif
         else if b > c
                 then max ← b
                 else max ← c
              endif
      endif
   end max
```

CASE STUDY 3.2 — REFINEMENT 2

Refinement 2 contains an example of a *nested* **if–then–else** statement; both the **then** and the **else** clauses of the outer **if–then–else** statement are themselves **if–then–else** statements.

Correctness

Since a complete program walkthrough would take too much space, we will just describe how to assure ourselves that function *max* is correct. First of all, since *max* is a function, its parameter types should be **in only,** as indeed they are, so this part of *max* is correct.

Turning now to the computation section of *max,* let's pick three typical values to test *max* with.

Let's pick $a = 3$, $b = 5$, and $c = 4$ as values for testing function *max*. In this instance, a is not greater than b, so the **then** clause of the outer **if** statement is skipped and the **else** clause of this **if** statement is executed, testing $b > c$. Since b is greater than c, the **then** clause of this nested **if** statement is executed, causing 5 to be assigned to *max*. Afterwards, the **else** clause of this nested **if** is skipped and the **endif** is reached. Then, the next **endif** for the outer **if** statement is encountered, followed by the **end** of function *max*. Thus the processor finishes execution of *max* and returns with the proper value in *max* (5) to the point in the initial procedure from which function *max* was called.

Example 3.2

Remember our admonition from the previous case study: there are three things to do to test function *max* for correctness.

1. Check that function *max* works for "typical" values of *a*, *b*, and *c*.
2. Check function *max* with different sets of values for *a*, *b*, and *c*, chosen so that each different path in *max* is executed at least once.
3. Determine which values (if any) for *a*, *b*, and *c* represent special values that might cause *max* to fail, and test *max* with these values.

The previous example shows that function *max* works for a set of values where *b* has the largest value. We should also test a set in which *a* has the largest value and one in which *c* is the largest.

Example 3.3 Along with the set of test values chosen for the previous example, we could choose *a* = 5, *b* = 3, and *c* = 4, and *a* = 3, *b* = 4, and *c* = 5 as two other sets of test values. By checking function *max* with these values, we can assure ourselves that *max* will compute the proper largest value regardless of whether it is in *a*, *b*, or *c*.

Notice that there are four paths in function *max*, one for each of the statements in which *max* is assigned a value. Thus, four different sets of test values must be chosen to ensure that each path in function *max* is executed.

Example 3.4 The three sets of values from the previous examples test three of the four paths in function *max*. The only path not tested is the first of the two assignment statements

max ← c

(Do you see why?) By including *a* = 4, *b* = 3, and *c* = 5 as a fourth set of values, all the paths in function *max* will be executed.

What special values do we need to be concerned about in checking function *max*? The only special values appear to be those in which two or three of *a*, *b*, and *c* have the same largest value.

Example 3.5 The sets

a = 5, b = 5, c = 4
a = 5, b = 4, c = 5
a = 4, b = 5, c = 5

represent the three cases where two of *a*, *b* and *c* are the same, and the set

a = 5, b = 5, c = 5

is an example where all three parameters have the same value. Adding these four sets of values to the four sets of test values in the previous two examples gives us eight sets of values with which function *max* should be tested.

We would consider these eight sets of test values to be sufficient to convince us that function *max* works. To be even more certain, we might wish to test function *max* with all the possible combinations of values for *a*, *b*, and *c* chosen from the numbers 3, 4, and 5 — there are 27 different combinations (can you explain why?). Even if *max* worked properly for all 27 of these sets of values, though, we would have no absolute proof that the program was totally correct, because these sets only check *max* with the values 3, 4, and 5. (If we allowed negative numbers, would the results differ?)

As you can see, picking good sets of values to aid in verifying programs is a tedious process. On large real programming projects there is usually a team of analysts whose sole responsibility is to generate a good set of test cases for this purpose. There are usually so many cases needing to be tested that a program walkthrough is done only with one typical set of data values and the rest of the test cases are executed on the computer after the program has been translated into a real programming language.

Second Solution — Use of a Local Variable

There is usually more than one way to design a program to solve a particular problem, and we often find that while we are working on one approach, a different (and perhaps easier) one comes to mind. In the last refinement we were really finding the larger of *a* and *b* and then comparing it with *c* to determine the largest. We can do this more directly as shown in refinement 3:

```
max : integer function
    {computes the maximum of a, b, and c}

    storage specification
        parameters
            a, b, c : in only integer
        variables
            large : integer
        end storage specification
    begin max
        if a > b
            then large ← a
            else large ← b
        endif
        if large > c
            then max ← large
            else max ← c
        endif
    end max
```

CASE STUDY 3.2 — REFINEMENT 3

Notice that a new variable, *large*, holds the larger of *a* and *b* so that this larger value can then be compared with *c*.

Is this refinement better than the previous one? Perhaps. Some would find this easier to read than the nested **if–then–else** of refinement 2. A good rule of thumb is: if it's easier for you to read and understand, then it is probably better. Later, when we begin studying the efficiency of programs, we will see cases where this rule does not hold; then we will modify this rule to say that when two procedures have the same efficiency, the more readable one is probably better.

You should pick some appropriate values for *a*, *b*, and *c*, and do a walkthrough of this version of *max* to convince yourself that it works.

Third Solution — Use Compound Conditional Expressions

Another thought comes to mind. If a direct solution is a good solution, what about this: If *a* is greater than both *b* and *c*, then *a* is the greatest; if *b* is greater than both *a* and *c*, then *b* is the greatest; if *c* is greater than both *a* and *b*, then *c* is the greatest. In chapter 1 we learned how to write compound conditions, which we use in the following refinement:

```
max : integer function
    {computes the maximum of a, b, and c}

    storage specification
        parameters
            a, b, c : in only integer
        end storage specification

    begin max
        if (a > b) and (a > c)
            then max ← a
            endif
        if (b > a) and (b > c)
            then max ← b
            endif
        if (c > a) and (c > b)
            then max ← c
            endif
    end max
```

CASE STUDY 3.2 — REFINEMENT 4

Here we have used the **if** statement without an **else** clause; this is entirely proper. If the condition is true, the processor executes the statements following the **then** and goes on to the next statement following the **if.** If the condition is false, the processor skips the statements following **then** and continues execution with the statement following the **if** (since there is no **else**).

Should we check this refinement of *max* for correctness? After all, we've designed max a few times now, and we are getting pretty good at it, so what could be wrong? Every programmer gets this feeling of confidence once in a while and then falls flat on his/her face as a result. *This refinement will not work.* If the maximum value occurs more than once in a, b, or c, this function fails to compute the maximum.

Example 3.6 Try refinement 4 with $a = 10$, $b = 15$, and $c = 15$. a is not greater than b and c, so the first **then** is skipped, and the processor goes on to the second **if**. b is not greater than a and c, so the second **then** is skipped and the third **if** is executed. Similarly, c is not greater than a and b, so function *max* terminates without assigning a value to *max*; this is an error.

Not considering special values is a very common type of error. We kept thinking that we wanted to find the greatest value of a, b, and c, but we overlooked what would happen if some of these values were the same. (A properly constructed set of test cases would have caught this error.) We can easily fix this problem by checking whether a is greater than *or equal to* b and c, and so on, replacing the $>$ sign with the $\geq$ sign to get

```
max : integer function
    {computes the maximum of a, b, and c}

    storage specification
        parameters
            a, b, c : in only integer
        end storage specification

    begin max
        if (a ⩾ b) and (a ⩾ c)
            then max ← a
            endif
        if (b ⩾ a) and (b ⩾ c)
            then max ← b
            endif
        if (c ⩾ a) and (c ⩾ b)
            then max ← c
            endif
    end max
```

CASE STUDY 3.2 — REFINEMENT 5

You should check this function as usual to be confident that it works.

In spite of the fact that it does work, this particular version of *max* is somehow not satisfactory. Consider what happens if *a*, *b*, and *c* all have the same value, say 5. Then certainly *a* is greater than or equal to both *b* and *c*, so the **then** following the first **if** is executed,

    then max ← a

setting *max* to 5. That finishes this **if** statement, so the processor goes on to the next statement — the second **if** statement. Even though *max* has already been set properly, this **if** statement is also executed. *b* is greater than or equal to both *a* and *c*, so the **then** of this second **if** is also executed:

    then max ← b

This sets max to 5 again, a wasted effort. Similarly, the third **if** is executed, and in the **then** clause 5 is again assigned to *max* in the statement

    then max ← c

In our previous refinements we did not have this problem. We could fix this particular refinement by putting each new **if** within the **else** clause of the previous **if,** but this would make the function much too cumbersome, so we will just abandon this train of thought.

Fourth Solution — Use Function Maximum

Let's review refinement 3. The method we used there was to first find the greater of the two values *a* and *b*, call it *large,* and then find the greater of the two values *large* and *c*. It suddenly dawns on us that in the first case study of this chapter we wrote a function called *maximum* that computes the greater of two values. This means that we can rewrite refinement 3 as

```
max : integer function
   {computes the maximum of a, b, and c}

   storage specification
      parameters
         a, b, c : in only integer
      variables
         large : integer
      end storage specification

   begin max
      large ← maximum(a, b)
      max ← maximum(large, c)
      end max

   where maximum computes the maximum value of two integers.
```

CASE STUDY 3.2 — REFINEMENT 6

How simple! If we use function *maximum*, function *max* becomes trivial. We can make *max* even more elegant by replacing the variable *large* in

max ← maximum(large, c)

with

maximum(a, b)

(because *large* is *maximum*(a, b)). We can use expressions, including other function references, as actual parameters when we invoke function *maximum*, because the parameters of *maximum* are **in only**. This gives our final refinement of function *max*:

```
max : integer function
   {computes the maximum of a, b, and c}

   storage specification
      parameters
         a, b, c : in only integer
      end storage specification

   begin max
      max ← maximum(maximum(a, b), c)
      end max

   where maximum computes the maximum value of two integers.
```

CASE STUDY 3.2 — REFINEMENT 7

One very nice feature of this design is that having already convinced ourselves that function *maximum* of case study 3.1 works, there is really no checking necessary here to assure ourselves that this new function *max* works, because all it does is call on function *maximum*.

Example
3.7   To be sure we see how refinement 7 of function *max* works, let's try it with $a = 5$, $b = 7$, and $c = 7$. In executing

max ← maximum(maximum(a, b), c)

the values of *a, b,* and *c* are first substitued to get

max ← maximum(maximum(5, 7), 7)

The processor first does the innermost function call, which is

    maximum(5, 7)

This evaluates to 7, making the original statement

    max ← maximum(7, 7)

which is 7. Thus 7 is stored into *max* and function *max* terminates.

We have gone to great pains here to explain our thoughts as we have developed various refinements of function *max*. We will not have the space to do this for very many case studies, so you should reread this case study carefully to understand how the various versions of the program were developed.

Summary — Case Study 3.2

In this case study we have taken several different approaches to developing function *max*. There is often no obvious "best" solution to a programming problem — once you have developed a solution, you should always consider the possibility of better alternative solutions.

We have again emphasized the importance of checking our programs carefully. A program should be checked with representative values, values that test all paths in the program, and special values. If errors occurring with unusual special values are not caught during the design stage, they may not appear until the program has been in use for some time.

Sort Three Integers

Case Study
3.3

> ***Problem Description:*** Given three integers in any order, print them out in ascending order.
>
> ***Input Specifications:*** An input line containing three integers.

The Solution — A Sorting Procedure

The initial procedure for this program should read the three input values into three variables, call on a procedure to rearrange the values of these variables by sorting them into ascending order, and then print out the variables:

```
sort : initial procedure
    {prints three input values in ascending order}

    storage specification
        variables
            a, b, c : integer
        end storage specification
    begin sort
        input a, b, c
        sort3(a, b, c)
        output a, b, c
        end sort

    where sort3 sorts a, b and c into ascending order

CASE STUDY 3.3 — REFINEMENT 1
```

Procedure *sort3* must rearrange the values of *a*, *b*, and *c* into ascending order. For example, if *a*, *b*, and *c* contain 13, 8, and 20, respectively, then after the call *sort3(a, b, c)*, *a* should contain 8, *b* should contain 13, and *c* should contain 20. We will now design *sort3* to accomplish this.

Let's call the formal parameters of procedure *sort3* *p*, *q*, and *r*, just to remind ourselves that formal parameter names and their corresponding actual parameter names need not be the same. The formal parameters will have to be of type **in out**, since we want to rearrange the values of the actual parameters supplied to *sort3*.

Let's begin designing *sort3*. Remember what we want to do — get the smallest value into *p*, the next smallest into *q*, and the largest into *r*. First, let's try to get the smallest value into *p*. We can start by comparing *p* and *q*. If *p* is larger than *q*, then the value of *p* doesn't belong in *p*, so we should swap the values in *p* and *q* to get *p* and *q* in the right order with respect to each other. This is equivalent to the statements

```
if p > q
    then swap(p, q)
    endif
```

Procedure *swap* was already written in case study 2.3, so we don't need to worry about designing it.

As we develop a complex routine, it is helpful to write down in comment form what we have accomplished so far. At this point we can be sure that regardless of what values were in *p* and *q* initially, *p* will be less than or equal to *q* after the processor executes this **if** statement. (If *p* was greater than *q* to start with, *p* and *q* will be swapped, otherwise no changes will be made to *p* or *q*.) We will use a special comment called an *assertion* to state this fact immediately after the **if** statement:

```
if p > q
    then swap(p, q)
    endif
    assert p ≤ q
```

The **assert** statement really adds nothing to the calculation of the desired result — it is for the benefit of us humans. In this case we are saying, "We assert that *p* will be less than or equal to *q* after this **if** statement is executed, regardless of the original values in *p* and *q*." Of course, asserting something doesn't make it true. The **assert** just makes us think harder about obtaining a correct solution, because in a sense, we are putting our reputation on the line. It means that we have given careful thought to our design and we believe that it is correct.

Continuing the design of procedure *sort3*, we should now compare *p* with *r* and place the smaller of these two values into *p*. This gives us

```
if p > r
    then swap(p, r)
    endif
    assert p ≤ q and p ≤ r
```

Notice the **assert** statement. Since we know that $p \leq q$ is true before this **if** statement is executed, we know that

$$p \leq q \text{ and } p \leq r$$

must be true after this **if** statement is executed, because if p is changed at all, it is changed to a smaller value than was there before.

At this point, we know that p contains the smallest value of the original three. We still don't know if q and r are in the correct order, but we can take care of them with

```
if q > r
    then swap(q, r)
    endif
assert p ≤ q and q ≤ r
```

After execution of this **if** statement, we know that $q \leq r$ is true, and we already know that p is at least as small as both q and r from the previous **if** statement, so we can safely say that

```
p ≤ q and q ≤ r
```

is true after the last **if** statement. This means that p, q, and r are now in ascending order as we wished, so let's combine these **if** statements into a complete procedure:

```
sort3 : procedure
    {sorts p, q, and r into ascending order}

    storage specification
        parameters
            p, q, r : in out integer
        end storage specification
    begin sort3
        if p > q
            then swap(p, q)
            endif
        assert p ≤ q

        if p > r
            then swap(p, r)
            endif
        assert (p ≤ q) and (p ≤ r)

        if q > r
            then swap(q, r)
            endif
        assert (p ≤ q) and (q ≤ r)
        end sort3

    where swap exchanges the two integer values supplied to it.
            It was defined in case study 2.3.

CASE STUDY 3.3 — REFINEMENT 2
```

Correctness

You should choose some typical input values for a, b, and c and do a program walkthrough of refinements 1 and 2 to be sure that you understand how this program works. (Have we chosen the right kind of formal parameters for this procedure?) A thorough set of test cases should also be developed along the lines given for case study 3.2. The set of test cases for this program should include all possible initial orderings of three input values such as 3, 4, and 5 (there are six such orderings) to test whether the values will be properly sorted in every case and to test the six different execution paths in *sort3* (can you locate these six paths?). Finally the special cases where any two or all three of the initial values are the same should be included in the test cases (there are seven of these). Thus a total of thirteen test cases would be a thorough test of this program.

Example   Using input values 3, 4, and 5, a good test of this program would be to execute the pro-
3.8   gram thirteen different times, using the following sets of input values for *a*, *b*, and *c*:

(1)	3	4	5
(2)	3	5	4
(3)	4	3	5
(4)	4	5	3
(5)	5	3	4
(6)	5	4	3
(7)	4	4	5
(8)	4	4	3
(9)	4	5	4
(10)	4	3	4
(11)	5	4	4
(12)	3	4	4
(13)	4	4	4

Remember, again, that even such a thorough test as this does not prove that the program will always work correctly. For example, cases we have not tested include negative input values.

Summary — Case Study 3.3

In this case study we have developed a simple sorting procedure. Sorting is an important and common application of computers, and we will study it in more detail in The Challenge section of chapter 5, after we learn how to manipulate arbitrarily long lists of values.

The **assert** statement was also introduced in this case study. Including **assert** statements in a program does not affect the execution of the program, but it does provide the reader with information about what the programmer intends at various points in the program. Such assertions greatly improve the readability of complex programs.

Case Study | Assigning Student Grades
3.4 |

> *Problem Description:* Given as input the lowest possible score for an A, B, C, or D letter grade, followed by a student score, compute and print the correct letter grade for the student.
>
> *Input Specifications:* First, four numbers giving the lowest possible scores to receive an A, B, C, and D, respectively, followed by a student's score; all of these will be real numbers.

The initial procedure for this program should input the four grade break points and the student's score, and then call on a procedure to output the grade:

---

assign grade : **initial procedure**
 {inputs grade boundaries and a student score and then prints
 a letter grade for the student}

  storage specification
    variables
       lowa, lowb, lowc, lowd, score : **real**
  end storage specification

  begin assign grade
    input lowa, lowb, lowc, lowd
    input score
    print grade(lowa, lowb, lowc, lowd, score)
  end assign grade

  where print grade computes and prints a student's grade

CASE STUDY 3.4 — REFINEMENT 1

Notice that we could have joined the two **input** statements into one, but for readability we prefer to separate them when they have different tasks.

First Solution — Nested If-Then-Else

We can use a nested **if–then–else** to design the procedure *print grade.* We first check to see whether the student score falls in the A range. If it does, then we output an A and quit, but if it does not then we use another **if–then–else** that checks which lower grade to assign. This will give us a strategy that looks like:

if {grade is an A}
  then {output an A grade}
  else {find the correct grade below A}
  endif

where we just use comments to indicate what is left to be done. Let's consider the last comment

  {find the correct grade below A}

At this point we know that the student didn't get an A, so we should check whether the student is to get a B:

if {grade is a B}
  then {output a B grade}
  else {find the correct grade below B}
  endif

Again, expanding the last comment

  {find the correct grade below B}

we see that it should be replaced by a statement which determines whether the student is to get a C (because at this point we know that the student did not get an A or a B):

```
if {grade is a C}
    then {output a C grade}
    else {find the correct grade below C}
    endif
```

Finally, the last comment here

```
{find the correct grade below C}
```

should replaced by

```
if {grade is a D}
    then {output a D grade}
    else {output an F grade}
    endif
```

since at this point the only two possible grades are a D or an F.

Putting these pieces together with the proper conditional expressions after each **if** and the necessary **output** statements gives the following complete refinement for procedure *print grade*.

```
print grade : procedure
    {computes and prints a student's grade}

    storage specification
        parameters
            lowa, lowb, lowc, lowd, score : in only real
        end storage specification

    begin print grade
        if score ≥ lowa
            then output 'grade is A'
            else if score ≥ lowb
                    then output 'grade is B'
                    else if score ≥ lowc
                            then output 'grade is C'
                            else if score ≥ lowd
                                    then output 'grade is D'
                                    else output 'grade is F'
                                    endif
                            endif
                    endif
            endif
        end print grade
```

CASE STUDY 3.4 — REFINEMENT 2

A problem with this refinement is that the nested **if–then–else** statements make it nearly unreadable. To make it more readable we introduce a new **elseif** clause, which can be used in any **if** statement.

Improved Solution — If Statement with Elseif Clauses

The **elseif** clause lets us restructure procedure *print grade*:

```
if {grade is an A}
    then {output an A grade}
    elseif {grade is a B}
        {output a B grade}
    elseif {grade is a C}
        {output a C grade}
    elseif {grade is a D}
        {output a D grade}
    else {output an F grade}
    endif
```

Basically, this statement allows a series of tests to be made without requiring nested **if–then–else** statements. This structure asks: is the grade an A? If so, print an A, but if not, is it a B? If so, print a B, but if not, is it a C? If so, print a C, but if not is it a D? If so, print a D. Otherwise if no grade has been printed yet, print an F.

The new form of procedure *print grade* is thus:

```
print grade : procedure
    {computes and prints a student's grade}

    storage specification
        parameters
            lowa, lowb, lowc, lowd, score : in only real
        end storage specification

    begin print grade
        if score ≥ lowa
            then output 'grade is A'
            elseif score ≥ lowb
                output 'grade is B'
            elseif score ≥ lowc
                output 'grade is C'
            elseif score ≥ lowd
                output 'grade is D'
            else output 'grade is F'
            endif
        end print grade
```

CASE STUDY 3.4 — REFINEMENT 3

This version of *print grade* is not only shorter than the one with nested **if–then–else** statements, it is also much simpler structurally — that is why it is easier to read.

Correctness

At this point you should do a program walkthrough with some typical values to check the basic design of the program. Have we chosen the proper type of formal parameters for procedure *print grade*? For test values for this program, we should pick five different scores such that each of the grades A, B, C, D, and F would be printed. These test values would also cause each path in procedure *print grade* to be executed once. Scores that are identical to *lowa*, *lowb*, *lowc*, and *lowd* are special values that should be tested to see if the program prints the correct grade (e.g., if *score = lowb*, then a B should be printed).

Summary — Case Study 3.4

For this problem we developed two different versions of procedure *print grade*, one using a nested **if–then–else** structure and one using the **elseif** clause to avoid nesting. The repetitive pattern of the conditional expressions in *print grade* made the use of the **elseif** clause appropriate, since its use results in a more readable program.

In general, an *mpl* **if** statement has the form

> **if** *condition*
> > **then** *statements*
> > *optional* **elseif** *clauses*
> > *optional* **else** *clause*
> > **endif**

where there can be any number of **elseif** clauses (including none). Each **elseif** clause has the form

> **elseif** *condition*
> > *statements*

Finally, there is the optional **else** clause, which has the form

> **else** *statements*

In any **if** statement there is at most one **else** clause, and in some statements it will be omitted altogether.

Procedure *print grade* is the first procedure we have developed that communicates no computed values back to the calling routine. Instead, procedure *print grade* accepts required values from the initial procedure, performs the necessary calculations with these values, and prints the letter grade itself. Recall from the In Retrospect section of chapter 2 that procedures are allowed to do this but that such actions are not recommended for functions.

Case Study 3.5 | Compute Ticket Costs

> **Problem Description:** Design a program for a football ticket office. The program will input a code representing a ticket type ($25, $20, or $15) and the number of tickets purchased and print the total cost of the tickets.
>
> **Input Specifications:** Two integers, the first being either a 1 (for tickets costing $25), a 2 (for tickets costing $20), or a 3 (for tickets costing $15), and the second an integer $n > 0$, giving the number of tickets purchased.

In this case study we will introduce a new kind of decision control structure, the **case** statement. This statement is really a restricted form of the **if–then–else** statement with **elseif** clauses; it can be used only when the actions to be performed depend on specific values of a variable or expression.

The initial procedure is simple. It must input the ticket code and the number of tickets ordered and then print the total cost of the tickets by calling on a function, *price,* to compute this amount.

```
tickets : initial procedure
    {inputs a coded ticket type and number of tickets. Prints
    the amount owed}

    storage specification
        variables
            code, n : integer
        end storage specification

    begin tickets
        input code, n
        output 'total amount owed = $', price(code, n)
        end tickets

    where price computes the total ticket cost
```

CASE STUDY 3.5 — REFINEMENT 1

We now turn our attention to the design of function price.

First Solution — If with Elseif Clause

We can use the **if** statement with **elseif** clauses (as in the last case study) to give us a direct solution for function *price:*

```
price : integer function
    {computes the total ticket cost for one of 3 kinds of tickets:
    code 1: $25, code 2: $20, code 3: $15}

    storage specification
        parameters
            code, n : in only integer
        end storage specification

    begin price
        if code = 1
            then price ← 25 * n
            elseif code = 2
                price ← 20 * n
            else price ← 15 * n
            endif
        end price
```

CASE STUDY 3.5 — REFINEMENT 2

Three quick program walkthroughs with three different code values should convince you that this program works.

Improved Solution — Case Statement

Function *price* of refinement 2 is a reasonable solution to our problem, but it can be improved by using a **case** statement instead of the **if** statement. Most modern programming languages provide a **case** statement, which is the reason we have chosen to model this statement in *mpl*. The **case** statement forces the processor to choose among various alternatives (cases) based on the value of a particular variable or expression. To demonstrate the **case** statement, we will use it in a new version of function *price:*

```
price : integer function
    {computes the total ticket cost for one of 3 kinds of tickets:
    code 1: $25, code 2: $20, code 3: $15}

    storage specification
        parameters
            code, n : in only integer
        end storage specification
    begin price
        case code is
            when 1 : price ← 25 * n
            when 2 : price ← 20 * n
            when 3 : price ← 15 * n
        endcase
    end price
```

CASE STUDY 3.5 — REFINEMENT 3

Notice how clean this version of function *price* looks compared to refinement 2.

As we can see in this refinement of function *price*, the first line of a **case** statement looks like

case *expression* **is**

where the *expression* is called the *case control expression*, or, if it is a variable, the *case control variable*. In this function the case control variable is *code*. The **case** statement works in the obvious way: the value of *expression* is compared to each **when** value, in order, looking for a match (i.e., a **when** value that is equal to *expression*). When a match is found, the statement on the right side of the corresponding **when** clause is executed. For example, if *code* is 2 when *price* is called from the initial procedure, the statement

price ← 20 * n

is executed by the processor, and all other **when** clauses are skipped.

Mpl **case** statements can also have an optional **otherwise** clause that follows all of the **when** clauses and has the form

otherwise *statements*

If none of the **when** values matches the case control expression, then the statements following the **otherwise** keyword are executed. For example, we could have used an **otherwise** clause in function *price* to assign a −1 to *price*, when a bad code value is received from the initial procedure (a bad code value is one not equal to 1, 2, or 3):

```
price : integer function
    {computes the total ticket cost for one of 3 kinds of tickets:
    code 1: $25, code 2: $20, code 3: $15}

    storage specification
        parameters
            code, n : in only integer
        end storage specification
```

```
      begin price
         case code is
            when 1 : price ← 25 * n
            when 2 : price ← 20 * n
            when 3 : price ← 15 * n
            otherwise price ← −1
         endcase
      end price
```

CASE STUDY 3.5 — REFINEMENT 4

With this version of function *price*, the person running the program would know that the code had been mistyped (i.e., a code number other than 1, 2, or 3 had been entered) if the initial procedure printed −1 for the cost of the tickets.

Correctness

A walkthrough of this program using either version of function *price* and typical input values for the type (*code*) and number (*n*) of tickets ordered would indicate that this program works properly. A comprehensive test of the program in some real programming language for a number of well-chosen sets of input data would lead to the same conclusion. We inadvertently uncovered (and fixed) one potential problem (invalid data) when we demonstrated the use of the **otherwise** clause in refinement 4. A program may be intended to work only for a specific range of input values, but that does not mean that those using the program will never enter invalid data. Indeed, typing a code other than 1, 2, or 3 would be a particularly easy mistake to make when using this program.

This problem of handling invalid data is of great concern in real programming situations. Normally, the person using a program is not a programmer, and it is important to make the program as *robust* as possible, so that regardless of what an uninitiated (or malicious) user might supply as data, the program will not terminate abnormally with an error. Thus we should extend our concept of a correct program and say that a program is not truly correct unless it is robust.

Examining our program in this light shows that function *price* of refinement 3 is particulary fragile (as opposed to robust), because if an invalid code were passed to this version of function *price*, none of the **when** clauses of the **case** statement would be executed, and the function name (*price*) would be left undefined. Later, when the processor tried to output *price(code, n)* in the initial procedure, the program would terminate abnormally with a program logic error. This kind of error would blow most users away. As we have shown, refinement 4 takes care of this problem by assigning a −1 to *price* whenever an invalid code is received. The directions on the use of the program could include a statement that tells the user to check the input values and reenter the correct ones whenever a −1 appears as output.

The input specifications stated that *code* should be 1, 2, or 3, and that $n > 0$. From now on, whenever the specifications place constraints like this on the input, the initial procedure will make sure that the actual inputs satisfy these constraints. If they don't, we will print a warning, as is done in the modified initial procedure below:

```
tickets : initial procedure
    {inputs a coded ticket type and number of tickets. Prints
    the amount owed}
    storage specification
        variables
            code, n : integer
        end storage specification
    begin tickets
        input code, n
        if (n ≤ 0) or (code < 1) or (code > 3)
            then output 'bad input data, n = ', n, ' code = ', code
            else output 'total amount owed = $', price(code, n)
        endif
    end tickets
    where price computes the total ticket cost
```

CASE STUDY 3.5 — REFINEMENT 5

This version of the initial procedure and the version of function *price* given in either refinement 3 or 4 constitute a correct, robust program.

Of course, it is impossible to protect users completely from their own mistakes. If a valid, but incorrect, code and/or number of tickets is entered, the program will print a proper, but incorrect, answer. It would help to have the program print the number and type of tickets ordered along with the total cost; this would serve as a check that proper values were input (we will leave this improvement as an exercise).

Summary — Case Study 3.5

In this case study we introduced the **case** statement. Its general form is covered in more detail in the In Retrospect section. The **case** statement is useful in situations when there are a number of different cases to be handled and the cases are identified by the value of a particular expression (the case control expression). In such situations the **case** statement is structurally simpler and therefore easier to design and read than the equivalent **if** statement. If you want to implement an *mpl* design containing a **case** statement in a real programming language that does not support the **case** statement, then you can use an **if** statement, as we did in refinement 2 of this case study.

The idea of a robust program was also introduced. In the future we will assume that our programs should all be robust.

**3.2
IN
RETROSPECT**

In the Getting Acquainted section we saw examples of each of the common decision statements found in real programming languages, the **if** statement and its variations (with **else** and **elseif** clauses) and the **case** statement. Not every real programming language includes all of these statements, but each of these statements can easily be simulated in any of the common procedural programming languages. When you design a program in *mpl*, you should use whichever of these statements is appropriate, since your design can be translated just fine into any real programming language you choose.

The decision statements are examples of *control structures*, statements that control the flow of a program based on the values of program variables.

No serious programs could be written without using a control structure. In fact, the **if** statement in conjunction with *recursive* procedure or function calls gives us enough expressive power to design any possible program. Some examples of recursive functions are given in The Challenge section. Before starting these challenging case studies, though, we will review the new concepts of this chapter.

THE IF STATEMENT

The general form of the **if** statement as modelled in *mpl* is

```
if condition
    then statements
    elseif condition
        statements
        ⋮
    elseif condition
        statements
    else statements
    endif
```

There can be as many **elseif** clauses as needed, including none at all, and the **else** clause is also optional.

The **if** statement is executed by the processor like this: the *condition* of the **if** is evaluated, and if it is true, the processor will execute the *statements* in the **then** clause and resume execution with the next statement following **endif.** If the *condition* of the **if** is false, the processor evaluates the *condition* of each **elseif** clause in succession. The first time an **elseif** condition evaluates to **true,** the processor executes the *statements* of that **elseif** clause, skips all remaining **elseif** clauses and the **else** clause, and resumes execution with the statement following **endif.** If neither the **if** *condition* nor any *condition* of an **elseif** clause is true, the processor will excecute the *statements* of the **else** clause and then continue execution with the statement following **endif** (if there is no **else** clause, no statements within the **if** structure would be executed, and the processor would continue execution with the statement following **endif**).

If–Then

An **if** statement may have only a single **then** clause, as shown in this example.

Examine the following **if** statement:

```
if x < y
    then swap(x, y)
    endif
```

If *x* is 4 and *y* is 5, the statement

```
swap(x, y)
```

would be executed, and then the processor would continue execution with whatever statement followed **endif.** If *x* is 5 and y is 4, the processor would not execute the **then** clause but would just resume execution with the statement following **endif.**

Example 3.9

The **then** clause of an **if** statement can contain more than one statement, as in

if x < y
   then output x, y
        swap(x, y)
        output x, y
   endif

If–Then–Else

The **if–then–else** statement controls which of two different groups of statements the processor is to execute, based on the value of the **if** *condition* when the **if** is encountered by the processor during program execution.

Example
3.10

The following program segment is a simple **if–then–else** with just one statement in both the **then** and **else** clauses:

if x < y
   then max ← y
   else max ← x
   endif

The **then** and **else** clauses can contain more than one statement, as in

if x < y
   then output x, y
        swap(x, y)
        output x, y
   else max ← y
        output max
   endif

If x is 4 and y is 5 in this example, the three statements of the **then** clause

output x, y
swap(x, y)
output x, y

would be executed, then the processor would resume execution with the statement following **endif**. If x is 5 and y is 4, only the two statements following the **else**

max ← y
output max

would be executed, then the processor would continue execution with the statement following **endif.**

If with Elseif Clauses

An **if** statement can include **elseif** clauses, which allow the programmer to avoid complicated nested **if–then–else** statements in some circumstances (see case study 3.4, for example).

An example of an **if** statement with **elseif** clauses is

Example 3.11

> **if** (1 ⩽ grade) **and** (grade ⩽ 6)
>   **then output** 'the student is in grade school'
>   **elseif** (7 ⩽ grade) **and** (grade ⩽ 9)
>   **output** 'the student is in junior high school'
>   **elseif** (10 ⩽ grade) **and** (grade ⩽ 12)
>   **output** 'the student is in high school'
>   **else output** 'this is an invalid grade: ', grade
>   **endif**

If *grade* is 4, only the statement

> **output** 'the student is in grade school'

would be executed before the processor moved on to the statement following **endif.** If *grade* is 10, only the statement

> **output** 'the student is in high school'

would be executed, and the processor would then execute the statement following **endif.** If *grade* is 14, only the statement

> **output** 'this is an invalid grade: ', grade

in the **else** clause would be executed. If the **else** clause of the above **if** statement is removed and *grade* is −3, then none of the statements within the **if** structure would be executed; the processor would just resume execution with the statement following **endif.**

The most important thing to remember about the **elseif** clause is that it is *not* another nested **if** statement. It can not have a **then** or **else** clause itself (however, any statement in an **elseif** clause can be an **if** statement). An **elseif** clause can contain more than one statement, and an **if** statement with **elseif** clauses need not have a final **else** clause.

The following example should underscore the usefulness of the **elseif** clause.

The previous example written without **elseif** clauses would be

Example 3.12

> **if** (1 ⩽ grade) **and** (grade ⩽ 6)
>   **then output** 'the student is in grade school'
>   **else if** (7 ⩽ grade) **and** (grade ⩽ 9)
>   **then output** 'the student is in junior high school'
>   **else if** (10 ⩽ grade) **and** (grade ⩽ 12)
>   **then output** 'the student is in high school'
>   **else output** 'this is an invalid grade: ', grade
>   **endif**
>   **endif**
>   **endif**

This version is more difficult to read than the previous version. Notice the difference between the

> **else if**

nested **if** construct and the use of the

elseif

clause of the previous example.

CASE STATEMENT

The **case** statement allows us to avoid using complex **if** statements when the decision about which action to perform is based on the value of some expression or variable. The form of the **case** statement is:

case *expression* **is**
    when *value, . . ., value* : *statements*
    when *value, . . ., value* : *statements*

      :

    when *value, . . ., value* : *statements*
    otherwise *statements*
    endcase

where *expression* is the *case control expression* or, when it is just a variable, the *case control variable*. There may be one or more **when** clauses, each of which has at least one *value*, called a *case clause label*, of the same type as the case control expression. The **otherwise** clause is optional.

The **case** statement is evaluated as follows: First, *expression* is evaluated. The **when** clauses are then scanned in order to see whether one of their case clause labels is the same as the value of the case control expression. If a matching value is found, the *statements* on the right-hand side of that **when** clause are executed, then the processor immediately skips to the statement after the **endcase** without executing any more **when** clauses or the **otherwise** clause. If the processor fails to find a *value* that matches the value of the *expression* in any of the **when** clauses, it will execute the **otherwise** clause; if there is no **otherwise** clause, the processor resumes execution with the statement after the **endcase** without executing any **when** clauses.

Example
3.13
    If the integer variable *class* contains the number of a college class (1 for freshman, 2 for sophomore, 3 for junior, and 4 for senior), then the following case statement is valid

    case class **is**
        when 1 : freshmen ← freshmen + 1
            output 'member of freshman class'
        when 2 : sophomores ← sophomores + 1
            output 'member of sophomore class'
        when 3,4 : **output** 'upperclassman'
        endcase

In this example, if *class* is 2, only the two statements

    sophomores ← sophomores + 1
    output 'member of sophomore class'

would be executed by the processor, and then the processor would resume execution with whatever statement followed **endcase.** If *class* is 5, none of the **when** classes would be executed; the processor would continue execution with the statement following **endcase.**

Including the optional **otherwise** clause in a **case** statement is a way to catch invalid data or to handle a large group of related case values. The following modification to the above **case** statement illustrates this concept:

> **case** class **is**
>   **when** 1 : freshmen ← freshmen + 1
>   **output** 'member of freshman class'
>   **when** 2 : sophomores ← sophomores + 1
>   **output** 'member of sophomore class'
>   **when** 3,4 : **output** 'upperclassman'
>   **otherwise output** 'bad class number: ', class
>   **endcase**

In this **case** statement, if *class* is 2, the two statements of the

> **when** 2:

clause would be executed as we described before, then the processor would resume execution with whatever statement followed **endcase.** If *class* is 5, the processor would execute the statement

> **output** 'bad class number: ', class

of the **otherwise** clause and resume execution with the statement following **endcase.**

If a **case** statement must be implemented with an **if** statement in an actual programming language that has no **case** statement, the best choice would be to use **elseif** clauses. The other choice would be to use nested **if–then–else** statements, which would be unreadable for a large **case** statement with many **when** clauses.

Translating the first **case** statement of the previous exercise into an **if** statement yields

Example 3.14

> **if** class = 1
>   **then** freshmen ← freshmen + 1
>   **output** 'member of freshman class'
>   **elseif** class = 2
>   sophomores ← sophomores + 1
>   **output** 'member of sophomore class'
>   **elseif** (class = 3) **or** (class = 4)
>   **output** 'upperclassman'
>   **else output** 'bad class number: ', class
>   **endif**

This **if** statement is not as elegant as the **case** statement.

Case statements should not be used with **real** case control expressions or **real** case clause labels, because of problems with *roundoff errors*, which occur because real computers cannot always represent decimal real values accurately.

Example
3.15   The following **case** statement would probably output B instead of A, because the computer will probably assign *x* the value 0.1999999 (or something similar) instead of 0.2, for reasons that we don't need to understand now.

```
x ← 1.0/5.0 {assume x is real}
case x is
    when 0.1, 0.2, 0.3 : output 'A'
    otherwise output 'B'
endcase
```

This is a special case of a general problem. We should avoid, where possible, checking to see whether two real values are equal, as roundoff problems will often introduce errors.

PROGRAM CORRECTNESS

As we develop more sophisticated programs, we find that it becomes more important to assure ourselves that the programs are correct. A program design is not complete until it is verified. Although it is impossible to show mechanically that every program is correct, we have introduced a number of methods that aid in the verification process.

Program Walkthrough

After the *mpl* design of a program is complete and before the program has been translated into some real programming language, one or more program walkthroughs should be made. A program walkthrough is done by the programmer (or preferably by a friend), who performs a careful hand execution of the program with some appropriately chosen input values. Most serious design errors can be detected by a careful program walkthrough.

Program Testing

Once an *mpl* program design has been thoroughly checked out by at least one program walkthrough, the program should be translated into a real programming language and executed a number of times with different input values. The results should be checked by hand to determine whether they are correct. Appropriate input values to test a program should be chosen as follows:

1. *Representative input values.* For example, if a program is to compute the largest of three input values, then the program should be tested with at least three different sets of input values in which the first, second, and third input values, respectively, are the largest. A more thorough test could be made over the six different sets of data representing all permutations of three given input numbers.
2. *Values that cause each path in the program to be executed.* Different sets of input values should be chosen so that each **then, elseif,** and **else** clause of an **if** statement or each **when** and **otherwise** clause of a **case** statement is executed at least once.
3. *Special input values.* For example, if a program is to award an A grade to a student with a score of 90 or higher, then 90 is an obvious special score that

should be used to check the program, because it lies on the boundary between As and Bs. Similarly, if a function is to compute the largest of three values, then the special cases to test would be those in which any two or all three of the input values are the same.

4. *Invalid data.* A robust program should not crash if invalid data is included — it should print an appropriate warning message and terminate normally. For example, if a program is to check for the four values 1, 2, 3, and 4 (meaning freshman, sophomore, junior, and senior, respectively) then an input of 5 should be detected as being invalid and an appropriate error message should be printed.

Program testing can become quite involved, requiring months of work for a large program whose reliability is crucial. The guidelines for the small programs we are developing here also apply to large real-life programs.

Program Comments

Any technique that makes a program more understandable will help in checking the correctness of a program. Comments can be used for this purpose. In top-down program design, where each procedure and function does some small integrated task, the comment just after the procedure or function header statement describing what the routine does is usually the only one necessary. Occasionally a comment may be needed to explain a rather complex calculation, but if explanatory variable names are chosen, such comments are usually unnecessary. (Remember, too, that whenever a calculation is particularly complex, it should be isolated in a separate procedure or function, anyway.)

A potentially negative effect of comments is that they state what we *think* a program does, not what it *actually* does. Therefore, comments should only be included in a program after the program has been designed and verified. Any necessary comments should be placed just in front of the group of statements being explained.

Program Assertions

Assertions were first used in case study 3.3. An assertion is a special comment that is used to declare the status of certain program variables immediately after a crucial computation has been performed. Assertions and comments are both ignored by the processor, but assertions and comments are used for different purposes. A comment is a general description of a particular calculation and is placed *in front of* that calculation after the program design is known to be correct. An assertion is placed *after* the calculation during the development of the program, to aid the programmer in the next stages of development.

After the **if** statement below has been executed, the trailing assertion will always be correct.

Example 3.16

```
if x < y
    then swap(x, y)
    endif
assert y ≤ x
```

The programmer can use the **assert** statement to determine what the next statements in the program should accomplish instead of having to look back at the (potentially long) **if** statement to see what the program has just done.

The most important point to remember about an **assert** statement is that it could be wrong. In the above example, a common mistake would be to write

assert $y < x$

which would not generally be true after execution of the **if** statement. So, although **assert** statements can be a useful aid in designing correct programs, they obviously need to be carefully formulated. The very act of writing an assertion in a program should make the programmer critically examine the program to make sure that the assertion is correct; thus, including assertions in the design of a program helps the programmer prepare a correct final version of the program. Assertions will play an increasingly important role in later chapters.

3.3 WARMUP EXERCISES

FOR REVIEW

3.1 Write down the general form of the **if** statement, then compare your version with that given in the book.

3.2 In your own words, explain the difference between using an **elseif** clause in an **if** statement and using a nested **if** statement.

3.3 Look at the following **if** statement:

if $x \geqslant y + 1$
    then output x
    else output y
    endif

What will be printed if

(a) $x = 6$ and $y = 9$

(b) $x = 6$ and $y = -7$

(c) $x = 6$ and $y = 5$?

3.4 Examine the following **if** statement:

if $x + 1 \geqslant y - 1$
    then $x \leftarrow x + 1$
        output x, y
    endif

What will be printed if

(a) $x = 6$ and $y = 8$

(b) $x = 6$ and $y = 7$

(c) $x = 10$ and $y = 100$?

3.5   List the criteria for constructing a set of input values to test a program.

3.6   Describe in your own words what the term *robust program* means.

3.7   Describe (a) the purpose of program comments, (b) where they should be included in a program, (c) when they should be included in a program, (d) the danger inherent in their use.

3.8   Describe (a) the purpose of formal **assert** statements in a program, (b) where they should be placed in a program, (c) when they should be included in a program, and (d) the danger inherent in the use of **assert** statements.

3.9   Does the use of comments affect execution of the program? Explain.

3.10   Does the use of formal assertions affect execution of the program? Explain.

3.11   Explain what is meant by an *execution path* of a program and why there can be more than one execution path in a program.

3.12   How many execution paths are there in the *mpl* program segment of exercise 3.3? Identify them.

3.13   How many execution paths are there in the *mpl* program segment of exercise 3.4? Identify them.

3.14   In the execution of a valid **if** statement with both a **then** and an **else** clause and possibly **elseif** clauses, are there any conditions that would result in none of the clauses being executed? If so, give an example; if not, explain why.

3.15   Give the general form of the **case** statement and then compare your definition with that given in this chapter.

3.16   Which is the more general statement, the **if** or the **case** statement? Explain.

3.17   Why should the case control expression and the case clause labels of a **case** statement not be real values?

3.18   Examine the following program segment

```
input n
case n is
    when 1 : output 'first class'
    when 2 : output 'second class'
    when 3 : output 'third class'
    otherwise output 'bad class number'
    endcase
output 'submit next class number'
```

(a)   If the input is 1, what will be printed?

(b)   If the input is −5, what will be printed?

(c)   If the input is 3, what will be printed?

(d)   If the input is 10, what will be printed?

(e) How many execution paths are there in this program segment? Identify them.

(f) Is this program segment robust? If so, explain why; otherwise explain how it could be modified to be made robust.

A DEEPER LOOK

3.19 Look at the following *mpl* segment, where x is assumed to be an integer test score between 0 and 100.

```
input x
if (0 ≤ x) and (x < 40)
    then output 'you fail, miserably'
    elseif (40 ≤ x) and (x < 50)
        output 'you fail, but not too badly'
    elseif (50 ≤ x) and (x < 70)
        output 'your grade is ', x
        output 'you did satisfactorily'
    elseif (70 ≤ x) and(x < 85)
        output 'your grade is ', x
        output 'you did well'
    elseif (85 ≤ x) and (x < 100)
        output 'your grade is ', x
        output 'outstanding, man'
    endif
output 'how did you do?'
```

(a) What will be printed if the input value is 0?

(b) What will be printed if the input value is 100?

(c) What will be printed if the input is 51?

(d) What will be printed if the value is −5?

(e) Is this *mpl* segment robust? If so, explain why. If not, explain how it could be fixed to be robust.

(f) How many execution paths are there in this *mpl* segment?

(g) Give a set of typical values for testing this program segment. Defend your choices.

(h) Give a set of values that would cause each path in this segment to be executed. Must this set be different from those in (g)?

(i) Give a set of special test values, and explain why the values you have chosen are special.

(j) Give a set of invalid scores for testing this program segment, and explain why the values are invalid.

3.20 Could the last exercise be written as a case statement? Defend your answer.

3.21 If you were told that you could use the *mpl* **case** statement, but that the **otherwise** clause is not available, how would you handle any case normally handled by an **otherwise** clause when designing an *mpl* program?

3.22   Examine the following *mpl* program segment:

if *condition*
    then t ← x
        x ← y
        y ← t
    endif
assert x ⩾ y

Which of the following could replace *condition* so that the assertion will always be true?

(a) x > y   (b) x ⩾ y   (c) x < y   (d) x ⩽ y

(e)   x = y   (f) (x > y) **or** (y ⩽ x)   (g) x > t

3.23   Develop a set of input values for testing the program designed in case study 3.4. Defend your choices.

3.24   Develop a set of input values for testing the program designed in case study 3.5. Defend your choices.

The next five questions refer to the following **case** statement, where *nuts* is an integer variable and *trunc* is a function that returns just the integer part of a value.

```
case trunc(nuts/5) is
    when 1 :          nuts ← nuts + 1
    when 10, −10 : output nuts
                      nuts ← nuts * 2
    when 50 :         output nuts ↑ 2
                      nuts ← nuts / 2
    otherwise         output 'nuts to you, bad value'
    endcase
```

3.25   What typical values should be chosen for variable *nuts* to test this case statement?

3.26   How many execution paths are there in this **case** statement? Is it the same number as the number of values that you used in the last exercise? If not, explain why.

3.27   Rewrite this **case** statement so that it computes the same results without using an **otherwise** clause (you may use an **if** statement along with the **case** statement).

3.28   Rewrite this **case** statement using only an **if** statement.

3.29   Rewrite this **case** statement using an **if** statement without **elseif** clauses.

TO PROGRAM

3.30   Design a program that inputs a real number and outputs its absolute value. Design your own absolute value function.

3.31   You drive through a police radar trap, and need to know how much (if anything) you owe in fines. You need to pay a fine if your speed is over 55 mph. For each mph between 56 and 60, you must pay $5; for each mph between 61 and 65, you must pay $10; and you must pay $20 for each mph over 65. Design a program that inputs your speed and outputs the fine. Design two different versions of your principal function, one based on an **if** with **elseif** clauses, and one based on a **case** statement. Select an appropriate set of test cases for your program and justify your selection.

3.32   A year is a leap year if it is exactly divisible by 4, unless it is exactly divisible by 100, in which case it is only a leap year if it is divisible by 400. For example, 1984, 1988, and 2000 are leap years, but 1990 and 1900 are not. Design a program that inputs a year number and determines whether or not it is a leap year.

3.33   In case study 3.2 we developed a number of different approaches for finding the maximum of three integers. Analyze each of these approaches and compare them, giving advantages and disadvantages for each one. Rank the solutions in your order of preference.

Extend each approach to an *mpl* function that returns the maximum of four integers. Does your solution to this part of the question change your ranking from the first part?

3.34   Describe and compare any strategies that you can think of to find the second largest of three real inputs. Design an *mpl* program for the best of these strategies. Develop a good set of test cases for your program, and justify your selection.

3.35   Modify case study 3.5 refinement 5 to print the number and type of tickets ordered along with the total cost. As discussed, this will make the program more robust.

**3.4
THE
CHALLENGE**

In this section we will see some advanced uses of **if** statements, including their application in recursive functions.

**Case Study
3.6**

Factorial

Problem Description: Given an integer *n* greater than or equal to zero, design a program that calculates its factorial (*n*!).

Input Specifications: One input line containing a value for *n* that is greater than or equal to zero.

Factorial is a function that can be applied to integer values greater than or equal to zero.

***Example
3.17***

The factorial of 4, written 4!, is just

$$4 * 3 * 2 * 1$$

which has the value 24.

The factorial of an integer *n* is computed by multiplying *n* times $n-1$ times $n-2$ times ... times 1. Since this is such a cumbersome definition, however, *n*! is usually defined *recursively* as

$$n! = \begin{cases} 1 \text{ if } n = 0 \\ n * (n-1)! \text{ if } n > 0 \end{cases}$$

This definition is recursive because if n is greater than 0, $n!$ is defined to be

$n * (n-1)!$

so we must apply the definition again to compute $(n-1)!$ If $n-1$ is greater than 0, then $(n-1)!$ is

$(n-1) * (n-2)!$

so we must compute $(n-2)!$, and so forth.

Applying the recursive definition to 4! gives

Example 3.18

4! = 4 * 3!

because 4 is not equal to 0. Since 3! now appears in our computation, we must apply the factorial definition again (recursively) to 3! This gives us

3! = 3 * 2!

so we now have

4! = 4 * 3! = 4 * 3 * 2!

Again, $2 \neq 0$, so

2! = 2 * 1!

which leads to

1! = 1 * 0!

We now have

4! = 4 * 3! = 4 * 3 * 2! = 4 * 3 * 2 * 1! = 4 * 3 * 2 * 1 * 0!

What is 0! ? By definition it is 1, so

4! = 4 * 3 * 2 * 1 * 1

which can now be multiplied (since there are no more calls to factorial) to yield 24.

Table 3–1 gives a short list of integers and their factorials. The values of $n!$ increase rapidly as n gets larger.

TABLE 3–1. VALUES OF $n!$

n	Definition	Value
0	1	1
1	1 * 0!	1
2	2 * 1!	2
3	3 * 2!	6
4	4 * 3!	24
5	5 * 4!	120
6	6 * 5!	720
7	7 * 6!	5040
8	8 * 7!	40320

The Solution — A Recursive Function

Let's design a program to calculate $n!$. The initial procedure in refinement 1 just reads in n and prints the value of the function *factorial*(n), first checking that n satisfies the input specifications, which state that $n \geqslant 0$.

---

factorial of n : **initial procedure**
    {inputs an integer n and prints n!}

  storage specification
    variables
      n, nfactorial : **integer**
    end storage specification

  begin factorial of n
    input n
    if n < 0
      then output 'negative input: ', n
      else nfactorial ← factorial(n)
        output n, ' factorial = ', nfactorial
    endif
  end factorial of n

  where factorial computes the factorial of n

CASE STUDY 3.6 — REFINEMENT 1

We can now design function *factorial* to compute the factorial of n. Look again at the mathematical definition of factorial:

$$n! = \begin{cases} 1 \text{ if } n = 0 \\ n * (n-1)! \text{ if } n > 0 \end{cases}$$

It is very easy to write this in *mpl:*

  if n = 0
    then factorial ← 1
    else factorial ← n * factorial(n − 1)
  endif

This **if** statement is a direct statement of the definition of factorial, and it is the computation section of function *factorial:*

---

factorial : **integer function**
    {computes n!}

  storage specification
    parameters
      n : **in only integer**
    end storage specification

  begin factorial
    if n = 0
      then factorial ← 1
      else factorial ← n * factorial(n − 1)
    endif
  end factorial

CASE STUDY 3.6 — REFINEMENT 2

We call function *factorial* a *recursive function* because within the computation section of function *factorial* is the statement

factorial ← n * factorial(n − 1)

which calls on function *factorial* again. Recursive functions and procedures are very useful programming tools. In some instances, they are so easy to write that they represent the most logical way of solving a problem. Factorial is a case in point: the function *factorial* is nearly identical to the formal definition of factorial. This suggests that if we are given a formal recursive definition of a function or procedure, we can often write it directly in *mpl* without having to design a different method of solving the problem. Many programming problems can be stated recursively, and writing the recursive programs to solve these problems is easy.

Since *factorial* is our first look at a recursive function, we might wonder how the processor handles it. Perhaps the best way to understand this is to think of the processor generating a new copy of the *mpl* function *factorial* each time *factorial* is called recursively. Thus, each time *factorial* is called, new storage cells are set aside for the formal **in only** parameter *n* and the function name *factorial*, and this new version of *factorial* is executed as if it were an entirely separate function.

Correctness

A program walkthrough will demonstrate that function *factorial* works.

In the previous example we showed how 4! is computed mathematically. Let's see now how our *mpl factorial* function computes 4!

Example 3.19

Assume that the initial procedure sets up storage cells for the variables *n* and *nfactorial*, and inputs 4 into *n*. It then calls *factorial(n)*. As the processor begins executing function *factorial*, a storage cell must be set aside for the function name, *factorial*, and another for the formal **in only** parameter, *n*, which contains a copy of the actual parameter 4. This gives the store

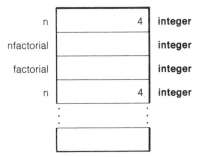

At this point the processor begins executing the **if** statement of function *factorial*. Substituting the value of the formal parameter *n* (4) into this **if** statement, we see that the processor is executing

```
if 4 = 0
    then factorial ← 1
    else factorial ← 4 * factorial(3)
    endif
```

Since 4 is not equal to 0, the statement of the **else** clause,

factorial ← 4 * factorial(3)

will be executed. Before the multiplication can be done, however, the function call

factorial(3)

must be evaluated by the processor. This causes a new call to function *factorial*. The processor will just assume that there is a brand new function *factorial* available and will send the actual parameter value, 3, to the formal **in only** parameter *n* of this new factorial function. Pictorially this can be represented as

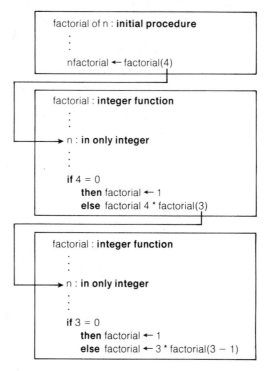

As the processor begins executing this new function *factorial*, one storage cell must be set aside for the function name *factorial*, and another for the formal **in only** parameter *n*, which receives a copy of the actual parameter 3. Thus, as the processor begins executing this new version of function *factorial*, the store looks like

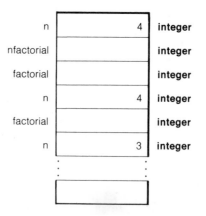

The processor is able to keep track of the fact that only the last two named cells in the store belong to this new version of *factorial*.

As the processor executes this latest *factorial* function, *n* has the value 3, so the computation section is (**endif** is omitted to conserve space):

if 3 = 0
    then factorial ← 1
    else factorial ← 3 * factorial(2)

As can be seen, execution of this **if** statement generates a new call to *factorial,* this time with actual parameter value 2.

The process continues. The new *factorial* function that was invoked in the statement

factorial ← 3 * factorial(2)

causes another new *factorial* function to be called in the statement

factorial ← 2 * factorial(1)

which in turn causes another new *factorial* function to be called in the statement

factorial ← 1 * factorial(0)

This statement causes the final call to function *factorial* with actual parameter 0. Pictorially, this entire series of recursive calls to *factorial* can be represented as

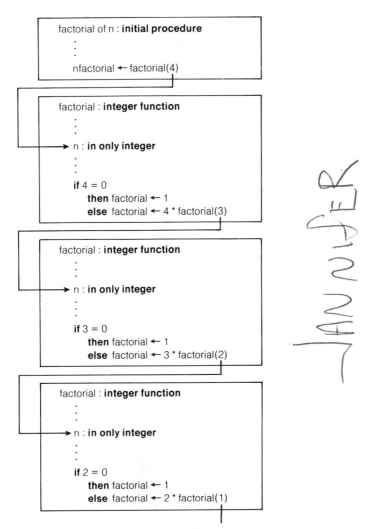

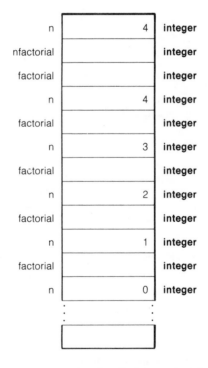

factorial : **integer function**
⋮
➤ n : **in only integer**
⋮

    if 1 = 0
       then factorial ← 1
       else factorial ← 1 * factorial(0)

factorial : **integer function**
⋮
➤ n : **in only integer**
⋮

    if 0 = 0
       then factorial ← 1
       else factorial ← 1 * factorial(−1)

At this point the store would look like

label	value	type
n	4	**integer**
nfactorial		**integer**
factorial		**integer**
n	4	**integer**
factorial		**integer**
n	3	**integer**
factorial		**integer**
n	2	**integer**
factorial		**integer**
n	1	**integer**
factorial		**integer**
n	0	**integer**

With this store the processor executes the **if** statement of the last *factorial* function called, where the formal parameter *n* has the value 0:

    if 0 = 0
       then factorial ← 1
       else factorial ← 0 * factorial(−1)

Since 0 = 0 evaluates to **true,** the **then** clause of the **if** statement is executed:

factorial ← 1

causing 1 to be stored into the function name (*factorial*) and the store to look like

n	4	**integer**
nfactorial		**integer**
factorial		**integer**
n	4	**integer**
factorial		**integer**
n	3	**integer**
factorial		**integer**
n	2	**integer**
factorial		**integer**
n	1	**integer**
factorial	1	**integer**
n	0	**integer**

This is the first time during execution of this program that the **then** clause of the **if** statement in function *factorial* has been executed. Before this, the **else** clause was always executed, causing a call to a new version of *factorial* before the **else** clause could completely finish executing. This time the **then** clause is executed, assigning the value 1 to *factorial*. Thus the **if** statement also finishes executing, the end of function *factorial* is reached, and the processor returns the value in the function name (*factorial*) to the place from which this version of *factorial* was called. This can be represented as

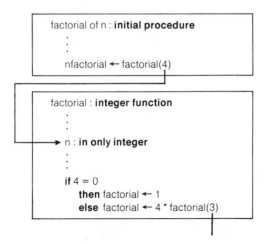

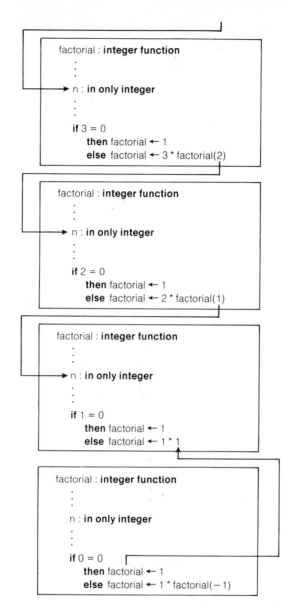

Compare this illustration of the recursive calls to function *factorial* with the previous one to see what has happened. The last function, instead of calling on *factorial* again, returns a value to the previous version, which called it.

Now, since the value 1 has been returned as the value of *factorial*(0), the **else** clause

    factorial ← 1 * factorial(0)

of the next to the last *factorial* function has become

    factorial ← 1 * 1

This is evaluated, causing a 1 to be stored in the function name (*factorial*) of this particular version of *factorial*. The store values associated with the last version of *factorial* have disappeared (because that version finished executing), so now the store looks like

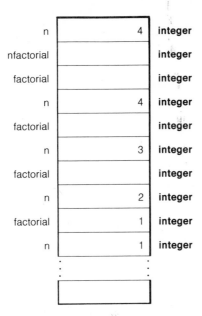

At this point the **else** clause of the current version of *factorial* has finished executing. Its execution was suspended while the recursive call to *factorial*(0) was made and the value of *factorial*(0) was computed and returned. Now that the **else** clause of the current version of *factorial* has finished executing, this version of *factorial* terminates, and the value in *factorial* is returned to the point in the previous version of *factorial* from which *factorial*(1) was called:

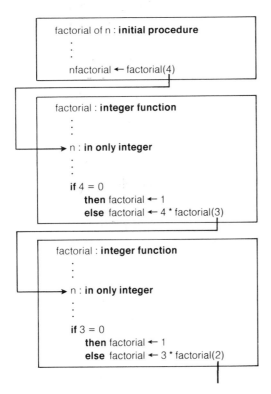

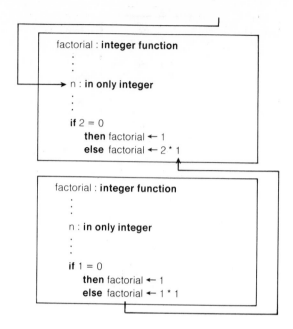

factorial ← 2 * factorial(1)

has become

factorial ← 2 * 1

which causes 2 to be stored into *factorial.* The store now looks like

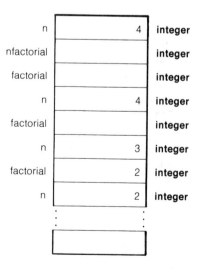

Again, the last cells in the store, which were associated with the previous version of *factorial,* have disappeared, since that version has finished executing.

This process continues. The current version of *factorial* finishes executing and the value in *factorial,* 2, is returned to the point from which this version of *factorial* was called:

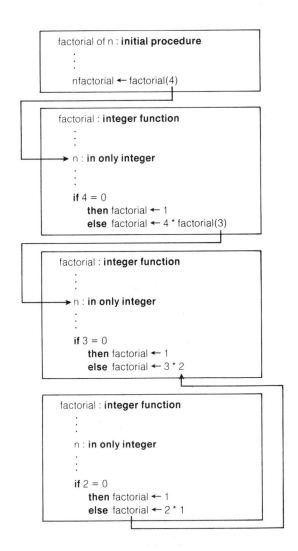

Now the **else** clause of the new current version of *factorial*

    factorial ← 3 * factorial(2)

has become

    factorial ← 3 * 2

causing 6 to be stored into *factorial* and resulting in the store

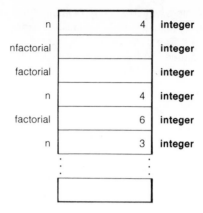

The current version of function *factorial* thus finishes executing, and the value in *factorial,* 6, is returned to the point from which this version of function *factorial* was called:

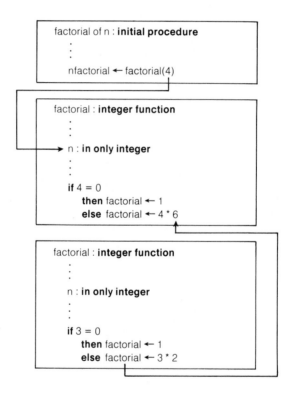

Again, the **else** clause in the new current version of *factorial* can finally finish executing now that the value of *factorial*(3) has been computed and returned. This **else** clause

factorial ← 4 * factorial(3)

has become

factorial ← 4 * 6

so 24 is stored into *factorial,* causing the store to look like

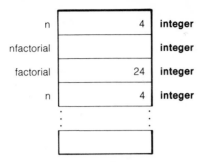

This current version of *factorial* now finishes executing, and the value in *factorial,* 24, is returned to the point from which this version of function *factorial* was called (it is returned to the initial procedure):

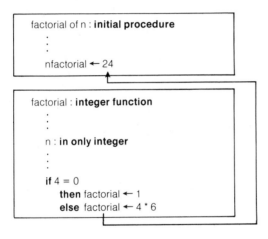

Now the statement

  nfactorial ← factorial(4)

in the initial procedure becomes

  nfactorial ← 24

so 24 is stored into the variable *nfactorial,* resulting in the store

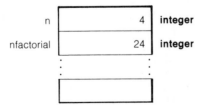

Notice that the store contains no trace of any of the recursive calls to *factorial.*

  At this point the only active routine remaining in the chain of calls to function *factorial* is the initial procedure, where the last statement to be executed is

output n, ' factorial = ', nfactorial

causing

4 factorial = 24

to be printed as we wished.

We explained this example of a recursive function in detail just to show how such functions are handled by the processor: you can consider that new copies of the function are made as each new recursive call is generated, and new storage cells are set aside for each new copy; when a return from a recursive version of the function takes place, the copy from which the return is being made disappears along with its storage cells. Once we have this picture in our minds, we don't need to concern ourselves much about the recursive call mechanism. As we stated at the beginning of this case study, recursive definitions and their translation into recursive *mpl* programs are usually very straightforward. If we know that the recursive definition is correct and we are careful in making the simple, direct translation of the recursive definition into *mpl*, we can be assured that our *mpl* program will compute the recursive problem correctly without the need to understand how the recursive calls work.

Summary — Case Study 3.6

In this case study we have introduced our first recursive function, *factorial*. Although many real programming languages do not allow recursion, good programmers need to understand the process involved. Recursive programs are usually structured as follows:

if *termination condition*
    then {handle termination case}
    else {handle recursive case}
    endif

Some readers will recognize the similarity between this structure and mathematical induction.

Even though the input specifications for this program stated that the input for the program was to be an integer greater than or equal to zero, we added the check

if $n < 0$

in the initial procedure to be sure that a user of the program does indeed supply proper values for n (thereby making the program robust). If we had not included this check and someone supplied a negative number as input to the program, function *factorial* would go into a *recursive loop*. For example, from the way function *factorial* is designed,

$$\text{factorial}(-2) = -2 * \text{factorial}(-3)$$
$$= -2 * -3 * \text{factorial}(-4)$$
$$= -2 * -3 * -4 * \text{factorial}(-5)$$
$$\cdot$$
$$\cdot$$
$$\cdot$$

The recursive calls to *factorial* are stopped only when the actual parameter sent to the function becomes 0, but this will never happen if we start with a negative number. In our model computer the computation would thus go on infinitely. On a real computer the program would eventually be terminated (perhaps by the computer operator), but only after a lot of computer time (and probably money) had been wasted — another good reason for making a program robust.

Fibonacci Numbers

Case Study 3.7

> **Problem Description:** Given an integer n greater than 0, compute and print the Fibonacci number of n.
>
> **Input Specifications:** 1 input line containing the integer n, where $n > 0$.

Before we even discuss what a Fibonacci number is, we can write the initial procedure shown in refinement 1. As we continue to stress, this is an advantage of top-down design: this same basic format for our initial procedure will work here regardless of what *fibonacci* does. If you compare this initial procedure with refinement 1 of case study 3.6, you will notice that there are no important differences between the two procedures.

```
fib : initial procedure
    {inputs an integer and outputs its fibonacci number}

    storage specification
        variables
            n : integer
        end storage specification

    begin fib
        input n
        if n < 1
            then output 'Input < 1, bad data: ', n
            else output fibonacci(n)
            endif
        end fib

    where fibonacci computes the fibonacci number of n
```

CASE STUDY 3.7 — REFINEMENT 1

Note that we have checked to make sure that we handle bad input with an error message. Integers < 1 are not allowed according to the input specifications.

The Solution — A Recursive Function

Fibonacci numbers are defined recursively by

$$fibonacci(n) = \begin{cases} 1 \text{ if } n = 1 \text{ or } n = 2 \\ fibonacci(n-1) + fibonacci(n-2) \text{ if } n > 2 \end{cases}$$

As we can see, for an integer larger than 2 the corresponding Fibonacci number is the sum of the Fibonacci numbers of the previous two integers. For example, $fibonacci(4) = fibonacci(3) + fibonacci(2)$, and $fibonacci(3) =$

fibonacci(2) + *fibonacci*(1). Since *fibonacci*(2) and *fibonacci*(1) are both equal to 1 by the definition, we have *fibonacci*(3) = 2 and *fibonacci*(4) = 3. A list of the smaller Fibonacci numbers is given in table 3–2.

TABLE 3–2. FIBONACCI NUMBERS FOR SMALL INTEGERS

n	fibonacci(n)	Value
1	1	1
2	1	1
3	fibonacci(2)+fibonacci(1)	2
4	fibonacci(3)+fibonacci(2)	3
5	fibonacci(4)+fibonacci(3)	5
6	fibonacci(5)+fibonacci(4)	8
7	fibonacci(6)+fibonacci(5)	13
8	fibonacci(7)+fibonacci(6)	21

As we said when working on the case study for $n!$, recursive procedures and functions are usually extremely easy to write once we know the mathematical recursive definition — there is no long design process as there was, for example, when we designed a program to find the maximum of three integers (case study 3.2). Instead we can translate the recursive definition directly into *mpl*, as we have done below for *fibonacci*:

```
fibonacci : integer function
    {computes the fibonacci number of n}

    storage specification
        parameters
            n : in only integer
        end storage specification

    begin fibonacci
        if n ≤ 2
            then fibonacci ← 1
            else fibonacci ← fibonacci(n − 1) + fibonacci(n − 2)
        endif
    end fibonacci
```

CASE STUDY 3.7 — REFINEMENT 2

This function will work, and in fact, it is the only way that we can write the function with the *mpl* language features that we know at this point, without using some fancy tricks (see exercise 3.42). But this function is spectacularly inefficient for large numbers. By *inefficient* we mean that this function does its calculations in a way that is so slow that even fast modern computers will not produce results quickly. Consider what happens if we call *fibonacci*(7). We can show the recursive function calls with the *tree* given in figure 3–1.

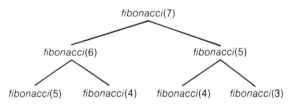

FIGURE 3–1. PARTIAL EXECUTION TREE FOR *fibonacci*(7)

Here we see that *fibonacci*(7) calls on *fibonacci*(6) and *fibonacci*(5); *fibonacci*(6) itself calls on *fibonacci*(5) and *fibonacci*(4); and so on (we have not shown the whole tree). Notice that even in this restricted tree some inefficiency has shown up. *fibonacci*(5) is evaluated twice, once when called by *fibonacci*(7) and once when called by *fibonacci*(6). It is clearly a waste of effort to call *fibonacci*(5) more than once, since the same value will be computed each time.

If we study the full function call tree given in figure 3–2, we will find that these inefficiencies increase as we descend the tree. We have used *f*(*n*) for *fibonacci*(*n*) throughout this figure to save space.

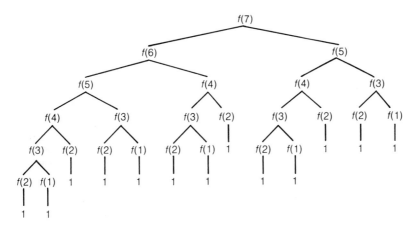

FIGURE 3–2. FULL EXECUTION TREE FOR *fibonacci*(7)

To show how much effort is duplicated in this function, count the number of times that *fibonacci*(*n*) is called, with *n* ranging from 7 down to 2. The count is shown in table 3–3. Notice that the number of calls follows the standard Fibonacci sequence, 1,1,2,3,5,8,.... . If we were to evaluate *fibonacci*(30), for example, *fibonacci*(2) would be evaluated *fibonacci*(29) times, which is over 500,000 times! Clearly this inefficiency is not acceptable, in the next chapter, when we have other programming options available, we will discuss a better solution.

TABLE 3–3. NUMBER OF CALLS FOR RECURSIVE
***fibonacci*(7) FUNCTION**

n	Number of Calls to *fibonacci* (*n*)
7	1
6	1
5	2
4	3
3	5
2	8

Summary — Case Study 3.7

In this case study we have developed another recursive function, *fibonacci*. Function *fibonacci* calls itself recursively twice in the assignment statement

fibonacci ← fibonacci(*n* − 1) + fibonacci(*n* − 2)

The two recursive calls are similar and will cause the same results to be computed over and over again, making this particular solution hopelessly inefficient. An efficient solution will be given in chapter 4.

Case Study 3.8 | Quadratic Equations

Problem Description: Design a program that finds the roots of the quadratic equation $ax^2 + bx + c = 0$.

Input Specifications: One input line containing three reals for a, b, and c.

The *roots* of the quadratic equation

$$ax^2 + bx + c = 0$$

are the values of x that make the left-hand side equal to zero. For example, the roots of the equation

$$2x^2 + x - 1 = 0$$

(where $a = 2$, $b = 1$ and $c = -1$) are $\frac{1}{2}$ and -1, since

$$2*(\tfrac{1}{2})^2 + \tfrac{1}{2} - 1 = \tfrac{1}{2} + \tfrac{1}{2} - 1 = 0$$

and

$$2*(-1)^2 + (-1) - 1 = 2 - 1 - 1 = 0$$

The Solution — Two Procedures

Before going into the details of how to find the roots of a quadratic equation, we need an initial procedure:

```
quadratic equations : initial procedure
    {inputs coefficients of a quadratic equation and calls a
     procedure to compute and print the roots of the equation}
    storage specification
        variables
            a, b, c : real
        end storage specification
    begin quadratic equations
        input a, b, c
        quadroots(a, b, c)
        end quadratic equations
    where quadroots computes and prints the roots of the quadratic
            equation ax↑2 + bx + c = 0
```

CASE STUDY 3.8 — REFINEMENT 1

Note that the input specifications don't put any constraints on a, b, and c, so we don't have to check for bad input data in the initial procedure. Also, we do not print any values in the initial procedure, since we will print the computed roots in procedure *quadroots*. We use a procedure rather than a function to compute *quadroots*, because a quadratic equation may have more than one root, and a function can return only a single value.

You may recall the formula for finding the roots of a quadratic equation. Given the equation $ax^2 + bx + c = 0$, there are, in general, two roots, given by the formulas

$$(-b + \sqrt{b^2 - 4ac})/(2a)$$

and

$$(-b - \sqrt{b^2 - 4ac})/(2a)$$

Let's look at the example given at the beginning of this case study to see how these formulas work. There we examined the quadratic equation

Example 3.20

$$2x^2 + x - 1 = 0$$

where $a = 2$, $b = 1$ and $c = -1$. We showed that the roots for this equation were ½ and -1. Putting the values of a, b, and c into the equations above should give us these same roots. The first equation becomes

$$(-1 + \sqrt{1^2 - 4*2*(-1)})/(2*2)$$

which is

$$(-1 + 3)/4 = 1/2$$

since

$$\sqrt{1^2 - 4*2*(-1)} = \sqrt{1 + 8} = \sqrt{9} = 3$$

The second equation has the same quantity inside the square root sign, so it becomes

$$(-1 - 3)/4$$

which evaluates to -1.

We can use these formulas in our first attempt at procedure *quadroots*, given below in refinement 2.

```
quadroots : procedure
    {computes and prints the roots of ax↑2 + bx + c = 0}

    storage specification
        parameters
            a, b, c : in only real
        variables
            root1, root2 : real
        end storage specification

    begin quadroots
        root1 ← (−b + sqrt(b↑2 − 4*a*c)) / (2*a)
        root2 ← (−b − sqrt(b↑2 − 4*a*c)) / (2*a)
        output root1, root2
        end quadroots

CASE STUDY 3.8 — REFINEMENT 2
```

Notice that we compute the square root of the expression $b^2 - 4ac$ using a function called *sqrt*. Most real programming languages include a set of powerful *built-in functions*, including *sqrt*, to compute commonly needed values. We will assume that a square root function is already available, so we will not design one.

Let's refine this procedure with a minor improvement. As we noted in example 3.20, the square root expression is the same for each root, and so it needs to be computed only once. We can save its value in a local variable called *squareroot* and then use that variable each time we compute a root. This is shown in refinement 3.

quadroots : **procedure**
　　{computes and prints the roots of ax↑2 + bx + c = 0}

　storage specification
　　parameters
　　　　a, b, c : **in only real**
　　variables
　　　　root1, root2, squareroot : **real**
　　end storage specification
　begin quadroots
　　squareroot ← sqrt(b↑2 − 4*a*c)
　　root1 ← (−b + squareroot)/(2*a)
　　root2 ← (−b − squareroot)/(2*a)
　　output root1, root2
　　end quadroots

CASE STUDY 3.8 — REFINEMENT 3

There is still a problem with refinement 3, however; it does not work well (or at all) for the following values of *a*, *b*, and *c*:

1. $a = 0$
2. Values of *a*, *b*, and *c* for which the discriminant, $b↑2 − 4*a*c$, is negative
3. Values of *a*, *b*, and *c* for which the discriminant, $b↑2 − 4*a*c, = 0$

To remedy these problems, we will first modify *quadroots* so that it recognizes the situations where $a = 0$ or $b↑2 − 4*a*c \leq 0$:

quadroots : **procedure**
　　{quadroots prints the roots of ax↑2 + bx + c = 0}

　storage specification
　　parameters
　　　　a, b, c : **in only real**
　　variables
　　　　root1, root2, squareroot, discriminant : **real**
　　end storage specification

```
    begin quadroots
        discriminant ← b↑2 − 4*a*c
        if (a = 0) or (discriminant ≤ 0)
            then badcase(a, b, c, discriminant)
            else squareroot ← sqrt (discriminant)
                    root1 ← (−b + squareroot)/(2*a)
                    root2 ← (−b − squareroot)/(2*a)
                    output root1, root2
        endif
    end quadroots

    where badcase handles the cases where a = 0 or b↑2 − 4ac ≤ 0
```

CASE STUDY 3.8 — REFINEMENT 4

Now we need to work on the procedure

badcase(a, b, c, discriminant)

There are three cases in which *badcase* will be called: $a = 0$, *discriminant* < 0, and *discriminant* $= 0$, where *discriminant* contains the value of $b\uparrow2 - 4*a*c$. Let's analyze these three cases.

If $a = 0$, then we don't really have a quadratic equation, since $ax^2 + bx + c = 0$ becomes the linear equation $bx + c = 0$ when $a = 0$. The only solution of this equation is

$x = -c/b$

unless b is also zero, in which case there is no solution (we can't divide by 0). Using these facts, we can begin the design of procedure *badcase*, as shown in refinement 5:

```
    badcase : procedure
        {called when a = 0 or b↑2 − 4ac ≤ 0}

        storage specification
            parameters
                a, b, c, discriminant : in only real
            end storage specification

        begin badcase
            if a = 0
                then if b = 0
                        then output 'no roots, a = b = 0'
                        else output 'single root at ', −c/b
                        endif
                else {handle discriminant ≤ 0}
            endif
        end badcase
```

CASE STUDY 3.8 — REFINEMENT 5

We must now decide how to handle the situation where *discriminant* ≤ 0. Remember that the two roots are

$(-b + sqrt(discriminant))/(2*a)$ and $(-b - sqrt(discriminant))/(2*a)$

If *discriminant* < 0, the square root function cannot return a real value (it will cause an error), so we should print an error message. If *discriminant* = 0, then *sqrt*(0) = 0, and both formulas will compute the same value:

$(-b)/(2{}^*a)$

This is called a *duplicate root*.

Using this discussion to complete refinement 5 gives us

```
badcase : procedure
    {called when a = 0 or b↑2 − 4ac ≤ 0}

    storage specification
        parameters
            a, b, c, discriminant : in only real
        end storage specification

    begin badcase
        if a = 0
            then if b = 0
                        then output 'no roots, a = b = 0'
                        else output 'single root at ', −c/b
                        endif
            elseif discriminant = 0
                output 'duplicate root at ', −b/(2*a)
            elseif discriminant < 0
                output 'no real roots'
            endif
    end badcase
```

CASE STUDY 3.8 — REFINEMENT 6

Note that there is no **else** clause in the main **if** statement. Procedure *badcase* is only called if $a = 0$ or *discriminant* ≤ 0, and we have handled these cases in the **then** clause (for $a = 0$) and the two **elseif** clauses (for *discriminant* = 0 and *discriminant* < 0). The final **elseif** clause

```
elseif discriminant < 0
    output 'no real roots'
```

could be replaced by the single **else** clause

```
else output 'no real roots'
```

The final procedure calling sequence is

```
quadratic equations (refinement 1)
            ↓
    quadroots (refinement 4)
            ↓
    badcase (refinement 6)
```

Correctness

The program of refinements 1, 4, and 6 is logically correct, as you could see by doing a code walkthrough. However, there are some small details of program design that are important to consider because of the nature of real computers. Observant readers will have noticed, for example, that twice in *quadroots* and three times in *badcase* we have broken one of our own rules by comparing real values for equality (including ⩽). The problem is that a small round-off error (due to the fact that real computers store real numbers with only finite accuracy) could cause, for example, an expression whose actual value should be 0 to be represented instead as a very small positive or negative number (e.g., 10^{-15}).

We can avoid these problems by assuming that whenever a real number gets close enough to some desired fixed real value, it actually is that value. This leaves two obvious questions: What is "close enough"? and How do we fix our program accordingly?

The answer to the first question obviously depends on the problem and the kind of inputs expected, but for our problem we will assume that if we are within 0.000001 of the desired value, we are close enough to that value. We will save 0.000001 in a variable called *epsilon*, which is the name of the Greek letter often used in mathematics to denote a very small number.

The solution to the second question assumes that *mpl* has another built-in function *abs(x)* that computes the absolute value of *x*. We use the built-in function *abs* along with the small value *epsilon* in the following revision of procedure *quadroots*:

```
quadroots : procedure
    {computes and prints the roots of ax↑2 + bx + c = 0}

    storage specification
        parameters
            a, b, c : in only real
        variables
            root1, root2, squareroot, discriminant, epsilon : real
        end storage specification

    begin quadroots
        epsilon ← 0.000001
        discriminant ← b↑2 − 4*a*c
        if (abs(a) < epsilon) or (discriminant < epsilon)
            then badcase(a, b, c, discriminant)
            else squareroot ← sqrt (discriminant)
                 root1 ← (−b + squareroot)/(2 * a)
                 root2 ← (−b − squareroot)/(2 * a)
                 output root1, root2
        endif
    end quadroots

    where badcase handles the case where a = 0 or b↑2 − 4ac ⩽ 0
```

CASE STUDY 3.8 — REFINEMENT 7

Procedure *badcase* is similarly modified:

```
badcase : procedure
    {handles the cases where a = 0, discriminant = 0, or discriminant < 0}
    storage specification
        parameters
            a, b, c discriminant : in only real
        variables
            epsilon : real
    end storage specification
begin badcase
    epsilon ← 0.000001
    if abs(a) < epsilon
        then if abs(b) < epsilon
                then output 'no roots, a = b = 0'
                else output 'single root at ', −c/b
            endif
        elseif abs(discriminant) < epsilon
            output 'duplicate root at ', −b/(2 * a)
        elseif discriminant < 0
            output 'no real roots'
        endif
end badcase
```

CASE STUDY 3.8 — REFINEMENT 8

Notice how we have used the small value *epsilon* in these two procedures. Whenever we must compare a real value x with some particular value y in a critical numeric calculation, we use the rules below

1. If x or y is real and we want to make the comparison $x = y$, then we use $abs(x - y) < epsilon$.

2. If x or y is real and we want to make the comparison $x \leqslant y$, then we use $x < y + epsilon$ instead.

3. If x or y is real and we want to make the comparison $x \geqslant y$, then we use $x > y - epsilon$ instead.

Summary — Case Study 3.8

This was the most involved case study we have seen so far. The original solution for *quadroots* in refinement 2 was simple enough, but we discovered that there were a number of potentially bad input values that needed to be eliminated to make the program robust. This led to the modified procedures of refinement 4 (*quadroots*) and refinement 6 (*badcase*). Even more modifications were needed, however. Because of round-off errors resulting from the fact that real computers must save arbitrarily long real numbers in relatively small storage cells, we must be careful not to check real numbers for equality: instead we must determine whether one real number is close enough to (within *epsilon* of) the other real number. This last problem is really separate from the problem of designing a correct program in the first place, so we were able to take the logically correct design of refinements 1, 4, and 6 and turn it into the practically correct design of refinements 1, 7, and 8 by checking against *epsilon* rather than checking against zero.

3.36 Design a recursive *mpl* function to compute $a \uparrow b$, where a is a real and b is a nonnegative integer (i.e., $b \geqslant 0$). Your function should not use the *mpl* $\uparrow$ operator. Notice that $a \uparrow b = a * a \uparrow (b-1)$ and that $a \uparrow 0 = 1$.

3.5
WORKING OUT

3.37 *Tower of Hanoi.* An old legend states that in a monastery in Hanoi there is a board with three large pegs on it. On these pegs there are 64 disks, all of different sizes, placed so that a larger disk is not on top of a smaller disk. Originally all 64 disks were on peg number 1, and the monks are attempting to move the disks one at a time to peg number 3. The top disk on any peg can be moved to another peg at any time, but a larger disk can never be placed on top of a smaller disk. Legend states that the world will end when the monks have finished their task. You must design an *mpl* program that tells the monks the correct moves to make.

Your initial procedure should call on another procedure, *hanoi*, with formal parameters *n*, *i*, and *j*, that prints the moves for moving the top *n* disks from peg number *i* to peg number *j*. So, for example, if *hanoi*(2, 1, 3) is called, the output should be:

$1 \rightarrow 2$
$1 \rightarrow 3$
$2 \rightarrow 3$

That is, to move the top two disks from peg 1 to peg 3, first move the small one from peg 1 to peg 2, then move the large one from peg 1 to peg 3, and then move the small one from 2 onto the large one on 3.

If we call *hanoi*(3, 1, 3), the best move sequence is:

$\left. \begin{array}{l} 1 \rightarrow 3 \\ 1 \rightarrow 2 \\ 3 \rightarrow 2 \end{array} \right\}$ hanoi(2, 1, 2)

$1 \rightarrow 3$ move large disk from peg 1 to peg 3

$\left. \begin{array}{l} 2 \rightarrow 1 \\ 2 \rightarrow 3 \\ 1 \rightarrow 3 \end{array} \right\}$ hanoi (2, 2, 3)

As we have noted on the right, the first three moves are *hanoi*(2, 1, 2), which move the two smaller disks from 1 to 2, then we move the remaining (largest) disk to peg 3, and then the last three moves move the two smaller disks from 2 to 3. Use this pattern to design *hanoi* recursively. You will probably find it useful to design an integer function *otherpeg*(*i*, *j*), which for any two pegs numbered between 1 and 3, returns the number of the remaining peg. Your initial procedure should read *n*, and if $n > 0$ should call *hanoi*(*n*, 1, 3).

3.38 Two hungry people decide to see who gets the last slice of a cake by flipping a coin, using the best of five flips, where the first player to win three flips wins the cake. There will be between three and five inputs, each giving the result of one coin flip. An input of 1 means player 1 wins a flip, and a 2 means player 2 wins a flip. Obviously, once a player has won three flips no extra flips are made, so there will sometimes be fewer than five inputs. Design an *mpl* program to determine who takes the cake. Select a good set of test cases for the program, and justify your selection.

3.39   Design an *mpl* program that inputs an integer $n > 0$, and then inputs and sums n more integers, printing the sum. So, for example, if the input is

4 6 −2 5 8

the output will be

17

Use only programming constructs that we have described so far, i.e., recursive functions and procedures and conditional statements.

3.40   When driving between two cities you estimate that each mile traveled costs 15¢. In addition, you are only willing to drive 300 miles in one day, after which you stay at a motel for $50 per night. (The trip will be less than 1000 miles.) Design an *mpl* program that inputs the number of miles to be traveled and calculates the trip cost.

3.41   In exercise 3.38 you designed a program to simulate a best-of-five coin flip contest, where the first player to win 3 flips wins the contest. Extend this program to first input an odd positive integer, n, and then simulate a best-of-n coin flip contest. Use only the programming features currently available to you. You will need to use recursion to control the input.

3.42   In case study 3.7 we gave an extremely inefficient recursive design for a Fibonacci function. Design an efficient recursive Fibonacci function that computes each Fibonacci value only once. (Hint: Generate the values recursively in ascending order, so that you first compute *fibonacci*(3), then *fibonacci*(4), and so forth.)

3.43   In spite of the many refinements to case study 3.8, it still contains a weak point. The value in *epsilon* is assigned in two different procedures, and could be mistakenly typed differently each time. Discuss ways to remedy this problem and then make the proper modifications to this case study.

| CHAPTER 4 |

Iteration

> **NEW CONCEPTS:** Loop control structures: While, Until, and Automatic indexing loops; Assertions; Correctness of loops; Statement counts; Time complexity

In the last chapter we learned to use the **if** and **case** control statements, whose function is not to perform calculations, but to provide a means of controlling the execution of programs. In this chapter we introduce a new control structure found in all common procedural programming languages — the *loop*. Loop constructs allow us to group a number of statements and direct the processor to execute these statements repeatedly until certain conditions are met; this process of repeated execution is called *iteration*.

There are many instances where iteration is called for — nearly every useful program contains a loop. The case studies of this chapter first introduce us to the **while** loop. This general loop form provides us with all the power of iteration we need. For convenience, a restricted form of the **while** loop, the *automatic indexing loop*, is also presented. Finally, we will look at the **until** loop. It is slightly less general than the **while** loop, but it proves useful in some applications.

4.1
GETTING
ACQUAINTED

We will now examine a number of case studies requiring loops.

Case Study
4.1

Sum a Series
of Integers

> *Problem Description:* Given a series of integers as input, compute and print their sum.
>
> *Input Specifications:* A list of integers.

On the surface, this simple case study appears to have little real-world value. However, it will explore two basic problems that arise in many applications: inputting a series of values and summing a series of numbers. Computing the balance in an account by adding the month's deposits and withdrawals, summing a set of scores in preparation for computing their average, and adding the day's receipts to determine gross sales are but a few applications of our case study. Learning how to handle these two problems in this simple case study will prepare us for similar but more complex problems that we will face later.

The Solution — A While Loop

In looking at our problem, the first thing to notice is that we are not told how many numbers there are in the input. If we were told that there were four integers to be added, we might think of solving the problem this way:

```
input number1, number2, number3, number4
sum ← number1 + number2 + number3 + number4
output sum
```

But what would we do if there were a million numbers in the input list? With this approach we would have to declare one million variables named *number1*, *number2*, ..., *number1000000* in a **variables** statement and then list all of these variables again in the **input** and *sum* statements. It would take about 115,000 lines of typing for the **input** statement alone! (This book is less than half that size.) Worse yet, if we later wanted to run this program for a different number of input values, we would have to rewrite it. This approach is not general and is hopelessly unwieldy.

The problem is best solved using iteration. The procedure that we wish to execute is very repetitive: input a number, add it to a running total; input a number, add it to a running total; input a number, add it to a running total; and so on, as long as there are more numbers left in the input. We need a loop structure similar to

```
sum ← 0
loop while ⎨there are more numbers⎬
    input number
    sum ← sum + number
endloop while
```

where we initialize the variable *sum* to zero before the loop starts, then each time through the loop we replace the value in *sum* with its current value plus the next number from the input. We want the processor to execute the statements in the **while** loop repeatedly as long as there are more numbers to be read in from the input device. We have written the condition {there are more numbers} as a comment, but we must actually express this as an *mpl* conditional expression.

As we can see, the general form of the **while** loop is

loop while *condition*
    statement
       ⋮
    statement
    endloop while

The processor executes a **while** loop in the following way: when the loop statement is first encountered the processor evaluates *condition* (just as it evaluates the condition of an **if** statement). If *condition* is false, the processor does not execute the statements in the loop but goes on to the statement following **endloop.** If *condition* is true, however, the processor executes each statement in the loop in succession until **endloop** is reached, then execution begins again at the **loop** statement. There *condition* is reevaluated, and this entire process is repeated. In other words, the processor executes the statements in the loop repeatedly *as long as*, or *while*, the loop *condition* is true. The *condition* may be false when the processor first encounters the **loop** statement — then the statements in the loop will not be executed even once. Of course, if *condition* is true when the processor first encounters the **loop** statement, the statements in the loop must in some way modify the values used in *condition*, or the loop will never terminate (*condition* will always be true). We call nonterminating loops *infinite loops.*

Let's return to our problem. Even though we now realize that we can handle the repetitive process of inputting each number and adding it to a running total with a **while** loop, we do not yet know how to write the loop condition, since we still do not know how many integers there are in the input list. There are three approaches to handling this problem: (1) we can specify that the first integer in the list indicate the number of integers which follow and which are to be added; (2) we can specify that the last value in the list be a uniquely identifiable value that signals the end of the input; (3) we can request that the processor check the input device and determine whether there are more numbers to be input. Each of these methods is used in practice and will be explored here.

Method 1 — Header Value

With this method, the first integer in the input must indicate how many values follow. For example, if we wished to add the numbers 35, −17, and 26, the input would have to be

    3 35 −17 26

where the 3 indicates that three integers follow in the input. This first number could be 0, indicating that no numbers are to be added, but it should never be negative. The following initial procedure inputs the first number and checks whether it is less than 0 before calling procedure *total*, which inputs the remaining numbers and computes their sum.

```
sum integers : initial procedure
    {prints the sum of a series of input values}

    storage specification
        variables
            n, sum : integer
        end storage specification

    begin sum integers
        input n
        if n < 0
            then output 'bad data, n < 0: ', n
            else total(n, sum)
                output 'sum of inputs : ', sum
        endif
    end sum integers

    where total inputs n integers and computes their sum
```

CASE STUDY 4.1 — REFINEMENT 1

Notice that we have decided to make *total* a procedure rather than a function. If we had designed *total* as a function we could have replaced the **else** part of the **if** statement in the initial procedure with

else output 'sum of inputs : ', total(n)

which is obviously simpler than the two-line **else** clause that we used. But remember the differences between procedures and functions that were discussed in chapter 1. Most good programmers follow the rule that a function should only perform calculations and return a single result and should not modify actual parameters or perform input or output. In this case we want *total* to perform input, so it should be a procedure.

As we can see, procedure *total* is sent the actual parameters *sum* and *n*. Parameter *sum* is initially undefined, but *n* contains the number of values in the input. Procedure *total* must input the *n* values, compute their sum, and return this sum to the initial procedure in parameter *sum*.

How can we use the value of *n* in designing the **while** loop of procedure *total*? If we input just one new value each time through the loop, we know that the loop must be iterated *n* times to handle all the values. We use a new variable, *i*, to ensure that this happens. We set *i* to 1 just before the loop starts; then in the last statement of the loop we add 1 to *i*. In this way *i* keeps track of the current iteration of the loop. As long as the value in *i* is less than or equal to the value in *n*, the loop must be iterated again to read the next input value. This gives us

```
sum ← 0
i ← 1
loop while i ≤ n
    input number
    sum ← sum + number
    i ← i + 1
    endloop while
```

Study this segment carefully. As the loop is entered for the first time, i has the value 1. Then, in the three statements in the loop, a new number is read from the input device, this number is added to the value in *sum*, and then 1 is added to i, giving i the value 2. Then **endloop** is reached, and the processor automatically continues execution with the **loop** statement at the top of the loop. If $i \leq n$ still holds, the loop statements are executed again with $i = 2$, and at the bottom of the loop one is again added to i, making $i = 3$, and the process reiterates. During the nth time through the loop, 1 will be added to i (making its value $n + 1$) in the last statement of the loop, just after the nth input value has been read in and added to *sum*. Now, when the processor evaluates the condition $i \leq n$ at the top of the loop, the condition will be false (i will no longer be less than or equal to n), so the processor will stop execution of the loop and resume with the statement following **endloop.**

Since loops are rather complex structures, it helps to include assertions that precisely describe what the loop is doing. There are two assertions in particular that should be included in most loops we design. One is the *loop goal assertion* that follows **endloop** and states what the loop has accomplished. In the **while** loop we have been constructing here, our goal is to have the variable *sum* contain the sum of all n input values upon termination of the loop. Thus the assertion

assert sum contains the sum of all n input values

should be included just after **endloop.**

The second assertion goes inside the loop just after the **loop while** statement and indicates that so far the goal assertion is being met for as many iterations of the loop as have been executed. Each time a new iteration is begun in the **while** loop we have been constructing, the value in variable i indicates that so far $i-1$ values have already been input and added to *sum* and that now the ith value can be input and added to *sum*. This fact can be stated as

assert sum contains the sum of the first i−1 input values

This assertion is called the *loop invariant assertion,* because it will be true (without varying) each time the loop is iterated. Including both the loop invariant assertion and the loop goal assertion within our **while** loop and incorporating this loop structure into a complete procedure gives us

```
total : procedure
    {inputs n integers and computes their sum}
    storage specification
        parameters
            n : in only integer
            sum : out only integer
        variables
            number, i : integer
        end storage specification
```

```
begin total
    sum ← 0
    i ← 1
    loop while i ⩽ n
        assert sum contains the sum of the first i−1 input values
        input number
        sum ← sum + number
        i ← i + 1
    endloop while
    assert sum contains the sum of all n input values
end total
```

CASE STUDY 4.1 — REFINEMENT 2

Variable *i* in this procedure has the special purpose of controlling the number of times the **while** loop is executed by keeping track of the number of iterations; each time the loop begins a new iteration, the value in *i* is the number, or index, of that iteration. For this reason we call *i* the *loop index variable*.

Notice also the **out only** designation of the formal parameter *sum* (**out only** parameters were discussed in the In Retrospect section of chapter 2). Parameter *sum* is undefined when *total* is called (so no value comes into procedure *total* in parameter *sum*), but *sum* will contain the total of the input values upon return to the initial procedure (so a value goes out of procedure *total* in *sum*).

Correctness

In the In Retrospect section we will discuss special ways to assure ourselves that a loop is correct, but for now we will do a program walkthrough. The walkthrough will also demonstrate how a **while** loop works.

Example 4.1   Assume that the input line is

    3 7 −2 6

when this program is executed. The initial procedure inputs the first value (3) and assigns it to *n*. The store then looks like

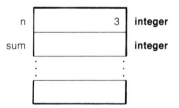

After verifying that the value in *n* is not less than 0, the initial procedure calls on procedure *total* to compute the sum of the three integers in the input. Immediately after the call to *total*, the store looks like

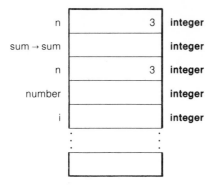

Remember that since the formal parameter *sum* is of type **out only,** it takes on the same storage cell as the actual parameter sent to it, in this case variable *sum* of the initial procedure.

The first two statements in the computation part of procedure *total* assign 0 to *sum* and 1 to *i,* causing the store to be

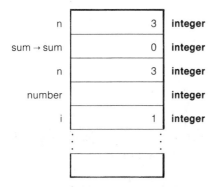

Then the processor reaches the **loop** statement. The condition $i \leq n$ is evaluated and found to be true, because *i* is 1 and *n* is 3. The processor thus begins execution of the loop. Notice that the assertion states that *sum* contains the sum of the first 0 inputs (since $i = 1$), which is true, since $sum = 0$. The **input** statement reads the next input value (7) and stores it into *number,* causing the store to look like

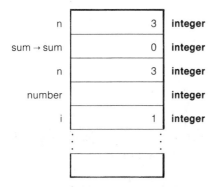

The next two statements in the loop add *number* to *sum* and increment *i* by 1, so the store becomes

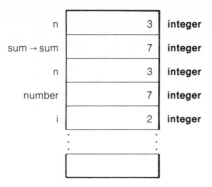

Then the processor reaches **endloop,** so it returns to the **loop** statement, where the condition $i \leqslant n$ is again evaluated. The condition is still true ($i=2$ and $n=3$), so the statements in the loop are executed again. Notice that the loop invariant assertion is again true on entering the loop. The **input** statement reads the next number (-2) from the input device and stores it into *number,* then *number* is added to *sum,* and 1 is added to *i,* giving

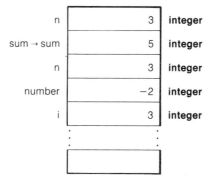

Once again **endloop** is reached and execution returns to the **loop** statement. By checking the condition $i \leqslant n$, the processor knows that the loop must be executed again. Once again the loop invariant assertion is true. The next (and final) value (6) is read into *number* by the **input** statement of the loop, then 6 is added to *sum,* and 1 is added to *i* to produce

Again, **endloop** is reached and execution returns to the **loop** statement. When the processor evaluates the condition in the **loop** statement this time, *i* is no longer less than or equal to *n,* so the loop statements are not executed. Instead the processor skips past the loop to execute whatever follows **endloop,** which in this case is the **end** of procedure *total* (the **assert** statement, remember, is not executed by the procedure). Notice that the loop goal assertion is true at this point; *sum* does contain the sum of all *n* input values. Procedure *total* is exited, its storage cells disappear, and the processor resumes execution with the **output** statement of the initial procedure. At this point the store looks like

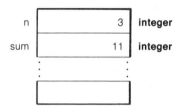

So the message

    sum of inputs : 11

is printed and the program terminates.

Study this example carefully to understand how the **while** loop works. As we have said, the problems of reading in data and summing numbers are common ones which crop up in various guises.

Method 2 — Trailer Value

The header method for reading in data values (refinement 2) is often less than ideal. For example, if you had to supply the data values (e.g., the receipts for a day's sales), you would need to count the receipts by hand and supply this number as the first data value. You would certainly make errors over the course of weeks, and besides, the job is tedious (there could be thousands of input items). The header method works best when the input data has been previously generated by a different computer program, or when there are only a few input values and the program is not run often. If another program generates this header number, the number should be correct, because counting is easily and accurately done by a computer. As a general rule, however, the header method for reading in data should not be used if a human is required to count the input numbers.

The trailer method avoids the "human intervention" problem of the header method by including a value that indicates the end of the input as the final entry in the input list. For example, if the numbers being input are all positive (e.g., exam scores), a negative value could be included as the last entry to indicate the end of the data. We call this unique last value a *trailer value*.

Assuming that all input values are nonnegative and that the end of the input is signaled by a negative number, a first attempt at writing a loop to input and sum a series of numbers might be

```
sum ← 0
loop while number ≥ 0
   input number
   sum ← sum + number
   endloop while
```

However, this won't work correctly — the first time the processor reaches the **loop** statement, the comparison

number $\geq$ 0

will cause an error because *number* is undefined (no value has yet been input for *number*). Instead, we need to input a value for *number* before the **loop** statement is first executed. Then, once inside the loop, the calculations involving *number* are done first; at the end of the loop, the next number is input in preparation for the next iteration of the loop. This ensures that the **while** condition is always checked with the proper value in *number* for the coming iteration:

```
sum ← 0
input number
loop while number ≥ 0
    assert sum contains the sum of all input numbers up to, but
            not including, the current value in number
    sum ← sum + number
    input number
    endloop while
assert sum contains the sum of all input numbers except the last
```

Notice the loop invariant assertion, which accurately describes the status of *sum* each time the loop begins a new iteration. This assertion will be true the first time the loop is executed (when *sum* = 0), and it will also be true after the loop is finished (we don't want *sum* to include the value in *number* upon termination of the loop, because that value is the trailer value, not one of the values to be added to *sum*).

The trailer method for inputting values should be carefully learned, because it, too, arises in many situations. Just remember that when loop termination is dependent on an input value, as it is here, the first value must be read in before the loop begins and each subsequent value must be read in at the end of the loop. As we can see, the trailer method also works if there is no input (i.e., the first input value is the trailer value). The entire procedure incorporating our new loop is

```
total : procedure
    {inputs a series of nonnegative integers and computes their sum}

    storage specification
        parameters
            sum : out only integer
        variables
            number : integer
        end storage specification
```

```
begin total
    sum ← 0
    input number
    loop while number ⩾ 0
        assert sum contains the sum of all input numbers up to, but
                not including, the current value in number
        sum ← sum + number
        input number
    endloop while
    assert sum contains the sum of all input numbers except the last
end total
```

CASE STUDY 4.1 — REFINEMENT 3

Procedure *total* in refinement 3 has only one parameter, the **out only** parameter *sum*. All values required by *total* are read from the input device. This means that we need a different initial procedure, since the one in refinement 1 also passed the parameter *n* to *total*:

```
sum integers : initial procedure
    {prints the sum of a series of input values}

    storage specification
        variables
            sum : integer
        end storage specification

    begin sum integers
        total(sum)
        output 'sum of inputs : ', sum
        end sum integers

    where total inputs a series of integers and returns their sum
```

CASE STUDY 4.1 — REFINEMENT 4

Correctness

You should do a walkthrough of the program defined by refinements 3 and 4 using the input

30 54 93 −1

to convince yourself that the program works.

Method 3 — The Moredata Condition

The trailer value method for inputting data values also has drawbacks. For some data sets we cannot pick a trailer value that could never be a valid input value. For example, if the input values to be added could be *any* integer values, then there would be no value we could pick as a trailer.

The method we will now explore is the best choice whenever it can be applied to reading in an indeterminate number of data elements. The loop structure is simple:

```
    sum ← 0
    loop while moredata
        assert sum is the sum of all input values up to, but
                not including, the next number to be input
        input number
        sum ← sum + number
        endloop while
    assert sum contains the sum of all input values
```

moredata is a special *mpl* keyword. When **moredata** is evaluated by the processor, the processor checks the input device: if there is at least one more item to be input, **moredata** is **true,** so the processor executes the loop; if there are no more data values, **moredata** is **false,** so the processor skips the loop and resumes execution with the statement following **endloop.**

Notice that the **input** statement is the first statement in the **while moredata** loop. Notice, too, how the loop invariant assertion is worded to account for this fact. Compare the **moredata** method carefully with methods 1 and 2 to understand the differences. The **moredata** loop gives us our final refinement for procedure *total:*

```
total : procedure
    {inputs a series of integers and computes their sum}

    storage specification
        parameters
            sum : out only integer
        variables
            number : integer
        end storage specification

    begin total
        sum ← 0
        loop while moredata
            assert sum is the sum of all input values up to, but
                    not including, the next number to be input
            input number
            sum ← sum + number
            endloop while
        assert sum contains the sum of all input values
        end total
```

CASE STUDY 4.1 — REFINEMENT 5

This version of procedure *total* also has just the one **out only** parameter *sum,* so the initial procedure of refinement 4 should be used with this version of *total* to form a complete program.

The **moredata** method cannot normally be used in interactive programs. As we discussed in chapter 2, execution of an **input** statement in an interactive program causes the processor to wait for the user to supply data at a terminal; if a **while moredata** loop were used, the processor wouldn't know whether the user was about to type more data, or whether all inputs were finished. The trailer method is the most common input loop used in interactive programs — the user, who is interacting with the program, can just type in the predetermined trailer value to signal the end of the data.

Correctness

Perform a walkthrough of the program made up of refinements 4 and 5 to convince yourself that it works. Use the input values

    60 −38 42

Efficiency

Until now, we have not been particularly concerned with how long it takes the processor to execute our programs or how much storage space our programs require as they are executed. These are questions of efficiency: if we can modify a program so that it uses less storage space or takes less time to execute, then we have increased the efficiency of the program.

Do we really need to concern ourselves with these questions? Our model computer executes as fast as we wish it to, and it has as much storage space as we will ever need, because, after all, it is just an abstract model. Real computers, however, work with real time and fixed storage space. Still, even they execute extremely quickly. Computation times on modern large computers are measured in *nanoseconds* (billionths of seconds), and an addition can be performed in less than 50 nanoseconds on many computers. In spite of this speed, we will see that questions concerning efficiency are very important considerations in programming.

Consider case study 4.1. We have used a **while** loop that will be iterated for each new input value. Therefore, as we increase n (the number of values to be input), the number of statements that the processor must execute in the **while** loop will grow proportionally. This, of course, means that the time required by the processor to execute the program will also grow.

To see this better, let's count the statements that the processor must handle as procedure *total* of refinement 2 is executed. Looking at the computation part only, we see that the statements

    sum ← 0
    i ← 1

will be executed once, because they lie outside the loop, whereas the five statements within the loop (counting the **loop** and **endloop** statements but not counting the **assert** statement, which is just a comment) will be executed n times, once for each new value to be input. In addition, the **loop** statement itself will be executed one more time when i finally equals $n + 1$, causing the processor to skip the loop and go on to the statement following **endloop.** Therefore, the number of statements executed in the computation part of procedure *total* is

    $2 + 5^*n + 1$

or

    $5^*n + 3$

This formula is the *statement count* of procedure *total.* The statement count is the number of statements (for any program, procedure, or function) that the processor must execute, based on the size of the input.

| *Example* | If there are 10 input values, then $n = 10$, and the number of statements executed in |
| *4.2* | procedure *total* would be |

$5*10 + 3 = 53$

If $n = 100$, the number of statements executed would be

$5*100 + 3 = 503$

and if $n = 10,000$ the number of statements executed would be

$5*10000 + 3 = 50,003$

Counting the statements executed in a routine gives us a feel for how much the time required to execute that routine (on a real computer) will change if the size of the input is changed. With the statement count we can answer general questions such as, If the input size is increased five times, how much longer will it take this routine to execute? and, If a new computer is ten times faster, how much more work can it do? Counting statements is certainly not a precise measure of how much time will be required to execute a program, because no distinction is made between statements like

$$x \leftarrow x\uparrow3 + 4^*x\uparrow2 - 13^*x + 5 \quad \text{and} \quad x \leftarrow 3$$

The first statement will definitely take more time to execute than the second. However, a simple statement count will be sufficient for our considerations of the execution time efficiency of our programs.

Example	Assume that it takes a computer 2 seconds to execute procedure *total* when there are
4.3	1000 values in the input. How long would it take this computer to execute *total* if there
	were 4000 values in the input? To answer this question, let's determine how many
	statements the processor executes when there are 1000 input values and when there
	are 4000 input values. We find this by plugging these values into the statement count
	formula. For $n = 1000$ we get

$5*1000 + 3 = 5003$ statements

For $n = 4000$ we get

$5*4000 + 3 = 20,003$ statements.

Since 20003 is nearly four times as large as 5003, it would take the computer about four times as long (i.e., 8 seconds) to execute *total* with 4000 input values. Increasing the input by a factor of 4 increases the run time by a factor of 4. Notice that the 3 statements executed outside the loop are so insignificant when n is large that we can ignore them.

As this example illustrates, if we increase the number of input values m times, then it will take the processor m times longer to execute procedure *total*.

Example	Assume that a computer can execute procedure *total* in 2 seconds with an input of
4.4	1000 values. If a new computer is five times as fast, how many input values can it han-
	dle in 2 seconds?

Since the old computer executed total with an input of 1000 values in 2 seconds, this means that

5*1000 + 3 = 5003

statements were executed by that computer in 2 seconds. The new computer is five times as fast, so it can execute five times as many statements (25,015) in 2 seconds. The question now is, How many input values can be handled if 25,015 statements can be executed? We answer the question again by using the statement count formula

5*n + 3 = 25,015

and solving for n. This gives us

n = 25012 / 5 = 5002.4

That is, the new computer can process *total* with about five times as much input in 2 seconds.

Notice again that the three statements executed outside the loop could have been neglected in calculating this general result.

Some readers will recognize that the results computed in the last two examples follow from the fact that the statement count formula for procedue *total* is a *linear function* of n. A linear function has the general form

a*n + b

where a and b are constants and n is a variable. In our present case study, n is the number of input values for procedure *total*. In general, n is called the *size of the input* — it can vary each time this program is run. In one sense, the statement count formula for procedure *total* is a measure of how "complex" *total* is with respect to how the time to execute *total* varies with the size of the input (n). For this reason we say that procedure total has *linear time complexity*, because its statement count formula is linear.

Whenever we determine that a procedure or function has linear time complexity, we know quite a bit about its behavior without even knowing the exact statement count formula:

1. If we increase the input size m times, it will take m times as long to execute the routine.
2. With a computer that is m times faster, we will be able to process m times as much data with this routine in the same amount of time.
3. As n (the size of the input) gets larger, the value of b (the number of statements executed just once) becomes insignificant.

To indicate that a routine has linear time complexity, we write O(n), which stands for "on the Order of n." This O notation doesn't tell us exactly how many statements are executed in a routine, but it tells us all we need to know to answer the general types of questions we have been asking.

Summary — Case Study 4.1

In this case study we have seen three methods for inputting a potentially long list of data items. In the header method, the first value input indicates how many values follow; this first number must be an integer, but, depending upon what is being computed, the remaining values may be of a different type. The trailer method requires that a unique trailer data item be used to indicate the end of the input; this value must have the same type as the other input values. In the **moredata** method, the processor itself determines when there is no data left at the input device. These various methods all find application in different settings. Whenever it can be used in batch programs, the **moredata** method is preferred, but in interactive programs a header or trailer value must be used.

This case study presented a task that is common to many programs — the summation of a series of values. The form of a summation loop is this: before the loop begins, the sum is set to 0; with each iteration of the loop, the next value is added to the current value of the sum; upon completion of the loop, the sum is the desired total.

The relative time required by the processor to execute a routine can be approximated by counting the number of individual statements the processor must execute. In this case study, procedure *total* contains a single loop that is iterated *n* times, resulting in a statement count formula that is linear in *n*. We say that procedure *total* has linear time complexity, which is abbreviated as $O(n)$. Any routine that has time complexity $O(n)$ will have the statement count formula

$$a^*n + b$$

Usually, this means that there are *a* statements inside a loop that executes *n* times and *b* statements outside the loop that are executed just once.

Case Study 4.2 | Sum the First n Even Integers

> *Problem Description:* Find the sum of the first *n* positive even integers. Print the running total as the sum is being computed.
>
> *Input Specifications:* One integer, $n \geqslant 0$.

This case study explores the *indexing loop*, a special form of the **while** loop that arises in numerous applications.

The Solution — An Indexing Loop

The value for *n* will be input by the initial procedure. No other values need to be input by the routine that computes the sum, but the running total is to be printed as the sum is being accumulated. Since the summing routine will perform output, we cannot use a function. Instead, we use a procedure, *sumeven*, which is called from the following initial procedure:

```
sum even integers : initial procedure
    {prints the sum of the first n even positive integers}

    storage specification
        variables
            n, sum : integer
        end storage specification
```

```
    begin sum even integers
        input n
        if n < 0
            then output 'bad data, n = ', n
            else sumeven(n, sum)
                    output 'the sum of the first ', n, ' even integers is ', sum
            endif
        end sum even integers

    where sumeven computes the sum of the first n even integers
```

CASE STUDY 4.2 — REFINEMENT 1

Procedure *sumeven* is different from procedure *total* of the previous case study, because in this program we know which numbers are to be added — the first n even integers: 2, 4, 6, ..., $2*n$. The value for n will be read from the input device, but we must generate the sequence 2, 4, 6, ..., $2*n$ ourselves. We can do this in a loop: on the first iteration we add 2 to the running total, on the second we add 4, on the third we add 6, and so on. In general, on the ith pass through the loop we add $2*i$ to our running total. Thus, we can compute the sum of the first n even integers with the loop

```
    sum ← 0
    i ← 1
    loop while i ⩽ n
        assert sum is the sum of the first i−1 even integers
        sum ← sum + 2 * i
        i ← i + 1
        endloop while
    assert sum is the sum of the first n even integers
```

Compare this loop with that of refinement 2 of case study 4.1. There the loop index variable i was used for one purpose only, to ensure that the loop was executed exactly n times. In this loop, which has the same form, the loop index variable i is used for *two* purposes: to ensure that the loop is executed n times and to provide the value that is added to the sum in each iteration. This loop forms the basis of procedure *sumeven*. We only need to include an **output** statement to print the running total.

```
    sumeven : procedure
        {computes the sum of the first n even positive integers}

        storage specification
            parameters
                n : in only integer
                sum : out only integer
            variables
                i : integer
            end storage specification
```

```
    begin sumeven
        sum ← 0
        i ← 1
        loop while i ⩽ n
            assert sum contains the sum of the first i − 1 even integers
            sum ← sum + 2 * i
            output 'the sum of the first ', i, ' even integers is ', sum
            i ← i + 1
        endloop while
        assert sum contains the sum of the first n even integers
    end sumeven
```

CASE STUDY 4.2 — REFINEMENT 2

Instead of running from 1 to *n*, the loop index variable *i* could take on the values 2, 4, ..., 2*n directly. This gives us the following equivalent refinement for *sumeven:*

```
sumeven : procedure
    {computes the sum of the first n even positive integers}

    storage specification
        parameters
            n : in only integer
            sum : out only integer
        variables
            i : integer
        end storage specification

    begin sumeven
        sum ← 0
        i ← 2
        loop while i ⩽ 2*n
            assert sum contains the sum of the first (i − 2)/2 even integers
            sum ← sum + i
            output 'the sum of the first ', i/2, ' even integers is ', sum
            i ← i + 2
        endloop while
        assert sum contains the sum of the first n even integers
    end sumeven
```

CASE STUDY 4.2 — REFINEMENT 3

There are a number of differences between refinements 2 and 3 because of the differences in the way the loops are set up. Compare these two until you understand these differences. Which one do you prefer?

Correctness

A program walkthrough will show how procedure *sumeven* works and help assure us that it is correct.

Example   Let's try the version of procedure *sumeven* in refinement 3 with a value of 3 for *n*. This
4.5   means that *sumeven* should sum the first three even integers, 2, 4, and 6. The result should be 12.

The initial procedure inputs the value 3 for *n* and calls on *sumeven; n* is **in only** and *sum* is **out only.** After the processor assigns 0 to *sum* and 2 to *i* in procedure *sumeven* the store looks like:

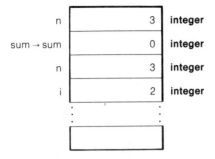

At this point the loop is reached. Since *i* is not larger than 2*n*, the statements in the loop are executed. Notice that upon entering the loop, the loop invariant assertion is true. First, *sum* is set to *sum + i*, which puts 2 into *sum*, then the **output** statement causes

the sum of the first 1 even integers is 2

to be printed, and finally *i* is incremented by 2, which gives

n	3	**integer**
sum → sum	2	**integer**
n	3	**integer**
i	4	**integer**

At this point **endloop** is reached, so the loop is attempted again. The loop condition is checked, and the processor determines that the value in *i* is still less than or equal to 2*n*, so the statements in the loop are executed again. Once again the loop invariant assertion is true. The value of *i* is added to *sum*, the line

the sum of the first 2 even integers is 6

is printed, and *i* is again incremented by 2, leaving both *sum* and *i* containing 6. When the loop condition is checked this time, it is still true, so the loop statements are again executed, and again the loop invariant assertion is true. The value of *i* is again added to *sum*, the **output** statement causes

the sum of the first 3 even integers is 12

to be printed, and 2 is once again added to *i*, which then contains 8. This time when the loop condition is checked, the value in *i* is no longer less than or equal to 2*n*, so execution of the loop terminates. The goal assertion is obviously true at this point. The processor now reaches the **end** of procedure *sumeven* and execution returns to the initial procedure, leaving the store looking like

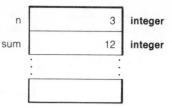

The next (and last) statement to be executed in the initial procedure is the **output** statement, which prints

the sum of the first 3 even integers is 12

You should check yourself whether procedure *sumeven* will work if the input value for *n* is 0.

Alternate Solution — An Automatic Indexing Loop

The **while** loop form we used in refinements 2 and 3 of this case study and in refinement 2 of case study 4.1 is so common that we give it a name. It is called an *indexing loop* because it uses a variable (the loop index variable) to keep track of the unique value (the index) associated with each iteration of the loop. The indexing loop has the general form

```
index ← starting value                          (1)
loop while index ≤ ending value                 (2)
    statement
        ⋮
    statement
    index ← index + increment                   (3)
    endloop while
```

In line (1) the loop index variable is set to some starting value, in line (2) it is compared with a preset loop ending value each time the loop is about to be iterated again, and in line (3) a constant increment is added to the loop index variable each time the end of the loop is reached. In other words, the loop index variable starts with some low value and works its way up to the ending value, being incremented by some positive amount each time through the loop. In the In Retrospect section we will also look at indexing loops that step backwards using a negative increment. These will use ≥ instead of ≤ in the **loop** statement.

The indexing loop is the most common loop type used. For this reason an *automatic indexing loop* is available in most real programming languages. The automatic indexing loop automatically performs the tasks of lines (1), (2), and (3) of the standard **while** indexing loop. Its form is

```
loop start index with starting value step increment to ending value
    statement
        ⋮
    statement
    endloop autoindex
```

When the processor first encounters the **loop** statement of an automatic indexing loop, it sets the loop index variable, *index*, to *starting value* (taking care of line (1) of the **while** loop form). Before executing the statements of the loop (the first time and each subsequent time) the processor compares the value in *index* with *ending value* (taking care of line (2) of the **while** loop form). If *index* is less than or equal to *ending value*, the statements of the loop are executed, otherwise the processor skips the loop and begins executing the statement after **endloop**. Whenever the processor reaches **endloop** after executing the loop statements, it automatically steps the value in *index* up by the *increment* amount before returning to the *loop* statement (taking care of line (3) of the *while* loop form). Thus the automatic indexing loop form shown here works exactly like the **while** indexing loop.

For example, the **while** loop of procedure *sumeven* in refinement 2,

```
sum ← 0
i ← 1
loop while i ⩽ n
    assert sum contains the sum of the first i − 1 even integers
    sum ← sum + 2 * i
    output 'the sum of the first ', i, ' even integers is ', sum
    i ← i + 1
    endloop while
assert sum contains the sum of the first n even integers
```

can be translated into the equivalent automatic indexing loop:

```
sum ← 0
loop start i with 1 step 1 to n
    assert sum contains the sum of the first i − 1 even integers
    sum ← sum + 2 * i
    output 'the sum of the first ', i, ' even integers is ', sum
    endloop autoindex
assert sum contains the sum of the first n even integers
```

In both loops *i* is the loop index variable. The phrase

start i **with** 1

in the **loop** statement of the automatic indexing loop is equivalent to the statement

i ← 1

appearing just before the **loop** statement of the **while** loop. Similarly, the phrase

to n

takes the place of the conditional expression

i ⩽ n

and the phrase

step 1

performs the same task as the statement

i ← i + 1

at the bottom of the **while** loop.

Using the automatic indexing loop in place of the **while** loop in refinement 2 gives us refinement 4 for procedure *sumeven*:

```
sumeven : procedure
   {computes the sum of the first n even positive integers}

   storage specification
      parameters
         n : in only integer
         sum : out only integer
      variables
         i : integer
      end storage specifiction

   begin sumeven
      sum ← 0
      loop start i with 1 step 1 to n
         assert sum contains the sum of the first i−1 even integers
         sum ← sum + 2 * i
         output 'the sum of the first ', i, ' even integers is ', sum
         endloop autoindex
      assert sum contains the sum of the first n even integers
      end sumeven
```

CASE STUDY 4.2 — REFINEMENT 4

Refinement 3 can also be rewritten using an automatic indexing loop:

```
sumeven : procedure
   {computes the sum of the first n even positive integers}

   storage specification
      parameters
         n : in only integer
         sum : out only integer
      variables
         even : integer
      end storage specifiction

   begin sumeven
      sum ← 0
      loop start even with 2 step 2 to 2*n
         assert sum contains the sum of the first (even-2)/2 integers
         sum ← sum + even
         output 'the sum of the first ', even/2, ' even integers is ', sum
         endloop autoindex
      assert sum contains the sum of the first n even integers
      end sumeven
```

CASE STUDY 4.2 — REFINEMENT 5

We have named the loop index variable *even* just to demonstrate that any integer variable can be used for this purpose.

Correctness

You should do a program walkthrough using the initial procedure of refinement 1 and either refinement 4 or refinement 5 of procedure *sumeven* to convince yourself that the program works. Use the same value for *n* (3) as was used in the earlier program walkthrough of refinement 3.

Efficiency

Using either refinement 2 or 3 we see that the number of statements executed by the processor will be

$5*n + 3$

because the five statements in the loop will each be executed n times, the **loop** statement will be executed one extra time, and the two statements outside the loop will be executed once. This statement count formula is again linear in n, which means that procedure *sumeven* has linear, or $O(n)$, time complexity. We should have recognized this fact immediately without even counting the statements in *sumeven*, since *sumeven* contains a single loop that is executed n times, where n is the size of the input. This always indicates linear time complexity, unless one of the statements in the loop either calls another procedure or function or is itself a separate loop, in which case the time complexity of this inner part would also have to be considered.

Now, consider refinements 4 and 5, which use automatic indexing loops. In both cases the statement count formula for procedure *sumeven* is

$4*n + 2$

because the four statements in the loop are executed n times, there is one statement outside the loop, and the **loop** statement will be executed one more time when the processor determines that the value in the loop index variable has gone past the ending value. From the statement count formulas it might appear that the versions of *sumeven* using automatic indexing loops will be executed faster than the corresponding versions using ordinary **while** loops. This isn't true, because the processor must perform the same operations for the automatic indexing loop form as it does for the **while** loop form. As we mentioned earlier, the statement count formula is not meant to be a precise measure of the actual run time required; it is only meant to help us determine the general time complexity of a routine. In this case, the statement counts are linear formulas regardless of whether automatic indexing loops are used, so all versions have linear time complexity.

Is there a way to make procedure *sumeven* substantially faster? Looking at refinement 2 we see that by removing the **output** statement, which is only used to print the running total, the number of statements executed in the loop would be reduced from five to four. This would reduce the statement count formula from

$5*n + 3$

to

$4*n + 3$

This is really quite an important gain in efficiency (assuming, of course, that we do not need to print the running total). If n is 4000, in the first case

$5*4000 + 3 = 20{,}003$

statements would be executed, whereas in the second case

$4*4000 + 3 = 16{,}003$

statements would be executed. That is, since the number of statements in the **while** loop is reduced from five to four, the new version will execute in about four-fifths the time of the old version (this is another consequence of the fact that *sumeven* has linear time complexity). This analysis leads to an important observation: removing statements from loops results in a substantial increase in efficiency.

Notice that although the second version is faster than the first, both versions still have $O(n)$ (linear) time complexity. In both cases, if we increase the input size m times, m times more execution time will be required. Thus, there are really two concepts of efficiency. One concerns real gains in execution time that can be achieved by modifying the program (e.g., removing statements from loops). The other concerns the general efficiency (time complexity) of a program in terms of its execution time behavior as the size of the input changes (e.g., the fact that *sumeven* has time complexity $O(n)$ in both of the above instances).

To see the difference between these two concepts of efficiency, consider this improvement to *sumeven:* if the **output** statement for printing the running total is no longer needed, then we should completely redesign *sumeven*, because there is a simple mathematical formula that computes the sum of the first n even integers without a loop. It is

$n*(n + 1)$

For example, the sum of the first three even positive integers is 12 (the same as 3 * 4) as we have seen before. Using this formula we could rewrite the entire computation part of *sumeven* as

```
begin sumeven
    sum ← n * (n + 1)
    end sumeven
```

This is truly a substantial improvement! Instead of executing a number of statements proportional to n, the processor needs to execute only one statement, regardless of the size of n. We have replaced a program with linear time complexity with one that runs in constant time! A program that always takes the same amount of time to run has *constant time complexity*, which is written in O notation as $O(1)$. Whenever we can replace a program of a certain time complexity class with one in a lower class we can feel proud of ourselves — the resulting savings in execution time (which translates to dollars) is worth the effort.

Summary — Case Study 4.2

In this case study we have seen the indexing loop in both its **while** form and its automatic form. The automatic indexing loop is convenient. It saves us from forgetting to initialize our loop index variable (which would cause the processor to halt with an error when it tried to check the loop condition the first time). It also saves us from forgetting to update the loop index variable at the bottom of the loop (forgetting this would cause the processor to continue executing the loop without ever terminating — an infinite loop). On the other hand, the **while** indexing loop gives us clear control over what we wish to express. Our advice is to use the automatic indexing loop wherever it seams natural to do so. For example, do not try to force the use of this loop when funny increments to the loop index variable are required — this usually leads to unclear programs. Automatic indexing loops are used almost exclusively for indexing up (or down) in increments of 1 (or −1). In these cases this loop is particularly useful. There are also numerous cases where automatic indexing loops cannot be used. We saw two of these in refinements 3 and 4 of case study 4.1. The automatic indexing loop is indeed less general than the **while** loop.

The problem of summing the first n even integers resulted in procedure *sumeven*, which contains a single loop that is iterated n times. Thus the time complexity for *sumeven* is linear, $O(n)$. This same procedure can be executed in constant time, written $O(1)$, if we are not required to print the running total.

Computing Average Scores

Case Study
4.3

> *Problem Description:* Compute the average score for each student in a class, where each student has the same number of scores, n. The class average (the average of all of the individual students' average scores) should also be computed.
>
> *Input Specifications:* The first input line contains the value for n. Then there is an input line for each student; each contains an identification number followed by n scores.

As a whole, this case study is considerably more complex than the earlier case studies of this chapter. However, as we break it down into smaller procedures by the top-down program design technique, we will see that it consists of simple parts that are already familiar to us.

The Solution — While Moredata and Automatic Indexing Loops

The initial procedure reads the value for n, the number of scores for each student. n should be larger than 0; if it is not, an error message is printed and the program terminates. Otherwise a procedure for computing the student averages is called.

```
scores : initial procedure
    {inputs the number of scores for each student in a class then
     calls a procedure to compute student averages and the class average}

    storage specification
        variables
            n : integer
        end storage specification

    begin scores
        input n
        if n ⩽ 0
            then output 'bad data, n ⩽ 0 : ', n
            else student averages(n)
            endif
        end scores

    where student averages computes the average of n scores for an
            indeterminate number of students and the class average for
            all students.
```

CASE STUDY 4.3 — REFINEMENT 1

In designing procedure *student averages* we need to consider what a typical set of input will look like:

```
4
75332  75  83  77  91
75761  80  90  95  93
       ⋮
       ⋮
73730  60  85   0  25
```

The first number is input into variable n by the initial procedure. It indicates that there are four scores for each student. The remaining lines are input when *student averages* is called. The first number on each line is a student identification number; the remaining four numbers are the scores for that student.

The structure of procedure *student averages* is thus

```
loop while moredata
    assert the average for each student up to, but not including,
            the next student in the input has been computed and printed
    input idnumber
    {input the n scores and compute the average for this next student}
    {print the idnumber and average for this student}
    endloop while
assert the average has been computed and printed for each student
{compute and print the overall class average}
```

The loop invariant assertion helps us design the proper loop structure, because it declares what the loop is to have accomplished up to the time it begins a new iteration. The program segment needed to replace

```
{input the n scores and compute the average for this next student}
```

must read in and sum the next n numbers. (Remember that n is the parameter containing the number of scores for each student; it is passed into procedure *student averages* by the initial procedure.) We developed procedure *total* in refinement 2 of case study 4.1 to do this same task — input and sum n numbers — so we will use it again here. Once the sum of these scores has been computed, dividing the sum by n will give the required student average:

```
total(n, sum)
average ← sum/n
```

Including an appropriate **output** statement gives the program segment

```
loop while moredata
    assert the average for each student up to, but not including,
            the next student in the input has been computed and printed
    input idnumber
    total(n, sum)
    average ← sum / n
    output 'the average for student ', idnumber, ' is ', average
    endloop while
assert the average has been computed and printed for each student
{compute and print the overall class average}
```

The last task to be handled by this procedure is

{compute and print the overall class average}

and it requires some modifications to the **while** loop. Computing the class average requires that a running total of the individual student averages be kept in the loop. Upon termination of the loop, this running total must be divided by the number of students to determine the class average. Since the number of students is not supplied directly in the input, we need to include a *counter* — a variable that will count each student — in the loop. Calling the variable that keeps the running total of individual student averages *averagetotal* and the counter variable *count*, and including these in procedure *student averages*, we get

```
student averages : procedure
    {student averages computes and prints the average scores for an
     indeterminate number of students, each of whom has n scores. The
     class average is also computed and printed}
    storage specification
        parameters
            n : in only integer
        variables
            averagetotal, average : real
            count, idnumber, sum : integer
        end storage specification
    begin student averages
        averagetotal ← 0
        count ← 0
        loop while moredata
            assert the average for each of the first count students has
                   been computed and printed; variable averagetotal
                   contains the sum of the averages of the first count
                   students
            input idnumber
            total(n, sum)
            average ← sum / n
            averagetotal ← averagetotal + average
            output 'the average for student ', idnumber, ' is ', average
            count ← count + 1
        endloop while
        assert the average for all students has been computed and printed;
               variable averagetotal contains the sum of all student
               averages; variable count contains the number of students
        output 'the class average is ', averagetotal/count
        end student averages
    where total inputs n integers and returns their sum

CASE STUDY 4.3 — REFINEMENT 2
```

Notice that the assertions have been modified to reflect the new computations done in the loop.

Correctness

In previous case studies of this chapter we just advised you to do a program walkthrough to familiarize yourself with the execution of a loop and to assure yourself that the procedure or function containing the loop worked as desired. However, all of the rules we gave in chapter 3 for choosing of good set of test data apply to programs with loops, too. In particular, the rule that test data should be chosen to cause each path in a procedure or function to be executed at least once should be applied to loops with the interpretation that some data may cause a **while** or automatic indexing loop not to be executed at all. This kind of data should be included in a test set along with data that causes the loop statements to be executed at least once. In this case study, if there are no students in the input, the **while moredata** loop of procedure *student averages* will not execute even once. Instead, the statement

> **output** 'the class average is ', averagetotal/count

will be executed immediately with *averagetotal* and *count* both still zero, causing program execution to terminate abnormally with a divide by zero error. We leave it as an exercise to modify procedure *student averages* to handle this case gracefully, making the program more robust.

Efficiency

As usual, we need to count the number of statements in the computation part of procedure *student averages* to determine its time complexity. There are three statements outside the **while** loop and eight statements within the loop, giving the statement count formula

> $8*m + 4$

where m is the number of students in the input. Thus, we might be tempted to say that procedure student averages has $O(m)$ (linear) time complexity, but watch out! One of the eight statements in the **while** loop is a call to procedure *total*, which in turn reads in n scores for a student in a loop that iterates n times. So in effect, this call to procedure *total* will cause

> $5*n + 3$

extra statements to be executed (this is the statement count formula for procedure *total*) each of the m times the **while** loop of procedure *student averages* is executed. Therefore, the statement count formula for procedure *student averages* is

> $(8 + (5*n + 3))*m + 4$

where each of the eight statements in the **while** loop of procedure *student averages* plus the $(5*n + 3)$ statements in procedure *total* are all executed m times in the **while** loop of *student averages*. This formula is equivalent to

> $5*m*n + 11*m + 4$

As both m and n get larger, procedure *student averages* will have an execution time that is much worse than if it were based on just m or n alone. Fortunately, there are usually relatively few students in a class and each student has relatively few scores (m and n are both small), so in most situations the computer could execute this program without requiring an excessive amount of time.

The key point in determining the time complexity of procedure *student averages* is this: there is a loop (the **while moredata** loop) that contains another loop (the **while** loop in procedure total). Both loops execute a number of times based on the size of the input. Each time the outer loop is executed once, the inner loop must be iterated to completion; thus the general run time complexity of procedure *student averages* is determined by multiplying the iteration factors of both loops. The run time complexity for procedure *student averages* is thus $O(m*n)$. The factor $m*n$ dominates the statement count formula as m and n both get larger.

Summary — Case Study 4.3

The problem of computing student averages in this case study has demonstrated one common programming situation: a particular computation that is relatively complex (such as computing student averages) must be iterated several times for a series of similar inputs. Computing the balance over a month's deposits and withdrawals for a number of bank accounts, computing the paycheck for each employee of a company, and printing the telephone bill for each subscriber are just a few more problems that have this form. For each account, employee, or subscriber, there must be a loop to input new data and perform the required calculations. If the procedure that performs the calculations also contains a loop that depends on the size of the input, then the resulting time complexity is $O(m*n)$.

Accumulating Interest

| Case Study
| 4.4

> *Problem Description:* Given an initial investment and an annual interest rate, determine the number of years required for the initial investment to reach a specified target balance. Do this for both simple and compound interest. For each year of the investment, print the accrued balance.
>
> *Input Specifications:* Three real input values — the initial investment, the annual interest rate, and the final target balance, all greater than zero.

In this case study we examine a problem in which the indexing loop cannot be used directly. Thus we will use both the general form of the **while** loop and the **until** loop, an alternative to the **while** loop that is useful in certain situations.

The Solution — The General While Loop

The initial procedure follows the usual pattern. We read in the three input values and check whether any of these values is zero or less. Also, we check whether the target balance is less than or equal to the initial investment, because this would indicate an error. If all of the input values are in the appropriate ranges, a procedure is called to compute the number of years for the initial investment to reach the target balance (*final*).

```
howlong : initial procedure
    {prints the number of years required for a given initial investment
     to accrue to a given final balance with a given interest rate}
    storage specification
        variables
            initial, annualrate, final : real
            years : integer
        end storage specification
    begin howlong
        input initial, annualrate, final
        if (initial ≤ 0) or (annualrate ≤ 0) or (final ≤ 0)
            then output 'bad data: negative or zero input'
            elseif final ≤ initial
                output 'bad data: final value ≤ initial investment'
            else numyears(initial, annualrate, final, years)
                output 'invest money for ', years, ' years'
        endif
    end howlong
    where numyears calculates the number of years required for the
                initial investment to accrue to the final balance
                with the given annual interest rate.
```

CASE STUDY 4.4 — REFINEMENT 1

As in case study 2.4, the initial procedure can be used regardless of whether procedure *numyears* uses simple interest or compound interest in its calculations. Only procedure *numyears* needs to be different for each case.

Procedure *numyears* is to return the number of years required for the initial investment to accrue to the final value. How can we compute this number? A straightforward approach is to keep a count of the number of years this process takes: we start with the initial investment as our accrued balance so far. Then, as long as our accrued balance is less than the final balance, we continue to replace our accrued balance with a newly accrued balance based on our interest calculations for a new year, adding one to a counter each time this is done. The value in the counter at the end of this process is the proper number of years. We can use a **while** loop and a counter variable for this approach:

```
years ← 0
loop while {the accrued balance is less than the final balance}
    assert years contains the number of years taken for initial
            to reach accrued balance
    {accrued balance ← accrued balance + new interest for this year}
    years ← years + 1
    endloop while
assert years contains the number of years for initial to
        reach final balance
```

The counter variable is called *years* here. Before this loop is entered for the first time, the accrued balance must be set to the initial invested value. If we name the accrued balance variable *accrued,* the program segment now looks like

```
accrued ← initial
years ← 0
loop while accrued < final
    assert years contains the number of years for initial to reach accrued
    accrued ← accrued + {new interest for this year}
    years ← years + 1
    endloop while
assert years contains the number of years for initial to reach final
```

Now we need to compute the new interest. Of course, this calculation depends on whether we use compound interest or simple interest. We recall from case study 2.4 that simple interest is calculated as

```
initial * annualrate / 100
```

because the interest is only computed on the initial investment. From case study 2.5 compound interest is calculated as

```
accrued * annualrate / 100
```

because the interest is computed on the accrued balance rather than the initial investment. These two minor differences give us two versions of procedure *numyears*, one for simple interest and one for compound interest:

```
numyears : procedure
    {computes the number of years (years) required for an initial
     investment (initial) to accrue to a final balance (final) based
     on a given interest rate (annualrate) for simple interest}

    storage specification
        parameters
            initial, annualrate, final : in only real
            years : out only integer
        variables
            accrued : real
        end storage specification

    begin numyears
        output 'the initial investment is ', initial
        accrued ← initial
        years ← 0
        loop while accrued < final
            assert years contains the number of years for initial to reach accrued
            accrued ← accrued + initial * annualrate / 100
            years ← years + 1
            output 'after ', years, ' years the accrued balance is ', accrued
            endloop while
        assert years contains the number of years for initial to reach final
        end numyears
```

CASE STUDY 4.4 — REFINEMENT 2

```
numyears : procedure
    {computes the number of years (years) required for an initial
    investment (initial) to accrue to a final balance (final) based
    on a given interest rate (annualrate) for compound interest}

    storage specification
        parameters
            initial, annualrate, final : in only real
            years : out only integer
        variables
            accrued : real
        end storage specification

    begin numyears
        output 'the initial investment is ', initial
        accrued ← initial
        years ← 0
        loop while accrued < final
            assert years contains the number of years for initial to reach accrued
            accrued ← accrued + accrued * annualrate / 100
            years ← years + 1
            output 'after ', years, ' years the accrued balance is ', accrued
            endloop while
        assert years contains the number of years for initial to reach final
        end numyears
```

CASE STUDY 4.4 — REFINEMENT 3

Notice that in both refinements we have added **output** statements to print the yearly accrued balance calculated in each iteration of the loop, as required by the problem description. This **output** statement must follow the count statement in which the parameter *years* is updated, in order to print the correct values.

The **while** loop used in procedure *numyears* is the most general we have seen so far. It is *not* an indexing loop. It has the form

```
loop while accrued < final
    statements
    endloop while
```

This loop will run as long as it takes for the condition (*accrued* < *final*) to become false. We do not know ahead of time how many iterations this will take. This is unlike most of our previous loops, where the loops were constructed to be iterated a specific number of times. Thus, the **while** loop in this case study cannot be replaced directly by an automatic indexing loop. This demonstrates the generality of the **while** loop.

An Alternative Solution — The Until Loop

We have just developed function *numyears* using the **while** loop form

```
loop while accrued < final
    statements
    endloop while
```

We read this "Continue to iterate the loop as long as *accrued* is less than *final*". Sometimes, however, we will find it easier to formulate our problems in the opposite way, such as, "Continue to iterate the loop *until accrued* becomes greater than or equal to *final*". In the first case we are saying that the loop is to be iterated as long as certain conditions still hold. In the second case we are saying that some desired condition has not yet been met and that the loop should be iterated until this condition is finally met.

Many programming languages have a control structure for stating loops in this new fashion — in our model programming language this structure is the **until** loop, which has the form

> **loop**
>   *statements*
>   **endloop until** condition

When the loop is first encountered, the statements in the loop are executed and at **endloop** the loop condition is checked. If it is false, the loop is iterated again and this process repeats. If the condition is true, execution of the loop is terminated and execution resumes at the statement following **endloop.**

The decision about whether to use a **while** loop or an **until** loop must be made carefully. For most loops we will want to ensure that the loop is not executed at all if certain conditions hold. This requires the use of the **while** loop, where the loop condition is checked at the top of the loop before any loop statements have been executed. In other cases we may wish to be sure that the loop statements are executed at least once regardless of the existing conditions. This suggests use of the **until** loop — the *statements* of an **until** loop will always be executed at least once, because the **until** loop condition is checked at the bottom of the loop after the loop statements have been executed. In still other situations conditions may be such that the loop will always be executed at least once anyway whether the **while** or **until** form is used. In this case we choose the loop form that seems to best express our intent.

In this case study the **while** loop of procedure *numyears* will always be executed at least once, because the initial procedure only calls *numyears* if *final* is greater than *initial.* That is, the first time the **while** condition

> accrued < final

is checked, it will be true, because the assignment

> accrued ← initial

is made before the loop. This means that we can replace the **while** loop with an **until** loop, which gives us the following refinement for *numyears* (for simple interest):

numyears : **procedure**
    {computes the number of years (years) required for an initial
     investment (initial) to accrue to a final balance (final) based
     on a given interest rate (annualrate) for simple interest}

    storage specification
        parameters
            initial, annualrate, final : **in only real**
            years : **out only integer**
        variables
            accrued : **real**
        end storage specification

```
begin numyears
    output 'the initial investment is ', initial
    accrued ← initial
    years ← 0
    loop
        accrued ← accrued + initial * annualrate/100
        years ← years + 1
        output 'after ', years, ' years the accrued balance is ', accrued
        assert years contains the number of years for initial to reach accrued
    endloop until accrued ≥ final
    assert years contains the number of years for initial to reach final
end numyears
```

CASE STUDY 4.4 — REFINEMENT 4

Notice the placement of the loop invariant assertion in the **until** loop. It goes just before the **until** condition, whereas in a **while** loop the loop invariant assertion goes just after the **while** condition.

Choosing an **until** loop instead of a **while** loop here is purely a question of style. You should use the loop that expresses best what you had in mind when you designed the loop. The **while** loop is still the most general loop, and as a result, it is used more often than the **until** loop.

Correctness

You should do program walkthroughs with some typical values to assure yourself that these various procedures work. In every case the loops will always execute at least once, because the initial procedure checks that *final* is greater than *initial* before calling procedure *numyears*.

Efficiency

The **until** and **while** versions of the program have the same time complexity. We will determine the time complexity of refinement 2. The time complexity is not as easy to determine as it was in earlier case studies, because, as we have mentioned, the **while** loop of this refinement is not iterated a specified number of times. However, if we look closely at procedure *numyears* we notice that each time through the **while** loop the same value.

    initial * annualrate / 100

is added to the accrued balance. Let's call this value *increment*. Since we start with an initial balance (*initial*) and work our way up to the final balance (*final*) by adding *increment* each time through the loop, it follows that the number of times the loop statements will be executed is the number of times we can add *increment* to *initial* before the result becomes larger than or equal to *final*. That is, the number of times the loop will be executed is the ceiling of

    (final − initial) / increment

(The *ceiling* of a value is the smallest integer greater than or equal to the value; for example the ceiling of 7.3 is 8, whereas the ceiling of 7.0 is 7.) We use the ceiling concept here, because *increment* may not divide the expression (*final* − *initial*) evenly, but the **while** loop in procedure *numyears* will always execute an integral number of times (until the accrued balance is larger than or equal to *final*).

These considerations show us that the execution time of procedure *numyears* is directly proportional to the difference between the initial investment and the final value. If we run the program for two different inputs where the second one has a five times greater difference between *initial* and *final*, the second run will be about five times longer than the first. Thus we can say that function *numyears* has time complexity $O(n)$, where

$n = (final - initial) / increment$

Determining the time complexity for procedure *numyears* of refinement 2 has been fruitful in another way. We have discovered that we are adding the expression

initial * interest / 100

to the accrued balance each time through the loop. That is, each time through the loop the processor must reevaluate this expression, even though the result is the same each time, since neither *initial* nor *interest* changes value throughout this function. What a waste! If the loop is executed 1,000 times we are forcing the processor to do 1,000 unnecessary multiplications and 1,000 unnecessary divisions. We can eliminate this wasted effort by setting a new variable *increment* to

increment ← initial * interest / 100

before entering the loop, and then adding *increment* to *accrued* inside the loop:

accrued ← accrued + increment

This gives us the refinement below.

```
numyears : procedure
    {numyears computes the number of years required for an initial
     investment (initial) to accrue to a final value (final) based on
     a given interest rate (annualrate) for simple interest}

    storage specification
        parameters
            initial, annualrate, final : in only real
            years : out only integer
        variables
            accrued, increment : real
        end storage specification

    begin numyears
        years ← 0
        accrued ← initial
        output 'the initial investment is ', initial
        increment ← initial * annualrate / 100
        loop while accrued < final
            assert years contains the number of years for initial to reach accrued
            accrued ← accrued + increment
            years ← years + 1
            output 'after ', years, ' years, the accrued value is ', accrued
            endloop while
        assert years contains the number of years for initial to reach final
        end numyears
```

CASE STUDY 4.4 — REFINEMENT 5

In this instance we have increased the efficiency of procedure *numyears* by moving an expression (not an entire statement) outside the loop. The statement count formula, which is left as an exercise to derive, will not show the added savings, because it only counts statements, not individual operations.

Calculating the time complexity of refinement 3 (compound interest) is similar to the calculations for refinement 2 (simple interest), but it requires a bit more mathematics. We leave it as an exercise. There is also an inefficiency in the loop for computing the accrued balance for compound interest; we leave it as an exercise to find and remove this inefficiency.

Summary — Case Study 4.4

The most general form of the **while** loop has been presented in this case study. It is

> **loop while** *condition*
>   *statements*
>   **endloop** while

condition is a general condition involving program variables that control execution of the loop. These variables must have values before the **loop** statement is first encountered, so that *condition* can be evaluated. They must also be modified within the loop statements so that *condition* eventually becomes false — otherwise an infinite loop results.

In the interest problems in this case study, the time complexities of the resulting procedures were somewhat more difficult to determine, because the loops were not written to be executed exactly *n* times for some input value *n*. However, careful analysis showed that the time complexity of the procedure using the simple interest computation was linear on

> (final − initial) / increment

In this case, the size of the problem is the difference between the final and initial investments, divided by the increment.

4.2 IN RETROSPECT

The common **while,** automatic indexing, and **until** loops available in most real programming languages were presented in the first section of this chapter. In this section we will summarize the use of these loops and the new concepts of time complexity and loop assertions.

LOOPS

Loop structures allow certain statements to be grouped together and repeatedly executed under specified conditions. The three common loop types are the **while** loop, the automatic indexing loop, and the **until** loop.

While Loops

The most general loop is the **while** loop. It has the form

loop while *condition*
   statement
     ⋮
   statement
  endloop while

The *condition* is any valid conditional expression, and each *statement* can be any valid statement, including **if** statements, **case** statements, and other **loop** statements (i.e., loops can be nested).

    The processor executes a **while** loop as follows: upon encountering the **loop** statement, the processor evaluates *condition.* If *condition* is true, each *statement* in the loop is executed in succession until **endloop** is reached. Then the processor immediately returns to the top of the loop and resumes execution with the **loop** statement, repeating the entire process. If *condition* evaluates to false when the processor executes the **loop** statement, the processor skips all statements in the loop and resumes execution with the statement following **endloop.**

    This last point is important: the **while** loop is never exited in the middle of the loop. Even though the loop statements may change variable values that would cause the loop *condition* to be false (this, indeed, must happen if the loop is to eventually terminate), the processor will not be aware of this until **endloop** is reached and execution returns to the **loop** statement where *condition* is reevaluated. Thus, the only point at which a **while** loop can be exited is the **loop** statement at the top of the loop.

    Since the **while** loop condition is evaluated at the top of the loop, the loop statements will not be executed even once if *condition* is false when the processor first encounters the **loop** statement. All of the case studies of the Getting Acquainted section of this chapter contain examples of **while** loops.

Indexing Loops

A very common special form of the **while** loop is one in which each iteration of the loop is associated with a unique value, a loop index. A loop index variable is used to ensure that the loop is executed some exact number of times. The value of the loop index variable is also often used in the calculations performed in the loop as well as in controlling how many times the loop is iterated. An indexing loop has one of two general forms

(1) *index* ← *starting value*
   loop while *index* ≤ *ending value*
    statement
      ⋮
    statement
    index ← *index* + *increment*
   endloop while

(2) *index* ← *starting value*
   loop while *index* ≥ *ending value*
    statement
      ⋮
    statement
    index ← *index* − *increment*
   endloop while

The difference between these two loops is that in (1) the loop index variable, *index,* starts with the *starting value* and works its way up to the *ending value* as a positive *increment* is added to *index* at the end of each loop iteration, just before **endloop;** in (2) *index* works its way from the *starting value* down to the *ending value* as a positive *increment* is subtracted from *index* at the end of each loop iteration. These differences are seen in the uses of ≤ and ≥ in the loop conditions of (1) and (2) and in the application of + and − in the increment statements before **endloop.** In both cases *index* is a simple integer variable, and *starting value*, *ending value*, and *increment* are integer arithmetic expressions, often just constants. The value of *increment* must always be positive, not zero or negative.

Example 4.6

Computing the sum of the first *n* odd integers in a loop could be done using either type of indexing loop:

(1) sum ← 0
    i ← 1
    loop while i ≤ n
        sum ← sum + 2 * i − 1
        i ← i + 1
    endloop while

(2) sum ← 0
    i ← n
    loop while i ≥ 1
        sum ← sum + 2 * i − 1
        i ← i − 1
    endloop while

Notice the differences between these two loops. The loop index variable *i* is initialized differently, the loop conditions are reversed, and in (1) index variable *i* is incremented by 1 whereas in (2) it is decremented by 1. You should do a walkthrough of these two loops (e.g., with *n* = 3) to see how they work differently.

Automatic Indexing Loops

Because the **while** indexing loop is so common, it has an automatic form in all procedural programming languages. The **while** indexing loop form

    index ← *starting value*
    loop while *index* ≤ *ending value*
        statement
            ⋮
        statement
        index ← *index* + *increment*
    endloop while

has the automatic indexing loop form

    loop start *index* **with** *starting value* **step** *increment* **to** *ending value*
        statement
            ⋮
        statement
    endloop *autoindex*

This automatic indexing loop works exactly like the **while** loop form it replaces; these two loops are completely interchangeable in any program (as long as no *statement* modifies *index ending value* or *increment*). The phrase

    start *index* **with** *starting value*

has replaced the statement

    index ← *starting value*

of the **while** loop; the phrase

    to *ending value*

has replaced the loop condition

index ⩽ ending value

of the **while** loop; and the phrase

step *increment*

has replaced the statement

index ← index + increment

appearing before **endloop** in the **while** statement.
Similarly, the **while** indexing loop form

index ← starting value
loop while *index ⩾ ending value*
   statement

     ⋮

   statement
   index ← index − increment
   endloop while

has the automatic indexing loop form

loop start *index* **with** *starting value* **step** *−increment* **to** *ending value*
   statement

     ⋮

   statement
   endloop *autoindex*

where *increment* is assumed to be some positive value.

In most real programming languages the value in *index* after an automatic indexing loop is unpredictable. If *index* is to be used after the loop, the **while** loop form should be used. Also, *index*, *increment*, and *ending value* are not allowed to be modified in any *statement* of an automatic indexing loop in most real programming languages.

The sum of the first *n* odd numbers can be computed using either of the following automatic indexing loops:

Example 4.7

```
sum ← 0
loop start i with 1 step 1 to n
    sum ← sum + 2 * i − 1
    endloop autoindex
```

or

```
sum ← 0
loop start i with n step −1 to 1
    sum ← sum + 2 * i − 1
    endloop autoindex
```

These two loops are identical to the two **while** indexing loops given in example 4.6 in the previous section on *indexing loops*. You should compare these two examples.

In any automatic indexing loop, you can determine the values that will be taken on by the loop index variable as well as how many times the loop will be iterated just by examining the **loop** statement.

Example
4.8

Examine the automatic indexing loops given below:

(a)   **loop start** i **with** 3 **step** 1 **to** 8
         {statements}
         endloop autoindex

(b)   **loop start** counter **with** 3 **step** 2 **to** 8
         {statements}
         endloop autoindex

(c)   **loop start** q **with** −1 **step** 3 **to** 8
         {statements}
         endloop autoindex

(d)   **loop start** i **with** 6 **step** −7 **to** −46
         {statements}
         endloop autoindex

(e)   i ← 3
         j ← 2
         loop start x **with** i **step** j **to** 4 * j
         {statements}
         endloop autoindex

(f)   **loop start** i **with** 3 **step** 1 **to** 2
         {statements}
         endloop autoindex

(g)   **loop start** i **with** 7 **step** 2 **to** 7
         {statements}
         endloop autoindex

(h)   **loop start** i **with** 5 **step** 1 **to** 3
         {statements}
         endloop autoindex

(i)   **loop start** i **with** −2 **step** −1 **to** 0
         {statements}
         endloop autoindex

(j)   **loop start** j **with** 5 **step** 0 **to** 8
         {statements}
         endloop autoindex

In loop (a) the loop index variable i is set to the starting value 3. Since 3 is not larger than the ending value (8), the processor executes the statements in the loop. At the end of the loop, the step factor 1 is added to the loop index variable i; this sets i to 4. Since 4 is not larger than the ending value (8) the processor executes the statements in the loop again. This process continues until the step factor (1) is added to i when i is 7. This sets i to 8. Still, i is not larger than the ending value (8), so the statements in the loop are executed again. This time when the loop is completed, 1 is added to i again, setting i to 9. Now, i is larger than the ending value of 8, so the processor does not execute the statements within the loop again. The statements following the loop are executed instead. At this point the value of i is 9. The loop index variable i has taken on the values 3, 4, 5, 6, 7, and 8 on successive iterations of the loop. The loop statements were executed six times, afterwards the value in i is 9.

In loop (b) the loop index variable is named *counter*. It takes on the values 3, 5, and 7, successively, as the loop statements are executed. Upon termination of the loop, *counter* has the value 9. The loop statements are executed three times.

In loop (c) the loop index variable is *q*. It takes on the values -1, 2, 5, and 8, successively. The loop statements are executed four times. The final value in *q* is 11.

In loop (d) the loop index variable is *i*, which is set successively to 6, -1, -8, -15, -22, -29, -36, and -43 as the loop statements are executed eight times. The value in *i* after the loop is -50.

In loop (e) the loop index variable is *x*, the starting value is *i* (which has the value 3), the step factor is *j* (which has the value 2), and the ending value is $4 * j$ (which evaluates to 8). Thus, this loop is identical to (b).

In loop (f) the step factor is 1, but the starting value for *i* is 3, which is already larger than 2, so the loop statements are not executed even once. The value in *i* remains 3 after the loop.

In loop (g) the starting and final values are the same, and so the loop statements will execute once, with $i = 7$. Upon completion of the loop, *i* will be 9.

Loops (h) and (i) are similar. In both cases the starting value for *i* meets the termination condition, and so the statements in the loop will not execute at all.

Loop (j) is illegal in *mpl* since the step factor is 0.

This example demonstrates that the automatic indexing loop can be used in relatively complex situations. As we have already stated, however, in practice it is used almost exclusively with a step factor of 1 or -1. For more complex cases the **while** loop is preferred.

Until Loops

The **until** loop has the form

loop
  statement
  .
  .
  .
  statement
  endloop until *condition*

Upon encountering the **loop** keyword, the processor executes each *statement* in succession until **endloop** is reached. At that point *condition* is evaluated. If it is true, the loop is terminated, and the processor resumes execution with the statement after **endloop.** If the condition is false, the processor continues execution at the top of the loop with the **loop** statement, and this process repeats.

Because the **until** *condition* is evaluated at the bottom of the loop, the statements in an **until** loop will always be executed at least once. This is in contrast to the **while** loop, in which the loop statements might not be executed even once, because the **while** *condition* is evaluated at the top of the loop. Also, whereas the **while** loop is executed as long as the **while** *condition* is true, terminating only when *condition* becomes false, the **until** loop is executed as long as the **until** *condition* is false, terminating only when *condition* finally becomes true. Therefore, the **until** loop form given above has the equivalent **while** loop form statement

$\vdots$

statement
loop while not (*condition*)
    statement

    $\vdots$

    statement
    endloop while

where the statements in front of the **loop** statement are the same as those in the loop, forcing them to be executed at least once, and the **not** logical operator has been applied to *condition*.

Example 4.9

The sum of the first n odd integers, for $n \geqslant 1$, can be written with the **until** loop form

```
sum ← 0
i ← 1
loop
    sum ← sum + 2 * i − 1
    i ← i + 1
endloop until i > n
```

Notice that this loop will execute once regardless of the value in n. This is the same as the **while** loop

```
sum ← 0
i ← 1
sum ← sum + 2 * i − 1
i ← i + 1
loop while not (i > n)
    sum ← sum + 2 * i − 1
    i ← i + 1
endloop while
```

(Of course, if you originally intended to write this particular loop as a **while** loop, you would design it differently.)

COMMON LOOP OPERATIONS

Inputting a series of data values, counting, and summing are three of the most common operations performed by loops.

Data Input in a Loop

There are three methods used for inputting a series of data values with a loop. One is the *header method*, in which the data values to be input are first counted, then this count is supplied as the first input value. This header number is first input into a variable, then as each subsequent value is input, it is counted (or, alternatively, 1 is subtracted from the header variable). When the count reaches the header value (or the value of the header variable reaches 0), all values have been input. The disadvantage of this method is that the data values must be counted first; counting is time-consuming and can be inaccurate if it is done by a human.

A second method is the *trailer method,* in which a uniquely identifiable value is included as the last data value. For example, if the input is a set of positive test scores, then any negative number can serve as the trailer value to indicate the end of the data. This method can also be used to separate groups of data from each other. The disadvantage of this method is that for some input no uniquely identifiable value can be chosen as a trailer value; for example, if the input can be any integer values, then there is no unique one that can serve as a trailer value.

A third method is the *moredata method.* In this method the processor itself checks whether there is more data before trying to read the next data value. The **moredata** keyword can be used as the loop condition to control execution of the input loop. The disadvantage of this method is that it cannot be used in interactive programs or when there are separate groups of data at the input device.

These three methods are discussed in detail in case study 4.1. You should review that case study for examples of these three methods.

Summing in a Loop

Summing a large number of values can be accomplished iteratively in a loop by adding one new value to a running total on each pass through the loop. The running total must be set to 0 just before the loop. The general form of a summation loop is thus

```
sum ← 0
loop while condition
    statements
    sum ← sum + new value
    statements
    endloop while
```

where *sum* is a variable of the proper type. Of course, an automatic indexing loop or an **until** loop can be used when they are appropriate.

Counting in a Loop

For various reasons, it will often be necessary to count the number of times a loop is iterated. This is done by including a *loop counter* in the loop. A loop counter is a simple integer variable that is initialized to 0 outside the loop and incremented by 1 inside the loop. A loop with a loop counter has the general form

```
counter ← 0
loop while condition
    counter ← counter + 1
    statements
    endloop while
```

where *counter* is a simple integer variable. At the completion of loop execution, *counter* will contain the number of iterations of the loop. Loop counters can also be used in automatic indexing loops and **until** loops.

PROGRAM EFFICIENCY

Since learning about loop constructs we have become more concerned about program efficiency. When a program is run, the number of times a loop is iterated (and thus the number of statements executed) usually depends on the input. Knowing how the execution time of a program is related to the size of the input helps us design efficient programs.

Statement Count

The most direct way to get a handle on the execution time requirements of a program is to count the number of statements that will be executed. This gives us the *statement count formula* for the program. Each statement in the computation section of a program (except the **begin** and **end** statements of the procedures and functions) is counted once for each time it would be executed. This means that each statement in a loop must be counted once for each iteration of the loop. In addition, in **while** and automatic indexing loops the loop statement will be executed one more time than the other statements in the loop since it will be executed once at the beginning of each loop iteration plus one more time when the loop condition is false and the loop is terminated. For **until** loops, the loop condition is checked at the bottom of the loop in the **endloop** statement, so all statements in the **until** loop, including the **loop** and **endloop** statements, will be executed the same number of times.

Example
4.10

The statement count formula for the section of program

```
sum ← 0
i ← 1
loop while i ≤ n
    sum ← sum + 2 * i
    i ← i + 1
    endloop while
```

is $4*n + 3$. The four statements of the loop will be executed n times each; this gives the factor $4*n$ in the formula. The two statements outside the loop will be executed just once, and the **loop** statement itself will be executed one more time when $i > n$ is true (causing loop termination); thus 3 is added to the formula. We say that the input size is n, because n is the variable whose value determines the value of the statement count formula (we are assuming $n \geq 0$).

For the loop

```
sum ← 0
loop start i with 1 step 1 to m
    sum ← sum + 2 * i
    endloop autoindex
```

the statement count formula is $3*m + 2$. The number 2 comes from the one statement outside the loop (which will be executed once) and the **loop** statement, which will be executed one extra time when i becomes larger than m, causing the loop to be terminated. In this case the input size is m.

For the loop

```
sum ← 0
i ← 1
loop
    sum ← sum + i
    i ← i + 1
endloop until i > x
```

the statement count formula is $4*x + 2$ and the input size is x. The **endloop** statement contains the loop condition, and it is executed only as many times as the other statements in the loop.

The loops given in the previous example were quite simple. Programs involving nested loops often have statement count formulas that depend on the square of the input size.

In the program segment

```
loop start i with 1 step 1 to n
    loop start j with 1 step 1 to n
        output i * j
    endloop autoindex
    output ' row ', i
endloop autoindex
```

the inner loop by itself has the statement count formula $3*n + 1$ (remember that the **loop** statement will be executed one extra time). But this inner loop is contained in an outer loop that also iterates n times. Each time the outer loop is executed once

$$3 + 3*n + 1 = 3*n + 4$$

statements will be executed, because there are three statements in the outer loop, in addition to the statements of the inner loop, which will be executed each time the outer loop iterates. So, the statement count formula for the entire segment is

$$(3*n + 4) * n + 1 = 3*n^2 + 4*n + 1$$

since the outer loop will be executed n times, with one extra execution of the outer **loop** statement.

Example 4.11

The statement count formula for a loop with k statements that iterates n times is

$$k*n + 1$$

The 1 comes from the fact that the **loop** statement will be executed one more time in **while** and automatic indexing loops; for **until** loops the 1 is not included. The factor k may be an expression also depending on external input if the loop being evaluated also contains an inner loop.

Whether loops are involved or not, the statement count formula of a procedure, function, or entire program must be determined based on the size of the input. This is usually a straightforward process, although it can sometimes be tricky. Studying the Efficiency sections of each case study in this and subsequent chapters will give you experience in doing statement counts.

Estimating the Execution Time of Programs

The statement count formula gives us a handle on the execution time requirements of a routine. The formula itself never tells us precisely how long a routine will take to execute, because that depends on the actual computer used, but it can be used to predict approximate execution times on a particular computer based on the past performance of that routine on the same computer. For example, if we know how long it took a program to execute for a given input size on a particular computer, we can estimate the execution time of the same program on the same computer for a new input size:

1. Plug the given input size into the statement count formula. This will give the number of statements that were executed for that input size in the known time. Call this the old statement count.
2. Plug the new input size into the statement count formula. This will give the number of statements that will have to be executed for this new input size. Call this the new statement count.
3. Divide the new statement count by the old statement count, and multiply by the known time required to execute the program with the old input size. This will give the approximate time required to execute the program with the new input size.

Example   Assume that the statement count formula for a program is
4.12

     15*x + 7

where x is the size of the input, and suppose we know from a previous execution of the program that it took 4 seconds to run the program with an input size of 1000. How long will it take the program to execute with an input size of 5000? Following our procedure, we first plug the given input size (1000) into the statement count formula to determine that

     15*1000 + 7 = 15,007

statements were executed in 4 seconds. Next we plug the new input size (5000) into the formula to discover that

     15*5000 + 7 = 75,007

statements will be executed when we run the program with the new input size. Finally, to determine how long it will take the program to execute with this new input size, we divide the new statement count (75007) by the old statement count (15007) and multiply by the time it took to execute the program with the original input size (4 seconds), giving

     4*75007/15007 = 20 seconds (approximately)

to execute the same program with the new input size.

     Similarly, if we wished to run the same program with an input size of 500 rather than 1000, the program would require

     4*7507/15007 = 2 seconds (approximately)

to run with this new input size.

     These figures should not surprise us. Since the statement count formula is linear, the number of statements processed as the program is executed will rise in proportion to the size of the input, so if the input is increased 5 times from 1000 to 5000, the execution time should also increase 5 times, from 4 seconds to 20 seconds. Similarly, if the input is decreased by half from 1000 to 500, the execution time should also decrease by half, from 4 seconds to 2 seconds. This is the nature of a linear function.

Suppose that a program has the statement count formula

Example 4.13

$$10^*y^2 - 2^*y + 3$$

where y is the size of the input, and suppose that for an input of size $y = 100$ the processor took 9 seconds to process this program. How long will it take the processor to execute this same program for an input size of 500? Again we can use the process outlined in this section to determine the answer. First plug the given input size (100) into the statement count formula to learn that

$$10^*100^2 - 2^*100 + 3 = 99{,}803$$

statements were executed in 9 seconds. Next find out how many statements would be executed if the input size were 500 by plugging 500 in for y to get

$$10^*500^2 - 2^*500 + 3 = 2{,}499{,}003$$

statements. Finally, to get the number of seconds necessary to execute these 2,499,003 statements, divide the new statement count by the old statement count and multiply by 9 seconds to get

$$9^*2499003/99803 = 225 \text{ seconds (approximately)}$$

Similarly, if we wanted to run the same program with an input size of 50 rather than 100 we would get

$$9^*24903/99803 = 2.25 \text{ seconds (approximately)}$$

Again, here, these figures should not surprise us. The dominant term of the statement count formula is n^2, so we would expect that if the input size is increased 5 times from 100 to 500, the execution time would rise 5^2 times from 9 to $9^*25 = 225$ seconds. Similarly, if the input size is decreased by half from 100 to 50, we would expect the execution time to decrease 0.5^2 times from 9 to $9^*0.25 = 2.25$ seconds. This is the nature of a quadratic function.

Suppose that the statement count formula for a program is

Example 4.14

$$7^*\log_2 n + 10$$

where n is the size of the input, and suppose that it took 2 seconds to process input of size 50,000. How long will it take to process input of size 100,000? First, we can determine that

$$7^*\log_2 50000 + 10 = 120 \text{ statements (approximately)}$$

were executed in 2 seconds when the input size was 50,000. When the input size is 100,000,

$$7^*\log_2 100000 + 10 = 127 \text{ statements (approximately)}$$

will be executed, so the time to execute this program with an input size of 100,000 will be

$$2^*127/120 = 2.1 \text{ seconds}$$

This result may seem strange if you are not familiar with logarithmic functions. Programs with logarithmic statement count formulas are very easy for a computer to handle, because doubling the input size only increases the value of the logarithm by 1! In other words, the input size can be doubled without a significant increase in the execution time. Graphing this formula would demonstrate its slow growth rate. We will encounter real problems with this statement count formula.

Example 4.15   Suppose that the statement count formula for a given program is known to be

$$5*2^n + n + 10$$

and that for an input size of $n = 10$ the program was known to take 3 seconds to execute. How long will it take for an input size of $n = 20$ to be executed? Following our procedure we first determine that

$$5*2^{10} + 10 + 10 = 5140 \text{ statements}$$

were executed in 3 seconds when the input size was 10. When the input size is 20,

$$5*2^{20} + 20 + 10 = 5,242,910 \text{ statements}$$

will be executed. So the time to execute these 5,242,910 statements will be

$$3*5242910/5140 = 3060 \text{ seconds (approximately)}$$

Doubling the size of the input has changed this program from a manageable one to one that is nearly impractical (3060 seconds is 51 minutes, which can be very expensive in terms of computer time). This is the nature of an exponential function. Increasing the input size by 1 causes the execution time to double, increasing the input size by 2 (not 2 times) causes the execution time to go up $2^2 = 4$ times. In general, increasing the input size by m (not m times, but from n to $n + m$) causes the execution time to go up 2^m times.

Another similar question that can be answered using the statement count formula is this: if it takes one hour to process a program with an input of size 5000 on the current computer and a new computer that is 10 times faster is purchased, what size of input can the new computer process in one hour with the same program? This is the same question as, What size of input can be processed if the execution time is raised from 1 hour to 10 hours on the current computer? To answer a question like this you must

1. Determine how many statements were executed with the original input size in the given time period. Call this the old statement count.
2. Multiply the old statement count by the speedup factor of the new computer (or the new time period divided by the old time period on the current computer). Call this the new statement count.
3. Set the statement count formula equal to the new statement count and solve for the proper input size.

Example 4.16   Suppose that the statement count formula for a program is

$$15*x + 7$$

where x is the input size, and that the program can process an input of size 1000 in 4 seconds. If we allow the program to run for 10 seconds, how large could the input size be made? First determine that

15*1000 + 7 = 15,007 statements

were executed in the original 4 seconds. So, in 10 seconds

(10/4)*15007 = 37,518 statements

would be executed. To find out what input size is equivalent to that many statements, we set

15*x + 7 = 37,518

and solve for x, which gives

x = 2500 (approximately)

This is not surprising, because the time increase from 4 to 10 seconds is a factor of 2.5; since the statement count formula is linear, we would expect the input that could be handled to increase by a factor of 2.5 also, from 1000 to 2500.

Suppose that a program has the statement count formula

$$10*y^2 - 2*y + 3$$

Example 4.17

where y is the size of the input, and that it can handle an input of size 100 in 9 seconds. What size of input could the program process in 9 seconds if we bought a computer that was 10 times faster? In 9 seconds on the old computer,

$$10*100^2 - 2*100 + 3 = 99,803 \text{ statements}$$

were executed. Since the new computer is 10 times faster, it will be able to execute

10*99803 = 998,030 statements

in 9 seconds. Solving for y in the formula

$$10*y^2 - 2*y + 3 = 998,030$$

shows us that y = 316 (approximately); that is, an input size of 316 can be handled in 9 seconds on the new computer.

This should not be surprising. Since the statement count formula is dominated by the term y^2, as the power of the computer (or the extra time on the old computer) rises by a factor of m, the amount of extra input that can be handled will only rise by a factor of the square root of m. Since the new computer was 10 times as fast in this example, we would expect that the amount of input that could be processed in the same 9 seconds would increase by the square root of 10 (3.16) times, from 100 to 3.16*100 = 316 times.

Suppose that the statement count formula for a program is

$$7*\log_2 n + 10$$

Example 4.18

where n is the size of the input, and suppose that in 2 seconds the processor can process an input of size 50,000. What size of input could be processed in 3 seconds? First we determine that

$$7*\log_2 50000 + 10 = 120 \text{ statements (approximately)}$$

were executed in the 2 seconds. In 3 seconds

(3/2)*120 = 180 statements

would be executed. The input size handled when 180 statements are executed is determined by solving for n in

$$7*\log_2 n + 10 = 180$$

or

$$\log_2 n = 24.3$$

so

$$n = 2^{24.3} = 20,655,200$$

Since the dominant term in this statement count formula is $\log_2 n$, we would expect that if the execution time of the program were increased m times, then the size of the input that could be handled would rise on the order of n^m. That is, if for an input of size n the statement count formula tells us that somewhere on the order of $\log_2 n$ statements will be executed, approximately m times that many statements, or $m*\log_2 n$ statements will be executed if the execution time is increased m times. But we know that $m*\log_2 n = \log_2 n^m$, which implies that an input size of about n^m can be processed if the execution time is increased m times. In this case, then we would expect that an input size of about

$$50,000^{1.5} = 11,180,300$$

would be handled. The actual increased input size turned out to be 20,655,200, which is about 1.8 times larger than 11,180,300; this increase is due to the constants 7 and 10 in the statement count formula.

Example 4.19   Assume that we have a program with statement count formula

$$5*2^n + n + 10$$

and that an input of size 11 requires 6 seconds to execute. If we let this program run 1000 times longer (i.e., for 6000 seconds, or 1.7 hours), how much input could be handled by the program?

First we determine that in 6 seconds

$$5*2^{11} + 11 + 10 = 10,261$$

statements were executed. In 6000 seconds, 1000 times as many statements (or 10,261,000 statements) will be executed. Solving for n in

$$5*2^n + n + 10 = 10261000$$

gives

$$2^n + n = 2,052,198$$

so n is approximately

$$\log_2 2052198 = 20.9$$

because n is insignificant compared to 2^n. Thus the size of the input cannot even increase twice to 22 even though the execution time increased 1000 times.

This is what we would expect, actually, because the dominant term in this statement count formula is

$$2^n$$

and an increase in execution time of 1000 will cause about

$$1000 * 2^n$$

statements to be executed, where 1000 is approximately 2 to the 10th power, meaning that

$$2^{10} * 2^n = 2^{n+10}$$

statements will be executed, showing that about 10 more statements can be handled if the execution time is increased 1000 times. So, instead of an input size of $n = 11$, an input size of $n = 21$ can be handled, as previously determined.

As these examples show, each statement count formula has a dominant term that has the greatest influence on execution time as the size of the input changes. The execution time closely follows the number of statements executed, and the dominant term of the statement count formula, especially for larger input sizes, causes the other terms to play an insignificant role. Thus we can isolate the dominant term of the statement count formula and use it alone as an indication of the execution time behavior of a routine. This leads to the idea of time complexity.

Time Complexity

For a general understanding of the execution time requirements of a program, a statement count analysis is more detailed than necessary. The dominant term of the statement count formula gives substantial insight into the run time behavior of a routine, and with practice we can usually identify this term by briefly examining the routine without doing a complete statement count. The dominant term shows the growth in the number of statements executed as the input size grows, and the number of statements executed is directly proportional to the time required for execution; thus the dominant term can also be used as an accurate predictor of general changes in execution time as the input size varies.

If the statement count formula for some routine has been determined to be

*Example
4.20*

$$5*n + 4$$

where n is the size of the input, then the dominant term is n. It is the only term in the formula that grows as the input size increases. Knowing that the dominant term is n tells us that the execution time grows proportionally to the size of the input, so, for example, if the input size is increased four times, then the time to execute the routine will also increase four times.

If we know that the dominant term of the statement count formula for another routine is

$$y^2$$

where y is the size of input, then we know that the execution time of that routine grows proportionally to the *square* of the size of the input. That is, if the input size is increased four times, then the time to execute the routine will grow about 16 times (4^2). We know this without even knowing the actual statement count formula, which may be

$$5*y^2 + 16*y + 3$$

or

$$5000^*y^2 + 1600^*y + 300$$

The observation that the execution time grows proportionally to the size of the dominant term

$$y^2$$

is true in both cases.

As shown in this example, the dominant term of the statement count formula for a routine indicates the general change in execution time as the size of the input changes; it is in one sense a measure of how "complex" a routine is, in terms of increases in execution time required as the size of the input increases. We would say, for example, that a routine whose dominant term in the statement count formula is n^2 is more complex than one whose dominant term is n (where n is the size of the input), because as n gets larger and larger the disparity in the execution times of these two routines would be tremendous. For this reason we like to categorize routines according to the dominant term of their statement count formulas, calling this term the *order of the time complexity* or just the *time complexity* of these routines. We use the "big O" notation (for *Order*) to indicate the order of the time complexity of any routine.

Example 4.21

If the statement count formula of a routine is

$$5^*n + 4$$

where n is the size of the input, we say that its time complexity is $O(n)$, because the dominant term is n. Since routines with time complexity $O(n)$ must have underlying statement count formulas that are linear in n (like the one shown above), such routines are also said to have *linear time complexity*.

If a routine has the statement count formula

$$5^*y^2 + 16^*y + 3$$

where y is the size of the input, we say that its time complexity is $O(y^2)$, or quadratic.

Classifying routines according to their time complexities gives us insight into the fundamental differences among routines with different time complexities as well as the similarities among routines with the same time complexity. On the other hand, the time complexity of a routine does not reveal much about its *actual* execution time. For example, two different routines with the same time complexity may have vastly different actual run time requirements.

Example 4.22

Given two different routines with time complexities $O(n^2)$ and $O(n)$, without knowing their statement count formulas we know that there are fundamental differences between the two routines. For example, if an input of size 1000 ($n = 1000$) requires 2 seconds to execute on a real computer for both routines, then making the input 4 times larger ($n = 4000$) means that the first routine will require roughly 32 seconds to execute (because its execution time increases about 4^2 (16) times) whereas the second routine will require only about 8 seconds to execute (because its execution time increases about 4 times).

Knowing that two different routines have the same time complexity, $O(n)$, for example, does *not* mean that they both require the same amount of time to execute for a given value of n (the input size). One routine may have statement count formula

$2*n + 5$

and the other

$1000*n + 5000$

Clearly, the second routine will always require much more time to execute. However, they both have linear time complexity, and so, for example, if the size of the input is increased 10 times for each routine, they will each require about 10 times as long to execute.

In determining the time complexity of an entire program it is important to consider the separate routines in the context of the program, because an individual procedure or function when viewed alone may have a higher time complexity than the entire program, as shown in the next example.

Consider the following procedure

Example 4.23

```
fudge : procedure
    storage specification
        parameters
            sum : out only integer
            n : in only integer
        variables
            i, j : integer
        end storage specification

    begin fudge
        sum ← 0
        loop start i with 1 step 1 to n
            loop start j with 1 step 1 to n
                sum ← sum + i + j
                output 'sum = ', sum
            endloop autoindex
        endloop autoindex
    end fudge
```

Examining this procedure by itself, we find that its time complexity is $O(n^2)$, because the nested loops are both dependent on n. (Since n is passed as a parameter to procedure *fudge*, n is treated as the input size for *fudge*.) Indeed, if *fudge* were called from the initial procedure

```
tryit : initial procedure
    storage specification
        variables
            sum, m : integer
        end storage specification
```

```
begin tryit
    input m
    fudge(sum, m)
    output 'the sum is ', sum
end tryit
```

then the entire program would have time complexity $O(m^2)$. If on the other hand *fudge* were called from the initial procedure

tryit2 : **initial procedure**

  storage specification
    variables
        sum : **integer**
    end storage specification

  begin tryit2
      fudge(sum, 5)
      output sum
  end tryit2

then the entire program has $O(1)$ time complexity (constant), because *fudge* is always passed the value 5 for *n*, so the loops in procedure fudge always iterate the same number of times.

The time complexity of a routine can always be determined from the statement count formula, but the statement count formula cannot be determined from the time complexity. As we have demonstrated, the most straightforward method of determining the time complexity of a routine is to do a statement count and then use the dominant term as the time complexity. However, with practice you will become so familiar with the usual sorts of time complexities that you will not need to do a statement count to determine the time complexity of a routine. The most common important time complexities are given in table 4–1.

TABLE 4–1. COMMON TIME COMPLEXITIES

$O(1)$	constant time complexity	Most Efficient
$O(\log_2 n)$	logarithmic time complexity	
$O(n)$	linear time complexity	
$O(n^*\log_2 n)$	linear times logarithmic time complexity	
$O(n^2)$	quadratic time complexity	
$O(n^3)$	cubic time complexity	
$O(2^n)$	exponential time complexity	Least Efficient

The common time complexities can be described as follows:

1. $O(1)$ — *Constant time complexity.* If a routine will only execute some maximum number of statements, regardless of the size of the input, then its time complexity is constant. That is, there is no growth in the maximum execution time as the input size changes. The $O(1)$ notation is used because 1 is a constant, indicating that the routine has constant time complexity. This does not mean that the same number of statements will always be executed regardless of the input; it just means that there will never be more than some maximum constant number of statements executed, regardless of the input size. For example, the routine could contain an **if** statement where the **then** clause has a

different number of statements than the **else** clause. For some inputs the **then** clause would be executed but not the **else** clause. However, as long as the *maximum* number of statements that could be executed is a constant, the routine would have $O(1)$ time complexity. The programs in chapter 2 and the nonrecursive programs in chapter 3 all have constant time complexity. Also, any program that does not perform input has $O(1)$ time complexity. (Why?)

2. $O(\log_2 n)$ — *Logarithmic time complexity.* This time complexity usually results from a single loop in which the size of the data being processed is cut in half on each pass through the loop. For input size n, the maximum number of times the loop can be processed under these conditions is $\log_2 n$. Case study 5.6 gives an example of a binary search routine with this time complexity.

3. $O(n)$ — *Linear time complexity.* Linear time complexity usually comes from a single loop that is executed a number of times proportional to the input size (e.g., n times, $n - 5$ times, $n/2$ times, or $5*n$ times). This chapter contains many programs with linear time complexity. It is important to note that some loops have constant time complexity, such as the loop below

```
loop start i with 1 step 1 to 5
    output i
    endloop autoindex
```

Some recursive functions and procedures (like function *factorial* of case study 3.6) may also have linear time complexity.

4. $O(n*\log_2 n)$ — *Linear times logarithmic time complexity.* This time complexity is important because of its significance in sorting, as demonstrated in case study 5.8.

5. $O(n^2)$ — *Quadratic time complexity.* This time complexity most often arises from nested loops, both of which iterate a number of times proportional to the input size, n. Each time the outer loop iterates once, the inner loop must execute to completion. You must be careful even when analyzing a loop that does not appear to have a nested loop in it. If the loop contains a call to another procedure or function, then that procedure or function must be included in the time complexity of the loop. If the called procedure or function also contains a loop, it acts like a nested loop. An example of a routine with this time complexity is given in case study 5.7. A similar time complexity is $O(n*m)$ resulting from an outer loop that executes a number of times proportional to n and an inner loop that executes a number of time proportional to m, where both n and m are input values. Case study 4.3 has this time complexity.

6. $O(n^3)$ — *Cubic time complexity.* Like quadratic time complexity, cubic time complexity usually arises from nested loops. A routine has cubic complexity when one loop contains a second loop which contains a third loop, and each loop is executed a number of times proportional to the size of the input. There aren't many applications requiring this level of nesting, and there are no examples of a routine with this time complexity in this book.

7. $O(2^n)$ — *Exponential time complexity.* This is a particularly bad time complexity that arises in some practical programs, such as one to determine the shortest path from one town through a specified group of towns back to the starting town, and in other interesting problems, such as playing chess with a computer. Case study 4.6 discusses one routine with exponential time complexity.

To really see the differences among the various time complexities you should graph them for different values of n and reread the examples at the end of the previous section on statement counts.

Example 4.24

Suppose that there are seven different programs with the seven different time complexities listed in table 4–1. Assume that each one of these programs can handle an input of size 1000 in 8 seconds. If we increase the execution time to 80 seconds and run each of these programs again, what is the maximum new input size that each of these programs will be able to handle?

First, the program with time complexity $O(1)$ will execute in a maximum time that is constant, so changing the input size does not affect the required execution time. That is, if 8 seconds is the maximum execution time required by this program, then it will take no longer than 8 seconds to execute, regardless of the size of the input.

For the program with time complexity $O(\log_2 n)$, increasing the execution time 10 times means that on the order of

$$10 * \log_2 1000$$

statements will be executed, where the old input size 1000 has been substituted for n in the formula. But

$$10 * \log_2 1000 = \log_2 1000^{10}$$

so the new input size which could be handled in 80 seconds is 1000^{10}, which is a huge value — 1 followed by 30 zeros. It is unlikely that such a large input size would ever be processed, so this program would never even come close to requiring 80 seconds of execution time. Routines with logarithmic time complexity are extremely efficient.

For the program with linear time complexity, $O(n)$, the size of the input that can be handled grows proportionally to the amount of additional execution time provided. Since the execution time was increased 10 times, the input size will rise about 10 times also, from 1000 to 10,000. Programs with linear time complexity are also considered to be very efficient, although they are much worse than those with logarithmic time complexity.

For the program with time complexity $O(n * \log_2 n)$, a little work with a calculator shows that the input size that can be handled in 80 seconds will be about 7600. This is not quite as good as the gain achieved by the program with linear time complexity, but as the input size n gets larger and larger, this program will begin to act like a program with linear time complexity, because the term

$$\log_2 n$$

will add less and less to the final result for large n.

For the program with quadratic time complexity, $O(n^2)$, the increase in input size that can be handled will grow as the square root of the increase in execution time. Since the execution time has been increased 10 times, we would expect the input size to increase only the square root of 10 times, or 3.16 times, from 1000 to just 3160. Programs with quadratic time complexity begin to tax even our largest computers as n becomes larger. Notice that we get barely a threefold increase in input size for a tenfold increase in execution time.

For the program with cubic time complexity, $O(n^3)$, the increase in input size will grow as the cube root of the increase in allotted execution time, so we would expect the input size to increase only about 2.15 times from 1000 to 2150. In this instance, increasing the execution time 10 times has barely doubled the input size that can be handled. Programs with cubic time complexity stretch the capabilities of even large supercomputers for input sizes of the type needed for such worthwhile tasks as weather prediction.

For the program with exponential time complexity, $O(2^n)$, the increase in input size that can be handled as the execution time increases 10 times can be determined as follows: since about 2^{1000} statements will be executed in 8 seconds with the original input size of 1000, it follows that in 80 seconds about 10 times as many statements, or

$$10 * 2^{1000} = 2^{3.32} * 2^{1000} = 2^{1003.32}$$

statements will be executed. This shows that the new input size is only about 1003, which is an increase of only 3 from 1000. In other words, a tenfold increase in the execution time has raised the input size by just 3. Programs with exponential time complexity are called *intractable* because no real computer will ever be able to process such programs even for moderate values of n. Unfortunately, there are a number of important and interesting programs that fall into this category. One, known as the traveling salesperson problem, is to determine the shortest path from the salesperson's hometown to all other towns on the sales route and back to the hometown. Another such problem is chess, if the game is played in the brute force method of examining every possible move and then choosing the best (this partially explains why a computer is not yet the world's best chess player). At least no one has found a faster program for either of these problems that does not rely on some "guessing" to take shortcuts leading to an approximate, but not perfect, solution.

As this example shows, programs with constant and logarithmic time complexities are trivial to execute on a computer, programs with linear or logarithmic-times-linear time complexities are manageable even for quite large input sizes, programs with quadratic or cubic time complexities pose serious problems for even modern large computers as the input size becomes large, and programs with exponential time complexity are hopeless, even when executed on the fastest supercomputers for small input sizes. Having an appreciation of the differences among the various commonly occurring time complexities will help you understand some of the fundamental properties of programs and aid you in the design of efficient programs. Other time complexities will also arise, but with practice they also will usually be easy to determine through inspection or a formal statement count.

Differences between Statement Counts and Time Complexity

The statement count formula and the time complexity formula serve different purposes, even though the time complexity can be determined from the statement count formula. The statement count formula is a precise picture of the execution time requirements of our procedures and functions, and changes in the statement count formula can indicate significant changes in the efficiency of these routines.

Assume that a particular procedure has the statement count formula

Example 4.25

$$5 * m + 4$$

where m is the size of the input, and say that this comes from the fact that this procedure contains a **while** loop with five statements that are executed m times, and three statements outside the loop that are executed once (remember that the **loop while** statement is executed one extra time). If we discover that one of the statements outside the loop is unnecessary and remove it, we get the formula

$$5 * m + 3$$

for the statement count, which is hardly more efficient than the original program, especially for large values of m. On the other hand, if we discover that we can remove one of the statements from the loop of the original procedure, the statement count formula becomes

$$4*m + 4$$

and the improvement we have made is truly significant; the modified procedure will run 20% faster than the original one.

Even though the improvement gained by deleting a statement from a loop is significant, as demonstrated in this example, the improvement is not fundamental, because the time complexities of the original and improved versions remain the same (in this example, both have $O(m)$ time complexity). A fundamental change usually comes not from just examining and modifying a routine but from reexamining the problem and discovering a completely new design with a lower time complexity.

Example 4.26　Assume that a function has been determined to have time complexity $O(y^2)$, where y is the size of the input. If we can design a new function to do the same task but with time complexity $O(y)$, we have made a fundamental improvement, because for larger and larger values of y the new version will be not just 20% better but y times better. (We know this without even knowing the statement count formula.)

By itself, the time complexity of a routine does not contain enough information to allow us to choose among various alternatives when trying to pick the most efficient for our purposes. This is true even when we have a choice between two routines with different time complexities.

Example 4.27　Assume that three people of various abilities write three different programs for doing the same task and that the routines have time complexities $O(2^n)$, $O(n^2)$, and $O(n)$.

Knowing only these time complexities, it is clear that the program with time complexity $O(n)$ should be chosen. However, if we also know that these programs have the statement count formulas

$$2^n + 15$$
$$10*n^2 + 15$$

and

$$500*n + 30$$

respectively, then for input sizes between 0 and 9 the program with exponential time complexity is the best. For input sizes between 10 and 50 the program with quadratic time complexity is the best, and for all input sizes greater than 50 the program with linear time complexity is the best. (You should plot these three formulas to see that this is so.) Thus the decision about which program to use should be made each time the program is to be run, after the size of the input is known.

In summary, the study of the time complexity of programs is a deep and active area of research in computer science. This textbook should provide you with an appreciation of the notion of time complexity and a simple and reliable method for determining the time complexity by using the statement count of any procedure, function, or program you may write. On the other hand you should be aware that comparing the efficiency of two different programs through their statement counts alone may lead to erroneous conclusions. Our method does not account for the fact that there is a wide range of capabilities among real computers — some can only do one single operation at a time, the way our model computer works, whereas large expensive computers can overlap some operations. Also, a statement count hides the fact that some statements take longer to execute than others.

The loop

Example 4.28

```
loop start x with 1 step 1 to n
    y ← 5*x↑3 − 3*x↑2 + 15*x −3
    output 'y = ', y
    endloop autoindex
```

has the statement count formula

$$4*n + 1$$

(the **loop** statement itself is executed one extra time to give the 1). On the other hand, the loop

```
loop start x with 1 step 1 to n
    a ← 5*x↑3
    b ← 3*x↑2
    c ← 15*x − 3
    output 'y = ', a − b + c
    endloop autoindex
```

has the statement count formula

$$6*n + 1$$

However, both loops compute the same thing, and they both have the same number of arithmetic operations to be evaluated, so in reality they would execute in about the same amount of time. The statement count formula of the first version hides the fact that a lot of individual operations occur in one statement.

In spite of this shortcoming, the statement count of a routine reveals much about its efficiency, including its time complexity, and you are encouraged to use the statement count formula to analyze the general execution time requirements of routines you design.

DETERMINING LOOP CORRECTNESS

Loops are one of the primary sources of errors in a program. It is easy to forget to initialize the relevant variables properly before entering a loop, forget to update these variables properly within the loop, or to write the loop so that it iterates the wrong number of times. It also takes practice to design a loop properly to compute the desired result, especially when you are not familiar with developing iterative solutions to problems. Carefully designing the loop allows us to avoid nearly all of the pitfalls mentioned above, and experience has shown that the design of loops around a loop invariant assertion leading to a loop goal assertion promotes error-free loop design.

Loop Invariant Assertions and Loop Goal Assertions

The most important concept to grasp in learning about loops is their iterative nature. A loop is intended to compute some goal result by building up a partial solution that on each iteration gets closer to the desired goal result until this partial solution finally becomes the goal result and the loop can be terminated. So, there are two very important points to be captured in the design of every loop:

1. *The loop goal assertion.* The loop goal assertion is a precise statement of the calculation performed by the loop (the purpose of the loop); it must be true when the loop has finished executing (immediately following **endloop**).
2. *The loop invariant assertion.* The loop invariant assertion is a statement declaring that the partial solution leading to the goal result is being properly computed on each iteration of the loop. This assertion is placed at the top of the loop just after the **loop** statement in **while** and automatic indexing loops, and at the bottom of the loop just before **endloop** in **until** loops.

The goal assertion for a loop should be carefully developed even before design of the loop begins. Since this assertion captures the purpose of the loop, the loop should not be designed until its purpose can be clearly stated as an assertion.

Example 4.29

Suppose that we have developed the following partial solution to a function to compute the sum of the first *n* even integers:

    sum ← 0
    {compute the sum of the first n even integers}
    sumeven ← sum

(*sumeven* is the name of the function we are designing.) Suppose now that we decide to use a loop to finish the part

    {compute the sum of the first n even integers}

The goal of this loop, regardless of whether we finally decide to use a **while** loop, **until** loop, or automatic indexing loop, is that variable *sum* contain the sum of the first *n* even integers. Thus, we can write our partial design as

    sum ← 0
    {compute the sum of the first n even integers}
    assert sum contains the sum of the first n even integers
    sumeven ← sum

even before we have the faintest idea how we will design the loop.

Once the goal assertion of a loop is formalized, the loop can be designed around this goal. We decide how we will calculate the goal result by computing a partial result on each iteration of the loop. This decision leads to formalization of the loop invariant assertion, which just states that the desired partial result is being properly computed on each pass through the loop.

Continuing with the partially designed function from the previous example, suppose that we decide to use an automatic indexing loop to complete the design, running the loop index variable i from 1 to n and ensuring that on the ith pass through the loop the ith even integer is added to *sum*. This means that just before each new iteration is begun, we must be sure that the sum of the previous $i-1$ even numbers is already in variable *sum* in preparation for adding the ith even number to *sum* during the current (ith) iteration. This gives us our loop invariant assertion, which must be placed immediately after the **loop** statement:

Example 4.30

> **assert** sum contains the sum of the first $i-1$ even numbers.

Placing this assertion in the loop gives the partial solution

```
sum ← 0
loop start i with l step 1 to n
    assert sum contains the sum of the first i−1 even integers
    ¦add the ith even integer to sum¦
    endloop autoindex
assert sum contains the sum of the first n even integers
sumeven ← sum
```

Notice that the loop invariant assertion will be true before each iteration of the loop (including the very first one when *sum* is 0 and i is 1) if we can finish the part

> ¦add the ith even integer to sum¦

properly. This is why this assertion is called an *invariant* assertion — it must be true, without varying, each time through the loop. Adding the ith even integer to *sum* is just a matter of including the statement

> sum ← sum + 2*i

in the loop giving

```
sum ← 0
loop start i with 1 step 1 to n
    assert sum contains the sum of the first i−1 even integers
    sum ← sum + 2*i
    endloop autoindex
assert sum contains the sum of the first n even integers
sumeven ← sum
```

which completes the design of the computation section of function *sumeven*.

As shown in example 4.29, the goal assertion states what the loop must accomplish, and it helps direct the initial design of the loop and the formulation of the loop invariant assertion. Then, as shown in example 4.30, the loop invariant assertion helps direct the completion of the loop design in such a way that the loop invariant assertion remains true.

For years, programmers have designed loops without formally writing down goal assertions and loop invariant assertions. However, whether they were conscious of it or not, they had to understand the concepts behind both of these assertions in order to design their loops properly, because these assertions are nothing more than formal statements of what the loops are doing anyway. Although we too could design loops without using assertions, taking the effort to identify and carefully state these two assertions has a number of benefits: it focuses our attention directly on the problem to be solved, making it clear whether or not we understand exactly what needs to be done; it gives us precisely stated goals to follow as we design the loop; and it leads to correctly designed loops.

This last point is an important one. We must continually stress that making an assertion does not automatically mean that it is correct. After carefully designing the loop using a loop invariant assertion, we must still show that the goal assertion will indeed be true after the loop has finished executing — we must convince ourselves that if the invariant assertion is true upon completion of the loop, the goal assertion has been fulfilled. This is usually not a difficult task, but it is slightly different for each of the three types of loops.

Verifying While Loops

The form of a **while** loop with loop invariant and goal assertions is

```
    (1)
loop while condition
    assert loop invariant assertion
    statement
        .
        .
        .
    statement
        (2)
    endloop while
        (3)
    assert loop goal assertion
```

To verify that such a **while** loop does indeed compute what is promised in *loop goal assertion*, there are three steps to follow corresponding to the three numbered lines in the **while** loop form given above.

1. Show that *loop invariant assertion* will be true *before* the loop is iterated the first time.
2. Knowing that *loop invariant assertion* is true *before* any given iteration of the loop, show that it will be true again *after* that given iteration, just in front of the **endloop** statement.
3. Knowing that *loop invariant assertion* is true when the loop has finished executing, immediately after **endloop,** and also knowing that the loop *condition* is false (otherwise the loop would still be iterating), show that these two facts imply that *loop goal assertion* will be true.

Example 4.31   Let's verify the correctness of the following loop, which computes the sum of the first n even integers, assuming that $n \geqslant 0$ holds:

```
sum ← 0
i ← 1
loop while i ≤ n
    assert sum is the sum of the first i − 1 even integers
    sum ← sum + 2*i
    i ← i + 1
    endloop while
assert sum is the sum of the first n even integers
sumeven ← sum
```

We first apply step 1. Will the loop invariant assertion be true before the first iteration of the loop? At that point *sum* is 0 and *i* is 1 (because of the two assignment statements before the loop), so the loop invariant assertion becomes

    assert sum is the sum of the first 0 even integers

and since *sum* does contain 0, this assertion is true. Notice that if the loop is not even executed once (because $n = 0$), the loop invariant assertion is still true.

Now we apply step 2. For an arbitrary iteration of the loop, we must show that knowing that the loop invariant assertion is true before that iteration is performed, then executing the two statements within the loop will cause the loop invariant assertion to be true again. Let's try it. Given that

    assert sum is the sum of the first i − 1 even integers

is true at the top of the loop, after executing the statement

    sum ← sum + 2*i

we could state

    assert sum is the sum of the first i even integers

because the *i*th even integer has just been added to *sum*. Then executing the next statement

    i ← i + 1

makes *i* one larger, so we could now only state

    assert sum is the sum of the first i − 1 even integers

which is the loop invariant assertion again, showing that the loop invariant assertion holds after executing the loop statements, given that it held before these statements were executed. This means that the loop invariant assertion will again be true at the top of the loop as the *next* iteration begins and as every subsequent iteration begins. Carrying out step 2 just once is enough to show that the loop invariant assertion will be true at the start of every loop iteration (except the first, which was checked in step 1).

Now, since we have shown in step 1 that the loop invariant assertion will be true on the first iteration of the loop or even if the loop is not iterated at all, and we have shown in step 2 that this assertion will always be true at the start of each iteration after the first, this implies that the loop invariant assertion will also be true just after **endloop** (the loop is terminated when the loop condition becomes false, but this does not affect the loop invariant assertion.) The loop terminates because the loop condition

    i ≤ n

is false; this means that $i = n + 1$ just after **endloop.** We can also state this as an assertion. The two facts,

    assert sum is the sum of the first i − 1 even integers

and

assert i now equals n + 1

imply that we can substitute $n + 1$ for i in the loop invariant assertion, getting the assertion

assert sum is the sum of the first n even integers

which is the goal assertion that we were hoping to prove true.

Putting all of these assertions into our loop gives us

```
sum ← 0
i ← 1
assert sum is the sum of the first i − 1 even integers
loop while i ≤ n
    assert sum is the sum of the first i − 1 even integers
    sum ← sum + 2*i
    assert sum is the sum of the first i even integers
    i ← i + 1
    assert sum is the sum of the first i − 1 even integers
    endloop while
assert sum is the sum of the first i − 1 even integers
assert i = n + 1
assert sum is the sum of the first n even integers
sumeven ← sum
```

This is quite unreadable at it stands, so we would never write our function in this form, but it does demonstrate how we verify that the loop goal assertion

assert sum is the sum of the first n even integers

really is met by the loop we have designed. Notice that by step 1 we have shown that the loop invariant assertion can also be placed just before the **loop** statement, where it must be true in order to be true when the loop is first entered. Step 2 has shown that the loop invariant assertion must be true just before **endloop** to show that it will be true on any subsequent iteration of the loop. Also, steps 1 and 2 assure that the loop invariant assertion will be true right after **endloop.** There, the fact that the loop condition is false can be combined with the loop invariant assertion to show that the desired goal assertion is true.

In looking back at the **while** loop form given at the beginning of this section and considering our example we see that verifying that the loop really does compute what the goal assertion states is a matter of showing that the loop invariant assertion can be placed at (1) by following step 1 of the verification process, and then showing that the loop invariant assertion can be placed at (2) by following step 2 of the verification process. Having done this, it follows automatically that the loop invariant assertion can be placed at (3). There, we must apply step 3 of the verification process to show that the loop invariant assertion, along with the additional known fact that the loop *condition* is now false, imply that the goal assertion is now true. If we find that we cannot apply any one of these steps this means that there is something wrong with our design.

Suppose that we had written the computation part of function *sumeven* this way:

Example 4.32

```
sum ← 2
i ← 1
loop while i ≤ n
    assert sum is the sum of the first i − 1 even integers
    sum ← sum + 2*i
    i ← i + 1
    endloop while
assert sum is the sum of the first n even integers
sumeven ← sum
```

To apply step 1 of the verification process, we would place the loop invariant assertion right before the **loop** statement giving

```
sum ← 2
i ← 1
assert sum is the sum of the first i − 1 even integers
loop while i ≤ n
    assert sum is the sum of the first i − 1 even integers
    sum ← sum + 2*i
    i ← i + 1
    endloop while
assert sum is the sum of the first n even integers
sumeven ← sum
```

We would notice right away that the loop invariant assertion is not true there, because *i* is 1 and *sum* is 2, so the assertion would be

assert 2 is the sum of the first 0 even integers

which is wrong. After a little thought we would realize that we would have to change the assignment statement

```
sum ← 2
```

to

```
sum ← 0
```

to make the loop invariant assertion hold true just before the **loop** statement. Continuing the verification process with steps 2 and 3 would then show the modified loop to be correct.

The examples of this section have shown how to apply the three steps of the **while** loop verification process. It takes a little time to verify that a **while** loop is correct, but it usually is not difficult, because this formal verification process is really no different than the informal method you would use anyway to assure yourself that a **while** loop you have designed is correct. Doing it formally is more thorough and safer. We will not have enough space in this book to verify all our case studies formally in this fashion. We will supply the loop invariant assertions and the goal assertions for our loops (in most cases) and leave the verification process as an exercise. Writing the loop invariant assertion and the loop goal assertion forces us to do a quick mental check of the three verification steps anyway, and this usually leads us to a correct design.

Verifying Automatic Indexing Loops

The form of an automatic indexing loop with a loop invariant assertion and a loop goal assertion is

loop start *index* **with** *starting value* **step** *increment* **to** *ending value*
    assert *loop invariant assertion*
    statement
        .
        .
        .
    statement
    endloop *autoindex*
assert *loop goal assertion*

Since the automatic indexing loop is equivalent to a **while** indexing loop, its verification process is similar. You must

1. Show that *loop invariant assertion* will be true the *first time* the loop is entered.
2. Knowing that *loop invariant assertion* is true before any given iteration of the loop, show that it will be true again before the next iteration of the loop.
3. Knowing that *loop invariant assertion* will be true just after **endloop** and also knowing that the value in the loop *index* has gone past *ending value* (causing termination of the loop), show that *loop goal assertion* will be true.

Example 4.33 Using the example of function *sumeven* again, suppose that we had written the computation section with an automatic indexing loop, assuming that $n \geqslant 0$ holds:

    sum ← 0
    loop start i **with** 1 **step** 1 **to** n
        assert sum is the sum of the first i−1 even integers
        sum ← sum + 2*i
        endloop autoindex
    assert sum is the sum of the first n even integers
    sumeven ← sum

To verify that this loop is correct we apply the three steps of the verification process. In step 1 *sum* will be 0 and *i* will be 1 when the loop is first entered. Substituting these values into the loop invariant assertion gives

    assert 0 is the sum of the first 0 even integers

which is certainly true.

Now we apply step 2. Given that the loop invariant assertion

    assert sum is the sum of the first i−1 even integers

is true before an arbitrary iteration of the loop begins, after the statement

    sum ← sum + 2*i

has been executed we could write

    assert sum is the sum of the first i even integers

because the *i*th even integer has now been added to *sum*. This brings execution to **endloop** where the increment 1 will automatically be added to *i* before execution returns to the **loop** statement, which means that

> **assert** sum is the sum of the first i−1 even integers

will again be true — this is our loop invariant assertion. Thus we have shown that if the loop invariant assertion is true before an arbitrary iteration of the loop, it will be true before the next iteration of the loop, satisfying step 2 of the verification process.

Verification steps 1 and 2 show that the loop invariant assertion will be true at the start of the loop, from the very first iteration to the last. Thus, this loop invariant assertion will also be true when *i* becomes *n* + 1, causing termination of the loop. So just after **endloop** we could write the two assertions

> **assert** sum is the sum of the first i−1 even integers

and

> **assert** i = n + 1

To satisfy verification step 3, we substitute the value *n* + 1 for *i* in the loop invariant assertion, which gives

> **assert** sum is the sum of the first n even integers

which is the goal assertion we wanted to show, so our loop is correct.

Including each of these new assertions in the loop gives

```
sum ← 0
loop start i with 1 step 1 to n
    assert sum is the sum of the first i−1 even integers
    sum ← sum + 2*i
    assert sum is the sum of the first i even integers
    endloop autoindex
assert sum is the sum of the first i−1 even integers
assert i = n + 1
assert sum is the sum of the first n even integers
sumeven ← sum
```

Again we stress that we would actually only include these extra **assert** statements as we were verifying that the loop is correct. It would make the function unreadable to include all these extra assertions in the final version.

In comparing this example with the one given for the **while** loop, notice that in the **while** loop the loop invariant assertion must hold true just before the **loop** statement and again just before **endloop.** This is not true of the automatic indexing loop, because the loop index variable is initialized and incremented in the **loop** statement. In both the **while** and automatic indexing loops, however, the loop invariant assertion will be true just after **endloop,** which allows us to show that the loop goal assertion will be true.

Verifying Until Loops

An **until** loop with a loop invariant assertion and a loop goal assertion has the form

```
loop
    statement
       .
       .
       .
    statement
    assert loop invariant assertion
    endloop until condition
assert loop goal assertion
```

An **until** loop verification is somewhat different than a **while** loop verification because of two features of the **until** loop: an **until** loop is always iterated at least once, and the check for loop termination is made at the bottom of the **until** loop. Thus, the three steps to follow in verifying that an **until** loop is correct are:

1. Show that *loop invariant assertion* will be true after the first iteration of the loop.
2. Given that *loop invariant assertion* is true just before **endloop,** and given that the **until** *condition* is not yet true, show that *loop invariant assertion* will again be true after the loop statements have been executed one more time, for any arbitrary iteration of the loop.
3. Given that *loop invariant assertion* and the **until** *condition* are true just after **endloop,** show that *loop goal assertion* is true.

Example Suppose that we have designed the computation section of function *sumeven* with an
4.34 **until** loop, assuming that n $\geq$ 0 holds:

```
sum ← 0
i ← 0
loop
    sum ← sum + 2*i
    i ← i + 1
    assert sum is the sum of the first i − 1 even integers
    endloop until i > n
assert sum is the sum of the first n even integers
sumeven ← sum
```

To verify that this loop is correct, we first apply step 1. Since *sum* and *i* are both 0 before the loop is iterated the first time, execution of the statement

sum ← sum + 2*i

will just cause a 0 to be reassigned to *sum,* and execution of

i ← i + 1

will cause 1 to be assigned to *i.* So, after the first iteration of the loop *sum* is 0 and *i* is 1. Substituting these values into the loop invariant assertion gives

assert 0 is the sum of the first 0 even integers

which shows that the loop invariant assertion will be true after the first iteration of the loop, as required by step 1 of the verification process.

Now we need to apply step 2. If the **until** condition is false (meaning that the loop must be iterated again) and the loop invariant assertion

> **assert** sum is the sum of the first i − 1 even integers

is true, then after the first statement of the loop,

> sum ← sum + 2*i

is executed we can state

> **assert** sum is the sum of the first i even integers

because the *i*th even integer was added to *sum,* which already contained the sum of the previous *i* − 1 even integers. Then, after *i* is increased by 1 in the statement

> i ← i + 1

we can assert that

> **assert** sum is the sum of the first i − 1 even integers

showing that the loop invariant assertion does indeed hold true again at the bottom of the loop, as required by step 2 of the verification process.

From verification steps 1 and 2 we know that the loop invariant assertion will always be true just before **endloop.** Therefore it must also hold true just after **endloop** when the loop terminates. So just after **endloop** we can make the two assertions

> **assert** sum is the sum of the first i − 1 even integers

and

> **assert** i = n + 1

which comes from the fact that the loop terminated. Substituting the value $n + 1$ into the loop invariant assertion gives us

> **assert** sum is the sum of the first n even integers

which is the goal assertion, meaning that we have completed step 3 of the verification process.

Including all of the new assertions we have generated while verifying this loop gives

```
sum ← 0
i ← 0
loop
    sum ← sum + 2*i
    assert sum is the sum of the first i even integers
    i ← i + 1
    assert sum is the sum of the first i − 1 even integers
    endloop until i > n
assert sum is the sum of the first i − 1 even integers
assert i = n + 1
assert sum is the sum of the first n even integers
sumeven ← sum
```

The loop given here could also be written as

```
sum ← 0
i ← 0
loop
    i ← i + 1
    sum ← sum + 2*i
    endloop until i = n
sumeven ← sum
```

if we assume that $n \geq 1$ holds. In this case the loop invariant assertion would be

assert sum is the sum of the first i even integers

You should go through the **until** loop verification process for this new loop to see the differences in the formulations of each added **assert** statement. The loop goal assertion, of course, remains the same.

A loop can only be verified if the loop goal assertion and the loop invariant assertion can be properly designed and located within the loop. The loop goal assertion belongs just after **endloop** in all three loop types. The loop invariant assertion belongs just after the **loop** statement in **while** loops and automatic indexing loops, and just before **endloop** in **until** loops. The reason for this difference is that the loop invariant assertion (which essentially states that the correct partial result is being properly computed on each iteration of the loop) must also be true upon termination of the loop, just after **endloop** (where the partial result is now the complete result, showing that the goal assertion is correct). So, locating the loop invariant assertion right next to the statement where loop termination is checked and showing that this assertion will always be true at that position in the loop means that this assertion will also be true when the loop finally terminates. In **while** and automatic indexing loops, the loop condition is checked in the **loop** statement at the top of the loop, so we include the loop invariant assertion right after the **loop** statement. In **until** loops the loop condition is checked at the bottom of the loop in the **endloop** statement, so we include the loop invariant assertion just before **endloop**.

Showing Loop Termination

Using a loop goal assertion and a loop invariant assertion to direct the design of a loop usually leads to an error-free loop. However, it is still possible to create a loop that will run infinitely for some inputs, even if the loop is carefully verified using one of the processes described in this chapter. Our verification processes do not address the problem of infinite loops — they just assure us that the goal assertion will be satisfied *if and when the loop terminates*. To show that the loop will indeed terminate is a separate step that is usually straightforward. We just need to show that there is a value that increases (or decreases) on each iteration of the loop and that the loop will no longer iterate after that value reaches a certain point.

Example 4.35   Procedure *numyears* of case study 4.4, refinement 2, has the computation section

```
output 'the initial investment is ', initial
accrued ← initial
years ← 0
loop while accrued < final
    assert years contains the number of years for initial to reach accrued
    accrued ← accrued + initial * annualrate / 100
    years ← years + 1
    output 'after ', years, ' years the accrued balance is ', accrued
    endloop while
assert years contains the number of years for initial to reach final
```

This loop can be verified by the process outlined for **while** loops, showing that the loop goal assertion will be true if and when the loop terminates. But how do we show that this loop will indeed terminate? Notice that this will happen when *accrued* is no longer less than *final*, that is, when

accrued ≥ final

is true. Therefore, we need to assure ourselves that *accrued* increases during this loop and that *final* doesn't change, because then we can be sure that *accrued* will eventually reach *final* and the loop will terminate. Looking at the initial procedure for this program (refinement 1 of case study 4.4) we see that *numyears* will not be called unless *initial* and *annualrate* are both larger than 0. So, in the statement

accrued ← accrued + initial * annualrate / 100

accrued will be incremented by some positive value on each iteration of the loop. Furthermore, no other statement in the loop modifies either *accrued* or *final*, so the loop will terminate.

Notice that we don't care how many times this loop iterates. By verifying the loop, we show that it does correctly compute what is stated in the loop goal assertion, if the loop terminates. Showing that the loop terminates completes the demonstration that the loop is correct.

Although it is usually not difficult to show that a loop terminates, there is no automatic way to do this. A famous problem called the *halting problem* essentially shows that no program can be written to check all programs and determine whether these programs have infinite loops.

Testing Loops

After verifying that a loop is properly constructed and then checking to be sure that the loop will terminate, we can be quite confident that it is correct. However, we cannot be absolutely sure, because these two checks are human checks and therefore subject to error. To be even more sure we must test each loop we design by doing a walkthrough of the finished program and by executing the program with appropriate input values. All of the testing methods we have developed previously also apply to loops. However, since we can never hope to test a general loop for all possible iterations, we need to choose test data carefully:

1. For **while** and automatic indexing loops, include test data (if possible) that will cause the loop not to execute at all (this data represents a special value).
2. For each type of loop, include test values (if possible) that will cause the loop to execute just once (these are also special values).
3. For all types of loops, include some representative test values.

Together with our previous methods for testing programs, these points should help determine whether loops are correct.

Debugging Loops

It will happen. After carefully designing some loop with a loop goal assertion and a loop invariant assertion, verifying the loop using one of the formal methods given, checking formally for loop termination, and then doing a walkthrough, you will finally test the loop and find that it doesn't work properly. At this point you need to locate and remove the bugs. It probably will do no good to reread the loop because you would have read it many times while following all the steps above to determine whether it was correct. The problem will most likely be a logic error, an error in which you assume that certain calculations are producing certain results that aren't actually being computed. For example, if you have mistakenly declared a variable to have type **integer** when you wanted it to be type **real,** you may be getting truncated values where you are expecting real values. If you have made such a wrong assumption (assuming all along that a particular variable is real rather than integer), then the loop verification step, checking for loop termination, and the walkthrough would all have been done with this false assumption in mind, and this is why the error escaped you. This shows why it is good to have a friend do the walkthrough for you.

What do you do now? The best thing to do is to include lots of **output** statements in the loop to print the values of the variables used in the loop on each loop iteration. Then run the program with the input values that are causing errors. Usually you will be able to figure out what is going wrong by looking at the printed results. The most important **output** statement to include is one that prints out the loop invariant assertion just after it is stated and just after **endloop.** This will frequently show you where your calculations are going wrong.

Example   In debugging function *sumeven* you should include at least the two **output** statements
4.36   shown below:

```
sum ← 2
i ← 1
loop while i ≤ n
    assert sum is the sum of the first i−1 even integers
    output sum, ' is the sum of the first ', i−1, ' even integers'
    sum ← sum + 2*i
    i ← i + 1
    endloop while
output sum, ' is the sum of the first ', i−1, ' even integers'
assert sum is the sum of the first n even integers
sumeven ← sum
```

If the loop is not functioning as you had planned (in this case sum is initialized to 2 rather than 0 as it should be), these **output** statements will show this fact. If, however, you still cannot determine *why* the error is occurring, including **output** statements after the statement

```
sum ← sum + 2*i
```

to print the value of *sum,* and after the statement

```
i ← i + 1
```

to print the value of *i* should pinpoint any error. Once the bugs have been fixed, the **output** statements should be removed.

We have previously stated that no function should include an **output** statement. If a function needs to be debugged, however, it is perfectly acceptable to include **output** statements in the function during the debugging phase.

The beauty of the top-down program design process, complete with the verification and testing methods presented, is that you will seldom need to expend much effort debugging your routines, because they will usually be correct when you finally get to the point of running them. The old style of programming taught that a program should be written quickly without applying any design methodology, program walkthrough, or loop verification. Then, most programming effort was spend debugging poorly designed programs that never seemed to be correct. All programmers succumb to the temptation to write a program this way sooner or later; when *you* do, you will discover that you spend far more time debugging your program than you would have spent on a careful design.

Summary of Determining Loop Correctness

In this section on loop correctness we have outlined six steps for you to follow to convince yourself that a loop is correct.

1. Design the loop around a loop goal assertion and a loop invariant assertion.
2. Verify that the loop is constructed properly using the appropriate process for the type of loop you have designed.
3. Show that the loop will eventually terminate.
4. Do a walkthrough of the loop (and the entire program that contains it).
5. Run the program on a computer with appropriate values to thoroughly test the loop.
6. If necessary, debug the loop by including **output** statements.

The three most common loop errors are (1) not initializing variables properly for the first pass of the loop, (2) using a loop termination condition that causes the loop to iterate one too many or one too few times, and (3) infinite loops, which should be caught by step 3. Other more serious logic errors caused by invalid assumptions about what is being computed will usually be uncovered by step 5, but may require step 6 to completely root out.

We will not have space to verify the case studies in this book completely. We will usually include loop goal assertions and loop invariant assertions in our loops, but we will leave verification of these loops up to you.

Formal verification of programs is another area of deep study in computer science, and it requires an understanding of mathematical logic. Here we have presented some of the most practical and easy-to-apply results from this research — the formulation and application of loop invariant assertions in the design of correct loops. Evidence has shown that careful design of a loop around a loop invariant assertion pays off in saved programmer time and reliable programs. You should use invariant and goal assertions in all loops you design.

**4.3
WARMUP
EXERCISES**

FOR REVIEW

4.1 What is the purpose of a loop?

4.2 There are three different loop types modeled in *mpl*. List them. Which is the most general loop type?

4.3 Give the general form of a **while** loop designed for summing a series of values.

4.4 Give the general form of a **while** loop in which the number of loop iterations is counted.

4.5 Repeat exercises 4.3 and 4.4 using an automatic indexing loop rather than a **while** loop.

4.6 Repeat exercises 4.3 and 4.4 using an **until** loop rather than a **while** loop.

4.7 Explain why a loop is called a control structure. Contrast the methods of control provided by **if** and **case** statements with those provided by **loop** statements.

4.8 What are the three methods for inputting a series of data values? Compare these methods in words and give the general form of the loop structure for each.

4.9 For each of the following automatic indexing loops, calculate the number of times that the statements in the loop are executed:

    (a)   **loop start** i **with** 10 **step** 1 **to** 20
            {statements}
          endloop autoindex

    (b)   **loop start** i **with** 5 **step** −2 **to** 0
            {statements}
          endloop autoindex

    (c)   **loop start** i **with** 30 **step** 5 **to** 33
            {statements}
          endloop autoindex

    (d)   **loop start** i **with** 5 **step** 2 **to** 3
            {statements}
          endloop autoindex

4.10 For each of the following automatic indexing loops, calculate the number of times that the statements in the loop are executed. This value could, of course, depend on the value of the integer variable j.

    (a)   **loop start** i **with** j **step** 1 **to** 2 * j
            {statements}
          endloop autoindex

    (b)   **loop start** i **with** j **step** j **to** 2 * j
            {statements}
          endloop autoindex

4.11 What is the statement count of a program, procedure, or function?

4.12 What is the time complexity of a program, procedure, or function?

4.13 Compare the meanings of the statement count and the time complexity of a routine.

4.14 Besides determining that a loop when exited will compute what was intended, what other determination must be made to show that a loop is correct?

4.15 What are the uses of the loop invariant assertion and the loop goal assertion? Compare the two.

A DEEPER LOOK

4.16 If the statement count of a routine is determined to be $4^*n + 3$, what is its time complexity?

4.17 If the statement count of a routine is $45^*n + n^2 - 5$ what is its time complexity?

4.18 If the statement count of a routine is $75^*\log_2 n + 5^*n + 6$ what is its time complexity?

4.19 If the time complexity of a routine is $O(n^3)$ what is its statement count?

4.20 Describe the differences among the following steps: testing a program, determining loop correctness, debugging a program, and performing a program walkthrough. In what order should these steps be done?

4.21 Assume that two different programs for doing the same task have time complexities $O(n)$ and $O(n^3)$. If these time complexities are all you know about these programs, which program should you choose? Are there any additional circumstances which, if known, would cause you to change your mind?

4.22 Write the following **while** loop structure using only **if** statements and **until** statements

```
i ← 1
loop while i ⩽ n
  j ← 1
  loop while j < m
    output i, j
    j ← j + 1
    endloop while
  i ← i + 1
  endloop while
```

What are the statement count and time complexity for the original **while** loop structure?

4.23 Calculate the statement count and time complexity of the compound interest version of function *numyears* from case study 4.4.

4.24 Is it possible to write an infinite loop using an automatic indexing loop? Explain why not or give an example showing an infinite loop.

4.25 Determine the time complexity of refinement 3 of case study 4.4.

4.26   In the Efficiency section of case study 4.4 it was pointed out that there is an inefficient repeated calculation in refinement 3. Find and remove this inefficiency.

4.27   We have always been careful to refer to the "size of the input" when speaking about statement counts and time complexity. How does this phrase differ from the "number of input values"? Are the two phrases ever the same? Are they ever different? Give examples.

4.28   The following procedure outputs the integers n, $n-1$, ..., 2. Write appropriate loop invariant and goal assertions and include them in the loop.

backloop : **procedure**

> **storage specification**
>> **parameters**
>>> n : **in only integer**
>> **variables**
>>> i : **integer**
>> **end storage specification**

> **begin** backloop
>> **loop start** i **with** n **step** −1 **to** 2
>>> **output** i
>>> **endloop** autoindex
>> **end** backloop

Now rewrite the loop using (a) a **while** loop, and (b) an **until** loop. (You will need an **if** statement in the **until** version of the procedure — explain why.) Include appropriate assertions in both versions.

4.29   Consider the following procedure:

statcount : **procedure**

> **storage specification**
>> **parameters**
>>> n : **in only integer**
>> **variables**
>>> i, j : **integer**
>> **end storage specification**

> **begin** statcount
>> **loop start** i **with** 2 **step** 1 **to** n
>>> **loop start** j **with** i+1 **step** 1 **to** n
>>>> **output** i*j
>>>> **endloop** autoindex
>>> **endloop** autoindex
>> **end** statcount

What is the statement count of procedure *statcount*? Use this count to find the time complexity of *statcount*. Would it be possible to design another procedure that produces the same output as *statcount* for any n but has a better time complexity? Defend your answer.

4.30   What is the time complexity of the following function?

```
twoloop : real function
    storage specification
        parameters
            x : in only integer
        variables
            i, j : integer
            sum : real
        end storage specification

    begin twoloop
        sum ← 1.5
        loop start i with 1 step 1 to x
            loop start j with i−1 step 1 to i+1
                sum ← sum + j/2
                endloop autoindex
            endloop autoindex
        twoloop ← sum
        end twoloop
```

Is it possible to design another function that computes the same value as *twoloop* for any x but has a better time complexity? State why.

4.31 In the summary section of case study 4.1 we stated that for the trailer value input method the trailer value must have the same type as all of the other input values. Explain why.

4.32 A potential problem in procedure *student averages* was uncovered in the Correctness section of case study 4.3. Fix the procedure in refinement 2 to take care of this problem.

4.33 In the discussion following refinement 3 of case study 4.4, it was pointed out that the **while** loops given could not be directly replaced with automatic indexing loops. Including some calculations in these programs just before the **while** loops, though, allows one to use automatic indexing loops in place of the **while** loops. Do this. (Hint: look at the Efficiency section.)

4.34 Pick any refinement of procedure *numyears* of case study 4.4 and determine its statement count formula.

4.35 In an attempt to make a program more efficient, which would be more important for you to know, the statement count or the time complexity of the program?

4.36 A state university with 15,000 students has developed a set of four programs for generating a number of different reports about its students. These reports have proved to be so useful that a state agency decides to use the programs to generate reports on all 75,000 students in the entire state college and university system. These four programs cost the university $5, $100, $200, and $500 each time they are run, and they have time complexities $O(\log_2 n)$, $O(n)$, $O(n*\log_2 n)$ and $O(n^2)$, respectively, where n is the number of students. Approximately how much will it cost the state agency to run these four programs for all 75,000 students?

4.37   A company is considering buying a new computer which is 16 times faster than the one they have. A survey of six programs with time complexities $O(1)$, $O(\log_2 n)$, $O(n)$, $O(n^2)$, $O(n^3)$, and $O(2^n)$ shows that the first program executes in 10 seconds, the second program executes with an input of size 10,000 in 2 seconds, the third program executes with an input of size 1000 in 5 minutes, the fourth program executes with an input of size 1000 in 5 minutes, the fifth program executes with an input of size 500 in 30 minutes, and the sixth program executes with an input of size 50 in an hour. How much time will it take each of these programs to run with the same input size on the new computer? What input size will be processed by each of these programs given the same amount of execution time on the new computer?

4.38   If there are three programs that do the same task with statement counts $100 * n + 15$, $4 * n^2 - n + 5$, and $2^n + 1$, which one should be chosen if only one program may be used? If all three may be used, show the input sizes for which each program is best.

4.39   For example 4.27, graph the statement count formulas for different values of n to demonstrate the results given in the example.

4.40   Formulate the loop invariant assertion and insert it into the proper position in the following **while** loop:

```
i ← 1
result ← 1
loop while i ≤ n
    result ← result * x
    i ← i + 1
    endloop while
assert result contains x to the nth power
```

4.41   Formulate the loop invariant assertion and insert it into the proper position in the following automatic indexing loop:

```
result ← 1
loop start i with 1 step 1 to n
    result ← result * x
    endloop autoindex
assert result contains x to the nth power
```

4.42   Formulate the loop invariant assertion and insert it into the proper position in the following **until** loop.

```
i ← 1
result ← 1
loop
    result ← result * x
    i ← i + 1
    endloop until i > n
assert result contains x to the nth power
```

Modify this program segment to first assign 0 to *result*, and exchange the order of the two statements inside the loop. Then do the exercise again.

TO PROGRAM

4.43 In the procedure *student averages* from case study 4.3, we called on procedure *total*. Rewrite *student averages* without calling procedure *total*. You will have to use an inner indexing loop inside the **while moredata** loop.

4.44 Design an *mpl* program that computes a↑b for any real *a* and integer *b*, without using either the *mpl* operator ↑ or recursion. What is the time complexity of your program?

4.45 Two teams play a soccer game. Design an *mpl* program that inputs the goals scored, in order, and reports the final score. An input of 1 represents a goal for team 1, and a 2 a goal for team 2. So, for example, an input of

1 2 2 2 1 2

would represent a 4–2 win for team 2. What is the time complexity of your program?

4.46 Design a checkbook balancing program in *mpl*. Compute the final balance given an initial monthly balance followed by a series of deposits and withdrawals in the input represented by positive and negative reals, respectively. If at any time the account is overdrawn after making a withdrawal, output a warning message and charge a penalty of $10.

4.47 If $0 \leqslant x < 1$, we can compute $\sin(x)$ using the series

$\sin(x) = x - x{\uparrow}3/3! + x{\uparrow}5/5! - \ldots$

Design an *mpl* program that inputs x and a small real number *epsilon* and continues adding in terms until the size of a term is less than *epsilon*. Then print the computed value of $\sin(x)$.

4.48 The greatest common divisor (gcd) of two integers larger than 0 is the largest integer which divides both evenly. Design a *gcd* function.

4.49 In the simple interest version of case study 4.4, one of the requirements of the problem was that the accumulating accrued balance be printed during each new iteration of the loop. If this requirement were removed, the results could be calculated without using a loop. Redesign procedure *numyears* to calculate the result without using a loop. What is the time complexity of your new procedure?

We will present two more case studies that use the loop structures introduced in this chapter. These two case studies give iterative solutions to the *factorial* and *fibonacci* functions from case study 3.6 and case study 3.7.

**4.4
THE
CHALLENGE**

Factorial Revisited

Case Study
4.5

> *Problem Description:* Same as case study 3.6.
>
> *Input Specifications:* Same as case study 3.6.

In case study 3.6 we designed a recursive function for computing the factorial of an integer. We now have the ability to design this function nonrecursively using loops. The initial procedure of case study 3.6 can still be used, so all we need to do is redesign function *factorial*.

The Solution — A Loop

The nonrecursive definition of factorial given in case study 3.6 was

$$n! = \begin{cases} n * (n-1) * \ldots * 1 \text{ if } n \geq 1 \\ 1 \text{ if } n = 0 \end{cases}$$

It should be clear now how to compute this function with a loop. We need to set up the loop body so that it keeps a running product of the decreasing integers, starting with n. Using the standard indexing loop gives us

```
i ← n
loop while i ≥ 1
    product ← product * i
    i ← i − 1
    endloop while
```

The value for n is supplied by the initial procedure (n is the formal parameter for function *factorial*). However, we must initialize variable *product* in function *factorial* before the loop is entered. Just as 0 is the *identity* for addition ($0+a = a = a+0$ regardless of what value is in a), 1 is the identity for multiplication ($1*a = a = a*1$ regardless of the value in a). As we have seen in previous case studies, we use the identity for addition when computing a running sum by setting the variable *sum* to 0 before entering the summation loop. Similarly, for our running product loop we need to set the variable *product* to 1 before entering the loop. This assures us that when the statement

```
product ← product * i
```

is executed in the first iteration of the loop, when $i = n$, we have

```
product ← 1 * n
```

which assigns n to product (which is what we want).

These considerations give us function *factorial*:

```
factorial : integer function
    {computes n!}

    storage specification
        parameters
            n : in only integer
        variables
            product, i : integer
        end storage specification
```

```
begin factorial
    product ← 1
    i ← n
    loop while i ≥ 1
        assert product contains 1 times the product of the integers
              from n down to, but not including, i
        product ← product * i
        i ← i − 1
        endloop while
    assert product contains n!
    factorial ← product
    end factorial
```

CASE STUDY 4.5 — REFINEMENT 1

Instead of using the **while** indexing loop, we could have used the equivalent automatic indexing loop shown in refinement 2:

```
factorial : integer function
    {computes n!}

    storage specification
        parameters
            n : in only integer
        variables
            i, product : integer
        end storage specification

    begin factorial
        product ← 1
        loop start i with n step −1 to 1
            assert product contains 1 times the product of the integers
                  from n down to, but not including, i
            product ← product * i
            endloop autoindex
        assert product contains n!
        factorial ← product
        end factorial
```

CASE STUDY 4.5 — REFINEMENT 2

Correctness

To assure ourselves that *factorial* works, we should consider what happens for various values of *n*. The initial procedure will never send an *n* with a value less than 0. For all values of *n* greater than 0, *factorial* appears to work well. What about $n = 0$? This is a special case that we did not consider when designing *factorial*. The first statement executed in function *factorial* of refinement 1, however, is

    product ← 1

regardless of the value of *n*. If *n* is 0, the **while** loop will not be executed even once, so the statement after the **while** loop

    factorial ← product

is executed, assigning a 1 to factorial before the function terminates. This is the correct value for 0!, so the function works. (Since the automatic indexing loop used in refinement 2 works exactly the same as the **while** indexing loop of refinement 1, refinement 2 also handles the case for $n = 0$ correctly.)

While checking that 0! is computed properly, we have noticed something else. Since we set *product* to 1 initially, there is no need to compute 1!, which is also 1. Therefore, we could replace the **loop** statement with

loop while i $\geqslant$ 2

Convince yourself that this works. (What would be the equivalent change to the automatic indexing loop of refinement 2?)

You should perform a detailed walkthrough of this version of function *factorial* with $n = 4$ and compare it to the walkthrough of the recursive version given in example 3.19 of case study 3.6; notice the differences between recursion and iteration.

Efficiency

The determination of the time complexity of function *factorial* is easy. In the recursive case, function *factorial* is called $n + 1$ times to compute $n!$. In the nonrecursive case (refinement 1) the loop computing the factorial of n is iterated n times (the difference is that *factorial*(0) is called in the recursive case, whereas in the nonrecursive case the loop is not executed for $n = 0$). In both cases the time complexity is $O(n)$ (linear).

There is, however, an important difference between the recursive and nonrecursive factorial functions. In example 3.19 each recursive call to *factorial* required that new storage cells be set aside for each new recursively generated version of function *factorial*. That is, the storage requirement also grows linearly with n in the recursive case. However, the storage requirement for the nonrecursive factorial function is constant. Thus, although both versions of function *factorial* require execution time proportional to n, the recursive function also requires space proportional to n, whereas the nonrecursive version does not.

Which version of *factorial* is better? The recursive version is cleaner and easier to read. The nonrecursive function is more space efficient. Even the execution time of the nonrecursive version would be faster on most real computers, because the processor requires a relatively large amount of time to make a function call, and in the recursive case, $n+1$ calls to *factorial* are made as *factorial*(n) is computed. (In the nonrecursive case, only one call to *factorial* is made as *factorial*(n) is computed.) These differences are not serious in this instance, though, so the choice between these two is really just a matter of taste.

Summary — Case Study 4.5

In this case study a nonrecursive factorial function was developed and compared with the recursive factorial function of case study 3.6. A simple indexing loop was used. Since this loop is executed n times, the time complexity of function *factorial* is $O(n)$. This is the same as the time complexity for the recursive *factorial* function. However, the recursive version also requires $O(n)$ storage; the nonrecursive function of this case study has $O(1)$ space complexity.

Fibonacci Revisited   Case Study
                                                        4.6

> *Problem Description:* Same as case study 3.7.
>
> *Input Specifications:* Same as case study 3.7.

The Solution — A Loop

The initial procedure of case study 3.7 can be used here. We want to redesign function *fibonacci* nonrecursively using a loop. Remember the definition of this function from case study 3.7:

$$fibonacci(n) = \begin{cases} 1 \text{ if } n = 1 \text{ or } n = 2 \\ fibonacci(n-1) + fibonacci(n-2) \text{ if } n > 2 \end{cases}$$

Except for $n=1$ and $n=2$, the Fibonacci value of a number is thus the sum of the previous two Fibonacci values. This means that to compute $fibonacci(n)$ nonrecursively we must have previously computed $fibonacci(n-1)$ and $fibonacci(n-2)$. This is our key: knowing $fibonacci(1)$ and $fibonacci(2)$ allows us to compute $fibonacci(3)$; then knowing $fibonacci(3)$ we can add it to $fibonacci(2)$ to get $fibonacci(4)$; knowing $fibonacci(4)$ and $fibonacci(3)$ allows us to compute $fibonacci(5)$; and so on. To compute the nth Fibonacci value, then, we need to build up to it. We will design a loop that uses the two previously computed Fibonacci values to calculate the new Fibonacci value until by this process it calculates the nth Fibonacci value. This gives us the first rough sketch of our loop:

```
loop while {not finished}
    newvalue ← sum of previous two fibonacci values
    endloop while
assert newvalue = fibonacci(n)
```

We notice immediately from this rough version that the first time through the loop we must have two previous values that were established before entering the loop. These are the first and second Fibonacci numbers, whose values are already defined to be 1. Thus, the first time through the loop we are really calculating the third Fibonacci value; the second time through the loop we calculate the fourth Fibonacci value; and so on. The loop thus computes the Fibonacci values for 3, 4, ..., n. If during each iteration of the loop we call our previous two values *oneback* and *twoback* (for example, when computing the Fibonacci value for 5, *oneback* is the already computed Fibonacci value for 4, and *twoback* is the already computed Fibonacci value for 3), we get the following loop structure:

```
twoback ← 1 {this is fibonacci(1)}
oneback ← 1 {this is fibonacci(2)}
newvalue ← 1
i ← 3
loop while i ⩽ n
    assert newvalue = fibonacci(i−1), oneback = fibonacci(i−1),
           twoback = fibonacci(i−2)
    newvalue ← oneback + twoback
    {update oneback and twoback}
    i ← i + 1
    endloop while
assert newvalue = fibonacci(n)
```

newvalue is assigned the value 1 before the loop to ensure that the loop invariant assertion will be true the first time through the loop.

In writing this section of the Fibonaci function we have come to another sticky point: each time the loop ends the values of *oneback* and *twoback* must be changed so that they contain the proper values for computing *newvalue* in the next iteration of the loop. For example, when *i* is 4 we calculate *newvalue* (the 4th Fibonacci value) from the previously computed 3rd and 2nd Fibonacci values. This means that *oneback* is the 3rd Fibonacci value and *twoback* is the 2nd Fibonacci value. To prepare for the next iteration of the loop (in which the 5th Fibonacci value is to be computed), *oneback* should become the 4th Fibonacci value (the number currently in *newvalue*) and *twoback* should become the 3rd Fibonacci value (the number currently in *oneback*). The solution is simple: at the bottom of the loop after calculating *newvalue*, put *newvalue* into *oneback* and *oneback* into *twoback*. This will prepare us for the next trip through the loop to compute the next *newvalue*. But be careful! If this is done in the straightforward fashion

```
oneback ← newvalue
twoback ← oneback
```

it will not work. (Why?) Instead, these assignments must be made in the opposite order. This gives us our new refinement for function *fibonacci*:

```
fibonacci : integer function
    {computes fibonacci(n)}

    storage specification
        parameters
            n : in only integer
        variables
            oneback, twoback, newvalue, i : integer
        end storage specification
    begin fibonacci
        twoback ← 1
        oneback ← 1
        newvalue ← 1
        i ← 3
        loop while i ≤ n
            assert newvalue = fibonacci(i−1), oneback = fibonacci(i−1),
                    twoback = fibonacci(i−2)
            newvalue ← oneback + twoback
            twoback ← oneback
            oneback ← newvalue
            i ← i + 1
        endloop while
        assert newvalue = fibonacci(n)
        fibonacci ← newvalue
    end fibonacci

CASE STUDY 4.6 — REFINEMENT 1
```

When the **while** loop of *fibonacci* is finished, the value in *newvalue* will be the *n*th Fibonacci number. This is what we wanted.

Correctness

Using the (partial) loop invariant assertion

assert newvalue = fibonacci(i−1)

helped us avoid one potential error. Since we wanted this assertion to be true the first time the loop was executed, as well as on all subsequent iterations, we included the statement

newvalue ← 1

before the **loop** statement. What would have happened if we had left this statement out? The program would have worked fine until *fibonacci*(1) or *fibonacci*(2) was calculated. (What would have happened then?) This underscores again the need to choose special data values when constructing test cases for a program.

Do a program walkthrough with 6 as the input value to convince yourself that function *fibonacci* works.

Efficiency

Our new version of function *fibonacci* contains a loop that is executed $n - 2$ times. (Since we are only concerned about the execution time of our programs when n is large, we can neglect the instances of $n = 1$ and $n = 2$ in this analysis.) The statement count when $n \geqslant 3$ is easily determined to be

6*(n −2) + 6 = 6*n − 6

so the time complexity of this iterative version of function *fibonacci* is $O(n)$.

This time complexity result is much better than that achieved for the recursive Fibonacci function. There, evaluating *fibonacci*(30) resulted in over 500,000 calls to *fibonacci*(2) alone. Using the nonrecursive function given here, evaluating *fibonacci*(30) requires executing the six statements of our loop just 28 times! We have replaced the recursive function, which has time complexity $O(2^n)$ (which is far, far worse than a linear function of n) with our nonrecursive function with time complexity $O(n)$ (linear). Being able to replace one program with an equivalent one in a lower time complexity class is always a significant achievement, as we have mentioned earlier.

Let's compare these two solutions another way. Using the recursive version to compute *fibonacci*(20) would take a certain amount of time; doubling that time would allow only *fibonacci*(21) to be computed (because $2*2^{20} = 2^{21}$ and the recursive version has time complexity $O(2^n)$). With the iterative program, doubling the time required to compute *fibonacci*(20) would allow *fibonacci*(40) to be calculated (because $2*20 = 40$ and the iterative version has time complexity $O(n)$).

Summary — Case Study 4.6

A nonrecursive Fibonacci function was developed here using a loop to replace the recursive function of case study 3.7. The recursive function is much cleaner and easier to read than the nonrecursive function and it was much easier to design, but the run time complexity of the recursive version makes it completely impractical. The loop in the Fibonacci function developed here is iterated $n - 2$ times for values of n larger than 2. This means that this version of *fibonacci* has time complexity $O(n)$, which is much better than the time complexity of the recursive Fibonacci function ($O(2^n)$).

4.5
WORKING OUT

4.50   Design an *mpl* program to find the winner of a baseball game between two teams, the Cougars (who bat first) and the Bobcats. The inputs are the number of runs scored in each half inning, in the order played. There should, therefore, be at least 17 inputs, and extra innings are played if the score is tied at the end of nine innings.

4.51   Nine people form a baseball team and play a series of games. For each game played there are nine pairs of integers input, representing the number of times at bat and the number of hits for *player1*, *player2*, ..., *player9*. Input the data for all games played, and output the overall individual batting averages, the team batting averages, and the top three batting averages. Describe the checks that you have made to ensure program robustness. What is the time complexity of your program?

4.52   Newton's method, which we saw in restricted form in exercise 2.26, can be used to attempt to find a root of an equation $f(x) = 0$. The method works as follows: given an approximation to a root, x, compute the expression

$x \leftarrow x - f(x)/f'(x)$

where $f'(x)$ is the derivative of $f(x)$. This becomes a new, and usually better, approximation to the root. Continue putting the new approximation for x into this expression until two consecutive approximations are within *epsilon* of each other, at which point the last approximation is the result returned. Design an *mpl* program that inputs an initial approximation and a positive real value *epsilon* and attempts to find a root of f given two **real functions** f and *fprime*. Perform a walkthrough of your program with $f(x) = x{\uparrow}2 - 2$, $fprime(x) = 2x$, an initial approximation $x = 1.0$, and *epsilon* = 0.01. Is your program robust? Consider $f(x) = (11x{\uparrow}4 - 23x{\uparrow}2 + 8)/2$, $fprime(x) = 22x{\uparrow}3 - 23x$, and an initial approximation of $x = 1.0$ or $x = 0.0$.

4.53   In the last exercise you designed a program to find a root of an equation $f(x) = 0$ using Newton's method. Design an *mpl* program that uses the *bisection method* to solve $f(x) = 0$. In this method we need two starting values, a and b, that bracket a root (i.e., a root lies between a and b) such that $a < b$, and one of $f(a)$ and $f(b)$ is positive and one is negative. Calculate the midpoint of a and b, (let's call it c) and then use c to replace one of the two bracketing points so that again one of the f values of the two bracketing points is positive and one is negative. Keep repeating this process until the two bracketing points are so close that the midpoint must be within *epsilon* of a root. Perform a program walkthrough with $f(x) = x{\uparrow}2 - 2$, $a = 1.0$, $b = 2.0$, and *epsilon* = 0.01. What is the time complexity of your program?

4.54 Redesign the iterative *factorial* function of case study 4.5 using an **until** loop. What condition on the value in the parameter n must hold in this case?

4.55 Redesign the iterative *factorial* function of case study 4.5 using an automatic indexing loop based on the loop invariant assertion

assert product = $(i-1)!$

4.56 Redesign the iterative *fibonacci* function of case study 4.6 using an automatic indexing loop. Does the loop invariant assertion change?

4.57 The decimal (base 10) number 362 means $3*10\uparrow2 + 6*10\uparrow1 + 2*10\uparrow0$. Similarly, the binary (base 2) number 1101 means $1*2\uparrow3 + 1*2\uparrow2 + 0*2\uparrow1 + 1*2\uparrow0$, which in decimal is $8+4+0+1$, which is 13. Design an *mpl* program to convert numbers from any base j, where $j \leqslant 10$, into decimal numbers. The input will consist of j on the first line followed by a list of base j numbers to be converted into decimal, each on a line by itself. Each base j number will consist of its digits (each of which is between 0 and $j-1$) separated by spaces and followed by -1. So, for example, if the input is

```
3
2 0 1 2 2 -1
0 -1
2 2 -1
1 1 -1
```

then the output values should be 179, 0, 8, and 4.

4.58 Design an *mpl* program that inputs an integer n and outputs the first n prime numbers. A prime number is a positive integer that is exactly divisible only by 1 and itself. For example, the first five prime numbers are 2, 3, 5, 7, 11. Your program should include appropriate assertions. What are the statement count and time complexity of your program?

4.59 Design a program that does not use loops for the problem of case study 4.1. That is, design three recursive programs to read and sum input values using (a) the header method, (b) the trailer method, and (c) the **moredata** method. Compare your programs to those of case study 4.1. You should find that the recursive versions of *total* are more concise, but less natural.

4.60 Explain why the recursive Fibonacci function has time complexity $O(2^n)$. (This is a difficult question.)

4.61 Show that the loop of exercise 4.40 is correct by properly including and verifying all assertions as described for **while** loops in the In Retrospect section.

4.62 Show that the loop of exercise 4.41 is correct by properly including and verifying all assertions as described for automatic indexing loops in the In Retrospect section.

4.63 Show that the loop of exercise 4.42 is correct by properly including and verifying all assertions as described for **until** loops in the In Retrospect section.

4.64   For exercises 4.40, 4.41, and 4.42, show that the loops will terminate.

4.65   Give an intuitive explanation for the fact that any program can be written without loops.

| CHAPTER 5 |

Maintaining Simple Lists: Arrays of One Dimension

NEW CONCEPTS: Simple lists, One-dimensional arrays, Searching, Sorting

Up to this point we have been occupied primarily with learning program structure. We now know that programs are collections of procedures and functions that are developed using the top-down design process. We have also become familiar with the **if, case,** and **loop** statements, which allow us to control the flow of statement execution. With so much of this book remaining, it may come as a surprise that these structures — procedures, functions, and the control structures — are all we will ever need to use in organizing and structuring programs. Every program we develop in future case studies will consist of statements we have already learned. In this chapter and the following ones, our new concepts will involve the structure and manipulation of *data* rather than the structure of *programs*.

Consider our previous case studies. There we have used just the simplest kind of data storage, single variables of type **integer, real,** or **truth value.** However, most useful programs involve more complex arrangements of data. For example, if we were to write a program to input an arbitrary series of numbers and then output these numbers in ascending order (that is, from smallest to largest), we could not design the program simply to input the numbers and then immediately output them. We would instead have to maintain a list of the numbers in the store and then manipulate this list by rearranging its values until the list elements were in ascending order. Then we could print the list. The organization and manipulation of this list would be the central issue of the program.

There are many ways of organizing data to make it easy to manipulate. The different organizing schemes are called *data structures*. In this chapter we introduce one of the most common data structures, the *simple list*. We can all think of examples of lists to be maintained by a computer — lists of names, lists of telephone numbers, lists of identification numbers, lists of scores, and so on. We need a simple way to store a list within a program to allow easy access to any element of the list. In the case studies of this chapter, we will learn about one-dimensional arrays, which are available for handling lists in most programming languages.

5.1
GETTING
ACQUAINTED

In this section we will examine the most basic operations performed on lists: input, output, and simple arithmetic.

Case Study
5.1

Printing a List
Forwards and Backwards

> *Problem Description:* Input a list of integers and print the list first in the order in which it was input and then in reverse order.
>
> *Input Specifications:* A list of integers.

This problem, as simple as it is, has the two basic ingredients common to nearly all programs involving lists: inputting and printing list values. In this problem, since we are to print the list values both in the order in which they appear at the input device and in reverse order, we must keep a copy of this list of values in the store. We cannot simply input a number, print it out, and then go merrily on to the next number as we have done in previous case studies. Instead we must somehow save these values in the store so that we can print them in reverse order. To do this we will use a *one-dimensional array,* or *1-D array.* A 1-D array is just a collection of storage cells, all of the same type, that can be used for storing a simple list. All programming languages of the type we are modeling provide 1-D arrays.

Example
5.1

The **variables** statement

> **variables**
>   alice : **1-D integer array** [1 → 100]

establishes a one-dimensional integer array in the store. The 1-D (one-dimensional) designation implies that this array is a list (single column) of integers. (In contrast, a 2-D array has two dimensions, rows and columns.) The declaration of array *alice* results in the store

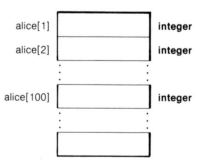

One hundred integer storage cells are established in the store; these cells are named *alice*[1], *alice*[2], . . . , *alice*[100], corresponding to the usual mathematical notation of subscripted names:

    $alice_1, alice_2, \ldots, alice_{100}$

The value in brackets is called a *subscript* or an *array index*. We can thus refer to specific array elements either directly with constant subscripts, as in the expression

3 * alice[2]

which means multiply the value in *alice*[2] by 3, or by using subscripts that are variables or expressions, such as

alice[i] * alice[j − 2]

In this example the value in *i* must be an integer between 1 and 100, inclusive, and the value in *j* must be an integer between 3 and 102, inclusive. For example, if *i* is 50 and *j* is 63, then this expression would cause the values in *alice*[50] and *alice*[61] to be multiplied.

The general form of an array declaration is

arrayname : **1-D** *type* **array** [*low* → *high*]

where *arrayname* is the name of the array being declared, *type* is any *mpl* data type, e.g., **integer, real,** or **truth value,** and *low* and *high* are integers that provide the array bounds. The array will have *high* − *low* + 1 elements named

arrayname[*low*], *arrayname*[*low* + 1], . . ., *arrayname*[*high*]

all of which have the specified *type*. Of course, *high* ≥ *low* must hold. In most cases *low* will be 1.

The Solution — 1-D Arrays

It is now clear how our program should be organized. First we need the initial procedure:

forward and back : **initial procedure**
  {inputs a list of integers, prints this list forwards and backwards}

  storage specification
    variables
      {declare an array called inputlist}
    end storage specification

  begin forward and back
    {input values into the array inputlist}
    {print the values of inputlist in input order}
    {print the values of inputlist in reverse order}
    end forward and back

CASE STUDY 5.1 — REFINEMENT 1

The first order of business is to decide how to declare the array *inputlist;* the declaration will have the form

  variables
    inputlist : **1-D integer array** [1 → ??]

The question is, what is the upper bound of the subscript range for *inputlist*? The problem description doesn't tell us how many input values there are, so we don't know how many storage cells to set aside for *inputlist.* This is a common problem. The usual solution is to make an educated guess about the maximum number of input values. For example, if a program is to be used to read in a set of scores for a class, and we know that there are no more than 100 students in any class, we can make the upper bound 100. In our case let's assume that 500 is a practical upper limit for the number of elements our array is likely to hold. Then we can declare *inputlist* as

variables
    inputlist : **1-D integer array** [1 → 500]

This statement would cause the store to look like

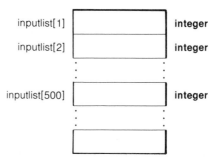

Having decided on the size of array *inputlist,* we can now turn our attention to the procedures for reading the input values into *inputlist,* printing the values of *inputlist* in the order in which they were read, and then printing these values in reverse order. First, we will design the input procedure. Recall from case study 4.1 that there are three ways to input an indeterminate number of values: the header method, the trailer method, and the **moredata** method. These three methods can also be used when reading an indeterminate number of values into an array.

Inputting Values into a 1-D Array by the Header Method

If we assume that the first value in the input is the number of input values for the array, then this first value should be input and checked by the initial procedure. If this number is less than zero, there is obviously an error, and there is also an error if this value is greater than 500, because we can assign at most 500 values to the array *inputlist.* This means that the initial procedure should contain the following statements:

```
input n
if (n < 0) or (n > 500)
    then output 'error in input, n < 0 or n > 500'
    else {input the n values into the array inputlist}
         {print the n values of inputlist in input order}
         {print the n values of inputlist in reverse order}
    endif
```

Although we are working with a particular array (*inputlist*) in this program, we want to make the procedures for inputting and outputting the array as general as possible, so that they can be used again in other programs involving 1-D arrays. In this case we want to input *n* values into *inputlist*[1], ..., *inputlist*[*n*], but in general we might want to input values into any subrange of an array, such as *a*[*low*], *a*[*low* + 1], ..., *a*[*high*]. Let's call our procedure for inputting the array values *read 1D integer*. Given any integer array *a* and the range of elements *low* through *high* to be input and stored into *a*, procedure *read 1D integer* should read the proper number of values from the input device and store them into successive elements of array *a*, from *a*[*low*] to *a*[*high*]. This means, among other things, that *a* should be an **out only** parameter (why wouldn't type **in only** work?).

Procedure *read 1D integer* will be invoked with the call

    read 1D integer(inputlist, 1, n)

meaning that *n* integers are to be read from the input device and stored into *inputlist*[1], ..., *inputlist*[*n*]. Procedure *read 1D integer* will thus look like

```
read 1D integer : procedure
    {inputs a list of integers into array a from a[low] to a[high]}

    storage specification
        parameters
            a : out only 1-D integer array
            low, high : in only integer
        variables
            i : integer
        end storage specification
    begin read 1D integer
        loop start i with low step 1 to high
            assert values have been input into a[low] through a[i−1]
            {input next value and store into a[i]}
            endloop autoindex
        assert values have been input into a[low] through a[high]
    end read 1D integer
```

CASE STUDY 5.1 — REFINEMENT 2

When the initial procedure for this case study calls *read 1D integer*, the actual array parameter *inputlist* will be passed to the formal array parameter *a*. Similarly, 1 will be passed to *low* and *n* will be passed to *high*.

In *read 1D integer* the parameter list *a* has been declared as

a : **out only 1-D integer array**

Notice that there is no range specified for the array subscripts (e.g., $1 \rightarrow 500$) in the declaration of the formal parameter *a*. Array *a* will take on the same subscript range as the actual array passed to *a* when *read 1D integer* is called. Thus procedure *read 1D integer* is general — it can be used in other programs to input integer arrays with different lengths.

To complete this procedure we will implement

    {input next value and store into a[i]}

simply as

input a[i]

That is, when *i* is *low*, the first input value is read and stored into *a*[*low*], when *i* is *low* + 1, the second input value is read and stored into *a*[*low* + 1], when *i* is *low* + 2, the third input value is read and stored into *a*[*low* + 2], and so on, exactly as we wish. This gives us our final refinement for *read 1D integer.*

---

read 1D integer : **procedure**
    {inputs a list of integers into array a from a[low] to a[high]}

    storage specification
        parameters
            a : **out only 1-D integer array**
            low, high : **in only integer**
        variables
            i : **integer**
        end storage specification

    begin read 1D integer
        loop start i **with** low **step** 1 **to** high
            assert values have been input into a[low] through a[i−1]
            input a[i]
            endloop autoindex
        assert values have been input into a[low] through a[high]
        end read 1D integer

CASE STUDY 5.1 — REFINEMENT 3

Notice the form of the loop invariant assertion

    assert values have been input into a[low] through a[i−1]

which just means "so far we have filled array elements *a*[*low*] through *a*[*i*−1] and we are now ready to input the next value into *a*[*i*]." This is what we wish to express, but the first time through the loop when *i* = *low* and no values have been input, this assertion reads

    assert values have been input into a[low] through a[low−1]

which makes no sense. However, there is no problem if we understand this statement to mean "so far, no values have been read into the array *a.*"

We will be able to use procedure *read 1D integer* whenever we need to input values into a 1-D integer array, as long as the number of values to be input is known. Virtually the same procedure will work for reading real numbers into a real array. If we copy *read 1D integer* and change

    a : **out only 1-D integer array**

to

    a : **out only 1-D real array**

and call the new procedure *read 1D real*, we get a procedure that works the same way and handles real numbers. In future case studies we will assume that both *read 1D integer* and *read 1D real* are available to us.

Printing a 1-D Array

The next procedure we will design is *write 1D integer* to do the task

{print the n values of inputlist in input order}

Procedure *write 1D integer* should also be general. It will be nearly identical to *read 1D integer,* except that the array values will be output rather than input:

```
write 1D integer : procedure
    {prints the values of array a from a[low] to a[high]}

    storage specification
        parameters
            a : in only 1-D integer array
            low, high : in only integer
        variables
            i : integer
        end storage specification

    begin write 1D integer
        loop start i with low step 1 to high
            assert a[low] through a[i − 1] have been printed
            output a[i]
            endloop autoindex
        assert a[low] through a[high] have been printed
        end write 1D integer
```

CASE STUDY 5.1 — REFINEMENT 4

Since the values of array *a* are not to be altered by *write 1D integer, a* has been declared to be of type **in only.**

Printing a 1-D Array in Reverse Order

Finally, we need to design the procedure to print the array elements in reverse order, as required by the task

{print the n values of inputlist in reverse order}

in the initial procedure. This procedure is identical to *write 1D integer* except that the loop runs from *high* to *low* (instead of *low* to *high*) as the array values are printed:

```
write 1D integer reverse : procedure
    {prints the values of array a from a[high] to a[low]}

    storage specification
        parameters
            a : in only 1-D integer array
            low, high : in only integer
        variables
            i : integer
        end storage specification
```

```
begin write 1D integer reverse
    loop start i with high step −1 to low
        assert a[high] through a[i+1] have been printed
        output a[i]
        endloop autoindex
    assert a[high] through a[low] have been printed
    end write 1D integer reverse
```

CASE STUDY 5.1 — REFINEMENT 5

Notice that the loop invariant assertion is different, since *i* is being decrement-ed on each pass through the loop rather than incremented.

We now have the three procedures required by this program. Procedure *read 1D integer* will input values for *a*[*low*], *a*[*low*+1], . . . , *a*[*high*] when sup-plied actual parameters for *a, low* and *high*. Procedure *write 1D integer* will output values in order from an integer array *a*, given actual parameters for *a, low,* and *high;* and procedure *write 1D integer reverse* is the same as *write 1D integer,* except that it prints the array values in reverse order. The initial procedure for this program will thus be

```
forward and back : initial procedure
    {inputs a list of integers, prints this list forwards and backwards}

    storage specification
        variables
            inputlist : 1-D integer array [1 → 500]
            n : integer
        end storage specification

    begin forward and back
        input n
        if (n < 0) or (n > 500)
            then output 'error in input, n < 0 or n > 500'
            else read 1D integer(inputlist, 1, n)
                write 1D integer(inputlist, 1, n)
                write 1D integer reverse(inputlist, 1, n)
        endif
    end forward and back

    where read 1D integer inputs values into inputlist[1], . . . , inputlist[n]
    where write 1D integer outputs the values inputlist[1], . . . , inputlist[n]
    where write 1D integer reverse outputs the values inputlist[n], . . . ,
            inputlist[1]
```

CASE STUDY 5.1 — REFINEMENT 6

Correctness

To be sure that this program works and that you understand how it works, we will do a program walkthrough.

Example 5.2   Assume that there are just three values to be read into the array *inputlist* and that the in-put is:

3 18 93 107

The first value, 3, tells us that there are three values following.

When the **variables** statement of the initial procedure is encountered by the processor, the store is organized as

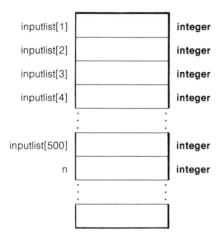

In the computation section of the initial procedure, the first statement executed is

input n

The first number in the input, 3, is thus read in and stored into *n*. Since 3 lies between 1 and 500, the procedures *read 1D integer, write 1D integer,* and *write 1D integer reverse* are called in order. Since the formal array parameter *a* is of type **out only** and the formal parameters *low* and *high* are of type **in only,** we have the following store just after the **storage specification** statement of *read 1D integer* is processed.

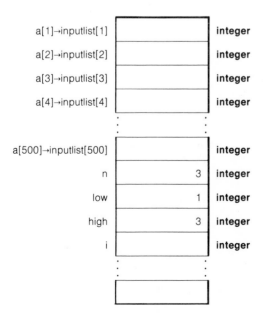

Notice that *inputlist* still has no values when *read 1D integer* is called. This is why array *a* is of type **out only** (the values are to be supplied to *a* in *read 1D integer* and these values go back out to the initial procedure upon termination of *read 1D integer*). Thus, the formal array parameter *a* takes the same subscript range and the same locations as the actual array *inputlist* passed to *a*. The formal parameters *low* and *high* of *read 1D integer* contain copies of the actual parameters 1 and *n* passed from the initial procedure because they are **in only** parameters. The cell named *i* is a local variable declared in the **variables** statement of *read 1D integer*.

The computation section of procedure *read 1D integer* consists of a single automatic indexing loop that should, by now, be very familiar. First *i* takes on the value 1, and then the statement

input a[i]

is executed. This reads in the next input number (18) and stores it into *a*[1], causing the store to look like

a[1]→inputlist[1]	18	integer
a[2]→inputlist[2]		integer
a[3]→inputlist[3]		integer
a[4]→inputlist[4]		integer
⋮	⋮	
a[500]→inputlist[500]		integer
n	3	integer
low	1	integer
high	3	integer
i	1	integer
⋮	⋮	

When the bottom of the loop is reached, 1 is added to *i* to make *i* equal to 2, and the loop is iterated again. This time, the statement

input a[i]

is the same as

input a[2]

since *i* is 2. Thus, the next value, 93, is input and stored into *a*[2], causing the store to look like

a[1]→inputlist[1]	18	**integer**
a[2]→inputlist[2]	93	**integer**
a[3]→inputlist[3]		**integer**
a[4]→inputlist[4]		**integer**
a[500]→inputlist[500]		**integer**
n	3	**integer**
low	1	**integer**
high	3	**integer**
i	2	**integer**

After the bottom of the loop is reached, the loop is attempted again with *i* equal to 3, which is still less than or equal to *high,* so the statement

input a[i]

is executed with *i* = 3. This causes 107 to be input and stored into a[3], resulting in the store

a[1]→inputlist[1]	18	**integer**
a[2]→inputlist[2]	93	**integer**
a[3]→inputlist[3]	107	**integer**
a[4]→inputlist[4]		**integer**
a[500]→inputlist[500]		**integer**
n	3	**integer**
low	1	**integer**
high	3	**integer**
i	3	**integer**

The bottom of the loop is reached again, and the loop is attempted again with *i* = 4. Since *i* is now greater than *high,* the loop statements are not executed. This causes termination of the procedure. The parameters and storage cells of *read 1D integer* disappear upon return to the initial procedure, so the store looks like

inputlist[1]	18	**integer**
inputlist[2]	93	**integer**
inputlist[3]	107	**integer**
inputlist[4]		**integer**
inputlist[500]		**integer**
n	3	**integer**

The first three elements of array *inputlist* contain the three input values as desired, and the storage cells set aside for the variables and parameters of *read 1D integer* have been released.

At this point in the initial procedure the call

write 1D integer(inputlist, 1, n)

is made. In *write 1D integer* the formal array parameter *a* (which matches the actual array parameter *inputlist*) is of type **in only**. The formal parameters *low* and *high* corresponding to the actual parameters 1 and *n* are also of type **in only,** and *i* is a local variable declared inside the procedure. After the call to *write 1D integer* is made, the store thus looks like

inputlist[1]	18	**integer**		a[3]	107	**integer**
inputlist[2]	93	**integer**		a[4]		**integer**
inputlist[3]	107	**integer**				
inputlist[4]		**integer**		a[500]		**integer**
				low	1	**integer**
inputlist[500]		**integer**		high	3	**integer**
n	3	**integer**		i		**integer**
a[1]	18	**integer**				
a[2]	93	**integer**				

All **in only** parameters in *write 1D integer,* including the array *a,* are assigned new cells with copies of the actual parameters, as required by the **in only** designation.

The procedure body of *write 1D integer* consists of the single loop

```
loop start i with low step 1 to high
    assert a[low] through a[i−1] have been printed
    output a[i]
    endloop autoindex
assert a[low] through a[high] have been printed
```

As we now know, this will cause the statement

output a[i]

to be executed three times — when *i* is 1, when *i* is 2, and when *i* is 3. This is equivalent to executing the three statements

output a[1]
output a[2]
output a[3]

So the values

18
93
107

are printed, and control returns to the initial procedure.

Finally, procedure *write 1D integer reverse* is called. A similiar analysis shows that the loop in that procedure has the same effect as executing the three statements

output a[3]
output a[2]
output a[1]

because the loop index variable *i* runs from *high* to *low* (3 to 1). Thus

107
93
18

are printed. This is the last procedure called, so the program terminates.

Notice that 497 elements of the array *inputlist* were left undefined. We just chose a small example here to demonstrate the array concept. However, this does remind us that our choice for the size of an array should be realistic. We don't want to leave an excessive amount of storage space unused. On our model computer we need not be concerned with wasted storage cells, because the store is as large as we want it to be, but on real computers storage space is limited and can be expensive to use.

Besides doing a walkthrough to help determine correctness, we should also develop a good set of data for testing the program on a computer, as we do for all programs. Special values would include input sizes of 0 and 500. Invalid sizes (e.g., −1 and 510) should also be included. (What will happen if the input size is 0?)

Inputting Values into a 1-D Array by the Moredata Method

If the number of input items for array *inputlist* is not known in advance, the **while moredata** loop can be used for reading the values into *inputlist*. This causes some additional concerns: first of all, we can no longer check in the initial procedure whether there are more values in the input than we have storage cells in *inputlist* (500); the procedure that inputs the values must make this check as the values are being input. Second, the input procedure will need to count the actual number of values input, since this number is not known ahead of time. If we call this input procedure *read 1D integer*, too, then the initial procedure could look like

```
forward and back : initial procedure
    {inputs a list then prints this list forwards and backwards}

    storage specification
        variables
            inputlist : 1-D integer array [1 → 500]
            n : integer
        end storage specification

    begin forward and back
        read 1D integer(inputlist, 500, n)
        if n > 500
            then output 'error, n > 500'
            else write 1D integer(inputlist, 1, n)
                write 1D integer reverse (inputlist, 1, n)
        endif
    end forward and back

    where read 1D integer inputs values into inputlist[1], . . . , inputlist[n]
    where write 1D integer outputs the values inputlist[1], . . . , inputlist[n]
    where write 1D integer reverse outputs the values inputlist[n], . . . ,
        inputlist[1]
```

CASE STUDY 5.1 — REFINEMENT 7

Procedures *write 1D integer* and *write 1D integer reverse* will remain exactly as before. Only *read 1D integer* will change.

In this refinement, *inputlist*, 500, and *n* are passed as actual parameters to the formal parameters *a*, *max*, and *n* of *read 1D integer*. Procedure *read 1D integer* reads values from the input device in a **while moredata** loop, counting the number of values input and returning this count in *n*. If there are more than *max* items in the input, *read 1D integer* is to signal this fact to the initial procedure by returning a number larger than *max* in *n*. Procedure *read 1D integer* has been designed to read in values into *a*[1], . . . , *a*[*n*], not into *a*[*low*], . . . , *a*[*high*] for some values of *low* and *high* (*low* and *high* cannot be determined before *read 1D integer* is called, as could be done in our last design).

```
read 1D integer : procedure
    {inputs values into a 1-D integer array and returns the number
     of values input in n}

    storage specification
        parameters
            a : out only 1-D integer array
            max : in only integer
            n : out only integer
        end storage specification
```

```
    begin read 1D integer
       n ← 1
       loop while moredata and (n ≤ max)
          assert values have been input into a[1] through a[n−1]
          input a[n]
          n ← n + 1
          endloop while
       assert values have been input into a[1] through a[n−1]
       n ← n − 1
       assert values have been input into a[1] through a[n]
       if moredata
          then n ← max + 1
          endif
       end read 1D integer
```

CASE STUDY 5.1 — REFINEMENT 8

Notice that both *a* and *n* are **out only** parameters in this procedure (why?). We subtract 1 from *n* at the end of the **while** loop to give the actual count of the values input. The fact that *n* is used both to count the number of input values and as the index of the array leads to a different loop goal assertion, too. Be sure you understand this. The third assertion has been included just to show that after subtracting 1 from *n* the desired result has been achieved.

There are two different conditions that will cause the **while** loop to terminate. One occurs when there is no more data (this is checked by the **moredata** keyword), and the other occurs when the number of values that have been input exceeds *max* (this is checked by the condition $n \leq max$). Upon termination of the loop, then, it must be determined whether the loop terminated because there was no more input data or because there were more than *max* input items. This is checked in the statement

```
if moredata
   then n ← max + 1
   endif
```

If there is more data at the input device, the loop was terminated because *n* exceeded *max* (that is, all array elements have been filled up). In this case *read 1D integer* is to return a value in *n* larger than *max* to signal to the initial procedure that an error occurred; this is accomplished by setting

```
n ← max + 1
```

in the **then** clause of the **if** statement.

This completes our second version of *read 1D integer*. Again we notice how much extra effort is required to check for error conditions. If we didn't have to worry about the possibility that there might be more input items than array elements, only *inputlist* and *n* would need to be passed to *read 1D integer* from the initial procedure, and the entire computation section of *read 1D integer* would look like

```
n ← 1
loop while moredata
    input a[n]
    n ← n + 1
    endloop while
n ← n − 1
```

This is indeed much simpler, but errors will result if there are more input values than array elements.

Before we continue, we should make a final observation about the form of the loop used in this procedure. 1 is subtracted from *n* upon termination of the loop to ensure that *n* contains the exact number of input values. We could avoid this subtraction by writing the loop differently. The reason we must subtract 1 from *n* after this loop terminates goes back to the way we defined the indexing loop in chapter 4. There we defined the indexing loop with the loop index variable set to the starting value just before the loop begins and updated by the increment at the bottom of the loop. (This pattern was originally given for the **while** indexing loop, because it is the underlying form of the automatic indexing loop.) In this case study, the loop index variable *n* is set to 1 just before the loop begins, then 1 is added to *n* at the bottom of the loop, according to that pattern, but it would be more natural to use the following loop:

```
n ← 0
loop while moredata and (n < max)
    assert values have been input for a[1] through a[n]
    n ← n + 1
    input a[n]
    endloop while
assert values have been input for a[1] through [n]
```

In this loop *n* starts at 0, and 1 is added to *n* just inside the loop when it is known that there is another value to read into *a[n]*. Notice also that the condition

$(n \leqslant max)$

has been changed to

$(n < max)$

in the **loop** statement (why?). The result of writing the loop this way is that *n* contains the exact number of values input into array *a* upon termination of the loop. Notice how this affects the loop invariant and goal assertions (what assertion could be placed just before **endloop**?).

You should compare this loop form carefully with the indexing loop given previously. They are different in important ways, and you should understand these differences so that you design loops properly.

Inputting Values into a 1-D Array by the Trailer Method

We could write another version of *read 1D integer* using the trailer method, where values are input and stored into the array *a* until a unique input item signals the end of the input. Again, we will have the problem that there may be more input items than there are array elements, and this possibility should be considered when designing this version of *read 1D integer*. We leave the design of this version as an exercise.

Efficiency

The different versions of *read 1D integer* are essentially identical as far as efficiency considerations are concerned, so we will look only at the program using the header method (refinements 3, 4, 5, and 6). The initial procedure of refinement 6 calls three other procedures in sequence: *read 1D integer, write 1D integer,* and *write 1D integer reverse*. Each of these three procedures contains a single loop, and these loops each contain three statements, so the total number of statements executed in these three procedures is

$$(3^*n + 1) + (3^*n + 1) + (3^*n + 1) = 9^*n + 3$$

In the initial procedure of refinement 6, six statements (counting the **if** condition, **endif** and the **else** clause but not the **then** clause) are executed, so the total number of statements executed is

$$9^*n + 9$$

The time complexity of our program is thus $O(n)$.

In this case study we have also used more than a constant number of storage cells, introducing a concern for the *space complexity* of our program. The idea of space complexity is similar to the idea of time complexity. Space complexity is just a measure of how much storage space is required by the program as the size of the input changes. In this case study we arbitrarily chose to declare the array *inputlist* with 500 elements. This looks like a constant, but it really is not. It is an estimation of n, the number of input values. If this estimation is too low, we would need to change our array declaration to include, say, 1000 elements. The important count is how many cells are actually used by the processor at any one time.

Looking at example 5.2, we see that the largest number of storage cells is used in procedures *write 1D integer* and *write 1D integer reverse*. There, n cells are in use in the actual array parameter *inputlist*, n cells are in use in the formal parameter array a, because a is of type **in only,** and there are four other cells reserved for the variable n, the **in only** parameters *low* and *high*, and the local variable i. So, the actual maximum number of cells in use at any one time during execution of this program will be

$$2^*n + 4$$

This is a linear expression, so we say that our program has linear ($O(n)$) space complexity.

In examining the space complexity of our program we have uncovered a particularly subtle inefficiency. Because we have declared the formal array parameter a to be of type **in only** in procedures *write 1D integer* and *write 1D integer reverse*, the processor must set aside new cells for a and copy the values of the actual array *inputlist* into a whenever these procedures are called. How does the processor do this? Essentially it must execute a loop that copies *inputlist*[1] into a[1], then *inputlist*[2] into a[2], then *inputlist*[3] into a[3], and so on. Even though we do not have to write this loop ourselves, this process is carried out by the processor. The result of this "hidden loop" is that two loops are actually executed when each of these two print procedures is called. Thus, the time complexity of the program is really

$$(3^*n + 1) + (6^*n + 2) + (6^*n + 2) + 6 = 15^*n + 11$$

rather than $9^*n + 9$. The terms $(6^*n + 2)$ reflect the fact that in both *write 1D integer* and *write 1D integer reverse* there is one explicit loop with statement count $(3^*n + 1)$ and one hidden loop that would have about the same statement count.

Is there a way to avoid this hidden loop? Yes, if we declare the formal array parameter *a* to be of type **in out**

a : **in out 1-D integer array**

rather than type **in only** in procedures *write 1D integer* and *write 1D integer reverse*, then *a* and *inputlist* would share the same locations whenever these procedures were called. The values in *inputlist* would not be copied to other locations. This, of course, would also conserve space, making the space used

$n + 4$

rather than

$2^*n + 4$

The danger in this approach is that if we were to make changes to the formal array parameter *a* in procedure *write 1D integer* or procedure *write 1D integer reverse*, corresponding changes to the actual array parameter *inputlist* would occur. A check of our program assures us that we make no changes to *a* in either of these procedures, so we are safe in using the **in out** designation for *a*.

In the future we will always declare formal array parameters to be of type **in out** whenever we are certain that undesired changes are not made to them. The **in out** designation will conserve both space and time. If changes are made to the formal array parameter that should not be reflected in the actual array parameter, we will use the **in only** declaration. Since **out only** parameters also share space with the actual parameters, we can declare arrays to be **out only** without wasting storage cells or time.

Summary — Case Study 5.1

The one-dimensional array was introduced. The most common procedure involving 1-D arrays — inputting a list of values into an array — was discussed in three forms. One form used the header method, the second used the **moredata** method, and the third (which was left as an exercise) used the trailer method. Two other procedures were developed, one for printing the values of a 1-D array in order from first to last and one for printing the array values in reverse order. In future case studies we may use these three procedures, *read 1D integer, write 1D integer*, and *write 1D integer reverse*, as well as the three corresponding real forms.

The time complexity of the entire program as well as each of the three called procedures was shown to be linear. The idea of space complexity was also introduced, and it was shown that this program has linear space complexity. Whenever possible, formal array parameters will be designated type **in out** to conserve storage space.

Computing Temperature Statistics

Problem Description: A local weather service provides information on recorded low temperatures for a year. The information consists of an integer giving the number of days when the low was below $-20°$ Celsius, followed by 51 integers giving the total number of days when the low was exactly $-20°$C, $-19°$C, $-18°$C, ..., $+28°$C, $+29°$C, and $+30°$C, respectively, finally followed by an integer giving the number of days when the low temperature was greater than 30°C. Design a program that computes and prints the total number of days when the temperature was less than or equal to n, for any n, $-21 \leqslant n < 31$.

Input Specifications: Fifty-three integers as described above, followed by a sequence of integers, each of which is $\geqslant -21$ and < 31.

In this case study we will see that array subscripts are not restricted to positive values. As long as the lower array bound is less than or equal to the upper bound, the bounds can take on any integer values.

The data structure of this problem is again a simple list, in this case a list of the number of days the temperature reached a specific recorded low, so we can use an array to hold this list. The interesting part of the problem is how to structure the array so that the list elements can be conveniently accessed.

The Solution — Arrays with Negative Bounds

To hold the list of data for this problem we will declare an array called *tempdays*, such that for a given temperature x, $-20 \leqslant x \leqslant 30$, *tempdays*[$x$] is the number of days when the low temperature was equal to x degrees Celsius. For convenience we will use *tempdays*[-21] to contain the number of days when the low temperature was less than $-20°$C, and *tempdays*[31] to contain the number of days when the low temperature was greater than $+30°$C. We can now design the initial procedure directly:

```
low temps : initial procedure
    {computes number of days at or below given temperatures}

    storage specification
        variables
            tempdays : 1-D integer array [−21 → 31]
            temp : integer
        end storage specification

    begin low temps
        read 1D integer(tempdays, −21, 31)
        loop while moredata
            input temp
            if (temp < −21) or (temp ⩾ 31)
                then output 'bad data — temperature < −21 or ⩾ 31'
                else output sumdays(temp, tempdays)
            endif
        endloop while
    end low temps

    where read 1D integer reads in tempdays[−21] through tempdays[31]
    where sumdays returns sum of tempdays[i] for −21 ⩽ i ⩽ temp
```

CASE STUDY 5.2 — REFINEMENT 1

Note that the test for bad data is

(temp < -21) **or** (temp $\geqslant 31$)

since we can compute the number of days the low temperature was *temp* or less if *temp* is between -21 and 30, inclusive, but not if *temp* is 31 (or larger) or below -21.

The first procedure called from the initial procedure is *read 1D integer,* which we designed in refinement 3 of case study 5.1. (You should review that procedure to convince yourself that it will work here, too.) We designed *read 1D integer* to make it general enough to input 1-D arrays with any valid subscript bounds.

The only routine we need to design, then, is function *sumdays. sumdays* will use an automatic indexing loop to sum the elements of array *tempdays* between *tempdays*[-21] and *tempdays*[*temp*]; this will compute the number of days for which the recorded low was *temp* degress or less.

```
sumdays : integer function
    {computes the number of days the temperature was
     temp degrees or below}
    storage specification
        parameters
            temp : in only integer
            tempdays : in out 1-D integer array
        variables
            i, sum : integer
        end storage specification
    begin sumdays
        sum ← 0
        loop start i with −21 step 1 to temp
            assert sum is tempdays[−21] + . . . + tempdays[i−1]
            sum ← sum + tempdays[i]
            endloop autoindex
        assert sum is tempdays[−21] + . . . + tempdays[temp]
        sumdays ← sum
        end sumdays

    CASE STUDY 5.2 — REFINEMENT 2
```

The formal array parameter *tempdays* has been declared to be **in out,** even though **in only** would be the natural choice. As we discussed in case study 5.1, it is inefficient in both time and space to make a formal array parameter **in only** unless changes will be made to the formal parameter that should not occur to the actual parameter.

Correctness

Do a walkthrough of this program to convince yourself that it works. What special values should you include when testing the program? To see that function *sumdays* works, you should apply the rules given in the In Retrospect section of chapter 4 for verifying that an automatic indexing loop is correct using the loop invariant and loop goal assertions. Notice that the first time through this loop, when *i* is −21, the loop invariant assertion reads

> **assert** sum is tempdays[−21] + . . . + tempdays[−22]

which we interpret to mean that *sum* is 0.

Alternate Solution — 1-D Arrays without Negative Bounds

Not all real programming languages allow arrays with negative or zero bounds. All modern programming languages do, but for older languages that don't, another solution to this problem is necessary. We would need to declare *tempdays* as

> tempdays : **1-D integer array** [1 → 53]

to hold all 53 values of the list. This declaration and the call

> read 1D integer(tempdays, 1, 53)

are the only changes that would need to be made to the initial procedure.

The changes to function *sumdays* are more interesting. Before, the array was set up so that it was easy to access the number of days the low temperature was, for example, −18°C: this value was stored in *tempdays*[−18]. Now, the number of days the low temperature was −21°C or less would be stored in *tempdays*[1], the number of days the low temperature was −20°C would be in *tempdays*[2], and so on. The number of days the low temperature was −18°C would now be in *tempdays*[4]. In general, given an input temperature, *temp*, the number of days the low temperature was *temp* degrees would be in *tempdays*[22 + *temp*]. This calculation to access the proper element of the list is our only recourse when negative array bounds are not allowed. The only change required in function *sumdays* is in the **loop** statement, which would become

> **loop start** i **with** 1 **step** 1 **to** 22 + temp.

Examine these needed changes to the program until you are satisfied that they work.

Efficiency

The time complexity for this program has some surprising new twists. We must analyze the initial procedure, procedure *read 1D integer*, and function *sumdays* in order to determine the time complexity of the program as a whole. Procedure *read 1D integer* was analyzed in the previous case study, where it was found to have linear time complexity. It would therefore be easy to jump to the conclusion that since this program calls *read 1D integer* it, too, must have at least linear time complexity. But there is an important difference between case study 5.1 and this one. There, the number of elements to be input, *n,* varied for different sets of data, and as *n* changed, the number of statements executed in *read 1D integer* changed proportionally. In this case study, however, *read 1D integer* is always called with *low* = −21 and *high* = 31. That is, regardless of the input data, procedure *read 1D integer* will input exactly 53 values. Therefore, the execution time of *read 1D integer* will be constant for this program.

This analysis tells us that up through the point where the initial procedure calls procedure *read 1D integer,* the time complexity of the program is constant. The next step is execution of the **while moredata** loop, which will iterate an indeterminate number of times, inputting a new temperature and calling on function *sumdays* each time. If there are *m* temperature values to be input, this **while** loop will iterate *m* times. As function *sumdays* is executed on each pass through this **while moredata** loop, it also contributes to the execution time of the program. But, like procedure *read 1D integer,* function *sumdays* contributes only a constant amount of execution time in spite of the fact that it contains a loop. The loop statement in function *sumdays* is

loop start i **with** −21 **step** 1 **to** temp

where *temp* lies between −21 and 30. That is, *temp* can be at most 30, so the loop will iterate at most 52 times.

We conclude that the time complexity of this program is linear, or $O(m)$, where *m* is the number of temperatures input in the **while moredata** loop of the initial procedure. Neither procedure *read 1D integer* nor function *sumdays,* both of which contain loops, contribute more than a known maximum number of statements to the statement count of the program. This analysis just reminds us that although a procedure or function may have one time complexity (e.g., linear) when viewed alone, it may contribute a different amount to the time complexity in the context of the program that contains it (e.g., constant).

You should do a statement count of this entire program to verify the analysis we have done here.

A count of the storage cells used shows us that the space complexity of this program is constant even though an array is used, because the size of the array is fixed at 53 elements regardless of the size of the input.

Summary — Case Study 5.2

A program was designed using an array whose lower index is a negative number. Although positive array bounds are the most common, you will occasionally design programs like this one where the natural solution using arrays does not fit the more common [1 → *n*] bounds.

Case Study 5.3 | **Computing Test Statistics**

Problem Description: A list of test scores has been generated for a class. Print this list, and compute and print the maximum score, the minimum score, the average, and the standard deviation. Finally print a list of scores below the average.

Input Specifications: The number of scores followed by a list of the scores is given.

In this case study we will carry out some of the arithmetic computations that are commonly required for lists of numbers.

The Solution — Statistics on 1-D Arrays

This case study presents a few of the usual computations carried out with test scores. While some of these calculations could be done without using arrays (e.g., finding the maximum and minimum values), others could not (e.g., printing the scores below the average, since the average must be computed on one pass through the list before making another pass to print all the scores below the average). If we plan to do each of the required computations in a separate routine, the organization of the program is simple:

```
test analysis : initial procedure
    {inputs student test scores and does statistical analysis}

    storage specification
        constants
            maxstudents : integer 300
        variables
            scores : 1-D integer array [1 → maxstudents]
            n : integer
            averagescore : real
        end storage specification

    begin test analysis
        input n
        if (n ≤ 0) or (n > maxstudents)
            then output 'error, n ≤ 0 or n > maxstudents'
            else read 1D integer(scores, 1, n)
                write 1D integer(scores, 1, n)
                output 'the maximum score is ', maximum(scores, n)
                output 'the minimum score is ', minimum(scores, n)
                averagescore ← average(scores, n)
                output 'the average is ', averagescore
                output 'the standard deviation is ',
                        standard deviation(scores, n, averagescore)
                print below average(scores, n, averagescore)
        endif
    end test analysis

    where read 1D integer inputs n values into an integer array
    where write 1D integer prints n values from an integer array
    where maximum finds the maximum value in an integer array
    where minimum finds the minimum value in an integer array
    where average computes the average of the values in an integer array
    where standard deviation computes the standard deviation of the
            values in an integer array
    where print below average prints all values in an integer array
            which are below the average value
```

CASE STUDY 5.3 — REFINEMENT 1

The organization of our program is straightforward. First the scores are read in and printed out using the procedures *read 1D integer* and *write 1D integer,* which we developed in case study 5.1. Then the functions *maximum* and *minimum* are called for determining the maximum and minimum elements of the *scores* array. Then the average is computed by a separate function that is called by the statement

averagescore ← average(scores, n)

The average is then printed in the statement

output 'the average is ', averagescore

These last two statements could be replaced by the single statement

output 'the average is ', average(scores, n)

but we do not do this because function *standard deviation* and procedure *print below averge* also require the computed average. Instead of recomputing the average for these two routines, the average is kept in the variable *averagescore* and passed to them.

One new feature in this initial procedure is the declaration of a *named constant* in a **constants** statement:

maxstudents : **integer** 300

The name *maxstudents* is assigned a storage cell just as if it were a variable name, and at the same time the constant value 300 is stored in this cell. Thus, after the **storage specification** statement has been processed, the store looks like

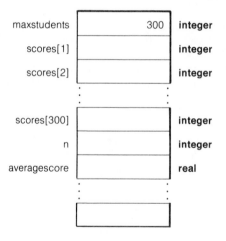

Named constants cannot change values. For example, the statement

maxstudents ← 500

could not be included in this program, because it represents an attempt to change the value of *maxstudents* (an error would be signaled).

Why would we use a named constant instead of using the constant itself (300 in this case)? Notice that in our initial procedure we have used the constant *maxstudents* twice, once in the array declaration

scores : **1-D integer array** [1 → maxstudents]

and once in the **if** statement

>   **if** (n ≤ 0) **or** (n > maxstudents)

Constant *maxstudents*, in other words, is our guess for the maximum number of scores we expect to process with our program; it is used to set up the array *scores* to be of the proper size and to check that there are not more input values than the array can hold. If we decide in the future that the program needs to handle a maximum of 500 rather than 300 scores, we just change the single line defining the named constant *maxstudents* to

>   maxstudents : **integer** 500

before running the program. This saves us from searching through the program for uses of the number 300 and deciding in each case whether that instance of 300 should be changed to 500. This is the important point: localizing the change to one statement removes many of the chances for error. Named constants should be used in cases where the constant is likely to change in future runs of the program. (However, some programming languages do not allow named constants.)

Let's now turn our efforts to designing the procedures and functions required in our program. As we have already seen in case study 5.1, the following pattern frequently arises in the processing of an array *a*:

>   **loop start** i **with** 1 **step** 1 **to** n
>   {process a[i]}
>   **endloop** autoindex

That is, we construct an automatic indexing loop in which the loop control variable (*i* in this example) runs from 1 to the number of array elements (*n* in this example). As *i* steps in succession from 1 to *n*, the array elements *a*[1] through *a*[*n*] are processed in succession. This pattern will repeat itself in each of the routines we design for this program.

Function *maximum* is typical. Here we wish to return the maximum value of the array. The parameters to *maximum* include an integer array and the number of values to be processed in the array. In function *maximum* we will call these formal parameters *a* and *n*, respectively, as in

>   **parameters**
>   a : **in out 1-D integer array**
>   n : **in only integer**

Even though *a* will not be changed in *maximum*, we make *a* to be of type **in out** rather than **in only** for the efficiency reasons discussed in case study 5.1.

To find the maximum value in the array *a*, we will step through the array comparing each successive element with the maximum value found so far (call this value *max*). Whenever we find an array value larger than *max*, we will replace *max* with this new value. When we have completed the pass through the entire array, *max* will then contain the largest value in the array. The loop goal assertion will thus be

>   **assert** max is the largest value in a[1] through a[n]

and the loop invariant assertion, which assures us that *max* is the largest of the array elements examined so far, will be (informally)

assert max is the largest value seen so far in array a

To start with, then, we might consider writing the loop to do this job as

```
loop start i with 1 step 1 to n
    assert max is the largest value in a[1] through a[i−1]
    if max < a[i]
        then max ← a[i]
        endif
    endloop autoindex
assert max is the largest value in a[1] through a[n]
```

There is, however, a problem with this. The first time through the loop, *max* has no value, so the loop invariant assertion will not be true at that point. We can remedy this situation by setting *max* to the first array value before the loop is entered and then running the loop from 2 to *n* rather than 1 to *n*. Making this change gives us function *maximum:*

```
maximum : integer function
    {computes the maximum value of an integer array}

    storage specification
        parameters
            a : in out 1-D integer array
            n : in only integer
        variables
            max, i : integer
        end storage specification
    begin maximum
        max ← a[1]
        loop start i with 2 step 1 to n
            assert max is the largest value in a[1] through a[i−1]
            if max < a[i]
                then max ← a[i]
                endif
            endloop autoindex
        assert max is the largest value in a[1] through a[n]
        maximum ← max
        end maximum

    CASE STUDY 5.3 — REFINEMENT 2
```

The next function to be developed is *minimum*, which is to find the smallest element of a 1-D integer array. Since function *minimum* is nearly identical to function *maximum*, we leave it as an exercise and instead turn our efforts to designing function *average*.

To compute the average of the values in a 1-D integer array, we must first sum the elements of the array and then divide by the number of array elements. This process is simple; we give function *average* without further explanation:

average : **real function**
{computes the average of the first n values of array a}

> **storage specification**
> > **parameters**
> > > a : **in out 1-D integer array**
> > > n : **in only integer**
> > **variables**
> > > i, sum : **integer**
> > **end storage specification**

> **begin** average
> > sum ← 0
> > **loop start** i **with** 1 **step** 1 **to** n
> > > **assert** sum is the sum of the first i − 1 elements of a
> > > sum ← sum + a[i]
> > > **endloop** autoindex
> > **assert** sum is the sum of the first n elements of a
> > average ← sum / n
> > **end** average

CASE STUDY 5.3 — REFINEMENT 3

The next function to be developed is to compute the standard deviation of an integer array. The standard deviation for *n* values is defined as

$$\sqrt{\frac{\displaystyle\sum_{i=1}^{n} (a_i - ave)^2}{n - 1}}$$

The mathematical symbol sigma (Σ) indicates that a sum is to be computed for *n* elements as *i* runs from 1 to *n*. This can always be translated into a loop in a programming language. In function *standard deviation*, the array *a*, the number of elements in *a* (*n*) and the average of the array values (*ave*) are each passed as parameters. There are three distinct parts to this formula. One is the summation

$$\sum_{i=1}^{n} (a_i - ave)^2$$

After this sum is computed, it is divided by *n* − 1. Finally, the square root of this result must be computed.

standard deviation : **real function**
{computes the standard deviation of the first n values of a

> **storage specification**
> > **parameters**
> > > a : **in out 1-D integer array**
> > > n : **in only integer**
> > > ave : **in only real**
> > **variables**
> > > sum : **real**
> > > i : **integer**
> > **end storage specification**

```
begin standard deviation
    sum ← 0
    loop start i with 1 step 1 to n
        assert sum = (a[1] − ave)↑2 +...+ (a[i−1] − ave)↑2
        sum ← sum + (a[i] − ave) ↑ 2
    endloop autoindex
    assert sum = (a[1] − ave)↑2 +...+ (a[n] − ave)↑2
    standard deviation ← sqrt(sum / (n − 1))
end standard deviation
```

CASE STUDY 5.3 — REFINEMENT 4

Notice that the way we have written the loop invariant assertion makes it read

assert sum = (a[1] − ave)↑2 +...+ (a[0] − ave)↑2

the first time through the loop; we just interpret this to mean *sum* is 0. Recall that *sqrt* is a built-in function.

The last procedure to be designed is the one that prints out all scores below the average. This is again a simple procedure. Each successive array value is compared to the average, and each value lower than the average is printed:

```
print below average : procedure
    {prints all values in an integer array which are below average}

    storage specification
        parameters
            a : in out 1-D integer array
            n : in only integer
            ave : in only real
        variables
            i : integer
    end storage specification

    begin print below average
        loop start i with 1 step 1 to n
            assert all values less than ave among the first i−1 elements
                    of a have been printed
            if a[i] < ave
                then output a[i]
                endif
        endloop autoindex
        assert all values in a which are below ave have been printed
    end print below average
```

CASE STUDY 5.3 — REFINEMENT 5

This completes the design of our program.

Correctness

You should do a walkthrough with a small set of test scores to check this program. You should also verify that the loops are correct using the methods given in the In Retrospect section of chapter 4.

To review the process of loop verification for an automatic indexing loop involving arrays, we will verify that the loop of refinement 2 works as described. The loop is

Example 5.3

```
max ← a[1]
loop start i with 2 step 1 to n
    assert max is the largest value in a[1] through a[i−1]
    if max < a[i]
        then max ← a[i]
        endif
    endloop autoindex
    assert max is the largest value in a[1] through a[n]
```

The first thing to show is that the loop invariant assertion is true the first time the loop is entered. At that point *i* is 2 and the assertion reads

max is the largest value in a[1] through a[1]

This is true, because *max* was set to *a*[1] just before the loop was entered.

The second thing to show is that given that the loop invariant assertion is true as an arbitrary iteration of the loop is begun, it will be true again when the next iteration of the loop starts. So, given that *max* is the largest value among *a*[1] through *a*[*i*−1], the **if** statement

```
if max < a[i]
    then max ← a[i]
    endif
```

checks whether *max* is less than *a*[*i*]. If it is, then *a*[*i*] must be larger than any previous value among *a*[1] through *a*[*i*−1], so after setting *max* to *a*[*i*] in the **then** clause, *max* is the largest of all array values through *a*[*i*]. If *max* is not less than *a*[*i*] then *max* must be at least as large as *a*[*i*] (as well as being the largest of all values through a[i−1]), and in this case *max* is left untouched. Upon completion of the **if** statement, then,

assert max is the largest value in a[1] through a[i]

is true. This is the end of the loop, so execution would resume with the **loop** statement, after 1 is added to *i,* making the loop invariant assertion

assert max is the largest value in a[1] through a[i−1]

true again at this point.

This finishes the application of step 2 of the verification process, which along with step 1 has shown that the loop invariant assertion will always be true at the **loop** statement from the first iteration on, which in turn means that the loop invariant assertion will be true at that point when the loop terminates with *i* equal to *n* + 1. But, when *i* is *n* + 1, the loop invariant assertion reads

assert max is the largest value in a[1] through a[n]

which is the loop goal assertion. This finishes step 3, thus verifying the loop.

Rewriting the loop with all these new assertions, we have

```
max ← a[1]
assert max is the largest value in a[1] through a[1]
loop start i with 2 step 1 to n
    assert max is the largest value in a[1] through a[i−1]
    if max < a[i]
        then max ← a[i]
        endif
```

           assert max is the largest value in a[1] through a[i]
          endloop autoindex
     assert max is the largest value in a[1] through a[i−1]
     assert i = n + 1
     assert max is the largest value in a[1] through a[n]

Notice again how each assertion after the first one holds true because of the previous assertions.

Following the simple steps needed for verifying that a loop is correct always results in a firm conviction that the loop is correct, which is why we suggest that you do this for all loops you design.

Efficiency

Each procedure and function in this program contains a simple indexing loop that runs from 1 to n (or, in the case of *maximum* and *minimum*, from 2 to n). None of these loops contain another loop or a reference to another procedure or function. Thus, each of these routines has time complexity $O(n)$. Since these procedures and functions are called in succession from the initial procedure, the entire program also has time complexity $O(n)$, where n is the number of students.

One inefficiency which we avoided, but which could easily have trapped a beginning programmer, could have occurred in function *standard deviation*. There the average of the array is subtracted from each array element in the loop. The easiest way to write this loop is as follows:

    loop start i **with** 1 **step** 1 **to** n
       sum ← sum + (a[i] − average(a, n)) ↑ 2
    endloop autoindex

If we were to do this, we would not have to pass *ave* as a parameter to procedure *standard deviation*, and so the program would be more concise. Although this would work, a call to function *average* would be executed each time the loop is iterated, and the same value would be computed each time! Since function *average* also has a loop that iterates n times, the time complexity of *standard deviation* would rise to $O(n^2)$! If the average was not previously computed and available as a parameter to procedure *standard deviation*, a much better solution would be

    ave ← average(a, n)
    loop start i **with** 1 **step** 1 **to** n
       sum ← sum + (a[i] − ave) ↑ 2
    endloop autoindex

This loop again has time complexity $O(n)$, since the average is computed only once, outside the loop. The same loop invariant assertion and loop goal assertion could be used here, too.

Summary — Case Study 5.3

In this case study we have studied some common operations on 1-D arrays. In each procedure and function the general form of the array operation was

loop start i **with** 1 **step** 1 **to** n
   {process array element i}
  endloop autoindex

That is, one pass through the loop handles each element of the array in succession. This is the form followed by most array operations. Such procedures and functions, because they have a single loop that iterates n times, have linear time complexity (if the time taken to process each element of the array is $O(1)$).

In this chapter we have learned how to store and manipulate simple lists of data using a one-dimensional array. All common procedural languages allow one-dimensional arrays similar to those modeled in *mpl*.

**5.2
IN
RETROSPECT**

SIMPLE LISTS

Many computer applications require the storage and manipulation of simple lists. A *simple list* is a data structure in which every element has the same type and the length of the list is fixed during execution of any program using the list. For example, a list of 500 names, a list of 300 test scores, and a list of 323 deposits and withdrawals from an account each represents a simple list, because each of these lists is *homogeneous* (all elements have the same type) and the length of each list is fixed. (Of course, the size of a simple list may be different from one program execution to the next, but the list does not grow or shrink during a single program execution.) In chapter 9 we will see examples of *dynamic* lists, which grow and shrink during program execution.

The one-dimensional (or 1-D) array is available in most programming languages for handling simple lists. The 1-D array is *not* the data structure, it is just the means provided for *implementing* some data structures, such as simple lists. 1-D arrays allow easy storage and manipulation of simple lists, including direct access to each list element.

THE 1-D ARRAY

The purpose of the 1-D array is to allow the programmer to establish in the store a homogeneous list of values that can be accessed and manipulated to perform a desired task. The primary considerations in handling 1-D arrays are

1. Declaring arrays to be of the proper size
2. Inputting values into arrays
3. Printing out array values
4. Accessing array elements

Declaring an Array to be of the Proper Size

An array must be declared with the proper subscript range, which determines the possible subscripts (or index values) the array can take on. For example,

  variables
    x : **1-D integer array** $[1 \rightarrow 30]$
    y : **1-D integer array** $[0 \rightarrow 17]$
    z : **1-D real array** $[-15 \rightarrow 30]$

are all proper declarations of 1-D arrays. The subscript range of an array, for instance

[−15 → 30]

specifies the low index bound, −15, and the high index bound, 30, for the array. The index bounds must be integers, and the low index bound must always be less than or equal to the high index bound (if the two are equal, the array has only one element). Some programming languages do not allow negative or zero index bounds, although most modern ones do.

The determination of the array bounds can sometimes be difficult; since most programs are designed to be executed many different times with different sets of data, the decision of how large an array should be is at best an educated guess. There are three alternatives for establishing the array size: numeric constants, named constants, and variables (dynamic arrays). Some actual programming languages allow only the first method, most of the modern ones allow the first two methods, but only a small number (e.g., Ada, Algol, and PL/I) allow the third method.

It is important to understand these three methods thoroughly in order to make the proper choice of array bounds in designing programs.

Use of Numeric Constants.   All of the usual procedural programming languages allow the use of numeric constants in establishing array bounds.

Example
5.4
Assume that we are designing a program to sort a list of integers into ascending order, (as we will do in case studies 5.7 and 5.8). Assume further that the number of items to be input and sorted is given as the first value of the input. Then the initial procedure for this program could be designed as follows.

```
sortit : initial procedure

    storage specification
    variables
        list : 1-D integer array [1 → 1000]
        n : integer
    end storage specification

    begin sortit
        input n
        if (n ⩽ 0) or (n > 1000)
            then output 'error, n ⩽ 0 or n > 1000 : n = ', n
            else read 1D integer(list, 1, n)
                write 1D integer(list, 1, n)
                sort(list, 1, n)
                write 1D integer(list, 1, n)
        endif
    end sortit

    where sort arranges list into ascending order
```

Notice that 1000, the upper bound on the array *list*, is used three times in this initial procedure. If for some future run of this program this array size should be 1500 instead of 1000, we would have to be sure to change all three occurrences of 1000 to 1500. In some programs there would be even more occurrences of the array bound to change, and these occurrences might be spread over many pages in complex programs. This is the chief disadvantage of the use of numeric constants.

Use of Named Constants.   A few of the more modern languages permit the use of named constants in declaring the size of an array. When they are permitted, named constants should always be used instead of numeric constants.

Using the initial procedure from the previous example but substituting named constants for the numeric constants gives

Example 5.5

sortit : **initial procedure**

    storage specification
      constants
        max : **integer** 1000
      variables
        list : **1-D integer array** [1 $\rightarrow$ max]
        n : **integer**
      end storage specification

    begin sortit
      input n
      if (n $\leqslant$ 0) **or** (n > max)
        then output 'error, n $\leqslant$ 0 or n > ', max, ': n = ', n
        else read 1D integer(list, 1, n)
            write 1D integer(list, 1, n)
            sort(list, 1, n)
            write 1D integer (list, 1, n)
      endif
    end sortit

    where sort arranges list into ascending order

If some future run of this program requires an array size of 1500, the line

    max : **integer** 1000

can be changed to

    max : **integer** 1500

before the program is executed. There is no need to search the entire program for occurrences of 1000. (We must merely be certain that in designing the program we never use 1000 anywhere that *max* should be used.) Localizing the change to one line significantly reduces the chance for error; this is the chief advantage of named constants over numeric constants.

Use of Variables — Dynamic Arrays.   If the input data gives the size of the input list, this value can be used to declare the array's size at execution time, as shown in the next example. This is permitted in only a few programming languages.

Using the same example with a dynamic array declaration, the initial procedure and an auxiliary procedure for declaring the list to be of proper size would be

Example 5.6

sortit : **initial procedure**

    storage specification
      variables
        n : **integer**
      end storage specification

```
      begin sortit
        input n
        if n ≤ 0
          then output 'bad data, n = ', n
          else setup(n)
        endif
      end sortit
```

where setup declares list to be length n

setup : **procedure**

storage specification
parameters
n : **in only integer**
variables
list : **1-D integer array** [1 → n]
end storage specification

```
      begin setup
        read 1D integer(list, 1, n)
        write 1D integer(list, 1, n)
        sort(list, 1, n)
        write 1D integer(list, 1, n)
      end setup
```

where sort arranges list into ascending order

The auxiliary procedure *setup* is needed to declare the array properly. The array list cannot be declared dynamically in the initial procedure, because the necessary value is input into *n after* the **variables** statement has been processed. Thus, *n* must be passed to another procedure, where the array is declared.

If it is possible to use dynamic arrays, this method is preferred. However, this method will only work if we know at execution time how many array values there will be. (In this example, we know how many input values there are.) We don't always know this information, as we have seen in some case studies.

Dynamic arrays should be used whenever possible. You never need to worry about having declared the array to be too small for some particular list of data if the program is executed many different times — with this method the array will always be exactly the right size. We will avoid using dynamic arrays in our case studies because so few programming languages allow them. You should be aware of them, however, because they are allowed in some languages you will encounter (e.g., Ada, Algol, and PL/I).

The following points summarize the methods for declaring the size of an array and should be memorized.

1. If the exact number of array elements is available in a variable, this variable should be passed to an auxiliary procedure and the array should be declared dynamically, if this is possible in the actual programming language you are using. The advantage of this approach is that the array will always have exactly the proper size without modifying the program. The disadvantage is that dynamic arrays can only be used if the exact array size is known. Many real programming languages do not allow dynamic arrays.

2. If the exact number of array elements will not be known at execution time, an educated guess of the size of the array must be made and the array declared

Beginning students are sometimes confused by the use of a variable such as *i* as an array index. Sometimes the confusion arises from thinking that the value in *i* is the value being referred to in an expression such as *x*[*i*] — this expression actually refers to the value in element *i* of array *x*. If *i* has the value 3, for example, then *x*[*i*] refers not to the value 3 but to the value in *x*[3], which might be 27.2. Another point of confusion is thinking that the variable name *i* has some special connection to arrays. This isn't so — any integer variable or expression can be used as an array index. For historical reasons, it just turns out that *i* is often chosen for this purpose.

FOR REVIEW

5.1   What is a control structure? What is a data structure?

5.2   Explain the difference between a simple list and a 1-D array.

5.3   Declare a **truth value** array which has 100 elements and a starting index of 0.

5.4   Explain the concept of space complexity. Does every program that contains an array have space complexity of at least $O(n)$?

5.5   Given the 1-D array

fuzzy : **1-D real array** [1 → 200]

write the standard loop form for processing the elements of *fuzzy* between 1 and 200 in succession.

5.6   Why do we choose to make formal array parameters have type **in out** in situations where type **in only** would be the usual choice?

5.7   What are the three methods for inputting values into a 1-D array? What special concerns must be considered to ensure program robustness?

5.8   List the rules governing the choice of an index range for a 1-D array. What practical considerations should be remembered?

5.9   What can be used as a valid array index when accessing an element of an array?

5.10 List the three methods for declaring array bounds. What are the strengths and weaknesses of each method?

5.11 How many elements are in each of the following arrays?

tom : **1-D real array** [0 → 5]
dick : **1-D integer array** [−3 → 0]
harry : **1-D real array** [−8 → 8]

A DEEPER LOOK

5.12 Find the time and space complexities of the following procedure:

```
complex : procedure
    storage specification
        parameters
            n : in out integer
        variables
            a : 1-D integer array [1 → 10]
            i, j : integer
        end storage specification
    begin complex
        loop start i with 1 step 1 to 10
            a[i] ← 1
            loop start j with 1 step 1 to n
                a[i] ← a[i] + i * j
                endloop autoindex
            output a[i]
            endloop autoindex
        n ← a[5]
        end complex
```

5.13   Is it possible for a procedure which only contains 1-D arrays to have space complexity $O(n^2)$ for some input size n? Explain.

5.14   What is the best possible time complexity for a function that sums all of the elements in an n-element integer array?

5.15   Are time complexity and space complexity related? In particular, is it possible to have a program with $O(n)$ time complexity that also has $O(1)$ space complexity? Is it possible to have a program with $O(n)$ space complexity that also has $O(1)$ time complexity? Explain your answers and give examples to back up your claims.

5.16   Can you think of any data structures which could not be implemented easily with 1-D arrays?

TO PROGRAM

5.17   Design an *mpl* function *firstnon* that finds the first non-zero value in an integer array. For example, if *a* is a 5-element array, where $a[1] = 0$, $a[2] = 0$, $a[3] = 14$, $a[4] = 2$, and $a[5] = 0$, then *firstnon(a, 5)* returns 14. As usual, make sure that your function is robust.

5.18   Design an *mpl* procedure *reverse(intarray, n)* that reverses the elements of a 1-D integer array whose length is *n*. If *a* contains 1, 5, 3, 2, for example, then *reverse(a, 4)* will leave *a* containing 2, 3, 5, 1. Give the time and space complexities of your procedure.

5.19   Design a program that computes the scalar product of an array: a procedure, *scalarproduct*, should be developed that takes a 1-D real array *a* and a real value *alpha* and multiplies each element of *a* by *alpha*.

5.20   Design a function, *lookup*, that takes an integer array *a* and a value in *a* and returns the index in *a* where the value is found. How should the function be modified if it is possible that the value is not in *a*? Would it help if *a* were in ascending order? Use time complexity analysis in your response.

5.21 Design an *mpl* function that returns the second largest element of a real array.

5.22 Design an *mpl* program that inputs two real arrays of equal size and sums their corresponding elements to form a new array with the same length. The input should be an integer n followed by n reals for the first array, and then n reals for the second array.

5.23 A town of 100 people uses a computer to keep track of which people are married and to whom. They use an array called *married* that is set up as follows: (a) If person i is not married, then $married[i] = 0$. (b) If $person[i]$ is married to $person[j]$, then $married[i] = j$ and $married[j] = i$. Design a **truth value** function $valid(married)$, which checks the validity of the array *married*, i.e., it returns **true** if whenever $married[i]$ is j, $(j \neq 0)$, $married[j] = i$. What are the time and space complexities of your program?

**5.4
THE
CHALLENGE**

Case Study
5.4

Computing the Dot Product
of Two Vectors

> *Problem Description:* Given two vectors of length n, compute their dot product.
>
> *Input Specifications:* A value for n, followed by one list of n real numbers corresponding to the first vector and another list of n real numbers corresponding to the second vector.

In this case study we examine the numerical problem of multiplying two vectors element by element. This operation has many uses in scientific computing, and it introduces programming techniques that will be developed further in chapter 7 for multiplying two matrices.

If we call the two vectors to be multiplied x and y, then the dot product of x and y is

$$\sum_{i=1}^{n} x_i * y_i$$

A vector is easily represented by a 1-D array. The dot product is just the sum of the products of corresponding vector components.

The Solution — 1-D Real Arrays

The form of the initial procedure is simple. The two vectors x and y are input using the procedure *read 1D real* defined in case study 5.1. Then the dot product of x and y is computed in a separate function (called *dot product*) and printed.

```
vector product : initial procedure
    {inputs two vectors x and y of length n and prints their dot product}
    storage specification
        constants
            maxsize : integer 100
        variables
            x, y : 1-D real array [1 → maxsize]
            n : integer
        end storage specification
    begin vector product
        input n
        if (n > maxsize) or (n ≤ 0)
            then output 'n larger than ', maxsize, ' or n ≤ 0 : ', n
            else read 1D real(x, 1, n)
                 read 1D real(y, 1, n)
                 output dot product(x, y, n)
        endif
    end vector product
    where dot product computes the dot product of vectors x and y
```

CASE STUDY 5.4 — REFINEMENT 1

The only function left to design is *dot product.* This function accepts two 1-D
real arrays of the same length (*n*) and computes their dot product. From the
definition of the dot product we see that a summing loop is involved. We have
seen many of these, so we give function *dot product* without further elabora-
tion.

```
dot product : real function
    {computes the dot product of two vectors x and y of length n}
    storage specification
        parameters
            x, y : in out 1-D real array
            n : in only integer
        variables
            i : integer
            sum : real
        end storage specification
    begin dot product
        sum ← 0.0
        loop start i with 1 step 1 to n
            assert sum = x[1] * y[1] + . . . + x[i−1] * y[i−1]
            sum ← sum + x[i] * y[i]
            endloop autoindex
        assert sum = x[1] * y[1] + . . . + x[n] * y[n]
        dot product ← sum
    end dot product
```

CASE STUDY 5.4 — REFINEMENT 2

Notice that the first time through the loop when *i* is 1, the loop invariant assertion will read

$$sum = x[1] * y[1] + \ldots + x[0] * y[0]$$

which we just interpret to mean that *sum* = 0.

Correctness

Do a program walkthrough and then use a calculator to check your results. You should also formally verify that the loop of function *dot product* is correct.

Efficiency

The loop of this function follows the simple form we have seen in many other functions and procedures. Just one pass from 1 to *n* is required to perform the required computations, so it is clear that the time complexity of the program *vector product* is linear. The space complexity is also easily seen to be $O(n)$.

Summary — Case Study 5.4

The dot product is a common numerical operation that is quite easy to write as a function using 1-D arrays. The time and space complexities of this function are both linear.

Searching an	Case Study
Unordered List	5.5

> *Problem Description:* Given a list of identification numbers in no particular order and a subsequent set of numbers from that list, find the position in the first list of each number in the second list.
>
> *Input Specifications:* A list of at most 1000 identification numbers, all positive integers, followed by the integer −1, followed by another list of identification numbers.

Searching a list for some specific value is a common application of computers. For example, all large businesses keep personnel information in computer files. In order to modify or print information about a particular employee, the record for that employee must first be located by searching through the file. There are many other examples involving searches. The underlying idea is simple: given a list of items in the store, find the position in this list of some particular value. Often, the list to be searched is in order (numerical or alphabetical), but sometimes the list is not in order. Different search techniques are used in these two cases. Here, we will study the case where the list is not in order.

The −1 in the input is used as *data separator*, to show the end of the list to be searched and the beginning of the numbers for which we will search. Each ID number in the second set of values must be compared with the ID numbers in the first list. When a match is found, its position in the first list must be printed.

Example 5.10

If the input is

79337 93321 37373 67666 −1 37373 93321

then the first number of the second list, 37373, is found at position 3 in the first list, and 93321 is found at position 2, so

3
2

should be printed by this program.

The Solution — Sequential Search

In designing a program to solve our problem, we first need to declare an array with 1000 elements for holding the list of ID numbers. Next, we need to input the values of this list and store them in the array. Then we need to design a loop that reads successive values from the second set of numbers and calls a procedure to search for these values in the array (the first list), printing the positions in the array where the matches are found. This general organization of the program is laid out in the following initial procedure:

```
searchlist : initial procedure
    {inputs a list of id numbers and then prints the location in this list
      of requested id numbers}

    storage specification
        constants
            listlength : integer 1000
        variables
            idlist : 1-D integer array [1 → listlength]
            id : integer
        end storage specification

    begin searchlist
        read 1D integer(idlist, −1, listlength, numids)
        if (numids = 0) or (numids > listlength)
            then output 'error: input size out of bounds'
            else loop while moredata
                    input id
                    {output position in idlist where id is found}
                    endloop while
        endif
    end searchlist

    where read 1D integer inputs a series of integers followed by a  −1
              into the array idlist
    where a function which locates and returns the position of a given id
              number in the array idlist must be designed
```

CASE STUDY 5.5 — REFINEMENT 1

We have again used a named constant (*listlength*) to define the size of an array (*idlist*) in this initial procedure. The version of procedure *read 1D integer* that uses a trailer value to signal the end of the inputlist has been discussed before (it was left as an exercise in case study 5.1). The only part left to design is the function that finds the position in *idlist* where *id* is found. We will call this function *lookup*. Notice that *lookup* will only be called if there are indeed values in *idlist*.

What parameters will *lookup* require? It needs an array of integers, a value to search for in the array, and the number of elements in the array. If we call these parameters *a*, *value*, and *n*, respectively, we will have the parameter list

parameters
    a : **in out 1-D integer array**
    value, n : **in only integer**

In this case *a*, *value*, and *n* all have values when *lookup* is called; since these values are not to be altered by *lookup*, they could all be of type **in only**. However, we have declared the array *a* to be of type **in out** for the usual reasons.

The loop in *lookup* that searches array *a* for *value* can be written as

```
i ← 0
loop
    i ← i + 1
    assert value is not among a[1] through a[i − 1]
    endloop until value = a[i]
assert value is at position i of array a
```

Here, *i* is set to 0 initially, then each time through the loop 1 is added to *i* until the values in *a[i]* and *value* are the same. This means that when the loop terminates, *i* is the position in the array *a* where the match with *value* was found. To complete the requirements for function *lookup*, then, we only need to return *i* as the value of *lookup*:

```
i ← 0
loop
    i ← i + 1
    assert value is not among a[1] through a[i − 1]
    endloop until value = a[i]
assert value is at position i of array a
lookup ← i
```

This program segment will work if *a* is not empty and if *value* is actually in the array *a* somewhere. We have ensured in the initial procedure that *lookup* will not be called if *a* is empty, so the first problem has been dealt with already. We still have the second problem, however. If *value* is not in the array *a*, then *i* eventually becomes larger than *n* as the loop is repeatedly iterated without finding a match; when this happens, evaluation of

```
value = a[i]
```

in the **until** clause will cause an error. We can remedy this situation by changing the **until** clause to force the loop to stop when a match is found (*value* = *a[i]*) or when *i* has stepped through all *n* defined elements of the array *a* ($i \geq n$). This gives us the loop

```
i ← 0
loop
    i ← i + 1
    assert value is not among a[1] through a[i − 1]
    endloop until (value = a[i]) or (i ⩾ n)
assert value is at position i of array a or value is not in array a
```

This causes the loop to terminate if either

    value = a[i]

or

    i ⩾ n

(or both) is true at the bottom of the loop. Both conditions would be true if the match with *value* occurred in the *n*th element of the array *a*. To complete this function, then, we need to check which of the two conditions in the loop goal assertion is true after the loop terminates. Was the loop terminated because a match was found or because no match was found and we ran out of array elements? We can check this with

```
if value = a[i]
    then lookup ← i
    else  lookup ← 0
    endif
```

If *value* = *a[i]*, then *i* contains the array position where *value* was matched. If *value* ≠ *a[i]*, the loop was terminated because the value in the loop index *i* had finally reached *n*, the number of elements in *a*, and no match was found. In the first instance *lookup* is set to *i* before the function terminates. In the second instance *lookup* is set to 0, to indicate to the initial procedure that no match was found.

The final version of *lookup* is given here.

```
lookup : integer function
    {computes the position in array a at which value is located;
        returns 0 if value is not in array a}

    storage specification
        parameters
            a : in out 1-D integer array
            value, n : in only integer
        variables
            i : integer
        end storage specification

    begin lookup
        i ← 0
        loop
            i ← i + 1
            assert value is not among a[1] through a[i − 1]
            endloop until (value = a[i]) or (i ⩾ n)
        assert value is at position i of array a or value is not in array a
        if value = a[i]
            then lookup ← i
            else  lookup ← 0
            endif
        end lookup
```

CASE STUDY 5.5 — REFINEMENT 2

Now that function *lookup* has been designed, we know how it should be used in the initial procedure; *lookup* should be called in the statements

```
position ← lookup(idlist, id, numids)
if position = 0
    then output id, 'is not in the list'
    else output id, ' is in position ', position
endif
```

where *position* needs to be declared as an integer. The initial procedure in its final form should thus look like

```
searchlist : initial procedure
    {inputs a list of id numbers and then prints the location in this list
     of requested id numbers}
    storage specification
        constants
            listlength : integer 1000
        variables
            idlist : 1-D integer array [1 → listlength]
            id, numids, position : integer
        end storage specification
    begin searchlist
        read 1D integer(idlist, −1, listlength, numids)
        if (numids = 0) or (numids > listlength)
            then output 'error: input size out of bounds'
            else loop while moredata
                    input id
                    position ← lookup(idlist, id, numids)
                    if position = 0
                        then output id, ' is not in the list'
                        else output id, ' is in position ', position
                    endif
                endloop while
        endif
    end searchlist
    where read 1D integer inputs a series of integers followed by a −1
            into the array idlist
    where lookup locates and returns the position of a given
            id number in the array idlist
```

CASE STUDY 5.5 — REFINEMENT 3

Correctness

In using the **until** loop verification rules to show that the loop of procedure *lookup* is correct, notice how the loop invariant assertion, which must be true just after **endloop,** and the loop termination conditions lead to the two assertions

```
assert value is not among a[1] through a[i − 1]
assert value = a[i], or i ⩾ n
```

being true just after **endloop.** Together, these two assertions imply the loop goal assertion

```
assert value is at position i of array a, or value is not in array a
```

The fact that the loop goal assertion gives two possible outcomes for the loop means that the actual outcome must be determined in an **if** statement; we included the proper **if** statement in function *lookup*. In this case the loop goal assertion was very helpful in directing what needed to be done upon termination of the loop.

Remember that the loop invariant assertion for an **until** loop goes just before the **until** statement. Notice that in the loop of function *lookup* the extra assertion

assert value is not among a[1] through a[i]

could be placed just after the **loop** statement.

Efficiency

Procedure *read 1D integer* will have a single loop that is iterated n times, where n is the final number of values stored in array a. Since in this case n truly depends on the input, procedure *read 1D integer* has $O(n)$ time complexity. Function *lookup* is somewhat more difficult. It takes a single value and checks whether that value is in the array a by iterating through the loop until a match is found. If the values sent to *lookup* are evenly distributed throughout array a, then on the average a match will be found halfway through a, at position $n/2$. This means that the loop will be iterated $n/2$ times on the average each time *lookup* is called. This loop thus has the general statement count formula

$c*(n/2) + d$

where c is the number of statements executed within the loop, which is iterated on the average $n/2$ times. It is still linear, because the formula can be rewritten in the standard form

$(c/2)*n + d$

Thus, function *lookup* also has time complexity $O(n)$.

Notice, however, that function *lookup* is called inside a **while moredata** loop in the initial procedure. This loop is executed m times, where m is the number of elements in the second part of the input data. This means that *lookup* will be called m times, so the actual time complexity of the **while moredata** loop in the initial procedure is $O(m*n)$. Since this is worse than the $O(n)$ time complexity generated by the single call to *read 1D integer*, the entire program has time complexity $O(m*n)$.

The space complexity of this program is $O(n)$, because an array containing n values (the size of the input) must be maintained in the store.

Summary — Case Study 5.5

We have designed a sequential search function that will be useful whenever a search for a value in a simple unordered list of values is required. The basic design of function *lookup* was very simple but, as is often the case, we were forced to put greater design effort into this function to ensure that it still worked for the special cases when the list was empty or when the value was not in the list. The time complexity of the resulting program was $O(m*n)$, because within the loop that inputs each new ID number to be matched with *idlist*, there is a call to function *lookup*, which in turn must (on the average) search halfway through *idlist* to find a match. The space complexity of the program is $O(n)$.

Searching an Ordered List

Case Study 5.6

Problem Description: Design a program that reads in a list of part numbers and a corresponding list of prices and then uses these lists to look up and print out the prices of a series of parts.

Input Specifications: First there will be *n* pairs of values, each pair consisting of a part number followed by its price. These pairs will be in order by part number (smaller part numbers always appear before larger ones). The list of pairs will be followed by a separator line containing −1 and −1.0. Finally, there will be a list of part numbers for which prices must be looked up in the price list and printed. All part numbers will be positive integers, and all prices will be nonnegative reals.

Programs for searching ordered lists have many uses, and a part number/price list program provides a convenient way of demonstrating the search process. Other practical uses include searching a personnel file for some information on an employee, finding a telephone number in a telephone directory, and looking up the meaning of an English word in a dictionary.

In case study 5.5 we implemented a simple list searching program, which just scanned down the list looking for a given value. That searching technique is called *sequential search*. In this case study we introduce a more sophisticated technique called *binary search*, which only works when the list to be searched is in order (it is much more efficient than a sequential search). We will design the program for this case study first using a sequential search and then using a binary search, so that the two techniques can be compared.

In tackling our problem we will first need to read in and save the part number list and the price list in two arrays,

```
part : 1-D integer array [1 → listsize]
price : 1-D real array [1 → listsize]
```

where *listsize* is a constant integer containing an estimate of the size of these lists. We will input the parts list and the price list so that *price*[*i*] is always the price of *part*[*i*]. So, for example, if *part*[42] contains part number 4867, then *price*[42] would contain the price of part number 4867.

First Solution — Sequential Search

The organization of our program is exceedingly simple. We first call on one procedure to read in the parts list and the price list as described and then call on a second procedure to input the second list of part numbers and print their respective prices. For this problem we cannot use our standard routine for inputting a 1-D array because the data for the two lists is intermixed. Such is the luck of programming! No procedure is ever general enough to handle all eventualities. However, having written a similar procedure before makes designing this one simpler. The initial procedure is

pricing : **initial procedure**
{inputs a parts list and a price list and then computes the
prices of a series of parts}

   storage specification
     constants
       listsize : **integer** 1000
     variables
       part : **1-D integer array** [1 → listsize]
       price : **1-D real array** [1 → listsize]
       n : **integer**
   end storage specification

   begin pricing
     read lists(part, price, n)
     if n = 0
       then output 'error, parts list is empty'
       else find prices(part, price, n)
       endif
   end pricing

   where read lists reads in the lists of parts and prices
   where find prices looks up the part prices in the price list

CASE STUDY 5.6 — REFINEMENT 1

Procedure *read lists* must read in the part/price pairs until the separator pair
$-1 -1.0$ is found.

read lists : **procedure**
{reads part numbers and prices into the arrays part and price}

   storage specification
     parameters
       part : **out only 1-D integer array**
       price : **out only 1-D real array**
       n : **out only integer**
     variables
       temppart : **integer**
       tempprice : **real**
   end storage specification

   begin read lists
     n ← 0
     input temppart, tempprice
     loop while temppart ⩾ 0
       assert the first n pairs of values have been read into
          the part and price arrays
       n ← n + 1
       part[n] ← temppart
       price[n] ← tempprice
       input temppart, tempprice
     endloop while
     assert n pairs of values have been read into the part
       and price arrays
   end read lists

CASE STUDY 5.6 — REFINEMENT 2

The loop in procedure *read lists* uses the trailer method for inputting the arrays.

After executing this procedure, *price*[1], *price*[2], . . ., *price*[n] will be the prices of the corresponding part numbers *part*[1], *part*[2], . . ., *part*[n]. This loop terminates when the trailer value pair −1, −1.0 is finally input. Actually, we only need to check the part number to see whether the trailer value has been found. Nonetheless, both of these negative trailer value pairs must be included, because both a part number and a price are input on each pass through the loop.

Procedure *read lists*, although now correct, is not robust. We leave it as an exercise to determine and correct the problem.

Procedure *find prices* has the following task: it is to input part numbers successively (as long as there is more data) and print each part number and its corresponding price. We can use function *lookup* of case study 5.5 to determine the position of a given part in the parts list. Since the price for any part occupies the same position in the price list, we can then output the price using the array index returned by *lookup*. Of course, we must check that the part was actually found in the list; remember that function *lookup* returns a 0 if the part isn't found. This gives us the following procedure for *find prices*:

```
find prices : procedure
    {finds and prints the prices of a series of part numbers}

    storage specification
        parameters
            part : in out 1-D integer array
            price : in out 1-D real array
            n : in only integer
        variables
            position, inputpart : integer
        end storage specification

    begin find prices
        loop while moredata
            input inputpart
            position ← lookup(part, inputpart, n)
            if position > 0
                then output 'the price of ', inputpart, ' is ', price[position]
                else  output inputpart, ' is not in the parts list'
                endif
            endloop while
        end find prices

    where lookup finds the position of inputpart in the part array

CASE STUDY 5.6 — REFINEMENT 3
```

This finishes our first attempt at this program. We have not included the usual loop assertions in *find prices*, because the **while moredata** loop used here is just a simple input loop.

Second Solution — Binary Search

The program we have just written uses the sequential search function *lookup*, which we designed in case study 5.5. This, of course, is one of the reasons for writing procedures and functions — to use them again whenever they are needed in other programs. Design time is saved by using these routines, and since these routines have (usually) been used and tested thoroughly, we are quite sure that they are error-free. However, sometimes it is worth the effort to reconsider a particular routine, especially in view of time or space complexity considerations, to see whether a substantially more efficient version could be designed.

In this case study the parts list has one important feature that was not present in the list for which *lookup* was originally designed: the parts list is in numeric order. If you were given a large parts-price book and were asked to look up the price of, say, part number 52631 you would not (we hope) start at the beginning of the book and search through it number by number the way function *lookup* searches. Instead, you would open the book somewhere in the middle and would check the part numbers there to see whether you had gone too far or not far enough. Then you would open the book again about halfway in the correct direction, and continue this process until the part number 52631 was isolated. This way you would find the part number in seconds, instead of spending many boring hours searching. You would apply this same technique to any large, ordered list of items (for example, a dictionary).

Similarly, we can use the fact that our array of part numbers is sorted in numerical order to write a function that uses this new *binary search* technique for finding *inputpart*. The basic idea is that we will maintain two variables, *low* and *high*, with values such that *part[low]* is always less than *inputpart* (*part[low]* comes before *inputpart* in the list) and *part[high]* is always greater than *inputpart* (*part[high]* comes after *inputpart* in the list). We will then repeatedly halve the distance between *low* and *high*, which will rapidly squeeze them together around *inputpart*. In mathematical terms, we will maintain the condition

$$part[low] < inputpart < part[high]$$

To state this process in more general terms, we want to design a new binary search procedure that takes a 1-D integer array *a* whose values are in ascending order, a value to be located in *a*, and the number of elements *n* in *a*, and returns the position in *a* where the value is found. Thus the formal parameters of this new function (called *binary search*) will be

parameters
    a : **in out 1-D integer array**
    value, n : **in only integer**

To begin the binary search process we must choose values for two variables *low* and *high* so that

    assert a[low] < value < a[high]

holds (this will be our loop invariant assertion). Function *binary search* will then work as follows: the number *mid* is picked such that *mid* is halfway between *low* and *high*. For example, if *low* is 1 and *high* is 10, then *mid* is 5. If *low* is 23 and *high* is 63, then *mid* is 43. We can use the formula

$$mid \leftarrow (low + high)/2$$

to get this value for *mid* (assuming that *mid* is of type **integer,** which, we recall, in *mpl* means that the value in *mid* will be the truncated integer portion of the expression on the right).

After computing the value for *mid* we must check whether we have a match by comparing *value* with *a*[*mid*]. If we do not have a match, then *value* is either between *a*[*low*] and *a*[*mid*] (*a*[*low*] < *value* < *a*[*mid*]) or *value* is between *a*[*mid*] and *a*[*high*] (*a*[*mid*] < *value* < *a*[*high*]). In the first case we set *high* ← *mid* (then *a*[*low*] < *value* < *a*[*high*] still holds) and repeat the process. In the second case we set *low* ← *mid* and continue similarly. This means that after setting *low* or *high* properly on each pass through a loop, effectively squeezing *low* and *high* closer together around *value*, the loop invariant assertion

assert a[low] < value < a[high]

will always be true.

A first (and incorrect) attempt at function *binary search* is shown below. We start with *low* set to 1 and *high* set to *n*. The **truth value** variable *found* is used to indicate when the searching loop should be terminated.

```
binary search : integer function
     {finds value in array a, and returns its position in a}
     storage specification
          parameters
               a : in out 1-D integer array
               value, n : in only integer
          variables
               low, high, mid : integer
               found : truth value
          end storage specification
     begin binary search
          found ← false
          low ← 1
          high ← n
          loop while not found
               assert a[low] < value < a[high]
               mid ← (low + high)/2
               if a[mid] = value
                    then found ← true
                    else if a[mid] < value
                              then low ← mid
                              else high ← mid
                         endif
               endif
          endloop while
          assert value is at position mid in array a
          binary search ← mid
     end binary search
```

CASE STUDY 5.6 — REFINEMENT 4

Correctness

In attempting to verify the loop of procedure *binary search* as it is written in refinement 4, we would first try to show that the loop invariant assertion will be true the first time through the loop. Can we always be sure that

assert a[low] < value < a[high]

will be true when the loop is first entered with *low* equal to 1 and *high* equal to *n*? What if *value* is either the first or last element of the list (i.e., *value* = *a*[1] or *value* = *a*[*n*])? In either of these cases the loop invariant assertion would be false the first time through the loop. This is a particularly subtle error, because function *binary search* would work fine for a potentially long period of time just as it is written, until it was finally used in an attempt to locate the first or last element of a list. Of course, a good set of test data (including the obvious special first and last values of the list) would have caught this error if it had slipped through the loop verification process; this is another argument for testing a program with special data values.

To fix this error, we can set *low* to 0 and *high* to *n*+1 before the loop is entered. Then, since there is no 0th or *n*+1st array element, if *value* is in the list it must lie between the 0th and *n*+1st array elements (exclusive). However, this too would make the loop invariant assertion

assert a[low] < value < a[high]

improper the first time through the loop (because *a*[*low*] and *a*[*high*] are invalid array elements when *low* is 0 and *high* is n+1). We will continue to use this assertion, though, considering it to mean "if *value* is in array *a*, it lies between array position *low* and array position *high*, exclusive."

A second problem with function *binary search* is that it does not handle the situation when *value* is not in the list (it would go into an infinite loop). Just as we did with the sequential search routine of function *lookup*, we should set the function name, *binary search*, to 0 if *value* is not found in array *a*. How can we determine that *value* is not in array *a*? Knowing that the loop invariant assertion

assert a[low] < value < a[high]

is true each time the loop is begun, we also know for sure that value is not in array *a* if there is *nothing* between array position *low* and array position *high*, that is, if

$$high - low \leqslant 1$$

Incorporating these changes into function *binary search* gives the correct version below. We have included all relevant assertions necessary to verify that the function is now indeed correct. For readability in an actual program, one might prefer to include only the loop invariant and goal assertions.

```
binary search : integer function
   {finds value in the array a, and returns its position in a;
    if value is not in array a, returns a 0}

   storage specification
      parameters
         a : in out 1-D integer array
         value, n : in only integer
      variables
         low, high, mid : integer
         found : truth value
      end storage specification

   begin binary search
      found ← false
      low ← 0
      high ← n + 1
      assert a[low] < value < a[high]
      loop while (high − low > 1) and (not found)
         assert a[low] < value < a[high]
         mid ← (low + high)/2
         if a[mid] = value
            then found ← true
            else if a[mid] < value
                    then assert a[mid] < value < a[high]
                         low ← mid
                    else assert a[low] < value < a[mid]
                         high ← mid
                 endif
         endif
         assert a[low] < value < a[high]
         endloop while
      assert (loop invariant) a[low] < value < a[high]
      assert (loop termination) high − low ≤ 1, or found is true
      assert (loop goal) value is not in array a, or value is at position mid

      {determine now whether the loop was terminated because value
       was found at position mid, or because high − low ≤ 1 and
       value is therefore not in array a}
      if found
         then assert a[mid] = value
              binary search ← mid
         else assert high − low ≤ 1
              binary search ← 0
      endif
   end binary search
```

CASE STUDY 5.6 — REFINEMENT 5

You should read this version of *binary search* carefully, assuring yourself that all assertions are correct. Remember that the loop invariant assertion

   assert a[low] < value < a[high]

is meant to be read, "If *value* is in array *a*, it lies between array position *low* and array position *high*, exclusive."

To use *binary search* in our program for case study 5.6, we need to go back to procedure *find prices* and replace

position ← lookup(part, inputpart, n)

with

position ← binary search(part, inputpart, n)

Efficiency

We have claimed that function *binary search* is much more efficient than the sequential search of function *lookup*. However, function *binary search* is more involved than the simple sequential search of function *lookup*. One might wonder whether the extra program design effort is worth it, since a computer is to be used to do the task anyway. To answer this question, we need to analyze and compare the two functions *lookup* and *binary search*.

There are n elements in the parts list. In the sequential search of function *lookup*, each given input part number is compared with the elements of the array *part* in sequence until a match is found. As we have seen in case study 5.5, this means that on the average, for a random input part number, the **until** loop of function *lookup* will be iterated $n/2$ times before a match is found. That is, if there are 10,000 entries in the array *part* ($n = 10,000$), then 5,000 trips through the **until** loop (on the average) will be required before a match for the input part number is found.

Now, consider function *binary search*. Here, each time through the **while** loop, the difference between *high* and *low* is cut in half. At first, when *low* = 0 and *high* = $n + 1$, the number of values between *high* and *low* is n. After one pass through the **while** loop, the number of values between *high* and *low* is $n/2$. After the second pass, the number is $(n/2)/2 = n/4$; after the third pass the number is $n/8$; and so on. In general, after m passes through the **while** loop, the number of values between *high* and *low* is $n/2^m$. The important question, then, is, "At most how many times must the loop be iterated before a match with the input part is made or it is determined that there is no match?" The answer is "m times", where m is the smallest number such that $2^m \geq n$. This is because in the most time-consuming case we continue looping until there is only one value (or no values if no match is found) between *high* and *low*, that is, m times until $n/2^m \leq 1$ holds. (Some readers may know that the formula for m is $\log_2 n$.) For example, if there are 10,000 elements in the array *part*, the question is, "What is the smallest value for m such that $2^m \geq 10,000$?" Since $2^{13} = 8,192$ and $2^{14} = 16,384$, the answer is 14. Instead of the *average* of 5,000 passes through the **until** loop in the sequential search of procedure *lookup*, at most 14 passes through the **while** loop of procedure *binary search* are required to match the input value! If we had to pay for the time consumed by the computer in performing these tasks, the savings achieved by using *binary search* would be well worth the effort of designing this function, especially if the list were searched often.

Using time complexity terminology, we have shown that the time complexity of sequential search is $O(n)$ and that the time complexity of binary search is $O(\log_2 n)$. When the complexities of two different routines for doing the same task differ like this, the extra effort needed to design the routine with lower time complexity is nearly always worthwhile.

Table 5-1 shows the *average* number of passes through the **until** loop of the sequential search function *lookup* and the *maximum* number of passes through the **while** loop of function *binary search* for different list sizes. The superiority of *binary search* is dramatic. Designing and analyzing function *binary search* was a little more difficult, but the results are rewarding.

TABLE 5-1. COMPARISON OF LOOP ITERATIONS FOR SEQUENTIAL AND BINARY SEARCH

	n = 100	n = 1,000	n = 10,000	n = 100,000	n = 1,000,000
sequential search	50	500	5,000	50,000	500,000
binary search	7	10	14	17	20

Now that we have determined the time complexities of the two functions *lookup* and *binary search*, we can figure out the time complexities of the two complete programs using these functions. In both programs the initial procedure calls procedure *read lists* and then procedure *find prices*. Procedure *read lists* has $O(n)$ time complexity, because it consists of a single loop for inputting the n part numbers and n prices into two lists.

Procedure *find prices* is the more time-consuming procedure. It contains a **while moredata** loop that reads in each new part number for which a price is to be determined. Inside this loop, a call to a function is made to determine the price of each part number. In refinement 3, this call is made to function *lookup*, which has time complexity $O(n)$, as we determined in case study 5.5. So if there are m part numbers to be input by the **while moredata** loop (and for each part number the corresponding price must be determined by function *lookup*), the time complexity of procedure *find prices* of refinement 3 is $O(m*n)$. The same analysis shows that procedure *find prices* of refinement 5, which calls function *binary search* rather than function *lookup*, has time complexity $O(m*\log_2 n)$.

For large values of m, then, procedure *find prices* contributes most to the time complexity of either program, so the program in which the sequential search function (*lookup*) is used has $O(m*n)$ time complexity, whereas the program using function *binary search* has $O(m*\log_2 n)$ time complexity. To see how much better the program using the binary search function is, assume that $m = n$ and graph the two time complexities $O(n^2)$ and $O(n*\log_2 n)$.

Summary — Case Study 5.6

Searching large lists is a very common application of computers. If the list to be searched is in order, a binary search can be employed using a loop that cuts the search space in half during each iteration. This leads to a time complexity of $O(\log_2 n)$ for completing a search for one item in a list of n items. If the list is not in order, a sequential search with a time complexity of $O(n)$ is required.

Sorting a List of Values

Case Study 5.7

> **Problem Description:** Read in a list of n integers, sort the integers into ascending order, and print them in this new order.
>
> **Input Specifications:** An integer n, followed by the n integers to be sorted.

Sorting is another common application of computers. In fact, studies have shown that almost one fourth of all computing time is spent sorting, since businesses often need to sort large files of information. It is therefore essential that all programmers understand efficient sorting techniques. Arranging identification numbers into ascending order (smallest to largest), names into alphabetical order, and scores into descending order (largest to smallest) are a few examples of problems requiring sorting routines.

Since sorting techniques are the same regardless of what data is to be sorted, we will examine this simply stated problem: sort a list of integers into ascending order. Our solution to this problem will involve the design of a sorting procedure commonly called *insertion sort*. In the next case study a faster sort called *quicksort* will be developed.

The Solution — Insertion Sort

To input the list of integers to be sorted, we use the standard procedure, *read 1D integer,* from case study 5.1. Once the list has been input, procedure *insertion sort* is called to sort the list of numbers into ascending order. Then the list is printed using procedure *write 1D integer* of case study 5.1. The initial procedure, which includes the usual checks to make sure that the list will fit into the array (called *list*), is

```
sort n numbers : initial procedure
    {inputs a list of numbers, then prints this list in ascending order}

    storage specification
        constants
            max : integer 1000
        variables
            n : integer
            list : 1-D integer array [1 → max]
        end storage specification

    begin sort n numbers
        input n
        if (n ≤ 0) or (n > max)
            then output 'bad data, ', n, ' out of range'
            else read 1D integer(list, 1, n)
                 insertion sort(list, n)
                 write 1D integer(list, 1, n)
            endif
        end sort n numbers

    where read 1D integer is the standard input procedure of case study 5.1
    where insertion sort sorts list into ascending order
    where write 1D integer is the standard output procedure of case study 5.1

    CASE STUDY 5.7 — REFINEMENT 1
```

The only routine we need to design is procedure *insertion sort*. The idea behind *insertion sort* is simple: it will contain a loop that steps through *list* from 1 to n, ensuring that the part of the list handled so far is in order. That is, using the loop index variable i, the loop invariant assertion will be

assert the first $i-1$ elements of list are in relative order

It will then be the task of the loop to make sure that $list[i]$ is set so that it is in relative order with respect to $list[1]$ through $list[i-1]$.

This is done as follows: when $i=1$, we have considered only $list[1]$, which is obviously in order relative to itself. When $i=2$, we compare $list[2]$ with $list[1]$. If $list[2]$ is less than $list[1]$, then the first two elements are out of order with respect to each other, so we swap them. Otherwise no changes need to be made. Now the first two elements are in order relative to one another. Then set i to 3 and compare $list[3]$ with $list[2]$. If $list[3]$ is at least as large as $list[2]$, the first three elements are in relative order. If $list[3]$ is less than $list[2]$, then the value in $list[3]$ must be inserted higher up in the list. (We use the word "higher" to mean "towards the front of the list;" if you think of the array as it appears in the store, our use of "higher" means "higher up in the store.") If this is the case, we swap the values in $list[2]$ and $list[3]$. This may not be enough, however, since the value now in $list[2]$ (which we found in $list[3]$) may also be less than $list[1]$, so we must now compare $list[2]$ and $list[1]$. If $list[2]$ is less than $list[1]$, their values are also swapped. In any case, when we have completed this process for these three list values and the value originally in $list[3]$ has been inserted into its proper position, we can say, "The first three values are in relative order." If we continue this process for all n list values, we can say "The first n values are in relative order," which means that the entire list is in order.

As an example of *insertion sort*, assume that the original array *list* is as shown in the store below:

Example 5.11

n	6	integer
list[1]	8	integer
list[2]	16	integer
list[3]	2	integer
list[4]	5	integer
list[5]	9	integer
list[6]	15	integer

We are using *insertion sort* to sort a six-element list. Assume now that we have finished iterating the loop of *insertion sort* with $i=3$ and are now about to iterate the loop with $i=4$. At this point the first three elements of *list* should be sorted with respect to one another, so the store should look like:

n	6	**integer**
list[1]	2	**integer**
list[2]	8	**integer**
list[3]	16	**integer**
list[4]	5	**integer**
list[5]	9	**integer**
list[6]	15	**integer**
i	4	**integer**

That is, the first $i - 1 = 3$ numbers have been sorted with respect to each other, and we now need to insert the value in *list*[*i*] ($i = 4$) into the correct place. Since *list*[4] is less than *list*[3] ($5 < 16$), we must move 5 up to its proper position in the list. We compare 5 against the number above it (16), and since $5 < 16$, we swap these values. We then re-peat the process, comparing 5 with 8, and again swapping the values. We keep doing this until we reach a value, in this case 2, that is less than or equal to 5; at this point the 5 has moved up as far as it should go, and the first four elements are now in order. Pic-torially, we first move 5 up once to get

n	6	**integer**
list[1]	2	**integer**
list[2]	8	**integer**
list[3]	5	**integer**
list[4]	16	**integer**
list[5]	9	**integer**
list[6]	15	**integer**
i	4	**integer**

and a second time to get

n	6	**integer**
list[1]	2	**integer**
list[2]	5	**integer**
list[3]	8	**integer**
list[4]	16	**integer**
list[5]	9	**integer**
list[6]	15	**integer**
i	4	**integer**

Now the indexing loop controlling *i* has finished the iteration with *i* = 4, implying that the first four list elements are in order. At this point *i* would be set automatically to 5 and the fifth list element (9) would be moved to its proper position above 16, so the first five elements of the list would be in order. Finally, with *i* = 6 the loop would execute for the last time, moving 15 up to its proper position. This would ensure that the first six elements of the list are in order. Since that is the entire list in this example, the list would now be sorted.

In general, then, we must establish an automatic indexing loop with loop index variable *i* that runs from 2 to *n* (we need not examine *list*[1], because it is trivially in order with respect to itself). For each value of *i*, we compare *list*[*i*] with *list*[*i*−1]. If *list*[*i*] is less than *list*[*i*−1], we call a procedure that moves the value in *list*[*i*] up to its proper position. If *list*[*i*] is at least as large as *list*[*i*−1], then it is at least as large as *all* previous list elements (since the list is in order to position *i*−1), so we do not need to move the value in *list*[*i*]. With this procedure, we know that each time we enter the loop with a new value of *i*, the previous *i*−1 values of *list* are in order. At the end of that pass through the loop, after comparing *list*[*i*] with *list*[*i*−1] and moving the value in *list*[*i*] up if necessary, we can assert that the first *i* elements of the list are in order for this value of *i*. These considerations assure us that the procedure works properly.

How do we move an element up to its proper position? In keeping with our top-down program design methodology, we don't worry about this problem right now. Instead we relegate it to a separate procedure. This gives us the following refinement for *insertion sort*.

```
insertion sort : procedure
    {sorts the array list into ascending order}

    storage specification
        parameters
            list : in out 1-D integer array
            n : in only integer
        variables
            i : integer
    end storage specification
```

```
   begin insertion sort
       loop start i with 2 step 1 to n
           assert the first i − 1 elements of list are in relative order
           if list[i] < list[i − 1]
               then moveup(list, i)
               endif
           endloop autoindex
       assert list is sorted in ascending order
       end insertion sort
   where moveup moves list element i up to its correct place
```

CASE STUDY 5.7 — REFINEMENT 2

For this problem, it is necessary to designate the array parameter *list* as type **in out.** The values in the formal array parameter *list* will be moved around, and we want to be sure that the same changes occur in the actual array parameter sent to *insertion sort* (since *insertion sort* is supposed to rearrange the original list).

Procedure *moveup* is called only when it is determined that the ith element of *list* is out of order relative to the previous $i − 1$ elements of *list* and must be moved up. The moving-up process is a loop that starts with i and steps backwards through *list*, moving the out-of-order value up one element at a time until its proper position is found. When procedure *moveup* is called, only the first $i − 1$ elements of *list* are in order. The goal assertion of the loop in procedure *moveup* will thus be

   assert list[1] through list[i] are in relative order

A first attempt at procedure *moveup* is given below.

```
moveup : procedure
    {moves the value in list element i up to its correct position}
    storage specification
        parameters
            list : in out 1-D integer array
            i : in only integer
        variables
            j : integer
        end storage specification
    begin moveup
        j ← i
        loop
            swap(list[j], list[j − 1])
            j ← j − 1
            assert list[1] through list[j − 1] are in relative order, and
                   list[j] through list[i] are in relative order
            endloop until list[j] ⩾ list[j − 1]
        assert list[1] through list[i] are in relative order
        end moveup
    where swap was defined in case study 2.3
```

CASE STUDY 5.7 — REFINEMENT 3

We can use an **until** loop here, because *moveup* is called only if the *i*th element is out of order, so at least one swap must take place. Notice the loop invariant assertion:

assert list[1] through list[j − 1] are in relative order, and
list [j] through list[i] are in relative order

Since *j* always points to the single element of *list* between positions 1 and *i* that may be out of order, we cannot be sure whether *list*[*j* − 1] and *list*[*j*] are in relative order, but we know that all elements between positions 1 and *j* − 1 are in relative order, as are all elements between positions *j* and *i* in *list*. But notice that the loop finally terminates when the **until** condition

list[j] ⩾ list[j − 1]

is true. This means that *list*[*j*] and *list*[*j* − 1] are in order with respect to each other. Since the loop invariant condition is also true at this point, *list*[1] through *list*[*j* − 1] are in relative order, *list*[*j* − 1] and *list*[*j*] are in relative order, and *list*[*j*] through *list*[*i*] are in relative order; thus our goal of forcing *list*[1] through *list*[*i*] to be in relative order has been met.

This analysis is fine, except that procedure *moveup* won't work correctly when the element to be moved up is the smallest number so far encountered in the list. In this instance, this number will eventually be swapped into *list*[1], and then *list*[1] will be compared with *list*[0] in the **until** condition, causing an error (because there is no *list*[0]).

We must therefore add a check to the loop of procedure *moveup* to determine whether the value being moved up finally has been placed into *list*[1]. This isn't as trivial as it appears. The obvious solution is to change the **until** condition to:

until (j = 1) **or** (list[j] ⩾ list[j − 1])

This would work correctly, except for the fact that most processors would always evaluate both parts of the **until** conditional expression, even when the first part is false. If *j* = 1, such processors would still compare *list*[1] with *list*[0], causing a probable error since *list*[0] doesn't exist.

There are two ways around this problem. One way is to just change the original definition of *list* in initial procedure *sort n numbers* to:

list : **1-D integer array** [0 → max]

and set *list*[0] to a value that is smaller than (or at least as small as) any other element in the list. Then no element of *list* could be moved into *list*[0], and procedure *moveup* would work without modification. The other solution is to use a **truth value** variable to stop the loop, as is shown in the final refinement for *moveup*:

```
moveup : procedure
   {moves the value in list element i up to its correct position}
   storage specification
      parameters
         list : in out 1-D integer array
         i : in only integer
      variables
         j : integer
         stop : truth value
   end storage specification
begin moveup {assume i ⩾ 2}
   j ← i
   stop ← false
   loop
      if list[j] < list[j − 1]
         then swap(list[j], list[j − 1])
              j ← j − 1
         else stop ← true
      endif
      assert list[1] through list[j − 1] are in relative order, and
             list[j] through list[i] are in relative order
   endloop until stop or (j = 1)
   assert list[1] through list[i] are in relative order
end moveup

   where swap was defined in case study 2.3
```

CASE STUDY 5.7 — REFINEMENT 4

In this solution *stop* is set to **true** if it is detected within the loop that the out-of-order value has been moved to its proper position (i.e., when *list[j]* is determined to be at least as large as *list[j − 1]*). The loop will terminate when *stop* is true or when $j = 1$ (the out-of-order value has been moved into *list[1]*).

Correctness

Remembering that *moveup* will never be called for values of i smaller than 2, you should follow the verification rules for **until** loops to determine that *moveup* is now correct. Step 3 is the interesting part — showing that the loop invariant assertion and the fact that the loop termination conditions are true imply that the loop goal assertion has been met. You should also verify procedure *insertion sort*.

Efficiency

Determining the time complexity of procedure *insertion sort* requires some thinking. If the list to be sorted happens to be in order already, the single loop in *insertion sort* is iterated $n-1$ times, for $i=2$ to n, with $list[i] \geqslant list[i-1]$ on each iteration. This means that no calls to *moveup* are made, so *insertion sort* runs in $O(n)$ time. On the other hand, consider what happens if the list to be sorted is in reverse order (from largest to smallest). Then, on each of the $n-1$ iterations (i running from 2 to n) of the loop in *insertion sort*, $list[i]$ will be less than $list[i-1]$ (if there are no duplicated values in *list*), and, as a result, *moveup* will be called each time. Furthermore, since the values are in reverse order, the value out of place will need to be moved all the way up to *list*[1]. That is, when $i=2$, the loop in *moveup* will be iterated one time. When $i=3$, this loop will be iterated two times. When $i=4$, the loop will be iterated three times, and so on, until $i=n$, when this loop will be iterated $n-1$ times in moving the last value in *list* up to *list*[1]. In this case, the total number of iterations of the **until** loop in *moveup* summed over each of the $n-1$ calls to *moveup* from *insertion sort* is

$$1 + 2 + 3 + \ldots + n - 1$$

This sum has the value

$$n * (n - 1) / 2$$

or

$$n^2/2 - n/2$$

Since the form of this expression is

$$an^2 + bn + c$$

where $a = 1/2$, $b = -1/2$ and $c = 0$, we say that *insertion sort* has quadratic, or $O(n^2)$, time complexity, since the n^2 term will dominate this expression for large values of n.

We have now determined that in the best case (when all elements are already in order) *insertion sort* has $O(n)$ time complexity, while in the worst case (when the elements to be sorted are in reverse order) *insertion sort* has $O(n^2)$ time complexity. Clearly, neither of these cases is likely. What would an "average" case be? The average case is when the numbers in the list are randomly distributed, that is, they are scattered through the list with no discernable pattern. Consider the ith element, *list*[i]. If this is the largest of the first i numbers, we won't call *moveup*(i), otherwise we will. How likely is it that *list*[i] is the largest of the first i numbers? Since the numbers are randomly distributed, any of these i numbers is equally likely to be the largest, and so each one of them, including *list*[i], has probability $1/i$ of being the largest of the first i values. So, when we reach *list*[i] in *insertion sort*, the probability that moveup will *not* be called is $1/i$, and the probability that it will be called is $1 - 1/i$, which is

$$(i - 1)/i$$

Now, assuming that *moveup* is to be called for a given value of i, how many iterations through the loop of *moveup* will be made on the average? There will be at least 1, and at most $i - 1$, and so the average is $(1 + (i - 1))/2$, which is

$$i/2$$

So, if the probability that we call *moveup* for any value of i is $(i - 1)/i$, and we make $i/2$ iterations through the loop in *moveup* when it is called, then the average amount of work (based on the number of iterations in *moveup*, and hence the number of calls to *swap*) when we handle *list*[i] in *insertion sort* is

$$((i - 1)/i) * i/2,$$

which is

$$(i - 1)/2$$

Summing this for $i = 2, \ldots, n$, which are the values taken by i in the indexing loop in *insertion sort* gives

$$1/2 + 2/2 + \ldots + (n - 1)/2$$

which is equal to

$$n * (n - 1)/4$$

or

$$n^2/4 - n/4$$

The dominant term in this expression for large n is $n^2/4$, and so we have shown that the average time complexity of *insertion sort* is $O(n^2)$. So, even though the average case is better than the worst case (it is about twice as fast, since the sum of the iterations was $n^2/2 - n/2$ in the worst case), it still exhibits general n^2 behavior, which is quite bad.

In determining the average time complexity of *insertion sort* we counted just the number of iterations of the loops in procedure *insertion sort* and procedure *moveup*. We did not count individual statements executed. As we have seen in previous case studies, it is the number of loop iterations that determines the general time complexity. We leave it as an exercise to give the formula of the statement count and show that this still leads to a time complexity of $O(n^2)$.

Is there any clue to tell us in general when a program has time complexity $O(n^2)$ without requiring such detailed analysis? Yes, there is: look for *nested loops*. Notice that procedure *insertion sort* has a loop that iterates $n-1$ times, and that inside this loop is a call to a procedure that also has a loop that executes a number of times dependent on n. So, on each of the $n-1$ iterations of the external loop of *insertion sort*, the internal or nested loop of *moveup* is executed a number of times also dependent on n. This means that the total number of iterations of the nested loop of *moveup* will be $O(n^2)$.

Since this case study has a single array *list* containing n elements, the space complexity of *insertion sort* is $O(n)$.

Summary — Case Study 5.7

Sorting is a common application of computers. The insertion sort was developed here, and we showed that this sort has $O(n^2)$ time complexity and $O(n)$ space complexity.

Case Study | Sorting a List
5.8 | of Values Faster

> **Problem Description:** Sort a list of n integers into ascending order.
>
> **Input Specifications:** An integer n, followed by a list of n integers to be sorted.

In case study 5.7 we designed a program to sort a list of integers into ascending order using *insertion sort*, which has time complexity $O(n^2)$. This means, for example, that if it takes 2 seconds to sort 1000 items, then to sort 4 times as many items (4000) will take about $4^2 = 16$ times as long, or 32 seconds, and to sort 1,000,000 items will take 2,000,000 seconds, which is about 23 days. This isn't very good, and other, faster sorting methods have been developed. In this case study we examine one of these methods.

To see how this new sorting method works, we will apply it to the same problem we tackled in case study 5.7.

The Solution — Quicksort

The sorting method we will develop here is called *quicksort*. The initial procedure that calls *quicksort* will be

```
sortit : initial procedure
    {inputs a list of n integers, then prints this list in ascending order}

    storage specification
        constants
            max : integer 1000
        variables
            list : 1-D integer array [1 → max]
            n : integer
        end storage specification

    begin sortit
        input n
        if (n ≤ 0) or (n > max)
            then output 'bad input: ', n
            else read 1D integer(list, 1, n)
                 quicksort(list, 1, n)
                 write 1D integer(list, 1, n)
        endif
    end sortit

    where read 1D integer is the standard 1-D array input procedure
            of case study 5.1
    where quicksort sorts list into ascending order.
    where write 1D integer is the standard 1-D array output procedure
            of case study 5.1
```

CASE STUDY 5.8 — REFINEMENT 1

In the initial procedure, array *list* is input and then procedure *quicksort* is called to sort this list into ascending order before the list is printed. The reason for passing the actual parameters *list*, 1, and *n* to *quicksort* will become clear later.

The idea behind *quicksort* is simple. We first rearrange the list of numbers in a "quick and dirty" fashion so that the first half of the list contains the smaller values and the second half of the list contains the larger values. That is, after rearranging the list, each value in the first half of the list is less than each value in the second half of the list. At this point neither the first half nor the second half of the list is in order. But, if we do eventually get the first half of the list in order, and then independently get the second half of the list in order, the whole list will be in order.

How do we get the two halves into order? Since we can handle them separately, we now treat the first half as a brand new list and the second half as a brand new list, and then pull the same trick on each of these new lists. That is, we partition each of these new lists into halves, and put the smaller numbers in the first half and the larger numbers in the second half of each new list. This partitions our original list into fourths. If we continue this process on each separate new list created, partitioning it into two new lists with the smaller elements in front and the larger elements in the rear, we create shorter and shorter lists, until each of the lists contains only one element. At this point the entire original list is in order.

Example 5.12

Assume that the original list looks like

3
7
6
2
1
8
5
4

After partioning the list into two halves such that the top half contains the smaller numbers and the bottom half the larger numbers, the list could look like

3
4
2
1

6
8
5
7

Notice that the top half is not sorted, but it does contain the numbers 3, 4, 2, and 1, each of which is smaller than the numbers 6, 8, 5, and 7 of the bottom half. We now repeat the partitioning process on each of these halves. Partitioning

3
4
2
1

might give us

2
1

4
3

where again the smaller elements (2 and 1) are in the first half and the larger elements (4 and 3) are in the second half. Repeating this process for the list

6
8
5
7

could give us the two new lists

    5
    6

    8
    7

The entire list now looks like

    2
    1

    4
    3

    5
    6

    8
    7

with four sublists. Applying the same partitioning process to each of these two-element sublists, the first sublist

    2
    1

becomes

    1

    2

after putting the smaller element into the first half of the list and the larger element into the second half. Each new sublist contains a single element — 1 is the first new sublist and 2 is in the second. Similarly, the partitioning process changes

    4
    3

into

    3

    4

The list

    5
    6

becomes

    5

    6

and

    8
    7

becomes

7

8

Now that we have continued this process until the sublists contain only one element, we are finished. The entire list now looks like

1

2

3

4

5

6

7

8

The list is sorted!

In this example we picked a special case where our lists were always divisible by two. What happens when we get lists that are not divisible by two? This process still works. For example, if the list is

3
7
5
9
1

the partitioning process could be designed to make the following two lists:

3
1

5
9
7

From the list

3
1

we get

1

3

From

5
9
7

we could get

5

7

9

The sublist containing just 9 is finished, but we still must partition the sublist containing 5 and 7, although in this case the order does not change. We get

5

7

and the entire list now looks like

1

3

5

7

9

which is sorted.

As we have stressed before, writing down our ideas as we did in this example helps us see what we need to accomplish. We can now give the general outline of *quicksort*, which will be a recursive procedure. Given a list we partition it into two parts such that each element in the first part is less than each element in the second part. Then we apply the same process to the first part and then to the second part. That is, we quicksort the first part and then quicksort the second part. Writing this down in general terms gives

```
quicksort : procedure
    .
    .
    .
begin quicksort
    {partition the list into two parts such that every element in the first part
     is less than every element in the second part}
    {quicksort the first part}
    {quicksort the second part}
    end quicksort
```

Notice the recursive calls to *quicksort* within *quicksort*. This is exactly what we meant when we said earlier that we would "apply the same process to the two parts of the list": applying the same process in this fashion requires recursion. Read the general form of *quicksort* above. Each time *quicksort* is called, it just partitions the sublist passed to it into two parts, then quicksorts the first part, and then quicksorts the second part. Quicksorting the first part is another call to *quicksort* where *that* first part is partitioned into two parts and then *those* two parts are quicksorted and so on. We can now see why the original call to *quicksort* in the initial procedure is

```
quicksort(list, 1, n)
```

We are indicating that *list* is to be quicksorted initially between *list*[1] and *list*[*n*]. Later, as the partitioning process breaks the list into smaller parts, *quicksort* will be called with different bounds; for example

    quicksort(list, 11, 24)

would apply the same process to the sublist between *list*[11] and *list*[24].

One problem with this rough version of *quicksort* is that we have not included a termination condition. We don't want to call *quicksort* when the part of the list we are trying to quicksort has just one element in it, because there is no way (and no need) to partition just one element. Including this check gives us

```
quicksort : procedure
    ·
    ·
    ·
begin quicksort
    if {the list contains more than one element}
        then {partition the list into two parts}
            {quicksort the first part}
            {quicksort the second part}
        endif
    end quicksort
```

Although this rough draft of procedure *quicksort* captures the intent of example 5.12, you should see that it doesn't cause the sorting process to proceed in the same manner as in the example. The reason is that after the original list has been partitioned into two parts in *quicksort*, the two recursive calls

    {quicksort the first part}
    {quicksort the second part}

are encountered, so the processor will first execute

    {quicksort the first part}

This causes a recursive call to *quicksort* where the first half of the list is partitioned into two parts by the process

    {partition the list into two parts}

and then the processor encounters the two recursive calls

    {quicksort the first part}
    {quicksort the second part}

again. Again, the first of these two calls,

    {quicksort the first part}

must be processed first. In other words, the order of the recursive calls to *quicksort* causes the first part of each partition to be processed first (and the first part of *that* first part, and so on) until the first part being processed does not contain more than one element. At that time, because of the **if** statement, a return is made to the last point in the recursive calling sequence from which *quicksort* was called. Since the calls were made from the first line of

{quicksort the first part}
{quicksort the second part}

the return would signal that

{quicksort the first part}

was now complete on whatever part of the list was being processed, so now the processor would execute

{quicksort the second part}

on that part. Notice that this recursive call to *quicksort* will cause this second part to be sorted in the same fashion: this second part will be partitioned into two parts, and the first of these parts will be passed to *quicksort* before the second of these parts, and so on.

The next example shows how procedure *quicksort* would process the first list given in example 5.12. You should compare these examples carefully to understand how *quicksort* works. Even though the process is different, it has exactly the same effect; once a list (or sublist) has been partitioned into two parts, it doesn't matter whether the first or second part is processed next. Since each part is treated as a separate list, when this process is complete, the entire list is in order.

The list of example 5.12 would be processed by procedure *quicksort* as shown below, where each new column of numbers represents a new call to quicksort.

Example 5.13

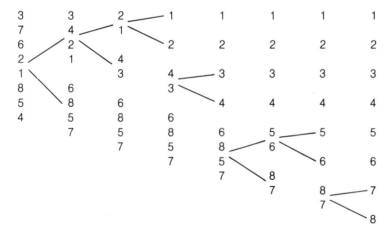

In these lists, the parts generated by

{partition the list into two parts}

are shown by the spaces between the sublists. You should apply the rough draft of *quicksort* to the first list and follow each step.

The heart of *quicksort*, as we now see, is the partitioning process, which takes a given part of a list (initially the entire list) and partitions it into two parts, with the lesser elements in the first part and the greater elements in the second part. We then apply this same partitioning procedure to these two parts by using recursive calls to *quicksort*. Partitioning the first part, as we saw in our examples, breaks it into two smaller parts, again with the smaller elements first and the larger elements last. Applying the partition procedure to the second part has the same effect, creating two smaller parts, with the smaller elements first and the larger elements last. As this process continues, the parts of the array get smaller and smaller, until they consist of only one element. At that point the entire array is sorted, because with each partition we have continuously moved the smaller elements up and the larger elements down.

Let's try to design the routine *partition*. It should work for any piece of the original list. That is, for an array a, partition is to rearrange the array between $a[low]$ and $a[high]$ into two parts, as we have described. It works like this: pick the median value from the elements between $a[low]$ and $a[high]$. The median value is the value such that half the elements between $a[low]$ and $a[high]$ are less than the median and the other half are larger than the median. Starting with $a[low]$, compare each element with the median value. When a value which is greater than or equal to the median is found, pause; this value belongs in the second part of the list. We can write this part as

```
i ← low
loop while a[i] < median
    i ← i + 1
    endloop while
```

This loop will terminate only when $a[i] \geqslant median$. When this happens, we know that the value in $a[i]$ belongs to the second part of this section of the array. We now need to find a value in the second part that is less than the median; then we will swap this value with the value in $a[i]$. That way we get the smaller value into $a[i]$ and the larger value down where it belongs. We find the smaller value by starting at $a[high]$ and working backwards towards $a[low]$ until we find a value that is less than the median. The following loop will accomplish this.

```
j ← high
loop while a[j] ≥ median
    j ← j − 1
    endloop while
```

When this loop terminates we have a value in $a[j]$ that is less than *median*. Thus,

```
swap(a[i], a[j])
```

will put the smaller value into $a[i]$ and the larger value into $a[j]$.

To continue this process until we have moved all larger elements to the lower part of this section of the list and all smaller elements to the upper part, we must continue on from where i left off, looking for the next value $a[i]$ that is larger than or equal to the median. When one is found, we resume where j left off, continuing backwards through array a until a value less than the median is found. Then we can swap $a[i]$ and $a[j]$ again. We just continue this procedure, alternately moving i forwards and j backwards, swapping $a[i]$ and $a[j]$ whenever $a[i] \geqslant median$ and $a[j] < median$ are found. When do we stop?

We stop when i and j meet ($i = j$). At that point, because of our swaps, all values between $a[low]$ and $a[i]$ are less than all values between $a[j]$ and $a[high]$. Writing this process in *mpl* gives

```
i ← low
j ← high
loop while i < j  {loop until i and j meet}

    {first move i forwards until i meets j or until a value a[i]
     larger than (or equal to) median is found}
    loop while (i < j) and (a[i] < median)
        i ← i + 1
        endloop while

    {next move j backwards until j meets i or a value a[j] less
     than the median is found}
    loop while (i < j) and (a[j] ⩾ median)
        j ← j − 1
        endloop while

    {now swap a[i] and a[j]}
    swap(a[i], a[j])
    endloop while
```

Notice that this design puts any values equal to the median in the lower part of the partition. We leave it as an exercise to include the proper loop invariant and loop goal assertions for the three loops given here.

There is still one problem to solve. How do we determine the median? That is, given a portion of an array between $a[low]$ and $a[high]$, how do we find the value (the median) such that half of the values between $a[low]$ and $a[high]$ are less than the median and half of the values are greater than or equal to the median? It could be done accurately, but it would add so much execution time to procedure *partition* that it wouldn't be worth it. Instead, we will just assume that $a[low]$, the first value in this portion of the array, is the median. In general, this will not be true, but if the array is in random order, this choice will be as good as any other. What will happen, however, is that the two parts of the list created by procedure *partition* will not in general have equal size. In the worst case we could think of, $a[low]$ might be the smallest value in this portion of the array. Then the two parts would wind up being just $a[low]$ alone as the first part and $a[low + 1]$ through $a[high]$ in the second part because there would be no values in $a[low + 1]$ through $a[high]$ less than the median ($a[low]$). A similar situation occurs if $a[low]$ turns out to be the largest element in this section of the array. Neither of these possibilities is very likely, however.

If we do choose $a[low]$ to be the median by setting

median ← a[low]

then we must change our procedure a little. We will start i at

i ← low + 1

so that we don't compare $a[low]$ with itself on the first pass through the first inner loop. Also, when i and j finally meet, we must move the median (the value in $a[low]$) to the proper position between the two parts just created. If the value in $a[i]$ when $i = j$ is greater than or equal to the median, then the value in $a[i]$ belongs with the larger elements, so we need to put the median at $a[i-1]$. We do this with the statement

    swap(a[low], a[i−1])

In this instance the median position is $i - 1$. We will assign this value to a variable named *medianposition*. Remember that by this time we know that the value in $a[i-1]$ is less than the median, otherwise i would not be advanced past this point. Similarly, if the value in $a[i]$, where i and j have met, is less than the median, this value must be included among the smaller elements. We put it there by swapping $a[i]$ with the median in $a[low]$:

    swap(a[low], a[i])

In this case the median position is i, so we will assign i to the variable *medianposition*.

After placing the median value in its proper position (determined by where i and j meet), we now have the following situation: between $a[low]$ and $a[medianposition - 1]$, all values are less than the median, which is now in $a[medianposition]$, (although they are usually not in order with respect to one another), and all the values between $a[medianposition + 1]$ and $a[high]$ are greater than or equal to the median value in $a[medianposition]$ (although, again, they are usually not in order with respect to one another). Thus, the value in $a[medianposition]$ is exactly where it belongs, and we now need to sort the part between $a[low]$ and $a[medianposition - 1]$ and then sort the part between $a[medianposition + 1]$ and $a[high]$. We do this by calling *quicksort* again twice and applying this partitioning process first to the part of the array between $a[low]$ and $a[medianposition - 1]$ and then to the part of the array between $a[medianposition + 1]$ and $a[high]$. This leads to our final version of *quicksort*:

```
quicksort : procedure
    {sorts a list of integers into ascending order}
        storage specification
            parameters
                list : in out 1-D integer array
                low, high : in only integer
            variables
                medianposition : integer
            end storage specification

    begin quicksort
        if high > low
            then partition(list, low, high, medianposition)
                quicksort(list, low, medianposition − 1)
                quicksort(list, medianposition + 1, high)
            endif
        end quicksort

    where partition divides the list such that for
                low ⩽ i ⩽ medianposition − 1,    list[i] < list[medianposition]
                i = medianposition,              list[i] = list[medianposition]
                medianposition + 1 ⩽ i ⩽ high,   list[i] ⩾ list[medianposition]
```

CASE STUDY 5.8 — REFINEMENT 2

Notice that the call to *partition* contains four parameters. The partition procedure needs to know the name (*list*) of the array it is to work on, and the low and high index positions (*low* and *high,* respectively) between which the partitioning process is to take place. In addition, after the partitioning process has taken place, *partition* must return the median position (in parameter *medianposition*) so that the recursive calls to *quicksort*

```
quicksort(list, low, medianposition − 1)
quicksort(list, medianposition + 1, high)
```

can quicksort the first and second parts of the partitioned list.

As mentioned before, we now see why the call to *quicksort* from the initial procedure was

```
quicksort(list, 1, n)
```

When *quicksort* is first applied, we want *partition* to act on the entire list between *list*[1] and *list*[*n*]. Subsequent calls to *quicksort* work on sublists.

Procedure *partition*, then, has the following form.

```
partition : procedure
    {partitions list between low and high so that it consists of
    numbers smaller than median, followed by median, followed
    by numbers greater than or equal to median; medianposition
    is set to the position of median in the array}

    storage specification
        parameters
            a : in out 1-D integer array
            low, high : in only integer
            medianposition : out only integer
        variables
            median, i, j : integer
        end storage specification

    begin partition
        median ← a[low]
        i ← low + 1
        j ← high

        loop while i < j
            loop while (i < j) and (a[i] < median)
                i ← i + 1
                endloop while
            loop while (i < j) and (a[j] ≥ median)
                j ← j − 1
                endloop while
            swap(a[i], a[j])
            endloop while

        if a[i] < median
            then medianposition ← i
            else medianposition ← i − 1
            endif
        swap(a[low], a[medianposition])

        end partition
    where swap was defined in case study 2.3

CASE STUDY 5.8 — REFINEMENT 3
```

Correctness

Performing a walkthrough of a recursive procedure can be quite complicated, even if the procedure is simple, because of the need to keep track of the recursive calls. Thus the design and testing phases become even more important. In *partition* the loop invariant assertion "*a[low+1]* through *a[i − 1]* are less than *median* and *a[j + 1]* through *a[high]* are greater than or equal to *median*" can be placed just after the outer **while** loop statement. The first inner **while** loop with index variable *i* has the loop invariant assertion "*a[low + 1]* through *a[i − 1]* are less than *median*", and the second inner **while** loop with loop index variable *j* has loop invariant assertion "*a[j + 1]* through *a[high]* are greater than or equal to *median*." We leave it to you to formulate the loop goal assertions and to show that these lead to the desired computation for procedure *partition* as stated in the comment under the procedure header statement (refinement 3). Notice also that this same result can then be stated just after the call to *partition* in procedure *quicksort*. Then after the first recursive call to *quicksort* the assertion "*list[low]* through *list[medianposition]* are sorted" can be included, and after the second recursive call to *quicksort* the assertion "*list[medianposition]* through *list[high]* are sorted" can be included. (Remember that *list[medianposition]* is in its proper position after *partition* is called.) These two assertions lead to the result assertion "*list[low]* through *list[high]* are sorted."

Example 5.14 To see how procedure *partition works,* assume that during the processing of *quicksort,* *quicksort* is called with

quicksort(list, low, medianposition − 1)

where *low* = 11 and *medianposition* = 25. This means that this call to *quicksort* is really

quicksort(list, 11, 24)

Now assume that at this point the storage cells for *list* look like

list[1]	5	**integer**
list[2]	8	**integer**
⋮	⋮	
list[10]	25	**integer**
list[11]	43	**integer**
list[12]	41	**integer**
list[13]	60	**integer**
list[14]	28	**integer**
list[15]	48	**integer**
list[16]	63	**integer**
list[17]	57	**integer**
list[18]	32	**integer**

list[19]	49	**integer**
list[20]	72	**integer**
list[21]	29	**integer**
list[22]	56	**integer**
list[23]	48	**integer**
list[24]	61	**integer**
list[25]	75	**integer**
⋮	⋮	
list[322]	562	**integer**

The array *list* has 322 elements (we have not shown all its storage cells or the other storage cells for *quicksort*).

From the way *quicksort* has been designed, there are some things we know already. The call to quicksort the first part of a given partition

quicksort(list, low, medianposition − 1)

is always made before the call to *quicksort* the second part of the partition

quicksort(list, medianposition + 1, high)

And, after the call to quicksort the first part, the next recursive call to *quicksort* handles the first part of *that* first part, and so on. Thus, since our example is calling *quicksort* for *list*[11] through *list*[24], it must be that *list*[1] through *list*[10] are already in order (see example 5.13). Also, because of the way the partitioning procedure works, none of the values from *list*[25] on are less than any of the values between *list*[10] and *list*[24]. So, if we sort the list between *list*[11] and *list*[24], these elements will be in their proper final positions.

Now let's see how the single call to *quicksort*

quicksort(list, 11, 24)

works. This call to *quicksort* sets the formal parameter *low* of *quicksort* to 11 and the formal parameter *high* to 24. The first thing that happens is that *partition* is called in

partition(list, low, high, medianposition)

Looking at procedure *partition,* we see that the formal array parameter *a* of procedure *partition* is matched with the actual array parameter *list* of *quicksort* as an **in out** parameter. Similarly, the formal parameters *low* and *high* of *partition* are passed the values 11 and 24, respectively, and the formal parameter *medianposition* of partition is matched with the actual parameter of the same name in *quicksort*. The parameter *medianposition* is of type **out only** because it does not have a value when it comes in; *partition* determines the value for *medianposition* and returns this value to *quicksort*. Before the outside **while** loop of procedure *partition* is begun, *median* is set to a[*low*] (43), the local variable *i* is set to *low* + 1 (12) and *j* is set to *high* (24). Thus, after the call to *partition* and just before the outer loop is begun, the store looks like the following one (where only the array elements 10 through 24 are shown to conserve space):

a[10]↔list[10]	25	**integer**	a[22]↔list[22]	56	**integer**
a[11]↔list[11]	43	**integer**	a[23]↔list[23]	48	**integer**
a[12]↔list[12]	41	**integer**	a[24]↔list[24]	61	**integer**
a[13]↔list[13]	60	**integer**			
a[14]↔list[14]	28	**integer**	low	11	**integer**
a[15]↔list[15]	48	**integer**	high	24	**integer**
a[16]↔list[16]	63	**integer**	medianposition → medianposition		**integer**
a[17]↔list[17]	57	**integer**	median	43	**integer**
a[18]↔list[18]	32	**integer**	i	12	**integer**
a[19]↔list[19]	49	**integer**	j	24	**integer**
a[20]↔list[20]	72	**integer**			
a[21]↔list[21]	29	**integer**			

At this point the outer loop of *partition* is begun. The first inner loop is executed, moving *i* down from its current position (12) until *i* meets *j* or until a[*i*] is larger than or equal to *median*. When *i* = 13, this loop terminates because a[13] = 60, which is greater than *median*. Then the next inner loop is begun, and *j* is moved up from its current position (24) until it takes on the same value as *i* or until a[*j*] is less than *median*. In this instance the loop quits when *j* = 21, because a[21] is less than *median*. Then a[*i*] and a[*j*] are swapped, moving the 29 to a[13] and the 60 to a[21].

After a[*i*] and a[*j*] (where *i* = 13 and *j* = 21) have been swapped, the store looks like

a[10]↔list[10]	25	integer
a[11]↔list[11]	43	integer
a[12]↔list[12]	41	integer
a[13]↔list[13]	29	integer
a[14]↔list[14]	28	integer
a[15]↔list[15]	48	integer
a[16]↔list[16]	63	integer
a[17]↔list[17]	57	integer
a[18]↔list[18]	32	integer
a[19]↔list[19]	49	integer
a[20]↔list[20]	72	integer
a[21]↔list[21]	60	integer
a[22]↔list[22]	56	integer
a[23]↔list[23]	48	integer
a[24]↔list[24]	61	integer

low	11	integer
high	24	integer
medianposition → medianposition		integer
median	43	integer
i	13	integer
j	21	integer

At this point, the processor reaches the end of the outer loop, where it checks for *i* < *j*, so the loop is attempted again. Since *i* is less than *j* the loop is iterated again. The first inner loop continues to move *i* down from 13 until *i* meets *j* or until a[*i*] is greater than or equal to *median.* This advances *i* to 15, where a[15] = 48 (which is greater than *median*). Then the next inner loop is executed, moving *j* up from 21 until *j* meets *i* or a[*j*] is less than *median.* The latter condition is satisfied when *j* = 18, since a[*j*] = 32, and so a[*i*] and a[*j*] are then swapped. After this pass through the outer loop of *partition,* the store looks like

a[10]↔list[10]	25	**integer**
a[11]↔list[11]	43	**integer**
a[12]↔list[12]	41	**integer**
a[13]↔list[13]	29	**integer**
a[14]↔list[14]	28	**integer**
a[15]↔list[15]	32	**integer**
a[16]↔list[16]	63	**integer**
a[17]↔list[17]	57	**integer**
a[18]↔list[18]	48	**integer**
a[19]↔list[19]	49	**integer**
a[20]↔list[20]	72	**integer**
a[21]↔list[21]	60	**integer**
a[22]↔list[22]	56	**integer**
a[23]↔list[23]	48	**integer**
a[24]↔list[24]	61	**integer**

low	11	**integer**
high	24	**integer**
medianposition → medianposition		**integer**
median	43	**integer**
i	15	**integer**
j	18	**integer**

Once again the outer loop is attempted, and since *i* is still less than *j*, this loop is iterated again. The first inner loop moves *i* to 16, where the loop quits because a[16] = 63, which is greater than *median* (43). Then the next inner loop is executed. This time this loop will terminate because *j* meets *i* without finding a value a[*j*] less than *median.* That is, *j* takes on the values 17 and then 16, where *j* = *i*, so this inner loop terminates because $i < j$ no longer holds. Now, since $i = j$, swapping $a[i]$ and $a[j]$ means that $a[i]$ is just swapped with itself, but this doesn't do any damage. This is the end of the outer loop; when the condition for this loop ($i < j$) is checked again it is found to be false, so the outer loop terminates.

Now procedure *partition* must place the median in $a[low]$ into its proper position, because the array indices i and j have met. The last **if** statement of procedure *partition* does this. Since $a[i]$ is not less than *median*, the **else** clause is executed, setting *medianposition* to $i - 1$. This just means that the median belongs just above the ith position ($a[i] = 63$, which is greater than *median*, so $a[i]$ belongs below the median). After the **if** statement has been executed, $a[low]$, the median, is swapped with $a[medianposition]$, putting the median, 43, in its proper position. Thus, at the completion of the partition procedure the store looks like

a[10]↔list[10]	25	**integer**
a[11]↔list[11]	32	**integer**
a[12]↔list[12]	41	**integer**
a[13]↔list[13]	29	**integer**
a[14]↔list[14]	28	**integer**
a[15]↔list[15]	43	**integer**
a[16]↔list[16]	63	**integer**
a[17]↔list[17]	57	**integer**
a[18]↔list[18]	48	**integer**
a[19]↔list[19]	49	**integer**
a[20]↔list[20]	72	**integer**
a[21]↔list[21]	60	**integer**
a[22]↔list[22]	56	**integer**
a[23]↔list[23]	48	**integer**
a[24]↔list[24]	61	**integer**

low	11	**integer**
high	24	**integer**
medianposition → medianposition	15	**integer**
median	43	**integer**
i	16	**integer**
j	16	**integer**

In this case *partition* has separated the array between a[11] and a[24] into two parts such that a[11] through a[14] are less than the median (43) and a[16] through a[24] are greater than or equal to the median, which is at a[15]. Because our choice of a[*low*] as the median was not perfect, the first part (between a[11] and a[14]) contains only four elements whereas the second part (between a[16] and a[24]) contains nine elements. That is, the partitioning process did not give us two partitions of equal size. This, however, doesn't matter for the success of the quicksort process.

Since procedure *partition* has terminated, control is returned to procedure *quicksort* with *medianposition* having value 15. After calling *partition,* procedure *quicksort* makes the two recursive calls

```
quicksort(list, low, medianposition − 1)
quicksort(list, medianposition + 1, high)
```

which are now the same as

```
quicksort(list, 11, 14)
quicksort(list, 16, 24)
```

This causes the partition procedure to be applied to the array *list* between *list*[11] and *list*[14] (which, in turn, causes other recursive calls to *quicksort,* as shown in example 5.13), and then to the array *list* between *list*[16] and *list*[24] (which causes more recursive calls to *quicksort*). Since *list*[15] is already in order with respect to these two parts, it no longer needs to be handled. Also, remember that all of the elements between *list*[11] and *list*[24] are in their proper positions, relatively speaking, with respect to the elements in *list*[1] through *list*[10] and the elements in *list*[25] through *list*[322], as the result of previous applications of the partition procedure. Thus, continuing to apply *partition* to smaller and smaller parts, moving the smaller elements in each partition up and the larger down, will leave them in order with respect to all preceding and all succeeding elements. After all the partitions of length 1 have been processed, then, the entire array will be in order.

Efficiency

To determine the time complexity for *quicksort,* let's see how fast *quicksort* runs in the best case. The best case occurs when the choice of the median is the true median; given the true median, partition will divide the list (or sublist) into two parts of the same size each time *quicksort* is called. How long can this process continue of dividing the entire list in half, then dividing each of these halves into halves (making them a quarter of the size of the original list), then dividing these quarters into halves (making eighths of the original sublist), and so on, until each sublist contains only one element? To rephrase this question, if the original list is n elements long, how many times can we divide by 2, starting with dividing n by 2 and then repeatedly dividing the quotient by 2, until the quotient finally is 1? Some readers will recognize that the number of times this can be done is given by the function $\log_2 n$.

Dividing the list into successive halves as described is illustrated by figure 5–1. The line on the far left represents the original list. The line just to the right shows the original list divided into halves. The next line to the right represents the original list divided into quarters. This process continues until the original list has been partitioned into sublists of one element each. From the discussion in the previous paragraph, we know that there would be $\log_2 n$ lines in this illustration if all lines were shown.

Now we must ask the question, how long does it take the quicksort procedure to generate these successive lists? To answer this question, just recall how *quicksort* works. To divide a sublist into halves, procedure *partition* works on the current sublist, moving the smaller elements to the top half and the larger elements to the bottom half. This is done by moving *i* down from the top of the sublist one element at a time and moving *j* up from the bottom of the sublist one element at a time until *i* and *j* meet. That is, each element of the sublist being partitioned is examined just once. Looking again at our illustration, we see that when partition works on the original list it must examine all *n* elements as *i* moves down from the top and *j* moves up from the bottom. The result of this pass of partition is represented in the second line; the smaller elements are in the top half and the larger elements are in the bottom half of the list rearranged by *partition*. Now the top half of the list is quicksorted and the bottom half is quicksorted. This means that the partition procedure will be applied to the top half of the list and then to the bottom half of the list. (Remember from example 5.13 that the bottom half actually will not be examined until the top half has been completely sorted, because of the way the recursive calls are generated. This does not matter in this discussion, however, because the bottom half will have to be examined sometime, and figure 5–1 is a good illustration of how the list elements are examined — not how the recursive calls are made.) In working on the top half of the list, *partition* will examine each of the *n*/2 elements there once, and in working on the bottom half of the list *partition* will examine each of the *n*/2 elements there once. Thus all *n* elements are examined again (this is not quite true, because as we have written *quicksort*, the median element of the previous partition is never examined again; however, we will neglect this minor detail in our analysis).

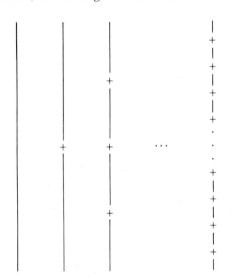

FIGURE 5–1. THE LOG$_2$$n$ SUCCESSIVE LIST ORGANIZATIONS WHEN QUICKSORTING A LIST

This process continues. When both parts of the list in the second line of our illustration are partitioned, the original list is in four equal parts with the first fourth containing the smallest elements, the second fourth containing the next smallest elements, and the third fourth containing the next smallest, and

the last fourth containing the largest elements. Each of these fourths is quick-sorted, that is, each of these fourths is handled by procedure *partition*. In each case the $n/4$ elements in the part being partitioned are examined once as i moves down from the top of the fourth and j moves up from the bottom of that fourth. So, considering that *partition* will be applied separately to each fourth, we see that all n elements will be examined once again. This gives us a new list divided into eighths, and the analysis continues until there is only one element in each sublist.

This analysis tells us that for each line in figure 5–1, all n elements will be examined once. Since there are $\log_2 n$ lines, the total number of examinations is $n*\log_2 n$. Thus, the time complexity of *quicksort* is $O(n*\log_2 n)$.

It might appear that the amount of time that we are spending on designing and looking at the complexities of our sorting algorithms is not worthwhile. However, as we have previously noted, it has been estimated that about 23% of all computing is spent sorting, mainly by businesses, which often need to keep large sorted files. Given this huge financial investment in sorting, it is essential that it be done efficiently.

The time complexity for *quicksort* was determined for the best case — we assumed that the list would always be partitioned into two equal parts on each call to *quicksort*. What happens in the average case? Studies have shown that the time complexity is still $O(n*\log_2 n)$. Of course, the constant multiplier for the actual time complexity will be larger in the average case. The worst case for *quicksort* will occur, ironically, when the list is already in order when it is passed to *quicksort*. In this case partition will break each sublist passed to it into two parts with the first part containing just one element and the second part containing the remaining elements. This leads to a time complexity of $O(n^2)$; calculation of this time complexity is left as an exercise.

Just how does *quicksort* with its $O(n*\log_2 n)$ time complexity compare with *insertion sort*, which has $O(n^2)$ time complexity? For large n, *quicksort* is clearly much better. To see this, just plot the values of $n*\log_2 n$ and n^2 on the same graph for increasingly larger values of n. For example, if $n = 1,000,000$, $n^2 = 1,000,000,000,000$, whereas $n*\log_2 n$ is only about 20,000,000, a remarkable difference.

Insertion sort does, however, have certain advantages over *quicksort*. Although it is beyond the scope of this book, it can be determined that for small lists of 11 or fewer elements *insertion sort* is faster than *quicksort*. How can this be? Don't forget that the $O(n^2)$ time complexity for *insertion sort* and the $O(n*\log_2 n)$ time complexity for *quicksort* just represent the orders, or relative growth rates, in the execution time for these two procedures. The actual times are closer to k_1*n^2 for *insertion sort* and $k_2*n*\log_2 n$ for *quicksort*, where k_1 and k_2 are constants determined by the number of statements that must be executed in these procedures. It turns out that $k_1 < k_2$ for two efficiently written versions of *insertion sort* and *quicksort*, and the difference between the two constants is enough to make *insertion sort* better than *quicksort* for average cases with lists smaller than 12 elements. As a result, the *quicksort* and *insertion sort* procedures are often combined. When *quicksort* is called for a sublist of 11 elements or fewer, instead of calling *partition* to split this list in half and then recursively quicksorting both halves, *insertion sort* is called. The resulting procedure is known as *quickersort*. We leave it as an exercise to modify and combine *quicksort* and *insertion sort* to produce *quickersort*.

To determine the space complexity of *quicksort* notice that in the worst case *quicksort* will be called recursively n times before a return from *quicksort* is encountered, and in the best case $\log_2 n$ times. Each time three cells will be required for the **in only** parameters *low* and *high* and the local variable *medianposition*. The array *list* is an **in out** parameter and thus requires just n cells. Therefore, in the worst case $n + 3 * n = 4 * n$ and in the best case $n + 3*\log_2 n$ cells will be required, so *quicksort*, like *insertion sort* (which uses $n + 4$ cells), has $O(n)$ space complexity.

Summary — Case Study 5.8

Procedure *quicksort* has been developed and shown to be much faster than *insertion sort* for large lists, and nearly as space efficient. Thus *quicksort* is the choice for sorting large lists.

5.5 WORKING OUT

5.24 In designing a program to search a list, when should sequential search be chosen instead of binary search?

5.25 Considering the time complexities of the sequential search, binary search, and quicksort routines, are there any conditions which would make it feasible to quicksort an unordered list in order to use the binary search on that list rather than the sequential search?

5.26 Do a statement count for the best case, average case, and worst case of *insertion sort*.

5.27 Redesign *insertion sort* so that it sorts the array a with subscript bounds between 0 and n rather than 1 and n, assuming that you can assign to $a[0]$ the smallest possible integer allowed on your computer. Does this make your program easier or more difficult?

5.28 An outlook test has been developed to determine whether a group of people has a generally optimistic, pessimistic, or neutral outlook on the economy. The integer test scores range from -10 to $+10$ with -10 being very pessimistic, $+10$ being very optimistic, and 0 being neutral. Design a program which inputs a series of test scores between -10 and $+10$ by the **moredata** method, keeping track of how many of each score there are. Then print this tabulation. Also, print the "outlook index" for the group as the sum of all the test scores, and print the score which occurred most often, the score which occurred least often, and the average score.

5.29 Design a procedure with nested loops to sort an integer array a where the outer loop satisfies the loop invariant assertion

assert $a[i-1]$ is the i-1st smallest element in a

and the inner loop satisfies the loop invariant assertion

assert $a[i]$ is the smallest element among $a[i]$ through $a[j-1]$

where i lies between 1 and n and j lies between $i+1$ and n. What are the best, worst, and average case time complexities of your program? Is this program better or worse than *insertion sort*? Explain your answer.

5.30   Would procedure *quicksort* work if the formal parameters *low* and *high* were changed from **in only** to **in out?** Explain.

5.31   The order of the recursive calls to *quicksort* is

quicksort(list, low, medianposition − 1)
quicksort(list, medianposition + 1, high)

If this order were reversed, would *quicksort* still work? Explain.

5.32   Make procedure *read lists* of refinement 2 of case study 5.6 robust as described there.

5.33   Design a *quickersort* procedure in *mpl* as described in the efficiency section of case study 5.8.

5.34   Prove that if *quicksort* is called on an array that is already in ascending sorted order, the time complexity is $O(n^2)$. What happens if the array is already sorted in descending order when *quicksort* is called?

5.35   If a large list is almost sorted, explain why *insertion sort* could be faster than *quicksort*. How could one define "almost sorted"? Write a **truth value** function which determines whether or not an array is almost sorted (using your definition), and discuss whether or not it should be used in a sorting program.

5.36   Design an *mpl* function *select(intlist, i, n)*, which returns the *i*th largest element of an integer array with *n* elements. Give the time and space complexities for your function.

5.37   Discuss possible strategies for finding the median value of an array of integers. Give the time and space complexities of each strategy discussed, and design an *mpl* program for the best strategy. (The median value is the value such that half the elements in the array are less than this value and the other half are greater than or equal to this value.)

5.38   Choose one of the functions and procedures that you have designed in these exercises and prove that it is correct.

5.39   The following two functions each find the maximum value in an integer array

```
maximum : integer function

    storage specification
        parameters
            a : in out integer array
            n : in only integer
        variables
            max, i : integer
        end storage specification

    begin maximum
        max := a[1]
        loop start i with 2 step 1 to n
            if a[i] > max
                then max ← a[i]
                endif
            endloop autoindex
        maximum ← max
        end maximum
```

maximum : **integer function**

storage specification
    parameters
        a : **in out integer array**
        n : **in only integer**
    end storage specification

begin maximum
    quicksort(a, 1, n)
    maximum ← a[n]
    end maximum

Assuming that *quicksort* is easily available, which of the two functions would you select to use? Why?

| CHAPTER 6 |

Character Data

NEW CONCEPTS: String variables, Character variables, Concatenation

Until now, all of our case studies have involved numbers (integers or reals). However, much of the data handled by real computers is alphabetic or *character* data. Every large business keeps computer files of personnel information such as names, addresses, and phone numbers. Universities keep similar files for students. Service companies keep files for their customers for monthly billings. And, of course, junk mail distributors maintain computerized mailing lists. Except for alphabetical sorting, character data does not require much manipulation; in most cases the information is simply read in and printed out.

An example of a more involved application is *word processing*. Word processing programs automatically arrange typed words into balanced lines, paragraphs, and pages. The pages can be numbered and tables of contents and indexes can be generated automatically. These programs are used with high quality printers for typing letters, manuscripts, and books; the manuscript for this book was prepared using a word processing program. The advantages are obvious. For example, if a new paragraph is inserted into a document, the document can be reprocessed by the program within seconds; the pages will all be renumbered properly, and a new, accurate table of contents and index will be generated.

The case studies of this chapter introduce character manipulation.

<table>
<tr><td>

6.1
GETTING
ACQUAINTED

</td><td>

In this section we will study simple character manipulation programs.

</td></tr>
<tr><td>

Case Study
6.1

</td><td>

Input and Output of Strings

</td></tr>
</table>

> *Problem Description:* Input and print a list of names.
>
> *Input Specifications:* A list of names.

The first case study of this section is simple. We wish to demonstrate that the string data type is no more difficult to master than the numerical data types we have used up to this point. Our first problem deals with input and output — how strings are read in and printed out.

Just as in case study 4.1, there are three possible ways to read in the list of names: the header method, the **moredata** method, and the trailer method. We will use the header method here.

The Solution — String Variables

To input character string data we will need a new variable type, which we will simply call type **string** in *mpl*.

**Example
6.1**

The **variables** statement

    variables
        phrase, name : **string**

causes the store to look like

phrase		**string**
name		**string**
	⋮	

After the assignments

    phase ← 'dog days'
    name ← 'J. D. Starkey'

the store looks like

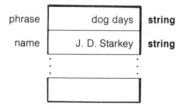

phrase	dog days	**string**
name	J. D. Starkey	**string**
	⋮	

Of course, since the storage cells of real computers have a fixed size, a single cell cannot hold arbitrarily long strings. However, we need not concern ourselves with this fact as we design programs in *mpl*.

To input strings, we simply list the desired **string** variables behind the **input** keyword just as we do with **integer** and **real** variables. For example, executing the statement

    input name, phrase

with the two strings

    'Mother Goose'
    'foggybottom'

at the input device, would give us the store

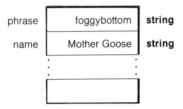

In all of these examples, single quotation marks (apostrophes) are required around the strings. These single quotes are not saved in the storage cells as part of the strings — they are used to *delimit* the strings (show where the strings start and stop). If an apostrophe is actually to be included as part of a string, it is indicated by two single quotes. For instance, the assignment

    phrase ← 'I don''t care'

would cause the store to look like

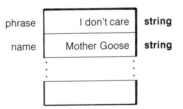

The processor recognizes that the string begins where the first quote mark is encountered. The end of the string is indicated by the next quotation mark not immediately followed by a second quotation mark. In between, two single quotes together indicate that one quotation mark is to be left in the string.

Following this example, we can assume that the input for our case study will have the form

    3
    'JONES, SAMANTHA M.'
    'O''MALLEY, CRUSTO C.'
    'GUMMIKOPF, GORSKI I.'

where the header value 3 tells how many names are in the input. The initial procedure, then, will be

```
names : initial procedure
    {reads and writes n names}

    storage specification
        variables
            n : integer
        end storage specification

    begin names
        input n
        if n > 0
            then readwrite names(n)
            else output 'bad data, n = ', n
        endif
    end names

    where readwrite names inputs and prints n names

CASE STUDY 6.1 — REFINEMENT 1
```

Notice the expression

'bad data, n = '

in the **output** statement. This is actually a string constant; we have been using such strings in our **output** statements since our earliest case studies.

The procedure *readwrite names* can now be written:

```
readwrite names : procedure
    {reads and prints n names}

    storage specification
        parameters
            n : in only integer
        variables
            name : string
        end storage specification

    begin readwrite names
        loop start i with 1 step 1 to n
            input name
            output name
        endloop autoindex
    end readwrite names

CASE STUDY 6.1 — REFINEMENT 2
```

Notice how simple this procedure is. Except for the declaration of *name* as type **string,** there is nothing to distinguish this procedure from similar ones we have designed involving numbers. We are now so familiar with this simple input/output loop, in fact, that we will omit the loop invariant and loop goal assertions.

Alternate Solution — Character Variables and Concatenation with the Header Method

There are a few drawbacks to the previous solution for reading and writing names. The first is that we must type single quotes around the strings to be input. In reality, character strings are seldom typed into the input with quotes delimiting each string. A more typical method of inputting names, for example, might require that the names be typed in the first 20 columns of each line, beginning in column 1, without surrounding quotation marks. With this method, the statement

    input name

where name is a **string** variable, cannot be used, because the processor cannot determine where to start and stop reading characters from the input into *name*. If quotation marks are not used to delimit input strings, a different input method must be developed.

Another drawback to using string variables for inputting character data is that delimiting the input strings with quotes is sometimes impractical. For example, the word processing program that formatted this book did not require us to put quotes around every word or every sentence as we typed the text. Clearly, this would have been an impractical and tedious process.

To solve these problems we need a way to read in character strings one character at a time. This requires introduction of *character variables*. If a variable is declared to be of type **character,** it can hold just a single character.

Assume that we have the following declaration:

    variables
      x : **integer**
      a, b, c : **character**

Example 6.2

Then we can make assignments like

    a ← '*'
    b ← 'b'
    c ← ' '

which assigns an asterisk to variable *a,* the letter "b" to variable *b,* and the blank to variable *c.* Notice that we still need the quote marks around the characters on the right side of ←. This is required in assignment statements, otherwise a statement like

    a ← c

would be ambiguous. Would this mean "assign the letter 'c' to the variable *a*" or "assign the contents of the variable *c* to the variable *a*"? Assigning a character to a character variable in an assignment statement thus requires the use of quotes.

When reading in characters with the **input** statement, however no quotes are required around the characters in the input. If the input contains

    −30 2ab

and the statement

    input x, a, b, c

is executed, the value in x will be -30, a will contain the character blank, b the character 2, and c the letter "a". This happens as follows: Since x is of type **integer,** the processor scans past all blanks in the input line until the first nonblank symbol is found (the "$-$"). The processor then assumes that between the "$-$" and the next blank symbol there is a number (if there isn't a number here, an error occurs), so the -30 is input into x. At this point the input pointer is at the blank between 0 and 2; the input pointer points to the character position following the last item input so that the next input operation can take up from that point. Since a is of type **character,** the character pointed to by the input pointer (the blank) is placed into a, then the input pointer is moved to the right one space to point to the 2. Thus, the character 2 is stored into the variable b and the pointer is moved again. Finally, the letter "a" is stored into the variable c and the pointer is moved to the right one more time. After this **input** statement has been executed, the input pointer is left pointing at the "b". The 2 in this example is treated as a character rather than a number, since it was input into a character variable.

If we are going to use character variables to input strings character by character, we need a mechanism to join characters and strings together to form larger strings. This operation is called *concatenation* (*catena* is the Latin word for *chain*) and is denoted by $\|$. For example,

'ab' $\|$ 'def'

is equal to

'abdef'

To build up strings a character at a time, we neeed to start with a special string called the *null string*. The null string is the string that contains no characters at all, not even a blank.

Example 6.3   If fuzz has been declared to be of type **string,** the assignment

fuzz $\leftarrow$ ''

assigns the null string to *fuzz*; there is nothing in between the two quote marks. Notice that this is *not* the same as

fuzz $\leftarrow$ ' '

which assigns a single blank character to *fuzz* or

fuzz $\leftarrow$ ''''

which assigns a single quote mark to *fuzz*.

Just as 0 is the identity for addition ($a + 0 = 0 + a = a$), the null string is the identity for concatenation (*fuzz* $\|$ '' = '' $\|$ *fuzz* = *fuzz*), because attaching the null string to either end of a string does not change the string.

The null string is the string of length 0 (in contrast, the string containing a single blank has length 1). This means, among other things, that the null string cannot be assigned to a variable of type **character,** since all character variables must be assigned a single character.

We can use the null string and concatenation to build up a string from the input one character at a time.

Assume that the input pointer is pointing to the first character of a word and the word is *Example* followed by a blank. You should convince yourself that the following segment will input *6.4* the word into the variable called *word,* assuming that *word* has type **string** and variable *ch* has type **character:**

```
word ← ''
input ch
loop while ch ≠ ''
    word ← word || ch
    input ch
    endloop while
```

To try this segment, suppose the input is

the quick brown fox

with the input pointer currently pointing to the "t" of the. When the loop is entered, *word* will contain the null string and *ch* will contain the first letter, "t". Within the loop, execution of the statements

```
word ← word || ch
input ch
```

will leave *word* containing "t" and *ch* containing "h". The next iteration of the loop will assign "th" to *word* and "e" to *ch.* The third loop iteration will assign "the" to *word* and " " to *ch,* which will cause termination of the loop.

Concatenation and character variables can be used to solve the version of this case study where each input name appears in the first 20 positions of a single line, without delimiting quote marks. In this case the initial procedure will be

```
names : initial procedure
    {inputs and prints n names}
    storage specification
        constants
            namelength : integer 20
        variables
            n : integer
        end storage specification
    begin names
        input n
        if n > 0
            then readwrite names(n, namelength)
            else output 'bad data, n = ', n
            endif
        end names
    where readwrite names inputs and prints n names
```

CASE STUDY 6.1 — REFINEMENT 3

In this version the actual parameter constant *namelength* must be passed to *readwrite names* to tell how many characters (in this case, 20) there are in each name. Procedure *readwrite names* is very similar to its form in refinement 2.

The major difference is that in place of the statement

   input name

the procedure call

   read string(name, namelength)

appears. Procedure *read string* reads in *namelength* characters, concatenating them to form *name*.

---

readwrite names : **procedure**
   {reads and prints n names}

   storage specification
     parameters
       n, namelength : **in only integer**
     variables
       name : **string**
       i : **integer**
     end storage specification

   begin readwrite names
     loop start i **with** 1 **step** 1 **to** n
       read string(name, namelength)
       output name
       endloop autoindex
     end readwrite names

   where read string inputs namelength characters, forming name

CASE STUDY 6.1 — REFINEMENT 4

Procedure *read string* contains a simple concatenation loop:

---

read string : **procedure**
   {inputs and concatenates n characters, returning the result in x}

   storage specification
     parameters
       x : **out only string**
       n : **in only integer**
     variables
       nextchar : **character**
       i : **integer**
     end storage specification

   begin read string
     x ← ''
     loop start i **with** 1 **step** 1 **to** n
       assert x is the concatenation of the previous i−1 input characters
       input nextchar
       x ← x ‖ nextchar
       endloop autoindex
     assert x is the concatenation of the previous n input characters
     end read string

CASE STUDY 6.1 — REFINEMENT 5

Alternate Solution — The Moredata Method

These two solutions (refinements 1 and 2 and refinements 3, 4, and 5) will work equally well using the **moredata** loop. Procedure *readwrite names* of refinement 2 would have no parameters and would consist of the loop

```
loop while moredata
    input name
    output name
    endloop while
```

In refinement 4 the loop would be

```
loop while moredata
        read string(name, namelength)
    output name
    endloop while
```

The initial procedure calling these two versions of *readwrite names* would need to be changed accordingly (*n* is not passed as a parameter).

Alternate Solution — The Trailer Method

The trailer value solution to reading in an unspecified number of names can also be applied to reading in strings. In this method the loop of refinement 2 could be replaced with

```
input name
loop while name ≠ '*'
    output name
    input name
    endloop while
```

Certainly, no name will be *, so if the last input line is just set to be a *, it can be used as the unique trailer value to signal the end of the data.

The loop of refinement 4 would be replaced similarly with

```
read string(name, namelength)
loop while name ≠ '*'
    output name
    read string(name, namelength)
    endloop while
```

Again, we would have to make other changes to make these procedures work properly in their respective programs. String comparisons like the one in the **while** condition

```
name ≠ '*'
```

are discussed in the In Retrospect section. In this case, the comparison will work properly as expected.

Correctness

The guidelines for verifying and testing program correctness apply to programs dealing with character strings. Programs using string data should be tested with special values, including the empty string. You should do a program walkthrough of both versions of this case study to convince yourself that they work. Also insert the proper assertions and show their correctness.

Efficiency

In the versions of procedure *readwrite names* that input a name as a single string, there is a single loop running from 1 to *n*, where *n* is the number of names in the input, so the procedure has linear time complexity. Since this is the only loop in the program, the entire program has linear time complexity.

In the versions of procedure *readwrite names* that use character input and concatenation, within the loop that runs from 1 to *n* (where *n* is the number of names in the input) there is a call to procedure *read string*, which also contains a loop. However, this loop runs from 1 to *stringlength* every time, where *stringlength* is a constant (20) that doesn't depend on the input. Thus *readwrite names* is linear, too. In fact, these two versions of *readwrite names* will have a negligible difference in execution time on a real computer, because when the statement

> **input** name

is executed (where *name* is a string variable), the processor still must read in *name* one character at a time even though the programmer does not specify this explicitly.

The space complexity of this program is constant since there are no arrays and no recursive procedure calls. However, strings of arbitrary length cannot be stored in a single cell in a real computer. Instead, strings must be spread out over a number of cells; typically there will be only 2 to 4 characters per cell. But even if each string takes up 10 cells, there are still only a constant number of cells required, since there are a constant number of strings declared in the **variables** statements.

One result of the way real computers must handle strings, spreading them out over a number of cells, is that the execution time for programs dealing with strings is higher than it is for similar programs handling only numbers. You do not need to know any of the details of how strings are actually handled internally by the processor, but you should be aware that programs involving strings will require more execution time than you might expect based on program structure and previous experience with similar programs dealing only with numbers.

Summary — Case Study 6.1

Strings are as easy to handle as numbers. The only added complexity is that strings must usually be input one character at a time, building up the input string using concatenation. Because of the way strings are stored on a real computer (the individual characters of the strings are spread over a number of cells), the storage requirements are greater than those of similar programs involving numbers. Also, since operations on strings require the processor to work on the strings one character at a time (even if the programmer doesn't specify these actions explicitly), more time is required to execute these programs than to execute similar programs involving numbers. The longer the strings are, the more noticeable the effect will be.

Counting Vowels

> **Problem Description:** Given an arbitrary text, count the number of occurrences of each vowel and compute the percentage of letters that are vowels.
>
> **Input Specifications:** An arbitrary text.

In the last case study we introduced two new variable types, **string** and **character.** In this case study we look at a simple problem requiring the use of character variables.

Although this problem is not typical of business or scientific applications, it is typical of many applications that a computer scientist might encounter. Word processing programs, for example, require that a text be input one character at a time as the text is reformatted into a pleasing form. This case study shows how a text can be processed one character at a time.

The Solution — Character Variables and the Case Statement

The form of the initial procedure for this case study should be clear. It should call a procedure that inputs the text one character at a time, keeping track of the total number of letters input as well as the number of occurrences of each vowel. Upon return to the initial procedure, the number of occurrences of each vowel can be printed, and the percentage of vowels in the text can be computed as the ratio of the total number of vowels to the number of letters.

---

vowel analysis : **initial procedure**
    {computes the number of occurrences of each vowel in a given
     text and the percentage of vowels in the text}

    storage specification
      variables
        letters, vowels, a, e, i, o, u, y : **integer**
      end storage specification

    begin vowel analysis
      count vowels(letters, a, e, i, o, u, y)
      output 'The vowel count is: '
      output 'a: ', a, 'e: ', e, 'i: ', i, 'o: ', o,
         'u: ', u, 'y: ', y
      vowels ← a + e + i + o + u + y
      output 'the percentage of vowels is ', vowels/letters * 100, '%'
      end vowel analysis

    where count vowels counts the number of letters and the number
         of occurrences of each vowel appearing in a text

CASE STUDY 6.2 — REFINEMENT 1

In the initial procedure we have chosen the variable name *a* to stand for the count of the letter "a" found in the input text, and similar variables represent the remaining vowels, "e", "i", "o", "u", and "y". These variables are of type **integer,** because they are counters.

We now design procedure *count vowels*. This procedure must contain a loop that on each iteration reads in a single new character from the input, counts it to keep track of the total number of characters input, and then checks to see whether the character is a vowel, adding one to the proper counter if it is. The only trick is this: in returning the total number of letters so that we can compute the percentage of vowels in the initial procedure, we certainly don't want to include the blanks and punctuation occurring in the input in the count of letters. This can be taken care of with an **if** statement that checks each character to see if it is a letter.

```
count vowels : procedure
    {counts the number of letters and the number of occurrences
    of each vowel in a given text}
    storage specification
        parameters
            letters, a, e, i, o, u, y : out only integer
        variables
            next : character
        end storage specification
    begin count vowels
        letters, a, e, i, o, u, y ← 0
        loop while moredata
            input next
            if (('a' ≤ next) and (next ≤ 'z'))
                or (('A' ≤ next) and (next ≤ 'Z'))
                then letters ← letters + 1
                    case next is
                        when 'A', 'a' : a ← a + 1
                        when 'E', 'e' : e ← e + 1
                        when 'I', 'i'  : i ← i + 1
                        when 'O', 'o' : o ← o + 1
                        when 'U', 'u' : u ← u + 1
                        when 'Y', 'y' : y ← y + 1
                        otherwise : {do nothing}
                    endcase
            endif
        endloop while
    end count vowels
```

CASE STUDY 6.2 — REFINEMENT 2

There are a few new twists to the way procedure *count vowels* is written. The first is the shorthand notation for initializing a number of variables to the same value as we did in

letters, a, e, i, o, u, y ← 0

It is clear that we wish to set each of the variables on the left of ← to 0, and this method is perfectly acceptable when using *mpl* to design a program. There are even a few real programming languages that allow this or similar shorthands.

Notice, too, that the labels of the **case** statement are single letters enclosed in quotation marks. This is because variable *next*, the case statement variable, is of type **character**, and so the case clause labels must be character constants. A character constant is just a single character delimited by quotation marks.

The **if** statement of procedure *count vowels* is

if (('a' ⩽ next) **and** (next ⩽ 'z'))
    or (('A' ⩽ next) **and** (next ⩽ 'Z'))

indicating that if the character *next* lies between a and z inclusive, or between A and Z inclusive, then it must be a letter. This check very much depends on how the various computer manufacturers decide to represent characters in their machines. This check will work for most computers and most input texts.

Correctness

We leave it as an exercise to design and include a loop invariant assertion in this program. In testing this program, a number of special cases come to mind: no input (empty text), text that contains no vowels, and text that contains only vowels. If the text is empty or contains only special characters (no letters), an error will occur in the initial procedure. We leave it as an exercise to uncover and correct this error.

Efficiency

The time complexity of this program is easy to determine. Each character of the text is input and handled once. Counting the statements executed in procedure *count vowels*, we see that there are seven statements executed outside the loop (we count the shorthand notation for zero initialization as seven separate statements), but we might at first be puzzled as to how to count the statements inside the loop because of the **case** statement. Actually, there are always just two statements executed within the **case** statement each time through the loop — the **case** line itself and the statement with the proper label (or the **otherwise** clause). Thus, within the loop there are seven statements executed each time (assuming that the **then** clause is executed on every iteration), so if there are *n* characters in the text, the number of statements executed is

$$7^*n + 8$$

(counting the extra loop check). Clearly, this procedure (and hence the entire program) has linear time complexity. Since there are no arrays and no recursive calls, the space complexity is constant.

Summary — Case Study 6.2

An example using a character variable was studied. Whenever a program is to read in and process an arbitrary text, the individual characters of the text will have to be input and processed separately. The time complexity of such programs is generally linear in the number of characters in the input.

Reading and Printing a List of Names

Case Study 6.3

> *Problem Description:* Input a list of names and print the list first in the order in which it was input and then in reverse order.
>
> *Input Specification:* A list of names.

Just as we did with numbers we must sometimes maintain a list of strings in the store in order to perform certain manipulations (e.g., sorting). We can maintain such lists by declaring a variable to be a string array.

Example 6.5

The declaration

name : **1-D string array** [1 → 1000]

declares an array of 1000 elements, each of which can contain a string. In this case we could make such assignments as

name[5] ← 'GUMMIKOPF, GORSKI I.'

As we recall from case studies 4.1, 5.1, and 6.1, there are three methods for reading in an indeterminate number of values: the header method, the trailer method, and the **moredata** method. We have seen many instances of each of these methods, so we will use only the **moredata** method here and leave the others as exercises.

The Solution — String Arrays

The initial procedure for this case study is trivial. It is

```
name list : initial procedure
    {prints a list of names forwards and backwards}
    storage specification
        constants
            max : integer 1000
        variables
            name : 1-D string array [1 → max]
            n : integer
        end storage specification
    begin name list
        read 1D string(name, max, n)
        if n ≤ max
            then write 1D string(name, 1, n)
                write 1D string reverse(name, 1, n)
            else output 'n is too large: ', n
        endif
    end name list

    where read 1D string inputs an array of strings
    where write 1D string outputs an array of strings
    where write 1D string reverse outputs an array of strings
        in reverse order
```

CASE STUDY 6.3 — REFINEMENT 1

Procedures *read 1D string*, *write 1D string*, and *write 1D string reverse* will be nearly identical to their counterparts for integer arrays in case study 5.1. One major consideration in *read 1D string* depends on whether the names in the input are delimited by quote marks. In this solution we will assume that they are, so this gives us the following version of *read 1D string*:

```
read 1D string : procedure
    {inputs a list of strings each delimited by quote marks}
    storage specification
        parameters
            a : out only 1-D string array
            max : in only integer
            n : out only integer
        variables
            i : integer
        end storage specification
    begin read 1D string
        i ← 0
        loop while moredata and i < max
            i ← i + 1
            input a[i]
            endloop while
        if moredata
            then n ← max + 1
            else n ← i
            endif
        end read 1D string
```

CASE STUDY 6.3 — REFINEMENT 2

Procedure *write 1D string* is the same as *write 1D integer* of case study 5.1, except that *a* must be declared

    a : **in out 1-D string array**

giving

```
write 1D string : procedure
    {prints a list of strings}
    storage specification
        parameters
            a : in out 1-D string array
            low, high : in only integer
        variables
            i : integer
        end storage specification
    begin write 1D string
        loop start i with low step 1 to high
            output a[i]
            endloop autoindex
        end write 1D string
```

CASE STUDY 6.3 — REFINEMENT 3

The only difference between procedures *write 1D string* and *write 1D string reverse* is that in the latter procedure the loop statement must be

       loop start i **with** high **step** -1 **to** low

so we will not write out the entire procedure here.

Alternate Solution — Character Variables and Concatenation

As we discussed in the first case study of this chapter, the strings that we wish to input in real life are rarely delimited by quote marks. When they aren't, the strings must be input one character at a time and built up by concatenation. In this case study, if the input names are not so delimited, changes will have to be made in the initial procedure and procedure *read 1D string*. In the initial procedure we must include the declaration

      constants
          namelength : **integer** 20

(assuming as in case study 6.1 that the names occur in the first 20 positions of each input line), and the call to *read 1D string* must include *namelength* as a parameter:

    read 1D string(name, max, n, namelength)

Procedure *read 1D string* will then be

```
read 1D string : procedure
    {inputs a list of strings by reading each input line a character
    at a time, building the strings by concatenation}
    storage specification
        parameters
            a : out only 1-D string array
            max : in only integer
            n : out only integer
            stringlength : in only integer
        variables
            i : integer
        end storage specification
    begin read 1D string
        i ← 0
        loop while moredata and (i < max)
            i ← i + 1
            read string(a[i], stringlength)
            endloop while
        if moredata
            then n ← max + 1
            else n ← i
            endif
        end read 1D string
    where read string inputs a string of length stringlength a character
            at a time, constructing the string by concatenation

CASE STUDY 6.3 — REFINEMENT 4
```

Procedure *read string* was developed in case study 6.1 for inputting a string of length *stringlength* one character at a time, building up the string by concatenation. This procedure will work in this case study without alteration, so we will not repeat it here.

Correctness

The inclusion of loop invariant and loop goal assertions have been left as an exercise. You should also do a program walkthrough and develop a set of test data for the various versions of these procedures.

Efficiency

Since each of the three procedures called by the initial procedure contains a single loop that iterates n times, n being the number of names in the input, the time complexity for this program is $O(n)$. We must constantly remind ourselves, however, that a program dealing with strings will usually take longer than a similar program dealing with numbers. Thus, the corresponding procedures of case study 5.1, which read and write integers, will be considerably faster than the string reading and writing procedures of this case study. This difference will be a constant factor (e.g., with the same number of input items, the program of this case study may take 10 times as long to execute as the program of case study 5.1).

At first glance the last refinement of *read 1D string*, where *read string* is called to read in the current string one character at a time, may appear to be more than linear. Procedure *read 1D string* calls *read string* from within a **while moredata** loop, and *read string* itself contains the loop headed by

loop start i **with** 1 **step** 1 **to** n

as seen by looking back at case study 6.1 (n is passed the value in *stringlength*). However, as we noted in case study 6.1, this loop executes a constant number of times (*stringlength*) independent of the input data. (You should reread the efficiency and summary sections of case study 6.1 if you do not recall this analysis.)

The space complexity of this program is also linear, because there is a single array, *name*, containing n input names. Again, this array will take up more space on a real computer than its counterpart in case study 5.1. As we have said, on real computers an arbitrarily long string cannot be stored in a single storage cell, so the names of this case study may be spread out over perhaps 5 storage cells. This would mean that $5*n$ cells would be required to store the n names in the array. The space complexity, of course, is still linear.

Summary — Case Study 6.3

Except for the fact that strings must usually be read in one character at a time, the procedure for inputting string arrays is no different from the procedure for inputting numbers. The time and space requirements of such programs are usually larger than similar programs dealing with numbers, because in real computers strings must be spread over several storage cells, depending on the lengths of the strings. These differences in the time and space requirements will be some constant factor depending on the string sizes.

6.2
IN
RETROSPECT

There are many computer applications involving character data. In the early days of computing, the primary applications were numeric, and computers were used almost exclusively for scientific purposes (this use of computers is usually called "number crunching"). As the price of computers fell, they were acquired by businesses and were used for maintaining company personnel files and other records involving large quantities of character data (names, addresses, and so forth). Now, with the price of small computing systems low enough to be practical for use in homes and offices, one of the fastest growing applications is word processing. Elaborate programs have been written to allow easy typing and modification of documents. Word processing programs format the text into balanced lines and paragraphs and, in some cases, can hyphenate words properly and check for spelling errors. Most newspapers and periodicals are compiled and typeset with such programs.

Even though the applications of computers to character data appear to be completely different from numeric applications, we have seen that programming for character-oriented applications is no different. It involves the same process of top-down design using procedures and functions, loops and decision control structures, and many of the same data structures. In fact, some programs that have been developed to handle numbers (e.g., searching and sorting) can be directly adapted for use with character data. So far, the only new features introduced in this chapter for dealing with character data are the data types **character** and **string** and the concatenation operator ||.

CHARACTER VARIABLES AND CONSTANTS

A character variable can hold exactly one single character, no more and no less.

Example
6.6

The declaration

> **variables**
> > letter : **character**

establishes a variable called *letter* that can contain a single character such as "a", "z", "*", or " ". A single character delimited by single quotation marks is called a *character constant.* Assignments of a character constant to a character variable are of the form

> letter ← '*'

If there are two variables of type **character,** x and y, then the assignment

> x ← y

is also proper as long as y is defined. Notice that this assignment is different from

> x ← 'y'

which assigns the character 'y' to the variable x; the previous statement assigned the contents of variable y to variable x.

A variable declared to be of type **character** is initially undefined (it does not contain a blank) and must be initialized in an assignment statement or via an **input** statement. As shown in the previous example, character constants must be enclosed in quotes to distinguish them from variables or to indicate that the character constant is indeed a blank.

STRING VARIABLES AND CONSTANTS

A string variable can hold an arbitrarily long string of characters.

The declarations

variables
    phrase1, phrase2 : **string**
    letter : **character**

Example 6.7

establish two string variables, *phrase1* and *phrase2,* and one character variable, *letter.* Assignments such as

    phrase1 ← 'The cow jumped'
    phrase2 ← 'cornflakes'
    letter ← '*'

are proper. The quote marks are needed to delimit the string constants assigned to *phrase1* and *phrase2*. The assignments

    phrase2 ← phrase1
    phrase1 ← letter

are legal; the contents of a string or character variable can be assigned to another string variable. Of course, the assignment

    letter ← phrase1

would be improper; a string cannot be assigned to a character variable (unless the string has length 1).
    Whenever a quote mark is to be included as part of a string, it must be indicated by two quotation marks side by side. The assignment

    phrase2 ← 'I don''t care'

causes the string

    I don't care

to be assigned to *phrase2*. Similarly, the assignment

    letter ← ''''

causes the single quotation mark, ', to be assigned to *letter.*

Every string variable or constant has a *length,* which is just the number of characters constituting the string. The null string is the special string consisting of no characters, the string of length 0. A variable declared to be of type **string** is initially undefined — an undefined string is different from the null string or a string of blanks.

Example 6.8   The declaration

> **variables**
>> apple : **string**

establishes an undefined cell named *apple* in the store. The assignment

> apple ← ''

assigns the null string to *apple,* which makes *apple* contain the defined string of length 0. This is different from

> apple ← ' '

which assigns the string of length 1 consisting of a single blank to *apple,* or

> apple ← ' '

which assigns a string of length 2 consisting of two blanks to *apple.*

Using string length terminology, we can say that a character constant is a string of length 1 and that a character variable can be assigned any string that has length 1 (and no others).

STRING OPERATIONS

Most programming languages that allow variables of type **string** provide concatenation and substring operations. Concatenation is the operation of combining two strings to obtain a new, longer string. Substring is the operation of creating a new string from part of an existing string.

Concatenation

The concatenation operator, written ‖, joins two strings to form a third.

Example 6.9   Suppose that we have the declarations

> **variables**
>> phrase1, phrase2, phrase3 : **string**
>> letter : **character**

Then, assuming that all four variables have been initialized, the assignments

> phrase2 ← phrase3 ‖ phrase1
> phrase1 ← phrase1 ‖ ' over the moon.'
> phrase3 ← phrase3 ‖ letter ‖ letter ‖ phrase2 ‖ 'the end.'

are all proper. Two or more string variables, character variables, and/or string constants can be concatenated to form a new string. If *phrase3* contained the string "The cow jumped over the moon.", *letter* contained "x", and *phrase2* was the string "This is ", then the last assignment statement shown above would assign

> The cow jumped over the moon.xxThis is the end.

to *phrase3.*

The null string is to concatenation what 0 is to addition and 1 is to multiplication: it is the identity. Thus, just as we have seen loops that compute a sum by first setting *sum* to 0 and then building the sum in a loop, as in

```
sum ← 0
loop {of some kind}
    input x
    sum ← sum + x
    endloop
```

and loops that build a product after setting *product* initially to 1, as in

```
product ← 1
loop {of some kind}
    input x
    product ← product * x
    endloop
```

so we will also see loops for building up strings from the input a character at a time, as in

```
line ← ''
loop {of some kind}
    input char
    line ← line || char
    endloop
```

where *line* is of type **string** and *char* is of type **character.**

Substring

The substring operation allows the programmer to extract part of a given string to form a new string. This operation is handled differently in every programming language that allows variables of type **string;** in some cases it is left to the programmer to design as a new procedure. In *mpl* we will model this operation as

string[*low:high*]

where *string* is any string variable and *low* and *high* are integers with *low* ≤ *high*. The result of this operation is that a new string will be formed from the characters in position *low* through position *high* of variable *string*.

Suppose that the declarations

variables
    sentence, phrase : **string**

were made along with the assignment

    sentence ← 'The cow jumped over the moon.'

Then

    phrase ← sentence[9:14]

Example 6.10

would assign "jumped" to *phrase.* Similarly,

> phrase ← sentence[5:5]

would assign "c" to *phrase.* The assignment

> sentence ← sentence[1:24] || 'rat.'

would cause *sentence* to contain

> The cow jumped over the rat.

The substring operation can also be used to examine the characters of a string one at a time.

Example 6.11

The loop

```
loop start i with 1 step 1 to length
    output sentence[i:i]
endloop autoindex
```

will print each character of the string variable *sentence* in succession, if variable *length* contains the number of characters in *sentence.*

INPUT AND OUTPUT OF STRING DATA

Reading in string data requires some new considerations, as we have seen in the previous case studies.

Inputting Strings

There are two methods of inputting strings. One is to place all input strings in single quotes and read in an entire string at one time. The other method requires reading in input strings one character at a time, building the strings up by concatenation. These two methods are used because of the way string data is handled by the processor during input. For example, in processing an input statement like

> **input** x, y

where x and y are two integer variables, the processor scans past all blanks in the input until a number is reached. It then inputs the number into variable x, stopping when it reaches the next blank. To input y, the processor must again scan past any blanks in the input, beginning with the one that followed the number input into x. When the next number is found, the processor places it into variable y, stopping when it reaches the first blank after y. This process will not work for inputting strings, because blanks are valid string characters, and the processor would not know whether intervening blanks were to be included in the string. Thus the statement

> **input** phrase

where *phrase* is a string variable, would require that quotes be placed around the string at the input device. The processor would scan past all intervening blanks until the first quote was found, and then it would include in the string all characters (including blanks and single quotes wherever two quotes are side by side) up to the next quotation mark not followed by another quotation mark.

Inputting strings this way can be a pain, however, because it requires that all strings in the input have quotation marks around them, and this is often impractical. The only other method inputs all the characters in the input, one character at a time. This allows you (the programmer) to decide where the desired strings start and stop. For example, in designing a program to process arbitrary text, you may wish to input one word at a time by picking up single characters and concatenating them to form a word until you encounter a blank. You should review case study 6.1 for more examples of this process.

Printing Strings

Printing string or character variables and constants poses no problem to the processor, since the lengths of the strings are known by the time they are to be printed.

STRING COMPARISONS

It is possible to compare two strings using the relational operators $<$, $\leqslant$, $>$, $\geqslant$, $=$, and $\neq$; we saw an example of this in case study 6.2. This capability allows us to search and sort lists of strings. Essentially, one string is less than another string if the first string precedes the second in a lexicographic (i.e., alphabetical) sense. If two strings being compared have different lengths, the shorter is padded on the right with a number of blank characters sufficient to make it as long as the longer one; the processor then compares the strings from left to right one character at a time. Since the blank character precedes all alphabetic characters on most computers, this comparison works as we would like.

Assume that the following assignments to string variables x and y are made:

Example 6.12

    x ← 'apples'
    y ← 'aardvarks'

The comparison

    x < y

evaluates to **false**. Comparison of x to y is made after "apples" is changed to the word "apples   " with three added blanks to make it as long as the string in y (this is not done in the variable x; x retains its original value). The comparison progresses from left to right. The first characters ("a") are the same in both strings, but the second characters do not match. Since the second character of y is "a" and the second character of x is "p", the processor knows without checking further that x > y (what is in x comes after what is in y alphabetically).

Similarly, in comparing the string "dog" with "dogs", the first string is extended with a blank to be "dog ". Each character matches until the last one; since the blank is less than any alphabetic character in a lexicographic ordering, the first string is recognized by the processor to be less than the second string, as we would expect.

Special symbols such as *, /, +, −, and punctuation marks can also be compared, but the results of these comparisons depend very much on the real computer being used. Whereas all computer designers know which letters precede other letters, there is no such single standard for special characters.

EFFICIENCY OF STRING HANDLING PROGRAMS

Computers are well adapted to handling character data, but, as we have discussed, programs that manipulate strings generally take longer and require more storage space than similar programs dealing only with numbers. The time and space requirements are increased because real computers cannot store arbitrarily long strings in a single cell — instead the strings must be spread out over a number of cells. The required execution time and space increase by a constant factor as the maximum size of the string increases; this increase may be noticeable for programs handling long strings, and it is a phenomenon you should be aware of.

CORRECTNESS OF STRING HANDLING PROGRAMS

The correctness of procedures and functions that process character data should be determined using the same methods we use for the other types of routines: careful top-down design, assertions where appropriate, loop verification, walkthrough, and testing with appropriate data (including special values).

6.3 | FOR REVIEW
WARMUP EXERCISES

6.1 Give some examples of string constants and character constants. Is every character constant also a string constant? Is every string constant also a character constant?

6.2 In our model computer we store arbitrarily long strings in individual storage cells. Explain why this would not be possible in a real computer.

6.3 Can a character value be assigned to a string variable? Can a string value be assigned to a character variable?

6.4 Explain the difference between the null string and the string consisting of a single blank.

6.5 Give the assignment statement that assigns the sentence

I said, "It couldn't be found."

to the string variable *sentence*.

6.6 What is the usual way to input textual data, a long phrase at a time into a string variable, or a character at a time into a character variable? Why?

6.7 Explain the use of the concatenation operator.

6.8 Give the standard loop for reading in a twenty-character line of text a character at a time into a string variable, *phrase*.

6.9   Explain why a program that manipulates character strings is likely to take longer than a similar program involving only numbers.

6.10 Do you suppose that character data is used much in real programs? Explain your reasoning.

6.11 Explain how two strings, possibly of different lengths, are compared by <. Is 'a' < 'b'? Is 'apple' < 'apples'? Is 'x   ' < 'x'?

6.12 Can you see any possible applications for character strings in business and scientific programming applications?

A DEEPER LOOK

6.13 Is there a difference between a string consisting of one blank and a string consisting of 10 blanks? Give examples to justify your answer. If these two strings were compared in an **if** statement, would they be equal?

6.14 How would you assign the apostrophe to a character variable?

6.15 Explain how the null string and the concatenation operator are related (in the same sense that 0 and + as well as 1 and * are related).

6.16 Addition and multiplication are associative. For example, $(5 + 7) + 2 = 5 + (7 + 2)$ and $(5 * 7) * 2 = 5 * (7 * 2)$. Is concatenation associative? Give an example. Addition and multiplication are also commutative. For example, $5 + 7 = 7 + 5$ and $5 * 7 = 7 * 5$. Is concatenation commutative? Give an example.

6.17 Explain why character strings that include special characters might compare differently on different real computers.

6.18 If two similar programs were written using the same strategy to print a list of integers and a list of names, respectively, which program would take longer to print an n element list? Would their time complexities be different? Explain your answers.

6.19 Explain how the substring operation of *mpl* works. If *phrase* contains the string

The cow jumped over the moon.

what are the values of the following expressions?

(a)   phrase[5:7]
(b)   phrase[15:15]
(c)   phrase[1:4] || phrase[25:28] || phrase[8:24] || phrase[5:7]
        || phrase[29:29] ||

6.20 Discuss ways in which the use of variable length character strings affects the analysis of the time and space complexity of a program.

TO PROGRAM

6.21 In case study 6.1 the header method for inputting character data was developed. Redesign the input procedures to work with the trailer method and the **moredata** method (both for inputting a string at a time and a character at a time).

6.22 In the Correctness section of case study 6.2 a potential problem was discussed. Locate and remedy the problem.

6.23 In case study 6.3 the **moredata** method for inputting a **string** array was developed. Modify the program to work for the header and trailer methods.

6.24 Design an *mpl* function *revstr* which results the reverse of a string given a string *s* and its length *n*. For example, if the variable *s* contains "abc", then *revstr(s, n)* will return "cba".

6.25 We have used < to compare two strings. Suppose that < only worked correctly between characters. For example, 'c' < 'f' would return **true,** but 'cat' < 'frog' would be undefined. Design a **truth value** function *lessstr(string1, n1, string2, n2)* which returns **true** if *string1* lexicographically precedes *string2*, where *n1* and *n2* are the lengths of *string1* and *string2*.

6.26 Design a program that inputs a text and counts the number of words that begin with the letter "z". Also, compute the percentage of words that begin with a "z".

6.27 Design an *mpl* function *duplicate(string, n)* which returns a string containing *n* copies of string. For example,

```
duplicate('ab', 3) = 'ababab'
duplicate('a', 5) = 'aaaaa'
duplicate('abcd', 0) = ''
```

6.28 Most programming languages which have a **string** data type also have a built-in function *length(s)*, which returns the length of a string *s*. Assume that *mpl* provides a *length* function and redo exercise 6.24 for *revstr(s)* rather than *revstr(s, n)*.

**6.4
THE
CHALLENGE**

We now turn to more challenging case studies involving strings.

**Case Study
6.4**

Sorting Names

> **Problem Description:** Given a list of names, sort the names into alphabetical order.
>
> **Input Specifications:** A list of names, last name first, given one per line in the first 20 positions and not delimited by quote marks.

The Solution — Insertion Sort

The initial procedure contains a few changes from case study 5.7, where insertion sort was first studied. A string array must be declared, and a constant indicating the length of the names must also be declared.

```
sort names : initial procedure
    {sorts a list of names into alphabetical order then prints the list}

    storage specification
        constants
            max : integer 500
            namelength : integer 20
        variables
            name : 1-D string array [1 → max]
            n : integer
    end storage specification

    begin sort names
        read 1D string(name, max, n, namelength)
        if (n ≤ 0) or (n > max)
            then output 'bad data, n out of bounds : ', n
            else insertion sort(name, n)
                    write 1D string(name, 1, n)
        endif
    end sort names

    where read 1D string inputs a list of strings
    where insertion sort sorts a list of strings into ascending order
    where write 1D string ouputs a list of strings
```

CASE STUDY 6.4 — REFINEMENT 1

Recall that procedures *read 1D string* and *write 1D string* were developed in case study 6.3.

The only change to *insertion sort* of case study 5.7 (and procedure *move-up* called by *insertion sort*) is that the declaration

list : **in out 1-D integer array**

must be changed to

list : **in out 1-D string array**

We leave this modification as an exercise.

Correctness

The techniques used for determining the correctness of case study 5.7 can be used here. In fact, since procedure *insertion sort* was carefully verified there, we can be sure that it will work here, too.

Efficiency

The time and space complexity of this program will be the same as for the numeric version of the program in case study 5.7, except that the string handling program will require a constant factor more actual time and space than its numeric counterpart. Thus, *sort names* has time complexity $O(n^2)$ and space complexity $O(n)$.

Summary — Case Study 6.4

Manipulating strings is so similar to manipulating numbers that often nearly identical programs can be used to do both. This is true of the searching and sorting programs of the previous chapter, as demonstrated by the insertion sort program developed for strings in this case study.

Case Study 6.5 | Blank Compression

Problem Description: The program must compress text lines by replacing all sequences of four or more blanks with the string &N&, where N is the number of blanks replaced.

Input Specifications: An arbitrary text consisting of 80-character text lines in which the character & does not appear.

One problem encountered on many computing systems involves the storage of large amounts of textual information. This information is not kept in the store but rather on *secondary storage devices*. These secondary storage devices cannot be used by the processor in the same way the store is used to hold the values of variables as a program is executed. Instead, secondary storage is used by the processor for storing information that is not in current use. When you write a program to be executed on a computer, for example, this program (and the data you supply for the program) might be stored on secondary storage devices so that you can retrieve it, modify it, and run it later without needing to retype it. You do not need to know how these secondary storage devices work, you just to need to know that they exist.

The problem we will examine here is this: when textual files are stored on secondary storage devices, a lot of space is often wasted because the text lines contain a large number of blanks. While these blanks may be necessary when the text is actually displayed for humans, space can be saved by compressing long sequences of blanks when a string is saved in secondary storage.

Example 6.13   On some computers, programs are considered to consist of a sequence of statements, each of which is 80 characters long. Since an average program line probably has no more than 15 to 20 nonblank characters, a substantial savings in storage space can be achieved by compressing unnecessary blanks out of these lines before·the program is stored on a secondary storage device. For example, a typical statement in a Fortran program might look like

20   DO 100 I = 1, N

We could save this line as

20&10&DO 100 I = 1, N&53&

which takes up only 25 characters rather than 80. In the positions where more than 3 blanks appeared together, the blanks have been replaced by &N& where N is the number of blanks that were there originally. Obviously, there is no reason to compress fewer than 4 successive blanks, since the replacement string would be at least as long as the string of blanks it replaced. Of course, we must be sure that the character & does not appear as a valid character anywhere in the text being compressed — if it does we will have trouble since we are using & to signal a compression sequence.

If a text is processed by a program that compresses the blanks as shown and is then stored on secondary storage, a second program can later input this text and replace the correct number of blanks in the text lines for display in its proper form.

Although we do not yet know how to input and output data on secondary storage devices, we can look at this problem anyway. (We will study secondary storage in chapter 10.) We will just use our usual input device to input an arbitrary text with lines 80-characters long, one line at a time, compress the blanks in the line, and output the line to our usual output device. The second program, which inputs an arbitrary compressed file and restores it to its original form, will be left as an exercise.

The Solution — String and Character Manipulation

Our initial procedure will be responsible for inputting the text one line at a time, compressing the blanks from each line input, and then printing each compressed line. The compression routine will require a parameter, which contains the contents of the current line; the compression routine will return this line with blanks compressed.

```
blank compress : initial procedure
    {compresses blanks from strings and prints the compressed strings}

    storage specification
        constants
            bufferlength : integer 80
        variables
            buffer : string
        end storage specification

    begin blank compress
        loop while moredata
            read string(buffer, bufferlength)
            output compress(buffer)
        endloop while
    end blank compress

    where read string inputs bufferlength characters from the input
            into buffer
    where compress compresses groups of 4 or more blanks.
```

CASE STUDY 6.5 — REFINEMENT 1

Recall that *read string* is the standard routine we developed in case study 6.1 for inputting a string one character at a time, building the string up by concatenation.

We are now left with the task of designing function *compress*. The basic strategy to be followed by this function is this: the characters of *buffer*, the string parameter containing the current input line, will be examined one at a time from left to right. As nonblank characters are input, they will be concatenated directly to the new compressed string being constructed. When a blank is encountered, a different tack must be taken; this blank cannot be simply concatenated to the compressed string as is done with nonblank characters. Instead, this blank and all subsequent blanks up to the next nonblank character must be counted. If fewer than four blanks are found in succession, then the exact number of blanks must be concatenated to the compressed string, otherwise the sequence &N& must be concatenated to this string, where N is the number of blanks just counted. An attempt at function *compress* gives

```
outstring ← ''
i ← 1
loop while i ≤ bufferlength
    {get the ith character from buffer}
    if {this new character is not blank}
        then outstring ← outstring || {the new character}
        else {handle blanks}
    endif
    {increment i properly}
    endloop while
```

This strategy raises a question: how are the characters retrieved one at a time from *buffer*? We will use the substring operation described in the In Retrospect section. It has the form

string[*low:high*]

where *string* is any string variable, and *low* and *high* are integers. The result of this expression will be a string whose length is $high - low + 1$, consisting of characters *low* to *high* of *string*. Obviously, it must be true that $high \geq low$, $low \geq 1$, and $high \leq$ the number of characters in *string*. The value of the substring operation if $high = low$, as in

string[*i:i*]

is a string of length 1 containing the *i*th character of *string*.

Example 6.14

Assume that the **string** variable *goodfield* is defined by

goodfield ← 'Computer Science'

Then the expressions below have the values shown

```
goodfield[1:7] = 'Compute'
goodfield[8:10] = 'r S'
goodfield[16:16] = 'e'
goodfield[12:10] = error, 12 > 10
goodfield[14:20] = error, 20 is too large
```

We can use this substring operation in our function *compress* to access each charcter of *buffer* one at a time by using

buffer[*i:i*]

inside an indexing loop that runs from 1 to *bufferlength*. Incorporating this feature into our design gives us the complete form of function *compress*:

```
compress : string function
     {removes all sequences of N ≥ 4 blanks from a string and
      replaces them with &N&}

  storage specification
     parameters
        buffer : in only string
        bufferlength : in only integer
     variables
        outstring : string
        char : character
        i : integer
  end storage specification

begin compress
  outstring ← ''
  i ← 1
  loop while i ≤ bufferlength
     char ← buffer[i:i]
     if char ≠ ' '
        then outstring ← outstring || char
             i ← i + 1
        else handle blanks(buffer, outstring, i, bufferlength)
     endif
  endloop while
  compress ← outstring
end compress

where handle blanks counts the blanks starting at buffer[i],
      and updates outstring and i accordingly
```

CASE STUDY 6.5 — REFINEMENT 2

Notice that we have replaced

else {handle blanks}

with a call to a procedure named *handle blanks*. Procedure *handle blanks* is passed the string *buffer* containing the current input line and the position *i* at which a blank has been encountered. As we discussed above, *handle blanks* must scan through parameter *buffer* starting at character *i*, counting blanks until either a nonblank character or the end of *buffer* (position *bufferlength*) is reached. Since we know that character *i* of parameter *buffer* is a blank whenever *handle blanks* is called, the basic loop could be:

```
count ← 1
i ← i + 1
char ← buffer[i:i]
loop while (char = ' ') and (i < bufferlength)
   count ← count + 1
   i ← i + 1
   char ← buffer[i:i]
endloop while
```

This program segment, however, has two problems, both associated with what happens when *i* reaches *bufferlength*. The first problem, which could be handled by including this segment in an **if** statement, is that if there is a

single blank at the end of *buffer* and we thus enter *handle blanks* with
i = *bufferlength*, this procedure will promptly attempt to access *buffer*[*buf-ferlength* + 1 : *bufferlength* + 1] before even entering the loop — this
will cause an error. Secondly, after the loop terminates, we must check to de-termine whether it terminated because a nonblank character was encountered
in *buffer* or because the end of *buffer* was reached. This check must be made
to ensure that *count* and *outstring* are handled correctly.

There are two ways around these problems. One is to check before the
loop whether *i* = *bufferlength* and then to check after the loop why the loop
terminated; we will leave this solution as an exercise. The other solution is
more subtle. Think how much easier this function would be if every string
buffer ended with a special nonblank character, which does not otherwise ap-pear in the input (for example, &); in this case procedure *handle blanks* would
not have to include the check that the last character in *buffer* is a blank, and
its form would simply be

```
count ← 1
i ← i + 1
char ← buffer[i:i]
loop while char = ' '
    count ← count + 1
    i ← i + 1
    char ← buffer[i:i]
    endloop while
```

If this function is so much simpler if there is an & in character position
bufferlength + 1 of *buffer*, let's put one there. We can do this easily in either
the initial procedure or function *compress* by including the statement

```
buffer ← buffer || '&'
```

We choose to modify the initial procedure to include this statement:

```
blank compress : initial procedure
    {compresses blanks from strings and prints the compressed strings}
    storage specification
        constants
            bufferlength : integer 80
        variables
            buffer : string
        end storage specification
    begin blank compress
        loop while moredata
            read string(buffer, bufferlength)
            buffer ← buffer || '&'
            output compress(buffer, bufferlength)
            endloop while
        end blank compress
    where read string inputs bufferlength characters from the input
            into buffer
    where compress compresses groups of 4 or more blanks
```

CASE STUDY 6.5 — REFINEMENT 3

We now design our final version of *handle blanks*. We have already designed the basic loop of *handle blanks*, so we just need to decide what must be done after the next nonblank character has been encountered in the loop, causing termination of the loop. At this point either the correct number of blanks (if there are fewer than 4) or the compressed blank code must be concatenated onto *outstring*. Notice that in the rough loop we have developed for *handle blanks*, variable *i* is incremented until it points to the next nonblank character in *buffer*. Thus, when *handle blanks* terminates and control is returned to function *compress*, *i* will be pointed to the proper character in *buffer* for the next iteration of the **while** loop in *compress*. Procedure *handle blanks* is given completely below:

```
handle blanks : procedure
    {concatenates the proper blank compression code onto buffer}

    storage specification
        parameters
            buffer : in only string
            outstring : in out string
            i : in out integer
        variables
            char : character
            count, j : integer
        end storage specification

    begin handle blanks
        count ← 1
        {count the number of contiguous blanks starting at position i}
        i ← i + 1
        char ← buffer[i:i]
        loop while char = ' '
            count ← count + 1
            i ← i + 1
            char ← buffer[i:i]
        endloop while

        if count < 4
            then {append the number of contiguous blanks found to
                    outstring, because fewer than 4 were found}
                loop start j with 1 step 1 to count
                    outstring ← outstring || ' '
                endloop autoindex
            else {append the blank compression code to outstring,
                    because more than 3 contiguous blanks were found}
                outstring ← outstring || '&' || converttostring(count) || '&'
        endif

    end handle blanks

    where converttostring is a built-in function which converts numbers
            to strings
```

CASE STUDY 6.5 — REFINEMENT 4

Notice that we no longer need the length (*bufferlength*) of parameter *buffer* in procedure *handle blanks*. This is because the **while** loop that checks for blanks will terminate if the & at the end of *buffer* is found. Thus, the call to *handle blanks* in function *compress* should be changed from

    else handle blanks(buffer, outstring, i, bufferlength)

to

    else handle blanks(buffer, outstring, i)

in order to make *compress* work properly.

Notice also that in the **else** clause of the **if** statement we have used the built-in function *converttostring* described in the **where** statement. When a number is to be treated as a string (as it is here, so that it can be concatenated to *outstring*), it must be converted to character form. This is because the processor treats numbers and the character representations of numbers differently. For example, the number 14 and the character string '14' are treated differently by the processor, for reasons that need not concern us at this point.

Correctness

The program developed for this case study is relatively complex. Furthermore, because strings are handled differently in different programming languages, there will undoubtedly be modifications necessary to this program as it is translated into a real programming language. Thus it is even more important to do a careful design, walkthrough, and testing of the program. We leave the inclusion of loop invariant and goal assertions as an exercise.

Efficiency

The main loop of concern is the **moredata** loop of the initial procedure. It reads in an undetermined number of text lines, say n. Each time through the loop there is a call to procedure *read string* and a reference to function *compress*. In procedure *read string* a loop that inputs the current line one character at a time, from 1 to *bufferlength*, is executed. Since *bufferlength* is a constant (80 in this case) a constant number of statements will be executed each time *read string* is called, independent of the input.

A similar analysis shows that the loop in *compress* will iterate a constant number of times also. In procedure *handle blanks* and function *compress*, the variable *i* runs from 1 to *bufferlength* + 1 (81), stepping alternately through the nonblank characters of *buffer* in the loop in *compress* and through the blank characters of *buffer* in the loop in *handle blanks*. Thus, since *read string* and *compress* both require only constant time, the only loop that depends on the size of the input is the **moredata** loop of the initial procedure. For n input lines, this loop has $O(n)$ time complexity. Function *converttostring* will also always execute in constant time (maximum) since 80 is the largest number that will ever be converted.

The space complexity is $O(1)$, constant. There are no arrays, and the largest data structures are strings with a constant maximum size of *bufferlength* + 1 characters.

Summary — Case Study 6.5

To perform data compression we needed to retrieve the individual characters of an input string character by character; this required the substring operation. This is a powerful feature that allows us to manipulate and reconstruct strings quite easily.

Another important programming concept was used for the first time in this case study. We modified the input data structure (string *buffer*) to have a special nonblank terminating character. This allowed us to design the loop of *handle blanks* much more simply than would otherwise have been possible. This trick of modifying a data structure to contain a special uniquely recognizable first (or last) element can often make it much easier to design procedures that must step through the data until the first (or last) element is reached. We suggested this as a solution to the problem of moving an element up past the beginning of a list when we developed procedure *moveup* in the insertion sort routine in case study 5.7.

A Simple Word Processor

Case Study
6.6

> **Problem Description:** Design a simple word processor that reads in words from an input text and outputs formatted text, where each output line contains as many words as possible.
>
> **Input Specifications:** First an integer that gives the length (number of characters) of the output lines, then an English paragraph to be printed. The beginning and end of the input text will be marked by # characters, which appear nowhere else in the input paragraph.

As we have previously mentioned, the use of computers in the area called *word processing* is growing. For example, all of the versions of this book, from the first rough drafts through the final typeset form, were produced using a computer text-formatting program. The term *word processing* refers to the area of computing that is involved with the organizing, formatting, and printing of documents.

Sophisticated word processing programs like the text formatter used in preparing this book provide enormous flexibility. The typist can type the text at a terminal with little regard for aesthetics; the individual lines can be very long or very short; numbering of chapters, sections, and pages is of no concern; and the placement of figures and tables is no worry at all when the text is being typed. The text-formatting program provides the aesthetics, balancing lines nicely within given margins, automatically numbering pages, chapters, and sections, positioning figures and tables appropriately, and even generating a table of contents and an index automatically. In other words, a text-formatting program inputs a rough text, along with values that indicate the margins for the page and keywords that indicate the start of new paragraphs, chapters, sections, tables, and figures. The program then processes this raw text one character at a time to produce the formatted text. Changing the text later is trivial: the typist simply retrieves the original draft, inserts new lines, deletes old lines, moves text around, and so forth, and then runs the text-formatting program again to produce a newly formatted draft.

In this case study we will develop a very basic word processing program. Its only task will be to take an input file of English text and output it in a format where as many words as possible are printed out on each line.

Before we start designing the program, we will give an example to make sure that the purpose of this case study is completely clear.

Example 6.15

Assume that the input to the program is:

```
30
#Design a simple word processor that reads in words from
an input text and outputs formatted text, where each
output line contains as many words as possible.#
```

The program should read in enough words to fill a 30-character long line, then it should print the line and start the process again by beginning a new line. In this example the output should be:

```
Design a simple word processor
that reads in words from an
input text and outputs
formatted text, where each
output line contains as many
words as possible.
```

These six output lines have lengths of 30, 27, 22, 26, 28, and 18 characters, and in all but the last line, the inclusion of the first word of the next line would cause the previous line length to exceed 30 characters.

The Solution — Text Manipulation

In our initial procedure we will first input *linelength* and then read in (and ignore) characters until a # is reached. Then we will call on a procedure named *format* to read in the text and output formatted lines.

```
text formatter : initial procedure
    {formats and prints a paragraph so that no more than linelength
     characters appear on a line}

    storage specification
        variables
            linelength : integer
            nextcharacter : character
        end storage specification

    begin text formatter
        input linelength
        if linelength ≤ 0
            then output 'bad line length: ', linelength
            else input nextcharacter
                loop while nextcharacter ≠ '#'
                    input nextcharacter
                    endloop while
        endif
        format(linelength)
        end text formatter

    where format inputs the text, and outputs lines which
            have length ≤ linelength and which are as long as possible
```

CASE STUDY 6.6 — REFINEMENT 1

After inputting characters until a # is found, as is done in the **while** loop of the initial procedure, the next character to be read will be the first character of the paragraph.

Now we need to develop the strategy for procedure *format*. The purpose of procedure *format* is to use the input text to construct and print output lines that contain as many words as possible but that are no longer than *linelength*. We will call the line currently being built up from the input *outline*. When *format* is first called, *outline* must be set to the null string. Then in a loop that iterates as long as there are more input words (that is, until the trailing # on the input paragraph is encountered), string *outline* is built up by continuously concatenating the next word from the input to *outline*, until a point is reached where concatenating the next input word to *outline* would make *outline* longer than *linelength*. At this point, *outline* is printed out as it is, then *outline* is reset to be just the input word that wouldn't fit on the last output line (that word is now the start of the *next* line of output), and the process of building a new output line continues.

These considerations lead to the following loop structure for *format*.

```
outline ← ''
loop while {there are more words in the input}
    {get the next input word (call it nextword)}
    if {the length of outline plus the length of nextword is less than linelength}
        then outline ← outline || nextword
        else output outline
            outline ← nextword
        endif
    endloop while
```

Close examination of this loop reveals that there are still some problems with it. In the **then** clause where outline is being built up by concatenation in the statement

```
outline ← outline || nextword
```

we are concatenating words without intervening blanks — the first line output would look something like

```
Designasimplewordprocessor
```

using this loop. We can fix this by changing the concatenation statement to

```
outline ← outline || nextword || ' '
```

which inserts one blank after each word concatenated to outline. Similarly, the statement

```
outline ← nextword
```

in the **else** clause must be changed to

```
outline ← nextword || ' '
```

to make sure that a blank follows the first word of each new output line being constructed.

There is another problem in our current design of the loop: what happens when there are no more words in the input? This would cause termination of the loop. But at this point *outline* probably contains some words that were not printed, because *outline* was in the process of being built up when the input was exhausted. It is also possible that *outline* is the null string at this point, as would be the case if the input were

  ##

(that is, the input paragraph contains no words). In either case, whether *outline* contains the last words of the paragraph or *outline* is the null string, printing *outline* upon termination of our loop will yield the desired result. If *outline* does contain the last words of the paragraph, then this last line must be printed, and if *outline* is the null string, then printing *outline* will be the same as printing a blank line, which causes no harm in this program.

  To finish procedure *format*, then, we will incorporate the changes noted above and include a call to another procedure, *getword. getword* returns the next word from the input, the length of that word, and whether the trailing # of the input was found as the next word was being read in. To keep track of the current line length, we will need integer variables *outlinelength* and *nextwordlength*. We will use the **truth value** variable *lastword* to indicate whether the end of the input has been reached.

```
format : procedure
    |formats a paragraph a line at a time putting as many words
     as possible in a line while keeping the line length ≤ linelength
     characters|

    storage specifications
        parameters
            linelength : in only integer
        variables
            outline, nextword : string
            outlinelength, nextwordlength : integer
            lastword : truth value
        end storage specification

    begin format
        lastword ← false
        outline ← ''
        outlinelength ← 0
        loop while not lastword
            getword(nextword, nextwordlength, lastword)
            if outlinelength + nextwordlength ≤ linelength
                then outline ← outline || nextword || ' '
                     outlinelength ← outlinelength + nextwordlength + 1
                else output outline
                     outline ← nextword || ' '
                     outlinelength ← nextwordlength + 1
            endif
        endloop while
        output outline
    end format

    where getword returns the next input word, its length, and whether
          it is the last word in the input

CASE STUDY 6.6 — REFINEMENT 2
```

We must now design procedure *getword*. At first glance it may apear that all we need to do is concatenate input characters until a blank is reached, at which point we have compiled a word from the input. While this idea will work well for picking up a word in the middle of an input line, there are other situations in which it will not work at all. For example, when the word we are inputting ends on the last character in a line, there is no blank following it (even though there might appear to be when the input line is written on paper); instead there is a special nonprinting end-of-line character at the end of each line. The processor will have to check whether the end of a line has been reached; we express this in our programs with the **endofline** keyword, which is used in a way similar to the way we use **moredata** to determine whether there is more data in the input.

Another situation in which a word may not terminate with a blank is when it is the last word of the input, in which case it may be followed immediately by a # (there may also, although not necessarily, be blanks between the last word and the terminating #). Thus we must consider three situations: a word may terminate with a blank, the end of line character, or the special symbol #. We must also remember that when we call *getword*, the input pointer might be pointing to blanks that appear before the next word. This will happen either if there are blanks immediately after the first # or if more than one blank appears between words.

These considerations give us the following version of *getword:*

```
getword : procedure
      {retrieves the next word from the input, returning this word,
       the length of this word, and whether this was the last word}

   storage specification
      parameters
         nextword : out only string
         nextwordlength : out only integer
         lastword : in out truth value
      variables
         char : character
      end storage specification

   begin getword
      input char
      loop while char = ' '
         input char
         endloop while
      nextword ← ''
      nextwordlength ← 0
      loop while (char ≠ ' ') and (char ≠ '#') and not endofline
         nextword ← nextword || char
         nextwordlength ← nextwordlength + 1
         input char
         endloop while
      if char = '#'
         then lastword ← true
         endif
      end getword
```

CASE STUDY 6.6 — REFINEMENT 3

Correctness

This is a relatively simple program, and it looks as though it should work well. Careful analysis of all expected inputs suggests a possible problem, however. What happens if the user puts some spaces between the last word and the #? The procedure will first return the last word, without setting the truth value variable *lastword* to **true.** The next time *getword* is called, any remaining spaces before the # will be skipped over. Once the # is reached, the assignments of the null string to *nextword* and 0 to *nextwordlength* are made. Since *char* = '#', the loop does not execute, and so the values returned are

nextword = '', *nextwordlength* = 0, *lastword* = **true**

As we can see, this causes no problems, because when execution returns to *format*, *nextword* (the null string) is concatenated onto the end of *outstring*, which will not change *outstring*.

There is one other possible problem with this procedure. What happens if a word whose length is greater than *linelength* is input? If *linelength* were set to 15, for example, the word "establishmentarian" would not fit on a single line, even by itself. If you check you will see that the program takes the reasonable course of printing the current line, and then printing the word that is too long on a line by itself, even though its length is greater than *linelength*.

Efficiency

The space complexity of this program is really determined by the number of characters in variable *outline*, which is determined in turn by the value in *linelength*, which is the first value input by the program. Thus, the space complexity is $O(k)$, where k is the value of linelength. However, it is unlikely that the length of any line would be more than a standard page width, so we would normally say that the space complexity of this program is $O(1)$, constant.

The time complexity of this program is determined by the fact that there is a loop in *format*, and within that loop a call is made to *getword*, which scans each character between the last word and the end of the next word in a loop. Thus we might say that the time complexity is $O(m*p)$, where m is the number of words to be output (this is how many times the loop of *format* will be executed), and p is the average number of characters in a word (this is the number of times the loop of *getword* will be executed). While this analysis is not wrong, we can see that it really boils down to this: these two loops simply ensure that every character of the input is read in formatting the output. The time complexity of the program is thus $O(q)$ where q is the number of characters in the input (notice that $q = m*p$).

Summary — Case Study 6.6

This simple line-formatting program demonstrates the type of tasks word processing programs must accomplish. Naturally, there would be many more routines in a comprehensive text-formatting program.

There are other considerations involved in designing a useful text-formatting program. With our program, if there is more than one blank between words in the input, there will be only one blank in the output text. Is this desirable? Special provisions are usually included to allow the typist to indicate when multiple blanks between words should be retained.

6.29 In case study 6.4 a program to sort a list of names was developed. Explain why this program would take much longer to sort n names than an equivalent program would take to sort n numbers. Would this difference be a constant factor or worse? Can you think of any technique that might be used to sort a list of names faster? (case study 8.2 solves a similar problem.)

6.30 Design a program to accept data of the form output by the blank compression program of case study 6.5 and restore it to its original form with all blanks in place.

6.31 The time complexity of the program of case study 6.5 was shown to be $O(n)$, where n was the number of input lines. We could have followed the argument used later when discussing the efficiency of case study 6.6 to show that the time complexity of the program in case study 6.5 is $O(k)$, where k is the total number of input characters. Explain why these two results are not contradictory.

6.32 Design an *mpl* function *index(str, n, ch)* which finds the first position of character *ch* in a string *str* of length *n*. If *ch* does not appear in *str*, the function should return 0. For example,

index('banana', 6, 'n') = 3
index('banana', 6, 'b') = 1
index('banana', 6, 'd') = 0

Design two versions of the function, one recursive and one iterative. Compare them.

6.33 Design an *mpl* function *find(subject, n1, substring, n2)* that finds the starting position of the first occurrence of the non-null string *substring* of length *n2* within the string *subject* of length *n1*. *find* should return 0 if *substring* does not appear as a substring of *subject*. For example,

find('banana', 6, 'an', 2) = 2
find('banana', 6, 'n', 1) = 3
find('banana', 6, 'banana', 6) = 1
find('banana', 6, 'ann', 3) = 0

6.34 Design an *mpl* function *replace(str, n1, ch1, ch2, n2)* that replaces all occurrences of certain individual characters in *str* (which has length *n1*) with different characters as follows. *ch1* is a string containing the individual characters to be located and replaced in *str* (so each character in *ch1* must be different), and *ch2* is the string of corresponding replacement characters (so *ch2* must have the same length *n2* as *ch1*). For example, if *ch1* = 'acd f' and *ch2* = 'eie-c' then each occurrence of a in *str* is replaced by e, each occurrence of c by i, each occurrence of d by e, each occurrence of a blank by -, and each occurrence of f by c. Example results of a call to *replace* are

replace('banana', 6, 'adn', 'xyz', 3) = 'bxzxzx'
replace('abcdefed', 8, 'abfg', 'bagf', 4) = 'bacdeged'

6.35 Design an *mpl* **truth value** function *nodup(str, n)* which returns **true** only if string *str* of length *n* contains no duplicate characters. For example,

nodup('banana', 6) = **false**
nodup('aced', 4) = **true**

6.36   Use function *nodup* from the last exercise in the design of function *re-place* of exercise 6.34 to ensure robustness (remember, *ch1* may not contain duplicated characters).

6.37   Modify the *mpl* text-formatting program of case study 6.6 so that the last word will be placed on an output line if placing it there will make the actual number of characters in the line as close as possible to *line-length*, even if this means exceeding *linelength* characters. In the example given in case study 6.6, this modification would produce the following output:

```
Design a simple word processor
that reads in words from an input
text and outputs formatted text,
where each output line contains
as many words as possible.
```

The advantage of such an approach is that the right margins will usually be less jagged; the disadvantage is that text will often overflow the expected right margin. In this example, the right margin was set to 30, but the line lengths are 30, 33, 32, 31, and 26. If a tie occurs (e.g., on the second line the length could have been 27 or 33 depending on whether or not "input" was included as the last word), the word should be included as the last word of the output line.

6.38   Design an *mpl* program (similar to the one in case study 6.5), that compresses any sequence of five or more identical characters as &cN&, where *c* is the repeated character, and N is the number of occurrences of this character in this sequence. For example, the line

```
******        EXAMPLE        ******
```

would become

```
&*6&& 6&EXAMPLE& 6&&*6&& 49&
```

6.39   In case study 6.5 we discussed two solutions to the procedure *handle blanks*. The solution implemented involved concatenating an & onto the end of *buffer*. Design a program for the solution that did not include concatenating a special character onto the end of *buffer*.

6.40   In case study 6.5 we used a built-in function *converttostring*, which converted an integer from number to string form. Design an *mpl* function to do this conversion (which would be necessary if the function were not built-in). Give a recursive and an iterative solution.

6.41   Modify case study 6.6 so that if an input word has length greater than *linelength* an error message is printed out.

6.42   Design an *mpl* program that prints out the longest word in a sentence. You may assume that the only punctuation in the sentence are commas and that the sentence ends with a period. Words are separated by 1 or more spaces. For example, if the input is

```
Go West young man, they said.
```

then the output should be

young

It is an error if there is a tie for the largest word, as in

Go to Idaho young man, they said.

and in these circumstances an error message should be output.

| CHAPTER 7 |

Multi-Dimensioned Arrays

NEW CONCEPTS: Tables, Matrices, 2-D arrays

In chapter 5 we learned how data structures in the form of simple lists could be stored and manipulated in 1-D arrays. In this chapter we will see how tabular data structures — data structures with rows and columns, such as tables and matrices — can be implemented using two-dimensional, or 2-D, arrays. All procedural programming languages allow 2-D arrays, and most allow arrays of even higher dimensions.

The case studies of this section will explore the use of 2-D arrays for implementing tables.

Case Study
7.1
Inputting and Outputting a Table

> **Problem Description:** Input a table of integer values with m rows and n columns. Print the table just as it was input.
>
> **Input Specifications:** Two integers representing m and n, respectively, will appear first, then the integer values for the table will be given one row at a time.

As has been our custom before when we introduced new data structures, our first case study will involve input and output. We will design general procedures for the input and output of tables, and we will use these procedures in future programs that involve tables.

The Solution — 2-D Arrays

The form described for the input is the common form for tabular data. The data for a table is usually given in *row major order*, that is, the elements are listed one row at a time rather than one column at a time. We leave it as an exercise to design an input procedure for data given one column at a time.

We could meet the specifications of this problem by just inputting the data and immediately printing it out, forming the proper output table. However, the purpose of this case study is to develop general input and output procedures that we can use elsewhere. In particular, we want to show how a 2-D array is declared and how the elements of a table are stored in a 2-D array and printed from a 2-D array.

The declaration of a 2-D array is similar to that of a 1-D array, except that two subscript ranges must be specified, one that gives the low and high index values for the rows and one that gives the low and high index values for the columns.

Example 7.1

If we declare a 2 by 3 table named *fred* as

variables
fred : **2-D real array** $[1 \rightarrow 2, 1 \rightarrow 3]$

six cells will be reserved in the store:

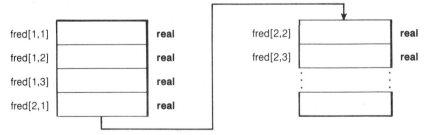

That is, we have created the equivalent of a 2-D table that looks like

fred[1,1]   *fred*[1,2]   *fred*[1,3]

fred[2,1]   *fred*[2,2]   *fred*[2,3]

Since the store is a sequential set of storage cells, the elements of the 2-D array must be stored sequentially. In this example we have assumed that a 2-D array is stored by the processor in *row major order,* which means that the rows of the array (represented by the first index) are stored one by one in the store, as is shown above. An alternative method is called *column major order,* in which the elements of the 2-D array are stored column by column. If column major order were used to store this 2-D array, the store would look like

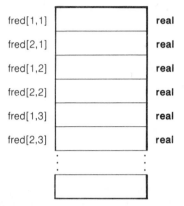

It depends upon the actual processor whether a 2-D array is stored in row or column major order. Except in obscure instances that we will not worry about here, there is no reason for the programmer to know which method a particular processor uses.

Using this description of a 2-D array we can now see how the initial procedure of this case study must be organized:

```
readwrite table : initial procedure
    {reads and prints a table of integers}

    storage specification
        constants
            max1 : integer 100
            max2 : integer 10
        variables
            table : 2-D integer array [1 → max1, 1 → max2]
            m, n : integer
        end storage specification

    begin readwrite table
        input m, n
        if (m > 0) and (n > 0) and (m ≤ max1) and (n ≤ max2)
            then read 2D integer(table, 1, m, 1, n)
                 write 2D integer(table, 1, m, 1, n)
            else output 'bad data, m = ', m, ' n = ', n
            endif
        end readwrite table

    where read 2D integer inputs a 2D integer array
    where write 2D integer outputs a 2D integer array
```

CASE STUDY 7.1 — REFINEMENT 1

Since the table has m rows and n columns, we declared the 2-D array *table* with enough rows and columns to handle the expected range of values for m and n. Here we have guessed that there would be no more than 100 rows and 10 columns, so we have used the constants $max1 = 100$ and $max2 = 10$ to declare the 2-D array *table* accordingly.

Example 7.2

Assume that the following values are at the input device:

```
4    3
25   36   71
32   31   30
71   61   13
36   60   97
```

This is no different from the single line of input values

4 3 25 36 71 32 31 30 71 61 13 36 60 97

which lists the table elements in row major order, with the first two values indicating the actual number of rows and columns in the table.

The initial procedure reads m and n first. The procedure that reads the table must then input 25 into *table*[1,1], 36 into *table*[1,2], and 71 into *table*[1,3]. This completes the first row of input, which consists of just 3 values, so *table*[1,4] up to *table*[1,10] will be left undefined. Similarly, 32 must be input into *table*[2,1], 31 into *table*[2,2], and 30 into *table*[2,3] to complete the input of the second row of *table*, leaving *table*[2,4] through *table*[2,10] undefined. This continues until the table has been completely read in; at this point rows 5 through 100 will still be undefined.

As we saw in this example, a table that is in row major order in the input is read in one row at a time. We will follow this approach in designing procedure *read 2D integer*. More specifically, we will design *read 2D integer* to accept any 2-D integer array, a the bounds on the rows to be input, *lowrow* and *highrow*, and the bounds on the columns to be read in, *lowcolumn* and *highcolumn*. Procedure *read 2D integer* will then input the table values into the formal array parameter a one row at a time from *lowrow* to *highrow*. The loop form for this process is

```
loop start row with lowrow step 1 to highrow
    assert rows lowrow through row – 1 have been input into array a
    {input the next row of a}
    endloop autoindex
assert array a has been input between rows lowrow through highrow in
        columns lowcolumn through highcolumn
```

The meaning of this *mpl* segment is clear. When *row* is *lowrow*, the first row is input; when *row* is *lowrow* + 1, the second row is input, and so on, until *row* is *highrow*, when the last row is input.

We now turn our attention to solving

{input the next row of a}

knowing that the number of the row to be input is in the loop index variable *row*. Again drawing on the previous example, we see that at this point a value is to be input into *a*[*row,lowcolumn*], then into *a*[*row,lowcolumn*+1], then *a*[*row,lowcolumn*+2], and so on, up to *a*[*row,highcolumn*]; this reads in all *highcolumn* − *lowcolumn* + 1 elements in the current row consecutively. We do this, of course, with a loop:

```
loop start column with lowcolumn step 1 to highcolumn
    assert elements a[row,lowcolumn] through a[row,column−1]
            have been input into the current row of array a
    input a[row,column]
    endloop autoindex
    assert the row of array a whose value is in loop index variable
            row has been input
```

Notice that we have assumed that the value of *row* is supplied by the outer loop. For example, when *row* is 3, this loop will input successive values for

a[3,*lowcolumn*], a[3,*lowcolumn*+1], . . . , a[3,*highcolumn*]

just as we wanted. We can substitute this loop for the line

{input the next row of a}

in the previous loop, and then incorporate these loops into a complete procedure:

```
read 2D integer : procedure
    {inputs a 2-D integer array in row major order between rows
     lowrow through highrow and columns lowcolumn through highcolumn}
    storage specifications
        parameters
            a : out only 2-D integer array
            lowrow, highrow, lowcolumn, highcolumn : in only integer
        variables
            row, column : integer
        end storage specification
    begin read 2D integer
        loop start row with lowrow step 1 to highrow
            assert rows lowrow through row − 1 have been input into array a
            loop start column with lowcolumn step 1 to highcolumn
                assert elements a[row,lowcolumn] through a[row,column−1]
                        have been input into the current row of array a
            input a[row,column]
                endloop autoindex
            assert the row of array a whose value is in loop index variable
                    row has been input
            endloop autoindex
        assert array a has been input between rows lowrow and
                highrow in columns lowcolumn through highcolumn   .
        end read 2D integer
```

CASE STUDY 7.1 — REFINEMENT 2

The procedure *write 2D integer* for outputting a 2-D array is the same as procedure *read 2D integer*, except that the 2-D array *a* must be output rather than input. This change is trivial to make, so we will leave the design of *write*

2D integer as an exercise. Remember, however, that in *write 2D integer* the array *a* should be declared as an **in out** rather than an **in only** parameter for the efficiency reasons discussed in chapter 5.

Correctness

Determining the correctness of a program utilizing 2-D arrays causes no new concerns. You should do a program walkthrough to convince yourself that the program works, and you should verify that the loops work correctly. Special values to be tested would include out-of-bounds values for *m* and *n* (less than 0, for example), and the values *m* = 1 (the array would have only one row), *n* = 1 (the array would have only one column), and *m* = *n* = 1 (the array would consist of just one element).

Efficiency

By now we are well aware that loops are the primary culprits where time complexity is concerned. Both *read 2D integer* and *write 2D integer* have a nested loop structure. This, of course, is the source of most of the execution time spent on this program. Let's examine these nested loop structures further. Each has the form

```
loop start row with lowrow step 1 to highrow
    loop start column with lowcolumn step 1 to highcolumn
        {single statement}
    endloop autoindex
endloop autoindex
```

For convenience, call the number of rows *m*, and the number of columns *n*. That is,

$$m = highrow - lowrow + 1 \text{ and } n = highcolumn - lowcolumn + 1$$

To determine the statement count of this loop structure, notice that the number of statements executed in the outer loop is

$$m * (2 + x) + 1$$

where *x* is the number of statements executed in the inner loop. The 2 comes from the **loop** and **endloop** statements of the outer loop, and the 1 comes from the fact that the outer **loop** statement will be executed one more time. The number of statements executed in the inner loop is

$$x = 3*n + 1$$

which can be substituted for *x* in the previous formula to give

$$m * (2 + 3*n + 1) + 1 = 3*m*n + 3*m + 1$$

as the true statement count formula, so the time complexity of procedures *read 1D integer* and *write 1D integer* is $O(m*n)$, where *m* is the number of rows and the *n* is the number of columns in the table. This is also the time complexity of the entire program.

The space complexity of this program is also $O(m*n)$ because given *m* rows and *n* columns in the table, the table fills *m*n* elements in the store. In addition, there are a maximum of ten other storage cells in use at any one time, giving a total of *m*n* + 10 storage cells.

We must make one final point concerning the time and space complexity of this program. What we choose as the size of the problem makes a big difference. In this case we have chosen the number of rows and the number of columns as the size of this problem, and this leads to a time complexity of $O(m*n)$. This is the usual way of measuring the time complexity of a program involving 2-D arays. However, a different measure of the size of the problem might be the total number of input elements, k (which is just $m*n$). This is the size we have often used for determining the time complexity of previous programs. In this case, since procedure *read 1D integer* handles each input element exactly once, we would say that is linear time complexity, $O(k)$. You should understand the differences between these two ways of determining the size of a problem. For programs using 2-D arrays, we will follow convention and treat the number of rows and the number of columns as the size.

Summary — Case Study 7.1

As we have seen, as m and n grow large, the time to process the elements of a 2-D array will generally approximate the square of the number of rows (if m and n are nearly equal). This, of course, is an unfortunate but inbred side effect of processing tabular data.

To input 2-D arrays we must know whether the input data appears in row or column major order. Usually the input will be in row major order. In this case we need an outer loop that steps through the rows of the array one at a time and an inner loop that steps through the columns (positions) of a given row, inputting each element encountered. In form, except for the need for nested loops, the procedures *read 2D integer* and *write 2D integer* are very similiar to their counterparts *read 1D integer* and *write 1D integer* of case study 5.1.

Operations on Tables

Case Study 7.2

> ***Problem Description:*** A company has five divisions. Given the gross quarterly earnings and the quarterly expenses of each division, calculate the quarterly profits of each division and the total company profit.
>
> ***Input Specifications:*** The quarterly earnings, with four consecutive values for each division, followed by the quarterly expenses with four consecutive values for each division. There will be 40 integers; all values are rounded to the nearest thousand dollars.

Tables find many applications in programs. We will look at an example in this case study.

The Solution — 2-D Arrays

The quarterly profits of each division are computed by subtracting the quarterly expenses from the quarterly earnings. Let's look at an example.

Example
7.3

Assume that the input values are

	78	85	69	100
	6	8	5	4
earnings:	61	58	56	57
	10	9	16	21
	23	28	40	35

	54	68	72	75
	7	7	7	7
expenses:	45	46	46	47
	12	12	11	12
	18	23	20	24

Each row corresponds to a division of the company, and the columns correspond to the four quarters. For example, the third division earned $61,000 in the first quarter and $56,000 in the third quarter. This same division spent $45,000 in the first quarter and $46,000 in the third quarter.

The quarterly profits table is computed by subtracting a division's quarterly expenses from its quarterly earnings. For example, since division 3 earned $61,000 and spent $45,000 in the first quarter, its first quarter profits were $16,000. The entire profits table looks like

24	17	−3	25
−1	1	−2	−3
16	12	10	10
−2	−3	5	9
5	5	20	11

The program for this case study should output the earnings, expenses, and profits tables along with the overall profit earned by the entire company; the overall profit is just the sum of the entries in the profits table. The last output line for this example should be

Company profit in thousands = $156

The data structure in this example is a table with rows and columns, so it can be implemented as a 2-D array. First, we will input the earnings and expense values into two 2-D arrays called *earnings* and *expenses*. Then we will compute and store the profits in a different array called *profits*. Each array will have dimensions

$[1 \rightarrow 5, 1 \rightarrow 4]$

which means that each will have 5 rows and 4 columns. From this description we see that the general form of the initial procedure must be:

```
company profit : initial procedure
    {computes company quarterly profits by division and overall}

    storage specification
        constants
            max1 : integer 5
            max2 : integer 4
        variables
            earnings, expenses, profits :
                2-D integer array [1 → max1, 1 → max2]
    end storage specification
```

```
begin company profit
    {input earnings table}
    {print earnings table}
    {input expenses table}
    {print expenses table}
    {compute the profits table from the earnings and expenses tables}
    {print the profits table}
    {compute the overall profit}
    {print the overall profit}
end company profit
```

CASE STUDY 7.2 — REFINEMENT 1

Notice that the constants ($max1$ and $max2$) used in declaring the array size are exact, since there are five divisions in the company and four quarters in a year. Although there will always be four quarters in a year, the company might someday sell a division or expand to include a new division, so it is a good idea to use named constants to declare the array size, as we have done here.

Each comment in this rough draft of the initial procedure will be a procedure or function (except for the last comment where the overall profits are printed). We designed the input and output procedures in case study 7.1, but we don't yet know what form the other procedures and functions will take, so we will design them first and come back later to replace the comments in the initial procedure with the proper calls and the right number of parameters.

We have one procedure and one function to design: a procedure for computing the quarterly profits of each division and a function for computing the overall company profit. The procedure that computes the quarterly profits must develop a profits table in which each of the entries is obtained by subtracting an entry of the expenses table from the corresponding entry of the earnings table. For example, to compute $profits[3,2]$ we subtract $expenses[3,2]$ from $earnings[3,2]$. (That is, to compute the profit made by division 3 in the second quarter, we subtract the expenses of that division in quarter 2 from the earnings of that same division in quarter 2.) In general, we can compute $profits[row,column]$ for any of the five values of row (the five divisions) and the four values of $column$ (the four quarters) by subtracting $expenses[row,column]$ from $earnings[row,column]$.

This is a special case of a more general problem: For three arrays a, b, and c, declared by

a, b, c : **2-D integer array** [lowrow → highrow, lowcolumn → highcolumn]

we will design a procedure called *array subtraction*, which subtracts each element of b from the corresponding element of a and puts the result into the corresponding element of c. That is

c[row,column] ← a[row,column] − b[row,column]

for all values of row between $lowrow$ and $highrow$ and all values of $column$ between $lowcolumn$ and $highcolumn$. The order in which these subtractions are done is not important, so we will use the loop form we designed for procedures *read 2D integer* and *write 2D integer* in case study 7.1. That is, we will do the subtraction one row at a time, and in each row we will subtract each column element in succession, as shown in procedure *array subtraction*:

```
array subtraction : procedure
    {subtracts array b from array a, producing a third array c}

    storage specification
        parameters
            a, b : in out 2-D integer array
            c : out only 2-D integer array
            lowrow, highrow, lowcolumn, highcolumn : in only integer
        variables
            row, column : integer
        end storage specification

    begin array subtraction
        loop start row with lowrow step 1 to highrow
            loop start column with lowcolumn step 1 to highcolumn
                c[row,column] ← a[row,column] − b[row,column]
                endloop autoindex
            endloop autoindex
        end array subtraction
```

CASE STUDY 7.2 — REFINEMENT 2

We leave the formulation and inclusion of the loop invariant and loop goal assertions for the two loops of this procedure as an exercise.

We must now design the function that computes the overall profit for the company. As we saw in our example, the company profit is computed by summing all the elements in the profits array. Again, this can be generalized to a function that takes any 2-D integer array a and returns the sum of the array elements. This function will have the same loop structure as all the other routines in this program.

```
sum 2D array : integer function
    {given an array a, computes the sum of the elements of a}

    storage specification
        parameters
            a : in out 2-D integer array
            lowrow, highrow, lowcolumn, highcolumn : in only integer
        variables
            row, column, total : integer
        end storage specification

    begin sum 2D array
        total ← 0
        loop start row with lowrow step 1 to highrow
            assert total is the sum of rows lowrow to row−1 of array a
            loop start column with lowcolumn step 1 to highcolumn
                assert total is the sum of rows lowrow through row−1,
                    plus the sum of columns lowcolumn through column−1
                    in the current row of array a
                total ← total + a[row,column]
                endloop autoindex
            assert total is the sum of the first row rows of array a
            endloop autoindex
        assert total is the sum of array a
        sum 2D array ← total
        end sum 2D array
```

CASE STUDY 7.2 — REFINEMENT 3

Now that all the necessary procedures and functions have been written, we return to our initial procedure and fill in the final details:

```
company profit : initial procedure
   {computes company profit by division and overall}

   storage specification
      constants
         max1 : integer 5
         max2 : integer 4
      variables
         earnings, expenses, profits :
            2-D integer array [1 → max1, 1 → max2]
         overallprofits : integer
   end storage specification

   begin company profit
      read 2D integer(earnings, 1, max1, 1, max2)
      write 2D integer(earnings, 1, max1, 1, max2)
      read 2D integer(expenses, 1, max1, 1, max2)
      write 2D integer(expenses, 1, max1, 1, max2)
      array subtraction(earnings, expenses, profits, 1, max1, 1, max2)
      write 2D integer(profits, 1, max1, 1, max2)
      overallprofits ← sum 2D array(profits, 1, max1, 1, max2)
      output 'Company profits in thousands = $', overallprofits
   end company profit

   where read 2D integer inputs a 2D integer array
   where write 2D integer outputs a 2D integer array
   where array subtraction subtracts two 2-D arrays, placing the result
      in a third array
   where sum 2D array sums all elements of an array
```

CASE STUDY 7.2 — REFINEMENT 4

Correctness

You should do a program walkthrough using the table values given in the example at the beginning of this case study. You should also verify the loops of each routine and supply loop invariant and goal assertions where they are missing. The fact that the loop structure of each routine is the same helps assure us that the basic designs of these routines are correct. Can you think of any special data values to be used in testing this program? Even though the arrays in this program have exactly five rows and four columns, each of the routines has been designed to be general, so they should be tested with special input values that cause them to consist of just a single row, just a single column, or just a single element.

Efficiency

The time complexity of this program is constant, $O(1)$. Each procedure and function in this program has the same nested loop structure as *read 2D integer*, so we might expect the time complexity of the program to be $O(m*n)$, but this is a special program. There will always be four quarters in a year, and the number of divisions in the company is essentially constant; it will seldom

— if ever — change. Thus the number of iterations of these loops does not depend on input values but is instead constant.

In general, however, we have seen that *read 2D integer* and *write 2D integer* have time complexity $O(m*n)$. Similarly, procedure *array subtraction* and function *sum 2D array* are generally $O(m*n)$. That is, in other programs, each of these procedures will have time complexity $O(m*n)$, where m is the number of rows and n the number of columns of the 2-D array passed to the procedure. In this particular program these procedures have $O(1)$ time complexity because of the nature of the program as a whole.

Similar considerations apply to the space complexity. If the number of divisions and reporting periods were input values, then the three arrays would each have $m*n$ elements, where m is the number of divisions and n the number of reporting periods, and so the space complexity would be $O(m*n)$. In this situation, however, the number of divisions is fixed at 5 and the number of reporting periods at 4, so the space complexity is constant, or $O(1)$. In fact, we can compute the exact maximum number of storage cells used in the program: it is 71 (it occurs inside the function *sum 2D array*) — 60 are used by the 3 arrays, 2 by the constants, and 1 for the integer variable of the initial procedure, plus 4 by the **in only** parameters, 3 by the local variables, and one for the function name in *sum 2D array*.

Summary — Case Study 7.2

In this case study the original problem was to use tabular data to compute the profits for various divisions of a company as well as the overall company profit. As we discovered, however, the underlying subproblems were much more general: reading and printing 2-D arrays, subtracting two 2-D arrays of the same size, and summing the elements of a 2-D array. In designing these general routines, we not only solved our specific problem, but we also wrote routines that will be useful in many programs.

The nested loop structure of the procedures for handling 2-D arrays results in $O(m*n)$ time complexity for these routines, which is the same as $O(n^2)$ when m and n have the same value. This means that as the size of n grows, the time to execute each procedure grows with n^2, a frightening prospect. The same complexity, $O(n^2)$, holds also for the amount of space required. While these complexity measures are true in general for the procedures and functions of this case study, the restricted nature of this particular program results in only $O(1)$ complexities.

7.2
IN
RETROSPECT

In this chapter we have seen examples of programs using two-dimensional (2-D) arrays. There are many programming problems where the data to be processed has a tabular structure and each data item has the same type (e.g., integer). 2-D arrays are ideally suited for implementing such data structures. Arrays of more than two dimensions are also allowed in most programming languages for implementing data structures that have a "natural" multidimensional organization. Once you understand the concepts of one- and two-dimensional arrays, arrays of higher dimensions are straightforward.

2-D ARRAYS

Each case study in this chapter uses a 2-D array, which has the general declaration form

variables
    arrayname : **2-D** *type* **array** [*firstrow* → *lastrow, firstcolumn* → *lastcolumn*]

where *arrayname* is any chosen name, *type* is one of the regular data types (e.g., **integer, real, truth value, character,** or **string**) and each of the subscript bounds *firstrow, lastrow, firstcolumn,* and *lastcolumn* is an integer constant or integer named constant. Of course, *firstrow* must be less than or equal to *lastrow,* and *firstcolumn* must be less than or equal to *lastcolumn.* Negative as well as positive subscript bounds can be used in declaring 2-D arrays.

    Processing (e.g., inputting or outputting) a 2-D array usually requires each element of the array to be handled in order. This is done with a nested loop structure of the form

loop start *row* **with** *lowrow* **step** 1 **to** *highrow*
    loop start *column* **with** *lowcolumn* **step** 1 **to** *highcolumn*
        {process element a [*row,column*] of the array}
        endloop autoindex
    endloop autoindex

where *a* is the name of the array being processed, the index variables *row* and *column* are of type integer, *lowrow* and *highrow* are integer variables or constants representing the rows of *a* to be processed, and *lowcolumn* and *highcolumn* are integer variables or constants representing the columns of *a* to be processed. The values in *lowrow, highrow, lowcolumn,* and *highcolumn* need not be the same as the values in *firstrow, lastrow, firstcolumn,* and *lastcolumn,* respectively, which were used in declaring the maximum size of the array, but in processing *a*[*row,column*] it must be ensured that neither *row* nor *column* is outside the bounds declared for the array, otherwise an error will occur.

    The loop form given above processes array *a* in *row major order* (a row at a time), which is the common way of processing an array. Sometimes a loop structure that processes the array a column at a time is needed and the following loop form would then be used

loop start *column* **with** *lowcolumn* **step** 1 **to** *highcolumn*
    loop start *row* **with** *lowrow* **step** 1 **to** *highrow*
        {process element a[*row,column*] of the array}
        endloop autoindex
    endloop autoindex

You should compare these last two loop structures until you understand the differences between them.

ARRAYS WITH MORE THAN TWO DIMENSIONS

Most programming languages provide arrays of three dimensions, and some provide arrays of arbitrary dimensions. Declaring and using such arrays is straightforward. The loop structures for handling each element of such arrays would have as many levels of loops as there are dimensions in the array, in a manner analogous to that described for 2-D arrays.

Example 7.4

We could declare a 3-D array using the declaration

found : **3-D integer array** $[1 \rightarrow 2, -1 \rightarrow 0, 0 \rightarrow 1]$

which would use eight storage elements:

found[1,−1,0]		integer
found[1,−1,1]		integer
found[1,0,0]		integer
found[1,0,1]		integer
found[2,−1,0]		integer
found[2,−1,1]		integer
found[2,0,0]		integer
found[2,0,1]		integer

In this case each reserved cell name has the form *found*[*i,j,k,*] such that $1 \leq i \leq 2$, $-1 \leq j \leq 0$, and $0 \leq k \leq 1$. The order of storage cells shown here is again row major order; the last index varies the fastest.

Arrays of more than three dimensions are seldom used in practice, and even 3-D arrays are quite uncommon.

CORRECTNESS OF PROGRAMS WITH MULTIDIMENSIONAL ARRAYS

Determining the correctness of programs using arrays of *n* dimensions follows the same guidelines we established in earlier chapters. In this case verifying the loops of a program will take more effort, because processing an *n*-dimensional array usually requires nested loops. However, verifying one loop at a time around the loop invariant and goal assertions is still normally a straightforward task.

In testing a program with arrays of multiple dimensions, special values should be included (where possible) to test what happens if any one of the dimensions is just one long. This would include the case where the array contains just a single element.

EFFICIENCY OF PROGRAMS WITH MULTIDIMENSIONAL ARRAYS

As we have mentioned earlier, the size of the input used for determining the time and space complexities of a program is a nebulous quantity. In some types of programs it is traditional to use the number of input values as the size, but for programs involving arrays the tradition is to use the number of values processed in each dimension of the array as the size of the input. This means, for example, that a loop that inputs k numbers into n rows and m columns of a 2-D array has $O(m*n)$ time complexity rather than $O(k)$ time complexity. The $O(m*n)$ time complexity is easy to determine because the loop structure would be nested, the outer loop iterating m times, and the inner loop iterating n times for each iteration of the outer loop. The reason for saying that the time complexity is $O(m*n)$ rather than $O(k)$, however, stems from the fact that for a table or matrix (the data structures most commonly implemented with 2-D arrays) increasing the input size means adding another row or column (or both) to the data structure; this in turn implies that either m or n (or both) is increased by 1. Such data structures never change size by just one element, so choosing the number of occupied rows and columns of a 2-D array is a fair measure of the size of the input for the routine processing that array.

Similarly, in a program using arrays of p dimensions, where $m_1, m_2, \ldots,$ m_p values are input into each of the p dimensions of the array, respectively, the size of the program (and therefore the time complexity) is determined from the values $m_1, m_2, \ldots, m_p$.

FOR REVIEW

7.1   What is the difference between a table and a 2-D array?

7.2   What do the terms row major order and column major order mean with respect to the input and output of a 2-D array?

7.3   Suppose that array a contains the following values:

a[1,1] = 5	a[1,2] = 6	a[1,3] = 7	a[1,4] = 8
a[2,1] = 9	a[2,2] = 10	a[2,3] = 11	a[2,4] = 12
a[3,1] = 13	a[3,2] = 14	a[3,3] = 15	a[3,4] = 16

How would the store look if a were stored in row major order? In column major order?

7.4   Suppose you have the following declarations:

storage specification
   constants
      max1 : **integer** 100
      max2 : **integer** 50
   variables
      table : **2-D integer array** [1 → max1, 1 → max2]
      rows, columns, i, j : **integer**
   end storage specification

(a)   Give the section of *mpl* program for inputting into variables *rows* and *columns* the number of rows and columns of data in the input and then inputting the data into *table* in row major order.

(b)   Repeat (a) for column major order.

(c)   Both (a) and (b) use the header method. What would the problems be with trying to implement the trailer or **moredata** methods for inputting a table into a 2-D array?

7.5   What types of special values should be tested on programs with 2-D arrays in determining robustness?

7.6   Give one possible loop form for processing each element of a 4-D array *fourd*, where the subscript range on each of the four dimensions is $[1 \to n]$. What is the time complexity of the loop?

7.7   Give the loop for printing just the diagonal elements of a 2-D array *a* that has the subscript range $[1 \to n]$ in both dimensions. What is the time complexity of this loop?

7.8   In what ways does the program design process change for problems with arrays of more than two dimensions?

7.9   How many elements are there in each of the following arrays?

   fred : **2-D integer array** $[-3 \to 5, -2 \to 0]$
   jet : **2-D real array** $[0 \to 0, 5 \to 5]$
   bigfoot : **3-D truth value array** $[1 \to 3, 2 \to 4, 3 \to 5]$
   tammy : **4-D real array** $[1 \to 1, 2 \to 2, 3 \to 3, 4 \to 4]$

7.10 Give an example of a problem for which it would be natural to use a 3-D array.

7.11 Give an example of a problem for which it would be natural to use a 4-D array.

A DEEPER LOOK

7.12 Suppose that a procedure prints each element of a 2-D array that has *m* rows and *n* columns. What are the differences in meaning between saying that this procedure has $O(m*n)$ time complexity and that it has $O(k)$ time complexity where *k* is the number of elements in the array? Which time complexity is more informative? Why?

7.13 Suppose that a procedure *whatsit* processes each element of a 2-D array with *m* rows *n* columns by calling a function for each element, where the function has time complexity $O(f)$. What is the time complexity of procedure *whatsit*?

7.14 Give examples of data structures that could not be implemented easily with 2-D arrays.

7.15 Explain why it is unimportant for general programming purposes to know how the processor actually stores an array in the store (e.g., in row or column major order, or in any other conceivable order).

7.16 If *mpl* allowed the instruction

   input arr

   to input all of the elements of a 2-D array *arr* without using loops, would this change your answer to the last exercise? Explain.

7.17 Include the appropriate loop invariant and goal assertions for procedure array subtraction (refinement 2 of case study 7.2).

7.18 If you are to design a program that is to access every member of an *n* by *n* array, where *n* is an input value, is it possible that the time complexity of the program will be better than $O(n*n)$? Could it be worse than $O(n*n)$?

7.19 Assume that you have to implement a program that uses a 2-D array declared as

arr : **2-D real array** $[1 \rightarrow m, 1 \rightarrow n]$

in a language that only provides 1-D arrays. Explain how you would do this, and how you would simulate access to an arbitrary element $arr[i, j]$.

7.20 Extend the last exercise to implement a more general array with bounds

$[m1 \rightarrow n1, m2 \rightarrow n2]$

7.21 Extend exercise 7.20, discussing how you would access an arbitrary element of a k-dimensional array, where the ith dimension has bounds $[mi \rightarrow ni]$. For example, how would you simulate access to the element:

arr[j1, j2, ..., jk]

TO PROGRAM

7.22 Modify case study 7.2 to work with real numbers (dollars and cents).

7.23 Design a procedure for inputting an integer table into a 2-D array in column major order. This procedure should be designed to take the place of procedure *read 2D integer* used in the programs of this chapter (for cases where the input is given in column major order).

7.24 Design a function to sum the elements of the diagonal of an n by n array.

7.25 Design *mpl* functions to find the largest and smallest values in any 2-D real array. What are the time and space complexities of these functions?

7.26 Design an *mpl* function to find the largest integer in any 3-D integer array. What are the time and space complexities of this function?

7.27 Design an *mpl* procedure *transpose(old, m, n, new)*, which assigns the transpose of an m by n array named *old* to an n by m array named *new*. Design an initial procedure that inputs values into an m by n array, calls *transpose*, and outputs the new array. The transpose of an array is the array whose columns were the rows of the original array. For example, the transpose of

2	4	6	is	2	8
8	3	5		4	3
				6	5

7.28 Design an *mpl* program that inputs an n by n table of reals, divides each element of each row by the diagonal element in that row, and outputs the resulting array. The input is a value for n followed by the array elements in row major order. For example, if the input is

```
4
2.0    6.1    0.0     4.2
0.0    7.3    7.3    14.6
1.9    2.7    1.0    51.8
2.0    4.1    0.0    -5.0
```

then the output should be

```
 1.0      3.05    0.0     2.1
 0.0      1.0     1.0     2.0
 1.9      2.7     1.0    51.8
-0.4     -0.82    0.0     1.0
```

Your program design should consider and handle any error situations.

**7.4
THE
CHALLENGE** | The two case studies of this section are numerical problems involving matrix multiplication. For each of these, the Correctness section has been left out, because their correctness is determined in the same manner as discussed in the case studies of the Getting Acquainted section.

**Case Study
7.3** | **Multiplying a Matrix
and a Vector**

> ***Problem Description:*** Multiply an m by n matrix by a column vector of length n.
>
> ***Input Specifications:*** Integers m and n, both > 0, followed by $m*n$ reals representing the matrix in row order, followed by n reals representing the vector.

A typical use of numerical arrays is in implementing vectors and matrices. A vector is implemented as a 1-D array and a matrix is implemented as a 2-D array. A matrix is just a rectangular collection of numbers, placed in m rows and n columns.

***Example
7.5*** Two matrices are given below:

$$\begin{bmatrix} -5.1 & 8.6 & 3.1 \\ 2.0 & 6.7 & 0.0 \end{bmatrix} \qquad \begin{bmatrix} 0.0 & 1.0 \\ 0.0 & 2.0 \\ -3.0 & 2.0 \\ 6.0 & -4.0 \end{bmatrix}$$

The first matrix is 2 by 3, as it has 2 rows and 3 columns, and the second is 4 by 2.

A column vector of size n is just an n by 1 matrix. That is , it consists of n numbers in a single column. For example, the following are 3- and 2-element column vectors, respectively.

$$\begin{bmatrix} -2.0 \\ 1.6 \\ -1.0 \end{bmatrix} \qquad \begin{bmatrix} -3.0 \\ 6.0 \end{bmatrix}$$

If we multiply an m by n matrix A by an n-element column vector B, we produce an m-element column vector C: the ith element of the product vector

C is found by multiplying each element of the ith row of A by the corresponding element of B and summing the results.

The result of multiplying a 3 × 3 matrix and a 3-element column vector is shown below.

Example 7.6

$$\begin{bmatrix} 1 & 2 & 3 \\ -1 & 0 & 2 \\ 0 & 0 & 1 \end{bmatrix} * \begin{bmatrix} -1 \\ 2 \\ 1 \end{bmatrix} = \begin{bmatrix} 1*-1 + 2*2 + 3*1 \\ -1*-1 + 0*2 + 2*1 \\ 0*-1 + 0*2 + 1*1 \end{bmatrix} = \begin{bmatrix} 6 \\ 3 \\ 1 \end{bmatrix}$$

A second example involves a 4 × 2 matrix and a 2-element column vector:

$$\begin{bmatrix} -2 & 3 \\ 1 & 2 \\ 6 & -6 \\ 1 & 3 \end{bmatrix} * \begin{bmatrix} 3 \\ 0 \end{bmatrix} = \begin{bmatrix} -2*3 + 3*0 \\ 1*3 + 2*0 \\ 6*3 + -6*0 \\ 1*3 + 3*0 \end{bmatrix} = \begin{bmatrix} -6 \\ 3 \\ 18 \\ 3 \end{bmatrix}$$

The Solution — 1-D and 2-D Arrays

The initial procedure for this program will declare three arrays, *matrix, vector,* and *result.* The array *matrix* is a 2-D array, whereas *vector* and *result* are 1-D arrays. The initial procedure inputs the actual numbers of rows and columns for *matrix,* checks to see whether these values are within bounds, and then inputs the two arrays *matrix* and *vector* using the input procedures of case studies 7.1 and 5.1. Finally, procedure *vectmult* is called to multiply *matrix* and *vector* to compute *result.*

```
matrix by vector : initial procedure
    {inputs a matrix and a vector and computes their product}
    storage specification
        constants
            rows, columns : integer 30
        variables
            matrix : 2-D real array [1 → rows, 1 → columns]
            vector : 1-D real array [1 → columns]
            result : 1-D real array [1 → rows]
            m, n : integer
    end storage specification
    begin matrix by vector
        input m, n
        if (m ≤ 0) or (n ≤ 0) or (m > rows) or (n > columns)
            then output 'bad data — too small or too large dimension'
            else  read 2D real(matrix, 1, m, 1, n)
                  read 1D real(vector, 1, n)
                  vectmult(matrix, vector, result, m, n)
                  write 1D real(result, 1, m)
        endif
    end matrix by vector
    where read 2D real is the standard 2-D array input procedure
    where read 1D real is the standard 1-D array input procedure
    where vectmult assigns the product of matrix and vector to result
    where write 1D real is the standard 1-D array output procedure
```

CASE STUDY 7.3 — REFINEMENT 1

We must now design *vectmult*, the procedure that multiplies the 2-D array *matrix* times the 1-D array *vector* to produce the 1-D array *result*. Recall from our example how this is done. The first element of the array *result* is computed by multiplying the first row of the array *matrix* by the corresponding elements of the 1-D array *vector* and summing the products. Similarly, the second element of the array *result* is computed by multiplying the second row of *matrix* by *vector* and summing the products, and so on. Since there are *m* rows in *matrix* the loop structure

```
loop start row with 1 step 1 to m
    {compute result[row] by multiplying the current row of
     matrix times vector and summing the products}
    endloop autoindex
```

can be used. To compute *result*[*row*] we first multiply

```
matrix[row, 1] * vector[1]
```

Then the second element in the current row of *matrix* is multiplied by the second element of *vector*,

```
matrix[row, 2] * vector[2]
```

and so on. In general, for each column in the current row of *matrix* the product

```
matrix[row, column] * vector[column]
```

must be computed, and then all of these products must be summed to get *result*[*row*]. That is,

```
result[row] ← matrix[row, 1] * vector[1]
             +matrix[row, 2] * vector[2]
             + ·
                 ·
                 ·
             +matrix[row, n] * vector[n]
```

This summing exercise is one we have done often. The loop to do this is

```
result[row] ← 0
loop start column with 1 step 1 to n
    result[row] ← result[row] + matrix[row, column] * vector[column]
    endloop autoindex
```

Inserting this section of code into our previous loop gives us the procedure *vectmult*.

```
vectmult : procedure
    {assigns the product of matrix and vector to result}

    storage specification
        parameters
            matrix : in out 2-D real array
            vector : in out 1-D real array
            result : out only 1-D real array
            m, n : in only integer
        variables
            row, column : integer
        end storage specification
    begin vectmult
        loop start row with 1 step 1 to m
            result[row] ← 0
            loop start column with 1 step 1 to n
                result[row] ← result[row] + matrix[row,column] * vector[column]
            endloop autoindex
        endloop autoindex
    end vectmult
```

CASE STUDY 7.3 — REFINEMENT 2

The inclusion of the loop invariant and goal assertions is left as an exercise.

Note that we have again used the **in out** designation for *matrix* and *vector*, even though the correct type would normally be **in only**. As we discussed in chapter 5, this avoids wasting storage and time caused by copying **in only** parameters. Since we do not alter either of these arrays within *vectmult*, the **in out** designation is fine.

Efficiency

The initial procedure calls four other procedures. Procedure *read 2D real* has time complexity $O(m*n)$, as we have determined before, where m is the number of rows and n the number of columns in the data being input. Similarly, *vectmult* has time complexity $O(m*n)$, because it contains a nested loop structure: the outer loop iterates m times and the inner one n times. The size of this problem is not the number of input items but rather the number of rows(m) and the number of columns (n) occupied in the array *matrix*.

We have previously determined that the other procedures called from the initial procedure have linear time complexity, either $O(m)$ or $O(n)$. Since these are lower time complexities than $O(m*n)$, we say that the overall time complexity for this program is $O(m*n)$.

By similar analysis we see that the largest data structure is stored in *matrix*, and it requires $m*n$ storage cells. Thus the space complexity for this program is also $O(m*n)$.

Summary — Case Study 7.3

Multiplying matrices and vectors is a common numerical computation. Although the reasons for performing such computations may be complex and require a deep knowledge of mathematics, the actual program is quite simple to develop. The nested loop structure has appeared in many diverse examples:

the rows of a 2-D array are stepped through in an outer loop, and each column element of a row is processed in an inner loop. The time complexity for this kind of nested loop is $O(m*n)$, where the outer loop is iterated m times and the inner loop n times.

Case Study 7.4 | Multiplying Two Matrices

> **Problem Description:** Multiply an m by n matrix by an n by p matrix.
>
> **Input Specifications:** Integers m, n, and p, all greater than 0, followed by $m * n$ reals representing the first matrix, and then $n * p$ reals representing the second matrix.

Multiplying two matrices is similar to multiplying a matrix and a vector. This problem also arises frequently in numerical computations.

The result of multiplying an m by n matrix by an n by p matrix is an m by p matrix. If we multiply two matrices named *first* and *second* to get a matrix called *result*, then for each row and column, *result[row,column]* is computed by pairwise multiplying *first[row,i]* times *second[i,column]* for all i between 1 and n and summing these products.

Example 7.7

Two 2 × 2 matrices are multiplied to get a 2 × 2 result matrix:

$$\begin{bmatrix} 1 & 2 \\ -1 & 0 \end{bmatrix} * \begin{bmatrix} 3 & 5 \\ -2 & 4 \end{bmatrix} = \begin{bmatrix} 1*3 + 2*-2 & 1*5 + 2*4 \\ -1*3 + 0*-2 & -1*5 + 0*4 \end{bmatrix} = \begin{bmatrix} -1 & 13 \\ -3 & -5 \end{bmatrix}$$

In the next example, a 3 × 2 matrix is multiplied by a 2 × 3 matrix to get a 3 × 3 matrix.

$$\begin{bmatrix} 1 & 0 \\ 0 & 1 \\ 1 & 2 \end{bmatrix} * \begin{bmatrix} 1 & 0 & 1 \\ 0 & 1 & 2 \end{bmatrix} = \begin{bmatrix} 1 & 0 & 1 \\ 0 & 1 & 2 \\ 1 & 2 & 5 \end{bmatrix}$$

Mathematically, the multiplication of two matrices is written

$$result[row,column] = \sum_{1 \leqslant k \leqslant n} first[row,k] * second[k,column]$$

The Solution — 2-D Arrays and Triply Nested Loops

The initial procedure is similar to that in case study 7.3:

```
matrix by matrix : initial procedure
    {inputs values into two matrices and computes their product}
    storage specification
        constants
            maxm, maxn, maxp : integer 30
        variables
            first : 2-D real array [1 → maxm, 1 → maxn]
            second : 2-D real array [1 → maxn, 1 → maxp]
            result : 2-D real array [1 → maxm, 1 → maxp]
            m, n, p : integer
    end storage specification
```

```
      begin matrix by matrix
        input m, n, p
        if (m ≤ 0) or (n ≤ 0) or (p ≤ 0)
                or (m > maxm) or (n > maxn) or (p > maxp)
        then output 'bad data – too small or too large dimensions'
        else  read 2D real(first, 1, m, 1, n)
              read 2D real(second, 1, n, 1, p)
              matrixmult(first, second, result, m, n, p)
              write 2D real(result, 1, m, 1, p)
        endif
      end matrix by matrix

    where read 2D real is the standard 2-D array input procedure
    where matrixmult assigns the product of first and second to result
    where write 2D real is the standard 2-D array output procedure
```

CASE STUDY 7.4 — REFINEMENT 1

Procedure *matrixmult* is the only one we need to design. For each row and column such that $1 \leq row \leq m$ and $1 \leq column \leq p$, *matrixmult* must compute *result[row,column]* by summing all products of the form *first[row,k]* * *second[k, column]* for $1 \leq k \leq n$. The computations in *matrixmult* are essentially the same as those in *vectmult* in the last case study. The difference is that in *matrixmult* we must multiply each row of *first* not by a single vector but by every column of *second* in succession (each column of *second* can be considered a separate vector). This implies that we need yet another loop, one for stepping through the columns of *second*. A top-down design of this three-loop nested structure is given below.

```
    loop start row with 1 step 1 to m
        assert rows 1 through row − 1 of result have been properly computed
        {Multiply the current row of first times each column
         of second to produce the current row of result}
        endloop autoindex
    assert rows 1 through m of result have been properly computed
```

The phrase "times each column of second" informs us that we need another loop that steps from 1 to *p*, where *p* is the number of columns in *second*.

```
    loop start row with 1 step 1 to m
        loop start column with 1 step 1 to p
            assert in the current row of result, result[row, 1] through
                    result[row,column−1] have been properly computed
            {compute result[row,column] by multiplying the current row of first
            times the current column of second and summing the products}
            endloop autoindex
        assert the current row of result has been properly computed
        endloop autoindex
```

From the previous case study and our examples in this case study, we recall that the computation of *result[row,column]* is

$$result[row,column] \leftarrow first[row,1] * second[1,column]$$
$$+ first[row,2] * second[2,column]$$
$$+ \vdots$$
$$+ first[row,n] * second[n,column]$$

This gives us the final loop structure

```
loop start row with 1 step 1 to m
    loop start column with 1 step 1 to p
        result[row,column] ← 0
        loop start k with 1 step 1 to n
            assert result[row,column] = first[row,1] * second[1,column] + ... +
                    first[row,k−1] * second[k−1,column]
            result[row,column] ← result[row,column] + first[row,k] *
                                         second[k,column]
        endloop autoindex {index k}
        assert result[row,column] = first[row,1] * second[1,column] + ... +
                first[row,n] * second[n,column]
    endloop autoindex {index column}
endloop autoindex {index row}
```

In each of the above segments we have included only the loop assertions for the new loop developed in that step. We use the final three-loop structure to write procedure *matrixmult*.

```
matrixmult : procedure
    {matrixmult multiplies two matrices, first and second, and puts  the product
    into result}

    storage specification
        parameters
            first, second : in out 2-D real array
            result : out only 2-D real array
            m, n, p : in only integer
        variables
            row, column, k : integer
    end storage specification

    begin matrixmult
        loop start row with 1 step 1 to m
            loop start column with 1 step 1 to p
                result[row,column] ← 0
                loop start k with 1 step 1 to n
                    result[row,column] ← result[row,column] + first[row,k] *
                                                 second[k,column]
                endloop autoindex {index k}
            endloop autoindex {index column}
        endloop autoindex {index row}
    end matrixmult
```

CASE STUDY 7.4 — REFINEMENT 2

We leave to you the inclusion of the loop invariant and goal assertions, which were developed as the loops were designed.

Efficiency

By now, our experience tells us that procedure *matrixmult* will be the most time-consuming routine in this program because of its three nested loops. All statements in the loop with index *row* will execute *m* times; all statements in the loop with index *column* will execute *p*m* times, because this loop lies in the *row* loop; and all statements in the loop with index k will execute $n*p*m$ times because this loop lies in the *column* loop, which lies in the *row* loop. Without further analysis, then, we can say that procedure *matrixmult* has time complexity $O(n*p*m)$, where the two arrays being multiplied have dimensions $n \times m$ and $m \times p$. Since all other procedures in this program have time complexity similar to $O(n*m)$, as derived earlier, we say that the entire program has time complexity $O(n*p*m)$.

Just how bad is this time complexity measure? In many instances the matrices involved are square (they have the same number, n, of rows and columns). In these cases the time complexity is $O(n*n*n)$ or $O(n^3)$. A 100×100 matrix is not uncommon in practice; multiplying two such matrices would mean that the statement

result[row,column] ← result[row,column] + first[row,k] * second[k,column]

in the innermost loop would be executed

100 * 100 * 100 = 1,000,000

times! Doubling the number of rows and columns in these matrices (to make 200×200 matrices) would result in 8,000,000 executions of that statement. Since the time complexity is $O(n^3)$, doubling the size of the problem results in not 2 times as many statements being executed but $2^3 = 8$ times as many statements. The number of statements executed rises proportionally to n^3.

Matrix multiplication is a real headache in practice. There are many applications involving very large matrices, so large, in fact, that the computations cannot be completed within practical time limits on real computers. The underlying reason is the triply nested loop.

The arrays used in this program are all 2-D arrays; the number of storage cells occupied in these arrays is $m*n$ for array *first*, plus $n*p$ for array *second*, plus $m*p$ for array *result*. If we have square $n \times n$ matrices, the space complexity becomes $O(n^2)$.

Summary — Case Study 7.4

The matrix multiplication problem is somewhat complex. Top-down program design methodology allowed us to break this problem into three simple, nested loops. The fact that these loops are nested, however, means that the program has a serious time complexity problem since the execution time grows rapidly as the size of the matrices increases. The time complexity for the problem is $O(n*p*m)$, or $O(n^3)$ if $n = m = p$.

7.29   The program for multiplying two matrices in case study 7.4 should be usable to solve the problem of multiplying a matrix times a vector (case study 7.3). Explain how.

7.5 WORKING OUT

7.30   Design an *mpl* program that inputs values into a 2-D array and sorts these values so that the smallest elements are in order in the first row, and next smallest in the second row, and so on. The number of rows and columns are placed at the head of the input data. For example, if the input is

```
 3   4
12   2    7    9
 3   2   17    1
 6   9   12    2
```

then the output should be

```
1    2    2    2
3    6    7    9
9   12   12   17
```

What are the time and space complexities of your program?

7.31 Design a program in *mpl* that solves the *traveling salesperson problem* (TSP) for a map containing five cities. The idea of TSP is that a salesperson starts in city 1, where he or she must ultimately return after visiting each of the other cities once. The salesperson is given the distance between each pair of cities, and must find the shortest route. The input consists of a 5 by 5 matrix called *distance* in which *distance[i, j]* is the distance between city i and city j. For example, if the input is

```
0   7   5   7   4
7   0   3   4   7
5   3   0   6   6
7   4   6   0   3
4   6   7   3   0
```

then the output should be

The best route is: 1   3   2   4   5   1
Distance = 19

Does your design take advantage of the fact that the distance around a route is the same in either direction? Determine the time and space complexities of your program.

7.32 In the previous exercise you designed a program to solve TSP. The input to that program was a 5 by 5 matrix of integers giving the distance between cities. Clearly, this matrix should satisfy certain properties: it should be symmetric (*distance[i, j]* = *distance[j, i]* for all i and j) and also distances should satisfy the triangle rule (*distance[i, j]* + *distance[j, k]* 9 *distance[i, k]* for all i, j, and k). In addition, *distance [i, i]* should be 0 for all i. Design a **truth value** function *legal(distance)* which checks to see whether or not an n by n integer array *distance* satisfies these properties. Incorporate this function into your program for exercise 7.31. Does this affect the overall time or space complexity of your program?

7.33 Design an *mpl* program which reads in an n by n matrix and calculates the value of its determinant. Find the time and space complexities of your program. (If you don't know what a determinant is don't worry, just ignore this exercise.)

7.34 Design an *mpl* program which uses Gaussion Elimination to solve a series of simultaneous linear equations. (If you don't know what Gaussion Elimination is don't worry, just ignore this exercise).

| CHAPTER 8 |

Records

NEW CONCEPTS: Records, Sorting records, Sorting records with an index array

Our study of data structures so far has shown that we can easily represent lists, tables, and matrices of *homogeneous values* (values of the same type, e.g., **integer**) using arrays. For example, a 1-D integer array can be used to store a list of integers, but it cannot be used to hold a list containing both integers and reals. So, while arrays serve quite well in many instances there are others where their use is quite cumbersome.

Consider the personnel office of a large company, where a record must be kept for every employee. Each record might contain an employee's name, social security number, salary, address, telephone number, and other information. If a computer program is designed to handle all this information, it would be desirable to keep the elements of a record together as a single unit. Modern programming languages provide this capability, which we model in *mpl* with the **record** data type, which is the topic of this chapter.

We will examine only two case studies involving records here, because there really aren't many practical uses for records within the context of the programming we have done so far. The largest application of records is in storing data in an *external file* (a file of data kept not in the store but in secondary storage). In chapter 10 we will describe secondary storage and delve into the external storage of data. Records are also used in constructing linked list representations of data structures, a topic covered in chapter 9.

8.1
GETTING
ACQUAINTED

The **record** data type in *mpl* is the equivalent of the filing card system used by companies before the advent of computers (pertinent employee information was kept on individual filing cards that were stored in alphabetical order in filing cabinets). An example will show how such records can be declared for use in a program.

Example
8.1

Suppose we have a filing cabinet containing cards that describe students in a university. Each card contains the following information:

> last name, first name
> ID number
> major
> grade point average

For example, the 50th card in the cabinet might contain

> Doe, John
> 3268215
> Business Administration
> 2.935

If we were to replace this card file with an equivalent computerized system, we would create a record for each student, declared by

> student : **record containing**
>   last : **string**
>   first : **string**
>   idnumber : **integer**
>   major : **string**
>   gpa : **real**
>   **endrecord** student

or the equivalent declaration:

> student : **record containing**
>   last, first : **string**
>   idnumber : **integer**
>   major : **string**
>   gpa : **real**
>   **endrecord** student

Either record declaration would set up the store to look like:

student.last		string
student.first		string
student.idnumber		integer
student.major		string
student.gpa		real

The student record is a structure with five *components*, *record items*, or *fields*, of which three are strings, one is an integer, and one is a real. As is shown in the store, a component of a record is referenced with the form

record name . component name

For example, the grade point average of the student described in this record (which we call *student*), has the name *student . gpa*, and references to this cell are made using this name. The information on the filing card described earlier can be saved in this record with the assignments

```
student.last ← 'Doe'
student.first ← 'John'
student.idnumber ← 3268215
student.major ← 'Business Administration'
student.gpa ← 2.935
```

In our example we have declared the idnumber component of the record to be of type **integer.** Since no arithmetic is performed on the idnumber, however, it could have been declared to have type **string.** This is often done in practice, reserving the **integer** and **real** data types for numeric values that will actually be used in calculations.

In the only case study of this section you will learn how to assign values to the fields of a record and how to print out these field values.

Constructing and Printing Employee Records

Case Study
8.1
in Pascal

> *Problem Description:* Read in an employee's name, social security number, hourly wage, address, and age into two records, one containing the employee's name, social security number, and hourly wage, and one containing the employee's name, address, and age.
>
> *Input Specifications:* Three character strings for the employee's first, middle, and last names, a 9-digit social security number, a real number giving the hourly wage, a character string address, and an integer age.

Personnel offices often maintain more than one file, with different types of data in each file. In this case the first record, which contains the employee's name, social security number, and hourly wage, might be a record of a finance file, whereas the second record, which contains the employee's name, address, and age, might be part of a personal information file. Of course, there would be many similar records making up these two files, but for this case study we will just examine how single records can be input and output.

The Solution — Simple Records

Our initial procedure will define the proper record structures and call on procedure *read records* to perform the input.

```
records : initial procedure
    {inputs and prints a finance record and a personal record}

    storage specification
        variables
            finance : record containing
                first, middle, last : string
                ssnumber : integer
                wage : real
                endrecord finance
            personal : record containing
                first, middle, last, address : string
                age : integer
                endrecord personal
    end storage specification

    begin records
        read records(finance, personal)
        output 'finance record:'
        output 'name —', finance.first, ' ', finance.middle, ' ',
            finance.last
        output 'social security number —', finance.ssnumber
        output 'hourly wage — ', finance.wage
        output ' '
        output 'personal record:'
        output 'name — ', personal.first, ' ', personal.middle, ' ',
            personal.last
        output 'address — ', personal.address
        output 'age — ', personal.age
    end records

    where read records inputs a finance and a personal record
```

CASE STUDY 8.1 — REFINEMENT 1

There are two record declarations in this refinement. The record named *finance* has five components called *first, middle, last, ssnumber* and *wage*. To access these fields of the record, we must refer to them as *finance.first, finance.middle, finance.last, finance.ssnumber,* and *finance.wage.* We read *finance.ssumber* as "field *ssnumber* in record *finance,*" for example. The **variables** declarations for records *finance* and *personal* will create 10 cells with the following structure:

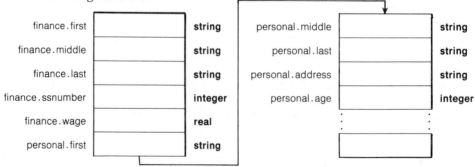

To design procedure *read records*, we need to know more about the input data. In nearly all cases involving record information, the data for the record is organized within very strict guidelines. For example, the name might appear as a single unit in the first 20 columns of an input line, followed by a blank, followed by 30 columns containing the address, and so on. This carefully organized structure makes the input routines much easier to design. In this case study we will assume that the data is organized as follows:

1. The first name appears in the first 10 positions.
2. The middle name appears in the next 10 positions.
3. The last name appears in the next 10 positions.
4. The social security number appears in the next 11 positions, including 1 leading and 1 trailing blank.
5. The hourly wage (a maximum of 5 digits including a decimal point) appears in the next 7 positions, with 1 leading and 1 trailing blank.
6. The address appears in the next 20 positions.
7. The age (a maximum of 2 digits) appears in the next 3 positions, including 1 leading blank.

The blanks are inserted around numbers because we assume that *mpl* inputs numbers from the preceding blank to the trailing blank. This gives us the following design for *read records:*

```
read records : procedure
    {inputs values into a finance and a personal record}
    storage specification
        parameters
            finance : out only record containing
                first, middle, last : string
                ssnumber : integer
                wage : real
            endrecord finance
            personal : out only record containing
                first, middle, last, address : string
                age : integer
            endrecord personal
    end storage specification

begin read records
    read string(finance.first, 10)
    read string(finance.middle, 10)
    read string(finance.last, 10)
    input finance.ssnumber, finance.wage
    read string(personal.address, 20)
    input personal.age
    personal.first ← finance.first
    personal.middle ← finance.middle
    personal.last ← finance.last
end read records

where read string inputs a string given the name of the string and
        the number of characters in the string; defined
        in case study 6.1.
```

CASE STUDY 8.1 — REFINEMENT 2

We have used procedure *read string* of case study 6.1 to input the necessary strings, so there are no other procedures to design here. Notice that the last three assignment statements of this procedure duplicate the employee name in the personal record.

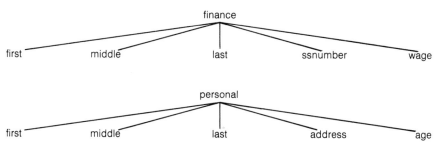

FIGURE 8-1. RECORD STRUCTURES

The finance and personal records declared in the initial procedure are illustrated in Figure 8-1. These record structures are satisfactory, but they can be organized better. The first record contains the employee's name, ssnumber, and wage, and the second contains the name, address, and age. The name has three parts, first, middle, and last. This information would be represented more meaningfully by the structures in Figure 8-2, which were created by replacing the three name components of each record (*first, middle,* and *last*) with an inner record called *name*, which has *first, middle,* and *last* as its components. In other words, the record declaration

```
finance : record containing
    first, middle, last : string
    ssnumber : integer
    wage : real
    endrecord finance
```

can be replaced by the declaration

```
finance : record containing
    name : record containing
        first, middle, last : string
        endrecord name
    ssnumber : integer
    wage : real
    endrecord finance
```

in which case the record named *finance* will have the structure shown in Figure 8-2. In this case we say that the finance record has three components. The first is *name*, which is also a record, and the second and third are the fields *ssnumber* and *wage*, respectively. This difference is important; we can no longer use the reference *finance.first* to refer to the first name. This reference must now be written *finance.name.first*, indicating "field *first* in record *name*, which is in record *finance*."

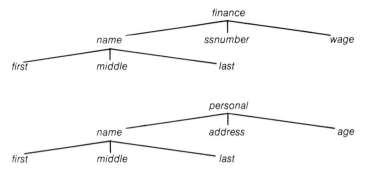

FIGURE 8-2. IMPROVED RECORD STRUCTURES

Using this new record form leads to the program shown in refinements 3 and 4:

```
records : initial procedure
    {inputs and prints a finance record and a personal record}

    storage specification
        variables
            finance : record containing
                name : record containing
                    first, middle, last : string
                    endrecord name
                ssnumber : integer
                wage : real
                endrecord finance
            personal : record containing
                name : record containing
                    first, middle, last : string
                    endrecord name
                address : string
                age : integer
                endrecord personal
        end storage specification

    begin records
        read records(finance, personal)
        output 'finance record:'
        output 'name — ', finance.name.first, ' ', finance.name.middle,
                ' ', finance.name.last
        output 'social security number — ', finance.ssnumber
        output 'hourly wage — ', finance.wage
        output ' '
        output 'personal record:'
        output 'name — ', personal.name.first, ' ', personal.name.middle,
                ' ', personal.name.last
        output 'address — ', personal.address
        output 'age — ', personal.age
        end records

    where read records inputs a finance and a personal record
```

CASE STUDY 8.1 — REFINEMENT 3

```
read records : procedure
    {inputs values into a finance and a personal record}

    storage specification
        parameters
            finance : out only record containing
                name : record containing
                    first, middle, last : string
                    endrecord name
                ssnumber : integer
                wage : real
                endrecord finance
            personal : out only record containing
                name : record containing
                    first, middle, last : string
                    endrecord name
                address : string
                age : integer
                endrecord personal
    end storage specification

begin read records
    read string(finance.name.first, 10)
    read string(finance.name.middle, 10)
    read string(finance.name.last, 10)
    input finance.ssnumber, finance.wage
    read string(personal.address, 20)
    input personal.age
    personal.name ← finance.name
    end read records

where read string inputs a string given the name of the string and
        the number of characters in the string; defined in case study 6.1.
```

CASE STUDY 8.1 — REFINEMENT 4

Note that since *finance.name* and *personal.name* have the same structure, we are able to use the single assignment statement

```
personal.name ← finance.name
```

in place of the three separate assignment statements we used before. The processor will automatically make the individual field assignments of the *finance.name* record (*first, middle, last*) to the corresponding fields of the *personal.name* record.

Correctness

Records have no unique features that affect the determination of program correctness; the process is the same for programs with records as it is for other programs. Common errors made with records include not declaring a record properly (for example, it is easy to forget a field in a large record) and not qualifying a field of a record properly (for example, writing *first* instead of *personal.name.first*).

Efficiency

This program has no loops and uses just a fixed amount of space, so both the time and space complexities are $O(1)$ (constant).

Summary — Case Study 8.1

We have learned how to use the *mpl* **record** type to implement data that is structured as a record with fields of various types. The components of a record can themselves be records, as we showed in refinements 3 and 4. Not every programming language allows records, but all modern ones do.

The **record** data type has been introduced in this chapter. To review how to declare a record in *mpl*, you should reread the introductory paragraphs of this chapter.

**8.2
IN
RETROSPECT**

SIMPLE RECORDS

In reviewing the case study of the previous section, we see that the primary purpose of records is really convenience. By using records, we can group items that logically belong together and treat these items as a single unit. If two records *a* and *b* have the same record structure, then the assignment

    a ← b

can be made, and the processor will automatically assign each record item of *b* to the corresponding record item of *a*. The alternative would be for the programmer to make the proper individual assignment for each field of *b* to *a*.

Real programming languages allow a number of shortcuts that make records more convenient to use. For example, we have been careful to fully qualify the various fields and subrecords of a declared record. For instance, in referring to the last name field of subrecord *name* of the personal record, we write

    personal.name.last

Some programming languages allow the programmer to use only as much qualification as is needed to uniquely distinguish the value being used. For instance, field *wage* only appears in the finance record, so the processor would be able to properly evaluate a reference to *wage* without the qualification *finance.wage*. However, using just the field *last*, or even *name.last* is not sufficient, because these fields appear in both the finance and personal records; the full qualification *finance.name.last* or *personal.name.last* is needed. In *mpl* we use full qualification for clarity.

A second shortcut that could be used in designing programs in *mpl* regards passing records as parameters. As seen in case study 8.1, each time a record is passed as a parameter to another routine, the entire record description is copied in the **parameters** list of that routine. We do this for completeness and clarity, but in reality it would be acceptable to just include a comment indicating that the record description used in the calling routine was to apply to the formal parameter. For example, in refinement 4 of case study 8.1 the **parameters** declaration could be written as

parameters
   finance : **out only record containing**
      {same description as in initial procedure}
   personal : **out only record containing**
      {same description as in initial procedure}

When translating this into an actual programming language, the information required by that language would then be included.

For examples of record declarations and their use, review case study 8.1.

ARRAYS OF RECORDS

Of course, single records of the type we declared in case study 8.1 have little use by themselves. It is only as we consider groups of records (for example, a set of employee records making up a personnel file for a company) that the use of records makes sense. In fact, as we shall see in chapter 10, a major application of records is in maintaining large files of data (e.g., personnel information) that must be kept available on external storage devices for daily processing by computer programs. To handle such files, it is often necessary to manipulate many records at once in the store. *Arrays of records* are used in these applications.

Example 8.2 In case study 8.1 we had two records, a personal record and a finance record. To declare an array of 200 personal records we could write

   personal : **1-D record array** [1 → 200] **containing**
      name : **record containing**
         first, middle, last : **string**
         endrecord name
      address : **string**
      age : **integer**
      endrecord personal

The store would be organized as follows to accommodate this array of records:

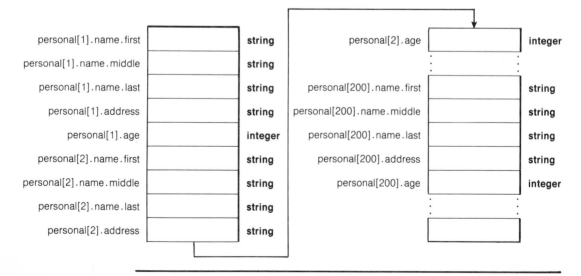

IMPLEMENTING RECORDS WHEN NO RECORD DATA TYPE IS AVAILABLE

Records have some advantages that can best be illustrated by looking at the alternative in some actual programming languages that do not have records; in these languages, separate arrays must be declared for each item when an array of records is to be implemented.

Most modern real programming languages have record data types, but some languages do not. Even when designing programs in languages that do not allow records, it is good to think of the data that logically forms a record (such as the personal information on an employee) as a single unit of information. However, this information must be kept in single 1-D arrays if records are not available. The personal record of the previous example would have to be simulated with five 1-D arrays:

Example 8.3

variables
firstname : **1-D string array** [1 → 200]
middlename : **1-D string array** [1 → 200]
lastname : **1-D string array** [1 → 200]
address : **1-D string array** [1 → 200]
age : **1-D integer array** [1 → 200]

The store would then be organized as follows:

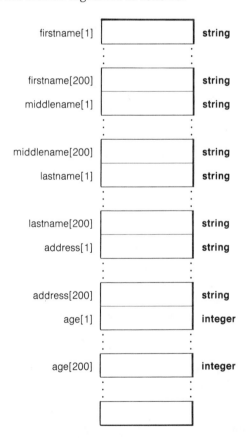

In the previous example, the *i*th record contained all of the information on the *i*th employee, that is, all of the personal information on employee *i* was in *personal*[*i*]. In this example, the personal information on employee *i* is contained in *firstname*[*i*], *middlename*[*i*], *lastname*[*i*], *address*[*i*], and *age*[*i*].

Consider how we would design programs to swap records in these two different cases. In the first case we would just define a new record, *temp*, with the same structure as *personal*, and then we could write

```
temp ← personal[i]
personal[i] ← personal[j]
personal[j] ← temp
```

to swap the entire *i*th and *j*th records of the array of personal records. If we wrote a procedure to do this swap, we would need to declare two **in out** parameters *x* and *y* with exactly the same record structure as a personal record, and then declare another record, *temp*, with the same record structure also. The body of this procedure (*swaprecords*) could then be written as follows:

```
begin swaprecords
    temp ← x
    x ← y
    y ← temp
end swaprecords
```

We could then swap the *i*th and *j*th records of the personal array by issuing a single call to *swaprecords*

```
swaprecords(personal[i], personal[j])
```

Now consider what happens when we want to swap records in the case where separate arrays are used to simulate the personal record structure. We would need to write a new procedure *swapstrings* for swapping two strings (it has the same basic design as our swap routine of case study 2.3, except that the two **in out** parameters and the variable *temp* would have type **string**). This new procedure *swapstrings* and our old procedure *swap* for swapping integer values would then be used as follows:

```
swapstrings(firstname[i], firstname[j])
swapstrings(middlename[i], middlename[j])
swapstrings(lastname[i],lastname[j])
swapstrings(address[i], address[j])
swap(age[i], age[j])
```

Here, unlike the case where a true record structure can be defined, the programmer must swap each element of the record individually, a tedious task.

In The Challenge section we will examine a case study that sorts arrays of records. Remember, if you are using an actual programming language that does not allow records, you must implement the array of records with as many 1-D arrays of the proper types as there are individual fields in the record being implemented.

CORRECTNESS OF PROGRAMS USING RECORDS

There is nothing unique to programs with records that requires special consideration when determining their correctness. Following the guidelines established in earlier chapters is sufficient. The most important thing to remember is that careful attention must be paid to the design of the records as well as to their use; it is sometimes easy to forget to handle each field of a record properly.

EFFICIENCY OF PROGRAMS USING RECORDS

The efficiency of programs that manipulate records is determined as usual by a statement count and a count of storage cells used. However, you must remember that operations on records can be much more time-consuming than operations on simple variables. For example, an assignment statement like

record1 ← record2

where *record1* and *record2* are two similar records containing (possibly) many fields, will obviously require much more time for the processor to execute than a statement like

a ← b

where *a* and *b* are simple integer variables. In other words, you must be aware that programs involving records will generally require more execution time than similar problems involving simple variables.

**8.3
WARMUP
EXERCISES**

FOR REVIEW

8.1 Give an example (different from those given in this chapter) of a real-world application in which a large set of identically structured records is needed.

8.2 What does the term homogeneous mean in the context of this chapter?

8.3 Declare a record *fraggle* which has an integer *number* field, a real *price* field, and subrecord *info* containing *ssnumber, id,* and *code,* all of type **string.**

8.4 Show how the store would be organized for the following declarations:

(a)   **storage specification**
          item : **record containing**
               partnumber : **integer**
               price : **real**
               description : **string**
               endrecord item
          end storage specification

(b)   **storage specification**
          newitem : **record containing**
               partnumber : **1-D integer array** [0 → 50]
               price : **real**
               description : **string**
               endrecord newitem
          end storage specification

8.5 For each field of the *item* and *newitem* records of the previous exercise give an example of how that field is accessed. For example, *item.partnumber* is an access of field *partnumber* in record *item.*

8.6   Give a loop that prints out each *partnumber* array element in (b) of exercise 8.4.

8.7   Under what conditions is it possible to assign one record to another directly?

8.8   Can two different records in the same program have identical field names? Explain your answer.

A DEEPER LOOK

8.9   Use the following record declaration in this exercise:

partlist : **record containing**
    type : **character**
    item : **record containing**
        partnumber : **1-D integer array** [0 → 5]
        price : **real**
        description : **string**
        endrecord item
    onorder : **truth value**
    inventory : **integer**
    endrecord partlist

(a)   How would this record appear in the store?

(b)   Give a loop to print the *partnumber* array.

8.10   Given the record declaration

partlist : **1-D record array** [1 → 100] **containing**
    type : **string**
    item : **record containing**
        partnumber : **1-D integer array** [0 → 5]
        price : **real**
        description : **string**
        endrecord item
    info : **2-D character array** [1 → 3, 1 → 3]
    onorder : **truth value**
    endrecord partlist

(a)   For each field of *partlist*, give an example of how that field is accessed.

(b)   How would this record appear in the store?

(c)   Give a loop structure to print the *partnumber* array for each record in *partnumber*.

8.11   Give reasons why a program designed to manipulate records might take substantially more execution time than a similar program designed to manipulate integers.

8.12   Discuss the way to implement a record data structure in a programming language which has no **record** data type, but has the other features studied so far in this book.

8.13   Give the declaration of a hundred element array of *item* records, where an *item* record is as given in exercise 8.4. Show how this declaration would organize the store.

8.14   In what ways does the program design process change to handle problems involving records?

TO PROGRAM

8.15   A business has a list of employee records each containing the following components:

name (character string length 10)
initials (2 characters)
age (integer)
salary (real)
sex (character, 'M' or 'F')
telephone extension (integer)

Design a program in *mpl* that reads this list of records and outputs all information on the highest paid woman in the company.

8.16   Modify the previous exercise to print all information on the highest paid man, the highest paid woman, the lowest paid man, the lowest paid woman, and the average salaries for men and for women.

8.17   A parts house has information in the following form on all parts it carries:

partname (character string, length 15)
partnumber (integer)
partprice (real)
inventory (integer — the number of parts of this type in the inventory)
threshold (integer — the inventory should not fall below this number)

Design a program using the **record** data type to input a list of record information in this form and print the following information: (1) the name and number of each part whose inventory is less than the threshold (to indicate that it is time to order new parts); (2) the total dollar value of the inventory for each part.

**8.4
THE
CHALLENGE**

Sorting Records

Case Study
8.2

> *Problem Description:* Given an array of personal records of the type in case study 8.1, print the names and addresses of all employees in alphabetical order by last name.
>
> *Input Specifications:* For each record the first name, middle name, and last name appear in the first 10 columns of three successive lines, the address appears on the next line in the first 20 positions, and the age appears on the next line.

As we have mentioned, it is often necessary to manipulate arrays of records. One common form of array manipulation is, naturally, sorting.

In case studies 5.7 and 5.8 we learned how to sort a simple list of homogeneous values stored in an array. How must we change these sorting methods (*insertion sort* and *quicksort*) to apply them to an array of records? One obvious difference is that we must exchange entire records when a swap is necessary instead of exchanging single elements. A second difference is that we must decide which field of the record is to determine the sorted order of the records. For example, if the records are to be ordered alphabetically by last name, then we would compare the last name fields to determine which records are to be swapped. These considerations will be illustrated in this case study.

First Solution — Insertion Sort Applied to Records

The initial procedure must call the procedures that input, sort, and print the personal record array.

```
sort personal : initial procedure
    {prints the personal record array sorted by last name}

    storage specification
        constants
            max : integer 500
        variables
            n : integer
            personal : 1-D record array [1 → max] containing
                name : record containing
                    first, middle, last : string
                    endrecord name
                address : string
                age : integer
                endrecord personal
    end storage specification

    begin sort personal
        read personal array(personal, n)
        sort personal array(personal, n)
        write personal array(personal, n)
        end sort personal

    where read personal array inputs the record elements of the
            personal array
    where sort personal array sorts the personal array into alphabetical
            order by last name
    where write personal array prints the names and addresses in each
            personal record

CASE STUDY 8.2 — REFINEMENT 1
```

Notice that the personal record array is declared with the first line

personal : **1-D record array** [1 → max] **containing**

which establishes an array with *max* records. As we discussed in the In Retrospect section, an element of this array is specified by placing the array index after the name of the record array, as in personal[i].age

which refers to the *age* field in the *i*th record of the personal array.

In previous chapters we constructed general input and output routines for handling similar types of data (for example, procedure *read 1D integer* for inputting one-dimensional integer arrays). General routines cannot be written for record arrays, however, because nearly every application using records requires a different record structure. That is, each time we construct a new 1-D record array, the record elements will undoubtedly have different fields than those of any previous record array. Thus we have named the procedures for reading, sorting, and writing the personal array of records *read personal array*, *sort personal array*, and *write personal array*, respectively. These names indicate clearly which records these routines are designed for.

Procedure *read personal array* is straightforward. It is

```
read personal array : procedure
    {inputs the records of the personal array}

    storage specification
        parameters
            personal : out only 1-D record array containing
                name : record containing
                    first, middle, last : string
                    endrecord name
                address : string
                age : integer
                endrecord personal
            n : out only integer
        end storage specification

    begin read personal array
        n ← 0
        loop while moredata
            n ← n + 1
            read string(personal[n].name.first, 10)
            read string(personal[n].name.middle, 10)
            read string(personal[n].name.last, 10)
            read string(personal[n].address, 20)
            input personal[n].age
        endloop while
    end read personal array

    where read string was defined in case study 6.1.
```

CASE STUDY 8.2 — REFINEMENT 2

When this procedure has finished executing, all of the records of the personal array will have been input, and *n* will contain the number of records in the array. As usual, we do not need to include the array bounds for the formal parameter array *personal*, because these bounds will be taken from the actual parameter.

Since the procedure *write personal array* is also quite simple, we include it next.

```
write personal array : procedure
    {prints the records of the personal array}

    storage specification
      parameters
        personal : in out 1-D record array containing
          name : record containing
            first, middle, last : string
            endrecord name
          address : string
          age : integer
          endrecord personal
        n : in only integer
      end storage specification

    begin write personal array
      loop start i with 1 step 1 to n
        output personal[i].name.first, ' ', personal[i].name.middle,
            ' ', personal[i].name.last
        output personal[i].address
        endloop autoindex
      end write personal array
```

CASE STUDY 8.2 — REFINEMENT 3

We now come to procedure *sort personal array*. Reviewing case studies 5.7 and 5.8 will make our first attempt at the design of this procedure quite easy. Our only choice, really, is whether to use the insertion sort of case study 5.7 or the quicksort of case study 5.8. In languages that allow recursion, the choice is clear; we have seen that *quicksort* is generally much faster than *insertion sort*. However, we have not yet described how a recursive procedure (*quicksort* in particular) can be designed to run nonrecursively in languages that do not allow recursion (we will do this in case study 9.6). So, we will first modify *insertion sort* so that it can handle records and then turn our attention to *quicksort*. Before doing this, however, we will design the new swap procedure for exchanging two personal records; this procedure will be used by both *insertion sort* and *quicksort*.

```
swap personal records : procedure
    {exchanges two records of the array personal}

    storage specification
      parameters
        personal1, personal2 : in out record containing
          name : record containing
            first, middle, last : string
            endrecord name
          address : string
          age : integer
          endrecord personal1, personal2
      variables
        temp : record containing
          name : record containing
            first, middle, last : string
            endrecord name
          address : string
          age : integer
          endrecord temp
      end storage specification
```

```
begin swap personal records
    temp ← personal1
    personal1 ← personal2
    personal2 ← temp
    end swap personal records
```

CASE STUDY 8.2 — REFINEMENT 4

Notice that most of the work in this procedure is in setting up the record structures. The swap in the computation section of the procedure looks as simple as it did in the original swap procedure of case study 2.3. But don't be fooled! The processor must do at least five times as much work here, because it must move the five fields in a record to different storage cells each time one of the assignment statements is executed.

Now, in modifying *insertion sort* to work with records, we must remember two things: (1) when we compare two records to determine whether one of them is out of place, we need only compare the last name fields, and (2) when a record is determined to be out of place, the entire record must be swapped (not just the name field). When we apply the first observation to procedure *insertion sort* (case study 5.7 — refinement 2) we get the following version, which has been modified to handle personal records. We will call the new procedure *sort personal array*.

```
sort personal array : procedure
    {sorts the personal record array into alphabetical order by last name}

    storage specification
        parameters
            personal : in out 1-D record array containing
                name : record containing
                    first, middle, last : string
                    endrecord name
                address : string
                age : integer
                endrecord personal
            n : in only integer
        end storage specification

    begin sort personal array
        loop start i with 2 step 1 to n
            if personal[i].name.last < personal[i−1].name.last
                then moveup personal(personal, i)
                endif
            endloop autoindex
        end sort personal array

    where moveup personal inserts the ith personal record into its proper position
```

CASE STUDY 8.2 — REFINEMENT 5

Notice that the only significant differences between this procedure and the original *insertion sort* are declaring the parameter array of personal records and using just the last name field of each record in the comparison in the **if** statement. Notice that *the same basic procedure works here*, even though the data structure is quite different.

To convert procedure *moveup* (case study 5.7 — refinement 4) to handle personal records, we must follow our second observation and swap entire records when an out-of-place record is moved up the list. Making this change in procedure *moveup* gives us procedure *moveup personal:*

```
moveup personal : procedure
    {moves the ith personal record up to its proper place}

  storage specification
    parameters
      personal : in out 1-D record array containing
        name : record containing
          first, middle, last : string
          endrecord name
        address : string
        age : integer
        endrecord pesonal
      i : in only integer
    variables
      j : integer
      stop : truth value
    end storage specification

  begin moveup personal
    j ← i
    loop
      if personal[j].name.last < personal[j−1].name.last
        then swap personal records(personal[j], personal[j−1])
            j ← j − 1
        else stop ← true
        endif
      endloop until stop or (j = 1)
    end moveup personal

  where swap personal records exchanges the jth and j − 1st records
```

CASE STUDY 8.2 — REFINEMENT 6

Again, we stress that we did not have to redesign our basic procedure to apply *insertion sort* to this case study. The only changes were in the data structures being manipulated. This is quite common — once we have made the effort to design a needed procedure, we can often apply the procedure to different data structures after making only minor modifications. This observation will also apply to procedure *quicksort*, which we will now examine.

Second Solution — Quicksort Applied to Records

It should now be clear how to modify *quicksort* to handle records. Comparisons are made between the same fields in two records, and when swaps are necessary the entire records are exchanged. The only major change we need to make in procedure *quicksort* (case study 5.8 — refinement 2) is in the **parameter** declarations.

---

quicksort personal : **procedure**
{sorts the personal record array into alphabetical order by last name}

    storage specification
      parameters
        personal : **in out 1-D record array containing**
          name : **record containing**
            first, middle, last : **string**
          endrecord name
          address : **string**
          age : **integer**
          endrecord personal
        low, high : **in only integer**
      variables
        medianposition : **integer**
    end storage specification

begin quicksort personal
    if high > low
      then partition personal(personal, low, high, medianposition)
          quicksort personal(personal, low, medianposition − 1)
          quicksort personal(personal, medianposition + 1, high)
      endif
    end quicksort personal

where partition rearranges the personal array such that for all i,
      low ≤ i ≤ medianposition−1,
      personal[i].name.last < personal[medianposition].name.last
      and for all i, medianposition+1 ≤ i ≤ high,
      personal[medianposition].name.last ≤ personal[i].name.last

CASE STUDY 8.2 — REFINEMENT 7

Since this procedure requires three parameters, the record array *personal* and the bounds *low* and *high* between which the array is to be sorted, the procedure call

    sort personal array(personal, n)

in the initial procedure (refinement 1) must be replaced with

    quicksort personal(personal, 1, n)

Procedure *partition* (case study 5.8 — refinement 3) must undergo similar modifications to turn it into procedure *partition personal* for this case study:

```
partition personal : procedure
    {partitions the personal array between personal[low] and
    personal[high] into two parts such that the last names
    in each of the personal records in the first part alphabetically
    precede the last name of the record in personal[low], and the
    last names in each of the personal records in the second part
    alphabetically follow (or are the same as) the last name of the record in
    personal[low]. The record in personal[low] is then swapped
    to be right between these two parts}
  storage specification
    parameters
      personal : in out 1-D record array containing
        name : record containing
          first, middle, last : string
          endrecord name
        address : string
        age : integer
        endrecord personal
      low, high : in only integer
      medianposition : out only integer
    variables
      median : string
      i, j : integer
    end storage specification
begin partition personal
    median ← personal[low].name.last
    i ← low + 1
    j ← high
    loop while i < j
      loop while (i < j) and (personal[i].name.last < median)
        i ← i + 1
        endloop while
      loop while (i < j) and (personal[j].name.last ≥ median)
        j ← j − 1
        endloop while
      swap personal records(personal[i], personal[j])
      endloop while
    if personal[i].name.last < median
      then medianposition ← i
      else medianposition ← i − 1
      endif
    swap personal records(personal[low], personal[medianposition])
    end partition personal
  where swap personal records swaps two personal records
```

CASE STUDY 8.2 — REFINEMENT 8

You should study this conversion carefully, comparing it with case study 5.8.

Third Solution — Sorting on Index with Insertion Sort

In both the modified *insertion sort* and the modified *quicksort* there is one point of gross inefficiency. Whenever a swap needs to be made, all the fields of two personal records are swapped. Since there are five fields in a personal record, the swap in procedure *swap records* will take at least five times as long as the original procedure swap of case study 2.3 (actually, swapping records will take considerably more than five times as long if strings are involved, as they are in the personal records).

Is there a way to avoid this problem? Yes, there is. We will use the following trick: instead of swapping records, we will maintain a simple integer list of indexes to indicate the desired order of the personal record array.

Assume that we have an array of five personal records in the store:

Example 8.4

personal[1].name.first	James	**string**
personal[1].name.middle	Alan	**string**
personal[1].name.last	Jones	**string**
personal[1].address	Harvard, Idaho	**string**
personal[1].age	25	**integer**

personal[5].name.first	Larry	**string**
personal[5].name.middle	Lawrence	**string**
personal[5].name.last	Lewis	**string**
personal[5].address	Princeton, Idaho	**string**
personal[5].age	53	**integer**

If the last names in the five records are Jones, Zumwalt, Adams, Stephens, and Lewis, respectively (for brevity we have not shown the records for Zumwalt, Adams, and Stephens), then the direct sorting methods of the first two solutions to this case study would rearrange the records so that the record for Adams appears first, followed by the records for Jones, Lewis, Stephens, and Zumwalt, in that order.

We can illustrate this better by representing each record by just the last name field of that record. Then originally the store looks like

personal[1]	[Jones]	**[record]**
personal[2]	[Zumwalt]	**[record]**
personal[3]	[Adams]	**[record]**
personal[4]	[Stephens]	**[record]**
personal[5]	[Lewis]	**[record]**

where each last name in a cell really stands for the *five* cells of the entire record — the brackets around the names are meant to remind us of this.

After the personal record array is sorted, the store would look like

personal[1]	[Adams]	**[record]**
personal[2]	[Jones]	**[record]**
personal[3]	[Lewis]	**[record]**
personal[4]	[Stephens]	**[record]**
personal[5]	[Zumwalt]	**[record]**

A number of record swaps would be required to transform the original store into this form. Each swap would take a considerable amount of time, since each of the five fields in each record would need to be swapped by the processor individually. The larger the records in a file, the more noticeable this effect would be.

The alternative to swapping these large records is to maintain another simple list of integers, which we will call *index,* such that running the sorting program would cause the store to look like

personal[1]	[Jones]	**[record]**
personal[2]	[Zumwalt]	**[record]**
personal[3]	[Adams]	**[record]**
personal[4]	[Stephens]	**[record]**
personal[5]	[Lewis]	**[record]**
index[1]	3	**integer**
index[2]	1	**integer**
index[3]	5	**integer**
index[4]	4	**integer**
index[5]	2	**integer**

In this case, none of the personal records have been swapped. Instead, the index array has been set up so that its elements indicate the correct order for the personal array: *index*[1] contains a 3, indicating that the first record in alphabetic order is in *personal*[3]; *index*[2] contains a 1, indicating that the record in *personal*[1] is the second record in alphabetic order, and so on. In general, if *index*[*i*] = *j,* then the *i*th record in alphabetic order is in *personal*[*j*].

To understand this better, look at the following loop.

```
loop start i with 1 step 1 to 5
    output personal[index[i]].name.last
    endloop autoindex
```

Executing this loop is the same as executing the five statements

output personal[index[1]].name.last
output personal[index[2]].name.last
output personal[index[3]].name.last
output personal[index[4]].name.last
output personal[index[5]].name.last

since *i* will take on the values 1, 2, 3, 4, and then 5 on successive iterations of the loop. Looking at the values of *index*[1], *index*[2], *index*[3], *index*[4], and *index*[5], we see that these five statements in turn are the same as

output personal[3].name.last
output personal[1].name.last
output personal[5].name.last
output personal[4].name.last
output personal[2].name.last

so the output will be

Adams
Jones
Lewis
Stephens
Zumwalt

just as it should be.

The advantage of using an index array is that its elements are simple integers that can be swapped much more quickly than large records. The real question, then, is how to establish and maintain such an index array. To start with, the index array would be initialized by the loop

loop start i **with** 1 **step** 1 **to** 5
    index[i] ← i
endloop autoindex

If we assume that the personal records are already in the store, this last loop will cause the store to look like

personal[1]	[Jones]	**[record]**
personal[2]	[Zumwalt]	**[record]**
personal[3]	[Adams]	**[record]**
personal[4]	[Stephens]	**[record]**
personal[5]	[Lewis]	**[record]**
index[1]	1	**integer**
index[2]	2	**integer**
index[3]	3	**integer**
index[4]	4	**integer**
index[5]	5	**integer**

Initializing the index array this way just says that we know nothing about the true sorted order of the personal records at this point.

Now, to rearrange the index array so that *index*[1] contains the number of the first personal record in alphabetical order, *index*[2] contains the number of second personal record in alphabetical order, and so on, we must compare the last name fields of two personal records through the associated index values and then if necessary swap not the two *records,* but the two *index values* for those two records. For example, assume that the store now looks like

personal[1]	[Jones]	**[record]**
personal[2]	[Zumwalt]	**[record]**
personal[3]	[Adams]	**[record]**
personal[4]	[Stephens]	**[record]**
personal[5]	[Lewis]	**[record]**
index[1]	3	**integer**
index[2]	1	**integer**
index[3]	2	**integer**
index[4]	4	**integer**
index[5]	5	**integer**

If we are now to compare the last name field of the record indicated by *index*[*i*] with the last name field of the record indicated by *index*[*i*+1] for *i* = 3, swapping if necessary, we do this with the statement

    if personal[index[i]].name.last > personal[index[i+1]].name.last
        then swap(index[i], index[i+1])
    endif

If *i* is 3, then *i* + 1 is 4, and the comparison in the **if** statement is

    personal[index[3]].name.last > personal[index[4]].name.last

or, since *index*[3] = 2 and *index*[4] = 4,

    personal[2].name.last > personal[4].name.last

which is

    'Zumwalt' > 'Stephens'

as we see by looking at the last name fields of *personal*[2] and *personal*[4]. Since this comparison is true, *index*[3] and *index*[4] are swapped, causing the store to look like

personal[1]	[Jones]	**[record]**
personal[2]	[Zumwalt]	**[record]**
personal[3]	[Adams]	**[record]**
personal[4]	[Stephens]	**[record]**
personal[5]	[Lewis]	**[record]**
index[1]	3	**integer**
index[2]	1	**integer**
index[3]	4	**integer**
index[4]	2	**integer**
index[5]	5	**integer**

Having swapped *index*[3] and *index*[4] we are just saying that the personal record indicated by *index*[3] (*personal*[4]) contains a last name field (Stephens) that alphabetically precedes the last name field (Zumwalt) in the record indicated by *index*[4] (*personal*[2]).

The main points in the design of a sorting procedure based on this method are the comparison of identical fields within two records by way of the index array and subsequent swapping of the index array elements where necessary. The standard sort procedures, *insertion sort* and *quicksort*, will otherwise work just the same.

This long example has described in detail how a sorting routine must be modified to use the index method. Accordingly, we will give *insertion sort* here, modified to use an index array, with little further explanation. In the initial procedure we include a new index array in the **variables** section, and although we can use the same procedure to input the records of the personal array, we must modify the procedures for sorting and printing the array of personal records.

```
sortindex personal : initial procedure
    {sorts an index array to represent the order of a
     personal record array alphabetically by last name}

    storage specification
        constants
            max : integer 500
        variables
            n : integer
            index : 1-D integer array [1 → max]
            personal : 1-D record array [1 → max] containing
                name : record containing
                    first, middle, last : string
                endrecord name
                address : string
                age : integer
            endrecord personal
    end storage specification
```

begin sortindex personal
    read personal array(personal, n)
    sortindex personal array(personal, index, n)
    writeindex personal array(personal, index, n)
    end sortindex personal

where read personal array (defined in refinement 2) inputs
    the records of the personal array using the **moredata** method
where sortindex personal array uses insertion sort to arrange
    the elements of the index array to indicate the proper
    alphabetical order on the last names of the records in
    the personal array
where writeindex personal array prints the names and addresses
    in each personal record in the sorted order given in the index array

CASE STUDY 8.2 — REFINEMENT 9

Procedure *sortindex personal array* will be a modification of procedure *sort personal array* in refinement 5. First, the index array must be set up so that *index*[*i*] = *i* for all *i*. Then, the last names of the records are compared through the index array.

sortindex personal array : **procedure**
    {uses insertion sort to arrange the elements of an index
    array to indicate the proper alphabetical order on the last
    names of the records in the personal array}

    storage specification
      parameters
        personal : **in out 1-D record array containing**
          name : **record containing**
            first, middle, last : **string**
            endrecord name
          address : **string**
          age : **integer**
          endrecord personal
        index : **out only 1-D integer array**
        n : **in only integer**
      variables
        i : **integer**
    end storage specification

    begin sortindex personal array
      loop start i **with** 1 **step** 1 **to** n
        index[i] ← i
      endloop autoindex
      loop start i **with** 2 **step** 1 **to** n
        if personal[index[i]].name.last < personal[index[i−1]].name.last
          then moveupindex personal(personal, index, i)
        endif
      endloop autoindex
    end sortindex personal array

where moveupindex personal inserts the value currently in index[i]
    into its proper position (so far) in the index array

CASE STUDY 8.2 — REFINEMENT 10

Procedure *moveupindex personal* will be a modified version of procedure *moveup personal* (refinement 6).

```
moveupindex personal : procedure
    {inserts the value currently in index[i] into its proper position
    (so far) in the index array}
    storage specification
        parameters
            personal : in out 1-D record array containing
                name : record containing
                    first, middle, last : string
                    endrecord name
                address : string
                age : integer
                endrecord personal
            index : in out 1-D integer array
            i : in only integer
        variables
            j : integer
            stop : truth value
        end storage specification
    begin moveupindex personal
        j ← i
        stop ← false
        loop
            if personal[index[j]].name.last < personal[index[j−1]].name.last
                then swap(index[j], index[j−1])
                    j ← j − 1
                else stop ← true
                endif
            endloop until stop or (j = 1)
        end moveupindex personal
    where swap, defined in case study 2.3, swaps two integer values

CASE STUDY 8.2 — REFINEMENT 11
```

Notice that the original integer *swap* routine of case study 2.3 can be used here, because we are swapping the integer values of the index array.

The last procedure to be designed is *writeindex personal array,* which is a simple modification of *write personal array* (refinement 3). The index array (which is now in sorted order representing the alphabetical order of the personal array) is used to print the names and addresses of the personal array in alphabetical order.

```
writeindex personal array : procedure
    {prints the names and addresses of the personal array in
    alphabetical order via the index array}

    storage specification
        parameters
            personal : in out 1-D record array containing
                name : record containing
                    first, middle, last : string
                    endrecord name
                address : string
                age : integer
                endrecord personal
            index : in out 1-D integer array
            n : in only integer
        variables
            i : integer
    end storage specification

    begin writeindex personal array
        loop start i with 1 step 1 to n
            output personal[index[i]].name.first, ' ',
                   personal[index[i]].name.middle, ' ',
                   personal[index[i]].name.last
            output personal[index[i]].address
        endloop autoindex
    end writeindex personal array
```

CASE STUDY 8.2 — REFINEMENT 12

You should review the index array modification of *insertion sort* until you understand it.

Fourth Solution — Sorting on Index with Quicksort

The conversion of the quicksort program to work with an index array is completely analagous to the conversion of *insertion sort* in the previous section, so we leave it as an exercise.

Correctness

Although we spent a considerable amount of time developing the various alternative programs for this case study, the insertion sort and quicksort methods were designed, verified, and tested in earlier case studies, so we can use them here with confidence. The only procedures that need to be scrutinized are those based on the index array, and we have already done a partial walkthrough for this method. In testing such a program it is sometimes helpful to output the values of the index and personal arrays on each pass through the loops in order to see what is happening (this is called a *program trace*).

Careful readers will have noticed that we have not included some standard checks in the initial procedures *sort personal* and *sortindex personal* as well as procedure *read personal array* for assuring robustness. We leave it to you to locate and remedy these problems.

Because we have previously verified each of the routines given here, we have excluded the loop invariant and goal assertions from all loops.

Efficiency

The time complexities of *insertion sort* and *quicksort* for sorting records either by straight record swapping or by the index method are the same as they were in case study 5.7 and case study 5.8, that is, $O(n^2)$ and $O(n*\log_2 n)$, respectively. The basic procedure, including the loop structure, is the same in all versions of *insertion sort* and all versions of *quicksort*. In the index method for both *insertion sort* and *quicksort* there will be an additional loop that will be executed just one time to initialize the index array:

```
loop start i with 1 step 1 to n
    index[i] ← i
    endloop autoindex
```

This loop has $O(n)$ time complexity, which is less than the $O(n^2)$ of *insertion sort* and the $O(n*\log_2 n)$ of *quicksort*, so it does not alter the general time complexities of these two programs.

Although the time complexities of these sorts are the same whether they are applied to simple integer lists, as they were in case studies 5.7 and 5.8, or to complex record arrays, as they were in this case study, we know that if entire records are swapped, it will actually take much more time to sort records than it would to sort integers. This analysis is a good lesson in the difference between the time complexity of a procedure and its actual required execution time. In all cases the general execution time behavior of *insertion sort* is n^2. That is, as n gets larger and larger, the time required to sort n integers or records will rise in proportion to n^2. However, depending on the size of the records, sorting n records may take, for example, five times as long as sorting n integers, regardless of the size of n.

Another time complexity comparison that should be made is the comparison between the straight record swapping method and the index method for sorting arrays of records. Both methods have the same time complexity, but the index method is clearly superior to the straight swapping method. Again, the fact that these two methods have the same time complexity just means that the growth in execution time for larger and larger values for n follows the same pattern for either method. However, the index method will be some constant times faster than the straight swapping method when large records are being sorted.

Summary — Case Study 8.2

Sorting arrays of records is a little more complicated than sorting simple numerical arrays. In particular, sorting arrays of records by swapping complete records is so inefficient that we use special routines in which only an index array (not the record array itself) is sorted. The added complication of sorting by index is more than made up for by the reduced program execution time.

8.5 WORKING OUT

8.18 Modify the design of the program for exercise 8.16 to also print a list of all women earning less than the average salary, a list of all men earning less than the average salary, and the ratios of the number of men above the average to the number of men below the average, and the number of women above the average to the number of women below the average.

8.19 Using the part records defined in exercise 8.17 design a program that inputs a list of partrecords already sorted in order by part number and then uses this list to look up information on parts. There will be a second input order list consisting of an undetermined number of lines, each containing an integer part number and the number of parts ordered (also an integer). For each of these input lines the program should look the part number up in the list and reduce the inventory by the number ordered. After all order input has been processed, a list of parts whose inventory has fallen below the threshold should be printed as well as the gross sales and the current dollar value of the total parts inventory. Be sure to make your program robust by including a way to handle the situation when the inventory drops below zero.

8.20 Repeat the previous exercise assuming that the orginal input list of part records is not in order. If your design of that program was well structured, you will only need to include a sorting routine and a call in the initial procedure to that sorting routine.

8.21 Repeat exercise 8.15 with the added restriction that you cannot use the **record** data type.

8.22 Explain the benefits of using an index sorting method, as in case study 8.2, for sorting a list of records. What are the costs incurred by using an index sorting method over a direct sorting method? At what point do you suppose the benefits outweigh the costs?

8.23 Redesign the solution in case study 8.2 that uses the index sorting method with the added restriction that you are not allowed to use the **record** data type.

| CHAPTER 9 |

Constructing Arbitrary Data Structures — Linked Lists

> **NEW CONCEPTS:** Dynamic data structures, Linked lists, Cell address variables, Queues, Stacks

In this chapter we examine ways of constructing arbitrary data structures. These data structures will be implemented by designing and maintaining explicit links among the data elements in the structure, hence this general implementation method is described by the term *linked lists*.

**9.1
GETTING
ACQUAINTED**

Consider the types of data structures we have so far encountered. Except for character strings and records, the data structures we have seen have been quite plain: simple lists, simple tables, and matrices. These data structures have two common features:

1. They are homogeneous. Each element of these data structures is of the same type, for example, integer. Even in a list of records, where each field in a record can have a different data type, all records in the list are nonetheless the same.
2. They are of predictable size. Once a simple list, table, or matrix is constructed in the store, its size does not change during execution of the program.

These two characteristics make arrays the ideal choice for implementing these data structures. As we have seen, an array must be declared so that each element of the array has the same type, as in

variables
    x : **1-D integer array** $[1 \rightarrow n]$

Also, once an array has been declared in a procedure to have a specific subscript range, for example, $[1 \rightarrow n]$, the size of that array is fixed for the entire time the procedure is in execution.

For some purposes it would be nice if we could declare arrays like

variables
    x : **1-D array**

where neither the type of the array elements nor the number of elements is specified. Then any type of value (**integer, real, character,** or **truth value**) could be stored in a particular array element, and the number of store elements reserved for the array would be determined by how many values were actually saved in the array.

Unfortunately, none of the programming languages of the kind we are modeling with *mpl* has such a flexible array definition, so arrays are awkward to use for implementing data structures with nonhomogeneous elements and unspecified sizes. While there are real examples of data structures with one or both of these characteristics, the most common of the two characteristics is unspecified size. Data structures that are homogeneous (all data elements in the structure are of the same type) but require unbounded room for growth are quite common.

---

*Example
9.1*

A performing arts coliseum box office specializes in phone-in ticket orders. A customer calling to order tickets must give his/her credit card number and the number of tickets he/she wishes to buy. The credit card number is entered into a computer program that maintains a list of ticket purchasers. Ordered tickets can be picked up at the time of the event, although some customers prefer to pick them up in advance. When tickets are picked up, the customer presents his/her credit card, and the number is entered into the program and checked against the list. If a match is made, the customer receives the tickets and the credit card number is deleted from the list. If no match is found, the current ticket purchaser list can be printed to determine if an error in entering the credit card number was made. Customers may also cancel their orders, up to some specified cutoff time.

As you can see, this situation poses some peculiar problems in the design of the data structure that maintains the list of ticket purchasers. This is not a simple list of the type we have seen in previous chapters. This list must constantly be maintained in numeric order by credit card number, because a printout of this list will be required often and at arbitrary times to settle problems (the list should be in order for easy visual checking). This means that credit card numbers will have to be inserted immediately in proper numeric order into the list as each ticket purchase is entered. Also, no gaps should remain when credit card numbers are deleted from the list.

For instance, at some particular time the list might look like

405   496   623   771

(we use small numbers and a short list to demonstrate this problem; this list could contain hundreds or even a few thousand elements). If credit card number 437 is to be entered into this list, it must go between 405 and 496, making the list look like

405   437   496   623   771

Similarly, if the holder of credit card number 496 picks up his/her tickets, 496 is deleted from the list, leaving

405   437   623   771

There is really no way to predict the maximum size this list might attain. Certainly the size is limited by the number of seats in the coliseum, but the size of the list will fluctuate enormously over the course of even one day. What problems would we have if we tried to implement this list with an array like the ones we used for the simple lists of earlier chapters? First of all, it would be difficult to guess the maximum size of the array; the guess would need to be high to ensure that the program would not run out of space as the list of ticket purchasers was built up, but this would waste storage space (many programs often share execution time on a real computer, and each program requires a portion of the store).

More serious problems would arise when inserting and deleting items. If a credit card number was to be inserted at position i in the array, all of the elements from position i on would first have to be moved down one position in the array to make room for this new credit card number. That is, a procedure would have to begin at position n (the last occupied position in the array) and move each element from the nth through the ith down one position, using a loop like

```
loop start j with n step −1 to i
    a[j+1] ← a[j]
    endloop stepping
n ← n + 1
a[i] ← new credit card number
```

where n is updated to reflect the new length of the list, and the new credit card number is inserted in the ith position of the list. Don't forget that position i, the location in the list where the new credit card number must be inserted, would also require some computation to determine in the first place.

Similarly, if the ith credit card number in the list were to be deleted, a procedure with a loop like

```
loop start j with i step 1 to n−1
    a[j] ← a[j+1]
    endloop stepping
n ← n − 1
```

would have to move all subsequent array elements up to fill the gap left by deleting the ith element; then n would have to be updated to reflect the new list size.

It is easy to see that an excessive amount of work would be required of the processor if an array were used to implement this list in the straightforward manner followed in previous chapters. Every time a person ordered or picked up tickets, half the list (on the average) would need to be recopied. It would also be very difficult to estimate the number of elements to reserve in the array.

These problems can be solved by using an explicitly linked structure to hold this dynamic list of credit card numbers. In this method the credit card number is stored in the list along with an explicit link to the next credit card number in the list. That is, a ticket purchase will be represented by a record that consists of two fields, a credit card number field and a link field. Pictorially, our original list would look like

The / used in the last list element indicates that no link is needed there. The insertion of credit card number 437 into this list would require only a redirecting of the link from 405 so that it linked to the new record containing 437, which in turn must be linked to the element containing 496:

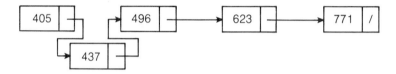

Similarly, deleting credit card number 496 from the list just requires redirecting the link from 437 to link to the element containing 623:

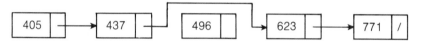

The space occupied by credit card number 496 could then be freed for later use by a different credit card number.

From this simple example it is clear that linked lists will take more storage space to maintain than simple lists, since a storage cell is required for each link as well as for each credit card number. However, it is also clear that arbitrary entries can be inserted and deleted much more easily and that the lists can grow and shrink arbitrarily. How linked lists are actually implemented in a programming language is the subject of this chapter.

As our example has shown, each list element in a linked list consists of a value part and a link part. The value part can be an arbitrary record containing as much information as required. For instance, each list element in our example could consist of the name, telephone number, and address of a ticket purchaser as well as the credit card number. The link part of a list element, on the other hand, must contain a special value that indicates where the next list element is located in the store. The whole purpose of using links is to avoid requiring list elements that follow each other *logically* to also follow one another *physically* in the store. A link is used to indicate where the next list element physically resides in the store, thus removing the requirement that the two elements actually follow one another in the store. Thus, when a new element is to be inserted into a list, the value and link information of this new element can be allocated to cells anywhere in the store. We must only ensure that (1) the link field of the new element is linked to the element that logically follows it, and (2) the link field of the element that logically precedes the new element is altered to link to the new element. Similarly, when an element of such a list is to be deleted, the link field of the element that logically precedes the one to be deleted must be altered to link to the element that logically follows the element to be deleted.

The question now is how to specify links in a program. To understand the answer to this question, we need to extend our abstract concept of the store. So far we have viewed the store as a series of cells to which we assign names in a **variables** declaration. However, each cell in the store actually has a *cell address* that uniquely identifies it. The store is thus more accurately pictured as

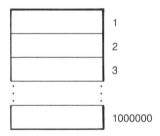

where the number to the right of each cell is that cell's unique address in the store. Here we have illustrated a store with 1,000,000 cells.

Until now, the fact that each cell in the store has a unique address has been transparent to us. There was no reason to know that cell addresses even existed, because we could just assume that the processor located a cell by the name we assigned to that cell. Now, however, understanding that cells do have addresses will clarify how we can maintain explicit links among data elements regardless of where those data elements are physically located in the store.

Recall the previous example where a list of ticket purchasers was to be maintained; each entry in the list consisted of a credit card number. To maintain this list as a singly linked list, each element in the list must contain a link field as well as a credit card number field. That is, each entry in the list will require two consecutive storage cells. The first cell will contain a credit card number and the second cell will contain the cell address of the credit card number of the *next* list element. The link field of an element is just the cell address of some other cell in the store. Using explicit cell addresses allows the storage cells for a new list element to be located anywhere in the store, because the list element that logically precedes the new list element can be linked to the new list element by assigning the cell address of the first cell of the new list element to the link field of the preceding list element.

Consider what happens the day tickets first go on sale. Suppose a person with credit card number 405 calls and orders some tickets. After credit card number 405 has been entered into the program, the store would look like

Example 9.2

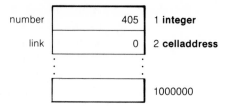

The first two cells of the store represent the list element for credit card number 405. The *link* variable contains 0, which is not a valid cell address. Since there are no other elements in the list, this element is not to be linked to any other element — this is represented by the 0, which is called the *null link*. In this example the null link indicates that the end of the list has been reached.

Now suppose that a person with credit card number 496 calls and orders some tickets. Since 496 follows 405 numerically, the element containing credit card number 405 must be linked to the new element containing credit card number 496. This results in the store:

number	405	1 **integer**
link	3	2 **celladdress**
number	496	3 **integer**
link	0	4 **celladdress**
	⋮	⋮
		1000000

The first element

number	405	1 **integer**
link	3	2 **celladdress**

now has 3 in the link field, since 3 is the cell address of the first cell of the next list element:

number	496	3 **integer**
link	0	4 **celladdress**

Notice that the link field of this new element is the null link (0), since this new element is now the last one in the list.

Suppose that the next two ticket purchasers in succession have credit card numbers 623 and 771, respectively. The same process will continue: the null link field of the list element containing 496 will be changed to indicate the address of the new element, which contains credit card number 623 and a link field of 0. When credit card number 771 is added, the null link associated with number 623 will be changed to point to the new list element containing credit card number 771, which will in turn have its link field set to the null link. At this point the store will look like

number	405	1 **integer**
link	3	2 **celladdress**
number	496	3 **integer**
link	5	4 **celladdress**
number	623	5 **integer**
link	7	6 **celladdress**
number	771	7 **integer**
link	0	8 **celladdress**
	⋮	
		1000000

We visualize the list like this:

where the diagonal slash in the list element containing 771 represents the null link. The links, which are represented by arrows, are nothing more than cell addresses in the actual representation of the list in the store.

What happens if the next ticket purchaser has credit card number 437? When 437 is entered into the computer program, the list should be modified to look like

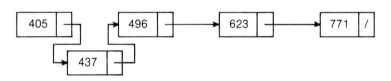

in order to maintain the numeric ordering of the list elements by credit card number. The link from the list element containing 405, which used to connect to the list element containing 496, must be modified to connect to the new list element containing 437. The link field of the new element containing 437 must now connect to the element containing 496. Addition of the new list element containing 437 will cause the store to look like

number	405	1 **integer**		number	771	7 **integer**
link	9	2 **celladdress**		link	0	8 **celladdress**
number	496	3 **integer**		number	437	9 **integer**
link	5	4 **celladdress**		link	3	10 **celladdress**
number	623	5 **integer**			⋮	
link	7	6 **celladdress**				1000000

Notice that the cells for the new list element

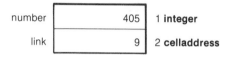

| number | 437 | 9 **integer** |
| link | 3 | 10 **celladdress** |

were taken from the next two available storage cells, those with addresses 9 and 10. The link field of this new element contains 3, which is the first cell address of the list element containing credit card number 496. The list element containing credit card number 405,

| number | 405 | 1 **integer** |
| link | 9 | 2 **celladdress** |

now has a link value of 9, which is the cell address of the newly allocated list element with credit card number 437. Even though the list elements containing credit card numbers 405 and 437 follow each other in our conceptualization of the list of ticket purchasers, they are actually far apart in the store. However, the link fields maintain the necessary connections between the list elements in spite of their physical separation in the store.

Finally, let's look at what happens when the purchaser with credit card number 496 stops by the coliseum box office and picks up his/her tickets. At this point the list element containing credit card number 496 should be removed from the list. Conceptually, the list would look like

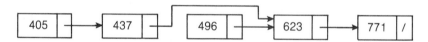

and the store would look like

number	405	1 **integer**
link	9	2 **celladdress**
number	496	3 **integer**
link	5	4 **celladdress**
number	623	5 **integer**
link	7	6 **celladdress**
number	771	7 **integer**
link	0	8 **celladdress**
number	437	9 **integer**
link	5	10 **celladdress**
		1000000

Notice that list element

number	496	3 **integer**
link	5	4 **celladdress**

no longer has any links *to* it, so it has effectively been removed from the list and can be reused by the processor later (e.g., for storing a different credit card number–link pair).

At this point, we would have a problem if we wished to print out the credit card numbers in the list: where is the first element of the list? Once we know where the first element is, we can follow the links to successive elements. However, there is nothing in the store to indicate where this first element is — it could be anywhere in the store after many insertions and deletions had occurred. To solve this problem, another link variable called *first* must be kept in the store. This variable must always point to the first list element. If the first list element changes as the result of inserting a new list element with a lower credit card number or deleting the first list element when those tickets are picked up, variable *first* must be changed to contain the address of the new first list element.

After incorporating variable *first,* the store might look like

first	2	1 **celladdress**
number	405	2 **integer**
link	10	3 **celladdress**
number	496	4 **integer**
link	6	5 **celladdress**
number	623	6 **integer**
link	8	7 **celladdress**
number	771	8 **integer**
link	0	9 **cellalddress**
number	437	10 **integer**
link	6	11 **celladdress**
	⋮	
		1000000

The pieces are now all in place for us to traverse the list, printing the credit card numbers in each list element. The address of the first list element is in the variable *first.* Since this address is 2, the first list element is

number	405	2 **integer**
link	10	3 **celladdress**

so 405 would be printed. The link field of this element states that the next list element begins at cell address 10, so it would be

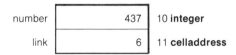

and 437 would be printed. The link field of this list element indicates that the next list element begins at storage cell 6, so the next list element is

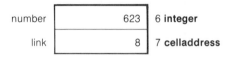

From this list element, credit card number 623 would be printed and the next list element would be determined. It begins at storage cell 8,

number | 771 | 8 **integer**
link | 0 | 9 **celladdress**

so credit card number 771 would be printed. At this point the null link is encountered, meaning that the end of the list has been reached.

As we have seen, carefully updating the links keeps the list elements in their proper logical order regardless of the physical positions of these list elements in the store.

This long example has indicated that some new programming features will be required in any programming language that supports linked lists. The first new feature is a type of variable that can contain storage cell addresses. Although these storage cell addresses may look like integers, they really are not. For example, storage cell addresses cannot be negative, and they do not have arithmetic performed on them. In *mpl* we will model variables that can contain cell addresses by declaring such variables to have type **celladdress.** The variable *first* in the previous example would be declared as

variables
    first : **celladdress**

A second feature that is necessary for representing linked lists is a way of specifying to the processor what a list element looks like. Since each list element will consist of at least two fields, a value field and a link field, it seems logical to describe such a list element with the *mpl* **record** declaration. This will be done in a new **listelement descriptors** section of the *mpl* **storage specification** statement. In our previous example, the list elements would be described as

listelement descriptors
    element : **record containing**
        number : **integer**
        link : **celladdress**
        endrecord element

A list element descriptor, like *element* above, cannot appear in the **variables** section, because it is not a variable. The descriptor *element* is nothing more than that: a descriptor. It is used by the processor when a new list element is to be allocated from the store; it tells the processor that two cells are needed for the new element, the first of type **integer** and the second of type **celladdress.**

This leads us to the third new programming language feature needed to support linked lists — a way of telling the processor that a new list element is to be allocated. In *mpl* we will model this statement as

getnew *listelement*

where *listelement* is the name of a list element descriptor given in a **listelement descriptors** statement. This tells the processor, as we have previously mentioned, how many cells to allocate and what type these cells are. It won't do us any good, however, if the processor allocates a new list element but does not provide the starting address of that element — we need to make the proper links to and from this new list element. Thus the full form of the **getnew** statement will be

getnew *listelement* **assign address to** *elementaddress*

where *elementaddress* is just any **celladdress** variable. Having the address of the new list element in variable *elementaddress* will allow the proper links to this new list element to be made.

We now need a way to refer to list elements. In *mpl* we will use expressions like

first:element . number

which we read as "the *number* field in the record named *element* whose address is in the variable *first*." The variable in front of the colon must therefore be of type **celladdress.** Thus, the statements

getnew element **assign address to** whereitsat
input whereitsat:element . number

would first allocate a new list element as described by the list element descriptor for *element* and assign the starting storage address of this new element to the **celladdress** variable *whereitsat*. Then the next value at the input device would be input and stored in the *number* field of the *element* record whose address is in *whereitsat*, i.e., in the *number* field of the new list element just allocated.

The final new programming language feature is a statement that indicates to the processor that a list element has been deleted and can be used for other purposes. This will be modeled in *mpl* with the **free** statement, as in

free whereitsat:element

which means, as you would guess, "free the list element called *element*, whose address is in variable *whereitsat*." Naturally, *whereitsat* would have to be declared to be a **celladdress** variable. Notice again that the processor would know exactly how many storage cells to free up because *element* has been described in a **listelement descriptors** statement.

To really understand the implementation of data structures as explicitly linked lists, we need to examine case studies involving linked lists. The first case study we present is a simple one using many of the features previously described. Just remember that these features only model the features of actual programming languages. Each programming language handles linked lists differently, but each of these features must be present in one form or another. If you understand the linked list concepts as presented here in *mpl*, you will have no trouble learning to use linked lists in an actual programming language.

Case Study 9.1 | Input and Print a Linked List of Integers

> *Problem Description:* input a series of integers, linking them together in a singly linked list in the order in which they were input, and print them out in this same order.
>
> *Input Specifications:* a list of integers.

In this first case study on linked list representations of data structures, we will follow our usual tack and design a very simple program for reading in a list, storing the list in singly linked form, and then printing the list. The list to be input is not dynamic; that is, arbitrary insertions and deletions of list elements will not occur. The list will be nothing more than the simple type of list we have seen in earlier chapters, and as we shall see now, the 1-D array representation of such a list is easier to handle than the linked list representation we will develop here. However, using a singly linked list to implement this simple list serves two purposes: first, it will allow us to compare the linked list representation with the 1-D array representation. Second, the basic strategies we develop here for constructing and printing a singly linked list will be applied in later case studies; the procedure for printing the values of a singly linked list in order will serve as a model for all similar output procedures in future problems.

The Solution — Singly Linked Lists

Solving this problem with a singly linked list will require more careful thought than other solutions would. As usual, however, the initial procedure will be quite straightforward:

```
readwrite list : intitial procedure
    {inputs a singly linked list and then prints this list}

    storage specification
        variables
            first : celladdress
        end storage specification
```

begin readwrite list
    readlist(first)
    writelist(first)
end readwrite list

where readlist inputs and constructs a singly linked list of input values
where writelist prints the values in the elements of a singly linked list

CASE STUDY 9.1 — REFINEMENT 1

The only variable in this initial procedure is *first*, which is of type **celladdress**. Variable *first* is to contain the store address of the first element of the linked list built up by procedure *readlist*. Since *first* is initially undefined, it is the responsibility of *readlist* to set *first* to contain the address of this first list element. The remaining list elements are to be linked together through a special link field in each element. Procedure *writelist* will print the values in the list starting with the list element whose address is in *first* and then following the link from each element to the succeeding element, until the null link is found.

One crucial point must be made about handling linked lists (as demonstrated in the initial procedure): *the lists themselves are never passed as parameters* to other procedures and functions. Only the *addresses* of these lists are passed by way of **celladdress** variables. The most important consequence of this fact is that there is no way to specify a list to be of type **in only** or **out only**. Thus, lists are treated as **in out** parameters, and changes made to a list within a procedure or function are permanent and are valid throughout the entire program. Of course, the **celladdress** variables passed as parameters can take any of the parameter types, **in only, in out,** and **out only.** However, you must understand clearly that changes to the list elements addressed by these **celladdress** parameters cause permanent changes in the list regardless of what type the **celladdress** parameters may be. For example, even if the **celladdress** parameter *first* were declared to be of type **in only** in procedure *writelist*, any changes to the list element addressed by *first* would result in a permanent change to the list.

These remarks about lists reflect the way lists are handled. Lists are usually referred to by a **celladdress** variable that contains the address of the first list element; only this variable is needed to specify the list. Notice that our initial procedure does not even have a description of the list elements. Since nothing is done to the list directly in the initial procedure, no description of the list elements is necessary there.

This brings us to the design of procedure *readlist*. Procedure *readlist* reads in the input values one at a time, stores each value into a new list element, ensures that each new list element is properly linked to the previous list element, and then returns in *first* the address of the first element of this list. For example, if the input is

30 45 50 25 19

then procedure *readlist* should input these numbers, construct the list

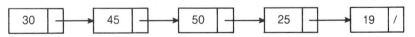

and return in *first* the address of the first list element (the one containing 30).

Each element in the list constructed by *readlist* contains an integer field and a link field, so the descriptor for these elements would be

> **listelement descriptors**
>   item : **record containing**
>   number : **integer**
>   link : **celladdress**
>   **endrecord** item

As we can see, this description fits our idea of what the list elements should look like: an element of the list is a record consisting of two fields, an integer field to hold the input number and a link field to point to the next list element. Recall that describing a list element in a **listelement descriptors** statement does not actually reserve any storage cells for a list element. This description only describes the format of a list element so that when a statement such as

> **getnew** item **assign address to** next

is executed, the processor can allocate a group of cells of the proper size from the store (in this case, two cells — one for *number* and one for *link*) and put the address of the first cell of this group into variable *next*. Of course, *next* would have to be declared to be a **celladdress** variable.

The computation part of procedure *readlist* will, naturally, consist of a loop that reads in the numbers one at a time, getting a new list element ⟨*item*⟩ for each new number and properly setting up the link to this new element from the previous element. The loop structure for this process is

> **loop while moredata**
>   {get new list element}
>   {input number and store into new list element}
>   {set up proper link to new list element from previous list element}
>   **endloop** while

A typical situation during iteration of the loop might be

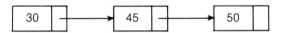

where the first three list elements have been constructed from the first three input values, and the link of the third list element is still undefined. Now, as the loop begins the fourth iteration, the statement

> **getnew** item **assign address to** next

would give us

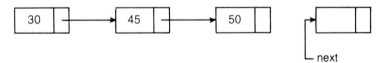

where we have a new list item with both the *number* field and the *link* field undefined. Variable *next* contains the address of this new list element, though, so the processor can now execute the statement

> **input** next:item . number

which means "input the next value from the input device and store it into the *number* field of the *item* record whose address is in *next*." After this statement has been processed, our list looks like

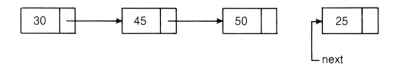

We now need to assign the *link* field of the element containing 50 to be the address of this new list element. The address of the new list element is in *next*, but how do we refer to the element containing 50? Remember, *a linked list element can only be referred to by address*, so somehow we must keep the address of the *previous* list element as well as the *next* list element. If we do this by including a new **celladdress** variable *previous*, our list at this point would really look like

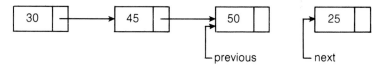

Now if the processor executes the statement

    previous:item.link ← next

meaning "assign the value in *next* to the *link* field of the record *item* whose address is in *previous*," the address in *next* (the address of our new element) will be assigned to the *link* field of the previous element, giving us the conceptual list

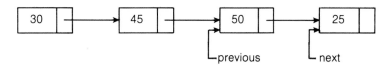

Since both *next* and the *link* fields of record *item* are of type **celladdress**, the assignment

    previous:item.link ← next

is proper.

One more thing must be done in the loop in preparation for the next iteration of the loop. In the next loop iteration, the list element now pointed to by *next* will be the previous element, so *previous* must be set to be the same address as *next* before that iteration starts. We can do this with the statement

    previous ← next

since both *previous* and *next* are of type **celladdress.** Thus at the end of the loop we have the list

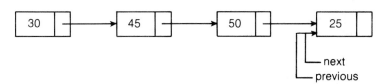

Putting all of these things together gives us the loop

> **loop while** moredata
> **getnew** item **assign address to** next
> **input** next:item . number
> previous:item . link ← next
> previous ← next
> **endloop** while

To summarize, the four statements inside the loop mean (1) get a new list element and put its address into variable *next*; (2) input a new value and put it into the *number* field of the list element whose address is in *next*; (3) set the link field of the previous list element to point to the next list element; and (4) set *previous* to be *next*, because the list element now pointed to by *next* will be the previous list element during the subsequent iteration of the loop.

As the loop begins its next iteration, the first statement executed is

getnew item **assign address to** next

which will cause our list to look like

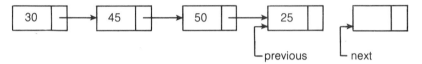

and then the process described above will be repeated.

As we well know by now, the design of the internal structure of a loop is only half the battle. We must ensure that the loop executes properly the first time, and we must also ensure that the loop terminates properly. First let's look at loop termination. If the input is

30 45 50 25 19

then our list upon termination of the loop (when **moredata** becomes false) will look like

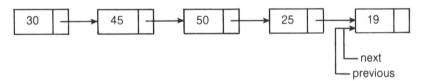

The *link* field of the last element is still undefined, so we will use the statement

next:item . link ← **null**

to assign the null link to the last list element, since no elements will follow this one in the list; the keyword **null** represents the null link. Executing this statement after the loop terminates will cause the list to look like

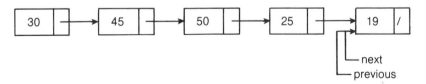

We must also set up the parameter *first* to contain the address of the first list element. It is clear that we cannot do this after the loop terminates, because we do not know where the first element is any more. Variables *previous* and *next* both contain the address of the last list element, and although this last list element is linked to all other list elements, these links are utterly useless at this point, because they link in only one direction. For example, from the element containing 25 we can get to the element containing 19, because the link field of the element containing 25 has the address of the element containing 19. However, there is no field in the element containing 19 that contains the address of any other element in the list, so we are stuck.

The solution to this problem is to assign *first* to be the address of the first list element allocated; we make this assignment *before* the loop is entered. This can easily be done; we must only be careful that the input is not empty.

```
if not moredata
    then first ← null
    else getnew item assign address to first
         input first:item.number
         previous ← first
         next ← first
         {loop given earlier}
         next:item.link ← null
endif
```

Notice that *first* is set to **null** if there is no input. This indicates that the linked list pointed to by *first* is also empty. If there is at least one value in the input, a new list element is allocated by the processor and *first* is assigned its address. Then the first value in the input is read in and assigned to the *number* field of record *item* of this first list element. The variables *previous* and *next* are also set up to point to this first list element in preparation for entering the loop. This gives us the following complete version of procedure *readlist*:

```
readlist : procedure
    {inputs and constructs a singly linked list of integers}

    storage specification
        parameters
            first : out only celladdress
        listelement descriptors
            item : record containing
                number : integer
                link : celladdress
            endrecord item
        variables
            next, previous : celladdress
    end storage specification
```

```
begin readlist
   if not moredata
      then first ← null
      else getnew item assign address to first
           input first:item.number
           previous ← first
           next ← first
           loop while moredata
              getnew item assign address to next
              input next:item.number
              previous:item.link ← next
              previous ← next
              endloop while
           next:item.link ← null
   endif
end readlist
```

CASE STUDY 9.1 — REFINEMENT 2

The last procedure we need to design is *writelist*. Given *first*, the address of the first element of the list, procedure *writelist* is to *traverse* the list, that is, examine each element in the list by following the link field in each list element, printing out the number stored in each element encountered. To do this traversal we will use a **celladdress** variable, *current*, to contain the address of the current list element being examined as we move through the list. The loop form will be

```
loop while {more elements in the list}
   {print the number in the list element whose address is in current}
   {update current to point to the next list element}
   endloop while
```

If *current* contains the address of the current list element, we can print the value in that list element with the statement

```
output current:item.number
```

which means "output the value in the *number* field of the *item* record whose address is in *current*." Similarly, updating *current* to be the address of the next list item (in preparation for the next iteration of the loop) is easy. The address of the next list element is in *current:item.link*, so the statement

```
current ← current:item.link
```

will accomplish this task. It means "replace the value in *current* with the address in the *link* field of the *item* record whose address is now in *current*." These considerations give us the following loop structure:

```
loop while {more elements in the list}
   output current:item.number
   current ← current:item.link
   endloop while
```

Now the question is, when should this loop terminate? (When can we tell that there are no more elements in the list?) Remember that the *link* field of the last list element is **null,** so when *current* finally becomes **null** after execution of the statement current ← current:item.link

we know that we are finished. This gives us the loop

```
loop while current ≠ null
    output current:item.number
    current ← current:item.link
    endloop while
```

The final point to resolve is what value *current* should have before the loop is entered the first time. Naturally, *current* must contain the address of the first list element, which is in parameter *first*. Setting *current* to *first* before the loop is entered the first time gives us

```
current ← first
loop while current ≠ null
    output current:item.number
    current ← current:item.link
    endloop while
```

This loop will now work even if the list is empty; in the case of an empty list, *first* is **null** (see procedure *readlist*), so *current* would be set to **null** and the list would not be executed even once, so no values would be printed.

This gives us our final refinement of procedure *writelist:*

```
writelist : procedure
    {prints the values in the elements of a singly linked list}

    storage specification
        parameters
            first : in only celladdress
        listelement descriptors
            item : record containing
                number : integer
                link : celladdress
                endrecord item
        variables
            current : celladdress
        end storage specification

    begin writelist
        current ← first
        loop while current ≠ null
            output current:item.number
            current ← current:item.link
            endloop while
        end writelist
```

CASE STUDY 9.1 — REFINEMENT 3

Notice that we must use exactly the same listelement descriptor for procedure *writelist* as we did when building the list in procedure *readlist*. This lets the processor know that each list element contains two cells, the first of type **integer** and the second of type **celladdress**; then these cells can be properly accessed in statements like

current ← current:item.link

When the processor executes procedure *writelist,* it has no way to remember the listelement descriptor given in procedure *readlist.*

Example 9.3   To see how procedure *writelist* traverses a singly linked list, assume that the linked list

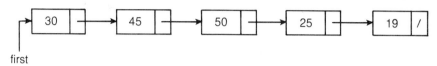

first

has been constructed by procedure *readlist.* The only parameter passed to *writelist* is *first,* which contains the address of the first list element. This is the only parameter needed by *writelist,* because once the address of the first list element is known, all other list elements can be reached through the links.

When *writelist* is called, the first statement executed sets variable *current* to *first,* giving

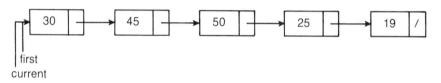

first
current

At this point the loop is entered for the first time, since *current* ≠ **null,** and *current:item . number* is printed, causing

30

to be printed at the output device. Then *current* is set to *current:item . link,* which contains the address of the list element with value 45 (remember that the links, which are represented in our diagrams with arrows, are really cell address numbers). This same address is now placed into *current,* giving

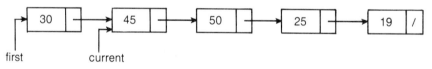

first   current

The loop is now iterated again, and *current:item.number* is printed, listing

45

at the output device. Then *current* is set to *current:item . link,* causing the list to look like

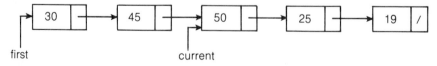

first   current

On this pass through the loop 50 will be printed and *current* will be set to point to the element containing 25. The following pass through the loop will print 25 and set *current* to point to the list element containing 19. At this point the list will look like

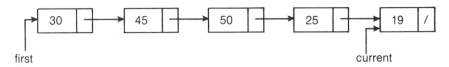

first   current

On the next pass through the loop *current:item . number* will be output, so

19

will be printed. Then *current* will be set to *current:item . link,* which has the value **null;** the loop will not be executed again because the loop statement is

loop while current ≠ **null**

so procedure *writelist* terminates.

This method for traversing a singly linked list will be used whenever a singly linked list is to be traversed.

This finishes the development of the program of this case study. Although actual programming languages treat lists in different manners, the basic strategy of updating the links of a list and accessing specific fields of a list element will be the same.

Correctness

The correctness of programs with linked lists is determined using the same methods we have used for other types of programs. You should do a program walkthrough with some typical data to learn how the program works. The most common errors in programs with linked lists come from setting the **celladdress** variables improperly: forgetting to keep a variable that points to the first list element, not properly updating **celladdress** variables that point to the current (and perhaps previous) list element, and forgetting to set the **celladdress** link fields of each list element properly (including setting the link field of the last list element to **null**).

For testing programs with lists, special values include the empty list and the list containing just a single element.

We have not included loop invariant or goal assertions in this program, because the loops involved are simple input and output loops of a kind we have seen many times. Also, assertions for loops involving linked lists can become quite long, as descriptions about the values in the **celladdress** variables keeping track of the list must be included. For this reason we will usually omit these assertions in this chapter. It is still a good idea for you to formulate these assertions for the programs given in this chapter and any programs you design. For example, the loop goal assertion for procedure *readlist* of refinement 2 could be

assert the input values are in a singly linked list in succession from the first input value to the last. Parameter first contains the address of the first element in this list

The loop invariant assertion could be

> **assert** all input values up to, but not including, the next input value have been input into individual list elements which are linked in succession from the first value input to the most recent value input. Parameter first contains the address of the first list element and variables previous and next both contain the address of the most recently allocated list element.

Including these assertions in procedure *readlist* would make *readlist* quite long. Similar assertions would be required in all programs of this chapter.

Efficiency

Procedure *readlist* contains a loop that iterates once for each new input value, so if there are n input values, its time complexity is $O(n)$. The same time complexity holds for procedure *writelist*, which contains a single loop that is iterated once for each list element.

Even though these procedures (and hence the entire program) have linear time complexity, they would run more slowly than similar procedures using only simple variables. When the processor executes a statement like

> **input** next:item . number

it must first get the cell address value in variable *next* and then use this value to find the location of *item . number* in the store in order to put the next input value there. This process takes at least twice as long to perform as the statement

> **input** x

where x is a simple integer variable. Additional time is also required whenever a new element is allocated by the processor in a **getnew** statement. The added time for executing this statement may be significant, and it is time not required in programs using only simple variables and arrays.

The space complexity of this program is also easily seen to be linear with n, where n is the number of input values. Each time a new value is input by procedure *readlist*, one new list element is allocated to hold this number. Since each list element also requires a cell for the link, the number of storage cells required is really $2*n$ (plus a few extra individual cells for variables such as *first*, *current*, and *next*). Remember, too, that the linked list is a "permanent" structure during the course of a program. When procedure *readlist* is finished, for example, the list elements generated by *readlist* do not disappear the way local variables and **in only** parameters do when a procedure terminates. The list generated by *readlist* is the same list used by *writelist*.

Extra cells are always required by a linked list. The list elements must each have at least one cell for the **celladdress** link field (there may be more than one link for each list element in some cases), so if a list contains n elements (each of which may contain many fields), at least n extra cells are required for the links. In our case study we needed twice as many cells to store the input items in a linked list as would have been required in an array! When lists are large, this extra space requirement can become crucial on real computers where the store is limited.

Summary — Case Study 9.1

This case study was a very simple example demonstrating how a list can be constructed by explicitly linking the list elements together and how such a linked list is traversed. Of course, the problem of the case study — reading in and printing out a list of integers — could have been done much more easily with the loop

```
loop while moredata
    input number
    output number
    endloop while
```

Procedures *read 1D integer* and *write 1D integer* of case study 5.1 could also have been used here, if we had stored the input list in a 1-D array. However, we chose to solve this simple problem with a linked list in order to contrast the extra effort involved in maintaining a linked list with the effort involved in using a 1-D array for this purpose. As we have seen, maintaining a linked list requires more design effort, longer execution time, and more storage space than similar programs using arrays.

On the other hand, linked lists are the most general means available to us for representing arbitrary data structures. We can arrange data in arbitrary ways with linked lists. The price we pay is a decrease in automation. Instead of having the processor keeping track of where each data element is (as it does in the case of arrays), the programmer must use links to maintain the proper relationships among the data items explicitly. We will see other examples of data structures where, unlike this case study, the linked list is the most logical and easiest way to implement the data structure.

Maintaining Several Order Lists

Case Study 9.2

Problem Description: A small cottage industry specializes in T-shirts. Whenever a new event warrants a new T-shirt with an appropriate com- memorative motto, orders are taken for the new shirts. The shirts come in only four colors: red, yellow, green, and blue. After the orders come in, the T-shirts are printed. A separate order list for each T-shirt color must be maintained.

Input Specifications: A sequence of orders where the first line of the order gives the color number (1 for red, 2 for yellow, 3 for green, and 4 for blue) followed by the quantity ordered, and the next line gives the name of the store placing the order as a twenty-character string.

A linked list representation of data is desirable when a list of information must be dynamically built up during the course of a program. The specific data structure might be similar to the simple list studied in chapter 5, where new list elements are always inserted at the end of the list, but it has the added condition that the list is allowed to grow arbitrarily as the program is executed. This added condition of dynamic growth makes it difficult to use a 1-D array to implement this list data structure, especially when the size of the store is limited and there are not just one, but many such dynamic lists that must be maintained at once in the store. Using 1-D arrays, if the size of these lists cannot be determined ahead of time, there is no way to provide for one list being larger than the others and still allow room for all of these lists to fit in the store (when arrays are used, the size of each array must be fixed by the programmer before the procedure or function using the arrays can be executed).

One example of a situation requiring more than one dynamic list is the construction of a concordance, which is a compilation of the precise locations (e.g., page and line numbers) of important words appearing in a text. In building a concordance it is impossible to predict how many times each word will occur, so arrays cannot easily be used to maintain the location lists associated with the words. Instead, linked lists can be used — as each new occurrence of a word is found in the text, a linked entry consisting of the page and line numbers of that occurrence is added to the end of the list associated with that word. After the text has been completely scanned, the concordance is printed a word at a time by listing the entries in the linked list for each word.

The problem chosen for this case study is similar, but simpler. There are only four dynamic lists to be maintained here as T-shirt orders are processed. A typical order might look like

```
2    20
J. C. Nickle
3    10
J. C. Nickle
1    7
Drug Farm
```

where J. C. Nickle has ordered 20 yellow T-shirts and 10 green ones, and Drug Farm has placed an order for 7 red T-shirts.

The Solution — Singly Linked Lists

The individual T-shirt orders will be entered at the input device in the order in which they are received. The program will build a separate list for each T-shirt color, with list elements containing the quantity ordered and the name of the ordering firm. Within each list the elements should be in the order in which they arrived, so that as the T-shirts are produced, they can be delivered to those who ordered them first.

We organize this process in the following initial procedure:

```
tshirts : initial procedure
    {inputs and prints a T-shirt order list}

    storage specification
        variables
            red, yellow, green, blue : celladdress
        end storage specification

    begin tshirts
        read orders(red, yellow, green, blue)
        output 'orders for red T-shirts: '
        print orders(red)
        output 'orders for yellow T-shirts: '
        print orders(yellow)
        output 'orders for green T-shirts: '
        print orders(green)
        output 'orders for blue T-shirts: '
        print orders(blue)
    end tshirts

    where read orders constructs four order lists from the input,
            one each for red, yellow, green, and blue T-shirts.
    where print orders prints the order list addressed by the parameter
            it is passed.
```

CASE STUDY 9.2 — REFINEMENT 1

As in the last case study, we see that the list elements are not described in the initial procedure. Procedure *read orders* is responsible for constructing the four lists, and only the pointers (cell addresses) to these lists (*red, yellow, green,* and *blue*) need to be returned to the initial procedure. After procedure *read orders* has constructed the lists, procedure *print orders* is called four times, each time with a pointer to a different order list.

Procedure *read orders* requires some extra thought in its design. The individual T-shirt orders are to be read in one at a time and connected to the end of the proper list, depending on the color of the T-shirts in each order. Although there are four different lists, the list elements in each list have the same description:

```
listelement descriptors
    order : record containing
        quantity : integer
        firm : string
        nextorder : celladdress
    endrecord order
```

Each element in an order list will contain the quantity ordered, the name of the ordering firm, and a link, called *nextorder,* to the next order in that order list. No field is included for the color of the T-shirts, because that is determined by the list in which an element is found. For example, all of the orders for red T-shirts will be placed in a separate list with **celladdress** variable *red* containing the address of the first element of that list.

Since the entries of each list have the same form, much of the processing will be the same for each order. In particular, a new order can be completely constructed from the input without regard to the T-shirt color. Separate processing must be done for each color only in determining what list the newly constructed list element belongs to. These considerations give us the general outline for procedure *read orders:*

loop while moredata

> {allocate a new order list element}

> {input the T-shirt color for the new order being constructed}

> {input the quantity ordered into order . quantity of the newly allocated list element}

> {input the ordering firm into order . firm of the newly allocated list element}

> {determine the list to which the newly allocated list element belongs, and add this new element to the end of that list}

> **endloop** while

To keep track of a newly allocated list element we will need a **celladdress** variable (let's call it *new*) to contain the address of the new list element. Also, since every new list element is added to the end of one of the order lists, **celladdress** variables pointing to the ends of these lists will be needed (otherwise, we would have to traverse the list from the first element to the last each time we added a new element, a highly inefficient process). This is the same method we used in case study 9.1 for including a new element at the end of the input list. With the declarations

> **variables**
>   new, endred, endyellow, endgreen, endblue : **celladdress**
>   color : **integer**

to establish the **integer** variable *color,* and the pointers for the newly allocated list elements and the last element in each order list, we can write the loop of procedure *read orders* in more detail:

```
loop while moredata
    getnew order assign address to new
    input color
    input new:order . quantity
    read string(new:order . firm, 20)
    case color is
        when 1 {red}    :   endred:order . nextorder ← new
                            endred ← new
        when 2 {yellow} :   endyellow:order . nextorder ← new
                            endyellow ← new
        when 3 {green}  :   endgreen:order . nextorder ← new
                            endgreen ← new
        when 4 {blue}   :   endblue:order . nextorder ← new
                            endblue ← new
        otherwise           output 'bad T-shirt color, order ignored for ',
                                new:order . firm, new:order . quantity
    endcase
endloop while
```

Notice that only two steps are required to link a newly constructed list element into one of the existing lists: (1) connect the link *nextorder* of the element currently at the end of the list (e.g., *endred:order.nextorder*) to the new list element and (2) update the variable indicating the end of the list (e.g., *endred*) to have the address of the new list element (which is now at the end of the list). We have used a **case** statement to determine the proper list for the new element, based on the T-shirt color of the current order. Also notice that we have used procedure *read string* of case study 6.1 to input the name of ordering firm.

As in every procedure involving loops, our work in designing this loop is not done until we make sure that the loop has properly initialized values when it is executed for the first time and until we have considered any special terminating conditions that must hold when the loop is finished. Let's look first at what happens when the loop is terminated. At that point the link field *order.nextorder* of the last element in each list is undefined. This is because the link in the last list element of each order list would have been set to the address of the next new element if another element had been added to that list. So when there are no new orders to be input, the link fields (*order.nextorder*) of the last element of each order list should be set to **null** to indicate the end of the list:

```
endred:order.nextorder ← null
endyellow:order.nextorder ← null
endgreen:order.nextorder ← null
endblue:order.nextorder ← null
```

(This will cause an error if there are no orders for some T-shirt color. Do you see why? This problem will be fixed in the final version of *read orders*.)

Initializing each list so that everything works properly the first time a new element is added to a list requires more thought. Remember that the **out only** parameters *red*, *yellow*, *green*, and *blue* are to contain the addresses of the first elements of the four order lists. Initially, these **celladdress** variables are undefined. The first solution that comes to mind is to set each of these variables to **null** and then, when the first order is added to any one of these lists, set the appropriate variable to the address of that new order element. Once *red*, *yellow*, *green*, and *blue* have each been set to the addresses of the first order elements in their respective lists, these parameters would not be used again in this procedure.

While this solution is workable, it is not entirely satisfactory, because each time a new order element is added to the list, we would have to check whether it is the first element or not. To do this, each case of the **case** statement would have to be modified, as shown here for the red order list:

```
when 1 {red} : if red = null
                  then red ← new
                       endred ← new
                  else endred:order.nextorder ← new
                       endred ← new
               endif
```

We see that whenever this segment of the **case** statement is executed, the **if** condition must be checked. But

red = **null**

would only be true the first time an element is added to the red order list. Then *red* would be set to the address of this new list element, as would *endred*, since this first element would also be the last element. From then on, only the **else** clause would be executed when a new element was added to this list. Nonetheless, the **if** condition would have to be checked each time.

There is a solution to this problem that allows us to avoid the use of the **if** statement in each case of the **case** statement. At the beginning of the procedure we can set up four dummy list elements, addressed by *red* and *endred, yellow* and *endyellow, green* and *endgreen,* and *blue* and *endblue.* These dummy list elements would not contain any order information, but they would serve as the first list elements of the order lists. Then, since every list starts with one element (the dummy element) no checking would be necessary for the special case of adding the first order element to a list. However, we must be sure to remember the dummy elements when we design the procedure *print orders,* because we don't want these elements to appear in the output.

```
read orders : procedure
    {constructs four order lists, one each for red, yellow, green, and
    blue T-shirts}

    storage specification
        parameters
            red, yellow, green, blue : out only celladdress
        constants
            firmlength : integer 20
        listelement descriptors
            order : record containing
                quantity : integer
                firm : string
                nextorder : celladdress
            endrecord order
        variables
            new, endred, endyellow, endgreen, endblue : celladdress
            color : integer
    end storage specification
```

```
        begin read orders
            {sets up the dummy first list element for each order list}
            getnew order assign address to red
            endred ← red
            getnew order assign address to yellow
            endyellow ← yellow
            getnew order assign address to green
            endgreen ← green
            getnew order assign address to blue
            endblue ← blue
            loop while moredata {builds the order lists}
                getnew order assign address to new
                input color
                input new:order.quantity
                read string(new:order.firm, firmlength)
                case color is
                    when 1 {red}    :  endred:order.nextorder ← new
                                       endred ← new
                    when 2 {yellow} :  endyellow:order.nextorder ← new
                                       endyellow ← new
                    when 3 {green}  :  endgreen:order.nextorder ← new
                                       endgreen ← new
                    when 4 {blue}   :  endblue:order.nextorder ← new
                                       endblue ← new
                    otherwise          output 'bad color, order ignored for ',
                                            new:order.firm, new:order.quantity

                endcase
            endloop while
            endred:order.nextorder ← null
            endyellow:order.nextorder ← null
            endgreen:order.nextorder ← null
            endblue:order.nextorder ← null
            end read orders

    where read string reads an input string one character at a time,
            defined in case study 6.1.
```

CASE STUDY 9.2 — REFINEMENT 2

We can now turn our attention to procedure *print orders*, which accepts just one parameter, the address of the first element of one of the order lists, and prints this list. Procedure *print orders* will be very similar to procedure *writelist* of case study 9.1, but we must remember that the first element of every order list is a dummy element that should not be printed. Otherwise, the order list will be traversed via the links in each list element, and the quantity ordered and the ordering firm in each order element will be printed.

```
print orders : procedure
    {prints the order list specified in the formal parameter current}
    storage specification
        parameters
            current : in only celladdress
        listelement descriptors
            order : record containing
                quantity : integer
                firm : string
                nextorder : celladdress
            endrecord order
    end storage specification
begin print orders
    {skips past dummy first element in list}
    current ← current:order . nextorder
    loop while current ≠ null {prints the list}
        output current:order . quantity, current:order . firm
        current ← current:order . nextorder
    endloop while
end print orders
```

CASE STUDY 9.2 — REFINEMENT 3

Notice that we have used the formal parameter *current* to step through the order list via the links. Since *current* is an **in only** parameter, however, changing the value of *current* in procedure *print orders* does not change the value of the actual parameter passed to *current* in the initial procedure; thus the value of the variable containing the address of the first element of the list remains intact in the initial procedure.

Correctness

You should do a walkthrough of this program with some simple input values to be sure that you understand how it works. Special values for testing this program would include values that would make each of the lists be empty or contain a single element.

Efficiency

The initial procedure contains no loops, but procedures *read orders* and *print orders* both contain loops. In procedure *read orders* the loop is executed as many times as there are orders in the input. Procedure *print orders* is called four times in the initial procedure, and each time its loop iterates as many times as there are elements in the list being printed. Summing the number of elements in each list, however, will give the number of original input orders, so the loop of procedure *print orders* will actually be executed as often as the loop in procedure *read orders*. Thus the program has $O(n)$ time complexity, where n is the total number of orders for T-shirts of all colors.

The space complexity of the program is also linear in n, since there will be as many list elements in the various lists as there are orders in the input. The dummy elements used to head the four lists and the other variables add only a constant number of extra storage cells, not affecting the general space complexity of $O(n)$.

In these considerations of time and space complexity, we must again recall that there will be extra time required to process the links of a linked list and extra storage space required for storing these links, making the program slower and larger than similar programs not using linked lists.

Summary — Case Study 9.2

Again we have seen that extra effort is required to implement a data structure with a linked list; this results from the need to keep careful track of the explicit links of the structure. However, the program itself still uses only the familiar looping and decision control structures we learned in the early chapters of this book. Our top-down style of programming pays off here, allowing us to concentrate on small, local portions of the problem in isolation from other problems.

In case study 9.1 we implemented a simple list data structure with an *mpl* linked list. As we pointed out in that case study, it is usually better to implement simple lists with arrays rather than linked lists. Arrays are generally more efficient in terms of storage space, since no explicit links need to be stored with array elements. Programming time is also normally lessened when arrays are used, because programs using arrays are somewhat easier to design than those using linked lists.

In this case study, however, we have seen an exception to that rule. Although the four order lists are each simple lists, when taken together they present a problem that is not easily solved with arrays: determining how large to declare the individual arrays. Consider what happens, for example, if we expect the total number of orders to be so large that nearly the entire store will be used to hold the four lists. It may be that on some occasions (e.g., St. Patrick's Day) an inordinate number of green T-shirts are ordered, while very few of the other colors are ordered. If we had designed our program so that the four lists were implemented as four arrays of equal size, there probably would not be enough room in the order list array for green T-shirts. Using linked lists to hold these orders, however, allows each list to grow arbitrarily long (within the constraints of the store) without our having to worry about which list might be the longest in any particular run of the program.

This situation — where there is more than one simple list to be maintained in the store and the sizes of these lists can vary dramatically during different executions of the program — calls for the use of linked lists. In later case studies we will see other instances where linked lists are the most logical method of representing a data structure.

A Dynamic Waiting Queue

Case Study 9.3

> **Problem Description:** A box office ticket sales organization must maintain a waiting list of phone numbers for customers trying to purchase tickets after all tickets have been sold. As cancellations come in, the persons whose phone numbers are at the front of the list are called and offered the tickets.

Input Specifications: A T will be input for a ticket request and a C for a cancellation; the Ts and Cs can be input in any order. Ts must be followed by the phone number of the ticket purchaser. The last input item will be a Q (for quit) to indicate that the program should be terminated.

In case study 9.1 we examined the construction and output of a simple list implemented as a linked list. That particular use of a linked list was shown to be generally inefficient, since a 1-D array can be used for the same purpose, requiring less storage space and probably less program development time. In fact, even using an array would be inefficient since each number could be input and then immediately output in a simple **while moredata** loop.

In case study 9.2 a more appropriate use of linked lists to implement simple lists was discussed; when more than one simple list is to be maintained in the store and the lists are of unpredictable size relative to one another, the lists should be implemented as linked lists. This allows each list to grow arbitrarily long (within the confines of the store) and still take up only as much space as needed.

In this case study we will use a linked list to implement another data structure — the *queue*. A queue (pronounced like "cue") is a line, like the one that forms at a ticket booth. The first person to get into such a line is the first one to be served and to leave the line. For this reason a queue is sometimes called a *first in first out (fifo)* data structure.

A queue can also be viewed as a list with a front and a back, with additions to the list allowed only at the back and deletions allowed only at the front. It is important to realize that queues are dynamic — they grow and shrink during program execution, in direct contrast to the simple lists we have studied so far. Simple lists are built up from the input until the input is exhausted, then their size remains fixed for the remainder of the program. Queues contain a varying number of elements during the course of a program, the number of elements changing dynamically as the program is executed.

Queues are quite useful data structures in many programs. For example, every large computing system has one very important program, the *operating system*, which executes intermittently whenever the computer is running. The operating system schedules the various programs that are submitted for execution by the users of the computer. The operating system may administer these many requests to run programs by placing each incoming request into a queue (at the end) and removing a request from a queue (from the front) when the necessary computer resources become available to run that program.

The particular problem we examine in this case study is a takeoff on the example of box-office ticket sales at the beginning of this chapter.

The Solution — Queues and Singly Linked Lists

To implement the waiting list of this problem effectively as a queue, we must make sure that it is easy to add new elements to the queue and delete old elements from it. These are the only two operations performed on a queue. Thus we must be able to (1) access the first element of the queue at any time — this is the element (phone number) that will be removed when a ticket cancellation occurs, and (2) access the last element of the queue in order to add new ticket request information.

Because of the dynamic nature of the waiting list queue, a linked list implementation will be best. To satisfy the first requirement a **celladdress** variable called *front* will continuously be updated to point to the first element of the queue. Similarly, a **celladdress** variable called *rear* will always point to the last element of the queue. The list will also have single links connecting each element of the list to the following one, from front to rear.

Suppose that there are currently three telephone numbers in the waiting queue. The queue will look like

Example 9.4

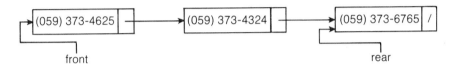

If a cancellation comes through, a C is input into the program, and the telephone number ((059) 373-4625) pointed to by the **celladdress** variable *front* is removed and printed so that the person at that number can be called and offered the ticket. The front pointer must then be changed to point to the next telephone number in the queue (the one to which the current front element is linked), so the queue would now look like

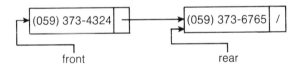

If someone else with telephone number (059) 373-9376 now requests tickets, a new list element must be allocated for this new telephone number. The link field of the last element in the queue (pointed to by *rear*), is now **null;** it must be changed to link to the new element and the rear pointer must be changed to point to this new rear element. Then the link field of the new rear element must be set to **null,** giving

As we can see, the front and rear pointers make the operations of adding and deleting queue elements quite easy. Notice what would happen, for example, if no rear queue pointer were maintained; to find out where a new element should be added, the links would have to be followed through each queue element, starting from the front, until the **null** pointer was found, indicating that the last list element had been reached. Then the new element could be linked in. This, of course, would be a very inefficient process for long queues.

A final point to consider is that we must be able to recognize when the queue is empty. Adding a new element to an empty queue will require special processing, because both variables *front* and *rear* will have to be set to point to the new single element (since that element will be both the first and last element in the queue). When the only element in a queue is deleted, *front* and *rear* must both be set to **null** to indicate that the queue is empty.

From this example we have a good idea how to design the program for this case study. The initial procedure will establish an empty queue and then read in the requests for tickets and cancellations, calling procedure *addtoq* when a ticket request comes in and procedure *removefromq* for a cancellation. Procedure *addtoq* will insert a new telephone number at the end of the queue, whereas procedure *removefromq* will return the first telephone number in the queue, updating the queue properly. The **celladdress** variables *front* and *rear* will have to be declared in the initial procedure, too, because they define the location of the queue in the store and will have to be passed to procedures *addtoq* and *removefromq*. These considerations give us our first attempt at the initial procedure for this program:

```
wait for tickets : initial procedure
    {maintains a waiting queue of ticket purchasers}

    storage specification
        variables
            front, rear : celladdress
            phonenumber : string
            type : character
        end storage specification

    begin wait for tickets
        {establish an empty queue}
        input type
        loop while {type indicates that the program is not done}
            case type is
                when 'T'    :   {ticket request}
                                output 'enter telephone number'
                                read string(phonenumber, 14)
                                addtoq(phonenumber, front, rear)
                when 'C'    :   {cancellation}
                                removefromq(phonenumber, front, rear)
                otherwise       output 'bad input, please retype'
            endcase
            input type
        endloop while
    end wait for tickets

    where read string was defined in case study 6.1
    where addtoq inserts a phone number at the rear of the queue
    where removefromq returns the phone number at the front of the queue
```

CASE STUDY 9.3 — REFINEMENT 1

Having declared the **celladdress** variables *front* and *rear*, which are to contain the addresses of the first and last queue elements, respectively, establishing an empty queue at the beginning of execution is easy. We just set both *front* and *rear* to **null**. A **null** address in either *front* or *rear* will be used to indicate that the waiting queue is empty.

Notice that the initial procedure has been designed as an interactive procedure; a message is printed prompting the user to enter a phone number each time a T is input. This is the only sensible way this program (with its dynamic queue) can be written, since ticket requests and cancellations will come in intermittently during business hours.

Since a Q will be entered to signal the end of processing, the **loop** statement should be

loop while type ≠ 'Q'

Inside the loop we first check whether *type*, which contains the character just input, has the value T (for ticket). If it does, a phone number is input and *add-toq* is called to add this new phone number to the queue. If type has the value C, procedure *removefromq* is called to remove and print the telephone number at the front of the queue. If an incorrect character (not Q, T, or C) is mistakenly typed, a printed message requests that the character be retyped.

One problem with our first attempt at the initial procedure is that we have called *removefromq* when a cancellation comes through without checking first whether the queue is empty. An error would result if we attempted to remove an element from an empty queue, so we correct this problem in the following version of the initial procedure. We also declare a new constant *phonesize* to hold the number of characters in a telephone number.

```
wait for tickets : initial procedure
    {maintains a waiting queue of ticket purchasers}

    storage specification
        constants
            phonesize : integer 14
        variables
            front, rear : celladdress
            phonenumber : string
            type : character
        end storage specification

    begin wait for tickets
        front ← null
        rear ← null
        input type
        loop while type ≠ 'Q'
            case type is
                when 'T'   :   {a ticket request must be queued}
                               output 'enter telephone number'
                               read string(phonenumber, phonesize)
                               addtoq(phonenumber, front, rear)
                when 'C'   :   {a ticket cancellation must be handled}
                               if front = null
                                   then {queue is empty}
                                       output 'no one in the waiting queue'
                                   else removefromq(phonenumber, front, rear)
                                       output phonenumber
                               endif
                otherwise      output 'bad input, please retype'
            endcase
            input type
        endloop while
    end wait for tickets

    where read string was defined in case study 6.1
    where addtoq inserts a phonenumber at the rear of the queue
    where removefromq returns the phonenumber at the front of the queue
```

CASE STUDY 9.3 — REFINEMENT 2

Although this initial procedure will now work properly, it will not be practical in an interactive program, because the statement

input type

is executed without printing a message to the user explaining what is to be input — the user will be staring at a blank terminal screen without a cue that something is to be typed. We need to add a statement like

output 'enter T, C, or Q '

in front of the **input** statements just before the loop and at the bottom of the loop. Actually, when we translate this program into a real programming language, a short description of the T, C, and Q codes should be included as part of the cue, so that the user knows what to type to get the desired results. An interactive program that explains the options available to a user at each step (so that the user does not need to spend time searching through a manual or seeking outside help to use the program) is said to be a *user-friendly* program.

The initial procedure we have designed here is already long and somewhat involved, and adding **output** statements to make it user-friendly may make it inconveniently long. In designing programs you will often discover, as we have in this case, that a small subproblem that originally could be nicely contained in a single routine has grown too large and unwieldy. When this occurs you should stop and break the newly designed routine into smaller procedures and functions. This will make the program more readable and therefore easier to understand and correct. In this case, one way to break up this initial procedure would be to make the options T and C of the **case** statement separate procedures. This is what we will do here, writing a new initial procedure as well as two new procedures, *request* and *cancel*, to handle the cases for T and C input codes, respectively.

```
wait for tickets : initial procedure
    {maintains a waiting queue of ticket purchasers}

    storage specification
        variables
            front, rear : celladdress
            type : character
        end storage specification
    begin wait for tickets
        front ← null
        rear ← null
        output 'enter T, C, or Q '
        input type
        loop while type ≠ 'Q'
            case type is
                when 'T'    :    request(front, rear)
                when 'C'    :    cancel(front, rear)
                otherwise        output 'bad input, please retype: '
                endcase
            output 'enter T, C, or Q '
            input type
            endloop while
        end wait for tickets

    where request queues a ticket request in the waiting queue
    where cancel removes and prints the first telephone number
            in the waiting queue, to be offered the cancelled tickets
```

CASE STUDY 9.3 — REFINEMENT 3

Notice that this new version of the initial procedure is much easier to read. Procedures *request* and *cancel* are simple, consisting only of the previously designed sections of the T and C case options:

---

request : **procedure**
    {queues a ticket request}

    storage specification
        parameters
            front, rear : **in out celladdress**
        constants
            phonesize : **integer** 14
        variables
            phonenumber : **string**
        end storage specification

    begin request
        output 'enter telephone number: '
        read string(phonenumber, phonesize)
        addtoq(phonenumber, front, rear)
        end request

    where read string was defined in case study 6.1
    where addtoq inserts a phonenumber at the rear of the queue

CASE STUDY 9.3 — REFINEMENT 4

---

cancel : **procedure**
    {processes a ticket cancellation by removing first telephone
    number in the waiting queue}

    storage specification
        parameters
            front, rear : **in out celladdress**
        variables
            phonenumber : **string**
        end storage specification

    begin cancel
        if front = **null**
            then {queue is empty}
                output 'no one in the waiting list'
            else {queue is not empty}
                removefromq(phonenumber, front, rear)
                output 'call this number: ', phonenumber
        endif
        end cancel

    where removefromq returns the phonenumber at the front of the queue

CASE STUDY 9.3 — REFINEMENT 5

We now turn our attention to the design of procedure *addtoq* called from procedure *request*. The parameters to *addtoq* are a telephone number of type **string** and two **celladdress** variables containing the addresses of the first queue element and the last queue element, respectively. The descriptor of the queue elements must be included in the **storage specification** statement; each list element will contain a phone number field and a link field used to point to the next element in the queue. Another **celladdress** variable, *new*, must be declared to contain the address of newly allocated list elements that are to be added to the end of the queue. The **storage specification** section of *addtoq* will thus be

```
storage specification
    parameters
        phonenumber : in only string
        front, rear : in out celladdress
    listelement descriptors
        waitinglistelement : record containing
            telephone : string
            link : celladdress
            endrecord waitinglistelement
    variables
        new : celladdress
end storage specification
```

To add a new telephone number to the queue, we must first have the processor get a new waiting list element and then assign the telephone number passed as a parameter to this new queue element. Since this new element will become the last one in the queue, its link field should be set to **null,** and the link element of the current last queue element (the one whose address is now in *rear*) must be updated to point to the new element. Finally, *rear* must also be assigned the address of the new last queue element. This gives us the following outline for the computation part of *addtoq:*

```
getnew waitinglistelement assign address to new
new:waitinglistelement.telephone ← phonenumber
new:waitinglistelement.link ← null
rear:waitinglistelement.link ← new
rear ← new
```

This program segment will work fine if the queue is not empty. What if the queue is empty? Then *rear* will contain **null,** and the statement

```
rear:waitinglistelement.link ← null
```

will cause an error, because *rear* does not contain a valid address of a waiting list element. Therefore, before executing the last two statements of the program segment just given, we must check whether *rear* is **null.** If *rear* is **null,** indicating that the queue is empty, then both *front* and *rear* must be set to contain the address of the new list element. These considerations lead us to the final refinement of procedure *addtoq:*

```
addtoq : procedure
    {adds a new telephone number to the end of the waiting queue}

    storage specification
        parameters
            phonenumber : in only string
            front, rear : in out celladdress
        listelement descriptors
            waitinglistelement : record containing
                telephone : string
                link : celladdress
                endrecord waitinglistelement
        variables
            new : celladdress
        end storage specification

    begin addtoq
        getnew waitinglistelement assign address to new
        new:waitinglistelement.telephone ← phonenumber
        new:waitinglistelement.link ← null
        if rear = null
            then rear ← new
                front ← new
            else rear:waitinglistelement.link ← new
                rear ← new
        endif
    end addtoq
```

CASE STUDY 9.3 — REFINEMENT 6

Procedure *removefromq* called from procedure *cancel* must retrieve the telephone number in the first queue element and return that number to procedure *cancel* via parameter *phonenumber*. In the process, the first queue element must be deleted and the parameter *front* set to point to the new first queue element (the one linked to by the current first queue element). If the current first queue element is the only queue element, then after it is removed *front* and *rear* must be set to **null** to indicate an empty queue. We know that there is only one element in the queue if *front* = *rear* (why?).

```
removefromq : procedure
    {returns the telephone number at the front of the waiting queue}

    storage specification
        parameters
            phonenumber : out only string
            front, rear : in out celladdress
        listelement descriptors
            waitinglistelement : record containing
                telephone : string
                link : celladdress
                endrecord waitinglistelement
        variables
            old : celladdress
        end storage specification
```

```
begin removefromq
    phonenumber ← front:waitinglistelement.telephone
    old ← front
    if front = rear
        then front ← null
                rear ← null
        else front ← front:waitinglistelement.link
    endif
    free old:waitinglistelement
end removefromq
```

CASE STUDY 9.3 — REFINEMENT 7

Here we have used a list operation — the **free** statement — that has not been needed until this case study. After deleting the first queue element, we must indicate to the processor that the storage cells used for this element are now free to be used for other purposes; we do this with the **free** statement. Since we lose the address of the original first list element when we update the queue pointer *front*, we save this address with the statement

old ← front

Thus we know the address of the list element being freed after *front* has been changed. The statement

free old:waitinglistelement

then causes the proper list element to be freed.

Correctness

As usual, you should do a program walkthrough to see how this program using a queue works. In testing the program, special values would include some that cause the queue first to grow, then shrink to one element, grow again, shrink to no elements, and then grow again; this will test whether the program will function properly with the empty queue and with a queue of one element.

Efficiency

Neither procedure *addtoq* nor procedure *removefromq* contains a loop and neither one is recursive, so both will run in constant time whenever called. However, the initial procedure contains a loop which iterates each time a new ticket order or cancellation comes in. If there are n such transactions processed during the course of executing the program, then the time complexity of the whole program must be $O(n)$. However, this is somewhat misleading, since the program will actually be in "continuous" execution, waiting at the **input** statement of the **while** loop in the initial procedure for the next order or cancellation. In terms of execution time, this is not the same as giving an input of size n to a program for a single run without pauses, as has been done in so many of our previous case studies. It is probably better to quantify the time complexity of this program by saying, "This program will be constantly ready to accept a new ticket transaction; each transaction (adding a new telephone number to the waiting queue or deleting a telephone number from that queue) takes constant time." The fact that each transaction takes a constant small amount of time independent of the input means that the program will process transactions faster than they can be entered. The program user does not need to worry that some transactions will take longer than others or that he/she will need to wait while the processor completes one transaction before another can be entered — these are the important time complexity considerations for such programs.

The space complexity of this program is another matter. It is impossible to predetermine the order in which ticket requests and cancellations will arrive, so there is no way of knowing how long the queue will grow. For some events the waiting queue might become quite large, while for others there may be no waiting list at all. The space complexity of the program, though dependent on the input, thus cannot be quantified. It must be approximated from past experience each time the program is run.

Summary — Case Study 9.3

In this case study we have seen our first example of a dynamic list, a list in which new elements are added to the list and old elements deleted from the list during the course of program execution. The dynamic list of this case study is called a queue because of its special form: new elements can be added only to the end of the list and old elements can be removed only from the front of the list; additions and deletions cannot be made at any other point in the list.

Queues have many applications in real life and, as a result, are extensively used in programs. Programs using queues are usually *online, interactive, real-time* programs. *Online* means that the program executes for an extended period of time (e.g., over the course of a week, perhaps, in the case of ticket sales). Such programs may be inactive much of the time, waiting for new input at an **input** statement, and continuing execution when input is received. *Interactive* means that the program interacts with the user, printing messages on the screen and accepting input from the keyboard when the user enters new values. *Real-time* means that the program is completing a task that is currently in progress in the real world, such as processing ticket requests and cancellations as these transactions are made. This is in contrast to other tasks, such as computing the average score for a test, which are done when convenient (i.e., not in real time as the tests are turned in).

The dynamic nature of the queue data structure makes a linked list representation of a queue the logical choice. A linked list allows the queue to grow as large as necessary (within the bounds of the store), an important consideration when it is virtually impossible to predict the maximum size of the queue.

A Dynamic Priority Stack

| Case Study
| 9.4

Problem Description: Design a program to maintain a priority list of interrupted telephone calls. Whenever S (for stack) is typed, it will be followed by the telephone number of an interrupted call, which must be stacked on top of the priority list. Whenever R (for return) is entered, the telephone number currently on top of the priority list must be printed, so that the call to that number can be returned.

> *Input Specifications:* The input will be a series of Ss and Rs in any order, the Ss followed by a telephone number of the form (209) 882-3732. An input of Q (quit) will signal that the program is to be terminated.

Another important data structure that arises in many computer programming applications is the stack. A *stack* is a dynamic list with only one access point, the top of the stack. The standard illustration of a stack is the plate dispenser found in many cafeterias. Clean plates are placed on top of a spring-loaded device that sinks down so that only the top plate can be seen and removed by a customer going through the line. As a plate is removed, the spring raises the stack so that the next plate is visible. The stack as a dynamic list data structure is similar. New list elements to be inserted must be added to the top of the stack. Only the element currently at the stack top can be removed from the list. This means that the last element added to a stack will be the first one removed, so a stack is sometimes called a *last in first out* (*lifo*) data structure. (Recall that a queue is a *first in first out* data structure.)

Although many of the applications for stacks as data structures are quite involved, we can think of simple everyday situations in which stacks occur, for better or for worse. Some people stack their mail as it arrives, answering the letter on the top of the stack when time permits. This might mean that the letter on the bottom of the stack never gets answered. Then there is the underwear drawer. After being washed, underwear is usually folded and stacked on top of clean underwear already in the drawer. Unless a person puts off washing until all the underwear is dirty, some clothes will wear out much faster than others, since clean underwear is always added to and chosen from the top of the stack.

A more appropriate use of stacks arises in a "priority interrupt" environment. If one task is in progress and a more urgent task suddenly presents itself, the first task must be interrupted while the second task is worked on. If a third yet more important task comes up, the second task will also have to be interrupted. If this third task is completed without interruption, then the second task will be resumed, since it is now the most important task again, and so on.

Example 9.5   Suppose an executive is involved in making an important decision for which supporting information is coming in via telephone. If the executive is involved in one conversation and a less important call comes in, the caller will be asked to call back. If a more important call comes in, the executive must write down the number of the person with whom he/she is now conversing, interrupt that call, and then take the new, more important call. The interrupted caller's phone number may be

(301) 356-2773

If during the second phone conversation, a third yet more important call comes in, the second call must also be interrupted. If the telephone number of the second caller is (301) 356-7371, the list of calls to be returned now looks like

(301) 356-7371
(301) 356-2773

where the most important interrupted call is on top.

This process could continue with the list building up to

(209) 475-6666
(512) 233-3633
(209) 475-1171
(301) 356-7371
(301) 356-2773

If the current call finishes without interruption, the next most important call must be returned. Since the list of calls to be returned has been maintained as a stack with the most recently interrupted caller's telephone number on top of the stack, the one on top of the stack will now be called, leaving the list of calls to be returned looking like

(512) 233-3633
(209) 475-1171
(301) 356-7371
(301) 356-2773

If this newly returned call is also finished without interruption, the next most important call to return is now on top of the list: (512) 233-3633. After this call is returned the list will look like

(209) 475-1171
(301) 356-7371
(301) 356-2773

Now suppose that another more important call comes in during the current call to (512) 233-3633; this number will have to be stacked again, giving

(512) 233-3633
(209) 475-1171
(301) 356-7371
(301) 356-2773

Thus the list of telephone numbers can grow and shrink arbitrarily. If calls come in continuously all day long, it is conceivable that those on the bottom of the stack will never be returned.

Of course, this example is oversimplified, but it serves as an illustration of how the stack of our current case study will be maintained.

The Solution — Stacks and Singly Linked Lists

Using the example of the telephone conversation interrupt stack, we can determine how to use a singly linked list to implement the stack for this problem. We will need a **celladdress** variable, *top*, which contains the address of the top element on the stack; the links between the elements will have to run from the top element of the stack to the bottom, as in

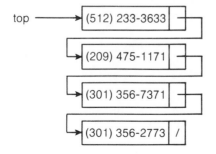

Why do the links run from top to bottom? Notice what happens when the top stack element is removed. We know where it is, because variable *top* points to it. But if it is removed, the one below it should become the new top stack element, as in

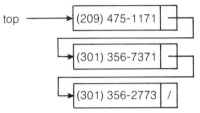

We know which element is next by following the link down from the current top element. Therefore, when a new element is to be added to the stack, the new element must be allocated, the phone number assigned to it, and then its link field set to point to the same place as *top*. If as this is done the address of the new list element is assigned to *new*, we get

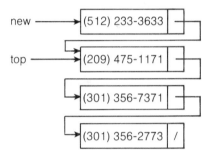

Then *top* must be set to point to the new top element (i.e., *top* should take on the same value as *new*):

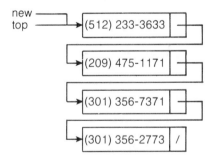

We will now design the program, implementing the stack as a linked list just as we have shown. In many ways, this program will be similar in its organization to the queue program in case study 9.3. Besides the initial procedure, we will need a procedure that adds a new element to the top of the stack and another procedure that returns the telephone number currently on top of the stack. Following the pattern established in case study 9.3, the initial procedure will use a loop with a **case** statement to process the three possible inputs, S to stack an interrupted telephone number, R to retrieve the top telephone number on the stack, and Q to quit the program. The actions to be taken when S or R is typed will be relegated to procedures *stacknumber* and *retrievenumber*, respectively. This gives us

```
stackcalls : initial procedure
    {maintains a stack of interrupted telephone calls}

    storage specification
        variables
            top : celladdress
            type : character
        end storage specification

    begin stackcalls
        top ← null
        output 'enter S, R, or Q'
        input type
        loop while type ≠ 'Q'
            case type is
                when 'S'    :    stacknumber(top)
                when 'R'    :    retrievenumber(top)
                otherwise       output 'bad input, please retype'
                endcase
            output 'enter S, R, or 'Q'
            input type
            endloop while
        end stackcalls

    where stacknumber inputs a phone number and places it on
            the top of the stack
    where retrievenumber removes and prints the phone number on
            the top of the stack

CASE STUDY 9.4 — REFINEMENT 1
```

Procedures *stacknumber* and *retrievenumber* are simple and are given next:

```
stacknumber : procedure
    {inputs and stacks the phone number of an interrupted caller}

    storage specification
        parameters
            top : in out celladdress
        constants
            phonelength : integer 14
        variables
            phonenumber : string
        end storage specification

    begin stacknumber
        output 'enter telephone number to be stacked: '
        read string(phonenumber, phonelength)
        stack(phonenumber, top)
        end stacknumber

    where read string was defined in case study 6.1
    where stack places a phone number onto the top of the stack

CASE STUDY 9.4 — REFINEMENT 2
```

retrievenumber : **procedure**
{retrieves and prints the top telephone number on the stack}

  storage specification
    parameters
      top : **in out celladdress**
    variables
      phonenumber : **string**
    end storage specification

  begin retrievenumber
    if top = **null**
      then {stack is empty}
        output 'no calls to be returned'
      else {stack is not empty}
        unstack(phonenumber, top)
        output 'return call to: ', phonenumber
    endif
  end retrievenumber

  where unstack returns the phone number on the top of the stack

CASE STUDY 9.4 — REFINEMENT 3

Procedure *stack* (called from procedure *stacknumber*) will place a new phone number onto the top of the stack, whereas procedure *unstack* (called from procedure *retrievenumber*) will return the phone number on the top of the stack. Before *unstack* is called, we make sure that the stack is not empty; the stack is empty when *top* has the value **null.**

The stacking operation is accomplished by allocating a new element, putting the telephone number to be stacked into that element, and then setting the link field of that element to have the address in *top* (remember that *top* contains the address of the element currently on the top of the stack). Finally, *top* is reset to point to the new element, since the new element is now the top element on the stack.

stack : **procedure**
{stacks a telephone number}

  storage specification
    parameters
      phonenumber : **in only string**
      top : **in out celladdress**
    listelement descriptors
      stackelement : **record containing**
        telephone : **string**
        link : **celladdress**
        endrecord stackelement
    variables
      new : **celladdress**
    end storage specification

  begin stack
    getnew stackelement **assign address to** new
    new:stackelement.telephone ← phonenumber
    new:stackelement.link ← top
    top ← new
    end stack

CASE STUDY 9.4 — REFINEMENT 4

In this refinement we haven't considered what happens if we try to add an element to an empty stack. In that case *top* will be **null,** and we need to set *new:stackelement.link* to **null,** since it will be the only element, and also set *top* to be *new.* If we carefully check the procedure, however, we find that this is exactly what it does when *top* is **null,** so the procedure needs no modification.

Procedure *unstack* is just as easy to design as procedure *stack.* Procedure *unstack* will not be called if the stack is empty (look at the procedure *retrievenumber*), so if the statement

phonenumber ← top:stackelement.telephone

is executed, the telephone number on the top of the stack will be assigned to parameter *phonenumber* of procedure *unstack.* Afterwards, the variable *top* must be reset to point to the new top stack element. The new top element will be the one linked to by the current top element (i.e., the new top element is the one whose address is in the link field of the element now pointed to by *top*), so

top ← top:stackelement.link

will cause *top* to point to the new top stack element. Notice that this will work properly even if there is only one element left on the stack when procedure *unstack* is called. In this case, *top:stackelement.link* will be **null** (indicating that no elements follow in the stack), so

top ← top:stackelement.link

will assign **null** to *top,* indicating that the stack is now empty.

This gives us procedure *unstack:*

```
unstack : procedure
    {returns the telephone number on the top of the stack}

    storage specification
        parameters
            phonenumber : out only string
            top : in out celladdress
        listelement descriptors
            stackelement : record containing
                telephone : string
                link : celladdress
            endrecord stackelement
        variables
            old : celladdress
    end storage specification
begin unstack
    phonenumber ← top:stackelement.telephone
    old ← top
    top ← top:stackelement.link
    free old:stackelement
    end unstack
```

CASE STUDY 9.4 — REFINEMENT 5

Notice that since we must free the element that is unstacked, we keep the location of that element in the **celladdress** variable *old.* You should compare this refinement with procedure *removefromq* of case study 9.3.

Correctness

A walkthrough using just a few telephone numbers will show you how this program works. As in the previous case study, you should pick test values that cause the stack to grow and shrink to one element and no elements.

Efficiency

Since this program is designed to be interactive, the comments concerning interactive, online, real-time programs in the Efficiency section of case study 9.3 apply here also. Essentially, the time and space complexities of this program cannot really be determined in their usual senses. We certainly cannot determine just how large the stack will become, so there is no way to pin down ahead of time how much storage space this program will require. The important question with regard to the time complexity is how long it takes to complete one transaction — the stacking of a new telephone number or the unstacking of an old telephone number. As in the queue of case study 9.3, each transaction involving the stack will take just a small constant amount of time that does not depend on the size of the input. Also, since additions and deletions are done only at the top of the stack and do not require searching through the stack, the size of the stack plays no role in the time required to stack or unstack an element.

Summary — Case Study 9.4

The stack data structure introduced in this case study is our second example of a dynamic list, a list that can grow and shrink arbitrarily during program execution (the first was the queue, which was discussed in case study 9.3).

A stack is a severely restricted form of a dynamic list, because insertions and deletions can only be done at one end of a stack, the top. Nonetheless, there are many situations in which a stack is the data structure required. A typical use for stacks is the "priority interrupt" list, in which tasks interrupted by more important tasks are kept in order so that they can be resumed later when the more important tasks are finished. Since the most recently interrupted task is the one that should be resumed, it is always placed on the top of the stack. This case study presented a simple priority interrupt list. Actually, on all but the smallest personal computers, the operating system (the special program that administers the execution of all other programs submitted to the computer) must maintain such a stack. For various reasons, the operating system must interrupt other running programs. Of course, the operating system must remember which programs were interrupted in order to resume their execution later.

Another common use for stacks arises in processing recursive function or procedure calls. For example, if we look back at example 3.19, where we showed the evaluation of *factorial*(4), we see that the two storage cells required by each call to *factorial* are allocated in stack fashion. The cells in use by the current version of *factorial* are on top of the stack, so that when this version of *factorial* ends, its storage cells disappear from the top of the stack, leaving the cells for the previous version of *factorial* on top of the stack. This is just what we want, since this previous recursive version of *factorial* should resume execution when the currently executing recursive version terminates.

We will see some of these advanced applications of stacks in The Challenge section of this chapter. Just remember that all of these applications, in spite of their seeming complexity, are based on the simple stack data structure.

As the case studies of this chapter have shown us, there are a number of real-world situations where explicit relationships among the values being kept in a program must be maintained. These include cases in which a number of simple lists must be constructed and it cannot be determined ahead of time how many items will be in each list. (You should read the introductory pages of this chapter for a review of the form of singly linked lists.) Dynamic data structures, which can grow and shrink wildly during the course of program execution, are even more important. Two of the most common dynamic data structures are the queue and the stack. These dynamic data structures require explicit links among data elements in the structure, and it must also be possible to allocate new storage cells for new items to be added to the data structure and free the storage cells no longer needed in the data structure.

CONSTRUCTING A LINKED LIST

In constructing a linked list, we must first describe the form of the list elements in a **listelement descriptors** declaration. A list element is a record that consists of at least two parts, the value to be stored in that element of the list, and a link to the next element in the list (the link is a variable of type **celladdress**). Each list element record can contain many values, for example, all of an employee's personnel information. For more advanced applications, a list element might have more than one link, for example, a list could have both forward and backward links. Since the link field of a list element is just the address of a storage cell, records with different **listelement descriptors** statements can be linked together in the store. In this book, however, we only deal with singly linked lists whose elements are all of the same type.

Once the elements of a list have been described in a **listselement descriptors** declaration, the list is constructed one element at a time. When a new element is to be added to a list, the statement

    getnew *listelement* **assign address to** *elementaddress*

must first be executed by the processor, which sets aside a group of unused cells large enough to hold the record described for *listelement* and places the address of the first cell of this group into variable *elementaddress*. After allocation of a new list element, the appropriate values must be saved in the proper fields of that list element, then the links to and from other list elements must be made in order to fit the new list element into the list in the proper position.

Suppose we have been constructing a list whose elements are described as

    listelement descriptors
        node : **record containing**
            value1 : **real**
            value2 : **integer**
            nextnode : **celladdress**
        endrecord node

*Example
9.6*

To set aside a new list element of this type we would have the processor execute the statement

> **getnew** node **assign address to** new

where *new* is a variable of type **celladdress.** To assign 5 to field *value2* of this node we could use the statement

> new:node.value2 ← 5

The processor uses the address in variable *new* to get to the first storage cell of the list element *node*, then it uses the **listelement descriptors** declaration of *node* to determine that field *value2* is one cell past the address in *new,* so 5 is stored in the cell whose address is one larger than *new.*

To link another list element to this newly allocated one we just store the value in *new* into the link field of that other list element, because *new* contains the address of the new list element. Similarly, linking this new list element to some other list element whose address is in **celladdress** variable *old* requires execution of the statement

> new:node.nextnode ← old

We can release a list element that is no longer needed so that its storage cells can be used again with the statement

> **free** *listelement*

where *listelement* is the name of the list element to be freed.

IMPLEMENTING LINKED LISTS WITH ARRAYS

All modern programming languages of the type modeled by *mpl* have the necessary features for implementing dynamic data structures. The *mpl* **getnew** and **free** statements as well as **celladdress** type variables have counterparts in most of the newer programming languages. In the older programming languages, such as Basic and Fortran, that do not have these special features, dynamic data structures must be implemented using arrays. Large arrays are declared and treated just like chunks of the store. The links, which we model in *mpl* with **celladdress** variables, are nothing more than integer values used as array subscripts in this scheme, and the programmer must keep explicit track of which array elements are free to be used (when new elements are to be allocated). While this method is cumbersome, arrays are the only way to handle dynamic data structures in these older programming languages.

PASSING LINKED LISTS BETWEEN ROUTINES

A linked list is never passed as a parameter to other routines, because the linked list itself is not a data type. Instead, for example, a **celladdress** variable containing the starting address of the list is passed as an actual parameter to any routine that is to manipulate the list; that routine can then access the list by beginning at the starting address given in the parameter and following the links in each list element. Thus, a list can never be an **in only, in out,** or **out only** parameter; whenever a list element is allocated by the processor in a **getnew** statement in any routine, that list element remains in the store for the duration of program execution or until released in a **free** statement. On the other hand, since the list starting address is passed as a parameter, this parameter can have any of the types **in only, in out,** or **out only,** but the parameter type does not affect the actual elements of the list. Of course, any particular element of a list can also be passed as a parameter to other routines.

Suppose that we have the declarations

Example 9.7

    listelement descriptors
        node : **record containing**
            value1 : **integer**
            value2 : **real**
            nextnode : **celladdress**
            endrecord node
    variables
        new : **celladdress**

and the processor has executed the statement

    getnew node **assign address to** new

Then in calling a procedure, say *traverse*, we could pass variable *new* as a parameter, as in

    traverse(new)

Similarly we could call a function, say *factorial*, with

    factorial(new:node.value1)

which just passes the value in the cell set aside for *value1* in the record *node* whose address is in *new.*

QUEUES, STACKS, AND GENERAL LISTS

There are some common data structures that lend themselves well to linked list representations, including queues (case study 9.3), stacks (case studies 9.4 and 9.6), and general lists (case study 9.5).

Queues

The queue data structure is a simple list in which additions to the list can be made only at the rear and deletions only from the front. These two operations are sometimes called *enqueue* (for entering an element into the queue) and *dequeue* (for deleting an element from the queue). Queues represent data that must be processed in the "first come first served" manner common to all sorts of waiting lines, as demonstrated in case study 9.3.

Stacks

The stack data structure is a simple list in which both additions and deletions are permitted only at one end of the list, usually called the stack top. Common terms for the addition of a new list element and the removal of the current top list element are *push* and *pop*, respectively. These two names are descriptive of the way the stack, which is sometimes called a *pushdown store*, operates.

Stacks are used to represent data that must be processed in the "last in first out" manner common to priority interrupt lists, as shown in case study 9.4.

General Lists

A general list is a list in which the addition of a new list element and the deletion of an old list element can occur anywhere in the list. Case study 9.5 uses a general singly linked list.

CORRECTNESS OF PROGRAMS WITH LINKED LISTS

The program verification, walkthrough, testing, and debugging methods of earlier chapters apply equally well to programs using linked lists. Errors in programs with linked lists usually involve improper values in the **celladdress** variables that are used for linking a list together and pointing to the start of a list. This is because the programmer must explicitly keep track of all link values, and details are sometimes overlooked. On one hand, linked lists allow the programmer more power, providing absolute control over all aspects of the organization of a data structure, but on the other hand, this added power comes at the expense of more program development time and attention to detail.

Another common error is forgetting to free list elements that have been deleted and are no longer in use. In this situation a program execution involving many insertions and deletions is likely to terminate abnormally because it runs out of storage cells.

In summary, very careful attention to detail must be paid when designing a program around linked lists. But you have been learning this style of programming from the start of this book, so you should have no trouble designing routines to handle linked lists.

EFFICIENCY OF PROGRAMS WITH LINKED LISTS

The time complexity of programs that manipulate linked lists is determined in the usual way. However, you must realize that such programs will take longer to execute than similar programs not using linked lists, because the **getnew** and **free** statements usually take an inordinate amount of time for the processor to execute. Also, references to values within a list element, such as

    new:node.value1

take longer to process than a reference to a simple integer variable. You must also consider the sequential nature of programs that process general linked lists — to get to an arbitrary element of the list, the links from the first element to the desired one must be followed in succession. All of these factors mean that the execution time for programs with lists will be greater than you might initially expect.

The space complexity of dynamic lists cannot be determined except from past experience, because in most programs the lists grow and shrink in unpredictable ways during execution. Since link addresses must be stored with every list element, more storage space is required for a linked list than for a similar array. The use of dynamic linked lists can lead to abnormal program termination for lack of storage space when too many **getnew** statements (and too few **free** statements) are executed.

FOR REVIEW

9.1 What are the two characteristics of arrays that make them unwieldy for implementing general lists?

9.2 Give an example of a list in real life which has non-homogeneous elements.

9.3 Give a real-life example (different from those given in the book) of a dynamic list.

9.4 What is meant by the terms logical location and physical location when describing the relative locations of list elements to one another?

9.5 Explain the concept of a cell address. What role do cell addresses play in linked list data structures?

9.6 We use arrows in our diagrams of linked lists to show the relationships among list elements. What do these arrows stand for in the actual linked lists of the program?

9.7 What does the term singly linked list mean? Can you think of situations in which a different kind of linked list would be valuable? Give examples.

9.8 How is the type **celladdress** different from type **integer?**

9.9 List and briefly describe each of the new *mpl* statements introduced for handling lists. Explain why each is needed.

9.10 Explain the use of **null.** In particular, a **celladdress** variable could be **null,** or undefined, or it could contain the value of a cell address. Explain the differences among these possibilities.

9.11 Explain why it is necessary to keep a **celladdress** variable which always contains the address of the first element of a singly linked list.

9.12 Given a singly linked list with elements defined as

listelement descriptors
    porkbarrel : **record containing**
        price : **real**
        quantity : **integer**
        nextpork : **celladdress**
        endrecord porkbarrel

do the following, assuming that **celladdress** variable *first* points to the first element of this list. You can assume that *nextpork* has the value **null** in the last element of this list.

(a) Give the statements which will print *price* and *quantity* in each element of the list in succession.

(b) Modify (a) so that at the end of listing these values, the total price (determined as the sum of *price* times *quantity* in each list element) is printed.

(c) Is there any way you could write these statements correctly if the *nextpork* field of the last list element were undefined instead of **null?**

9.13   What does the term traverse a list mean?

9.14   Explain how the loop condition in

loop while {more elements are in the list}

will always be implemented in a singly linked list.

9.15   What are some special situations to be tested when verifying that a singly linked list has been implemented properly in a program?

9.16   In what ways does the program design process change when working with linked lists?

9.17   What efficiency considerations must be accounted for in programs with linked lists?

9.18   Explain the terms dynamic, online, and real time as they refer to programs involving linked lists.

9.19   Why is the space complexity of a program that manipulates linked lists generally difficult (or impossible) to determine?

9.20   Describe and contrast a queue and a stack. How do they differ from a general list?

9.21   Explain how linked lists are communicated among the various routines of a program.

9.22   Explain under what circumstances you would use a linked list implementation of a data structure instead of an array.

9.23   Why do we use the **free** statement in *mpl* (storage will be released for other users when the program finishes anyway)?

9.24   If you wanted to maintain a list of 100 numbers in a program, would you expect an array or a linked list representation to use more storage. Why?

9.25   It can be said that a linked list is dynamic and an array is not. What does this mean? Is this an advantage?

A DEEPER LOOK

9.26   The added flexibility and power resulting from implementing general data structures as linked lists are not without cost. List and explain some of these costs.

9.27   Some computer scientists who specialize in programming methodology and programming languages believe that linked lists are not a good programming language feature. Can you think of reasons why this might be true?

9.28   A 1-D array is much like the store itself: it contains a number of contiguous locations, and the array indices act as cell addresses. Could a single 1-D array therefore be organized to implement a general linked list? Explain your answer.

9.29 Explain why a record descriptor given in a **listelement descriptors** declaration is not the same as a record declared in a **variables** declaration.

9.30 Explain why a linked list cannot be passed as a parameter to a routine. In particular, consider what problems would arise in trying to declare a linked list as a formal **in only** parameter. Also, what are the differences between passing a linked list as a parameter and passing a list element as a parameter?

9.31 What is the important time complexity measure in an online, real time program? How does this differ from the time complexity measures we usually use for programs?

TO PROGRAM

9.32 Design an *mpl* function that finds the largest value in a singly linked list of integers.

9.33 Design a procedure *removeall* which removes all elements from a singly linked list of integers starting at the first occurrence of the integer parameter x. If x does not appear in the list, print an error message.

9.34 Modify *removeall* in the last exercise so that it works for a singly linked list of reals. What important change needs to be made in addition to changing all occurrences of **integer** to **real?**

9.35 Design an *mpl* procedure *remove* to search a singly linked list of integers and delete all elements containing the value in an integer parameter x.

9.36 Design an *mpl* procedure *deleteafter* to delete the element after the first occurrence of the value in an integer parameter x in a singly linked list of integers.

9.37 Design an *mpl* function to find the length of a singly linked list of reals.

9.38 Design an *mpl* procedure to merge two singly linked lists of reals into a new list. You can assume that the two original lists are in ascending order by value from smallest to largest. The resulting list (constructed by the merge procedure) should contain all of the values in the two original lists and be linked in order by value from smallest to largest. You may assume that you won't need the original two lists again in your program.

9.39 Design an *mpl* function to compute the number of occurrences of the integer x in a singly linked list of integers.

In the challenge section of this chapter we continue to restrict our attention to data structures involving only singly linked lists. In the first case study we will design a program to solve the box office ticket reservation problem of example 9.2. In the second case study we will see how to design the quicksort routine to run nonrecursively by using a stack.

**9.4
THE
CHALLENGE**

Case Study | A General Dynamic
9.5 | Order List

> *Problem Description:* A coliseum box office ticket sales operation is to be automated. Customers can phone in ticket orders that are to be charged to a credit card. The customer's credit card number and the number of tickets ordered are entered into a list of ticket orders in numeric order by credit card number. A customer can pick up his/her tickets at any time by presenting the credit card under which the tickets were ordered.
>
> *Input Specifications:* Whenever an order for tickets is placed, T (for tickets) is entered, followed by a credit card number and the number of tickets ordered. Whenever tickets are picked up, P (for pickup) is entered, followed by a credit card number. L (for list) will be entered whenever the current list of ticket orders is to be listed (printed). Q (for quit) will be entered when the program is to be terminated. A credit card number will always be a 16-character string, for example,
>
> 7993 456 746 333
>
> and the number of tickets ordered will be an integer.

In this case study we develop a program for the ticket reservation system of examples 9.1 and 9.2 — you should reread those examples before proceeding with this case study. A good understanding of case study 9.3 and case study 9.4 in which the queue and the stack data structures, respectively, were studied, will also be a help in the design of this program.

The Solution — A General Singly Linked List

In this case study deletions and insertions will be made at arbitrary times and in arbitrary places in the ticket order list — this is really the distinguishing characteristic of this case study. However, we can draw on our previous experience in designing programs with linked lists to make this design as simple as possible.

First of all, we must remember that our data structure, the ticket order list, is the central issue of this program. Our job will be easier if we put careful thought into how we implement this data structure with a singly linked list *before* we get started. In particular, the special cases (which are always a pain to handle and which always seem to arise in dealing with such a data structure) should be considered now, before the linked list representation is fixed. What are the special cases? The ones that seem to cause the most headaches are the ones that concern the empty list. When we insert a new element into the list, we must always check first whether the list is empty, because inserting an element into an empty list requires special processing. Similarly, if the only element in the list is to be deleted, making the list empty, this will require special processing.

Even when we do not have to worry about the empty list, there are other aggravating conditions to consider. For example, if we insert or delete an element at the front of the list, we must change the **celladdress** variable that contains the address of the first list element, because there will now be a new first list element. Inserting or deleting an element at the rear of the list causes similar problems, because the last element of the list must contain **null** in its link field.

The upshot of these special cases is that every time we insert a new ticket order element into the list we must first check (1) whether the list is empty, (2) whether the insertion is to be made at the front of the list, and (3) whether the insertion is to be made at the end of the list. And each time we are to delete an element from the list we will need to check (1) whether it is the only element in the list, (2) whether it is the first element of the list, and (3) whether it is the last element of the list. Not only will these checks make the insertion and deletion procedures more difficult to design, they will also increase their execution time, because the three checks will have to be made *each time* we make an insertion or deletion.

Fortunately, there is a simple way to avoid these problems: ensure that the list is *never* empty and that an insertion or deletion can *never* be made at the front or rear of the list. We do this by initializing the list with a unique first element (a credit card number smaller than any possible real credit card number) and a unique last element (a credit card number larger than any possible real credit card number). Then the list will never be empty, and no insertion or deletion will ever be made at the front or rear of the list. We will use this approach for the list in this case study to make the design of our program easier.

The organization of the program is outlined in the following general description of the initial procedure:

```
{initialize the ticket order list with bogus first and last elements}
output 'enter T, P, L, or Q'
input {code letter}
loop while {code letter} ≠ 'Q'
    case {code letter} is
        when 'T'   :   {A ticket order has been received. Get the credit
                        card number of the ticket purchaser and the number
                        of tickets requested. Call a procedure to insert
                        this new order information into the list of ticket
                        orders.}

        when 'P'   :   {A ticket order is being picked up. Get the credit
                        card number of the person picking up the tickets. Call
                        a procedure to verify the number of tickets in this
                        order and delete the corresponding entry from
                        the ticket order list. If no such ticket order is found,
                        print an appropriate message.}

        when 'L'   :   {The ticket order list is to be listed. Call a
                        procedure to do this.}

        otherwise      {A bad code letter has been entered. Print
                        a message asking that the letter be retyped.}
    endcase
    output 'enter T, P, L, or Q'
    input {code letter}
endloop while
```

Initializing the list to have bogus first and last elements will be done in a procedure called *initialize list*. If parameters giving the credit card values for the bogus first and last list elements are sent to procedure *initialize list*, this procedure will allocate two list elements, link them properly and return the address of the first list element in another parameter, *front*. Thus, the call to procedure *initialize list* should look like

    initialize list (lownumber, highnumber, front)

where *lownumber* and *highnumber* are the bogus credit card numbers to go in the first and last list elements, respectively.

Following the pattern established in the initial procedures of case studies 9.3 and 9.4, the calculations required to process the T, P, and L instances of the **case** statement will be done in separate procedures. We can now write the initial procedure, *box office:*

```
box office : initial procedure
    {maintains a list of ticket orders}

    storage specification
        constants
            lownumber : string '0000 000 000 000'
            highnumber : string '9999 999 999 999'
        variables
            front : celladdress
            codeletter : character
        end storage specification

    begin box office
        initialize list(lownumber, highnumber, front)
        output 'enter T, P, L, or Q'
        input codeletter
        loop while codeletter ≠ 'Q'
            case codeletter is
                when 'T'  :   ticketpurchase(lownumber, highnumber, front)
                when 'P'  :   pickuptickets(lownumber, highnumber, front)
                when 'L'  :   printlist(front)
                otherwise    output 'bad code letter, please retype'
            endcase
            output 'enter T, P, L, or Q'
            input codeletter
        endloop while
    end box office

    where initialize list initializes the ticket order list with bogus first
            and last elements
    where ticketpurchase enters the information on a ticket purchase
            into the list
    where pickuptickets locates, removes from the list, and prints the
            information on a ticket order
    where printlist prints the list of ticketorders
```

CASE STUDY 9.5 — REFINEMENT 1

The first procedure to design is *initialize list*. It will have the three parameters

```
parameters
    lownumber, highnumber : in only string
    front : out only celladdress
```

as we can see from the initial procedure. Since *initialize list* must construct the two bogus list elements for the ticket order list, this procedure will need a **listelement descriptors** section. We already know that each ticket order consists of a credit card number, the number of tickets ordered, and a link to the next ticket order in the list, so we can describe an element of the ticket order list with

> **listelement descriptors**
> ticketorder : **record containing**
> cardnumber : **string**
> numberordered : **integer**
> nextorder : **celladdress**
> **endrecord** ticketorder

The actions taken by procedure *initialize list* will be simple. They are

getnew ticketorder **assign address to** new

{assign lownumber to the cardnumber field of this new ticket order}

{assign 0 to the numberordered field of this new ticket order}

{set front to the value in new, so that front contains the address
 of the first ticket order}

getnew ticketorder **assign address to** new

{assign highnumber to the cardnumber field of this new ticket order}

{assign 0 to the numberordered field of this new ticket order}

{set the link field (nextorder) of this new ticket order to **null,** since
 it will always be the last ticket order in the list}

{set the link field of the front ticket order element to have the value
 in new, so that the first ticket order element is linked to the last
 ticket order element to start with}

Following this outline will set up the ticket order list with the bogus first and last elements.

The entire procedure *initialize list* is given below.

```
initialize list : procedure
    {initializes the ticket order list with bogus first and last elements}
    storage specification
        parameters
            lownumber, highnumber : in only string
            front : out only celladdress
        listelement descriptors
            ticketorder : record containing
                cardnumber : string
                numberordered : integer
                nextorder : celladdress
                endrecord ticketorder
        variables
            new : celladdress
    end storage specification
```

```
    begin initialize list

        getnew ticketorder assign address to new
        new:ticketorder.cardnumber ← lownumber
        new:ticketorder.numberordered ← 0
        front ← new

        getnew ticketorder assign address to new
        new:ticketorder.cardnumber ← highnumber
        new:ticketorder.numberordered ← 0
        new:ticketorder.nextorder ← null

        front:ticketorder.nextorder ← new

    end initialize list
```

CASE STUDY 9.5 — REFINEMENT 2

We can now design procedure *ticketpurchase*, which is called in the **when** 'T' clause of the **case** statement in the initial procedure. The primary purpose of procedure *ticketpurchase* is to place a new ticket order into the list of ticket orders. This will be done by a new procedure, *insert*. Before *insert* can be called, however, the credit card number of the purchaser and the number of tickets to be ordered must be input. The credit card number is first checked to see whether it is within bounds before the number of tickets is input and procedure *insert* is called. As usual, we must include output messages to cue the user what to type.

```
ticketpurchase : procedure
    {a ticket order is processed and entered into the list}

    storage specification
        parameters
            lownumber, highnumber : in only string
            front : in only celladdress
        constants
            cardlength : integer 16
        variables
            creditcard : string
            tickets : integer
        end storage specification

    begin ticketpurchase
        output 'enter credit card number: '
        read string(creditcard, cardlength)
        if (lownumber < creditcard) and (creditcard < highnumber)
            then output 'enter number of tickets requested: '
                    input tickets
                    insert(creditcard, tickets, front)
            else output 'bad credit card number, please retype'
            endif
        end ticketpurchase

    where read string was defined in case study 6.1
    where insert inserts a new ticket order into the ticket order list
```

CASE STUDY 9.5 — REFINEMENT 3

We now turn our attention to procedure *insert.* As we can see from its call in procedure *ticketpurchase,* procedure *insert* will have three parameters: *creditcard, tickets,* and *front:*

parameters
    creditcard : **in only string**
    tickets : **in only integer**
    front : **in only celladdress**

Furthermore, since procedure *insert* will deal with the elements of the ticket order list, the elements of this list must also be described in *insert* just as they were in procedure *initialize list:*

listelement descriptors
    ticketorder : **record containing**
      cardnumber : **string**
      numberordered : **integer**
      nextorder : **celladdress**
      endrecord ticketorder

The strategy for procedure *insert* will be to first allocate a new list element and assign as the values of this new element the credit card number and number of tickets passed as parameters to procedure *insert.* Once this has been done, it must be determined where this new element is to be inserted:

getnew ticketorder **assign address to** new
new:ticketorder . cardnumber ← creditcard
new:ticketorder . numberordered ← tickets
loop while {the next order element in the ticket order list has a
      credit card number less than the credit card number of
      the new element}

   {follow the link from the current list element to the next
   list element}

   endloop while

{insert the new order element before the next order element in
  the ticket order list}

As described here, the **while** loop traverses the list, looking for the place in which the new element is to be inserted. This is done on each iteration of the loop by looking ahead to the next element in the list to see whether the new element should be inserted before the next list element. If the new list element does not belong there, the link is followed from the current list element to the next, and the process reiterates.

Using small numbers for the credit card numbers in the list, assume that the list looks like *Example 9.8*

front

where the top number in each element is the credit card number and the bottom number is the number of tickets ordered. If the new element

is to be inserted into the list, we can find where it belongs by traversing the list, using a **celladdress** variable called *current* to keep track of the location of the current list element during each iteration of the loop. A **celladdress** variable called *next* simultaneously keeps track of the location of the next list element. So, at the start, we have

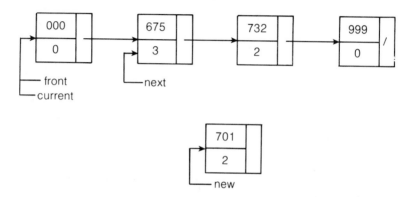

Comparing the credit card number (701) of the new list element with the credit card number of the element pointed to by *next*, we see that the new element does not go before the element indicated by *next*. So, *current* is assigned the value in *next*, and *next* is assigned the value in the link field of the element now pointed to by *next*, giving

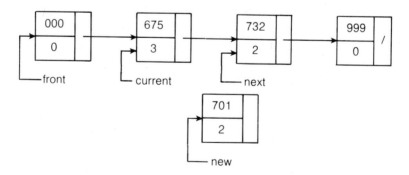

This time when the new credit card number (701) is compared with the credit card number in the list element indicated by *next*, it is seen that the new element should be inserted between *current* and *next*. That is, the link field of the list element whose address is in *current* should be changed to be the address of the new list element (i.e., the value in the **celladdress** variable *new*), and the link field of the new list element should be assigned the value in *next*, giving

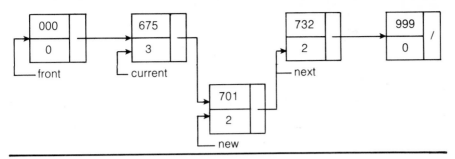

From this example we can see that the general form of the **while** loop for procedure *insert* should be

```
loop while next:ticketorder.cardnumber < new:ticketorder.cardnumber
    current ← next
    next ← next:ticketorder.nextorder
    endloop while
assert the new order element belongs between the current element
        and the next element
current:ticketorder.nextorder ← new
new:ticketorder.nextorder ← next
```

In this loop we have included a loop goal assertion but no loop invariant assertion because the statement about what the loop is doing is completely contained in the loop condition

```
next:ticketholder.cardnumber < new:ticketholder.cardnumber
```

No calculations are done in the loop except those necessary for moving pointers *current* and *next* through the ticket order list as the loop condition is continuously checked. Because it is known that *new:ticketorder.cardnumber* is greater than the credit card number in the bogus first element and less than the credit card number in the bogus last element (this was checked in the procedure *pickuptickets*), the loop will terminate at the point where the loop goal assertion holds.

We still need to ensure that variable *current* points to the first element of the list and that variable *next* points to the second element of the list before the loop is entered for the first time. Remember that because of our bogus first and last elements, there will always be at least two elements in the list.

This gives us the following refinement for procedure *insert*:

```
insert : procedure
    {inserts a new ticket order element into the ticket order list}

    storage specification
        parameters
            creditcard : in only string
            tickets : in only integer
            front : in only celladdress
        listelement descriptors
            ticketorder : record containing
                cardnumber : string
                numberordered : integer
                nextorder : celladdress
                endrecord ticketorder
        variables
            new, current, next : celladdress
        end storage specification
```

```
        begin insert
            getnew ticketorder assign address to new
            new:ticketorder.cardnumber ← creditcard
            new:ticketorder.numberordered ← tickets
            current ← front
            next ← front:ticketorder.nextorder
            loop while next:ticketorder.cardnumber < new:ticketorder.cardnumber
                current ← next
                next ← next:ticketorder.nextorder
            endloop while
            assert the new order element belongs between the current element
                    and the next element
            current:ticketorder.nextorder ← new
            new:ticketorder.nextorder ← next
        end insert
```

CASE STUDY 9.5 — REFINEMENT 4

Returning to the initial procedure, we see that we must now design procedure *pickuptickets*, which will search the ticket order list for a given credit card number, print the number of tickets ordered with that credit card, and then delete that ticket order from the list. This means that a credit card number must first be input and checked for validity in *pickuptickets*. Then a new procedure, *delete*, will be called to search for and delete a ticket order, returning the number of tickets ordered in the process. Of course, it is possible that a wrong credit card number may be given, in which case procedure *delete* will not be able to find a corresponding order in the ticket order list. For this reason we must include a **truth value** variable *found*, which *delete* will set to **true** if the ticket order was found and **false** otherwise. This gives us the following procedure:

```
pickuptickets : procedure
    {retrieves and prints a ticket order from the list}
    storage specification
        parameters
            lownumber, highnumber : in only string
            front : in only celladdress
        constants
            cardlength : integer 16
        variables
            creditcard : string
            found : boolean
            tickets : integer
    end storage specification
```

```
begin pickuptickets
    output 'enter credit card number: '
    read string(creditcard, cardlength)
    if (lownumber < creditcard) and (creditcard < highnumber)
        then delete(creditcard, tickets, front, found)
            if found
                then output 'credit card holder ', creditcard,
                                ' is to receive ', tickets, ' tickets'
                else output 'credit card number ', creditcard,
                                ' not found'
                endif {found}
        else output 'bad credit card number, please retype'
        endif {lownumber...}
    end pickuptickets

where read string was defined in case study 6.1
where delete removes a ticket order from the list and
        returns the order information
```

CASE STUDY 9.5 — REFINEMENT 5

This finishes the design of procedure *pickuptickets*, and we can now design procedure *delete*. In procedure *delete* we must examine successive elements of the ticket order list, looking for the credit card number that matches the value in parameter *creditcard*, which is passed to *delete*. The search is complete when we find an order element with credit card number larger than or equal to the one we are searching for (since the ticket order list is in numeric order by credit card number). If the search stops because a credit card number match is found, then parameter *tickets* is to be set to the value in the *ticketorder.numberordered* field of the matching ticket order list element, and parameter *found* is to be set to **true.** Then the matching ticket order element is to be deleted. However, if the search stops because the next ticket order element contains a credit card number larger than the one being searched for, there is no match in the list, so parameter *found* is to be set to **false.**

Deleting an element from a list means that the link field of the list element just in front of the one to be deleted must be connected to the list element just after the one to be deleted. For this reason we will use two **celladdress** variables, *current* and *next*, just as we did in procedure *insert*, to keep track of where we are in the list. Variable *next* will always point to the list element with which a match is being attempted. That way, if a match is made, the link field of the list element pointed to by *current* can be set to the same value as is in the link field of the list element pointed to by *next*; this will effectively remove the element pointed to by *next* from the ticket order list.

This gives us the following refinement for *delete*, which we give in its final form, since it is much like procedure *insert:*

delete : **procedure**
  {searches for an element in the ticket order list, returning the number of
  tickets in that element and deleting that element if found}
  storage specification
    parameters
      creditcard : **in only string**
      tickets : **out only integer**
      front : **in only celladdress**
      found : **out only truth value**
    listelement descriptors
      ticketorder : **record containing**
        cardnumber : **string**
        numberordered : **integer**
        nextorder : **celladdress**
        endrecord ticketorder
    variables
      current, next : **celladdress**
    end storage specification

begin delete
  current ← front
  next ← front:ticketorder. nextorder
  loop while next:ticketorder. cardnumber < creditcard
    current ← next
    next ← next:ticketorder. nextorder
  endloop while
  assert either creditcard matches the card number in the list
          element pointed to by next, or creditcard is not in the list
  if next:ticketorder. cardnumber = creditcard
    then tickets ← next: ticketorder. numberordered
        found ← **true**
        current:ticketorder. nextorder ← next:ticketorder. nextorder
        free next:ticketorder
    else found ← **false**
  endif
end delete

CASE STUDY 9.5 — REFINEMENT 6

Once again we see that this procedure is made much simpler because of
the bogus first and last elements in the ticket order list. Because of the check
made in procedure *delete*, we know that the credit card number we are
searching for is between the first and last elements of the ticket order list, if it
is in the list at all. There is no need to worry about deleting the first or last element of the list or about what happens if we search past the end of the list,
since neither of these situations will occur. These same considerations show
that the loop must terminate and that the loop goal assertion will be true when
it does. No loop invariant assertion is included for the same reasons mentioned in the development of refinement 4.

Procedure *printlist* is the last procedure left to design. We have already decided that we will go ahead and print the bogus list elements along with the
other elements of the ticket order list, so this will be an easy procedure to develop. In fact, we designed a similar procedure in case study 9.1, so we will
give procedure *printlist* without further discussion:

```
printlist : procedure
    {prints the ticket order list}
    storage specification
        parameters
            front : in only celladdress
        listelement descriptors
            ticketorder : record containing
                cardnumber : string
                numberordered : integer
                nextorder : celladdress
                endrecord ticketorder
        variables
            current : celladdress
        end storage specification
    begin printlist
        current ← front
        loop
            output 'credit card number ', current:ticketorder.cardnumber,
                    ' ordered ', current:ticketorder.numberordered, ' tickets'
            current ← current:ticketorder.nextorder
        endloop until current = null
    end printlist
```

CASE STUDY 9.5 — REFINEMENT 7

It is safe to use an **until** loop in procedure *printlist* because of the bogus first and last elements in the list. That is, the loop statements must be executed at least once, and an **until** loop always executes at least once.

Correctness

We have already discussed the correctness of the *insert* and *delete* loops of refinements 4 and 6. To make procedure *insert* truly robust we should handle the situation where a credit card number is entered more than once; we leave this as an exercise. The usual program walkthrough and testing should be done for this program.

Efficiency

Both procedure *insert* and procedure *delete* use a sequential search. Therefore, if there are n elements in the list, each new ticket order and each ticket pickup will require searching through $n/2$ list elements on the average. Since the ticket order list is dynamic, however, there is no way to predict how large the list will be at any time.

In case study 5.6 we discussed a much faster searching method, the binary search, which could be used on an ordered list. The ticket order list of this case study is in order by credit card number, so we might be tempted to consider using the binary search here. It cannot be done. The binary search depends on the ability to immediately access any element of any sublist of the original list. This is easy to do if the list is implemented as an array. In a singly linked list, however, we can get to the middle element of the list only by following the links through all other intervening list elements, so there would be no point in using a binary search.

Summary — Case Study 9.5

The ticket order list data structure of this case study is the most general list data structure we have encountered so far. The fact that it requires dynamic insertions and deletions of data items at arbitrary points in the list is what makes this list so general.

A major problem with dynamic lists is the large number of special cases that must be handled: inserting the first element into an empty list, deleting the last element from a list, inserting an element at the front of the list, deleting an element from the front of the list, inserting an element at the end of a list, and deleting the last element of a list are the usual special cases. Because the list grows and shrinks dynamically throughout the course of program execution, these special cases could arise many times. For example, this list could become empty many times. The best solution to these problems is the one we used in this case study: initialize the list to contain bogus first and last elements in such a way that none of these special cases can arise. The extra design effort in the initial procedure and the two extra list elements required in this solution are more than made up for by the easier design of procedures *insert* and *delete* as well as in execution efficiency, since no checks for the special cases are required.

Case Study 9.6 | Nonrecursive Quicksort

> **Problem Description:** Implement quicksort nonrecursively.
>
> **Input Specifications:** Same as case study 5.8.

In case study 9.4 we used a stack data structure in a simple problem. Stacks have a number of uses in more complex problems, too. The solution to this case study uses a stack to implement a recursive procedure nonrecursively. As we have learned, some real programming languages (such as standard Fortran and Basic) do not allow recursive procedures, so it is important to know how to change a program that has been designed recursively to run nonrecursively. In case study 5.8 we designed a fast sorting program called *quicksort*. Procedure quicksort embodies a very important sorting technique, but its design is recursive. It will be useful to see how to implement *quicksort* nonrecursively.

Since procedure *quicksort* was the only recursive procedure in the original sorting program of case study 5.8, replacing *quicksort* with a nonrecursive version will make the entire program nonrecursive. The other procedures of case study 5.8 can then be used in their original form with the new version of *quicksort*.

Notice that the problem says "implement *quicksort* nonrecursively," not "design *quicksort* nonrecursively." *Quicksort* is most easily and naturally designed recursively, as we did in case study 5.8:

```
quicksort : procedure
     ⋮
     ⋮

     {partition the list to be sorted into two parts with the smaller
      elements of the list in the first part and the larger elements
      in the second part}

     quicksort {the first part}
     quicksort {the second part}
```

Since this is the natural way to design *quicksort*, it is the way it *should* be designed. In other words, a program should be designed recursively if the recursive design is the easiest and most natural to accomplish, regardless of whether recursion is allowed in the actual programming language in which a program will eventually be written. Once the recursive design is correct, we can then apply a transformation like the one we will show here to turn the recursive design into an equivalent nonrecursive design.

Not only is *quicksort* a naturally recursive procedure, it is really quite difficult to design *quicksort* directly in a nonrecursive fashion. The transformation of *quicksort* we give here uses a stack to keep track of the recursive calls of the original version. The transformation is really quite simple, but it does require a thorough understanding of how the recursive version of *quicksort* works. We suggest that you review case study 5.8 before proceeding with this case study.

The Solution — Simulating Recursive Calls with a Stack

To see how a stack can be used to implement *quicksort* nonrecursively, it will help to see the recursive *quicksort* procedure again as it was given in refinement 2 of case study 5.8:

```
quicksort : procedure
    {sorts an array of integers into ascending order}

    storage specification
        parameters
            list : in out 1-D integer array
            low, high : in only integer
        variables
            medianposition : integer
        end storage specification

    begin quicksort
        if high > low
            then partition (list, low, high, medianposition)
                quicksort (list, low, medianposition − 1)
                quicksort (list, medianposition + 1, high)
        endif
    end quicksort

    where partition divides the list such that for
            low ⩽ i ⩽ medianposition − 1,  list[i] < list[medianposition]
            i = medianposition,            list[i] = list[medianposition]
            medianposition + 1 ⩽ i ⩽ high, list[i] ⩾ list[medianposition]
```

The important thing to notice in this recursive version of *quicksort* is how the recursive calls are made. The first time *quicksort* is called (from the initial procedure) it will be called for the entire array, *list*, as in

```
quicksort(list, 1, n)
```

assuming that there are n elements in the list. In procedure *quicksort*, *list* will first be passed to procedure *partition*, where *list* will be partitioned into two parts so that all of the elements in the first part are less than all of the elements in the second part, and so that the element between these two parts (the median) is in its proper position. Procedure *partition*, you will remember, is not recursive. After this partitioning has been accomplished, the two recursive calls

```
quicksort(list, low, medianposition − 1)
quicksort(list, medianposition + 1, high)
```

are made in succession (where *low* is 1 and *high* is *n*). Of course, the first of these calls to *quicksort* must be completed before the second call to quicksort is initiated. This first call to *quicksort* generates two more recursive calls to *quicksort*, and these calls must be completed before the original second call to quicksort (shown above) is reached. Thus the first call to *quicksort*, along with the recursive calls it generates, must be completely finished before the second call is made — the underlying mechanism for accomplishing this is the stack. We can think of this process like this: as a call to *quicksort* is made, the two new recursive calls generated by the first call are stacked, and the top call on the stack is the one processed next. This ensures that the first call to *quicksort*, and all recursive calls generated by that first call, will be finished before the second call is processed.

**Example
9.9**

Assume that the array list to be sorted is

     35   90   25   20   43   67   12   5   87   16   71

Since there are 11 elements in this list, the first call to *quicksort* will be

     quicksort(list, 1, 11)

From the way *partition* works (see case study 5.8), we see that list will be partitioned as

     [12   16   25   20   5]   35   [67   43   87   90   71]

where the sublists in brackets are the parts of the list remaining to be sorted. 35 is the median element, and it has been placed in its proper position by *partition*. Notice that all the elements in the first part are less than the median and all of the elements in the second part are greater than or equal to the median.

     After this partitioning process has been completed, *quicksort* is called recursively on the first part and the second part:

     quicksort(list, 1, 5)
     quicksort(list, 7, 11)

That is, the original call

     quicksort(list, 1, 11)

has been processed and has been replaced by the two stacked calls

     quicksort(list, 1, 5)
     quicksort(list, 7, 11)

after procedure *partition* has finished (element 6 of *list* is now in order and must no longer be handled). To continue the process, the top call on the stack is processed:

     quicksort(list, 1, 5)

The portion of the list between elements 1 and 5 is partitioned, giving

     [5]   12   [25   20   16]   35   [67   43   87   90   71]

After the partitioning process is complete, two new calls to *quicksort* are made to process the two new parts of the list just generated by *partition*. That is, the call *quicksort(list,* 1, 5) is replaced by

     quicksort(list, 1, 1)

and

     quicksort(list, 3, 5)

making the stack of calls waiting to be processed

    quicksort(list, 1, 1)
    quicksort(list, 3, 5)
    quicksort(list, 7, 11)

Notice that the call *quicksort(list,* 7, 11) has been pushed farther down the stack.
    Now the top call on the stack is

    quicksort(list, 1, 1)

This call is processed next, but since *low* and *high* are both 1 (the last two actual parameters, 1 and 1, in this call to *quicksort* correspond to the formal parameters *low* and
high, respectively, in *quicksort*), *high* is not greater than *low,* so this call to *quicksort* terminates without calling *partition* or generating any new recursive calls to *quicksort.* To
see this, just look at the **if** statement of procedure *quicksort.* Since *low* and *high* are
both 1, this call to *quicksort* actually means "quicksort the elements of the array *list* between *list*[1] and *list*[1]." There is, of course, nothing to sort — the single element *list*[1]
is already in order with respect to itself — so this call to *quicksort* leaves the list unchanged:

    5   12   [25   20   16]   35   [67   43   87   90   71]

We have removed the brackets from the first element, 5, to note that it has been taken
care of by the last call to *quicksort,* which essentially did nothing (the bracketed sublists
show which pending calls to *quicksort* are on the stack at any time). The stack of calls
to *quicksort* now looks like

    quicksort(list, 3, 5)
    quicksort(list, 7, 11)

    Continuing in the above fashion, the top call on the stack,

    quicksort(list, 3, 5)

is now processed. First the list is partitioned between *list*[3] and *list*[5] to give

    5   12   [16   20]   25   []   35   [67   43   87   90   71]

In this case the procedure *partition* breaks up the list between *list*[3] and *list*[5] so that
16 and 20 are in the first part, the median is 25, and there is nothing in the second part
(this is indicated by the empty bracket pair []). The two new recursive calls to *quicksort*
to handle the two new sublists are placed onto the stack, giving

    quicksort(list, 3, 4)
    quicksort(list, 6, 5)
    quicksort(list, 7, 11)

Notice that the second call to *quicksort*

    quicksort(list, 6, 5)

corresponding to the empty sublist [], has parameter *low* (6) greater than *high* (5).
    Again, the top call to *quicksort* is processed, with *partition* breaking the sublist
[16, 20] into [] 16 [20] (16 is the median), giving

    5   12   []   16   [20]   25   []   35   [67   43   87   90   71]

and a stack of

    quicksort(list, 3, 2)
    quicksort(list, 4, 4)
    quicksort(list, 6, 5)
    quicksort(list, 7, 11)

Now, when the top call to *quicksort* is processed, *low* is not less than *high* (3 is not less than 2), so nothing happens. The list can now be represented as

5   12   16   [20]   25   []   35   [67   43   87   90   71]

and the stack is

    quicksort(list, 4, 4)
    quicksort(list, 6, 5)
    quicksort(list, 7, 11)

Again the top call on the stack is processed, and again *low* is not less than *high* (4 is not less than 4), so nothing happens. The list is now

5   12   16   20   25   []   35   [67   43   87   90   71]

and the stack looks like

    quicksort(list, 6, 5)
    quicksort(list, 7, 11)

Once again the top call on the stack is processed, and once again *low* (6) is not less than *high* (5), so once again nothing happens. The list can now be represented as

5   12   16   20   25   35   [67   43   87   90   71]

and the stack is

    quicksort(list, 7, 11)

We have finally gotten around to processing the last half of our array! This call to *quicksort,* which is now on top of the stack, was generated back at the beginning when the first call to *quicksort* was made and procedure *partition* broke the original list into two parts; the call now on top of the stack is the second of those original two parts. This call to *quicksort* could not come up for processing until the first part had been processed, including numerous recursive calls to *quicksort* that in turn caused the stack to grow, and then shrink, until this call

    quicksort(list, 7, 11)

is finally the next call to be processed.

Stepping quickly through the rest of this example, then, the list between *list*[7] and *list*[11] is partitioned, giving a list of

5   12   16   20   25   35   [43]   67   [87   90   71]

and a stack of

    quicksort(list, 7, 7)
    quicksort(list, 9, 11)

Since the top call on the stack has *low* (7) not less than *high* (7) the list becomes

5   12   16   20   25   35   43   67   [87   90   71]

and the stack becomes

    quicksort(list, 9, 11)

Processing the top (only) call on the stack gives the list

5   12   16   20   25   35   43   67   [71]   87   [90]

and the stack

    quicksort(list, 9, 9)
    quicksort(list, 11, 11)

Now the top stack element has *low* (9) not less than *high* (9), so nothing is done; the list looks like

    5   12   16   20   25   35   43   67   71   87   [90]

and the stack looks like

    quicksort(list, 11, 11)

Again, since the top call on the stack has *low* (11) not less than *high* (11), nothing is done. The list looks like

    5   12   16   20   25   35   43   67   71   87   90

and the stack is now empty, since no new recursive calls to *quicksort* were made. The empty stack implies that *quicksort* is now finished — all recursive calls have been processed. Indeed, the list is now sorted as we wished.

This example shows that one easy way to simulate the *quicksort* procedure nonrecursively would be to maintain a stack of pending calls to *quicksort*. After all, the processor really uses the stack mechanism automatically when handling recursive calls (actually, the stacking mechanism used by a real processor is usually different than the one in our example, but our example does demonstrate how to use a stack to implement recursion nonrecursively). Using this idea we can replace the recursive calls in procedure *quicksort* with a loop:

    {place the representation of the very first call to quicksort,
     quicksort(list, 1, n), onto an empty stack}

loop
        {retrieve the top stack element, which represents
         a call to quicksort, quicksort(list, low, high)}

    if low < high

        then {partition list between list[low] and list[high];
                  procedure partition returns the position of the
                  properly placed median value in medianposition}

                 {place the representation of the second of the two new
                  recursive calls to quicksort generated after procedure
                  partition is finished, quicksort(list, medianposition + 1, high),
                  onto the top of the stack}

                 {place the representation of the first of the two new
                  recursive calls to quicksort generated after procedure
                  partition is finished, quicksort(list, medianposition − 1, high),
                  onto the top of the stack}

        endif
    endloop until {the stack is empty}

Remember from our example that we are finished when the stack finally becomes empty.

Notice that after procedure *partition* has created two new parts to be quicksorted, we first put the information about the second part on top of the stack and then place the information about the first part on top of that. Because of the way a stack operates, the information for the first part will be on top of the stack and will therefore be processed first, as we wish. However, the order in which these elements are placed on the stack actually makes no difference as far as sorting the list is concerned (can you explain why?).

Each element on our stack will represent a call to *quicksort*, such as,

     quicksort(list, 5, 15)

where *low* is 5 and *high* is 15. If *low* is less than *high*, we call *partition* to partition the list between *list*[*low*] and *list*[*high*] into two parts. We then stack the information necessary to quicksort the two new parts created by procedure *partition*, and the loop reiterates. On some passes through the loop, the stack element removed will have values such that *low* is not less than *high*. In these cases the **if** condition will be false, so no action will be taken (just as we saw in our example) and the loop will begin again; that is, the top stack element will be unstacked and no new calls to *quicksort* will be stacked, so the stack will shrink.

What information do we need to put onto the stack to represent a call to *quicksort*, such as

     quicksort(list, 5, 15)?

The only information really required is the *low* and *high* index values (5 and 15 in this case) between which the partitioning process is to take place. There is certainly no reason to stack the name of the procedure (*quicksort*), and the array (*list*) will always be available to us, so there is no reason to save *list* on the stack, either.

We now see how to finish the nonrecursive *quicksort* procedure (which we will just refer to as *quicksort*). We will need the same parameters and variables as were required in the recursive version, but we will also need a **celladdress** variable (*top*) to keep track of the address of the top stack element at all times. Procedure *stack* will stack a new *low* and *high* value pair onto the stack, and procedure *unstack* will return the current *low* and *high* value pair from the top of the stack.

```
quicksort : procedure
    {sorts a list of integers into ascending order}
    storage specification
        parameters
            list : in out 1-D integer array
            low, high : in only integer
        variables
            medianposition : integer
            top : celladdress
    end storage specification
```

```
begin quicksort
    top ← null
    stack(top, low, high)
    loop
        unstack(top, low, high)
        if low < high
            then partition(list, low, high, medianposition)
                 stack(top, medianposition + 1, high)
                 stack(top, low, medianposition − 1)
            endif
        endloop until top = null
    end quicksort
```

where stack places a new low, high pair representing the rescursive
　　　call to quicksort(list, low, high) onto the stack
where unstack returns the top low, high pair representing the
　　　recursive call to quicksort(list, low, high) from the top
　　　of the stack
where partition was defined in case study 5.8: it divides list so that for
　　　low ≤ i ≤ medianposition − 1,　list[i] < list[medianposition];
　　　i = medianposition,　　　　　　list[i] = list[medianposition];
　　　medianposition + 1 ≤ i ≤ high,　list[i] ≥ list[medianposition]

CASE STUDY 9.6 — REFINEMENT 1

As usual, we denote the empty stack by setting *top* to **null.** Therefore, we
must set *top* to **null** at the beginning of the procedure before stacking the first
low and *high* values. We check whether the stack is empty in

endloop until top = **null**

at the bottom of the loop.

Procedure *stack* will be very similar to the one of the same name developed
in case study 9.4, so we will give it here without further explanation:

```
stack : procedure
    {stacks a low, high value pair}

    storage specification
        parameters
            top : in out celladdress
            low, high : in only integer
        listelement descriptors
            stackelement : record containing
                lowvalue, highvalue : integer
                link : celladdress
            endrecord stackelement
        variables
            new : celladdress
    end storage specification

begin stack
    getnew stackelement assign address to new
    new:stackelement.lowvalue ← low
    new:stackelement.highvalue ← high
    new:stackelement.link ← top
    top ← new
end stack
```

CASE STUDY 9.6 — REFINEMENT 2

The design of procedure *unstack* for this case study also parallels that of procedure *unstack* in case study 9.4, because the unstacking method is the same. We will also give this procedure without further explanation:

```
unstack : procedure
    {unstacks a low, high value pair}

    storage specification
        parameters
            top : in out celladdress
            low, high : out only integer
        listelement descriptors
            stackelement : record containing
                lowvalue, highvalue : integer
                link : celladdress
                endrecord stackelement
        variables
            old : celladdress
        end storage specification

    begin unstack
        low ← top:stackelement.lowvalue
        high ← top:stackelement.highvalue
        old ← top
        top ← top:stackelement.link
        free old:stackelement
    end unstack
```

CASE STUDY 9.6 — REFINEMENT 3

There is no need to worry about trying to unstack an element from the empty stack, because, as we can see in procedure *quicksort*, unstack will never be called if the stack is empty. The loop of procedure *quicksort* is entered only after the first *low, high* pair has been stacked. Thereafter, the loop is iterated again (and an *unstack* performed) only if the stack is not empty.

Correctness

The same test cases generated for testing the recursive *quicksort* of case study 5.8 could be used here. You should also do a walkthrough of the program using the list given in example 9.9.

Efficiency

The strategy for sorting the values in array *list* is the same as the one used in the recursive quicksort procedure of case study 5.8 — the only difference is that here we had to "fake" recursion by using a stack. Since the stacking and unstacking procedures developed in this case study require only constant time each time they are called, our nonrecursive version of *quicksort* has the same average time complexity as the recursive version, $O(n^*\log_2 n)$, where n is the number of elements in the list to be sorted.

The space complexity of our nonrecursive version of *quicksort* is also the same as it was for the recursive version. Both require that the list of values to be sorted be kept in the store, and both require a stack to keep track of the parts of the list left to be sorted. In the recursive version, this stack was hidden, because it was maintained automatically by the processor. In the nonrecursive version, we have to maintain the stack explicitly.

One glaring inefficiency in our nonrecursive version of *quicksort* comes to light when we examine example 9.9 again: after procedure *partition* has completed its work in breaking the list between *list*[*low*] and *list*[*high*] into two parts, two new recursive calls to quicksort, say,

```
quicksort(list, 7, 7)
quicksort(list, 9, 11)
```

are generated and placed on the stack of pending calls to *quicksort*. When the processor gets around to processing

```
quicksort(list, 7, 7)
```

we know that nothing will happen, because *low* (7) is not less than *high* (7). The same is true of a call like

```
quicksort(list, 6, 5)
```

since *low* (6) is not less than *high* (5).

We have faithfully followed this scheme in implementing *quicksort* nonrecursively. If the call

```
quicksort(list, 7, 7)
```

would be generated in the recursive version, we dutifully place the *low*, *high* pair

```
7    7
```

onto the stack, *even though we can determine right now that nothing will happen* when this pair is unstacked. The condition in

```
if low < high
```

will be false for these cases, so the **then** part of the **if** statement will not be executed.

This inefficiency can be removed by stacking only *low*, *high* pairs representing a call to

```
quicksort(list, low, high)
```

when *low* < *high* is true. This will save a lot of unnecessary calls to *stack* and *unstack*. We leave these changes to the nonrecursive version of *quicksort* as an exercise.

Summary — Case Study 9.6

This case study involves the use of a stack, but the stack is not the primary data structure of the program. The 1-D array *list* that holds the values to be sorted is really the primary data structure involved. The stack is just the vehicle for changing the recursive version of *quicksort* into a nonrecursive version.

All recursive procedures and functions can be implemented nonrecursively with stacks. In this case study the only values we had to keep on the stack were a couple of the parameters. In other nonrecursive implementations of recursive routines, it may also be necessary to keep some of the values of the local variables (besides parameters) for the routine on the stack. In any case, since there are some easily obtainable, useful routines with inherently recursive designs, it is nice to know that these recursive routines can be transformed directly and easily into nonrecursive routines by using a stack. The same time and space complexities will be maintained by this transformation.

We have mentioned before that most of the programs that need dynamic structures such as queues, stacks, and general lists are online, real-time, interactive programs. This case study is an exception to that rule. To the person wishing to sort a list of integers, this program acts no differently than the program using the recursive quicksort procedure. The sorting is done in one shot. There is no interaction with the user, no need for the program to respond in real-time to events occurring in the world (it could be run at night, while the user is asleep), and no reason that the program be online (that is, in a constantly running state).

9.5 WORKING OUT

9.40 Design an *mpl* procedure to reverse the order of the elements in a singly linked list of integers (by reversing the appropriate links). You should design two versions of the program, one recursive and one nonrecursive.

9.41 Design a procedure *midout* which determines whether a singly linked list of integers has an even number of elements, and if so, removes the middle two elements.

9.42 A list of single characters can be considered to be a character string. Design a program that reads an input string a character at a time into a singly linked list, one character per list element. Your program must then determine whether or not the string is a palindrome (a palindrome is a character string that reads the same forwards and backwards). Input strings will be terminated by a $, which is not considered part of the input. For example, given the inputs shown below, the program should output the messages given:

input	output
DEED$	YES, A PALINDROME
ABLE WAS I ERE I SAW ELBA$	YES, A PALINDROME
COMPUTER$	NO, NOT A PALINDROME
HAHA$	NO, NOT A PALINDROME

9.43 Use a stack to implement the recursive design of the function *factorial* from case study 3.6 nonrecursively.

9.44 Design an *mpl* procedure to sort a singly linked list of integers so that the list elements are in ascending order. Discuss possible strategies and implement the best one. Give the time complexity of any strategy discussed.

9.45 Redesign the solution to case study 9.5 using a doubly linked list instead of a singly linked list. That is, in each list element there are to be two links, one linking to the next element in the list and one linking to the previous element. Does this design of the linked list make your *insert* and *delete* procedures easier? Are there any reasons why you should not consider using a doubly linked list?

9.46   Design a new solution to case study 9.5 under the restriction that linked lists may not be used. (Hint: use arrays to hold the values in the list elements and a separate integer array to hold the index of the next element of each element in the list. You will have to devise methods for maintaining a list of free array slots to simulate the **getnew** and **free** statements.)

9.47   Design an *mpl* program for the queue problem of case study 9.3 under the added restriction that linked lists cannot be used. (Hint: use a large 1-D array which you think of as a ring. When inserting an element into the queue, add the element to the next free index position in the array and when removing an element from the queue take it from the first occupied index position in the array. When the end of the array is reached as a new element is added to the queue, continue by wrapping around to the first array position, which should have been vacated earlier as list elements were removed from the front of the queue. Use two integer variables to contain the indices of the first and last queue elements in the array.) What special situations must be considered?

9.48   Design an *mpl* program to solve the stack problem of case study 9.4 under the added restriction that linked lists may not be used. (Hint: use a large 1-D array with an integer variable *top* containing the index value of the top stack element in the array. When a value is to be pushed onto the stack, add 1 to *top* and place the value into the array at position *top*. If a value is to be popped off the stack, remove the value in the array at position *top*, and then subtract 1 from *top*. How do you know when the stack is empty in this scheme?)

9.49   Some programming languages that allow linked lists do not have an equivalent of the *mpl* **free** statement, because maintaining a list of free list elements can often be done more efficiently by the programmer. Design your own free list element management scheme for either case study 9.3 or 9.4. Remember, whenever a list element is to be freed, it must be added to the list of free elements; whenever a new list element is to be allocated, the list of free elements is first checked for an available element, but if there are none there, the new element must be acquired by use of the **getnew** statement.

| CHAPTER 10 |

External Files

NEW CONCEPTS: Secondary storage devices, External files,
Processing external sequential files

We now introduce one more programming language feature that is available in all common procedural programming languages: the ability to read and write external files. To understand this new feature and to appreciate why it is necessary, we must reconsider our computer model (see figure 10-1), which consists of a processor, a store, an input device, and an output device. Throughout this book we have seen how each of these components is used: the processor executes programs one statement at a time; the store holds named constants and variable values as the program is executed; the **output** statement causes values to be displayed at the output device; the **input** statement causes values to be retrieved from the input device and stored into variables.

These components of the model computer represent real components of actual computers. All computers have a processor responsible for carrying out program instructions. The input and output devices might be a combined keyboard and video screen where the programmer (or program user) types in program statements or data required by a program on the keyboard and views the results on the screen. The printed output of a program can be routed to the same screen, or alternatively, the output could be sent to a completely separate hard-copy device that prints the output on paper (i.e., the hard copy). The actual form of these components in a real computer is of little importance in the design of a program — that's why we have just abstracted these features in our model computer. We do need to know that the processor has only simple arithmetic and comparison units in order to understand why we must design programs using these simple

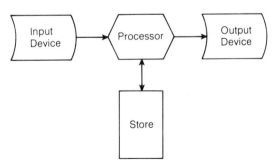

FIGURE 10-1. ORIGINAL MODEL COMPUTER

operations. Also, knowing that the store is composed of individual cells helps us understand the need for variables — the names that stand for storage cells. We have learned that **input** and **output** statements let a program communicate with the program user. In other words, we have described the parts of our model computer in just enough detail to help us understand why we must design programs the way we do.

Although our model computer has served us well until now, it lacks one feature absolutely necessary on any real computer — secondary storage. Recall how the store of the model computer is used: when the processor begins executing a procedure or function, it sets up the store according to the **storage specification** statement and then stores values into the cells of the store as directed by assignment and **input** statements. When the routine has finished execution, the values in the storage cells used locally in that routine disappear. As a result, when execution of the initial procedure is finished, none of the values used anywhere in the store by the program remain. All of the data input into the program and all of the computed values are gone, and all that remains is what we may have directed the processor to print on paper at some output device. This means that each time this program is run, someone must supply new input values. For our purpose, (which has been to demonstrate the principles of program design), this method of operation has been sufficient, but in many real-world problems it would be woefully inadequate. Consider the time and effort involved in retyping records for every employee of a large company every month just to run the payroll, or retyping this entire book just to correct one mistake, so that a document-processing program could reformat it nicely in book form. Such requirements would, of course, be ludicrous.

These examples demonstrate the need for something that all computers have: *secondary storage devices*, where information can be stored and retrieved by a program each time the program is executed. This secondary storage cannot be the same as the primary store for at least two reasons: (1) on real computers there is not enough room in the primary store for permanent storage of all necessary data, and (2) the primary store is electronic, so when the power goes off (accidentally or otherwise), everything in the store is usually lost. Secondary storage is most often based on magnetic principles; data is stored on magnetic devices in much the same way that music can be recorded and kept on magnetic tape. In fact, *magnetic tapes* and more sophisticated *magnetic disks* are used for storing data on computers. It is not important at this time to understand how these tapes and disks function, but you should realize that there is a virtually unlimited number of such storage devices. Just as cassette tapes in a tape recorder can be changed at will to record or play a new song, so the magnetic tapes and disks of a computer's secondary storage can be changed to provide access to an old set of data or space in which to store newly generated data. Also, just as music tapes can be erased and rerecorded, so the tapes and disks of a computer's secondary storage can be erased and replaced with new data. Large libraries of such tapes and disks keep data (and programs) available for use at any time.

We thus need to extend our model computer to include secondary storage, as illustrated in figure 10–2. There are many methods for storing and retrieving data from secondary storage; some are simple and some are quite complex. We will examine only the sequential storage scheme — it is the simplest storage scheme and it is the one most frequently used for moderate-sized data sets. This storage scheme is adapted to the nature of the secondary storage devices themselves. Just as music must be recorded and played back sequentially on cassette tapes, so data is recorded and read sequentially from

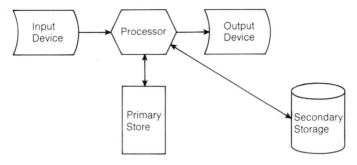

FIGURE 10-2. MODEL COMPUTER WITH SECONDARY STORAGE

magnetic computer tapes. That is, to get to the middle of a song on a music tape, the tape must be wound past the first half of the song — there is no way to position the tape immediately to the middle of the song. Magnetic tapes holding data work the same way: to get to the third data item stored on the tape, for example, the preceding two data items must first be scanned over. Data stored on magnetic disks, however, is more like music stored on a long-playing record. Just as we can place the playing arm at the beginning of the third song on a record, skipping the first two, we can also (in a similar way) go directly to the beginning of any file on an external disk. Once we have reached the beginning of that file, however, we must scan through its data item by item in sequential fashion.

Assume that the personnel file of a company is stored in secondary storage. This file contains a record for each employee, consisting of the employee's name (last name first), social security number, hourly wage, and address. The records are in order alphabetically by name. Such a file would usually be stored on tape or disk one record at a time. For example, the file might look like

Example 10.1

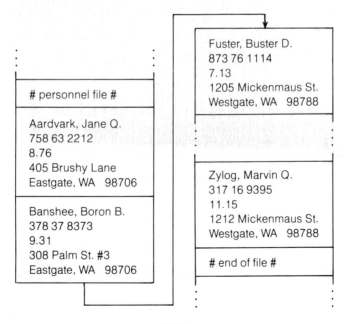

523

Notice that each record has the same form, except for the first and last records, the *header record* and the *trailer*, or *end-of-file record*, respectively. The header record contains the name of the file, and the trailer record indicates the end of the file. There are generally many different files on a magnetic tape or disk, so a header record is used to allow the processor to search through the tape or disk until the right file name is found; then the processor knows that the records of that file follow. The end-of-file trailer record tells the processor when the last record of the file has been processed. Of course, for this scheme to work, every file name in secondary storage must be different, and it is the programmer's responsibility to pick unique names.

A set of data stored on an external storage device is called a *file*, or an *external file*. A file consists of a number of *records* that are all similar; the records may be quite simple, containing just a single integer, for example, or they may be larger groupings of data. The records of a file follow each other sequentially on the secondary storage device.

To use a file the programmer must first tell the processor to locate the file by giving its file name as it appears in the header record; once the processor has positioned the external storage device to the first record of the desired file, the records of the file can be accessed sequentially by the program, one at a time. In the previous example, if the secondary storage device is a tape, the processor would have to start at the front of the tape and scan through all intervening files until the header record of the personnel file was found. At this point, if the programmer wanted to retrieve information from this file on employee

Jones, John R.

then the program would need to scan through all of the records in the personnel file appearing before that of Jones, John R.

Actually, it makes no difference to the programmer whether an external file is on tape or on disk, even though disks are more sophisticated than tapes. As previously stated, disks are constructed so that the processor can access a file without scanning through all intervening files. In both cases, however, the programmer must first direct the processor to locate the desired header record of the file by giving the processor the name of the file. After the file has been located by the processor, it must be processed sequentially, one record at a time. This is in contrast to the primary store, where each storage cell can be accessed directly by the processor without scanning all preceding cells.

Example 10.2 The primary store of a computer, which we have simply been calling the "store," is a sophisticated electronic device that allows the processor to access any individual cell as quickly as any other cell. If the store looks like

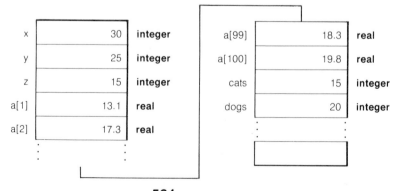

during execution of some program, and the statement

$y \leftarrow (z + a[50])$ * dogs/cats

is executed, the processor can access the values in z, $a[50]$, *dogs*, and *cats* immediately. The processor does not need to scan through x, y, z, $a[1]$, $a[2]$, ..., $a[49]$ before finding $a[50]$, for example. Such capabilities do not exist in secondary storage.

Because any random cell of the primary store can be accessed as quickly as any other cell, the primary store is often called *random access memory* or *RAM*.

In summary, we have extended our concept of computers and programs to include secondary storage. Although secondary storage devices are complex, we have abstracted just the fundamental features that are important to a beginning programmer. Each set of data stored in the secondary store is called a *file*, and each file consists of a sequential list of identical records. A file must have a unique name recorded in the first record (the header record), and every file ends with a trailer record that acts as an end-of-file marker. In the following section we will see how to build and manipulate such files.

10.1 | The first thing we need to know is how to construct a file and save it in secon-
GETTING | dary storage. A simple case study will demonstrate these processes.
ACQUAINTED |

Case Study | Construct an External File
10.1 |

> **Problem Description:** Construct an employee file in secondary storage.
>
> **Input Specifications:** A record of information on each employee will be given at the standard input device. The name, social security number, hourly wage, and address will be given, one value per line. The name will appear last-name-first in the first 20 positions of one line, followed by an 11-character social security number on the next line, then the hourly wage on the next line, followed by the address on the next four lines — the street address in the first 20 positions of the first address line, the city address in first 15 positions of the second line, the 2-character state code on the third line, and the 5-digit zip code on the last line. The names will be given in alphabetical order.

Whenever a permanent file is to be constructed and stored in secondary storage for the first time, someone must first type the data in at the standard input device (or the data must be created by another program), then a program must read this data and store it in the secondary store. After this has been done, the data can be read from this permanent file, which is now in the secondary store. Constructing and saving such a file in the secondary store is the topic of this case study.

The Solution — Saving a File in the Secondary Store

Several things must be considered when constructing and saving a new file in secondary storage:

1. The processor must be told that a new file is to be created in the secondary store and it must be told the name of this new file.
2. The records to be saved must be described to the processor.
3. Each record must be successively read from the standard input device and then put into the secondary store.
4. After the last record of the file has been stored in the secondary store, the processor must be directed to mark the end of the file with the end-of-file marker.

Every actual programming language must provide a way to do each of these tasks, so we will have *mpl* statements to model these actions.

The first task, directing the processor to create a new file in the secondary store, will be done in *mpl* with the statement

create new *filename* **file**

where *filename* is the name we choose to give the new file. This file name must be unique — there cannot be an existing file by that name in secondary storage — or an error will result.

If we want to start a new file called *personnel* in the secondary store, we use the statement

create new personnel **file**

The processor will record the header record for this file as

personnel

to distinguish this file from the others already in secondary storage.

Example 10.3

In order for the processor to build the desired personnel file in secondary storage, we must provide a description of this file somewhere in our program. We must first declare the name of the file and indicate that the file is to be saved in secondary storage. This is done in an **external files** declaration within the **storage specification** statement of an *mpl* program. For this case study the **external files** declaration would be

```
external files
     personnel : file of records
          employee : record containing
               name, ssnumber : string
               wage : real
               address : record containing
                    street, city, state, zip : string
                    endrecord address
               endrecord employee
          endfile personnel
```

This declaration informs the processor that the program will be using a file named *personnel* in secondary storage (**external** indicates secondary storage) and that each record of this file is an *employee* record. The *employee* record is defined immediately following the **file of records** statement.

When we declare the *personnel* file, we cause storage cells to be set aside in the primary store for a single record of the type found in the *personnel* file. That is, in the primary store we will have an internal template (or picture) of a sample record. This internal record has a special use: for each employee, we will input each item of information on that employee given at the standard input device and store this information in the internal employee record one item at a time until all of the data for this particular employee has been input. Then the internal employee record will be full, and we can cause this entire record to be placed into the *personnel* file in secondary storage with the statement

put personnel.employee **record into** personnel **file**

This statement causes the processor to copy the internal *employee* record from the primary store into the *personnel* file in the secondary store.

This process continues until the entire *personnel* file has been constructed: the data on each employee is input into the internal *employee* record, and then this record is placed into the *personnel* file immediately following the previous record (or following the header record if this is the first *employee* record), thus constructing a sequential *personnel* file.

The final step in the process of creating a file in secondary storage comes after the last record has been written. At this point the file must be marked with the special trailing end-of-file record. In *mpl* we model this process with the **terminate file** statement, as in

terminate personnel **file**

When the processor executes this statement it will automatically write the end-of-file trailer record as the last record of the *personnal* file and then close the file.

We now have enough information to design the program for this case study. We will usually design all of our file-handling programs as follows: whenever a procedure is to perform some action on a complete file, such as constructing, printing, copying, or sorting the file, that procedure will be responsible for all operations necessary for using the file, such as creating the file, terminating the file, and so on. This means that our initial procedure in this case study will do nothing but call on another procedure, *transfer records* (which will construct the new file), passing the name of the new file as the only parameter.

```
construct file : initial procedure
    {builds a new external personnel file}

    storage specification
        external files
            personnel : file of records
                employee : record containing
                    name, ssnumber : string
                    wage : real
                    address : record containing
                        street, city, state, zip : string
                    endrecord address
                endrecord employee
            endfile personnel
    end storage specification

    begin construct file
        transfer records(personnel)
    end construct file

    where transfer records inputs and moves records to the personnel file

    CASE STUDY 10.1 — REFINEMENT 1
```

Procedure *transfer records* is quite simple. Its design follows the discussion just given on the placing of new records into an external file.

```
transfer records : procedure
   {fills the personnel file with records from the standard input device}

   storage specification
      parameters
         personnel : in out file of records
            employee : record containing
               name, ssnumber : string
               wage : real
               address : record containing
                  street, city, state, zip : string
                  endrecord address
               endrecord employee
            endfile personnel
      end storage specification

   begin transfer records
      create new personnel file
      loop while moredata
         read string(personnel.employee.name, 20)
         read string(personnel.employee.ssnumber, 11)
         input personnel.employee.wage
         read string(personnel.employee.address.street, 20)
         read string(personnel.employee.address.city, 15)
         read string(personnel.employee.address.state, 2)
         read string(personnel.employee.address.zip, 5)
         put personnel.employee record into personnel file
         endloop while
      terminate personnel file
      end transfer records

   where procedure read string was defined in case study 6.1
```

CASE STUDY 10.1 — REFINEMENT 2

Recall that procedure *read string* inputs a string one character at a time, building up the string by concatenation when given the name of the string and the length of the string.

As we can see, the loop of procedure *transfer records* just fills the internal *employee* record by reading in each item of a record from the input device. Once the internal *employee* record is full, it is put into the external *personnel* file. In this case we use the **in out** parameter designation for the *personnel* file parameter so that the internal *employee* record occupies the same cells of the primary store in procedure *transfer records* as in the initial procedure. To access each element of the *employee* record being constructed, we use the prefix.

personnel.employee

We will see the importance of this notation in later case studies when more than one file with the same record type is used.

Correctness

Beyond the usual considerations for determining program correctness, there are some special concerns when an external file is written. The programmer must be sure to **create** the file before putting records into it and **terminate** the file when finished. Sometimes a program that writes an external file will quit abnormally if the file being written does not fit in the external storage device in the chosen location. This can usually be corrected by using a new disk or tape or by using a special routine supplied with your computer for reorganizing the files already stored on the disk or tape to make more room for your file.

For the simple type of output loop given in procedure *transfer records*, we do not include loop invariant or goal assertions.

Efficiency

Our previous experience tells us that this program is linear on the number of records to be constructed, that is $O(n)$, where n is the number of records in the personnel file. It is important to recognize, however, that programs that deal with external files are in general much slower than equivalent programs for which all of the data is in the primary store; this is due to the physical characteristics of the external storage devices. Compared with a real computer's all-electronic primary store with no moving parts, the secondary storage devices, which do have moving parts, are much slower. This fact must be taken into consideration when working with external files.

The space complexity of this program is $O(n)$ since there are n records in the *personnel* file (we count all storage cells used in the primary and secondary stores).

Summary — Case Study 10.1

In this case study we have seen our first example of a program that deals with external files. These files must be specified in an **external files** statement by giving the names of the files and descriptions of the records of the files. A new file is started with the **create new file** statement, which generates a new file in the external store with a special header record containing the name of the file. File names must all be unique. A new file is ended with the **terminate file** statement, which generates the special end-of-file trailer record.

There are substantial differences in the way external files are treated in real programming languages. In some cases, special operations such as creating a new file must be done *before* the program is run, using special processor commands that give the name of the file and also an estimate of the amount of space required by the file — then the processor can choose a position in the external store with enough room to contain the file. Although you may need to learn a particular method of dealing with files peculiar to your actual language and the real computer you are using, the basic operations on files presented here will arise in one form or another.

Case Study 10.2 | Print an External File

Problem Description: Print the external *personnel* file of case study 10.1.

Input Specifications: The *personnel* file of case study 10.1 in secondary storage.

Printing a file is perhaps the simplest application involving an existing file in secondary storage. As simple as it is, however, it is very common; often just a listing of the records in a file is needed for review. This problem introduces a few new concepts necessary for getting records from an external file, but the program developed here is otherwise very similar to the one in case study 10.1.

The Solution — Getting Records from an External File

The first thing we need is the name of the external file that is to be printed. Since there are usually many extenal files in secondary storage, we must refer to a file by its unique name whenever we wish to use it. In this case study we will use the external file *personnel* from case study 10.1. Calling the procedure for printing the *personnel* file *printfile*, we can thus design the initial procedure for this case study; it will be very similar to the initial procedure of case study 10.1.

---

printer : **initial procedure**
  {prints an external personnel file}

  storage specification
    external files
      personnel : **file of records**
        employee : **record containing**
          name, ssnumber : **string**
          wage : **real**
          address : **record containing**
            street, city, state, zip : **string**
            endrecord address
          endrecord employee
        endfile personnel
    end storage specification

  begin printer
    printfile(personnel)
    end printer

  where printfile prints the records of the personnel file

CASE STUDY 10.2 — REFINEMENT 1

To design procedure *printfile*, we need to learn how to gain access to the records in an external file and how to indicate to the processor that we wish to retrieve records from such a file. We can make an analogy to a file in a filing cabinet to understand this process: to get information from a filing cabinet, we open a drawer, examine the necessary records of the file, and then close the drawer. We will use the **open file** and **close file** commands in *mpl* to model this process for external files. In particular, we will use the statement

  open personnel **file**

to tell the processor to locate the file named *personnel* in secondary storage and prepare to get records for processing from that file. Similarly, we will use the statement

  close personnel **file**

to indicate that we have finished processing the *personnel* file.

After the *personnel* file has been opened, procedure *printfile* will get each *employee* record of the *personnel* file in succession, printing each record after it has been retrieved from the external file. The process of retrieving the next *employee* record from the *personnel* file will be accomplished with the **get record** statement:

> **get** personnel.employee **record from** personnel **file**

Notice that this is just the opposite of the **put record** statement introduced in case study 10.1. The processor keeps track of the last record retrieved from the file, so that it knows which record is next. (Remember that in our model of secondary storage, records can be retrieved only in sequential order, one at a time.) Each time a **get record** statement is executed, the next record in line to be input will be brought in and placed into the internal *employee* record in the primary store. Notice that the entire record is retrieved at once — the individual elements of the record are not brought in one at a time.

Procedure *printfile*, then, looks like

```
printfile : procedure
    {prints each record of the personnel file in succession}
    storage specification
        parameters
            personnel : in out file of records
                employee : record containing
                    name, ssnumber : string
                    wage : real
                    address : record containing
                        street, city, state, zip : string
                    endrecord address
                endrecord employee
            endfile personnel
    end storage specification

    begin printfile
        open personnel file
        get personnel.employee record from personnel file
        if personnel.employee is end of file record
            then output 'file is empty'
            else loop
                    output personnel.employee.name
                    output personnel.employee.ssnumber
                    output personnel.employee.wage
                    output personnel.employee.address.street
                    output personnel.employee.address.city, ' ',
                        personnel.employee.address.state, ' ',
                        personnel.employee.address.zip
                    get personnel.employee record from personnel file
                endloop until personnel.employee is end of file record
        endif
        close personnel file
    end printfile
```

CASE STUDY 10.2 — REFINEMENT 2

Notice that before the printing loop is entered we check whether the first record input is the special end-of-file record, indicating that the file is empty. If it isn't the end-of-file record, the first record is a valid record, so we can go ahead and print it. This is why we are able to use an **until** loop. The last step of this loop is to get the next record, which is checked by the **until** condition

> **endloop until** personnel.employee **is end of file record**

to determine whether it is the special end-of-file record before starting through the loop again.

In our procedures and functions for handling an external file, the parameter required is the *name* of the file, complete with the description of the records in the file. The actual file, which is in the secondary store, is *not* the parameter (its name — along with the associated internal record — is really the parameter). For example, in procedure *printfile* the processor uses the formal **file** parameter name *personnel* to access the proper file in the external store. When an *employee* record is input from the external storage device, it is stored in the primary store in the internal *employee* record associated with the *personnel* file formal parameter. The **in out** designation on the *personnel* file simply means that the *employee* record of the formal file parameter takes on the same cells as the internal *employee* record of the actual *personnel* file parameter sent by the initial procedure. In this case the **in out** designation would also have worked.

Correctness

Reading values from an external file is very similar to reading values from the standard input device. The only point to be particularly careful about is using the **open** and **close** statements to get the file ready for input and to indicate that processing of the file has finished. Again, because just a simple input loop is employed in procedure *printfile*, no loop invariant or goal assertions are included.

Efficiency

Refinement 2 of this case study contains a single **until** loop, which reads each record in the *personnel* file once. The time complexity of this procedure is therefore $O(n)$, where n is the number of records in the *personnel* file. The space complexity of this program is also $O(n)$, since the external *personnel* file contains n records.

Summary — Case Study 10.2

Whenever we access an existing external file we must first open it with the instruction

> **open** *filename* **file**

and when we have finished with it we must close it again with the instruction

> **close** *filename* **file**

Once a file has been opened, we can access records from the file, in order, using the instruction

> **get** *recordname* **record from** *filename* **file**

Each time this instruction is used, it retrieves the next record from the named external file and stores it in the associated internal record in the primary store.

Case Study 10.3 | Searching an External File

> **Problem Description:** Given the *personnel* file of case study 10.1 and a subsequent list of names, print the name, social security number, and wage of each person whose name appears in the second list.
>
> **Input Specifications:** The *personnel* file of case study 10.1 in secondary storage and a list of names at the standard input device.

Many of the routines we presented in earlier chapters for handling arrays of data can be applied to external files, but many cannot. For example, the sequential search routine can be applied to external files, but the binary search routine cannot be applied at all, because it assumes that the middle element of the list being searched is immediately accessible. (In external files of the simple type we are discussing, all records must be retrieved in sequential order.) In this case study we will apply a sequential search to an external file.

The Solution — Sequential Search

One way to solve this problem is to input each name from the standard input device and search through the external *personnel* file from the start, comparing the name in each record with the name for which we are searching. This introduces a new problem: how do we tell the processor to reset the external store to the start of the *personnel* file each time a new name is to be searched for? Each real programming language has a way to accomplish this; we will model this action with the *mpl* **reset** statement, as in

> **reset** personnel **file**

When the processor executes this statement, it causes the external storage device to be reset at the *personnel* file header record, ready to start scanning the file again from the beginning.

We need an initial procedure that uses a loop to process each name input from the standard input device. The loop should cause the *personnel* file to be searched for each name and then print the name, social security number, and wage associated with that name or print an appropriate message if the name is not found in the *personnel* file.

```
search a file : initial procedure
    {searches a personnel file for given names, then prints the
    corresponding information in matched records}
    storage specification
        external files
            personnel : file of records
                employee : record containing
                    name, ssnumber : string
                    wage : real
                    address : record containing
                        street, city, state, zip : string
                    endrecord address
                endrecord employee
            endfile personnel
        variables
            inputname : string
            found : truth value
    end storage specification
```

```
      begin search a file
         open personnel file
         loop while moredata
            read string(inputname, 20)
            search(personnel, inputname, found)
            if found
               then output personnel.employee.name
                    output personnel.employee.ssnumber
                    output personnel.employee.wage
               else output inputname, ' not in personnel file'
            endif
         endloop while
      close personnel file
      end search a file

   where search attempts to find inputname in the personnel file
```

CASE STUDY 10.3 — REFINEMENT 1

Notice that file *personnel* is opened at the start of the initial procedure and closed at the end. This varies from our rule of having the procedure which manipulates the file do all of the file operations. In this instance, procedure *search* will be responsible for resetting the *personnel* file to the front with the **reset** statement each time *search* is called.

Procedure *search* will work as expected. The *personnel* file will be **reset** and then searched from the beginning for *inputname*. If and when a match is made, the matched record will be in the primary store in the internal *employee* record so a return can be made to the initial procedure, where the appropriate information is printed from the internal *employee* record. If a match is not made with *inputname* (that is, if the trailing end-of-file record in the *personnel* file is reached before a match is made), the **truth value** variable *found* will be set to **false,** otherwise it will be set to **true.**

```
   search : procedure
      {searches for an occurrence of inputname in the personnel file}

      storage specification
         parameters
            personnel : out only file of records
               employee : record containing
                  name, ssnumber : string
                  wage : real
                  address : record containing
                     street, city, state, zip : string
                     endrecord address
                  endrecord employee
               endfile personnel
            inputname: in only string
            found : out only truth value
      end storage specification
```

```
begin search
    reset personnel file
    found ← false
    get personnel.employee record from personnel file
    loop while (personnel.employee not end of file record)
            and (not found)
        if personnel.employee.name = inputname
            then found ← true
            else get personnel.employee record from personnel file
        endif
    endloop while
end search
```

CASE STUDY 10.3 — REFINEMENT 2

Notice that the **out only** (or **in out**) designation on the formal *personnel* file parameter is necessary here. The records from the external storage device are input in succession into the internal *employee* record, and when procedure *search* finds the employee being searched for, a return to the initial procedure is made, where the values in the internal *employee* record must be the same as those input in procedure *search*.

For the sake of clarity, we have been including the entire description of the file records in each procedure and function to which we pass an external file name as a parameter. To save time while designing programs in *mpl*, it is certainly acceptable to describe these records simply as comments. For example, the **parameters** section of procedure *search* could have been written as

parameters
    personnel : **out only file of records**
        {employee record as described in the initial procedure}

Most real programming languages provide a shortcut that does not require copying all this information in every routine.

Not all real programming languages allow a file which has been opened to be reset to the front as we have designed procedure *search* to work. In these cases the **open** and **close** statements must be taken out of the initial procedure and placed in procedure *search* — the **open** statement should be placed just after **begin** *search* and the **close** statement just before **end** *search*. That way the *personnel* file will be opened each time *search* is called and closed each time *search* terminates, which will be equivalent to the way *search* is designed here.

Correctness

Procedure *search* is a standard sequential search. The fact that the search is being performed on an external file adds only the complication that the file must be **reset** each time a new search is begun and then closed only when the program is complete. The loop invariant and goal assertions for procedure *search* can be determined from those given in the sequential search routine of chapter 5 (case study 5.5).

Efficiency

By now we recognize that the time complexity of this program is $O(m*n)$, where m is the number of names at the standard input device (the number of times the loop in the initial procedure will iterate) and *n* is the number of records in the *personnel* file (on the average, *n*/2 records will be searched before a match with *inputname* is found). Also, it is clear that the space complexity is $O(n)$.

Alternate Solution — Single Pass through the External File

Another approach to this problem is to read all the names from the standard input device into a **string** array, and then compare the name in each record in the *personnel* file against all the names in the array. This would be a simple program to design, and it would again have a time complexity of $O(m*n)$. It would, however, be a much better solution than our first one, since it only requires a single pass through the *personnel* file; the tradeoff is that multiple passes through the **string** array in the primary store would now be required. This tradeoff would be worthwhile, because it is much faster for the processor to access values in the primary store than to access records in the secondary store.

We can even improve on this new solution by taking advantage of the fact that the records in the *personnel* file are in alphabetical order by the *name* field. If we read the input names into a **string** array (as we described above) and then sort this array into alphabetical order, too, we can read the records from the external *personnel* file one at a time, comparing the *name* component in each record against just the first element in the array. Once a match is made, or once we reach a name in the file that is alphabetically greater than the first name in the array, we can resume comparing the names in the file against the second name in the array, and so on. As we shall see, for large files this strategy results in an $O(n)$ routine. This solution requires one of the sorting routines, *insertion sort* or *quicksort*, developed in The Challenge section of chapter 5 (modified to handle strings as described in case study 6.4). If you did not study either of those sorting routines, you may wish to skip this alternate solution.

First, we need a new initial procedure.

```
search a file : initial procedure
    {inputs a list of names, sorts them into alphabetical order, then
     searches a personnel file (already in alphabetical order by name)
     for occurrences of the names in the list, printing the appropriate
     information in matched records}

    storage specification
        external files
            personnel : file of records
                employee : record containing
                    name, ssnumber : string
                    wage : real
                    address : record containing
                        street, city, state, zip : string
                    endrecord address
                endrecord employee
            endfile personnel
        constants
            maxnames : integer 500
        variables
            names : 1-D string array [1 → maxnames]
            count : integer
    end storage specification
```

```
        begin search a file
            read 1D string(names, maxnames, count)
            if count > maxnames
                then output 'too many input names'
                else sort(names, 1, count)
                      searchfile(personnel, names, count)
            endif
        end search a file

    where read 1D string reads all input names into the array names
            (case study 6.3)
    where sort sorts the array names (either insertion sort
            or quicksort may be used — see case study 6.4)
    where searchfile attempts to find each input name in the personnel file
```

CASE STUDY 10.3 — REFINEMENT 3

We have already designed procedure *read 1D string*, and either *insertion sort* or *quicksort* can be used for procedure *sort*, so we can concentrate on procedure *searchfile*. Before we write down the details of the procedure *searchfile*, we should think about its design. We will need an integer variable (*currentname*) to tell us which element of the array *names* we are looking at. We will also need a **while** loop to read records from the *personnel* file and compare their name components against *names*[*currentname*]. We want this loop to stop either when we have read all of the records in the file *personnel* or when we have processed all of the names in the *names* array. When we compare *employee.name* of the current internal *employee* record against *names*[*currentname*] there are three possibilities:

1. *employee.name* = *names*[*currentname*]. In this case, we have a match, so we can print the required output. We then need to add one to *currentname* so that we look at the next name in the *names* array, and we need to retrieve the next input record from the *personnel* file.

2. *employee.name* > *names*[*currentname*]. This means that we have gone past the current name alphabetically, so it is not in the file. We must output a message to the user, and we must remember not to read in a new record from the personnel file, since the name now in *employee.name* might match *names*[*currentname* + 1] (we must therefore add 1 to *currentname*).

3. *employee.name* < *names*[*currentname*]. This means that no match has been found yet, so the next employee record from the external *personnel* file must be input.

It is now easy to write our procedure. The main structure will be a **while** loop that continues executing as long as the current internal record of the personnel file is not the special end-of-file record (meaning that some records of the personnel file have not yet been examined) and as long as

currentname ⩽ *count*

(meaning that there are still some names left in the sorted *names* array). Within this loop there will be an **if** statement that checks the three possibilities described above and performs the actions discussed. Finally, upon completing the loop, if there are still names remaining at the end of the *names* array that were not matched in the *personnel* file, these names and appropriate messages must be printed. The result is given below.

```
searchfile : procedure
    {finds records in the personnel file whose name components match
    the names in the array names and prints the corresponding
    information in matched records}

    storage specification
        parameters
            personnel : in out file of records
                employee : record containing
                    name, ssnumber : string
                    wage : real
                    address : record containing
                        street, city, state, zip : string
                    endrecord address
                endrecord employee
            endfile personnel
            names : in out 1-D string array
            count : in only integer
        variables
            currentname : integer
        end storage specification

    begin searchfile
        open personnel file
        get personnel.employee record from personnel file
        currentname ← 1
        loop while (personnel.employee not end of file record)
                    and (currentname ≤ count)
            if personnel.employee.name = names[currentname]
                then output personnel.employee.name
                    output personnel.employee.ssnumber
                    output personnel.employee.wage
                    currentname ← currentname + 1
                    get personnel.employee record from personnel file
                elseif personnel.employee.name > names[currentname]
                    output names[currentname], ' not in file'
                    currentname ← currentname + 1
                else get personnel.employee record from personnel file
            endif
        endloop while
        loop while currentname ≤ count
            output names[currentname], ' not in the file'
            currentname ← currentname + 1
        endloop while
        close personnel file
    end searchfile
```

CASE STUDY 10.3 — REFINEMENT 4

The last **while** loop takes care of the possibility that some names may remain in the *names* array after the *personnel* file has been exhausted. These names are printed with the message "not in the file."

Correctness

There is nothing new in this case study, but this program is certainly more complicated than the first ones of this chapter, so careful program testing is in order. One obvious special value to test is a list containing one input name that is not in the file (or even a list of names where none of the names are in the external file). Because of the nature of the main **while** loop of procedure *searchfile* the loop invariant and goal assertions would have to be quite long (they would have to reflect much of what is in the **if** statement), so we will leave them out here to save space. The *sort* routine (whichever is used, *insertion sort* or *quicksort*) was verified when it was designed in chapter 5.

Efficiency

Our latest design has three procedure calls in the initial procedure, to *read 1D string*, *sort*, and *searchfile*. If we assume, as before, that there are n records in the *personnel* file and m input names, then we already know that *read 1D string* is $O(m)$. If we use *insertion sort* of case study 5.7 for the *sort* procedure, then the time complexity of procedure *sort* is $O(m^2)$. If we use *quicksort* of case study 5.8, then the time complexity of procedure *sort* is $O(m*\log_2 m)$. The main loop in procedure *searchfile* is executed at most $m+n$ times, because each time through the loop either a new record is retrieved from the *personnel* file, or *currentname* is increased by 1, or both. The time complexity of *searchfile* is therefore $O(m+n)$. Since m is less than both $m*\log_2 m$ and $m+n$, we can ignore the time complexity of procedure *read 1D string*. Thus the time complexity of the program if we use *quicksort* is the maximum of $O(m*\log_2 m)$ and $O(m+n)$, which is usually written

$$O(m*\log_2 m + m+n)$$

which can be simplified to

$$O(n + m*\log_2 m)$$

since once again m is smaller than $m*\log_2 m$. If we use *insertion sort*, the time complexity of the program is $O(m^2+m+n)$ or $O(m^2+n)$ since m^2 is larger than m.

Assume now that n is much larger than m. This will usually be true — the values of n and m might be 1,000,000 and 100 respectively. If this occurs, then n is also much larger than $m*\log_2 m$ or m^2, so the time complexity will be $O(n)$, or linear in the number of records in the external file. Remember, too, that n refers to the number of records input from the *personnel* file, and that retrieving records from the secondary storage device is very slow compared to operations applied to values in the primary store. So, even if $n = 10,000$ and $m = 100$ (i.e., $m^2 = 10,000$) the time required to process the *personnel* file will be substantially longer. The time to access a value in the primary store can often be measured in *nanoseconds* (billionths of a second); the time to access a value in secondary storage is measured in *milliseconds* (thousandths of a second), which is 1,000,000 times slower!

Summary — Case Study 10.3

A search of an external file must be sequential, since in our model the secondary storage devices do not allow individual records of a sequential file to be accessed randomly. Even the fact that the file is in a particular order (e.g., alphabetical) does not permit a binary search of the file.

To improve the efficiency of programs that access an external file, we should minimize the number of passes that are made through that file, because accessing a record in an external file generally takes much more time than accessing a record in the primary store.

<table>
<tr><td>

Deleting Records
from an External File
</td><td>

Case Study
10.4
</td></tr>
</table>

> *Problem Description:* Given the *personnel* file of case study 10.1, update this file by deleting terminated employees.
>
> *Input Specifications:* The *personnel* file of case study 10.1 and a list at the standard input device of employee names whose records are to be deleted from the *personnel* file.

Many files kept in external storage undergo frequent change. In a personnel file, for example, a new record must be inserted for each new employee hired, records must be deleted as employees resign or are fired, and records must be updated whenever employees' wages or addresses change. Because of the sequential nature of our secondary storage devices, there is really only one way to modify an external file: the file must be input one record at a time, each individual record is then changed (if necessary) after it is brought into the primary store, and a new temporary external file is constructed simultaneously from the modified records. At the completion of this process, the newly constructed temporary file must be renamed with the name of the original file.

This problem will demonstrate just one of the common file manipulation problems — deleting records from a file. The other types of file manipulations will be left as exercises.

The Solution — Use of a Temporary File

To delete records from the *personnel* file, we will construct a new temporary file consisting only of the good records and then rename this temporary file with the original file name. If there was just one record to delete, we would input each record from the external personnel file one at a time and compare the name in each record with the name of the employee whose record is to be deleted. If the names did not match, we would immediately transfer the record into the temporary file. When the names finally did match, we would leave the matched record out of the temporary file, copy the remaining *employee* records from the *personnel* file into the temporary file, and finally rename the temporary file to be the *personnel* file (this would free the secondary storage space occupied by the old *personnel* file). The time consumed by this process would be $O(n)$, where n is the number of records in the *personnel* file, because each record of the *personnel* file must be examined once.

We could proceed in this fashion when we have more than one record to be deleted, copying the *personnel* file into a new temporary file each time we delete one record, but this approach would be horribly inefficient — it would require recopying the entire *personnel* file every time a name is processed. A typical personnel file is very large, whereas the number of deletions from the file in a given week or month would be relatively small.

Example 10.4   Suppose this inefficient method for deleting records from a file is used for a personnel file containing 10,000 records. If 100 records are to be deleted, the employee file will have to be copied 100 times. That is, 1,000,000 records will have to be moved in the secondary store when the program following this deletion scheme is run.

A better solution is to input all of the names to be deleted into an array (in the primary store) first and then sort these names into alphabetical order, as was done in case study 10.3. Since the *personnel* file is also in alphabetical order, we can then just copy the *personnel* file once, leaving out each record in which the name matches the next name in the array of employee names whose records are to be deleted. In The Challenge section of chapter 5, we developed two different procedures for sorting an array of integers into ascending numeric order, *insertion sort* and *quicksort*. These procedures can be used to sort an array of strings into alphabetical order by changing the **integer** array parameters to type **string** parameters in the appropriate places. If you did not study these particular case studies, you can still use the program we develop here by deleting the call to procedure *sort* in the initial procedure and supplying the names to be deleted in alphabetical order to begin with at the input device.

The initial procedure is given below. First the array of names to be deleted, *deletenames*, is input from the standard input device. Then, after checking whether this array is empty or whether too many names to fit in *deletenames* were given at the standard input device, the array is sorted and passed to procedure *delete*, where the *personnel* file is reconstructed by omitting the records to be deleted.

```
delete records : initial procedure
    {inputs a list of names, sorts the list into alphabetical order, and then
    searches a personnel file (already in alphabetical order) for occurrences
    of names in the list. Whenever a match is found, the corresponding
    record is deleted}
    storage specification
        external files
            personnel : file of records
                employee : record containing
                    name, ssnumber : string
                    wage : real
                    address : record containing
                        street, city, state, zip : string
                    endrecord address
                    endrecord employee
            endfile personnel
        constants
            maxnames : integer 100
        variables
            deletenames : 1-D string array [1 → maxnames]
            n : integer
        end storage specification
```

```
begin delete records
    read 1D string(deletenames, maxnames, n)
    if (n > maxnames) or (n = 0)
        then output 'bad data, n = ', n
        else sort(deletenames, 1, n)
                delete(deletenames, personnel, n)
        endif
    end delete records

where sort is either insertion sort of case study 5.7 or quicksort of
        case study 5.8, modified to sort strings
where read 1D string is as given in case study 6.3 for inputting
        an array of strings
where delete removes the records in the personnel file of employees
        whose names are in the array deletenames.
```

CASE STUDY 10.4 — REFINEMENT 1

The procedure *read 1D string* has been previously presented and will not be covered here. The procedures *quicksort* and *insertion sort*, either of which could form the basis for procedure *sort*, have also been given earlier. As we have mentioned, if you did not study either *quicksort* or *insertion sort*, you can replace the **else** clause with

    else delete(deletenames, personnel, n)

removing the call to procedure *sort*; be sure you then supply the list of names to be deleted in alphabetical order at the input device. Thus the only procedure left to design is *delete*, which will be similar to procedure *searchfile* in case study 10.3.

```
delete : procedure
    {creates a new personnel file with all records deleted which
    contained a name appearing in the array deletenames}

    storage specification
        parameters
            deletenames : in out 1-D string array
            personnel : in out file of records
                employee : record containing
                    name, ssnumber : string
                    wage : real
                    address : record containing
                        street, city, state, zip : string
                        endrecord address
                    endrecord employee
                endfile personnel
            n : in only integer
        external files
            deletefile : file of employee records
        variables
            i, j : integer
        end storage specification
```

```
begin delete
    open personnel file
    create new deletefile file
    i ← 1
    get personnel.employee record from personnel file
    loop while (personnel.employee not end of file record)
                and (i ≤ n)
        if personnel.employee.name = deletenames[i]
            then i ← i + 1
                get personnel.employee record from personnel file
            elseif personnel.employee.name < deletenames[i]
                put personnel.employee record into deletefile file
                get personnel.employee record from personnel file
            else output deletenames[i], ' is not in personnel file'
                i ← i + 1
        endif
    endloop while
    loop while personnel.employee not end of file record
        put personnel.employee record into deletefile file
        get personnel.employee record from personnel file
        endloop while
    loop start j with i step 1 to n
        output deletenames[j], ' is not in the personnel file'
        endloop autoindex
    destroy personnel file
    rename deletefile file to be personnel file
    end delete
```

CASE STUDY 10.4 — REFINEMENT 2

This case study has demonstrated how an external sequential file is modified: the file must be copied into a temporary file one record at a time, and the individual records must be modified after they are input into the primary store from the original file and before they are copied into the temporary file in the secondary store. In this case the only modification to the file was leaving records out (not copying them into the temporary file) if their names matched one of the names in the list of names to be deleted. The same strategy is used to add new records to a file (copy the records from the original file into a temporary file until the position is found where the new record is to be inserted, put the new record into the temporary file, then continue copying records from the original file, and so on) or to update items within individual records (get each record individually from the original file, check whether it needs to be modified, put it directly into the temporary file if it does not need to be modified, otherwise modify the proper item in the record and then put the record into the temporary file).

When all of the required records have been moved into the temporary file, we discard our old file using the command

destroy *old* **file**

and then rename the temporary file to replace the old file using

rename *temp* **file to be** *old* **file**

We did not assume that all of the input names actually appeared in some record of the *personnel* file. In a typical situation the list of names to be deleted would be typed in by humans, and typing mistakes, misspellings, and entries of completely invalid names would commonly occur. Thus, to make our program practical, procedure *delete* prints an *exception report* of names for which no match was found in the *personnel* file.

As will be described in the In Retrospect section, great care should be taken that an important file is not destroyed by mistake. In this program, for example, we may not actually want to **destroy** the old personnel file, because we may want to check first whether the new personnel file was constructed properly. In fact, the **destroy** statement is not even included directly in most programming languages. We have included it in *mpl* to make you aware that old external files which are no longer needed must somehow be deleted.

Correctness

Obvious special values to use for testing this program include a list of names to be deleted that includes some "bad" names. Again, the loop invariant and goal assertions for procedure *delete* are long and have not been included; they are not difficult to formulate, however, so we leave them as exercises.

Efficiency

The time complexity analysis for this case study is identical to the analysis that we did in case study 10.3: if the number of records in the *personnel* file, n, is much larger than number of entries to be deleted, m, the time complexity will be linear, $O(n)$. Only one pass is made through the *personnel* file. Similarly, the space complexity is $O(n + m)$ because an array of m elements is maintained in the store and there are n records in the *personnel* file. Since n is usually much larger than m, we can say that the space complexity is just $O(n)$.

Summary — Case Study 10.4

The underlying strategy involved in developing a program to manipulate an external sequential file has been discussed and demonstrated. Even though this case study dealt with deleting records from a file, it demonstrated the basic steps necessary in modifying a sequential file: each record must be brought one at a time into the primary store, any modifications to the record are to be made there, and then the record must put into a temporary file. When this process has been completed, a modified copy of the original file will exist in the temporary file. At this point the temporary file must be renamed to have the name of the original file, so that it now becomes the official file, and the old original file must be deleted (so that its space in the secondary store is free to be used for other purposes).

SECONDARY STORAGE

**10.2
IN
RETROSPECT**

There are two principal reasons for using secondary storage: it keeps data available for future use, and it allows us to manipulate data files that are too large to fit in the primary store of the computer. The primary store is limited in size on real computers, and it is usually *volatile* — if electrical power to the primary store is lost, the contents of the primary store are lost, too. For these and other reasons, the primary store cannot be used for long term storage of information. Secondary storage is not volatile (it retains the information stored there even when the power fails), and it is otherwise well suited to storing information over long periods of time.

Secondary storage, though, is not as convenient to use as the primary store. The individual records of an external file cannot be retrieved at random, as they could be if the data was in the primary store. Instead, to get to any particular record of an external file, all previous records of the file must first be retrieved — this is true at least for the sequential storage of files as discussed in this chapter. For some applications, more elaborate schemes have been devised for storing data in the external store, but these, too, are limited by the sequential nature of the storage devices themselves (we will not look into any of these more elaborate schemes, which are beyond the scope of this book). Sequential files are the most common.

OPERATIONS ON EXTERNAL FILES

There are a number of basic operations associated with files: creating a new file with the **create** statement, which starts a file with a header record containing the name of the new file; putting records into a new file with the **put** statement; terminating a new file with the **terminate** statement, which causes a trailing end-of-file record to be placed at the end of a new file; opening an existing file with the **open** statement; getting records from a file and bringing them into the primary store with the **get** statement; resetting a file with the **reset** statement to the first record again during processing of the file; indicating that processing of an existing file is finished with the **close** statement; renaming an existing file with the **rename** statement; and removing an existing file with the **destroy** statement.

The most important points to remember about external sequential files are their restrictions, which can be boiled down to just two issues: you can only **get** records from an *existing* file, and you can only **put** records into a *new* file. The **get** and **put** operations cannot be used on the same file simultaneously — you cannot **get** a record from a file, modify it, and then **put** it back into the same file, for example. All modifications to an existing external sequential file must be made by copying that file one record at a time into a new file, using the **get** statement to retrieve each record from the existing file and place it into the primary store, and using the **put** statement to copy each record from the primary store into the new file after modifications are made to the record. (Remember that the only way to modify a record is to bring it into the primary store and modify it there.) At the end of this copy/modification process, the **rename** statement must be used to rename the new file with the name of the original file, after the original file has been destroyed.

Note that in situations where the records of a file are modified, only one record at a time is usually ever in the primary store. The description of that record is given in the **record containing** declaration, which appears after the **file of records** statement used for declaring the file. The processor uses this record description to reserve the proper number and types of cells in the primary store; a record retrieved from the secondary store by a **get** statement will then fit into these reserved cells of the primary store, where the elements of the record can be directly manipulated. (You can, of course, declare an array of internal records into which you can store a group of records from the external file, but most external files are so large that only a relatively small number of records from an external file can fit into the primary store at once.)

No actual programming languages have all of the file-handling statements modeled in *mpl*. Also, the statements that destroy and rename existing files are often not allowed within a programmng language; instead, these two actions must usually be specified directly to the processor as separate actions outside of any program. This is done because of the way the processor must handle a potentially large number of files used by numerous programs (perhaps written in different programming languages). Chaos would result if a programmer could destroy an important file accidentally (or maliciously) by running a program containing a **destroy** statement with the name of some large file! Nonetheless, all of the operations we have described must be possible in any computing environment, and the way we have modeled these operations in *mpl* should make you aware of the necessary tasks for dealing with external files in an actual programming language.

HEADER RECORDS, TRAILER RECORDS, AND CHECKING FOR END-OF-FILE

Each external file has a special first record called the header record and a special last record called the trailer or end-of-file record. The records in between are the actual records of the file (if the file is empty, it has only a header and an end-of-file record). When an **open** or **reset** statement is executed, the processor locates the file by its header record and then positions the file so that the first **get** statement executed will retrieve the first record after the header record (if the file is empty, this next record will be the end-of-file record). The easiest way to process a file with an unknown number of records is to **get** each record of the file in succession until the end-of-file record is retrieved. Since even the first **get** might get the end-of-file record (if the file is empty), the standard external file processing loop has the form

```
open filename file
get filename.record from filename file
loop while filename.record not end of file record
    statement
        :
        :
    statement
    get filename.record from filename file
endloop while
```

where *filename* is the name of the file being processed, and *filename.record* is that file's internal record. The first **get** statement is positioned just before the **loop** statement to ensure that the loop will not be executed even once if the first record of the file is the end-of-file record. If the first record is not the end-of-file record, the loop is entered, that record is processed, and the last statement of the loop **gets** the next record in preparation for the next pass through the loop.

Notice the difference between this kind of loop for processing data from an external file and the **moredata** loop for processing data from the standard input device. When we use the **moredata** loop, we assume that the processor checks whether there is more data at the input device *before* an **input** statement is issued; for external files we assume that the processor can only determine that there is no more data in a file *after* the **get** statement retrieves the end-of-file record. Thus, the **moredata** loop, which processes each input item from the standard input device in a manner analogous to the loop given above for processing the records of a file, has the form

```
loop while moredata
    input data
    statement
       .
       .
       .
    statement
    endloop while
```

This loop will not be executed even once if there is no data at the input device, and it will only be entered for a new iteration if there is data at the input device; this means that the first statement of the loop can be the **input** statement, which is then followed by the statements for processing the data. You should compare these two input loops to understand their differences.

The following two *mpl* **truth value** expressions are used to determine whether the internal file record of the file being processed is empty:

> *filename.record* **is end of file record**

and

> *filename.record* **not end of file record**

where *filename.record* is the name of the internal record of the file being processed.

EXTERNAL FILES AS PARAMETERS

An external file cannot be a parameter, because it does not reside in the primary store and therefore could not be declared in the usual fashion with type **in only, in out,** or **out only** designations. Instead, the *name* of the file along with its record description is passed as a parameter to procedures and functions using that file. The file record descriptor can be treated as an **in only, in out,** or **out only** parameter, because it actually resides in the primary store. These considerations show that changes made to an external file in a procedure where **get record** or **put record** statements are executed are permanent changes, affecting the entire program.

CORRECTNESS OF PROGRAMS WITH EXTERNAL FILES

Programs using external files are really no different from other programs, so the same verification, walkthrough, testing, and debugging methods should be used. The only added complications are details: remembering to **open** a file before using it, **close** it when done, **reset** it to start processing it from the front again, **destroy** old files, **rename** new ones, and so on. You must pay careful attention to such details, because disastrous results may otherwise occur. For example, if you destroy an old file without renaming the new file (the modified version of the old file), you could lose irreplaceable data. For this reason, *backup files* are usually kept for all important files. A backup file is just a recent copy of an important file. For example, files that undergo frequent change might be backed up (copied) once a week, so that if the original file is destroyed somehow, the backup copy can be used with at most a week's worth of modifications required to bring it up-to-date. As a result, one of the most widely used programs for processing external files is one that copies one file to a new file.

EFFICIENCY OF PROGRAMS WITH EXTERNAL FILES

The time complexity of programs with external files is determined as usual. However, a program that deals with external storage requires much more time to execute than a similar program not using external storage (this difference in execution time will be a constant factor, albeit a large constant factor). For example, a procedure to find the maximum value in an unordered list of integers might require 10,000 times as much execution time if the list is stored in an external file instead of in an array. Also, the sequential nature of external files makes application of some elegant time-saving routines (e.g., binary search) impossible.

The space complexity of a program using external files is calculated from the number of storage cells required both in external storage and in the primary store.

FOR REVIEW

**10.3
WARMUP
EXERCISES**

10.1 What is an external file?

10.2 Diagram the model computer as extended to include secondary storage devices, and then compare your diagram with the one in the book.

10.3 In your own words, explain why secondary storage devices are needed. In particular, compare secondary storage with the primary store, explaining the key differences.

10.4 What are the physical properties of external storage devices and the primary store that make the two fundamentally different?

10.5 What are the similarities and differences between tape and disk external storage devices?

10.6 The primary store is often called RAM. Explain this term and state why this term does not apply to secondary storage.

10.7 Explain the meaning of the term *volatile* as it applies to storage devices. Is the primary store volatile? Why? Is secondary storage volatile? Why?

10.8 List the new *mpl* statements required for working with external files and briefly explain the use of each statement.

10.9 Every external file has a special header and trailer record. Explain their use.

10.10 Which is faster in speed of accessing arbitrary stored values, secondary storage or the primary store? Why?

10.11 Discuss briefly how an existing record is deleted from an external file and how a new record is inserted into an external file.

10.12 Give the general loop form used for processing each record of an external file in sequence.

10.13 Explain the concept of a backup file.

10.14 Explain briefly how each program developed in the case studies of the first section of this chapter works.

10.15 Explain the important differences between a file and an array of records.

10.16 Explain why programs that manipulate files generally take much longer to execute than similar programs that manipulate similar internal data structures.

A DEEPER LOOK

10.17 The delete procedure developed for external files will cause problems if two employees have the same name. Explain why and what can be done to fix the problem.

10.18 Would a program to print an array of records (from the primary store) be faster or slower than a similar program to print a file of the same records (from secondary storage)? Explain your reasoning. Would this difference in execution time be a constant factor (regardless of the number of records to be printed) or a fundamental difference in time complexity?

10.19 An external file cannot be read from and written to at the same time: a particular file is either open for reading or writing, but not both. List any reasons for this you can think of.

10.20 We have developed many data structures and many good routines for accessing these data structures in this book. Explain why many of these routines cannot be applied directly to data stored in external files. Give examples of routines we have designed earlier which can be directly applied to files and examples of routines which cannot. Explain your reasoning.

10.21 The *mpl* **destroy** statement represents an important needed operation on files. Explain why most programming languages do not have the equivalent of this statement.

10.22 Continuing with the previous exercise, most programming languages also do not have equivalents of the **rename** or **create file** statements, even though these operations must be available. List any reasons you can think of why this is so.

10.23 If each value of an unsorted list in the primary store is to be looked up in an existing external file, which of the following would be more efficient? (1) For each value in the primary store, scan through the external file from the front looking for a match. (2) For each value in the external file, search through the list of values in the primary store looking for a match. Is the time complexity different in these two cases? Explain your answers to both questions.

10.24 Discuss how files are handled as parameters.

10.25 Discuss the special considerations required for determining the correctness of programs with external files. In this respect, what are backup files, and what is their use?

10.26 In case study 5.1 we chose the simple problem of printing a list forwards and backwards to demonstrate the concept of the 1-D array. Would this be a simple problem to solve with external files? What does this tell you about the differences between secondary storage and the primary store?

10.27 Explain the differences between the **while moredata** loop used for inputting values from the standard input device and the **while not end of file record** loop used for inputting records from an external file.

10.28 Assume that the primary store of your computer can contain at most 1000 records of a particular external file at a time. Is it possible to manipulate this external file if it contains 100000 records? Say instead that each record of the external file is so large that two records cannot be contained in the primary store at one time. Specify some of the kinds of problems that can and cannot be solved in this case. What would happen if even one record of this file could not fit in the primary store?

TO PROGRAM

10.29 Design a program to insert records into the file of case study 10.1.

10.30 Design a program to insert records into the file of case study 10.1, but check for duplicates and do not insert a new record if it is already in the file.

10.31 In exercise 8.15 you designed a program to print out the record of the highest paid woman in a personnel file. Repeat this program, but instead of getting the input from the standard input device, get it from an identical external file called SALARY.

10.32 Design a program which takes a list of social security numbers and prints the employee names in matching records of the file given in case study 10.1. Would it help if the list of social security numbers were in numeric order?

10.33 Design an *mpl* program which updates the file of case study 10.1 by increasing the wages of all employees by 5% if their current wage is less than $12.50, and by 10% if their current wage is greater than or equal to $12.50.

In this section we will study just one important file processing procedure which is central to many programs dealing with external files: merging. The merge procedure developed here can be adapted to the problem of sorting an external file, as discussed in the Working Out exercises (10.40) in the following section.

10.4 THE CHALLENGE

Case Study | Merging Two External Files
10.5 |

> **Problem Description:** Merge a *personnel* file with a file of new employees and call the resulting file the new *personnel* file.
>
> **Input Specifications:** A *personnel* file as described in case study 10.1 and a *new employee* file containing the same type of records, in alphabetical order by employee name.

In this case study we will examine the problem of merging two files to form one new file. The purpose of a merge routine is to take two files with the same record format and the same order (e.g., two personnel files where all records are in alphabetical order by name) and create one new file with the same order.

The input specifications show that both the *personnel* file and the *new-employee* file are sorted alphabetically by name. We can assume that the *personnel* file is always maintained in alphabetical order by each program that manipulates this file. The *new employee* file, on the other hand, would normally be typed in from a list of new employees generated as the employees arrived. It would not be in alphabetical order and would have to be sorted. For this case study, however, we will assume that the *new employee* file is already sorted (sorting an external file is the subject of exercise 10.40).

The Solution — Merging Two Files

Since both files are in alphabetical order by name, a new file can be created by a simple process called *merging:* one record from each file is brought into the primary store. The names in these records are compared, and the record with the smallest name (alphabetically) is copied into the output file; if this record came from the *personnel* file, then a new record from the *personnel* file is brought into the primary store; otherwise a new record from the *new employee* file is brought into the primary store.

Example A simple example will illustrate how this merge process works. Instead of using a large
10.5 personnel file, assume that file 1 contains simple records consisting of just one integer each

        12   15   18   20   *

and that file 2 contains similar records

        16   17   21   *

where the * represents the end-of-file record. Notice that both files are sorted. To merge these two files into file 3, we start by getting the first record from each file:

        from file 1: 12   from file 2: 16

Then the following process is repeated until one of the files becomes empty: (1) compare the two numbers; (2) put the smaller number into file 3; (3) replace the record just copied into file 3 with the next record of the file from which that record was taken.
    Using ↑ to indicate the current positions in file 1 and file 2, we start with

```
primary store:  12            16
file 1:             12    15    18    20    *
                    ↑
file 2:             16    17    21    *
                    ↑
file 3:
```

Following the three steps listed above, 12 is compared with 16; since 12 is smaller, it is put into file 3 and replaced with next record from file 1 (the file from which 12 originally came). This gives us

```
primary store:  15            16
file 1:             12    15    18    20    *
                          ↑
file 2:             16    17    21    *
                    ↑
file 3:             12
```

Now 15 is compared to 16, and since 15 is smaller, it is put into file 3 and the next record from file 1 (where 15 originated) is brought into the primary store:

```
primary store:  18            16
file 1:             12    15    18    20    *
                                ↑
file 2:             16    17    21    *
                    ↑
file 3:             12    15
```

When the two numbers now in the primary store are compared, the number 16 (from file 2) is smaller, so it is copied from the primary store into file 3 and the next record from file 2 is retrieved, giving

```
primary store:  18            17
file 1:             12    15    18    20    *
                                ↑
file 2:             16    17    21    *
                          ↑
file 3:             12    15    16
```

This process continues until the end-of-file record is retrieved from one of the files. Then the remaining numbers in the file that is not empty are simply copied into file 3 (until that file's end-of-file record is retrieved), since these numbers belong at end of file 3. The result would be

```
primary store:  *             *
file 1:             12    15    18    20    *
                                      ↑
file 2:             16    17    21    *
                                ↑
file 3:             12    15    16    17    18    20    21    *
```

After the merge process is complete, file 1 and file 2 might no longer be necessary, in which case they should be destroyed. It may also be necessary to rename file 3.

Even though this example deals with simple numbers, it demonstrates how two files containing larger records would be merged. Instead of bringing two numbers from the two files into the primary store, two records would be brought in, the fields by which these records are ordered (e.g., the name fields if the file is in alphabetical order by name) would be compared, and the proper record would be copied into the new merged file. Then the next record from the proper file would be brought in for the next comparison.

For this case study, we need an initial procedure that declares three files, the *personnel* file, the *new employee* file, and *mergedfile*. The procedure *mergefiles* is called to merge the *personnel* and *new employee* files, forming *mergedfile*. Afterwards, the *personnel* and *new employee* files are destroyed, and *mergedfile* is renamed to be the *personnel* file.

merge two files : **initial procedure**
　{merges a personnel file and a new employee file to produce an
　　updated personnel file}

　storage specification
　　external files
　　　personnel, new employee, mergedfile : **file of records**
　　　　employee : **record containing**
　　　　　name, ssnumber : **string**
　　　　　wage : **real**
　　　　　address : **record containing**
　　　　　　street, city, state, zip : **string**
　　　　　endrecord address
　　　　endrecord employee
　　　endfile personnel, new employee, mergedfile
　　end storage specification

　begin merge two files
　　mergefiles(personnel, new employee, mergedfile)
　　destroy personnel **file**
　　rename mergedfile **to be** personnel **file**
　　end merge two files

　where mergefiles merges the personnel and new employee files to form
　　　mergedfile

CASE STUDY 10.5 — REFINEMENT 1

This initial procedure assumes that the *new employee* file was already created by some other program — this is quite common. Many different programs are generally used for maintaining a personnel file and performing various operations on the file.

Procedure *mergefiles* will proceed essentially as we described it in example 10.5. It will use a procedure named *shift* to move the smaller record from the primary store into *mergedfile* and get a new record from the proper file. Procedure *mergefiles* will also use a procedure named *clear* to move all leftover records from the remaining file into *mergedfile* when the other file becomes empty.

```
mergefiles : procedure
    {merges file1 and file2 into mergedfile}

    storage specification
        parameters
            file1, file2, mergedfile : in out file of records
                employee : record containing
                    name, ssnumber : string
                    wage : real
                    address : record containing
                        street, city, state, zip : string
                    endrecord address
                endrecord employee
            endfile file1, file2, mergedfile
        end storage specification

    begin mergefiles
        open file1 file
        open file2 file
        create new mergedfile file
        get file1.employee record from file1 file
        get file2.employee record from file2 file
        loop while file1.employee not end of file record
                and file2.employee not end of file record
            if file1.employee.name < file2.employee.name
                then shift(file1, mergedfile)
                else shift(file2, mergedfile)
                endif
            endloop while
        if file1.employee is end of file record
            then clear(file2, mergedfile)
            else clear(file1, mergedfile)
            endif
        close file1 file
        close file2 file
        terminate mergedfile file
        end mergefiles

    where shift moves a record into mergedfile and gets a new record from
            the proper file.
    where clear moves the remaining records of a file into mergedfile.
```

CASE STUDY 10.5 — REFINEMENT 2

Notice the parameter names *file1*, *file2*, and *mergedfile*; these names show the generality of this procedure, which can be used to merge any two files of the proper type (*file1* and *file2*) into a new file (*mergedfile*).

The procedure *shift* is straightforward and is given below.

```
shift : procedure
    {moves the current record from infile into outfile, then gets
    the next record from infile}

    storage specification
        parameters
            infile, outfile : in out file of records
                employee : record containing
                    name, ssnumber : string
                    wage : real
                    address : record containing
                        street, city, state, zip : string
                    endrecord address
                endrecord employee
            endfile infile, outfile
    end storage specification

    begin shift
        put infile.employee record into outfile file
        get infile.employee record from infile file
    end shift
```

CASE STUDY 10.5 — REFINEMENT 3

Notice the use of the general formal parameter name *infile;* both *file1* and *file2* will be passed as the first actual parameter to *shift* at different times from procedure *mergefiles.*

Now we need to design procedure *clear,* which is to empty out whichever file still has remaining records.

```
clear : procedure
    {moves the remaining records in infile to outfile}
    storage specification
        parameters
            infile, outfile : in out file of records
                employee : record containing
                    name, ssnumber : string
                    wage : real
                    address : record containing
                        street, city, state, zip : string
                    endrecord address
                endrecord employee
            endfile infile, outfile
    end storage specification

    begin clear
        loop while infile.employee not end of file record
            put infile.employee record into outfile file
            get infile.employee record from infile file
        endloop while
    end clear
```

CASE STUDY 10.5 — REFINEMENT 4

Correctness

We have not included loop invariant or goal assertions in refinement 2, but they can easily be formulated. Essentially, the loop invariant assertion must state that the records remaining in *file1* and *file2* are in order alphabetically by the name field, the records now in *mergedfile* are in order alphabetically by the name field, and that the last record in *mergedfile* alphabetically precedes the first record in both *file1* and *file2*. This ensures that the merge process is going along properly.

Efficiency

The time complexity of this program is quite easy to determine without even examining the loop structure of *mergefiles*. Each record of the *personnel* file and each record of the *new employee* file is handled exactly once as *mergedfile* is created from the records of both files. Thus, if the *personnel* file contains k_1 records and the *new employee* file contains k_2 records, then the time complexity of this program is $O(n)$, where $n = k_1 + k_2$, or linear on the total number of records in the *personnel* and *new employee* files.

Summary — Case Study 10.5

Merging two files requires time proportional to the total number of records in the files to be merged. Merging is a common process that is applied not only when new records must be added to a file but also when an external file is to be sorted, as discussed in exercise 10.40.

A possible additional requirement of a merge procedure would be checking whether any of the new records being merged were already in the established file. If duplicate records existed and no check were made, the new merged file would end up containing these duplicate records, which would be undesirable. Modifying the merge procedure of this case study to handle duplicate records is left as an exercise.

10.5 WORKING OUT

10.34 Describe a tactic which could be used for applying a routine designed to work only on a list of data in the primary store to an external file which cannot fit in the primary store all at once. Can you think of an example application where this tactic would not work very well?

10.35 Explain briefly how the merge program of case study 10.5 works.

10.36 Discuss strategies for designing a program to reverse an external file. For example, how would you process a personnel file that is in alphabetical order by the last name field to produce a new file that is in reverse alphabetical order by last name? Give the time complexity for any approach that you consider and program the best solution in *mpl*.

10.37 Assume that for some problem which manipulates a large external file with n records you are considering two possible programs. The first has $O(n*\log_2 n)$ time complexity and makes n passes through the file. The second has $O(n^2)$ time complexity but only makes 1 pass through the file. Which program would you choose? Discuss the factors that you would consider.

10.38 In the program of case study 10.5 a new employee file is merged into a personnel file; we did not check there to ensure that the new employees were not already in the personnel file. Design a new merge routine that detects such duplications and does not include them in the new file and also prints out an exception list of duplications.

10.39 Modify the requirements of case study 10.4 by changing the assumption that the records in the file *personnel* are in alphabetical order by their name components. Assume instead that they are ordered by wage. Design an *mpl* program which solves this more complex problem in $O(n*\log_2 m)$ time while making only one pass through the n record *personnel* file (m is the number of input values and n is the size of the file). Your program should print an exception list of all input names that are not in the file.

10.40 The *personnel* file used in all case studies of this chapter is in alphabetical order by the name field. This is not the best order because there could be two employees with the same name. This would create problems for searching, updating (e.g. deleting), and merging procedures. It would be better if the file were in numerical order by social security number, because the social security number is unique for each employee. Design an *mpl* program to sort the *personnel* file into numerical order by social security number (the *ssnumber* field) assuming that the entire *personnel* file will not fit into the primary store at once. There are two ways to do this: (1) Start with an initially empty file called *sortedfile*. Design a loop which reads successive chunks from the *personnel* file into an array in the primary store, sorts this internal array of records using *quicksort* (case study 5.8) modified to sort on index (case study 8.2), and then merges the sorted array with *sortedfile*. By this method, *sortedfile* will start out empty but will continue to grow as each sorted chunk of the *personnel* file is merged with *sortedfile* until the entire *personnel* file is in *sortedfile*, sorted by social security number. This program will have time complexity $O(n^2)$, where n is the number of records in the *personnel* file. (2) The second method is similar, except that as each chunk of the *personnel* file is input and sorted, it is not immediately merged with *sortedfile*. Instead, each sorted chunk is stored in its own external file; the first chunk is stored in *sortedfile*[1], the second in *sortedfile*[2], and so on (notice that this requires an extension to *mpl* to allow *arrays of files*). After the entire *personnel* file has been processed this way there will be k new files *sortedfile*[1], *sortedfile*[2], . . ., *sortedfile*[k] in secondary storage, each containing a separate chunk of the original *personnel* file sorted by social security number. These should now be merged pairwise — *sortedfile*[1] with *sortedfile*[2] to produce a new *sortedfile*[1] with twice as many records, then sortedfile[3] with *sortedfile*[4] to produce a new *sortedfile*[2] with twice as many records, and so on. After this step there will be half as many files, each with twice as many records. This step should be repeated until only one file remains, which will be the original *personnel* file sorted by social security number. If *quicksort* is used to sort the original chunks of the *personnel* file, this program will have $O(n*\log_2 n)$ time complexity, so it will generally be better than the first method described.

10.41 Prove that the time complexity of the method you chose for doing exercise 10.40 (method 1 or method 2) has the stated time complexity ($O(n^2)$ or $O(n*\log_2 n)$, respectively).

| APPENDIX A |

Answers to Selected Exercises

1.1 See page 4.

1.2 See pages 4–8.

1.3 See pages 8–10.

1.4 Arithmetic operators: ↑, *, /, +, −
Relational operators: $<, \leqslant, >, \geqslant, =, \neq$
Logical operators: **and, or, not**

1.5 See page 29.

1.6 The model processor can only perform the operations listed in the solution to exercise 1.4. Any more complicated processes must be described by the programmer in terms of these simple operations.

1.7

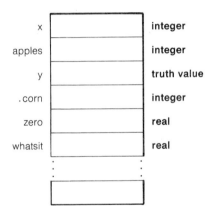

1.8 (a) 3 + 2 − 5   (c) 3 + 7 / 4

(e) (3 + 7) / 4   (g) 3 ↑ 2 + 4 ↑ 2

1.9   (a)   ((5.2 + 7.3) * 3.2) / 5.0   (c)   5.2 + 7.3 * 3.2 / 5.0

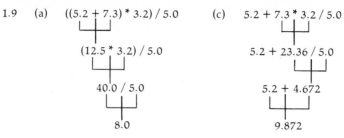

(12.5 * 3.2) / 5.0   5.2 + 23.36 / 5.0

40.0 / 5.0   5.2 + 4.672

8.0   9.872

(e)   (5.2 + 7.3) * (3.2 / 5.0)

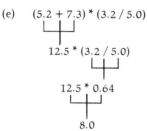

12.5 * (3.2 / 5.0)

12.5 * 0.64

8.0

1.10   (a)   3 < 5   (c)   (3 ≠ 6) or (7 > 7)

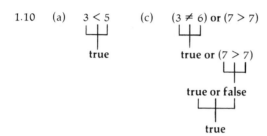

true   true or (7 > 7)

true or false

true

1.11   (b)

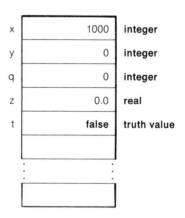

x	1000	integer
y	0	integer
q	0	integer
z	0.0	real
t	false	truth value

1.12   (a) $3.14159 * r \uparrow 2$ or $3.14159 * r * r$

(c) $a * x \uparrow 3 + b * x \uparrow 2 - c * x + 5.37$

(e) $(a + b + c) / 3$

1.13   The divide and conquer program design strategy is also called *stepwise refinement*, *top down design*, or *modular design*. The idea is that whenever you are designing an initial procedure or other procedure or function, you never attempt to directly implement a complex subprocess or calculation. Instead, you just call on another procedure or function to do this task, leaving the design of the new routine for later. Thus you conquer a problem by dividing it into smaller pieces which can be solved more easily.

1.14 A procedure extends the statement set of the language by performing a certain series of operations whenever it is called. A function extends the operator set of the language by calculating and returning a value whenever it is called. More differences are given in chapter 2.

1.15 It provides the organization for the program of which it is a part, calling on the other procedures and functions of the program to perform the necessary calculations.

2.1 See pages 73–76.

2.2 (a) True   (c) True   (e) False (almost everywhere; a function call cannot appear on the left side of the assignment operator ←)
    (g) False (**in only**)

2.3 See page 75.

```
square : integer function
    {computes the square of an integer}

    storage specification
        parameters
            x : in out integer
        end storage specification

    begin square
        x ← x * x
        square ← x
    end square
```

Now, if z = 4, and we include in the initial procedure the statements

```
y ← square(z)
output 'the square of ', z, ' = ', y
```

then the output would be

the square of 16 = 16

due to the side effect that *square* changes the **in out** parameter *x*.

2.4 See pages 58, 61 and 77–79.

2.5 See pages 79–87.

2.6

	in only	in out	out only
(a)	False	True	True
(c)	False	True	True
(e)	False	False	True
(g)	False	True	True
(i)	True	False	False

2.7 See pages 69 and 87.

2.8 See pages 87–88.

2.9 In general, walkthroughs and tests cannot check all possible inputs to a program, but only a hopefully representative set of sample data and test cases.

2.10 See pages 88–89.

2.12 (b) 2   4   6
        10   4   6   14
    (c) Error: **out only** parameter w is used before it is given a value.

2.13 (a) −4.5   2.0   1.5

CHAPTER 3

3.2   See pages 128–130.

3.3   (a)   9

3.4   (a)   7   8   (c)   nothing will be printed

3.5   See pages 132–133.

3.6   A robust program is one which gives reasonable output even if the inputs are unreasonable. This usually means that if invalid data is input an error message is output rather than allowing the program to crash.

3.7   See page 133. A well designed program should be largely *self commenting*. That is, if each function and procedure has a descriptive comment in its header, that should usually be sufficient. If a piece of program is so complex that it needs a comment, it should probably be replaced by a procedure or function call.

3.8   See pages 133–134.

3.10   No, unless they are checked by the processor, as in Pascal VS or Ada.

3.11   See page 132. For example, there are two paths for each **if–then–else,** two for each **if–then,** and one for each **case** clause.

3.12   2 — each **output** statement.

3.16   The **if** is more general. It can be used for tests other than equality, and can also be used for **real** comparisons.

3.17   Because of potential roundoff errors. See pages 131–132.

3.18   (a)   first class   (b)   bad class number
                submit next class number   submit next class number

3.19   (a)   you fail miserably
                how did you do?

        (c)   your grade is 51
                you did satisfactorily
                how did you do?

        (e)   no: it ignores $x < 0$ and $x \geqslant 100$. Include an **else** clause to handle these cases.

        (g)   20, 45, 60, 80, 90 — these are typical of all expected grades.

        (i)   0, 40, 50, 70, 85, 100 — these check the boundary values.

        (j)   −5, 105 — these are unexpected inputs.

3.21   By replacing it with the structure:

        if {the **case** control expression evaluates to one of the **case** labels}
            then {include the **case** statement here}
            else {include the **otherwise** clause here}
            endif

3.22   (a)   no   (c)   yes   (e)   no   (g)   no

3.24   1 5;   1 0;   1 −2;   2 5;   2 0;   2 −2;   3 5;   3 0;   3 −2;   4 2;
        −1 2;   0 2;   −1 0.

3.25   1, 10, −10, 50

3.27   **if** ((5 ⩽ nuts) **and** (nuts ⩽ 9)) **or**
        ((50 ⩽ nuts) **and** (nuts ⩽ 54)) **or**
        ((−54 ⩽ nuts) **and** (nuts ⩽ −50)) **or**
        ((250 ⩽ nuts) **and** (nuts ⩽ 254))
        then case trunc(nuts/5) **is**
        when 1 :   nuts ← nuts + 1
        when 10, −10 :   **output** nuts
                         nuts ← nuts * 2
        when 50 :   **output** nuts ↑ 2
                         nuts ← nuts / 2
    endcase
        else output 'nuts to you, bad value'
        endif

3.42   We will give the solution to this programming problem. Look at it carefully, and then explain how and why the program works. The two functions below replace the single *fibonacci* function of case study 3.7.

    fibonacci : **integer function**
      {computes fibonacci(n) efficiently, using recursion}

      storage specification
        parameters
          n : **in only integer**
        end storage specification

      begin fibonacci
        if n ⩽ 2
          then fibonacci ← 1
          else fibonacci ← fib(n, 3, 1, 1)
          endif
      end fibonacci

    where fib computes fibonacci numbers in ascending order

    fib : **integer function**
      {computes fibonacci numbers in ascending order}

      storage specification
        parameters
          n, i, oneback, twoback : **in only integer**
        end storage specification

      begin fib
        if n = i
          then fib ← oneback + twoback
          else fib ← fib(n, i + 1, oneback + twoback, oneback)
          endif
      end fib

CHAPTER 4

4.1   Loops allow the programmer to perform repetitive actions. For example, computing the payroll for each employee in a large organization will require a loop that executes once for each employee. Loops also permit the programmer to compute values by repetitively calculating a partial result which eventually becomes the desired complete result. For example, summing a series of inputs by adding the next value to a running total on each iteration of a loop computes a desired sum.

4.2   In order of decreasing generality, the **while** loop, the **until** loop, and the automatic stepping loop.

4.3   sum ← 0
        loop while {more numbers to be summed}
            number ← {next number to be summed}
            sum ← sum + number
        endloop while

4.4   count ← 0
        loop while {some condition}
            count ← count + 1
            {statements of loop}
        endloop while

4.7   Loops control how many times, if any, their inner statements will be executed, whereas **if** and **case** statements control which of their inner statements will be executed.

4.8   Header value, trailer value, and **moredata.** See case study 4.1.

4.9   (a)   11   (c)   1

4.10   (a)   If $j \geqslant 0, j + 1$ times
               If $j < 0$, 0 times

4.11   See pages 208–209.

4.12   See pages 215–223.

4.13   See pages 221–223.

4.16 $O(n)$

4.18 $O(n)$

4.19 $a*n^3 + f(n)$ where $f(n)$ is less complex than n^3, and a is a constant. In general, the exact statement count cannot be determined from the time complexity.

4.21   The $O(n)$ program. If n is very small the $O(n^3)$ program could be faster; the statement counts would help us determine this.

4.24   No, as we don't allow a step factor of 0, and don't allow the statements of a loop to change any of the loop controlling variables. So, if the final value is on the correct side of the starting value ($\geqslant$ if step > 0, $\leqslant$ if step < 0) then ultimately the loop control variable will pass the final value, and the loop will stop. Conversely, if the final value is on the other side of the initial value, the loop statements will not execute at all.

4.28   backloop : **procedure**

            storage specification
                parameters
                    n : **in only integer**
                variables
                    i : **integer**
                end storage specification

            begin backloop
                loop start i **with** n **step** −1 **to** 2
                    assert the integers n down to i+1 have been output
                    output i
                    endloop autoindex
                assert the integers n down to i+1 have been output
                assert i = 1
                assert the integers n down to 2 have been output
                end backloop

4.31   The loop will keep inputting values into some variable, say x, until the trailer value has been input into x. Therefore, all of the inputs and trailer value must have the same type as x, since they are read into that variable.

4.35   The statement count. With this you can easily obtain the time complexity if needed, and it also allows an analysis of the efficiency gains that can be achieved by, for example, moving a statement out of a loop.

4.36   We assume that the cost of executing a program rises in direct proportion to the number of statements executed. For example, if the number of statements executed rises k times, then the cost to execute the program also rises k times. Since the time complexity of a program gives the rate of growth of the number of statements executed as the input size changes, we can discover the multiplication factor k for this problem by dividing the time complexity formula with the new input size (75,000) by the time complexity formula with the old input size (15,000). We then multiply this result times the cost to run the program with the old input size to get the new approximate cost. This gives us

1. $(\log_2 75000/\log_2 15000) * \$5 = \$5.84$
2. $(75000/15000) * \$100 = \$500$
3. $(75000*\log_2 75000)/(15000*\log_2 15000)) * \$200 = \$1,167$
4. $(75000^2/15000^2) * \$500 = 25 * \$500 = \$12,500$

4.40   **assert** result contains x to the (i − 1)st power.

Place this assertion above the statement $result \leftarrow result * x$.

4.61   The loop complete with all assertions is:

```
i ← 1
result ← 1
assert result contains x to the 0th power                          (1)
loop while i ⩽ n
    assert result contains x to the (i − 1)st power                (2)
    result ← result * x
    assert result contains x to the ith power                      (3)
    i ← i + 1
    assert result contains x to the (i − 1)st power                (4)
    endloop while
assert result contains x to the (i − 1)st power                    (5)
assert i = n + 1                                                   (6)
assert result contains x to the nth power                          (7)
```

We must now prove each of the following.
(1) is true after $i \leftarrow 1$ and $result \leftarrow 1$.
(1) implies (2) when the loop is first entered with $i = 1$.
(2) and $result \leftarrow result * x$ imply (3).
(3) and $i \leftarrow i + 1$ imply (4).
(4) is the same as (2).
(4) is the same as (5).
    Loop termination implies (6).
(5) and (6) imply (7).
Fortunately, each of these eight proofs is trivial.

4.64   In each loop, i increases by 1, and since n is not changed in the loop, i must eventually become $\geq n$, causing termination of the loop.

4.65   Consider just the **while** loop, since this is the most general loop type. The **while** loop

> **loop while** *condition*
>   *statements*
>   **endloop** *while*

can be replaced by a call to a recursive procedure named, say, *whilerep(parameters)*, whose computation part is

> **if** *condition*
>   **then** *statements*
>   whilerep(*parameters*)
>   **endif**
> **where**   *parameters* includes everything needed for *condition*
>   and *statements* to be processed.

CHAPTER 5

5.1   A control structure is used to control the execution of statements in a program. The **if** and **case** statements are control structures that control which of various groups of statements will be executed, and the **loop** statements are control structures which control how many times a group of statements will be executed. A data structure is a set of logically related data, such as a list of ID numbers or a table of conversions from pounds to kilograms, that includes a particular structure or relationship among the values.

5.2   A 1-D array is a programming language feature that can be used to store a simple list, which is a data structure.

*5.3   newarray : **truth value array** [0 → 99]

5.4   The space complexity of a program is a measure of how the storage needs of the program increase as the size of the input increases. Just as the time complexity of a program indicates the increase in the time required by a program as the input size increases, so the space complexity indicates the increase in the number of storage cells used by a program as the input size increases.

No. For example, see case study 5.2, which was shown (page 274) to have $O(1)$, (constant), space complexity.

5.5   **loop start** i **with** 1 **step** 1 **to** 200
                {process fuzzy[i]}
                endloop autoindex

5.6   To conserve storage space and also to save the time required to copy the array. See case study 5.1 pages 269–270.

5.8   The index range that most naturally fits the problem should be used. If the exact value of either the lower bound or the upper bound is not known, then an index range that includes all likely values for these bounds should be used. So, for example, if likely values for the lower bound are between -8 and $+5$ and for the upper bound are between $+3$ and $+82$, then declare the array to have a range of $[-8 → 82]$. Practical considerations include not requesting more storage cells than are available and not requesting an excessive number of cells. Whenever it is possible that more array elements may be needed than you planned for, it is essential that you include program checks to detect if and when you are about to fall out of the array bounds.

5.9   Any integer valued expression.

5.10   Using numeric constants, named constants, and variables (dynamic arrays). See pages 283–287.

5.11   *dick* has four elements: *dick*[−3], *dick*[−2], *dick*[−1], *dick*[0].

5.13   Yes. For example, a program that inputs a positive integer, *n*, and then computes, stores in an array, and manipulates the first n^2 prime numbers.

5.15   Case study 4.1 has $O(n)$ time complexity but $O(1)$ space complexity. All usual programs that have $O(n)$ space complexity will have at least $O(n)$ time complexity, since it will take $O(n)$ input or computation steps to fill the $O(n)$ cells.

5.24   Only when the list is not sorted or is very short.

5.25   Only if the list must be searched a large number of times. For example, if the list must be searched about *n* times, where *n* is the length of the list, then a quicksort followed by *n* binary searches has time complexity $O(n*\log_2 n)$ + $O(n*\log_2 n)$, which is just $O(n*\log_2 n)$, while *n* calls to sequentially search an *n*-element list would require $O(n^2)$ time.

CHAPTER 6

6.1   String constants: 'Cpt S 150', 'a', '$', '32', '5'
       Character constants: 'a', '$', '5', 'A'

       All character constants are string constants, but not all string constants are character constants.

6.2   A computer storage cell is a finite device that can only store a fixed amount of information.

6.3   Yes.   No.   (See the answer to the last part of exercise 6.1.)

6.4   The null string is a string constant of length 0. It is not a character constant. The string consisting of one blank is both a string constant of length 1 and a character constant.

6.5   sentence ← 'I said, ''''It couldn''t be found'''''

6.6   Usually a character at a time. This does not require that the user put quotes around the strings to be read in.

6.7   The concatentation operator is used to join strings together to make longer strings. For example, input characters can be joined to make words, words joined to make sentences, sentences joined to make paragraphs, paragraphs joined to make chapters, and chapters joined to make a book. All of these joining operations are just concatenations of strings.

6.8   phrase ← '' {initialize to null string}
```
loop start i with 1 step 1 to 20
        assert phrase contains the first i−1 input characters
        input ch
        phrase ← phrase ǁ ch
        endloop autoindex
assert phrase contains the first 20 input characters
```

6.13   Yes. For example, if the **output** statement

       output 'a' ǁ blankstring ǁ 'b'

       is executed, then if *blankstring* contains ten blanks

       a   b

       will be printed, while if *blankstring* contains one blank

       a b

       will be printed. Because of the way strings are compared, however, a string of one blank would be equal to a string of 10 blanks.

6.15   See page 359. The null string is the identity for concatenation.

6.19   (a)   cow   (b)   a single blank

7.1   A 2-D array is a programming language feature which can be used to store a table, which is data structure.

7.2   In row major order values are input (or output) row by row, whereas in column major order values are input (or output) column by column. See pages 384–385.

7.3   Row major:

a[1,1]	5	integer
a[1,2]	6	integer
a[1,3]	7	integer
a[1,4]	8	integer
a[2,1]	9	integer
a[2,2]	10	integer
a[2,3]	11	integer
a[2,4]	12	integer
a[3,1]	13	integer
a[3,2]	14	integer
a[3,3]	15	integer
a[3,4]	16	integer

7.4   (a)

```
input rows, columns
loop start i with 1 step 1 to rows
    loop start j with 1 step 1 to columns
        input table[i, j]
    endloop autoindex
endloop autoindex
```

7.5   1. An array with only one row.
       2. An array with only one column.
       3. An array with one row and one column.
       4. An array each of whose entries is a special value, e.g. 0.
       5. Input which would cause the array to have no rows or columns.
       6. Input which would cause the array to exceed one or both bounds.

7.6
```
loop start i with 1 step 1 to n
   loop start j with 1 step 1 to n
      loop start k with 1 step 1 to n
         loop start m with 1 step 1 to n
            {process fourd[i, j, k, m]}
         endloop autoindex
      endloop autoindex
   endloop autoindex
endloop autoindex
```

The time complexity is $O(n^4)$.

7.8 There are no changes in the top-down design process we have stressed from the beginning.

7.9 fred : 27.   jet : 1.

7.10 A company which sells ten products has twenty salespeople. Record the number of items of each product sold by each salesperson in each month of a year. Use a 20x10x12 integer array, named *sales* such that *sales[person, product, month]* gives the number of items of the specified product sold by the named salesperson in the given month.

7.12 Both versions are accurate and acceptable. The first is slightly more informative since it gives a better picture of the structure of the problem. So, for example, it is clearer that if you double the number of rows while keeping the number of columns fixed, the execution time will double. Furthermore, most of the data structures implemented by a 2-D array are such that increasing the input size by one does not mean that a single new element is added to the array but that an entire new row or column is added. In this case the first expression is more informative.

7.15 Because programmers usually explicitly use automatic stepping loops to access the elements of the array in the order that they want to use, ignoring the internal order. As long as the processor knows where any particular element is, for example $a[i, j]$, the programmer need not be concerned with where this element is stored.

7.18 1. No.
2. Yes, if the operation performed on each access is not $O(1)$.

8.1 A library's book catalog. Typical entries include title, author, publisher, catalog number, number of copies, date checked out, etc.

CHAPTER 8

8.2 In a homogeneous data structure every entry has the same type.

8.3
```
fraggle : record containing
   number : integer
   price : real
   info : record containing
      ssnumber, id, code : string
   endrecord info
endrecord fraggle
```

8.4   (a)

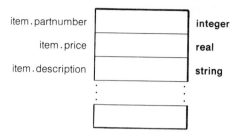

item.partnumber		integer
item.price		real
item.description		string

8.5   (a)   *item.partnumber, item.price, item.description*

8.6   **loop start** i **with** 0 **step** 1 **to** 50
          output newitem.partnumber[i]
          endloop autoindex

8.7   If both records have identical components, item for item.

8.8   Yes. For example, item and newitem from exercise 8.4 could appear together in a program. Both contain price as a component. Items with the same name in different records are distinguished by the processor by the record name. For example, *item.partnumber* is different from *newitem.partnumber*.

8.9   (a)

partlist.type		character
partlist.item.partnumber[0]		integer
partlist.item.partnumber[1]		integer
partlist.item.partnumber[2]		integer
partlist.item.partnumber[3]		integer
partlist.item.partnumber[4]		integer
partlist.item.partnumber[5]		integer
partlist.item.price		real
partlist.item.description		string
partlist.onorder		truth value
partlist.inventory		integer

8.11   The difference is that a record will usually contain a large number of components, and so if, for example, one record must be assigned to another, the assignment must be made component by component by the processor, which obviously takes more time than a simple integer assignment.

8.13   itemlist : **1-D record array** [1 → 100] **containing**
          partnumber : **integer**
          price : **real**
          description : **string**
          endrecord itemlist

itemlist[1].partnumber		**integer**
itemlist[1].price		**real**
itemlist[1].description		**string**

⋮ ⋮

itemlist[100].partnumber		**integer**
itemlist[100].price		**real**
itemlist[100].description		**string**

⋮ ⋮

9.1 Arrays are homogeneous and have fixed length.

9.2 A list of orders received and placed by a company could be kept in order of processing. Orders received by customers could include the customer's name and address, the description of the item ordered, the quantity ordered, the unit price, the total price, and the unit identification number. Orders placed by the company for raw materials could have a completely different format, for example, just the name and address of the firm with which the order was placed, a description of the ordered material, and the quantity ordered. Because the list contains both types of records intermixed, the list is non-homogeneous.

9.3 A list of students waiting to add a popular class. If a new section is opened up or if other students drop, then names will be removed from the list and added to the class, with seniors having the highest priority.

9.4 The logical locations of the list elements are their relative positions in the list data structure. So, the logical location of the first element of the list precedes the logical location of the second element, and so on. The physical locations of the elements are their actual positions in the store, which may have no relationship to their logical locations.

9.5 See pages 445–450. In a linked list, cell addresses are used to physically link the list elements together to match the logical arrangement of the data structure being implemented in the linked list.

9.6 Cell addresses, which allow the next elements to be located.

9.7 In a singly linked list each element is linked to exactly one other list element. Consider a list of lists. For instance, the T-shirt example from case study 9.2 could be represented as a single list of lists.

9.8 Variables of type **celladdress** can only be used to contain storage cell addresses. As such they are more restricted than variables of the **integer** type since values of **celladdress** variables cannot be negative, and since none of the usual arithmetic operations can be performed on such variables.

9.9 **listelement descriptors** and **celladdress** declarations, and **getnew** and **free** statements (see pages 450–452).

9.10   If a **celladdress** variable is undefined it has no value and cannot be referred to as an address. On the other hand **null** is a legitimate value for a **celladdress** variable and has the special meaning "a link to nowhere." If a **celladdress** variable contains a defined, non-null value, it is treated as the address of an actual cell in the store. The expression **if** $x.link = y.link$ will result in an error if either $x.link$ or $y.link$ is undefined; if both are defined with an address or the null link, the expression will be evaluated properly.

9.11   Without it, it is impossible to access the beginning of the list. All other elements in the list are accessed by following the links from the first element.

9.12   (a)   current ← first
            loop while current ≠ **null**
                output   current:porkbarrel.price,
                            current:porkbarrel.quantity
                current ← current:porkbarrel.nextpork
            endloop while

9.13   Move through a singly linked list, element by element, from the first element to the last.

9.14   The structure will be

current ← {address of first list element}
loop while current ≠ **null**
    {process current element}
    current ← {link component of current list element}
    endloop while

so the loop condition essentially checks whether the list is empty or whether the link field of the last list element processed was **null.**

9.15   Empty list; list with one element; list missing important values; values appearing more than once in the list; important values in first element of list; important values in last element of list; and so forth.

9.16   The programmer must pay closer attention to details, but the careful top-down program design strategy does not change.

9.17   The fact that all of the elements of the list are not immediately accessible (as they are in an array), means that some efficient algorithms (e.g., binary search) cannot be used with lists. Because of the links the space expended when using linked lists will usually be more than the space expended when using arrays.

9.18   See page 481.

9.19   Lists are usually only used in highly dynamic environments. That is, elements will be constantly added to and deleted from the list, making it difficult to estimate the maximum number of cells in use at any time. In cases where it is possible to make a good estimate of the maximum size, arrays can usually be used (more efficiently) instead of lists.

9.20   In a queue elements are always added to one end of the list and removed from the other. In a stack all additions and deletions are made at one end of the list. In a general list, elements can be added and deleted at any place in the list.

9.21   A list cannot be a parameter; instead a **celladdress** variable that contains the address of an element in the list (usually the first element) must be sent as an actual parameter in communicating information about a list from one routine to another.

9.22 A linked list would normally be used in highly dynamic circumstances, where it is difficult to estimate the number of storage cells in use at any time, and where the number of updates (additions and deletions) become more important than the number of other accesses to the data. Also, for data structures containing non-homogeneous elements a linked list implementation may be necessary (there are no examples of such a data structure in this book).

9.23 The **free** statement is used so that storage can be released for use again by *this* program. Without it, so much storage would be wasted that many programs would quickly use all of the available cells in the store.

9.24 A linked list will use more storage because of the **celladdress** fields in each list element that are required to link the elements together.

9.26 There is the potential storage cost of the **celladdress** link fields used in elements of linked lists, which must be balanced against the potential storage saved due to the fact that the user does not need to estimate the maximum array size for any problem using arrays instead. There is also the potential time cost caused by the linked list traversals required to access arbitrary elements of the data structures. Program design time will also usually increase because the links needed to implement the data structures as linked lists must be planned and analyzed by the programmer. This also means that extra careful attention must be paid to ensuring that the program uses and updates the links properly. These are not considerations when a data structure can be implemented directly with an array.

9.29 A record declared in a **variables** statement causes cells to be reserved in the store for that record. A record declared in a **listelement descriptors** statement does not cause any storage cells to be reserved. Such a record is just a *descriptor* of a list element, so that whenever a **getnew** statement is executed to get a new list element of that type, the processor can — *at that point* — reserve the proper number and type of cells for the record.

10.1 An external file is data that is stored on a secondary storage device, typically as a sequential list of records.

CHAPTER 10

10.2 See page 523.

10.3 Primary store is limited in size, and is relatively expensive. It is also usually volatile, so that data kept in the primary store will be lost when the power is turned off. Tapes and disks are non-volatile, and are relatively cheap. Typical relative storage sizes on the central computer at a large university are: primary store, 16 megabytes (million characters); secondary store (disk), 20 gigabytes (billion characters); secondary store (tape), 500 gigabytes.

10.4 (a) The primary store is volatile, secondary storage is not.
(b) The primary store is random access, secondary storage is not.
(c) The primary store is much faster than secondary storage.

10.5 Tapes are much slower and cheaper than disks. For access differences see pages 522–523.

10.6 RAM means *Random Access Memory*. In RAM each storage cell is equally quickly accessible. In secondary storage one must search through data sequentially to find a particular item.

10.7   A storage device is volatile if its data will be lost when the power is turned off. Primary storage is usually volatile because it depends on a constant current source to keep the data stored there. Secondary storage is usually based on magnetic properties and therefore retains what is stored there even if the power is turned off.

10.8   See page 546.

10.9   The header record identifies the file. The trailer record acts as an end-of-file marker.

10.10 Primary storage is much faster.

10.11 In either case the file is copied, record by record, into a temporary file until the points of deletion or insertion are reached. Records to be deleted are simply not copied into the temporary file. Records to be inserted are constructed and then added to the temporary file at the proper point. In either case, the rest of the original file is copied, record by record, into the temporary file. Finally, the original file is destroyed, and the temporary file is renamed to the name of the original file.

10.12 See page 547.

10.13 A backup file is a copy of an important file that is saved in case the original gets destroyed accidentally.

10.15 A file is a large list of records saved on an external storage device. An array is a list of records in the primary store. Arrays are random access, files are sequential access.

10.18 It takes a long time (relatively speaking) to retrieve data from secondary storage. Printing the external file will, therefore, take much longer. In both cases the time complexity will be $O(n)$ where n is the number of records in the file or array, so the execution time difference between the two print routines would be a large constant factor, regardless of the size of n. Of course, if by "printing" we mean that we want to see the results on paper, then we would notice no differences in the time required by either print routine, because the printer will print slower than data can be retrieved from secondary storage.

10.21 It would be too easy to make programming errors and accidentally destroy an important file.

10.24 The file name and description, not the file itself, is passed as a parameter. See page 548.

10.26 It would not be easy. Since a file is not random access, a copy of the file in reverse order would have to be constructed (see exercise 10.36), and then both files would be printed.

10.27 See pages 547–548.

Index

†